A Search for Power

A Search for Power

The "Weaker Sex" in Seventeenth-Century New England

LYLE KOEHLER

UNIVERSITY OF ILLINOIS PRESS

Urbana   Chicago   London

Library of Congress Cataloging in Publication Data

Koehler, Lyle, 1944–
   A search for power.

   Bibliography: p.
   Includes index.
   1. Women—New England—History—17th century.
2. Sexism—New England—History—17th century—Sources.
3. Women's rights—New England—History—17th century—
      Sources.   4. Deviant behavior.   I. Title.
HQ1438.A11K63   305.4'0974   80-16666
               ISBN 0-252-00808-1

Acknowledgments

THE PROCESS OF MANUSCRIPT PREPARATION IS LONG AND, AT TIMES, exasperating. I have incurred many more debts than I can possibly acknowledge. I must, however, list those persons and institutions who have provided the most assistance.

Most historians owe a special, although sometimes unexpressed, debt to librarians. I received valuable help from the personnel at the Maine Historical Society (Portland), Essex Institute (Salem, Massachusetts), New Hampshire State Archives (Concord), Lynn Public Library (Massachusetts), Boston Public Library, Massachusetts Historical Society (Boston), Massachusetts State Archives (Boston), Pilgrim Society (Plymouth), Redwood Library and Atheneum (Newport, Rhode Island), Newport Historical Society, John Carter Brown Library (Providence), Rhode Island Historical Society (Providence), Widener Library (Harvard University), Houghton Library (Ann Arbor, Michigan), and Connecticut State Library (Hartford). I am especially beholden to Thomas L. Gaffney, curator of manuscripts at the Maine Historical Society, who spent several hours sorting through old documents for me. The Providence Friends Meeting gave me access to the extensive manuscript records at the Friends Library in a wing of the Rhode Island Historical Society. Also helpful were innumerable employees at the clerks of court offices in the Suffolk, Essex, Hampden, Hampshire, Middlesex, Dukes, and Bristol County Courthouses in Massachusetts; the York County Courthouse in Alfred, Maine; and the Newport and Providence County Courthouses in Rhode Island.

Zane Miller provided needed structural commentary and aided me with many practical suggestions. John Alexander contributed his considerable knowledge of colonial history to a painstaking analysis of the manuscript's coherence and accuracy. Henry Shapiro recommended several important changes in the chapters he took time to go through. I am much obligated to all three. Most of all, I am grateful to Karin Rabe for her generous and invaluable contribution of time and effort in reading, discussing, and abundantly contributing her editing expertise to my revisions of the original manuscript. Whatever the manuscript's virtues, its errors, miscalculations, or excesses are, however, my own.

—L. K.

Contents

Introduction

> History records but few of their deeds. It is not unusual to read of the early pioneers that *he* came to the woods of Maine; *he* felled trees; *he* cleared this five-acre lot; *he* built his log cabin; *he* reared his large family of children; and *he* died. Not even the name of the mother recorded.
> —Helen Coffin Beedy, *Mothers of Maine*

EACH PASSING DECADE BRINGS EVER MORE STUDIES OF THOSE SOME-times enigmatic but always fascinating seventeenth-century Calvinists who helped carve an English society out of the New World terrain. Yet, despite the perennial interest in John Winthrop, William Bradford, Thomas Hooker, Roger Williams, and their male associates, only minimal attention has been paid to a certain numerically significant New England group: women. Three of the most prominent Puritan ladies have become the subjects of biographies (Anne Hutchinson, Anne Bradstreet, and Margaret Winthrop[1]); witches, most of whom were female, have also received a good deal of consideration. Edmund S. Morgan's important work on *The Puritan Family* contains a valuable chapter on relationships between husbands and wives, and some material about the position of New England women appears in works by John Demos and Roger Thompson.[2] Three excellent general studies, by Elizabeth Dexter, Julia Cherry Spruill, and Mary Sumner Benson,[3] have added an important dimension to our knowledge about the female sex in colonial America, but none of these deals very extensively with New England women. Although Puritanism has, rather too flippantly, been credited with either emancipating or subordinating women, no one has examined in much detail the female experience in the northeastern colonies.

Some of the hypotheses advanced for the alleged liberating effects of Puritanism and a New World environment on the "weaker sex" have been too easily formulated. The argument that America provided numerous occupational opportunities for all persons willing to work does not necessarily suggest any degree of female emancipation. Indeed, such an argument might suggest quite the reverse, since employing women at low-status, low-paying jobs could have freed men, *not* women, from society's dirty work. Opening schools to the "weaker sex," usually viewed as a liberating measure, might rather have served a conservative purpose—as an institutional way to ensure that woman would remain tied to her home and husband. What instructors teach women is ultimately more important than the fact that women are taught. Many women may have behaved more freely because they were *not* molded by schooling into proper ladies. Similarly, the Puritan belief in marital love need not have had an emancipating effect, unless Puritans defined love in egalitarian terms. In all likelihood, love meant something different to seventeenth-century men and women than it does to modern ones. Moreover, the celebration of love may have offered women an illusion which made their oppression more tolerable. In the final analysis, all the claims made for the Puritans as liberators may prove accurate; I have merely been presenting a cynical point of view to illustrate the complexity of the issues involved. Such claims stand or fall only when we pay careful attention to collecting hard data and analyzing the total context in which early Puritans lived.

We can never really understand what the Puritan experience meant—either vis-à-vis other parts of the world, especially England, or in terms of the considerable inter-colony differences, or even in its intrinsic reality for individual women—unless we pore over the wealth of available records: the letters, court transcriptions, poems, tax lists, diaries, and contemporary accounts in which women's stories have been buried. Such records are, of course, incomplete—letters are few, some court logs are missing, and diaries are often frustratingly limited. But enough evidence remains to give the researcher a reasonably valid sense of the times. Juxtaposing literary evidence against insights drawn from anthropology, sociology, and psychology can add much to our understanding of Puritan and non-Puritan women.

In such a search, it is important to recall that cultures differ in their definitions of male and female status, as do the individuals who comprise any given culture. At the same time, male domination of females has been qualitatively different, or even absent, in some neighboring cultures. The patriarchal Pequod Indians, for example, treated women quite differently from the more egalitarian Iroquois. One might also expect some difference in the way heretical Rhode Islanders reacted to women, when compared to orthodox Puritans or Maine frontiersmen. Even in the general context of male social advantage, the existence of variations, whether minor or profound, clearly calls for a comprehensive analysis. Surely one significant factor must be that women have been active participants in every society, as well as frequent victims of their own biology and of male domination. In any given society it is not simply how men see women that is important, but how women see themselves: the extent to which they accept or even contribute to the male view of them, and the extent to which they in fact abide by that view. Since people are marvelously complex, we can expect to find any number of female reactions. Puritan men and women were by no means homogeneous; urban shopkeepers, Connecticut farm people, servants, English travelers, Anglicans, Presbyterians, Anabaptists, and Congregationalists all had their own definitions of reality. So, too, within the Puritan family, one husband or father might be lenient, encouraging, and caring, while another might reveal a more self-seeking, authoritarian bent.

Whatever the impact of "personality," however, the ideological and practical dimensions of a society—its entire worldview, its consistencies and inconsistencies, its psychological and social *modus operandi*—have their own impact upon individual behavior. The way New Englanders construed sex roles reflected their views on basic human issues such as individualism versus conformity, sexual restraint versus permissiveness, religious salvation for the many or for the few, and kindliness as opposed to punitiveness in child-rearing. Puritan culture's ideals, reinforced by school and church, were so firmly implanted in children that anyone who rejected them became a rebel—a social deviate.

In some sense, a rebel—whether a woman rebelling against the limitations of her sex role, or a Puritan man rebelling against the authority of the Anglican Church—is involved in a search for power. In its most basic form, power is the ability to affect one's physical and social environment, to control one's own life. Increasingly, psychologists are recognizing that one of the most dif-

ficult barriers to individual happiness involves failure to feel in
control of one's life.[4] The person made insecure because of early
and prolonged frustration by people or events will often try to
control others in compensation, as a kind of proof of potency
and expression of accumulated anger. Such efforts to control may
involve interfering with the freedom of others, or compelling
them to act in particular ways. Men's and women's searches for
power take varying forms; some are benign, others more antagonistic, if not self-destructive. Spouse-beating, rape, condemning
the authorities, infanticide, covert manipulation, killing Indians,
witchcraft accusations, adopting heretical religious attitudes (and,
in more contemporary times, "doing one's own thing") are some
of the manifold ways in which people search for power.

This search often has subterranean characteristics. Many of the
"rebellious" actions in the seventeenth century were highly individualized—sometimes impulsive, rather than carefully and rationally thought out. Although the woman who violates a prevailing
sex-role stereotype need not necessarily have a philosophical or
political justification for her action, that action is pointed nevertheless, revealing her frustration with one or more aspects of her
life—frustrations which are often tied to either her image of herself
as a woman, or to the expectations placed upon her by others in a
sexually polarized society. She is a rebel, albeit not always a self-
aware one. What she does is at least as important as what she thinks
about it, especially since the Puritan woman rarely left letters,
journals, or published works to enable us to better understand
her thoughts.

This book approaches New Englanders' search for power from
three perspectives. First, it attempts to describe the cultural stereotype of the proper woman within the context of the English background and the worldview of early American Puritanism. Here the
major emphasis is on the institutionalization of the male-dominant
Puritan value system, on societal ideals which—notwithstanding
considerable pressure for change at different times—remained
essentially static throughout most of the century. The orthodox
female role posited in 1630 was the same as that celebrated by many
of society's leaders in 1692.

Realities, however, only approximate ideals. The second part of
this work therefore analyzes female variation from and adjustment
to the feminine stereotype, describing some of the ways in which
Calvinist women coped with male dominion and sought to exercise
influence over their own and others' lives—in short, how they

searched for power. Here the emphasis shifts away from Puritan (and, to some extent, English) society and roles, instead focusing on reacting individuals, resulting in a wider perspective that includes effect as well as cause, social realities as well as social forms, Women as well as Woman.

Finally, this study further broadens its focus to include non-Puritan New Englanders, examining how stereotypes and behaviors varied at different times and places: from the sparsely populated hills of Maine to the southerly shores of Narragansett Bay, from the urban coast of Massachusetts to the interior reaches of Connecticut. While mainstream Puritanism dominated in seventeenth-century New England, it was not the only religious and cultural force among the colonists; moreover, Puritans themselves were affected by the influx of outsiders into their society later in the century. Comparisons in time and place are necessary to any complete depiction of woman in seventeenth-century New England. No large group can be adequately studied without reference to the broader changes occurring in society as a whole, without some examination of the frustrations and anxieties afflicting a certain people at a certain time. The social environment profoundly affects the extent to and means by which people search for power. As society is assailed by agents of change, both external and internal, so too are human expectations modified.

In sum, then, this exploration of women's roles and realities will reveal aspects of the New England woman's situation which contradict the fairly common assumption that Puritanism liberated the "weaker sex." It will further show the range of possibilities and limitations experienced by women throughout New England, analyzing the dynamics of conflict and accommodation that occurred as New England women dealt with their expected social role. Finally, it will tie increasing numbers of non-traditional women late in the century to the social changes then fragmenting Puritan society. The information yielded by such analyses should help us understand what was happening with seventeenth-century women, and I hope this understanding will make the book a fruitful source for women's studies scholars today.

1. Curtis, *Anne Hutchinson*; Rugg, *Unafraid*; Kenyon, *Scarlet Anne*; Ellis, "Life of Anne Hutchinson"; Berryman, *Homage to Mistress Bradstreet*; Campbell, *Anne Bradstreet & Her Times*; Piercy, *Anne Bradstreet*; Earle, *Margaret Winthrop*.

2. Morgan, *Puritan Family*; Demos, *Little Commonwealth*; Thompson, *Women in Stuart Eng. & Am.*

3. Dexter, *Col. Women of Affairs*; Spruill, *Women's Life & Work*; M. Benson, *Women in 18th Cent. Am*.

4. Seligman, *Helplessness*, is the best empirical exposition of this theme.

I

The Creation of a Puritan Mode

Calvinist doctrine, the idea of the antisocial nature of instinctual impulses and the necessity of using force to condition the unreasoning mind, the fear of "spoiling" by permissiveness—these are some of the rationalizations which make a virtue of an evil.
—Joseph C. Rheingold, *The Fear of Being a Woman*

The Commercial Revolution and Puritanism

THE ENGLAND WHICH CREATED THE PURITANS WAS A LAND EXPERIencing profound social change, as both poor and rich strove to benefit from the opportunities spawned by the Commercial Revolution. A competitive spirit defined human relations in expanding urban centers. Roads everywhere were clogged with prospective opportunists—wealthy merchants, peddlers, laborers, debt-plagued farmers, country squires, and common thieves. In the cities, morality often seemed to take a back seat to the greed of "hell-hound tradesmen" whose chicanery "sticks plaguely in the gizard."[1] Things were no better in rural areas, where there existed "such pressing and oppressing . . . about farms, trade, traffic, etc. so as a man can hardly anywhere set up a trade but he shall pull down two of his neighbors." More than one observer complained, "Was there ever more suits in law, more envy, contempt, and reproach than nowadays? . . . Even the most wise, sober, and discreet men go often to the wall, when they have done their best."[2]

While some profited enormously from the changed circumstances of English economic life, others found their high expecta-

tions all too readily dashed. Bejeweled and elaborately dressed
merchants lived in sharp contrast to the "vulgar sort" who resided
in "allies stuft with poor." When jobs were not available, "the
jeering, cunning courtesan, the rooking, roaring boy" attempted to
wheedle and bully "naive newcomers." Beggars and prostitutes
multiplied. Needy widows and runaway wives helped swell the
London populace to thirteen women for every ten men, but these
former usually found work only at the poorly paid "housewives'
trades" of cooking, baking, or service. In "the monster London"
vagabonds, pickpockets, drunkards, and idlers seemed to be
everywhere, particularly in the new tenements arising "over stables, in gardens and other odd corners." Disaster often struck unexpectedly. Storms and pirates could plunge a merchant into
bankruptcy. Economically slow periods put numerous dockhands
and Jack Tars out of work indefinitely. Highway robbers exacted
their toll from people of all social classes. The Thirty Years War
(1618–48) caused a contraction in the English textile trade, impoverishing both investors and laborers in that business.[3]

Political turmoil existed as well. The sixteenth-century Tudor
rulers had clipped the wings of the powerful nobles, but had neglected to establish their own viable bureaucracy over villages,
boroughs, and shires controlled by the local nobility. Leaders
emerged, many from the gentry, to zealously defend local autonomy. Stuart efforts at centralization in the 1620s and 1630s
confronted this "persistent localism" head on, as T. H. Breen has
pointed out, pitting "small congregations against meddling
bishops, incorporated boroughs and guilds against grasping
courtiers, local trainbands against demanding deputy lieutenants,
and almost everyone in the realm against the collectors of uncon-
stitutional revenues."[4]

For many it appeared that the world was fragmenting socially,
economically, politically, and morally. The ceaseless pursuit of
"honour, credite, welthe, jollitie etc." threatened to undermine the
traditional belief that people, like the "heavens themselves, the
planets and the centre/ Observe degree, priority, and place."[5] While
lords and ladies enjoyed "the delights of the palate," town officials
complained of the burden of aiding the unemployed poor.[6] Open
lasciviousness on the streets, play-going, gambling, and corruption
in high office convinced many English people, especially those of
conservative temperament, that conditions had gone morally hay-
wire. Religious division spiraled, assisted by the isolation of local

congregations. Catholics, Anglicans, Presbyterians, Congregationalists, and Anabaptists vied for ascendancy throughout Britain.

Englishmen and women who wished to "purify" the Church of
England felt particularly hard pressed by the changes in late sixteenth and early seventeenth century society. To convert seeming
chaos into stability, these Puritans called for a widespread cleansing
of the entire society. Relying on independent local congregations
for support, they sharply castigated the twin evils of idleness and
extravagance, denouncing their church opponents as "Dumme
Doggs, Unskilful sacrificing priests, Destroyeing Drones," and the
"Catholic Whore at Rome." Their crispness encountered Anglican
stubbornness, with the result that King James I, and then a decade
later Archbishop of Canterbury William Laud, decided either to
make Puritans "conform themselves" or to "harry them out of the
land." Between 1604 and 1611 and in the late 1620s Puritans were
frequently imprisoned; some were branded on the forehead with a
"B" for Bible-worshiper, and others had their tongues clipped, their
noses slashed, and their ears cut off. Universities were purged of
Puritan lecturers, and an occasional Separatist died on the hang-
man's gibbet. Puritan women faced the sting of the constable's
lash, while their children bore the ridicule of neighboring youngsters. Indeed, James I called anyone who attended a Separatist
meeting "a rat to be trapped and tossed away." Many a separating
and non-separating Puritan felt, like Captain Edward Johnson, that
"every corner of England was filled with the fury of malignant
adversaries."[7]

Such persecution, coupled with the anxieties produced by a
changing English lifestyle (including the significant loss of fortunes
in the decaying textile industry), led discontented Puritans to search
for stability in new, fearsome lands—Holland, that "cage of unclean
birds," and America, that land of "hideous Thickets," wild beasts,
and pagan "savages."[8] In the isolated soil of the New World they
believed it would be possible to reconstruct a "little Israel," an
uncorrupted place where Puritans could build again the Biblical
Commonwealth of Old Testament times. In America, after all, unholy rogues, foul drunkards, brazen-cheeked whores, beggars, and
covetous merchants did not exist.

That reform-minded Puritans should adopt the theological ideas
of John Calvin makes complete sense. Much concerned with the
backsliding reality of an increasingly self-seeking world, Puritans
denounced their contemporaries for failing to snuff out a prelapsar-

ian "natural pride." Suspicious and distrustful, they easily accepted Calvin's contention that the human heart was no more than "a meer nest, root, fountain of Sin, and wickedness; an evil Treasure from whence proceed evil things, viz. Evil Thoughts, Murders, Adulteries, &c."[9] Like Calvin's, the imaginative life of Puritans focused graphically upon the horrors of sin and searing hellfire. At a time when exotic foods, silk dresses, fine wines, public flirtations, and bawdy theatrical presentations threatened to overwhelm more spiritual considerations, English Calvinists reacted by condemning the "mere toys" of material existence. They shared the Geneva reformer's moral distaste for sensual pleasure.

Puritans believed English society and the Anglican Church had mistaken form for substance, thereby filling life with rituals of empty self-aggrandizement. Deviously worded business contracts, inflated prices, and usurious practices often thinly veiled unscrupulous avarice. Anglican sermons choked with "grammatic subtleties, and tortuous language" hid ministerial pomposity.[10] Curbing social and personal hypocrisy was one of the most frequently reiterated concerns in Puritan sermons. These reformers wished all speech to be plain, easily comprehensible to the unlearned peasant, and lacking affectation. Religion must be simply yet not simplistically rendered, in literal accordance with biblical principles. Apprehensive lest corrupt institutions estrange men and women from their proper humility before God, Puritans came to believe that the individual could work out his or her own reckoning with the Creator. True churches could be formed only by those who had undergone the conversion experience, and who thereby felt reasonably sure that they were among the fortunate recipients of divine grace.

Fortified by the conclusion that they were probable members of God's elect, Puritans found the emotional and ideological support necessary to cope with the evils emerging from the growth of materialism. But that same materialism had a patent appeal. Puritan divines reiterated the need for each individual to harness any tendency toward exploitation, gluttony, "promiscuous dancing," card-playing, dressing in gorgeous attire, and "the Vomits, and Quagmires" of premarital sexual intercourse.[11] Personal struggle and community watchfulness were both assumed absolutely necessary to keep Satan's hot breath in check. (By the end of the seventeenth century Puritans had, of course, bound the material and spiritual sides of life more closely, at least in terms of viewing one's "material" position in society as a reflection of one's inclusion among God's elect. However, in the pre-colonization years a sharp separation was drawn between the world of the "spirit" and the world of the "creature.")

"Saving" the Child

The Puritans who set up the New World colonies of Plymouth, Massachusetts, Connecticut, and New Haven attempted to create a carefully regulated society, one in which sin could be kept to a minimum. Various courts penalized the offender with a fine or, more publicly, with a whipping, a stocking, or time in the cage. Law codes circulated widely, especially the capital laws concerning murder, incest, bestiality, homosexuality, adultery, treason, blasphemy, etc. Churches excommunicated members for drunkenness, fornication, and disorderly speech.[12]

Calvinists in England and in America expected each person to keep his or her proper place in God's social design. They placed virtually everyone on a grid of inferiority and superiority—servant before master, non-church-member before church member, idler before working man, wife before husband, child before adult. Such a system facilitated supervision, because each master was legally accountable for overseeing the behavior of designated subordinates.

Crucial to the maintenance of religious and social order was the Puritans' attention to proper child-rearing. Godly parents were to make sure that their "unstaid and young" charges did not become addicted to the "greasy sensuality" of play—to "rattles, baubles, and such toyish stuff."[13] Pilgrim pastor John Robinson described the difficulty of such a task:

. . . surely there is in all children . . . a stubborness, and stoutness of mind arising from natural pride, which must, in the first place, be broken and beaten down; that so the foundation of their education being laid in humility and tractableness, other virtues may, in their time, be built thereon. . . . For the beating and keeping down of this stubborness parents must provide carefully . . . that the children's wills and wilfulness be restrained and repressed, and that, in time; lest sooner than they imagine, the tender sprigs grow to that stiffness, that they will rather break than bow. Children should not know, if it could be kept from them, that they have a will in their own, but in their parents' keeping; neither should these words be heard from them, save by way of consent, "I will" or "I will not."[14]

As Robinson indicated, the parent was to crush the child's drive or desire for self-assertion or independence, for such feelings might advance the child's "natural pride." Instead, adults were to inculcate in youngsters a sense of virtual helplessness before parental whim and God's authoritarian will.

In America, as in English Puritan locales, the ideal child was expected to serve the parent in a spirit of "all faithfulness and thankfulness." "Undutiful children soon become horrid Creatures," Cotton Mather asserted, and might well "commit the most Unnatural Murders." Rather, youngsters' minds must be "Struck with some awful Apprehension" of their parents' superiority and "see an awful Image of God" in that "Superiority." Saucy and clownish talk to parents, verbal defamations, and back-biting were anathema, even if parents had wrongfully injured their children.[15] If children cursed or struck their parents—except "to preserve themselves from Death or Maiming"—Puritan law specified the death penalty. New Hampshire and Connecticut also prescribed hanging for any son who refused to heed his mother's or father's voice after chastisement.[16] The authorities neglected to prosecute youngsters under such capital laws, but they did use the laws to inspire fear. In 1647 the authorities also expended some time and effort attempting to revive "the ancient practice in England of children asking their parents' blessing upon their knees,"[17] which would presumably symbolize the child's "Obedience unto the commands" of his or her parents.[18] Ipswich minister Thomas Cobbett went still further, explaining that children "should rise up and stand bare [headed] before their Parents when they come to them, or speak to them. . . . It stands not with Parents' Honour for children to sit and speak, but rather they should stand up when they speak to Parents."[19]

Puritans argued that obedience better enabled a child to control sinful impulses. It could help raise a lad's mind above play's "debasing Meannesses," and prevent that idleness in youth which "is scarcely healed without a scar in age."[20] It could substitute a sense of utter despicableness before God for "inborn" egocentricity. The father could use images of a fiery Hell to convince his offspring that, as Mather phrased it, "tis a Folly for them to pretend unto any Witt and Will of their own; they must resign all to me, who will be sure to do what is best; *my word must be their law.* . . . To be chased for a while out of my Presence I would make to be look'd upon, as the sorest Punishment in the Family."[21]

The archetypal Puritan patriarch kept his children in a state of repressive bondage. He was a classic example of what clinical psychologist Diana Baumrind calls the authoritarian parent,[22] who

values obedience as a virtue and favors punitive, forceful measures to curb self-will at points where the child's actions or beliefs conflict with what he or she thinks is right conduct. He or she believes in keeping the child in his place, in restricting his autonomy, and in assigning household responsibilities in order to inculcate respect for work. This parent regards the preservation of order and traditional structure as a highly valued end in itself. He or she does not encourage verbal give and take, believing that the child should accept the parents' word for what is right.

Such a parent believed that "too much doting affection" distracted children from thoughts of God, or led them to consider themselves their parents' equals. Minister Thomas Cobbett warned that "fondness and Familiarity breeds . . . contempt and irreverence in children." Robert Cleaver believed "cockering" children with affection could only ruin them: "For as the Ape doth with too much embracings, well neer kill her young whelpes: so likewise some indiscrete parents, through immoderate love and over-much pampering and cherishing do utterly despoil and mar their children. Therefore, if parents would have their children live, they must take heed that they love them not too much."[23]

Puritans stressed discipline more than affection. In English Puritan households, according to one scholar, "the rod was most favored" as a punitive device. In America, the Massachusetts *Body of Liberties* (1641) prohibited "unnaturall severitie" toward the young, but did not specify when punishment became "severe" or "unnatural."[24] The adult faced prosecution when he broke a child's bones, endangered the child's life, or delivered a cudgeling with "a walnut tree plant, big enough to have killed a horse"[25]—but only three of nearly three dozen such offenders received more than an admonition or a very small fine.[26] Still, New England Puritans did not oppose the use of the "Rod of Correction"; in fact, they considered it "an ordinance of God," suitable to inspire "love and fear."[27] Cotton Mather stated it simply: "Better whipt, than Damn'd."[28]

Not only parents, but society's leaders also reinforced constraint and submissiveness in children. Ministers prepared catechisms which attacked self-confidence and emphasized the need for youngsters to honor, respect, and obey all "Superiors whether in Family, School, Church, and Common-wealth."[29] Schoolmasters freely used the rod to beat down individual will.[30] The authors of the *New England Primer* warned their readers: "From Death's Arrest no Age is free,/ Young Children too may die," and urged them to make eleven basic promises—four of which directly enjoined reverence, obedience, and submission to "superiors."[31] "Grave and sober" overseers disciplined youngsters who became unruly during the long Sunday sermons.[32] Town selectmen periodically checked up on families to make sure children were taught religious principles at home.[33] If, in the selectmen's judgment, a child was not receiving proper religious training, said child might be taken away from his or her parents and placed with a more holy family.[34]

Growing up in a Puritan home was certainly painful. Strict control through the family and all other social institutions often created a feeling of profound helplessness in children. This phenomenon had wide-ranging impact, for, as psychologist Martin Seligman has shown, repeated and sustained perceptions of an inability to control one's outcomes can lead to a state of chronic despair.[35] Many boys and girls, in true Puritan fashion, lamented their own despicability and great sinfulness. Elizabeth Butcher, aged two and one-half, purportedly asked herself often from the cradle "the question, What is my corrupt Nature? and would make answer to herself, It is empty of Grace, bent into Sin, and only to Sin, and that continually."[36] Jerusha Oliver, "While her infancy was hardly yet expired," professed many sins. Depressed by her backsliding, at age twelve she began sequestering herself for entire days, so that she could repent.[37] Sarah Derby "set up almost all night, crying to the Lord, that he would please apply unto her, by His own Holy Spirit, a Promise, which might Releive the Disconsolations of her Soul."[38] Recurrent melancholia assailed Samuel Sewall's daughter Elizabeth between the ages of seven and fifteen.[39] One minister's son, Nathaniel Shrove, hoped for death, that he might avoid sin—and then decided he was too despicable to deserve even that.[40]

These were anxiety-ridden, insecure, unhappy children—the products of a culture which devalued independent thought, self-satisfaction, exuberance, and real closeness. A consideration of their anguish and preoccupations can help us to understand the Puritan psyche, particularly as it affected attitudes toward the female sex. With good cause, Erik Erikson has written, " . . . if we should choose to overlook or belittle the phenomena of childhood, along with the best and worst of our childhood dreams, we shall have failed to recognize one of the eternal sources of human anxiety and grief."[41]

The Child as "Father of the Man"

Boys and girls who had to be submissive and self-condemning could hardly have abandoned their deep-seated insecurities in the relative freedom of adulthood. Nor were they magnificently transformed by the conversion experience, by the grand feeling of God's grace operating upon their own souls. The manifold tensions and frustrations, agitated by innumerable sermons and by the disquieting complexities of Puritan theology, continued to fester like spiritual sores, defining and constricting the Puritan's inner life. Although men could exercise real control over many aspects of their individual lives, they had trouble accepting the reality of that control; their childrearing had predisposed them, both psychologically and intellectually, to think in terms of their own virtual powerlessness before God and their own sinful nature. Since the *belief* that one has (or lacks) power governs subjective experience, and thus objective behavior, a theology of ultimate powerlessness almost certainly had a profound effect on the psychological well-being of individuals—no matter what possibilities for freedom and self-realization a New World might have to offer.

Although an occasional Puritan—a woman like Anne Bradstreet, for example—could conquer the helplessness ingrained in childhood, the diaries of many of her contemporaries testify to the problems Puritans experienced, as adults, in reconciling their own material needs with their supposedly inherent sinfulness, their own childhood patterns of religious anxiety with their conversion experiences, their own feelings of despicableness and powerlessness before God with their continuing human need to feel self-control and personal value. Melancholy ran deep through the Calvinist character; ministers frequently urged their parishioners to "look to your Coffins, and walk to your gravesside often, and so stand there and hear the cry and see the Lord acoming."[42] Such sermons surely had an effect, because they emphasized the gravity implicit within the Calvinist worldview. A man like Philip Pain held himself to be "but dust," daily composed depressing "considerations of death and eternity," and often walked in cemeteries, asking God to utterly terrify him each day as a reminder that death and the probable "cursed Doom" of hell were nigh. Puritans, unable to become absolutely assured of their salvation and morally crippled by a belief in their natural depravity, "were possessed of an intense, overt fear of death"—whereas other contemporary Christians more often viewed it as "an outlet from sin and misery, and an in-let to Glory both in Holiness and Happiness."[43]

Puritan diaries are filled with references to inner religious turmoil.[44] Watertown minister John Baily's diary is the woeful account of his fears concerning salvation. One day he wrote, "I was almost in the suburbs of hell all day; . . . I saw death and sin full of terror: I thought I never [really] sought the glory of God: Oh! what a matchless wretch am I: Oh! that I could love above all things, and seek the glory of God, and live contentedly on him alone!" Baily criticized himself for feeling too cheerful, and castigated himself for the loathsome sins of "unadvised words," being "too forgetful of God," "exceeding in tobacco," and "prayerlessness." He sometimes spent the hours between 8 A.M. and 3 P.M. in constant prayer; when he flagged after five hours in one session, he upbraided himself for not continuing the full seven hours with equal ardor.[45]

Michael Wigglesworth likewise felt himself inexorably sinful. As a youngster he, in his own words, lacked "natural affection and pity" for his "afflicted parents." Constantly haunted by "creature comforts" and assailed by pride, passionate "distempers," vain thoughts, and lustful longings, he often fell into fits of melancholy.[46] His "stirrings of fleshly lusts" and periodic wet dreams filled him with so much personal guilt that he considered himself a beast before God and developed an apparently psychosomatic penile discharge.[47] Wigglesworth spent a tremendous amount of time lamenting his vileness and condemning himself for being a "viper" in God's nourishing bosom. Hopelessly frustrated in his need for some genuine sense of power over his own life, he attempted to treat his students as harshly as he felt God had treated him.[48] In his widely read poem Day of Doom Wigglesworth described a horrifying God who punished sinners with an unquenchable wrath and placed justice, hard and cold, before mercy. A stern, threatening figure, He held a schoolmaster's rod over a cringing audience.[49] Wigglesworth's God became an incarnation of his not unaccountable but extreme needs. With apparent envy, the minister described an omnipotent, all-controlling authoritarian. Wigglesworth's own feelings of inadequacy, of despicableness, led him to devalue his own actual power as a religious leader in the community; thus that power became a purely negative, unconsciously vengeful force, rather than a positive source of self-esteem.

Edward Taylor's conception of God was somewhat different, although his God too disliked man's fascination with material things. Taylor feared lest worldly "sweets," like card-playing, bowling, riches, and sex, tempt him into hell. He asked God to help him break the material "Garison" in which he felt trapped: "Oh! let the Clouds of they sweet Vapours rise,/and both my Mammularies Circumcise." Taylor's choice of images here was precise, for he realized that the particularly sensitive parts of the body, the phallus and the nipples, corrupted the sweetness of God. To cut out the nipples—those symbolic sustainers of the material world—brought greater consciousness of the spiritual alternative, God's sweetness.[50] Yet Taylor continued to worry about his own sensuality. Unable to circumcise his mammularies, he did the next-best thing —he spiritualized his unacceptable materiality by describing the interaction between God and man in vividly sensual terms. He wished Christ to "kiss me with the Kisse of his mouth," for Christ is the "Fairest among Women," one whose "Flame" of "rich Grace" "do ravish with delight." He requested God to put the savior's "nibbles then my mouth into/ And suckle me therewith I humbly pray,/ Then with his milk thy Sprituall Babe I'st grew."[51] Taylor's Christ was the consoling wife-mother,[52] the virgin drawing her lover to the baptism of purity,[53] both the one seduced and the awe-inspiring, magnificently endowed seducer,[54] as well as the fertilizing sperm.[55]

The world's riches—silver, gold, pearls, precious stones, apparel, and perfume—plagued Taylor's imaginative life. Here, too, he abstracted his own impulses and projected them onto the Lord. His descriptions of Christ and heaven were ornamental in the extreme; Christ had cheeks like "a Bed of Spices," lips like "Lillies, dropping sweet smelling Myrrh," legs like pillars of marble on bases of fine gold, and a belly like "bright Ivory overlaid with Saphires." In heaven itself mansions abounded, and the streets were composed of transparent gold.[56]

Edward Taylor, a man of extremely fertile imagination, enjoyed a rather close relationship with his God, at least on some abstract level. As was true for Michael Wigglesworth, Taylor's God became a reflection of his own anxious needs. Desiring the world's riches and the joy of sexual fullfillment, Taylor saw his God as an idealized representation of those same sinful longings. Presumably if God

justified them, albeit only on a metaphorical level, their actual despicableness was less; if so, then they became more tolerable on a
material level. Yet Edward Taylor did not rest content in his relatively self-affirming theology. Like so many other Calvinists, he
agonized over the state of his soul and his feelings of worthlessness. This Westfield pastor realized all too well that lasciviousness,
blasphemy, murderous impulses, malice, tyranny, wrath, and
atheism could easily slip into the unwary mind to "bed and board,"
thereby making "the heart a sty/ Of all Abominable Brothlery."[57] Apparently his heart slipped into such abominations quite frequently,
because Taylor constantly demeaned himself. His verbal self-
portrait would have frightened children as much as Wigglesworth's
Day of Doom did, for his positive, spiritualized sensual imagery gave
way to its negative counterpart of material decay and loathsome-
ness. In his poetry Taylor describes himself as

a dirt ball, a muddy sewer, a tumbrel of dung, a dung-hill, a dot of dung, a
varnished pot of putrid excrements, drops in a closestool pan, guts, garbage, and rottenness. He wears a crown of filth, his cheeks are covered with
spider's vomit, and he is candied over with leprosy. He is also a pouch of
passion, a lump of loathesomeness, a bag of botches, a lump of lewdness;
and he gives off a nauseous stink. He is wrapped in slime; pickled in gall; a
sink of nastiness; and a dirty, smelly dish cloth: he is, in short, "all blot."[58]

The extremity of Edward Taylor's self-abuse and the gloom of
Michael Wigglesworth's experience were in some degree duplicated
in the Mather family. As a youngster, Increase Mather "Swam
quietly in a Stream of Impiety and Carnal Security" until he, at age
fifteen (1654), fell ill with "a sore Disease," repented, and had the
conversion experience. Absorbed with introspection and ridiculed by his companions for his "strictness," he bewailed his "pride,
passion, sloth, selfishness, sensuality, earthly mindedness, and
unbelief." Increase was tormented by sinful dreams and, reflecting
his own sense of helplessness, asserted his "failings in every place"
where he had lived, as well as "in every relation" he had sustained.
He and his wife, Mary, observed a rigid fast more than once a
month, spending entire days in their closet to express before God
the "Extremity of Anguish" in their souls. Increase sometimes
found himself "Desirous to Dy," but ultimately decided to live "that
I may Glorify GOD in my Lord Jesus Christ."[59]
The example of Increase Mather was not without effect on his

family. His son Nathaniel expressed much guilt over his own whit-
tling on the Sabbath; "for fear of being seen, I did it behind the
door," he later lamented, "A great reproach of God! A specimen
of that atheism that I brought into the world with me!"[60] Nathaniel's brother, Cotton Mather, "began to pray almost as soon as to
speak"[61] and throughout his life spent a good deal of time groveling
in the dust of his closet. By smearing his face in that dust, he
attempted to demonstrate his "Inexpressible Self-Abhorrence."[62]
Cotton swung between exalted and depressed moods, often loath-
ing himself for excessive pride, slothfulness, envy, selfishness,
"earthly-mindedness," and, in particular, lust. Having feared the
dreadful possibility of masturbation in his twenties, Mather again
experienced severe temptation to sexual "Impurities" when he
neared age forty. (His first wife had died.) Only at forty-eight
could he state emphatically, "I renounce the FLESH. . . . I rebuke,
I restrain, I deny the Flesh in its irregular Inclinations."[63]

Struggling with manifold temptations, Cotton Mather often
lamented his own vileness. Even the most unexpected moments
could be turned into times of reflection upon his own debasement.
For example, on a June day in 1700, after he had emptied the
chamber pot, Mather began urinating against a wall. A nearby dog
soon copied the minister's example, and Mather began to wail,
"What mean, and vile Things are the Children of Men, in this mortal
State! How much do our natural Necessities abase us, and place us
in some regard, on the same level with the very Dogs!" In the
fearsome and anxiety-ridden world of Calvinism, it was difficult for
a man even to urinate without feeling enslaved by his condition
of beastliness.[64]

Cotton Mather was a strong minister, measured by the society in
which he lived. His writings were read in New England and abroad.
His name was well respected by his Puritan compatriots. Still, he
had an uneasy sense of his own power. Often he complained of
"Peoples' Cheating and Starving their Ministers (which they horribly do)" and believed that "a numerous Crue in this Town" raised a
"Storm of Clamour and Slander against mee."[65] Any little criticism
was intolerable to this man who felt so insecure about his own
relationship to God. He wrote nearly four hundred religious tracts
and sermons—approximately one-fourth of all the works published
in New England before his death—in an obsessive effort to prove his
ability and communicate *his* truth. Still, Mather was a kindly man;
he kept pennies, fruits, and paints upon his person to treat little

children, sometimes gave away a thousand books a year to bed-ridden women, and aided countless other needy people.[66] Yet he was also a man who reflected the peculiar tensions of his culture. Like so many of his contemporaries, he suffered attacks of what modern psychologists would call clinical depression—that state characterized by a devastating loss of self-confidence, a deep sense of personal failure, a severe feeling of despair, and profound helplessness.

Baily, Wigglesworth, Taylor, and the Mathers were exceptional men. However, they all shared in the anguish which the Puritan way foisted upon young children. Self-hatred and feelings of powerlessness, a need to separate themselves from the joys of the material world, and fear of sex characterized both their childhood training and their adult behavior, at great emotional cost. Struggling for a sense of power and control, Puritans sought not just to guide but to order the lives of their offspring. In turn, those sons and daughters, fighting their own feelings of worthlessness, desired to regiment and regulate all aspects of their own children's lives. So was the culture carried on. In the process, the child became little more than a projection of the adult's own fears. When an unsupervised youngster fell into the fire or was otherwise injured, the father, in particular, distanced himself from any complicity in the injury (e.g., for leaving the child alone) and avoided expressing any real empathy for the child's distress. Instead, he perceived the event as a providential punishment of himself.[67]

For Puritans, hierarchical social roles conveyed a sense of significance and order in an insecure world threatened by satanic chaos. Because they remembered English conditions, Calvinists in the New World tended to rigidify the age and sex roles that had prevailed there, so that those roles became not only enforceable but, from their perspective, inevitable. Belief in the importance of a rigid hierarchy helped magistrates and ministers to conquer their personal feelings of ineffectuality, as they became the hawk-like, punitive guardians of the Biblical Commonwealth. In the family the Puritan male found a small niche where he was granted the nearly absolute authority with which he found himself constantly confronted elsewhere. There he could exercise a power not his own, not spontaneous or creative, but built into the position which he had "earned" by submitting to and internalizing the social system. Having little control over his own religiously conditioned inner life of spiritual anguish, the man compensated by "thrashing down natu-

ral pride" in his children and dominating his wife. Not that this gave
him inner satisfaction, for his childhood training and many contemporary sermons reminded him of his own emotional helplessness
before God. His wife was in an even worse situation, since she was
subject to her husband's direct control and could exercise only
limited authority over her children.

The Need to Keep Women Down

Puritan males in England on the eve of colonization had good
reason to believe that, as John Milton later put it, "God's universal
law gave to man despotic power/ Over his female in due awe."[68]
Such men were suffering from a profound sense of their own powerlessness, arising from James's and Archbishop Laud's persecution, Charles I's dissolution of the pro-Puritan Parliament, the depression of the Puritan-dominated textile market, and the increasing
materialism of English life. Unable to have much concrete effect on
the sinfulness of the contemporary world, they overcompensated
by ruling that one thing which lay within their purview: the home.

Puritan males were appalled that some of the "weaker sex" responded positively to the materialism then saturating English culture. Calvinist divines attacked women who drank all too freely,
engaged in maypole-dancing, painted their faces, enticed men,
adorned themselves in the latest fashions, and vainly spent "their
golden daies in filthie idlenesse and sinne."[69] Especially detestable
were those females who spent "a good part of the day in tricking and
trimming, pricking and pinning, pranking and pouncing, gir-
dling and lacing, and *brauing* up themselves in most exquisit manner . . . whereupon they do so exceedingly swell with pride, that it
is to be feared, they will burst with it as they walk in the streets."
"It seemeth," opined one Puritan, "that such women are altogether
a lumpe of pride, a masse of pride, euen altogether made of pride,
and nothing else but pride, pride."[70] According to another observer,
the use of cosmetics was a preliminary to adultery and witchcraft.[71]

Although Puritan men opposed contemporary arranged marriages, the sale of wives, and husbands who treated their wives like
whores, male Calvinists felt threatened by the growing momentum
of the feminist movement in Elizabethan and Jacobean England.[72]
At a time when some praised women's strength of intellect, Puritans attacked female education as corruptive because it created an
"unnatural" interest in amorous classical poetry and voluptuous

love stories. In 1616 Robert Anton contended that some educated women went so far as to compose bawdy verse.[73] Both Puritans and Anglicans inveighed against those "Masculine-women" who cut off their long hair, put on men's hats and plumes, and then went about with "a Leaden-Hall Dagger, a High-Way Pistol . . . and behauior sutable or exceeding euery repeated deformitie."[74] Desiring to keep sex roles separate, Calvinist ministers denounced stage plays partly because male actors dressed in women's garments to play female roles.[75]

Puritan males particularly disliked the egalitarianism of men like Daniel Tuvill and William Austin. In *Asylum Veneris, Or a Sanctuary for Ladies* (1616) Tuvill asserted that man's presumption of superiority derived from self-conceit, while Austin's *Haec Homo, Wherein the Excellency of the Creation of Women Is described* (1637) argued that the sexes differed only in body, having the "same reasonable soule," the "same mind," and the "same understanding."[76] Puritan divines, on the contrary, affirmed the "natural" superiority of husband over wife and urged wives not to become too familiar with their mates. The Reverend William Gouge went so far as to recommend that wives call their spouses "Husband," avoiding such pet names as "Sweet, Sweeting, Heart, Sweet-heart, Ioy, Deare, &c" or even using their Christian names.[77] Order in the home was a clearcut Puritan priority, for "Such as Families are, such at last the Church and Commonwealth must be."[78]

From parent, husband, and pulpit, Puritan women learned that they were supposed to submit to male rule. If a wife tried to exercise much self-government, she had to confront the fact that her own expression of freedom threatened to destroy the God-created hierarchy of her own family and Puritan society. Although the Puritan woman might feel (as Flavia summed it up in the play *Albumazar*) that "Our sex is most wretched, nurs'd up from infancy in continual slavery,"[79] she had little opportunity to rebel while still maintaining the integrity of her belief system.

Did moving to a New World change all that, providing a fertile soil where women could become self-supporting and comparatively free from male dominion? Elizabeth Wade White argues as much when she declares:

During the first cruel winters when famine, disease, the lurking Indians and the inescapable cold were ever-present enemies, the men and women fought shoulder to shoulder, and when the worst battles were over the survivors looked at one another as tested human beings, rather than as members of a superior and inferior sex.[80]

Roger Thompson maintains that the perennial shortage of laborers drew women out of their homes, that the frontier ethos made novelty in male-female relationships more acceptable, and that the shortage of available wives curbed male arrogance.[81] Other scholars speculate just the opposite,[82] but neither group supplies much evidence for its contentions. Certainly, the male Puritans who came to New England's shores and grew up in the various Biblical Commonwealths had great needs for power, since the impotence and repressed vitality of childhood remained with them throughout their lives. Enforced church attendance and catechism lessons served to remind Puritan men and women of their despicableness and helplessness before God. School discipline helped deprive children of any sense of their own independence. Unlike most of their English counterparts, New England magistrates were Puritans and could easily punish improper role behavior whenever they observed it. Community watchfulness made deviation from Puritan norms less likely. Yet, at the same time, these transplanted English men and women were in a new environment, a wilderness which could conceivably enshroud time-trusted social forms and institutions. A more comprehensive examination of Puritan sex roles in theory and in practice is needed before we can even begin to understand the social conditions and frustrations experienced by maidens, goodwives, and widows in seventeenth-century New England.

1. Quoted in Bridenbaugh, *Vexed & Troubled Eng.*, p. 164; Rowse, *Eng. of Eliz.*, pp. 81–85, 110–11.

2. C[ushman], "Reasons & Considerations," in *Mourt's Rel.*, pp. 101–8.

3. Bridenbaugh, *Vexed & Troubled Eng.*, pp. 27, 59, 162–64, 167, 183.

4. Breen, "Persistent Localism."

5. See John Winthrop, quoted in Morgan, *Puritan Dilemma*, p. 16; Ulysses in Shakespeare's *Troilus & Cressida*, I:iii, ll. 85–86.

6. C[ushman], "Reasons & Considerations," in *Mourt's Rel.*, p. 107; Winthrop, "Fragmentary Letter, 1629," in A. Forbes, ed., *Winthrop Papers*, II, 123, 139.

7. Morgan, *Visible Saints*, pp. 7–9; Leynse, *Preceding the Mayflower*, pp. 42, 52, 59, 66, 69, 77; E. Johnson, *Wonder-Working Prov.*, p. 23. Descriptions of early Puritan difficulties appear in Collinson, *Eliz. Puritan Movement*; Frere, *Eng. Church*; Haller, *Rise of Puritanism*.

8. Fisk, *Beginnings of N. Eng.*, p. 74; W. Bradford, *Of Plym. Plant.*, pp. 25–26.

9. Calvin, *Institutes of Christian Rel.*, I, 314–16; Wadsworth, "Nature of Early Piety," p. 10.

10. Miller & Johnson, eds., *Puritans*, p. 70.

11. For Puritan concerns, see sermons in Chandos, ed., *In God's Name*, pp. 87–92, 109, 151–96, 225–28, 245, 250–51. Stubbes, *Anatomy of Abuses*, contains a very detailed list of those English activities which Puritans considered particularly sinful.

12. Powers, *Crime & Punishment in Mass.*, and Oberholzer, *Delinquent Saints*, are essential to understanding how Puritans controlled sinful behavior.

13. C. Mather, *Help for Parents*, p. 29; W. Bradford, "Descriptive Account of N. Eng. in Verse," p. 82; A. Bradstreet, "Four Ages of Man," in *Works*, p. 54.

14. Robinson, *Works*, I, 246–47.

15. C. Mather, *Early Rel.*, pp. 115–16; T. Shepard, "Letter," pp. 193, 196; J. Janeway, *Token for Children*, preface.

16. Shurtleff, ed., *Mass. Rec.*, II, 179; Trumbull, ed., *Conn. Rec.*, I, 515; *New-Haven's Settling in New-England and Some Lawes for Government* (London, 1656), in Hoadly, ed., *Rec. of N. Haven 1653–Union*, p. 576; Bouton, ed., *Prov. Papers of N. Hamp.*, I, 385.

17. Winthrop, *Journal*, II, 324.

18. C. Mather, *Family Well-Ordered*, pp. 60–61.

19. Cobbett, *Fruitfull Discourse*, p. 94.

20. C. Mather, *Diary*, I, 536; Norton, *Abel Being Dead*, p. 9.

21. C. Mather, "Some Special Points Relating to the Education of My Children," in Mather, *Diary*, I, 535.

22. Baumrind, "From Each According to Her Ability," p. 179. Baumrind juxtaposes the authoritarian parent against the permissive parent. The latter behaves in "an affirmative, acceptant, and benign manner toward the child's impulses and actions." Such a parent gives the "child as much freedom as is consistent with the child's physical survival. Freedom to the permissive parent means absence of restraint."

23. Wigglesworth, *Diary*, p. 328; Cobbett, *Fruitfull Discourse*, p. 96; Cleaver, *A godlie forme of govt.*, p. 296. David Stannard has observed that, in a century of high childhood mortality, the creation of "due distance" between parent and child served to insulate the parents against the potential shock of their offspring's death ("Death & Puritan Child," pp. 463–67).

24. Calhoun, *Social Hist. of Am. Family*, I, 40; "Coppie of Liberties of Mass.," p. 230.

25. See, e.g., "Rec., Ct. of Assts., 1665–77," in "Conn. Rec.," LVI, 4–5; G. Dow, ed., *Essex Ct. Rec.*, I, 257; VI, 141, 299–300; VIII, 295–96, 341; Winthrop, *Journal*, I, 310–14.

26. Winthrop, *Journal*, I, 310–14; G. Dow, ed., *Essex Ct. Rec.*, I, 202; Libby, Allen, & Moody, eds., *Maine Ct. Rec.*, II, 351.

27. Boston Rec. Cmrs., *Rep. Containing Dorchester Town Rec.*, p. 56; C. Mather, *Diary*, I, 535–36; C. Mather, *Family Well-Ordered*, pp. 22–23; T. Hooker, *Soules' Humiliation*, p. 188.

28. C. Mather, *Help for Parents*, p. 28.

29. John Cotton, *Spiritual Milk*, pp. 4, 7, 19. Cotton's and at least three

other catechisms went into three editions before the seventeenth century ended. Between 1641 and 1660 alone, eight different ministers prepared catechisms.

30. Boston Rec. Cmrs., *Rep. Containing Dorchester Town Rec.*, p. 56; Winthrop, *Journal*, I, 310–14; C. Mather, *Diary*, I, 535–36; Barnard, "Autobiography," p. 178.

31. *N. Eng. Primer*, I, 381–83. The other seven "promises" were pledges to love friends, hate no man, forgive enemies, keep the commandments, respect the Lord's Day, learn the catechism, and revere God's sanctuary.

32. Shurtleff, ed., *Mass. Rec.*, V, 61; Boston Rec. Cmrs., *Rep. Containing Boston Town Rec., 1630–59*, p. 31; Boston Rec. Cmrs., *Rep. Containing Dorchester Town Rec.*, p. 230; W. Bliss, *Side Glimpses*, pp. 97–98.

33. Shurtleff, ed., *Mass. Rec.*, II, 6–7; Axtell, *School upon a Hill*, pp. 21–26; Murphy, "Mass. Bay Col: Role of Govt. in Educ."

34. Pulsifer, trans., "Rec. of Middlesex Ct.," I, 89; III, 87–88, 290; Hamp. Ct. of "Gen. Sessions," pp. 36, 100, 145–46.

35. Seligman, *Helplessness*. The traumatic effects of a feeling of helplessness, which Seligman documents on laboratory animals and in human life, appear to be particularly disabling and lasting when they occur in childhood. Motivation, cognition, and emotional affect can all be impaired by that trauma, so that a self-perpetuating state of chronic despair or passivity results. Because Seligman's data consist of rather extreme cases, he does not discuss the likelihood that some degree of reaction formation, or even overcompensation, may occur when the traumatic conditioning is less severe or absolute. This response was particularly available to the adult Puritan male, placed as he was in a socially defined position of automatic dominance over women and children.

36. Quoted in Caulfield, "Pediatric Aspects," p. 799.

37. C. Mather, *Memorials of Early Piety*, pp. 4–6.

38. C. Mather, *Early Rel.*, pp. 109–12.

39. Sewall, *Diary*, I, 308, 419–20, 422–23, 437.

40. C. Mather, *Early Rel.*, pp. 85–94.

41. Erikson, *Identity, Youth, & Crisis*, p. 120.

42. T. Shepard, *Parable of Ten Virgins*, II, 49.

43. Pain, *Daily Meditations*, pt. 1, p. 6; Stannard, "Death & Dying in N. Eng.," pp. 1305–30.

44. Preparing the heart to receive God's grace involved a long and agonizing personal struggle. Even the Puritan who reached the stage of assurance continued to be assailed by lingering doubts. As Edmund S. Morgan has explained, "If they ceased, that would be a sign that he had never had faith to begin with, but had merely deluded himself and had not entered into the covenant of grace." See Morgan, *Visible Saints*, p. 69; Pettit, *Heart Prepared*; Feinstein, "Prepared Heart," pp. 167–76.

45. Baily, "Diary," pp. 504–7.

46. Wigglesworth, *Diary*, pp. 322–24, 332–33, 344, 365–66, 371–72, 378, 400. Warren, *N. Eng. Conscience*, gives a short but good description of the particular neurotic concerns of Wigglesworth (pp. 66–75) and Cotton Mather (pp. 76–87).

47. Wigglesworth, *Diary*, pp. 323–25, 369, 380, 388–91, 399, 402–6.

48. *Ibid.*, pp. 323, 326, 328, 345–46, 350, 376.

49. Wigglesworth, *Day of Doom*, ll. 55–114.

50. E. Taylor, "Med. 40, 2:97, 38, 3" in his *Poems*, pp. 64, 250, 62, 8.

51. "Meds. 2:96, 2:128, 2:150," "God's Determinations," *ibid.*, pp. 254, 315, 354, 414.

52. "God's Determinations," *ibid.*, p. 414.

53. "Med. 2:70," *ibid.*, p. 211.

54. "Med. 5," *ibid.*, p. 16.

55. "Med. 2:80," *ibid.*, p. 230.

56. "Meds. 2:119–2:127, 23, 2:97, 2:89, 3," *ibid.*, pp. 300–314, 39, 256, 242, 8.

57. "God's Determinations," *ibid.*, p. 410.

58. Grabo, *Edward Taylor*, p. 53. See also Bach, "Self-Depreciation in Taylor's *Sacramental Meds.*," pp. 45–59.

59. C. Mather, *Parentator*, pp. 7–10, 24, 41, 69; Murdock, *Increase Mather*, pp. 5, 89–90, 99; I. Mather, "Autobiography."

60. C. Mather, *Magnalia*, I, 216.

61. Marvin, *Life & Times of C. Mather*, p. 6, quoting Mather's son Samuel.

62. C. Mather, *Diary*, I, 237.

63. *Ibid.*, I, 15–18, 38, 43, 45–46, 79–80, 110, 224, 457–58, 467, 475–77, 484, 492; II, 119.

64. *Ibid.*, I, 357.

65. *Ibid.*, I, 338, 351; II, 707.

66. *Ibid.*, II, 46, 85, 102, 160, 213–14, 278, 344, 349, 364, 589.

67. De Mause's "Evol. of Childhood," pp. 1–73 in his *Hist. of Childhood*, details the inability of parents to relate to children empathetically, in the seventeenth century and at other times.

68. Quoted in K. Rogers, *Troublesome Helpmate*, p. 157.

69. G. Bradford, *Eliz. Women*, pp. 64–65, 72–73; Wright, *Middle-Class Culture*, p. 503; Ashley, *Stuarts in Love*, p. 7.

70. Dent, *Plaine Man's Path-way to Heauen*, pp. 45–46.

71. Tuke, *Treatise against Painting*.

72. Dusinberre, *Shakespeare & Women*, pp. 110–11; G. Bradford, *Eliz. Women*; Wright, *Middle-Class Culture*, pp. 217–18, 465–507; Heinrich, "Frauenfrage."

73. Wright, *Middle-Class Culture*, pp. 112–13.

74. Knappen, *Tudor Puritanism*, p. 495; Wright, *Middle-Class Culture*, p. 493.

75. Notestein, *Eng. People on Eve of Coloniz.*, pp. 154–55.

76. Notestein, "Eng. Woman 1580–1650," p. 93; Wright, *Middle-Class Culture*, pp. 218, 502–3, 495.

77. Wright, *Middle-Class Culture*, pp. 222–23.

78. James Fitch, quoted in Greven, *Four Generations*, p. xx. The English Puritan Daniel Rogers explained how important the institution of marriage was, in Calvinist thinking: "Marriage is the Preservative of Chastity, the Seminary of the Common-wealth, seed-plot of the Church, pillar (under God) of the world, right-hand of providence, supporter of lawes, states, orders and offices, gifts and services: the glory of peace, the sinews of warre, the maintenance of policy, the life of the dead, the solace of the

living, the ambition of virginity, the foundation of Countries, Cities, Universities, succession of Families, Crownes and Kingdomes" (Rogers, *Matrimonial Honour* [1642], quoted in Haller & Haller, "Puritan Art of Love," pp. 246–47).

79. Quoted in Notestein, "Eng. Woman 1580–1650," p. 85.

80. E. White, "Tenth Muse," p. 376.

81. Thompson, *Women in Stuart Eng. & Am.*; P. Smith, *Daughters of Promised Land*, pp. 37–57, argues the same position.

82. E. Davis, *First Sex*, pp. 286–93; Sinclair, *Emacipation of Am. Woman*, pp. 3–8; Flexner, *Century of Struggle*, pp. 7–12.

II

Sex-Role Stereotyping in Puritan Ideology and Practice

. . . the things that most women mean when they speak of "happiness," that is, love and children and the little republic of the home, depend on the favour of men, and the qualities that win this favour are not in general those that are most useful for other purposes.
—Emily James Putnam, *The Lady*

"The Weaker Sex" in Puritan Ideology

LIKE SO MANY OF THEIR EUROPEAN CONTEMPORARIES, NEW ENGLAND'S male Puritan leaders assumed that the obvious physical differences between the sexes had important social consequences. Throughout the seventeenth century these authorities argued and acted as if they believed anatomy alone determined destiny. In virtually all avenues of behavior Puritans affirmed the differences and deemphasized the similarities between the sexes—a practice which usually worked to the disadvantage of women. Because Puritan men had a high need to prove that they wielded some sort of power, in the face of the impotence inculcated in childhood and a theology of man's ultimate powerlessness before God, they tended to exaggerate prevailing notions of male superiority. While such men referred to themselves as the "Magnanimous, Masculine, and Heroicke sexe," every woman became a "poore fraile" creature—the "weaker sex."[1] As Elnathan Chauncy scrawled in his commonplace book, "Y^e soule consists of two portions inferior and superior[;] the superior is masculine and aeternal. Y^e inferior foeminine and mortal."[2] Custom meshed with psychological need for Puritans and non-Puritans alike—with sometimes bizarre results.

Beginning with conception and birth, profound developmental differences were assumed between male and female infants. Some physicians hypothesized that the male child was conceived earlier than the female because the male, as a higher, more sophisticated form of life, needed more time to develop in the womb.[3] On the other hand, some religious leaders asserted that the male embryo, in recognition of its ultimate superiority, received his soul on the fortieth day, while the female embryo had to wait until the eightieth day before she acquired hers. When a woman had conceived twins of each sex, those twins supposedly occupied segregated uterine chambers to breathe into them the "laws of chastity."[4] When the twins or a single child was ready to enter the outside world, the birth of a male was easier, according to the English obstetrical expert Thomas Raynalde. The reason for this was simple: babies were presumed to find their way into the outer world under their own power, and boys, being more vigorous than girls, got out faster. After delivery, the attending midwives cut a girl's navel string shorter than a boy's, "because they believe it makes . . . [females] modest, and their [genital] Parts narrower, which makes them more acceptable to their husbands."[5]

Daughters were "less long'd for" than sons,[6] perhaps in part because English obstetrical guides asserted that mothers who were carrying boys enjoyed fair complexions, red nipples, and white milk, while girls gave them "a pale, heavy, and swarth[y] countenance, a melancolique eye," black nipples, and watery bluish milk.[7] At birth Puritan daughters, in particular, often received names which providentially reminded them of the limitations of their feminine destiny: Silence, Fear, Patience, Prudence, Mindwell, Comfort, Hopestill, and Be Fruitful. No Calvinist girl would ever bear an impressive name such as Freeborne, Fearnot, or Wrestling.

Puritan males, like so many of their English contemporaries, valued those characteristics in women which would insure submissiveness. The ideal woman blushed readily and chose "to be seen rather than Heard whenever she comes." She held her tongue until asked by her father or husband to speak; then only good, comforting words flowed from her mouth.[8] "The greatest Nuisance in Nature," Joseph Beacon unequivocatingly wrote, "is an immodest impudent Woman."[9] The ideal female displayed "an Eminence in Modesty, reserve, purity, temperance, humility, truth, meekness, patience, courtesie, affability, charity, goodness, mercy, [and] compassion," taking special care to avoid the "monstrous" decorative habit of painting the face with "varnish."[10] Tender, consoling, and in need of careful direction, she was viewed as a defenseless creature, "that naked Sex that hath no arms but for imbraces."[11]

In Puritan terms, women needed men, not only for physical protection and financial support but also to prevent themselves from going intellectually astray. Since the woman was presumed less able to ground her spiritual development in the cold logic of reason, Puritan divines told her to consult her father, her husband, or a minister whenever she wished to comprehend a theological issue.[12] In fact, too much intellectual activity, on a theological or any other plane, might overtax her frail mind and thereby debilitate her equally weak body. In 1645 Emmanuel Downing claimed his wife, Lucy, made herself sick "by trying new Conclusions"; he suggested riding as a cure. In the same year Downing's brother-in-law, Massachusetts Governor John Winthrop, asserted that Ann Hopkins, the wife of the Connecticut governor, had lost her understanding and reason by giving herself solely to reading and writing. This statesman commented that if she "had attended her household affairs, and such things as belong to women, and had not gone out of her way and calling to meddle in such things as are proper for men, whose minds are stronger etc., she had kept her wits, and might have improved them usefully and honorably in the place God had set her."[13]

Weak-minded women ostensibly had little talent for letters. Joseph Tompson included the poems of his sister Anna Hayden in a manuscript journal, since they had "love & . . . Christian spirit breathing in them," but at the same time he pointed out that her poems lacked literary merit. Some of Tompson's contemporaries were reluctant to extend Anne Bradstreet much recognition for her own obviously superior poetic efforts. Nathaniel Ward was quick to state that men—Du Bartas, Chaucer, and Homer—had laid the basis for the poetry of a thirty-eight-year-old "girl" whose achievement was notable, because women did not do "good" things; even though Ward recognized Bradstreet's talent, her finest efforts could only "half" revive him. "R. Q." wrote an introduction to the first volume of Bradstreet's poetry (1650) in which he rather snidely concluded that her verse seemed only superficially dangerous to male supremacy:

Arme, arme, Soldado's arme, Horse, Horse, speed to your Horses,

Gentle-women, make head, they vent their plots in verses;

They write of Monarchies, a most seditious word,
It signifies Oppression, Tyranny, and Sword:
March amain to London, they'l rise, for there they flock,
But stay a while, they seldome rise till ten a clock.[14]

In the same year when Bradstreet's first edition appeared, Thomas Parker, the Newbury pastor, reacted to his own sister's writing with particular sharpness. "Your printing of a Book," he wrote, "beyond the custom of your sex, doth rankly smell."[15]

The Puritan divines celebrated woman's divinely prescribed destiny to exist for and through man. William Secker emphatically explained God's design as follows: "She must be so much, and no less, and so much, and no more. Our Ribs were not ordained to be our Rulers: They are not made of the head to claim Superiority. . . . They desert the Author of nature that invert the order of nature. The Woman was made for the mans comfort, but the man was not made for the womans command. Those shoulders aspire too high, that content not themselves with a room below the head."[16]

Many English and American Puritans believed the virtuous woman should walk in the shadow of her male masters from the cradle to the grave. A daughter owed almost complete allegiance to her father's wishes. He was to supervise whom she might choose as friends, direct her to the service of others, and remind her to keep constant watch over the state of her soul. He was expected to reprimand her for tending to become a "Busie-Body" or "Pragmatical." Whatever he commanded (with exception of something sinful), she was to obey. His pleasure was her goal, and "her heart would melt/ When she her Fathers looks not pleasant felt." The ideal daughter was like "a nun unprofest," a girl who never read lust-inducing plays and romances, who avoided the comb and the looking glass, and who relished serving her parents with a demeanor of "Virgin Modesty."[17] When she reached a marriageable age, a daughter should "do nothing" without her father's approval; in marriage matters, she should be "very well contented . . . to submit to such condition[s]" as her parents "should see providence directing."[18] In every familial relation the father, that "soul of the family," served as "governor of the governed." Apparently to emphasize the potency of such paternal overlordship, John Cotton in 1641 actually suggested hanging any maiden who allowed a lover to have sexual intercourse with her in her father's house.[19]

In marriage the woman traded her father's surname for her husband's, in a symbolic transferral of the male right to "govern, direct, protect, and cherish" her. Her lack of an independent name accented the fact that she could not exist independent of men: as daughter she was to give "Reverence, subjection & Obedience" to her father, and as wife she was to give the same to her marital "master."[20] Since he possessed more "quickness of witte . . . greater insight and forecast," that "Prince and chiefe Ruler" deserved her assistance, "reuerand awe," and silent submission—if not outright fear. Massachusetts Governor John Winthrop wrote, "a true wife accounts her subjection her honor and freedom[?], and would not think her condition safe and free, but in her subjection to her husband's authority, even if he were an unbeliever." A wife should so need to please her husband, Cotton Mather asserted, that she would utterly fear his frowns and be "loth in any way to grieve him, or cause an Head-ake in the Family by Ofending him." Her personal identity so completely depended upon him that for a "Woman to be Praised, is for her to be Married." She could shine only "with the Husbands Reyes," deserving no praise "except she frame, and compose herself, what may be, unto her husband, in conformity of manners."[21]

Theologians directed the "true wife" to be constantly concerned for her husband's welfare, even at the expense of her own. In Cotton Mather's words:

When she Reads, That Prince Edward in his Wars against the Turks, being stabbed with a poisoned Knife, his Princess did suck the Poison out of his Wounds, with her own Royal Mouth, she finds in her own Heart a principle disposing her to shew her own Husband as great a Love. When she Reads of a woman called Herpine, who having her Husband Apoplex'd in all his Limbs, bore him on her Back a thousand and three Hundred English Miles to a Bath, for his Recovery, she minds herself not altogether unwilling to have done the Like.

Mather urged the wife to address her husband by the appropriate title of "My Lord." If she felt any "passion" against her mate, she left it unexpressed; but when he was in a passion, she quickly strove to mollify it. The virtuous wife was to "carry her self so to her husband as not to disturb his love by her contention, nor to destroy his love by her alienation." She was to be at his beck and call, acting "as if there were but One Mind [His] in Two Bodies."[22]

The utterly selfless Calvinist woman who aspired to carry her husband 1,300 miles to a bath was an economic asset; certainly she could be relied upon to maintain her husband's estate. Women who worked long and hard could advance their husbands financially, instead of being like despicable "Moths . . . spending when they should be sparing." Although wives received no direct remuneration for their services, Puritans expected them to assume the appearance of "labouring Bees" about the household hive, so that the home would exist as a functional economic unit, like a hive overflowing with honey.[23]

A wife's major purpose in life, besides working on religious salvation, was to minister to her husband's needs. Her personal identity and social rank were derived through him. She was his appendage, as Cotton Mather explained in a letter to his sister-in-law, Hannah Mather. To be the "best of women in the American World," he urged Mistress Mather, "Go on to love him [her husband], and serve him, and felicitate him, and become accessary to all the Good which *he* may do in the world."[24]

The need to define all women as weak and dependent was so deeply embedded in the character of American Puritanism (and English conservatism in general) that even the anti-feminine prototypes could not exercise much self-direction, and what little they did exercise got them into trouble. A witch willfully signed, usually in blood, a covenant with Satan to acquire the power to kill by sorcery and to afflict individuals with awesome fits. Yet the being whence these powers supposedly derived was a male figure, who often appeared to the witch as a tall dark man and to whom, in return for such powers, she was to pledge her submission. Without Satan's presumed assistance there could be no fits, no mysterious deaths, and no witchly suspensions of the law of gravity. In addition, the status hierarchy of Satan's kingdom reflected the male-focused hierarchy of seventeenth-century society. Male witches, or wizards, were considered the closest confederates of the tall, dark man. They allegedly killed more people than the female witches could dream of, and presided over the large-scale gatherings of witches.[25]

Quite in tune with the belief that women were dependent by nature was the Puritan contention that female activities ought to be largely limited to the home's safe environment, even though many non-Puritan women worked in various English agricultural pursuits.[26] William Perkins wrote, "The woman is not to take libertie of wandring, and staying abroad from her owne house, without the man's knowledge and consent." Considering her an ineffective manager of "outward business and affairs," Puritan leaders urged the wife to busy herself with cooking, cleaning, spinning, child care, and other household tasks. Indeed, worldly concerns constituted a potential threat to her health in a way that monotonous household activities did not. A woman achieved respect largely by the extent to which "She looks well to the Wayes of her Household."[27]

In Puritan theory, men could better face the challenges and dangers of life in an insecure wilderness plagued with fierce nor'easters, crop-destroying insects, and sometimes warlike red men. Women could be better protected and more easily supervised in the relative isolation of the home, where they could also bear and nurture children, fulfilling a role for which Puritans believed they were divinely designed. The need for children to populate the growing settlements gave that particular function great importance in the New World.

Of course, childbirth was associated with age-old, biblically ordained risks and difficulties.[28] John Oliver's *Present for Teeming Women,* the standard pregnancy guide in England and America, directed women to prepare diligently before their delivery for their own possible death. If they did not do so, Oliver warned, God would deliver them "in anger not in favour," making death even more probable.[29] Mather considered severe delivery pains a divine sign that a woman needed to cleanse her soul; conversely, he asserted that the easily delivered mother was "a [God-] Praising One."[30]

After giving birth, the mother properly exercised her nurturant function by suckling her child. At a time when many Englishwomen employed wet nurses for their infants, Cotton Mather warned, "You will Suckle your Infant your self if you can; Be not such an Ostrich as to Decline it, merely because you would be One of the Careless Women, Living at Ease."[31] The "prudent" mother was one who took good care of her child, dressing it in short, uncumbersome garments to prevent falls and injuries.[32] She also strove to dress her youngster's soul in the garments of God, becoming "very uneasy" whenever she witnessed or heard about her little one's sins, however inconsequential they might be. She was expected to encourage her children to listen to their father's conversation so that they might procure wisdom.[33]

The desire to bear and rear children was so pervasive that the woman who lost a youngster was often viewed as a fit subject for the devil's wooing. More than one frustrated mother reportedly became a witch when Satan "drew [her] in by appearing to her in the likeness . . . of a child of hers then lately dead, on whom her heart was much set."[34] Barrenness was viewed as a particularly lamentable state, but even that could not destroy woman's reputed nurturance. Such a condition allegedly prepared the afflicted woman "to be more Fruitful in all the good works of Piety and Charity."[35]

When an older woman no longer had any children at home, the divines urged her to continue giving herself to others while remaining in a dependent capacity. At age sixty, women became eligible to serve under the supervision of male deacons in "administering to the sick."[36] Since ministers assumed the world could no longer flatter such elderly women "with its Promises & Prospects of Pleasures, Profits & Glories, as when they were younger," deaconesses were purportedly suited to "teach the Young women to be Sober, to love their Husbands, to be discreet, chaste, keepers at home, good, Obedient, & c." Their final station, after a lifetime of dependency and nurturance, was, in Benjamin Colman's words, to have their blood "chill'd in their Veins, their Senses & Relishes decay'd."[37]

In the final analysis, the spokesmen for the several Biblical Commonwealths posited an ideology of female weakness, deference, patience, and nurturance. Sex roles were sharply separated, with the male viewed as the stronger, ruling sex, one more protective than nurturant. As much as and perhaps more than their English contemporaries, the Puritan spokesmen of New England viewed male characteristics as expressions of their own "obvious" superiority. Michael Wigglesworth held that women's weakness made them "generally more ignorant, and Worthless."[38] Nathaniel Ward found it hard to view women as anything other than "feather-headed" spendthrifts and "Squirrel-brained" friskers after the latest fashions, ladies "fitter to be kickt . . . then either honour'd or humour'd." He called "these nauseous shaped gentlewomen" no more than "gant-bar-geese, ill-shapen-shotten-shell-fish, Egyptian Hyeroglyphics, or at the best . . . French flurts of the pastery." This acerbic minister maintained that "The world is full of care, much like unto a bubble/ Woman and care, and care and Women, and Women and care and trouble."[39] Another minister, William Hubbard, believed women to be little better than property; concerning a case wherein two men claimed the same woman as wife, he wrote that it took much time "to find who was the right *owner* of the *thing* in controversy."[40]

Misogyny in New England had its limits, however. Although they affirmed the need for women to seek male theological advice, Puritans did allow women to work out their individual reckonings with God in the isolation of their closets. Some ministers attacked their male associates for refusing to recognize female worth. Cotton Mather wrote:

> Monopolizing HEE's, pretend no more
> Of Wit and Worth, to hoard up all the store.
> The Females too grow Wise & Good & Great.

This divine informed his readers, "It is a Common, but Causeless report that women's tongues [wag ceaselessly] and are frequently not governed by the fear of God."[41] Similarly, John Cotton asserted that those men who viewed women as "a necessary Evil" were "Blasphemers." Yet another man, John Saffin, in a poem entitled "Cankers touch fairest fruites" directed his male readers away from the belief that women were "Woe to men."[42]

The hatred toward women which some Puritan ministers either expressed or described was similar to the venom hurled at the "weaker sex" by many of the English.[43] Other Puritans, also like a number of their English contemporaries, needed not so much to hate women as to dominate them. Notoriously absent from the New England sources, however, is any Puritan mention of the reforms endorsed by English feminists, including men like Daniel Tuvill and William Austin.[44] Puritans would not countenance an egalitarian relationship between the sexes. Future examination of seventeenth-century attitudes toward women may enable us to describe more precisely the differences between Puritans and other English groups; for the time being, we can only say that the celebration of dependency, subordination, modesty, and weakness was common in England and America, without reference to any particular sect. It should also be pointed out, however, that Puritans appeared more preoccupied with defining the attributes of proper femininity. After all, almost all the Englishmen who prepared treatises on the "weaker sex" were Calvinists; these divines, more than their Anglican contemporaries, hammered home the theme that men should rule. Since a cross-cultural study of seventeenth-century English attitudes remains to be undertaken, the present work will largely limit its comparative comments to the differences between Calvinists and their neighbors in non-Puritan areas of New England.

The Dynamics of "Love" in Marriage

The reader may object that I have been painting too bleak a picture of the Puritans' ideas about the "weaker sex." After all, many scholars have pointed out that these religious reformers emphasized the importance of love—an attitude which theoretically facilitated the liberation of women from the shackles of male dominion. On the surface this argument seems plausible, as some Puritans indicated their approval of affection and the emotional closeness which sometimes develops with physical closeness. John Winthrop addressed his wife Margaret as "My Chiefe Ioye in this World" and, when away from her on business, wrote letters containing the following affectionate remarks:

[April 28, 1629] I kisse and loue thee with the kindest affecion and rest Thy faithful husbande,

[May 8, 1629] the verye thought of thee affordes me many a kynde refreshinge, what will then the enioyinge of thy sweet societye, which I prize aboue all worldly comforts,

[February 5, 1629/30] My sweet wife, Thy loue is such to me, and so great is the bonde betweene vs, that I should neglect all others to hold correspondencye of lettres with thee.[45]

Edward Taylor viewed his relationship with his wife as "the True-Love Knot, more sweet than spice/ And set with all the flowre of Graces dress." To this divine, the wedding knot was the place "Where beautious leaves are laid with Honey Dew./ And Chanting Birds Cherp out sweet Musick true."[46] Thomas Hooker described the ideal husband very romantically, as "The man whose heart is endeared to the woman he loves, he dreams of her in the night, hath her in his eye and apprehension when he awakes, museth on her as he sets at table, walks with her when he travels and parlies with her in each place where he comes." Such a husband cradled his wife's head on his bosom and "his heart trusts in her . . . the stream of his affection, like a mighty current, runs with ful Tide and strength."[47] Thomas Thatcher wrote poetically to Margaret Sheafe, his betrothed, in the 1660s:

> Thy Joy I seek, thy comfort's my desire
> Whilst to enjoy thy bosom I aspire;

. . . .

My heart still ravish'd with your love, to be
  In the glad duty whereto I am bound,
And true Solaces therein I shall see
  Whilst interchanged joys with us abound.
    And we in one do laugh and weep together,
    Firmly conjoyned in both, disjoyned in neither.[48]

Puritans like Thatcher, Hooker, Taylor, and Winthrop certainly
expressed loving sentiments, quite in accord with those English
Puritan divines who described "setled affection," "companionship," and "tender loue" as the "glue" between marital "yoke-
fellows." Many a divine directed the husband to support his wife,
praise her virtues, honor her, and "bee not bitter, fearce, and cruell
vnto her."[49] Yet, when ministers celebrated the mutual delight and
concord existing in "louing" union, they considered love "not so
much the cause as . . . the product of marriage." A "duty" owed
one's spouse and God, it became "nothing but Christian charity,
and marriage supplied the chief form for the exercise of that charity."[50] As one minister explained, love was "the Sugar to sweeten
every addition to married life *but not an essential part of it. Love was
Condition in the married Relation.*"[51] Since a couple need not love
to marry, either sex could wed for less romantic considerations.
A young man could legitimately search for a "goodly lass with
aboundation of money" or a "very convenient" estate, as long as he
had a desire to respect his wife-to-be and did not keep his motives
from her. And a maiden could accept the hand of a suitor for equally
mercenary motives, as long as she was honest about it.[52] Such
marriages had little to do with love; it magically appeared at some
later date, if at all.

Nor did Puritans view love in egalitarian terms. Although a couple "are combined together as it were in one," Calvinists agreed
that, even in the closest human relationship, "one is alwaies higher,
and beareth rule, the other is lower, and yeeldeth subjection."
Ministers concluded that the wife, of all "inferiours," "commeth
nearest to a paritie" with her mate, and then ranked "Submission; or
Subiection" as her "maine dutie." William Gouge pointed out that a
couple "are yoak-fellows in mutuall familiaritie, not in equall authoritie. . . . If therefore he will one thing, and she another, she may
not thinke to haue an equall right and power. She must giue place
and yeeld," even if he be "a drunkard, a glutton, a profane swag-
gerer, an impious swearer, and blasphemer."[53] Gouge and his

contemporaries urged the wife, as a specific manifestation of her love, "to guid the house &c. not guid the Husband."[54] The male-centered nature of such love becomes particularly clear in admonitions for her "wholly to depend on him, both in judgment and will."[55] When the husband brought home unexpected dinner guests or failed to take her moods seriously enough, the enduring wife was to grin and bear it, for discontentment over such matters "argueth not a louing affection, nor a wiuelike subiection." Love meant that she empathized with his moods, in a nurturant manner, but that he did not need to reciprocate. In fact, even if she were "wiser, more discreete, and prouident then the Husband," those traits could not "overthrowe the superioritie of the man." The wise wife could advise him, but only with "humilitie and reuerence; shewing her selfe more willing to heare, then to speake."[56] Given the Puritan need to affirm male superiority in love, as well as in other matters, the disobedient or contentious wife became one of the world's most despicable creatures—not only "an heart-sore to him that hath her," but no better than a wolf, a wart, a cancer, a gangrene, or even excrement. (By comparison, the harsh or churlish husband became only "a wild beast."[57]) Quite revealingly, Puritan Alexander Niccoles explained the prevailing notion of male-centered love: a man "not only unitest unto thy selfe a friend," a "comfort for society" and "a companion for pleasure," but "in some sort a servant for profite too." Thomas Gataker went a step further, referring to the wife as a form of the husband's property. She "must resolue to giue herselfe wholly to him," Gataker wrote, "as her Owner, on whom God hath bestowed her."[58] Still, in their effort to maintain security within the familial unit, as a counterpart to the insecurity occurring in the world outside, many Puritans disliked calling the wifely role "servitude" or "slavery." However, their overt endorsement of female subjection, coupled with affirmations of the husband's "superiority" and "authoritie" in "all things" at home, revealed that Puritans perceived marriage as servitude, although in a slightly different cast.

The Puritan notion of love served, then, not to liberate women; instead, it institutionalized sex-role oppression for both men and women. Whatever the realities of any particular interaction, as an idea it reinforced female submission and made it difficult for males to be anything other than controlling.

Such a concept of love fed male egocentricity. The Puritan male tended to emphasize what his wife could do for him, rather than

what he could do for her. He loved her not for her uniqueness but
for the extent to which she fulfilled the role expectations of the ideal
female, including a self-sacrificing concern for his needs. Joseph
Thompson cared for his wife because she studied how "to make my
life Comfortable to me, as far as she could." Similarly, Richard
Mather's wife was accounted "a Woman of singular Prudence"
when she managed his secular affairs so well that he could devote
himself totally to his own studying and "Sacred Imployments."[59]
Thomas Shepard applauded his mate for her "incomparable meekness of spirit, toward myselfe especially." Edward Taylor's wife,
Elizabeth Fitch, was, in his opinion, "a Tender, Loving, Meet,/
Meecke, Patient, Humble, Modest, Faithful, Sweet/ Endearing
Help," a woman "Whose Chiefest Treasure/ of Earthly things she
held her Husbands pleasure." If she "spi'de displeasure in his face,/
Sorrow would spoile her own, and marr its grace."'[60] Noticeably
absent from almost all Puritan accounts is any mention of the husband freeing his wife for study and sacred employments, behaving
meekly toward her, or being quick to salve her displeasure.

If Puritans had conceived of love as free, unlimited emotional
sharing, love might still have operated to liberate women. However, in assuming a fundamental disjunction between matter and
spirit, Puritans could not tolerate such a view; they argued instead
that too much material love for a spouse weakened the spiritual love
which was God's due. Winthrop's letters to his wife contained
frequent reminders of the preeminence of the love of God over their
more earthly love, suggesting that he had difficulty constraining his
own deep affection for Margaret Tyndal. Edward Taylor reminded
his own sweetheart of the need to subordinate their feelings to
"Gods Glory," even though his passion for her was as "a Golden
Ball of pure Fire." Thomas Shepard lamented during his wife's
four-day agony in childbirth, "I began to grow secretly proud and
full of sensuality, delighting my soul in my dear wife more then in
my God."[61] Puritans could not agree with the Antinomian and
Quaker belief that an intense feeling between husband and wife
served as a reflection of, instead of a danger to, love for God. When
Antinomian William Hutchinson said he thought more of his wife
than of their church, the Puritans could only call him a man of "weak
parts," one incapable of constraining his own affection or of regulating his wife's behavior.[62]

Despite the Puritan desire to limit the genuine, earthly love that
could develop between two people by subordinating it to the love of

God and to demands arising out of sex role dominance and submission, some couples did marry for love and enter into very close relationships. That closeness developed not because of, but in spite of Puritanism. Ideologically, the egalitarian impulse of pure affection was undercut by the Puritan need to regard love first and foremost as duty—not as deep feeling brought to a marriage by the couple, but as a network of obligations imposed upon the couple by God. Such a notion of love, coupled with a belief system which accentuated male superiority, constituted an effort not only to be true to biblical prescriptions and to the sometimes conservative ethos of English culture, but also to countermand the Puritan male's peculiar feelings of impotence, as outlined in the last chapter.

Practical Implementation of Sex-Role Ideology

An important issue arises at this point: Was Puritan sex-role ideology consistent with Puritan practice, or simply an unenforceable vision? Was it a purely intellectual identification with a glorified biblical past, or the genuinely descriptive adjunct of socially institutionalized sex roles? Such questions necessitate an examination of the extent to which the prevailing sex-role ideology was implemented.

Puritan society was organized in a way that explicitly affirmed the belief in sex segregation as a reminder of men's and women's different destinies. In church the men, women, maidens, and youths all sat separately, with the most prominent men sitting in the foremost, highest-status pews. Each sex also entered the meetinghouse by a separate door.[63] Male and female youngsters met in catechism classes at different times.[64] The little girls who went to help the town herdsmen watch cattle on the commons were barred, by legislative fiat, from conversing with the little boys who were likewise occupied.[65] When the little girl attended a dame school to learn the rudiments of education, she studied at a curriculum somewhat different from that of the boys; while the latter grappled with Latin, penmanship, spelling, reading, and religion, the former learned cooking, weaving, and spinning, as well as reading, writing, and religion.[66]

A few years in dame school constituted the typical girl's formal education, since many of the town fathers and school trustees agreed that educating girls was "Improper and inconsistent with such a Grammar Schoole as ye law injoines."[67] Walter Small's search of colonial town records revealed that only seven of nearly two hundred towns specifically permitted girls to attend the town schools; the records of another five towns implied such permission.[68] Segregated classes may have been the rule in those few grammar schools which the "weaker sex" could attend. James Trumbull, for one, has suggested that boys and girls attended classes at different times.[69]

Of course, girls could receive some schooling at home, but the quality of that education depended upon the knowledge and will of their parents, or of the masters to whom they had been apprenticed. A minister like Cotton Mather, for example, taught his daughters a number of subjects, but the daughters of the poor had no such advantages. Whatever limited education women did receive, either at home or in school, tied them to a domestic sphere. While male education was a vehicle for social advancement, a way to prepare youths "for ye Colledge and publique service of ye Country in Church, & Commonwealth,"[70] female education was not designed to create college students, magistrates, or ministers. Instead, girls were taught the tasks of good wives: "Brewing, Baking, Cookery, Dairy, Scouring, Washing, Dinner matters, Afternoon works, Evening works, Supper matters, After supper matters," knitting, and embroidery. In addition to subjects like reading, writing, and religion, a girl also learned ciphering and accounting, so that she might assist her father in his business and her prospective husband in his.[71] When the courts provided for the education of a deceased parent's children, they sometimes directed that sons be instructed how "to write plainly and read distinctly in the Bible, and the daughters to read and sew sufficient for the making of ordinary linen."[72] School and home thus complemented one another in creating different lifestyles for men and women.

Dress also taught men and women their respective places in society. Ministers pointed out that donning the garb of the opposite sex was an "abomination to the Lord thy God." As Nicholas Noyes explained, breeches were for men because they testified to male superiority; the more cumbersome dress was a token of female subjection.[73] Both men's and women's clothing therefore bore witness to the male's relative freedom. While men had unimpaired movement in their shirts and leather pants, women had to cope with voluminous skirts and petticoats. Not only did their folds get in the way if a woman wanted to run, but the easily muddied skirts kept her inside on wet days.

Puritan authorities prosecuted those who wore the wrong apparel. In 1677 the Essex County magistrates ordered Dorothy Hoyt to be severely whipped or her father to pay a £2 fine after she put on men's clothing. (She escaped a lashing only by fleeing Massachusetts.) Fourteen years later, the Suffolk County Court sentenced Deborah Byar to submit a £10 bond for good behavior and to stand for an hour on a stool in a public place, with a paper on her breast which read "For putting on man's apparrell." In 1697 Mary Cox was summoned before the next Court of General Sessions for wearing men's clothing upon the Boston streets. One man was also prosecuted, in 1652: Joseph Davis of Haverhill, Massachusetts, paid a ten-shilling fine for donning female dress and going from house to house in the middle of the night. Not until 1695, however, did the Massachusetts authorities actually enact a law against wearing opposite-sex clothing. Offenders could be fined up to £5 or corporally punished.[74]

Long hair became yet another "token of Women's Subjection." Considered a cocoon of modesty, it became an "Ornament" and sign of gracefulness on women. Any woman who cut off her long hair and then framed it into a wig for men was guilty of perverting "the End God gave for her" and degrading "her self unto the rank and quality of a beast."[75] The dangers of long hair on men were equally severe. Michael Wigglesworth warned his associates that a mane might lead its male bearer to assume "soft and womanish spirits," or to become "filthy and full of vice." Nathaniel Ward even went so far as to suggest that long-haired King Charles I was effeminate.[76] Perhaps no one better illustrated the prevailing anxiety over sex-role differentiation than Nicholas Noyes, when he rhetorically queried, "What a mad World would it be, if women should take the same affection to wearing of Men's beards; as Men do to Women's hair? Would they not be accounted meer Viragos, or virile Housewives?"[77] No record exists of any court action being taken against either a long-haired man or a short-haired woman, although one male offender was promised a remission of half of his ten-shilling fine if he would cut his long hair "into a seuill frame" (1637).[78] The Massachusetts General Court on May 10, 1649, directed all church elders "to manifest their zeal" against the "uncivil and unmanly" wearing of long hair, but specified no penalty save public censure for the offense. Six years later the trustees of Harvard College prohibited any student from wearing "Long haire, Locks or foretopps" and from "Curling, crisping, parting or powdering their haire."[79]

Although no actual legal sanctions were used against people who

wore their hair improperly, in other realms Puritans used institutional prohibitions to distinguish between the respective roles of
men and women. Both spinsters and widows could own property,
but neither could vote for public officials. Puritans considered the
franchise an important means for protecting of civil liberties, but for
men only—as Nathaniel Ward wrote, without such protection,
"men are *but* women."[80] Nor could women vote in church affairs,
prophesy, or even ask questions in church, for in all such cases
"speaking argues power." A woman could speak only when singing
hymns or, in a few churches, when she made a public request for the
privilege of membership.[81] Male members not only reserved full
participation in church affairs for themselves, but also were reluctant to admit to membership women who were "full of sweet affection" but "a little too confident."[82]

Puritan society provided virtually no avenues for women to seek
fulfillment outside marriage. The school curriculum emphasized the
importance of the woman staying in the home, and the apprenticeship system trained girls for no trade other than housewifery.
There is no record of any New England mercantile establishment
hiring a maiden to work outside the home until after King Philip's
War, although in England a daughter could receive apprenticeship
training as a shopkeeper. Maidens, wives, and widows could not
hawk or peddle goods throughout the countryside, as was true
in their Puritan homeland.[83] An unwed woman could attempt to
build some savings by working as a domestic servant, a doctor,
or a schoolmistress; however, such occupations were very poorly
paid.[84] Without marriage, a woman could hardly expect to have any
financial security.

Even if a woman did manage to accumulate a sizable estate or
income (through an inheritance, for example), she faced great social pressure to marry. If a lass remained single until age twenty-
three, neighbors called her a "spinster."[85] If she was still unwed
at twenty-six, she received the more odious appelation of "thornback."[86] Bookseller John Dunton remarked in 1686 that "an old (or
Superannuated) Maid, in Boston, is thought such a curse as nothing
can exceed it, and [look'd] on as a Dismal Spectacle."[87] Some of
Dunton's Puritan contemporaries believed that deceased old maids
could do no better than to lead apes in Hell.[88]

Men were expected to marry also, but community gossip did not
focus on the bachelor as it did on the spinster. There was, in fact, no
term of opprobrium comparable to "spinster," "thornback," or "old

maid." The church members of at least one town, Salem, chose a thirty-six-year-old bachelor, Nicholas Noyes, as their minister (1683). Puritans did, however, establish vehicles for the regulation of bachelors' behavior, since Satan reportedly loved to provide erotic fantasies to tempt the minds of unwed males. Medfield, Massachusetts, set aside segregated housing, a special Bachelors' Row, to facilitate their supervision. The Middlesex County magistrates prosecuted many "singlemen" who failed to place themselves under family government between 1665 and 1679, while Plymouth, New Haven, and Connecticut colonies required bachelors to live with "licensed families." The Connecticut enactment actually specified that bachelors living alone pay a £1 fine each week[89]—which undoubtedly helps to explain why Madame Knight wrote in 1704 that half of Connecticut's males were married by the time they reached twenty years of age.[90]

Despite such pressures to marry, the prospective suitor could not simply court any girl he wished. He first had to secure the permission of the maiden's father, or face prosecution on a charge of "inveigling" the girl. All Puritan-controlled locales except Maine punished by a £5 fine or a whipping any man who "stole away" the affections of a maiden by "speech, writing, message, company-keeping, unnecesary familiarity, disorderly night-meetings, sinful dalliance, gifts, or in any other way."[91] The severity of the punishment for inveigling suggests that Puritans took very seriously the father's right to convey his overlordship to another male, thereby depriving the daughter of any initial decision about whom she wished to woo her. A father could not "wilfullie and unreasonably deny any childe timely or convenient" marriage, but he could largely determine whom she married.[92] The daughter could, of course, reject any suitor allowed to court her, but she then had to deal with the consequences of her decision. For example, when Lucy Downing refused to wed a candidate of whom her parents approved, her mother informed her that such behavior was unwise and disreputable.[93] When a depressed Betty Sewall withdrew from Grove Hirst's suit, her father reminded her that such action would "tend to discourage persons of worth from making their Court" to her.[94] A young woman capable of such independence could hardly be expected to transform herself into a submissive, obedient wife, a fact which further restricted her marital possibilities.

Young men had fewer limitations. Even though a father might attempt to "control" his sons by refusing to give them any of his property,[95] they could hire themselves out to artisans, become fishermen, or enter a number of other occupations. Once a young man decided he wanted to marry, he could secure the appropriate paternal permission to court one or more lasses. His father did not need to approve of his choices, although certainly that was the preferred route.

Once a couple had wed, no law specified that the wife had to obey her husband's every wish. However, the law did give him great supervisory control over her property and behavior. At marriage, a wife had to relinquish control over whatever real estate she possessed or income she received. She could, through a prenuptial contract, attempt to retain some control over her own property, but the English Court of Chancery and the Massachusetts Assistants did not recognize the validity of such an agreement.[96] Not until 1762 did the Bay Colony accept prenuptial contracts as binding, although Connecticut had done so as early as 1673.[97] The authorities of New Haven, New Hampshire, and Plymouth never heard a case concerning the legitimacy of such a contract. Whatever their position on prenuptial agreements, all of the colonies respected the husband's "right" to regulate his wife's realty. Only some of her personal estate—her dresses, quilts, needles, and so on —remained in her hands after marriage.

Puritan legal practice reinforced the notion that a husband was his wife's overseer, and therefore held him accountable if she stepped out of line. When a woman commited a minor crime, the courts usually ordered her husband to pay for it, in a fit punishment for his indiscretion in allowing her to break the law. If a wife did not attend Sabbath services, for instance, her husband was held responsible for failing to bring her to the meetinghouse. If she sold alcoholic beverages without a license, he paid £5 to £10 for tolerating her behavior.[98] With the husband lay the decision of whether to pay a fine assessed against his wife, or to subject her to a whipping instead. In one case the Plymouth General Court actually allowed the husband to punish his wife "att home" after she had beaten and reviled him (1655).[99] The wife had almost no opportunity to discharge a fine by enlisting the aid of her family or a charitable neighbor. Of course, no woman received a trial by a jury of her female peers.

Although, as in English local and customary law, a wife could sue in court for wrongs done her (provided she had her husband's permission), usually her husband brought suit in her behalf.

Whenever a wife hurled scurrilous remarks at a neighbor, both she and her husband automatically became parties to the suit. If the husband neglected to take civil action when his spouse was the injured party, her parents might bring suit on her behalf (in a slander suit, for example). Without husbandly or parental allowance, a wife could not seek damages for any injury, irrespective of its severity.[100] Her honor belonged to her father or her husband, who protected it at his discretion. Under no circumstances could a woman sue her own husband for tortious acts (e.g., slander, assault) against her, although she could give evidence against him in a criminal case.

A wife's activity in "outward matters" was always contingent upon her husband's approval. She could contract for rents and wages, sell goods, and collect debts, but only if her husband had authorized her activity. Since Puritans believed the "weaker sex" had little ability in such dangerous matters, they wished to keep women within the home's protective confines. To prevent weak Puritan wives from unwarily responding to some sinner's solicitations, the Massachusetts General Court in 1674 barred any wife, in the absence of her husband, from entertaining any traveler without the allowance of the town selectmen, under the penalty of a £5 fine or ten lashes.[101] She also had to busy herself with household tasks, in order to avoid prosecution on a charge of idleness.

Whatever free time a woman possessed was to be spent not for her own enjoyment, but in charitable work or in spinning linen, cotton, or woolens during times when clothing was in short supply. In 1656 the Massachusetts General Court ordered that "all hands not necessaryly imployd on other occasions, as woemen, girles, and boyes" must spin three pounds of cloth per week for thirty weeks of each year or pay a fine of 12 pence for each pound lacking. The deputies directed town selectmen to keep careful watch over all families, encouraging the diligent and reproving the negligent, ostensibly to remedy a clothing shortage by delegating the necessary work to those persons considered the most idle. The law made no mention of compensating the spinners for their labor.[102]

In Puritan ideology and practice, a wife could have few outright belongings. Neither her premarital possessions (with the exception of some personalty) nor her subsequent acquisitions, nor the use of her free time, nor even her criminal sentences were hers alone. Her status seemed quite like that of a servant, even though the latter's period of servitude was limited by contract.[103]

Woman's Disadvantages Qualified and Placed in Context

Practically speaking, the Puritans attempted to keep women subordinate and dependent by limiting their educational opportunities, separating the sexes whenever possible, providing no possibility of female economic security outside marriage, censuring "old maids," depriving women of the vote in church and commonwealth, forcing wives to relinquish control over their realty, and placing married women under the effectual supervision of their husbands. Still, despite such disadvantages, women were not completely under male control in Puritan New England. Single, widowed, or divorced women of means could open mercantile shops, own land, and maintain inns.[104] These women could sue on their own behalf in court. Three extant petitions indicate that women attempted to have some political impact by petitioning the Massachusetts General Court or a Connecticut magistrate.[105] In half of all cases where a deceased husband left a widow, she received the right to act as the executor of his estate—a position of some administrative importance.[106]

Even though the husband could restrict his wife's activity in many ways, she retained certain legitimate claims on him (based not on her "rights" but on her supposed weakness, or need for protection). In Plymouth and New Haven, a wife's permission was necessary before a husband could sell their house or any of their land. In contrast, however, Connecticut and much of Massachusetts conceded that property transferral was the husband's prerogative. In his will the Connecticut husband usually referred to the couple's acquisitions as "my" lot or "my" dwelling house.[107] When a husband made his will, he could not leave his wife penniless. In Massachusetts before 1649, Connecticut before 1696, Plymouth, and New Haven, the law reserved to the widow a dower right of one-third of the lands, houses, tenements, rents, and hereditaments her husband possessed. This widow's third was free from all debts, rents, judgments, and executions against her deceased mate's estate. Plymouth and New Hampshire also allowed the widow either all or part of her husband's personal estate, while in Massachusetts after 1649 the magistrates determined what portion she would receive.[108]

A husband's legal responsibilities toward his wife included assuming her prenuptial debts and fines, although he could discharge that obligation if she gave up whatever property she possessed and married him while attired only in her shift or in clothing of his providing.[109] Predictably, the husband was expected to supply his wife with appropriate victuals, clothing, and firewood; if he did not do so, the court justices either ordered him to reform his ways,[110] lodged him in prison,[111] directed him to provide a bond for his wife's maintenance (5 shillings per week or £20 per year),[112] or sequestered a portion of his estate for the use of his wife and children.[113] A husband could not live in the woods away from his wife, nor could he legally leave her in foreign parts for longer than two years without incurring a monthly fine of £2 in Connecticut or a flat £20 fine in Massachusetts.[114] Public disapproval of the husband who refused to keep his wife by his side was great: at Boston in 1705 there was serious discussion about tearing down the house of a man who asserted that he had a basic right to live apart from his spouse.[115]

A husband could not beat his wife in order to reduce her to abject submission. As early as 1599 the English Puritan Henry Smith asserted, "If hee cannot reform his wife without beating, he is worthy to be beaten for choosing no better."[116] Almost a century later Cotton Mather agreed that for "a man to Beat his Wife was as bad as any Sacriledge. And such a Rascal were better buried alive, than show his Head among his Neighbours any more."[117] The Bay Colony's initial law code, the "Body of Liberties," in 1641 freed the wife from "bodily correction or stripes by her husband, unlesse it be [given] in his owne defence upon her assalt." Nine years later the Massachusetts General Court specified a fine of up to £10 or a whipping as punishment for any man who struck his wife, or for any woman who hit her husband.[118] None of the other four Puritan colonies enacted such a law, although they did lightly penalize husbands who abused their wives too readily.

Some scholars have asserted that New World Puritanism fostered "an increasing tendency to treat women as individuals before the law" by prohibiting wife-beating, allowing divorce for several causes, and granting wives the proprietary, contractual, tortious, and evidentiary rights denied them under English common law. Such claims are rather short-sighted. The defenders of Puritan legal freedom for women neglect to mention that only one colony actually barred spouse-beating; nor do they examine court records to determine whether wife-abusers actually faced prosecution or received significant penalties for their indiscretions. Also ignored is the central fact that wives who entered contracts, sued in court, and managed estates had to first secure their husbands' consent.[119]

Comparisons between English realities and New England Puritan practice have been too facile. Massachusetts authorities prohibited wife-beating, but so did the non-Puritan King Charles II. Furthermore, some Anglicans agreed on the need to curb husbandly abuse, and ecclesiastical courts had for more than three centuries punished violent husbands.[120] Puritans allowed separation or divorce for adultery, impotence, bigamy, incest, refusal to have intercourse, and desertion—a seeming gain over English practice, where only ecclesiastical courts or (later) parliamentary enactment could end a marriage. Although the ecclesiastical courts granted only annulments or separations on complaints of cruelty, desertion, or adultery, Chilton Powell asserts that the English paid little attention to prohibitions on remarriage. And civil magistrates "unofficially" allowed divorce for a large number of different reasons, including, in some areas, "mutual consent." Thomas Ridley wrote in 1607 that divorce was increasing in the mother country, particularly because of "Adultery, deadly hatred . . . intolerable cruelty, neernesse of kindred and affinitie in degrees forbidden, impotencie on one side or the other."[121] The Puritan attitude represented a continuation, rather than a liberalization, of English practice. In at least two respects the Puritans were more conservative: they did not allow remarriage after a separation, and they did not permit divorce on grounds of mutual consent.

Puritan women possessed certain "rights" unavailable to women under English common law, but this evidence, too, has been wrongly used. Puritan law was based not on common law, but on local, customary, and statutory law.[122] Alice Clark has noted that in England "'Common Law' was the law of the nobles, while farming people and artizans alike were chiefly regulated in their dealings with each other by customs depending for interpretation and sanction upon a public opinion which represented women as well as men."[123] The English legal historian W. S. Holdsworth has enumerated many of the traditional privileges that wives lost at common law.[124] Moreover, if Puritan legal practice is compared with that of the English equity courts, little difference is apparent. Equity courts—arising to guarantee fairness in the face of common law —respected customary law and granted wives proprietary, tortious, and evidentiary rights. Not until the late seventeenth century did common law fully supplant local privileges of wifely freeholdship, the franchise for propertied women, and female membership on juries.[125] However, from their earliest years of settlement New

England Puritans made no efforts to carry such local privileges to the New World. Puritans brought with them only those elements of local and customary law which did not threaten the male need for power. Perhaps this explains, in part, why Puritans designated their wives as executors of their estates only half of the time, while testators in rural England almost always did so.[126]

The assumption that women were weak vitalized the patriarchal family and society by decreasing the possibility that women would search for independence, assertive impact, and self-dominion. Still, membership in the weaker sex did give certain practical benefits. Women who applied for church membership confessed their wrongdoings in private to preserve their feminine modesty, while men had to make a public confession before the entire congregation.[127] In court, "weak" women usually received five or ten fewer lashes than men for equivalent offenses, although in serious cases the penalties were similar.

Ideological and practical confirmation of female weakness readily suited the woman for an unassertive, nurturing role. Although a woman could not legitimately pursue her non-nurturant needs, nurturance did provide her with her one source of strength: an active caring for and management of the children who depended upon her, and the needy people whom she aided. She could mold and shape her children's habits, play with them, sustain them, teach them, or even push them to fullfill her own desires and mock her husband's hopes. Since the Puritan wife exercised little control over most areas of her life, her positive nurturant virtues of kindness and sustenance may sometimes have yielded to a need to dictate her children's affairs and to order servants about.

Wives probably did not exchange domestic power for public submission, because the husbands could legitimately undercut female authority, even in the home. Even the power over children was theoretically disproportionate, as Samuel Willard indicated in his *Compleat Body of Divinity*. Willard began by stating, "If God in his Providence hath bestowed on them [husband and wife] Children or Servants, they have each of them a share in the government of them." Willard continued: "tho' there is an inequality in the degree of this Authority, and the Husband is to be acknowledged to hold a Superiority, which the wife is practically to allow." So, even though the wife "is vested with an Authority" over children and "her Husband is to allow it to her," his authority was superior; no "equality" was affirmed or implied. More specifically, the English divine William Gouge wrote, "A wife may not simply without, or directly against her husbands consent, order and dispose of the children in giuing them names, apparelling their bodies, appointing their callings, places of bringing vp, mariages, or portions."[128]

We cannot know the extent to which wives possessed real "private power" or derived satisfaction from the marital power arrangement. We do not know how many men sought to circumvent their wives' orders to children or servants. We cannot say how many husbands who worked at home—as shoemakers, shopkeepers, innkeepers, and so forth—actually interfered in their wives' supervision of domestic affairs. Nor do we know how many strong-willed children objected to their mothers' efforts to guide or "control" them, especially since properly modest wives reportedly found it difficult to whip errant offspring.[129] We can, however, get some sense of the widespread occurrence of marital friction, as Chapter 5 will specify. All we can state with any certainty is that, theoretically, the wife's authority was subordinate to her husband's. Whatever compensatory power a wife may have sought through controlling her children was probably eroded by her limited role in Puritan society. As a general rule, the specter of male overlordship is so apparent in institutional, intellectual, economic, and family life throughout the seventeenth century that it leaves little room to doubt women's difficulty in achieving, much less exerting, a sense of their own assertive independence. All of woman's protections and the few privileges she enjoyed as a widow did not, in the final analysis, facilitate her development beyond the limitations imposed by her sex-role conditioning.

Real Women as Ideal Women

Human behavior can best be understood by probing the characteristics that define the man's or woman's ideology, sentiments, beliefs, and so on—in short, his or her identity. The skeptical scholar might argue that, in the "free aire" of the New World, deep-seated conventions faced severe tests and ultimate disruption, that women neither listened to what the authorities had to say nor drew the proper inferences from separation of the sexes. However, such a claim ignores the fact that an individual woman's identity is largely a product of her experiences in society. The person she becomes, and her response to events in her environment are highly conditioned by her cultural milieu. "Becoming a woman" was measured primarily by the degree to which females adopted or possessed the distinguishing characteristics that the Puritan community had defined as necessary for the status of womanhood.

Some sex-role changes occurred in New England between 1620 and 1700; however, such changes ought to be considered against Puritanism's potent, often immobilizing psychological impact on women. Puritan men, combatting a generalized sense of their own inadequacy, viewed disobedience on the part of a child, servant, or wife as a dire threat, a potentially mortal blow to the integrity and viability of the Biblical Commonwealth. As N. Ray Hiner has pointed out, "Puritans viewed enculturation, the process by which the central values of a culture are internalized by a child, as more critical than socialization, the process by which a child learns the ways of a society so that he can function within it."[130] The repeated emphasis on guilt to compel both child and adult, male and female, to think, feel, and act in acceptable ways made female rejection of the ideal role very unlikely. Even if a woman thought for herself, she then had to confront the sheer force of her sex-role conditioning, community censure, the many legal checks on her behavior, and her lack of training for any occupation other than that of housewife and mother.

Puritan sex-role stereotyping had great impact. Young girls apparently felt that they should not actively pursue learning, for few girls attended the town schools in those regions where they were allowed to do so. At Northampton in 1674, for example, 30 or 40 boys but only 11 girls attended classes, while at Hatfield in 1700 only four girls—8.7 percent of the students—appeared on the schoolmaster's class list.[131] Nor did most females obtain rudimentary educations through dame schools. The number of women who signed deeds with a mark, instead of a signature, suggests that female education in home or school was hardly adequate. William Kilpatrick has reported that 11 percent of the 179 men who made deeds in Suffolk County, Massachusetts, between 1653 and 1656 made marks, as did 11 percent of 199 men deeding property between 1686 and 1697. By contrast, 58 percent of 48 and 38 percent of 130 women in those time intervals signed deeds only with a mark.[132] Kenneth Lockridge's examination of 75 women's wills (1650–70) in Massachusetts, Connecticut, New Hampshire, and Maine yields corroborative results. Fewer than one-third of the female but 60 percent of the male testators could sign their names.[133]

Given their educational disadvantages, the prevailing censorship of the press, and the potency of their sex-role conditioning for non-intellectual activity, women chose not to seek fulfillment through writing. Only four women are among the authors of the 911 works published in seventeenth-century New England. Anne Bradstreet's *Several Poems Compiled with Great Variety of Wit and Learning* appeared in 1678. Four years later, Mary Rowlandson's account of her captivity among the Indians was published under the title *The Soveraignty & Goodness of God, Together With the Faithfulness of His Promises Displayed.* In 1694 M. Hooper's *Lamentations for Her Sons, Poisoned by Eating Mushrooms, August 1, 1693* was published. The fourth book, a *Valedictory and Monitory-Writing,* was a private journal kept by Sarah Goodhue of Ipswich, Massachusetts. It appeared in print only after her death (1682).[134]

Women did not express themselves in print on any of the important issues of the day; nor did they keep private journals, like so many Puritan men, or attempt to write poems for their own private satisfaction. I have found only two women, Mistress Goodhue and Elizabeth White, who wrote accounts of their personal religious turmoil; in addition, only two of the fifty-seven seventeenth-century New Englanders listed in William Matthews's *American Diaries* were women.[135] Of more than a hundred known poets, Anne Bradstreet and her sister Mercy Woodbridge are the only females.[136] Women's lack of education indeed affected their desire to create and to wield influence through the pen.

The young woman looked to marriage for security and fulfillment, just as many ministers suggested she should. Maidens sometimes "toyed" with fortune-telling devices to find out "what trade their sweet harts should be of."[137] They often rushed into marriage; statistics for Plymouth, Dedham, and Andover indicate that the typical bride was between 19 and 22.5 years old, five to eight years younger than her English counterpart. Men, on the other hand, wed at 25 to 27, like their English contemporaries.[138] More than 99 percent of all women married at least once. Even the widow reportedly "has one Eye weeping for her Departed Husband, [while] she . . . has the other open to see, who comes next," since remarriage was often her only realistic alternative to poverty.[139]

A mere handful of women possessed the will and means to become shopkeepers, doctors, schoolteachers, or innkeepers. Instead, most became housewives, for which they received great praise. Benjamin Tompson, for example, could think of no higher accolade for his deceased wife Mary than to accent her role in beautifying their house, and her charitable willingness to minister to the sick and the poor. Edward Taylor similarly boasted of his mate, "She was a neate good Huswife every inch."[140]

Many wives deferred to their mates. Elizabeth, the wife of John Winthrop, Jr., described herself in a letter to her husband as "thy eaver loveing and kinde wife to comande in whatsoeaver thou plesest so long as the Lord shall be plesed to geve me life and strenge." Lucy Downing, a sister of the elder John Winthrop, ended her letters to her brother with a deferential "Your sister to commaund." Governor Winthrop's own wife, Margaret Tyndal, considered herself "faythfull and obedient" to him and felt she had "no thinge with in or with out" worthy of her husband. She depended completely upon his care for her own security; she valued herself only because he valued her. In one letter she told him, "I will be a seruant to wash the feete of my Lord, I will doe any seruice whearein I may please my good Husband." Tyndal blushed to hear herself commended by her mate and left all important decisions to him, even when she had definite preferences of her own.[141]

Another Puritan wife, much later in the century, was equally obedient, although she did not consider her husband as Christ-like as Margaret Tyndal did. Boston printer Bartholomew Green's wife "was so exactly observant" to her husband's will "that he cou'd not be more ready to Command, then she was to obey." When some of Green's "Commands seem'd not to be as kind as she might have expected," she would obey them nevertheless, objecting only by asking him to extend humane "Compassion to a meek sufferer." Like Elizabeth Winthrop, Lucy Downing, and Margaret Tyndal, she put into practice the ideal of dutiful wifely compliance.[142]

Female dependence was so much a part of Puritan life that women undergoing spiritual stress sometimes asked men to intercede with God on their behalf. In 1640 Mary Cole, plagued with a "corrupt hart, and strong inclinations to sinne, and weaknesse to resist temptation," asked John Winthrop to "plead hard with the lord for me." Similarly, Hannah Jones wrote in 1681 to Increase Mather: "Sometimes I feel myself so under the pres of unbeleav that it makes me cry, mournfully, More fath, more fath. O that the Lord would moue your hart & the harts of the rest of the desipills to intreat the Lord for me & many more."[143] Men in times of religious turmoil were much more inclined to work out their own reckoning with God; although they occasionally sought the comfort of other men, they did not ask those men to intercede with the Lord on their behalf.

A deferential attitude did not accord well with high self-esteem. Hannah Jones, for one, called herself "bold to present a few lynes" to the "worthy" Mather. She had to justify even writing her letter by explaining, "Now, Sʳ, tho I am a worm, not worthy to be regarded by God or by men, yet senc it is put into my heart to ventur to give you the trubell of these scrales [i.e., scrolls], exorsise pasience so far as to read them, & if you can desern anything of the spirit of God, I beleaue you will not reject it."[144] Anne Bradstreet, in so many respects an unusual woman, also questioned her own "weak" abilities, when faced with the desire to imitate poetically the "sugared lines" of Guillaume Du Bartas. Bradstreet felt her pen was too "mean" to write of "superior things": songs "of wars, of captains, and of kings,/ Of cities founded, commonwealths begun,/ . . . / Or how they all, or each their dates have run." By her own admission too "simple" to write anything as well as Du Bartas, Anne Bradstreet told her readers that women could not compete poetically with men. Yet, at the same time, she urged men to extend to her and other poetesses a small measure of recognition:

> Let Greeks be Greeks, and women what they are
> Men have precedency and still excel,
> It is but vain unjustly to wage war;
> Men can do best, and women know it well.
> Preeminence in all and each is yours;
> Yet grant some small acknowledgement of ours.

Although she wrote ambitious poems about "masculine" subjects, Bradstreet was embarrassed to find the "ill-formed offspring of my feeble brain" published "by friends less wise than true."[145]

For a woman to feel that she was a complete person, seventeenth-century ideology specified that she must bear and rear children. That concern was pervasive among newlywed women. Bradstreet, married at sixteen, lamented, "It pleased God to keep me a long time without a child, which was a great grief to me and cost me many prayers and tears, before I obtained one."[146] (Her first child came after five years.) Midwife Jane Hawkins did a flourishing business by distributing fertility medicines among Boston women in the 1630s. Other New England women used a common potion (dried beaver testicles grated in wine) in an effort to facilitate conception, prevent miscarriages, and moderate delivery pains.[147]

The woman willing to conceive a child must also be willing to endure the "bearing pangs . . . which cann't be told by tongue" and the possibility of her own death in delivery. John Oliver told of prospective mothers who were subject to "accidental melancholy from obstructions, hysterical vapours, many pains and illnesses, and sad apprehensions of the burthen they carry and the hazard they are in, under all which 'tis impossible to be in so good a humour as at other times."[148] Women's severe discomfort in pregnancy and childbirth was undoubtedly aggravated by the divines' reminders that such pain served as a providential censure of female sinfulness. Unfortunately, such divines failed to specify criteria for determining when delivery pains were intense enough to constitute such a censure, thereby probably causing any woman to feel that her soul, as well as her life, was endangered.

The examples of two women can illustrate the problems of a Puritan orientation for women facing pregnancy and childbirth. The first, Jerusha Oliver, worried daily about impending annihilation during the fifth through ninth months of her pregnancy. "I am of a very fearful disposition naturally, and am much afraid of death," she admitted. She thanked God for her pain because she felt her fears were "a Sign that I am not Fit for Death." By wanting to be a good Puritan, she had placed herself in a hopeless psychological state: the more she feared, the more she was not conscious of her salvation; the more she questioned her salvation, the more she feared. Yet her fears were well founded, or self-fulfilling. In 1710, at age twenty-six, Jerusha Oliver died in childbirth.[149]

The second case, of Mary Onion of Roxbury, Massachusetts, illustrates the impact of Puritan ideology on a woman of independent spirit. The "very stubborn and self-willed" Mistress Onion reportedly "proved very worldly, aiming at great matters" beyond her sex. She became pregnant but would not give herself up to the pain of delivery. However, when her first child was stillborn, she did a complete about-face, interpreting her misfortune as a sign that she had "neglected her spiritual good for a little worldly trash." Filled with "dreadful horror of conscience," she affirmed that "now she must go to everlasting torments." Rejecting any consolation, Mary Onion died a few hours later (1643). At a particularly difficult time, her susceptibility to Puritanism had helped to kill her by depriving her of the will to continue living.[150] In childbirth, that time when women needed support, affirmation, sympathy, and a good deal of courage, Puritanism offered only fear and censure. Quite understandably, pregnant women took a number of concoctions (including beaver testicles, basil, and dittany) to assure easy delivery. Dr. Zerobabel Endicott of Salem copied into his notebook one interesting remedy "For Sharpe and Difficult Trauel in Woman with Child:"

Take a Lock of Vergins haire on any Part of ye head, of half the Age of ye Woman in trauill Cut it very Smale to fine Powder then take 12 Ants Eggs dried in an ouen after ye bread is drawne or other wise make them dry and make them to pouder with the haire, giue this with a quarter pint of Red Cows milk or for want of it giue it in strong ale wort.[151]

Although difficult to come by, such a potion ostensibly saved women from the "odious" sin of "bewailing" pregnancy.[152] Presumably these remedies did have some placebo effect.

After the child was born, Puritans expected the mother to breastfeed it. Although the quality and quantity of milk is often diminished in women who are nervous, large, sickly, emotionally upset, malnourished, under eighteen, or over forty,[153] New England mothers quite probably felt guilty when they faced "the Calamity of Dry Breasts."[154] Dr. Endicott indicated that women suffering from that "malady" might snuff the juice of the anemone plant to increase the flow.[155]

Many a Puritan mother wished to take good care of her children, nurturing them with kindness and religious concern. In her old age such a woman might have desired, like Anne Bradstreet, to be remembered by her children as

> . . . a dam that loved you well,
> That did what could be done for young,
> And nursed you up till you were strong,
> And 'fore she once would let you fly,
> She showed you joy and misery;
> Taught what was good, and what was ill,
> What would save life, and what would kill.[156]

Since New England men wrote very few biographical accounts of their wives and mothers,[157] we cannot determine the extent to

which women adhered to the feminine ideal. Still, the occasional
ministerial eulogy is revealing. Mary Brown, a casualty of childbirth
in 1703, is one such case in point; she learned or did some good thing
every day, attentively perused her Bible, prized Sundays, dressed
modestly, abhorred face paint, and exhibited much industry. She
possessed several traits particularly praiseworthy in a member of
the "weaker sex": complete lack of self-confidence, obedient submissiveness to her tutors and husband, inability to bear hearing the
least indecency, and a capacity to blush "Red with Modesty."[158]

Particularly appalling to the historian is the absence of information on how sex-role stereotyping worked at home. Only the diary
of Hetty Shepard, a maiden who resided both in Plymouth Colony
and in Boston during the 1670s, provides a glimpse of the effect of
familial pressures on one young girl's developing sense of her own
sinfulness and insignificance. On December 6, 1675, her fifteenth
birthday, Hetty faced censure for wearing a "fresh kirtle [dress] and
wimple [head-covering], though it be not the Lord's day." As Hetty
related, "my Aunt Alice coming in did chide me and say that to pay
attention to a birthday was putting myself with the world's people.
It happens from this that my kirtle and wimple are not longer
pleasing to me, and what with this and the bad news from Boston
[about sickness and Quaker troubles] my birthday has ended in
sorrow."[159]

Hetty Shepard's relatives urged her to assume an attitude of
religious sobriety, especially when faced with life's little pleasures.
At Christmas in 1675 her cousin Jane told her "much of the merry
ways of England upon this day, of the yule log, and plum pudding,
till I was fain to say that I would be glad to see those merry doings."
Jane informed her, however, that "it was better to be in a state of
grace and not given over to popish practices." Such reminders had
their effect; two years later Hetty sharply reproved herself after she
lay awake all night, anticipating the merry entertainment at an
upcoming militia training. "This is a sin," she wrote. "I repented at
morning prayers with many tears. Why am I so prone to sin? The
devil goeth about like a roaring lion, seeking whom he may
devour."[160]

Hetty Shepard heeded her elders. She was quick to blame herself
for innocently encouraging others to sinful behavior, and for questioning some of the authorities' actions. When she smiled at her
beau during prayer time and he responded by whispering "that he
would rather serve me than the elders," she chastised herself for

enticing him. Although she could not understand how the divines could wish to sell the captured nine-year-old son of King Philip into slavery "or even worse," she then felt that "perhaps it is a sin to feel this." In February, 1677, Hetty considered it unjust that her uncle had been voted into the first (most prestigious) seat in the meeting-house, but her aunt only into the third seat. After she expressed that concern to her aunt, the latter "bade me consider the judgment of the Elders and the tithing-man as above mine own." And so Hetty did.[161] Hetty Shepard's brief diary indicates that the women in her extended family helped create feelings of guilt over her desire for some merriment, pretty dress, and independent thought. Submis-sively, she took to heart the words of her female elders.

The existence of women like Hetty Shepard, Mary Brown, and Margaret Tyndal Winthrop demonstrates that the posited female role had great impact on the behavior of Puritan women. The fragmentary records of their lives suggest that many, if not most, Puritan women conformed to the ideological expectations of their culture and respected the institutional checks on female indepen-dence. Although we can draw no definitive conclusion about the extent to which the typical woman fulfilled the attributes of the ideal female role, we can reasonably speculate that Puritan women ex-isted primarily through others, not as individuals who acted for themselves. As in more modern times, the woman spent a lifetime bestowing her energies, skills, talents, and services on her family or on society's needy. This is not to dismiss her impact on society, in the broadest sense; as homemaker, nurturer, and creator of the child's environment, the woman filled an important (but too often undervalued) function. However, that sole function was obscured, if not positively injured, by her need to maintain proper deference, dependency, and non-assertiveness. Puritan males, possessing the power needs of men of their religion and their century, would generally have it no other way. Puritan women, even more power-less than their male "overlords," may have acted in an ideal way; however, we cannot assume that they totally accepted the con-straints on their behavior. The evidence is simply too sparse to allow such a claim. Still, enough material does exist to refute the widely reiterated contention that Puritanism served as a liberating experi-ence for women; those women who struggled to express their freedom in seventeenth-century New Enrland generally did so in spite of Puritanism, not because of it. Before we consider these struggling women in some detail, we should examine how Puritanism defined the woman as a sexual being and as a self-supportive worker, for such definitions are central to a comprehensive understanding of the dimensions of Puritan sexism.

1. "Nicholas Noyes on Wigs, Jan. 15, 1702/3," pp. 120–28 of "Sewall & Noyes on Wigs"; "John Winthrop to Margaret Tyndal, March 1618," in A. Forbes, ed., *Winthrop Papers*, I, 222.

2. Chauncy was quoting T. Vaughan's *Anthroposophia Theomagica*, p. 30. See Kittredge, "Harvard Salutary Oration," p. 11.

3. Cianfrani, *Short Hist. of Obstet. & Gynec.*, p. 174.

4. Lewinsohn, *Hist. of Sexual Customs*, p. 178; Findley, *Priests of Lucina*, p. 133.

5. Cianfrani, *Short Hist. of Obstet. & Gynec.*, p. 139; *Aristotle's Compleat Masterpiece*, p. 73.

6. C. Mather, *Ornaments for Daughters of Zion*, p. 90.

7. Axtell, *School upon a Hill*, p. 59.

8. "Margaret Winthrop to John Winthrop, Nov. 22, 1627, and ca Nov. 15, 1637," in A. Forbes, ed., *Winthrop Papers*, I, 329, III, 510; C. Mather, *Ornaments for Daughters of Zion*, pp. 20, 73–74; Welde, *Answer to W. R.*, p. 19; Peter, *Dying Father's Legacy*, p. 47.

9. Beacon, "Solitary Meditations," p. 217 (no. 171).

10. Colman, *Duty & Honour of Aged Women*, p. 11; Calvin, *Commentary on Epistle to Corinthians*, I, 352.

11. C. Mather, *Ornaments for Daughters of Zion*, p. 94; Secker, *Wedding ring*, n.p.

12. John Cotton, "Psalm-Singing a Godly Exercise," p. 266.

13. "Emmanuel Downing to John Winthrop, August 1645," in A. Forbes, ed., *Winthrop Papers*, V, 39; Winthrop, *Journal*, II, 225.

14. Murdock, ed., *Handkerchiefs from Paul*, p. xxxviii; Nathaniel Ward, "Introductory Verse," in A. Bradstreet, *Works*, p. 4; R. Q. in [A. Bradstreet,] *Tenth Muse*, introductory dedication.

15. T. Parker, *Coppy of a Letter*, p. 63.

16. Secker, *Wedding ring*, n.p.

17. Peter, *Dying Father's Legacy*, pp. 3, 5, 7, 10, 22, 26, 33; C. Mather, *Ornaments for Daughters of Zion*, p. 78; Fiske, *Watering of Olive Plant*, p. 71; Dunton, *Letters*, pp. 98, 100–101.

18. Lawson, *Duty & Property of Rel. Householder*, pp. 30–31; "J. Winthrop, Jr., to F. Winthrop, Sept. 9, 1658," pp. 45–49; C. Mather, *Ornaments for Daughters of Zion*, p. 75.

19. John Cotton, *Abstract of Lawes*, p. 11. Fortunately, Cotton's recommendation was never enacted into law.

20. Fiske, *Watering of Olive Plant*, p. 71; Man, "Advice to Children," p. 39.

21. Perkins, *Oeconomie*, p. 700; Pricke, *Doctrine of Superioritie*, p. K2; Cleaver, *A godlie form of govt.*, pp. 115, 214; Gataker, *Marriage Dvties*, p. 11; Demos, *Little Commonwealth*, pp. 83, 91; Winthrop, *Journal*, I, 239; C. Mather, *Ornaments for Daughters of Zion*, pp. 30, 37, 78.

Gataker described the requisite fear not as "a seruile or slavish dread, but a liberall, free and ingenuous fear; (like that feare that the godly beare vnto

God)." It consisted of "a desire to doe euery thing so as may please her husband and giue him contentment." Such explanations seemed little more than efforts to perfume a skunk, for ministers never linked "fear" to the husband's "duty" to avoid displeasing his wife.

22. C. Mather, *Ornaments for Daughters of Zion*, pp. 77, 79, 81; Secker, *Wedding ring*, n.p.

23. Secker, *Wedding ring*, n.p; C. Mather, *Ornaments for Daughters of Zion*, p. 85.

24. C. Mather, *Diary*, II, 325.

25. E.g., see Woodward, ed., *Rec. of Salem Witchcraft* and "Salem Witchcraft—1692."

26. A. Clark, *Working Life of Women*, pp. 42–92.

27. Perkins, *Oeconomie*, p. 692; Earle, *Home Life*, pp. 34, 123–52; C. Mather, *Ornaments for Daughters of Zion*, p. 74; Wigglesworth, "Letter"; C. Mather, *Family Well-Ordered*, p. 37.

28. In Genesis 3:16, God tells Eve after her sin, "I will greatly multiply thy sorrow and thy conception; in sorrow thou shalt bring forth children; and thy desire shall be to thy husband and he shall rule over thee."

29. Oliver, *Present for Teeming Women*, n.p. This work went into one American and three English (1663, 1669, 1688) editions in the seventeenth century.

30. C. Mather, *Ornaments for Daughters of Zion*, pp. 47, 92.

31. C. Mather, *Eliz. in Holy Retirement*, p. 35. See also Wadsworth, *Well-Ordered Family*, p. 45. Seventeenth-century people considered mother's milk good not only for infants, but also for sick persons of riper years. Animal milk, on the other hand, was presumed dangerous, because it might cause the infant to take on the character of the animal. Similarly, a wet nurse could reportedly communicate her "natural Inclinations," "irregular Passions," or "some secret Disease." See Wickes, "Hist. of Infant Feeding," pp. 157, 232; McCoy, "Hygienic Recommendations of *Ladies Lib.*," p. 368.

32. A. Bradstreet, "Meditations Divine and Moral," in her *Works*, p. 279.

33. C. Mather, *Ornaments for Daughters of Zion*, pp. 94–95.

34. N. Mather, "Letter to I. Mather, Dec. 31, 1684," p. 58; "Salem Witchcraft—1692."

35. C. Mather, *Ornaments for Daughters of Zion*, p. 89.

36. John Cotton, *Way of Cong. Churches Cleared*, p. 39; Leynse, *Preceding the Mayflower*, p. 57.

37. Colman, *Duty & Honour of Aged Women*, pp. 15–30.

38. [Wigglesworth,] "On Wearing Hair," p. 371.

39. [N. Ward,] *Simple Cobler*, pp. 19–22.

40. Hubbard, *Gen. Hist. of N. Eng.*, VI, 382. Italics mine.

41. C. Mather, *Ornaments for Daughters of Zion*, pp. 1–2, 49–50.

42. John Cotton (II), *Meet Help*, p. 15; Saffin, "Cankers touch fairest fruites," p. 93.

43. For illustrations of misogyny in late Tudor and seventeenth-century England, see Notestein, "Eng. Woman 1580–1650," pp. 69–107; Wright, *Middle-Class Culture*, pp. 431, 458, 465–507, 652–53; K. Rogers, *Troublesome Helpmate*, pp. 135–59; Masters & Lea, eds., *Anti-Sex*, pp. 20–25, 219–42; Powell, *Eng. Domestic Rel.*, pp. 147–69.

44. On English feminism, see Wright, *Middle-Class Culture*, pp. 218, 495, 502–3; Notestein, "Eng. Woman 1580–1650," p. 93; Gagen, *New Woman*; Hilda Smith, "Private Tyranny."

45. "John to Margaret Winthrop, 1629–30," in A. Forbes, ed., *Winthrop Papers*, II, 196, 85, 89, 201.

46. E. Taylor, "Upon Wedlock & Death of Children," in his *Poems*, p. 468.

47. Hooker is quoted in Morgan, *Puritan Family*, pp. 61–62.

48. Thomas Thatcher, "Love Letter to Elizabeth Thatcher," in Meserole, ed., *Seventeenth-Century Am. Poetry*, pp. 406–7. Thatcher's great-grandson named this poem, erroneously thinking that it was written to Thatcher's first wife, Elizabeth Partridge.

49. Pricke, *Doctrine of Superioritie*, pp. K1–K4; Cleaver, *A godlie form of govt.*, pp. 92, 169; Gataker, *Wife Indeed*, pp. 38–43; Perkins, *Oeconomie*, p. 691; Gouge, *Of Domesticall Dvties*, p. 197.

50. Morgan, *Puritan Family*, p. 54; Morgan, "Light on Puritans," p. 100.

51. Sewall, *Diary*, II, 403. Italics mine.

52. Morgan, *Puritan Family*, pp. 56–59, 81–84; Demos, *Little Commonwealth*, pp. 160–62; Hoadly, ed., *Rec. of N. Haven 1653–Union*, pp. 134–36. Roger Thompson argues that mercenary marriages were less common in America than in England, indicating that there was little outcry against such marriages in the colonies (*Women in Stuart Eng. & Am.*, pp. 122–23). This may be true, but a lack of outcry cannot be construed to mean lack of practice. Certainly, if Puritans approved of openly mercenary marriages, as Edmund Morgan has pointed out, we should not expect much outcry against them.

53. Perkins, *Oeconomie*, p. 670; Gouge, *Of Domesticall Dvties*, pp. 271, 303, 273; Gataker, *Marriage Duties*, p. 7.

54. Fiske, *Notebook*, pp. 27–28; E. Morgan, "Light on Puritans," 99–100.

55. Perkins, *Oeconomie*, p. 692.

56. Gouge, *Of Domesticall Duties*, p. 263; Pricke, *Doctrine of Superioritie*, p. K4; Cleaver, *A godlie form of govt.*, pp. 221–22.

57. Gataker, *Wife Indeed*, pp. 9–11.

58. Niccoles, *Discourse of Marriage*, p. 5; Gataker, *Good Wife Gods Gift*, p. 22.

59. Murdock, ed., *Handkerchiefs from Paul*, p. xxiii; I. Mather, *Life of R. Mather*, p. 25.

60. [T. Shepard,] *God's Plot*, p. 70; E. Taylor, *Poems*, pp. 474–75.

61. Goodman, "Taylor Writes His Love"; Morgan, *Puritan Family*, p. 61; [T. Shepard,] *God's Plot*, p. 55.

62. Winthrop, *Journal*, I, 299.

63. Earle, *Sabbath in Puritan N. Eng.*, pp. 47, 52, 54.

64. Axtell, *School upon a Hill*, pp. 31, 40.

65. Shurtleff, ed., *Mass. Rec.*, II, 6.

66. Earle, *Customs & Fashions in N. Eng.*, pp. 29–30.

67. "Rules of N. Haven Hopkins School," p. 297; Slafter, *Rec. of Educ.*, p. 20.

68. Small, "Girls in Col. Schools," pp. 532–34.

69. J. Trumbull, *Hist. of Northampton*, I, 222.

70. "Rules of N. Haven Hopkins School," pp. 296–98.

71. Woody, *Hist. of Women's Educ. in U.S.*, I, 160–61; Sewall, *Diary*, I, 436; C. Mather, *Family Well-Ordered*, p. 37, and *Diary*, II, 51.

72. Small, "Girls in Col. Schools," p. 534.

73. "Nicholas Noyes on Wigs, Jan. 15, 1702/3," pp. 121, 126 of "Sewall & Noyes on Wigs."

74. G. Dow, ed., *Essex Ct. Rec.*, VI, 341; Hist. Rec. Survey, *Abstract & Index of Suffolk Ct. Rec.*, p. 137; "Ct. Files—Suffolk Co.," XLVI (1696–97), no. 4347; O. Hammond, ed., *N. Hamp. Ct. Rec.*, p. 96; *Acts & Resolves of Mass.*, I, 210.

75. "Nicholas Noyes on Wigs, Jan. 15, 1702/3," pp. 120–28 of "Sewall & Noyes on Wigs."

76. [Wigglesworth,] "On Wearing of Hair," p. 369; [N. Ward,] *Simple Cobler*, p. 23. See also Scheick, "Widower Narrator of Ward's *Simple Cobler*," pp. 92–94.

77. "Nicholas Noyes on Wigs, Jan. 15, 1702/3," p. 121 of "Sewall & Noyes on Wigs."

78. Perley, *Hist. of Salem*, I, 444–45.

79. Morison, *Harvard Col. in Seventeenth Century*, I, 86, 88.

80. John Cotton, *Discourse about Civil Govt.*, p. 5; Bradford & Allerton, "Letter," p. 299; [N. Ward,] *Simple Cobler*, p. 34.

Roger Thompson (*Women in Stuart Eng. & Am.*, pp. 224–25) attempts to make a case for women voting in town elections, but his evidence is questionable. He asserts that one woman "voted on the question of dividing woodland in Dedham in 1645." However, his source, B. Katherine Brown's "Puritan Democ. in Dedham," pp. 387–88, only mentions that the town "voted to divide a stretch of woodland 'according to the number of persons and mens estates,'" then distributed lands to 83 persons, including one woman. Nowhere does Brown claim that any woman participated in deciding which persons would receive what properties. Thompson's reference to two widow landowners at Sudbury who cast their ballots on an issue involving land allotments is more substantial. I have been unable to check out the manuscript source for that claim, but even if landowning widows were allowed to vote on matters of land distribution, that fact cannot be construed to suggest that they could vote on other town issues or for town officers. Nor does it indicate that any women could exercise the franchise on a colonial level, or that wives (i.e., most women) were able to vote. Neither is there any way to determine whether the Sudbury situation is representative or unique.

Thompson's catalogue of four influential women and six female petitioners cannot be used as evidence for women voting. (One also wonders why there were *only* four influential women and six petitioners.) Nor can the extension of the franchise to women at the Brattle Street Church be used to prove that "*some* churches did indeed allow the female elect a say in their affairs," for that institution was a radical departure from, rather than a continuation of, previous events. Moreover, it cannot be reasonably assumed that the democratization of the franchise after the 1680s had, as Thompson believes, the effect of opening up the ballot to women—unless or until some evidence suggests that. None does.

Thompson does not mention Puritans like John Cotton, Nathaniel Ward, and William Bradford, who maintain that women did not vote. It seems unreasonable to question their word, since no concrete evidence exists to invalidate it.

81. C. Mather, *Magnalia*, II, 180; Fiske, *Notebook*, p. 4; John Cotton, "Psalm

Singing a Godly Exercise," p. 266; Lechford, *Plain Dealing*, p. 68.

The prohibition on women speaking in church was based on Paul's statement in 1 Timothy 2:11–2: "Let your women keepe silence in the Churches, for it is not permitted vnto them to speak: but they ought to be subiect, as also the Law sayth. And if they will learne any thing, let them aske their husbands at home: for it is a shame for women to speake in the Church."

82. Boston Rec. Cmrs., *Rep. Containing Roxbury Rec.*, p. 53.

83. A. Clark, *Working Life of Women*, pp. 200–201, 206; Bridenbaugh, *Vexed & Troubled Eng.*, pp. 169–70.

84. Ch. 4 contains a full analysis of women's work in early Puritan New England.

85. Savage, "More Gleanings," p. 100. Lucy Poyett, age 23, was identified on one shiplist as a spinster (Banks, *Planters of Commonwealth*, p. 182).

86. Dunton, *Letters*, p. 99. John Higginson wrote of some maidens, they "are like to continue ancient maids, Sarah being 25 or 26 years old" (quoted in Thoms, "Beginnings of Obstet.," p. 668).

87. Dunton, *Letters*, p. 99.

88. Earle, *Customs & Fashions in N. Eng.*, p. 38.

89. *Ibid.*, pp. 36–37; Shurtleff & Pulsifer, eds., *Plym. Rec.*, XI, 233; Hoadly, ed., *Rec. of N. Haven 1653–Union*, p. 608; J. Trumbull, ed., *Conn. Rec.*, I, 8; Pulsifer, ed., "Rec. of Middlesex Ct.," I-III.

90. Knight, *Private Jour.*, p. 53.

91. Earle, *Stage-Coach & Tavern Days*, p. 216.

92. "Coppie of Liberties of Mass.," p. 230.

93. "Lucy Downing to John Winthrop, ca. Feb. 1648/9," in A. Forbes, ed., *Winthrop Papers*, V, 309.

94. Sewall, "Letter-Book," p. 213.

95. Philip Greven, after studying land distribution in colonial Andover, Massachusetts, asserts that only one-fourth of those sons who had settled on their father's land actually owned that land before their father's death; 56% of Andover patriarchs (14 of 25) retained title to *all* their lands until they died, a fact which gave fathers great influence over their children's lives in a community where land was a basis for economic self-sufficiency. Such paternal control may well have been a factor prompting the younger generation to found new communities. John Demos, however, maintains that there is evidence in Plymouth Colony to support just the opposite point of view: "that for most people a real and decisive measure of economic independence came rather early in their adult lives, and that if they remained at all beholden to their parents it was for reasons more psychological than material." Demos does acknowledge that the effort of fathers to control lands until their deaths is reflected in some wills, but in other cases fathers conveyed lands outright to their sons. Nowhere, though, does Demos tell us how many fitted into either category, and in another place he does state that in "some of the wills bequests to certain children were made contingent upon their maintaining the proper sort of obedience." Although Andover practice may have been different from that in Plymouth, Greven's position is the more sound statistically. See Greven, *Four Generations*, pp. 77–83; Demos, *Little Commonwealth*, pp. 164–70, 103, 106.

96. Morris, *Studies in Am. Law*, p. 136; Holdsworth, *Hist. of Eng. Law*, V,

311–12. Between 1581 and 1638 the English chancery courts upheld only two premarital agreements. All other cases were dismissed. In fact, "the court sometimes seems to have regarded devices used by the wife to withdraw her property from her husband's control, as frauds upon the husband's legal rights, unless the husband had received consideration for the abandonment of his rights."

97. Morris, *Studies in Am. Law*, p. 138; J. Trumbull, ed., *Conn. Rec.*, II, 198–99. In 1673 the Connecticut General Court allowed £200 to be set aside from Thomas Fairchild's estate to satisfy his prenuptial obligations. For a Massachusetts case in which the magistrates ruled against a prenuptial contract, see *Rec. of Suffolk Ct.*, I, 5–8, 98–99.

98. E.g., see Libby, Allen, & Moody, eds., *Maine Ct. Rec.*, I, 289; Scales, ed., *Hist. Memoranda Concerning Dover*, I, 38; O. Hammond, ed., *N. Hamp. Ct. Rec.*, p. 186.

99. Shurtleff & Pulsifer, eds., *Plym. Rec.*, III, 75.

100. Morris, *Studies in Am. Law*, pp. 186–92.

101. Shurtleff, ed., *Mass. Rec.*, V, 4.

102. *Ibid.*, III, 396–97; see also *ibid.*, I, 294. Not all parties spun the full amount; the selectmen determined each individual's capacity and then accordingly assigned quarter or half work assignments.

103. Edmund S. Morgan, in his generally well researched and lucidly written study of *The Puritan Family*, takes an opposing point of view. However, the one case he cites to prove his contention that the wife was not her husband's slave or servant is not convincing: "When Daniel Ela told his wife Elizabeth that 'shee was none of his wife, shee was but his Servantt,' neighbors reported the incident to the authorities, and in spite of the abject Elizabeth's protest 'that I have nothinge Agenst my husband to Charge him with,' the Essex County Court fined him forty shillings." Morgan's statement implies that Elizabeth Ela had, in point of fact, nothing to charge against her husband except his assertion of her servitude, and the court fined him specifically for that offense.

A closer reading of the case indicates that Morgan has created an inappropriate impression. In early 1681 Daniel and Elizabeth Ela had argued over his neglecting to pay a laborer for work performed. After that quarrel, Mistress Ela went to the barn and was there seen by a witness "crying and sniffling." Sometime later she appeared at a neighbor's explaining that her husband had beaten her about the head and that she feared he would kill her. When several neighbors visited Mr. Ela as intermediaries for his wife, he told them "his wife was his servant and his slave and he would have her whipped but that would be a disgrace to him, for he would never have a quiet hour until she died." He refused to allow her at home unless she would humble herself before him "for what wrong she had done him both in person and estate by her tongue." Calling her "but a devil in woman's apparel," Ela took the oath that, "if he ever had her come home without an humble acknowledgment, he hoped his hands might rot off or his legs never carry his body more." He also threatened to get even with anyone who harbored his wife, saying "he was Lord paramount in his owne house; hee might [there] doe or say w^t hee would & none should controle him." When Elizabeth Ela did make some effort to return home, he came at her with a stick. Later he refused to give up her Bible and spectacles to a neighbor who requested them on her behalf.

Neighbors brought the Elas' difficulties before the Essex County Court, but Mistress Ela, apparently abject and not desiring further trouble, would not press charges against her husband. Enough of their neighbors did, however, testify that Daniel Ela's abusive behavior could not be doubted, and he was duly fined £2. We cannot assume that the authorities punished Ela because he called his wife a servant. His offenses were many: beating his wife, saying she was a devil, depriving her of her Bible, threatening the neighbors, and generally making a public nuisance of himself. Despite all this, the Essex County authorities let him off with a rather small fine. See Morgan, *Puritan Family*, p. 45; G. Dow, ed., *Essex Ct. Rec.*, VIII, 272–73.

104. R. Morris, *Studies in Am. Law*, p. 128. Although unattached women could sometimes own property, it was difficult for them to acquire realty. Salem became one of the few towns to establish "maids lotts," but some residents considered this an "evil" precedent ("Town Rec. of Salem," IX, p. 28).

105. Corey, *Hist. of Malden*, p. 145; Gallop, "Letter," p. 104; *Watertown Third Book of Rec.*, p. 74.

106. See Chart 11.1 for a comparative breakdown of designated executors.

107. In Suffolk County before 1652 and in Middlesex County, Massachusetts, the husband alone conveyed property, but after 1652 the wife's allowance was deemed necessary in the former locale. See Pulsifer, trans., "Rec. of Middlesex Ct.," III, 238; *Suffolk Deeds*; Shurtleff & Pulsifer, eds., *Plym. Rec.*, XI, 52; Hoadly, ed., *Rec. of N. Haven 1653–Union*, p. 303; Calhoun, *Social Hist. of Am. Family*, I, 95–96; Manwaring, ed., *Digest of Conn. Probate Rec.*

108. J. Trumbull, ed., *Conn. Rec.*, IV, 167; Shurtleff & Pulsifer, eds., *Plym. Rec.*, VIII, 13; "Coppie of Mass. Liberties," p. 229; *New-Haven's Settling in New England and Some Lawes for Government* (London, 1656), in Hoadly, ed., *Rec. of N. Haven 1653–Union*, p. 586; Page, *Judicial Beginnings of N. Hamp.*, p. 154; Shurtleff, ed., *Mass. Rec.*, II, 281.

109. Hoadly, ed., *Rec. of N. Haven 1638–49*, pp. 334, 382–83; Manwaring, ed., *Digest of Conn. Probate Rec.*, p. 183.

In 1673, for example John Betts wed a woman "in clothes of his own providing to her, Shift & Stareless [*i.e.*, on a starless night], being Stript" by four female witnesses. Then he in court "Renounenced all Claymes & Interest to her estate, both Debts and Credits."

110. G. Dow, ed., *Essex Ct. Rec.*, III, 218; Shurtleff & Pulsifer, eds., *Plym. Rec.*, V, 10; Manwaring, ed., *Digest of Conn. Probate Rec.*, I, 301.

111. G. Dow, ed., *Essex Ct. Rec.*, II, 57.

112. *Rec. of Suffolk Ct.*, II, 1063; Noble & Cronin, eds., *Rec. of Mass. Assts.*, I, 60.

113. G. Dow, ed., *Essex Ct. Rec.*, VIII, 344; Shurtleff & Pulsifer, eds., *Plym. Rec.*, V, 25.

114. Shurtleff & Pulsifer, eds., *Plym. Rec.*, III, 102; J. Trumbull, ed., *Conn. Rec.*, I, 350; plus virtually all Massachusetts County Court records.

115. Sewall, *Diary*, II, 125–26.

116. Henry Smith, *Sermons*, p. 31.

117. C. Mather, *Ornaments for Daughters of Zion*, pp. 87–88.

118. "Coppie of Mass. Liberties," p. 299; Shurtleff, ed., *Mass. Rec.*, III, 212.

119. Thompson, *Women in Stuart Eng. & Am.*, p. 165; see also pp. 161–86 passim. For more comparisons of "progressive" colonial with "traditional" common law, see Stevenson, "Marital Rights in Col. Period"; Cobbledick, "Property Rights of Women in N. Eng."; R. Morris, *Studies in Am. Law*, pp. 126–200.

120. Schlatter, *Social Ideas of Rel. Leaders*, pp. 20–21; Hair, ed., *Before the Bawdy Court*, pp. 44, 244.

121. Schlatter, *Social Ideas of Rel. Leaders*, pp. 24–28; Powell, *Eng. Domestic Relations*, pp. 61–100. Ridney quoted on p. 87.

122. Stevenson, "Marital Rights in Col. Period," p. 84; Goebel, "King's Law & Local Custom."

123. A. Clark, *Working Life of Eng. Women*, pp. 236–37.

124. Holdsworth, *Hist. of Eng. Law*, III, 520–33.

125. *Ibid.*, V, 310–15; VI, 644–48. Lundberg & Farnham, "Destruction of Women's Legal Rights," in Appendix VII of their study *Modern Woman*, pp. 422–41, argue that jurist Edward Coke misrepresented the contemporary legal status of women in his widely read *Institutes* because he wished to justify taking away the extensive properties owned by his own "wildcat" wife.

126. Barbara Todd has discovered that, in Berkshire during the 1550s, male testators designated their widows as executors (76%) or co-executors (19%) in 95% of all wills. In 1608–9 the corresponding figure was 86%. See Todd, " 'In Her Free Widowhood.' "

127. Winthrop, *Journal*, I, 120; *Plym. Church Rec.*, I, 145. The Wenham congregation served as an exception to this general rule. There it was argued that women "should make their relations personally in public" because "this kind of speaking is by submission where others are to judge." The Wenham church members agreed that confessions were a special case, while for a woman even to ask a question in public was forbidden as imparting too much power to the speaker (Fiske, *Notebooks*, p. 4).

128. Quoted in Morgan, *Puritan Family*, pp. 45–46; Gouge, *Of Domesticall Dvties*, p. 309.

129. Eliot, *Harmony of Gospels*, p. 29; C. Mather, *Help for Distressed Parents*, pp. 8–9.

130. Hiner, "Cry of Sodom Enquired Into," pp. 6–7.

131. J. Trumbull, *Hist. of Northampton*, I, 222; Small, "Girls in Col. Schools," p. 533.

132. Kilpatrick, *Dutch Schools of N. Neth.*, p. 229. Roger Thompson considers these signatures an invalid measure of literacy because he confuses deeds conveying property with wills signed in a weak and dying condition. However, even if the Suffolk County deeds had been wills, Thompson's criticism remains inappropriate. He supplies no evidence to prove that wills were, in fact, usually made by persons on their deathbeds; nor does he explain why so few men but so many women should be debilitated. He also fails to indicate why there should be a difference in female signatures between 1653–56 and 1686–97. Kenneth Lockridge's conclusion, based on a

thorough study of 3,100 wills made between 1650 and 1762, is quite the reverse of Thompson's. Lockridge contends that "most wills seem to have been made before impending death could palsy a literate hand." See Thompson, *Women in Stuart Eng. & Am.*, pp. 220, 210; Lockridge, *Literacy in Col. N. Eng.*, p. 8.

133. Lockridge, *Literacy in Col. N. Eng.*, pp. 38, 13.

134. Published titles are compiled from listings in Evans, *Am. Bibliog.*, I & II, and Bristol, *Supplement to Evans*.

135. These two women were Hetty Shepard of Plymouth Colony and Mehetable Chandler Coit of Connecticut. See Matthews, *Am. Diaries*, pp. 7, 10.

136. Jantz, "First Century of N. Eng. Verse," contains a bibliographical listing of seventeenth-century poets, including four women and 164 men.

137. "Salem Witchcraft—1692," I, n.p.

138. E. A. Wrigley's compilations from parish records at Colyton in the Axe Valley, East Devon, England, give a mean age at marriage for 507 females (1560–1719) of 27.7 years; in the years 1647 to 1719 the mean was 29.6 years. For 367 Colyton men the average age at marriage was 27.3. Like Wrigley, American statisticians have found that the mean age increased for brides. John Demos recorded a mean marital age of 20.6 for Plymouth Colony women born between 1600 and 1625, and of 27 years for Plymouth men. For those born between 1675 and 1700 the corresponding ages were 22.3 and 24.6 years. At Andover, Philip Greven found an increase in mean age for women, while the male mean age remained constant. See Wrigley, "Family Limitation in Pre-Industrial Eng.," pp. 53–99; Demos, "Notes on Life in Plym. Col.," p. 275, and *Little Commonwealth*, p. 193; Greven, *Four Generations*, pp. 33–35, 117–20; Lockridge, "Pop. of Dedham," p. 330; S. Norton, "Pop. Growth in Ipswich," p. 445.

139. C. Mather, *Ornaments for Daughters of Zion*, p. 101.

140. Murdock, ed., *Handkerchiefs from Paul*, p. 4; E. Taylor, *Poems*, p. 474.

141. "Elizabeth to John Winthrop, Jr., ca June 1636," in A. Forbes, ed., *Winthrop Papers*, III, 267; Downing, "Letters," pp. 20, 25, 27; "Margaret to John Winthrop, 1624–30," in A. Forbes, ed., *Winthrop Papers*, I, 354–55, 369; II, 165, 199.

142. Dunton, *Letters*, p. 103.

143. "Mary Cole to John Winthrop, May 2, 1640," in A. Forbes, ed., *Winthrop Papers*, IV, 235; Jones, "Letter," p. 605.

144. Jones, "Letter," pp. 604–5.

145. A. Bradstreet, "The Prologue" and "The Author to Her Book," in her *Works*, pp. 15–16, 221.

146. A. Bradstreet, "To My Dear Children," *ibid.*, p. 241.

147. Shurtleff, ed., *Mass. Rec.*, I, 224, 329; E. Ward, *Trip to N. Eng.*, p. 64.

148. A. Bradstreet, "Before the Birth of One of Her Children," in her *Works*, p. 224; Oliver, *Present for Teeming Women*, n.p.

149. C. Mather, *Memorial of Early Piety*, pp. 23, 40, 42.

150. Winthrop, *Journal*, II, 93; Boston Rec. Cmrs., *Rep. Containing Roxbury Rec.*, p. 171.

151. G. Dow, *Everyday Life in Mass.*, pp. 191, 193, 185.

152. C. Mather, *Eliz. in Holy Retirement*, pp. 3, 6, 8.

153. DeLee & Greenhill, *Principles & Practice of Obstet.*, pp. 317–19.

154. Quotation appears in Caulfield, "Infant Feeding in Am.," p. 676.

155. G. Dow, *Everyday Life in Mass.*, pp. 191, 193.

156. A. Bradstreet, "In Reference to Her Children, 23 June 1659," in her *Works*, p. 234.

157. Governor Winthrop's account of his wife's death is typical of the few words written about Puritan wives. He stated simply that Margaret Tyndal was "a woman of singular virtue, prudence, and piety, and especially beloved and honored of all the country" (Winthrop, *Journal*, II, 327).

158. [C. Mather,] *Eureka.*

159. [H. Shepard,] "Puritan Maiden's Diary," p. 20.

160. *Ibid.*, pp. 20, 24.

161. *Ibid.*, pp. 21–24.

III

SEX AND SEXISM

Boston Puritans did not want anyone to be happy. And although many of them seem to have acted pretty naturally they did not enjoy it, because that fierce thing called conscience kept them awake nights.
—Eleanor Early, *New England Sampler*

. . . in matters of sex the Puritans showed none of the blind zeal or narrow-minded bigotry which is too often supposed to have been characteristic of them.
—Edmund S. Morgan, "The Puritans and Sex"

MANY WOMEN'S RIGHTS ADVOCATES OF THE LAST FEW DECADES HAVE pointed out that sexism is closely tied to male attitudes about female sexuality, women's bodies, and their own sexual identity. Puritan journals certainly attest to New England Calvinists' fears about the acceptability of their sexual desires—fears which often determined how men related to women, and vice versa. In this most intimate area of interaction, women faced problems other than unwanted pregnancies. Before examining female disadvantages, we should consider the sexual context in which Puritan sexism functioned.

That Problem of Sex

Like many of their non-Puritan English contemporaries, Puritans believed that sexual intercourse was "a base & contemptible thing in it selfe, naught and vncleane, so farre that all beasts would naturally abhorre it, if there should be no pleasure in it." The act of "Venery" had such a "filthie and vncleane" character that every living creature was reportedly sad after performing it. Too much sexual pleasure was especially dangerous for Puritans, because it might lead the individual away from the spiritual closeness to God. Each person must therefore struggle against the imperious nature of his or her "affections," taking care lest "noysom lusts . . . carry and command the head, and send up dunghill streams which distemper the mind, and disturb it." Despite the careful scrutiny of the public, as well as innumerable laws and sermons against it, lust continued "boyling and burning,"[2] often breaking through the barriers erected to restrain it. As William Bradford explained, after an outbreak of "wickedness" among the Plymouth Separatists in 1642,

> . . . it may be in this case as it is with waters when their streams are stopped or dammed up. When they get passage they flow with more violence and make more noise and disturbance than when they are suffered to run quietly in their own channels; so wickedness being here more stopped by strict laws, and the same more nearly looked unto so as it cannot run in a common road of liberty as it would and is inclined, it searches everywhere and at last breaks out where it gets vent.

Bradford did believe some inroads had been made by constant vigilance, with the result that there was "nothing near so many [offenses] by proportion as in other places." According to the governor, the relative lack of thickets and dense forests in Plymouth Colony made it possible to apprehend most offenders.[3]

Puritans thought sex was a river of fire that had to be banked and cooled by a hundred restraints if one was to preserve the individual soul. Anything which might fan that fire must be avoided. For a man and a woman to simply lie in bed together, even though the man's wife was also present, was grounds for prosecution.[4] Lewd behavior, lasciviousness, fornication, indecent exposure, masturbation, adultery, bestiality, "even sodomy and buggery (things fearful to name)" were all penalized, usually corporally; the last four merited capital punishment. Ministers warned their congregations about letting the genitals rule the mind. After Benjamin Goad was executed for bestiality, Samuel Danforth addressed his congregation sharply: "For any to go on in the sin of uncleanness, after such a solemn warning as this, is to sin in contempt of the Holiness of

God, in contempt of the Jealousie of God, in contempt of his fierce
Wrath and Indignation"—to, in effect, shut oneself "out among
the Dogs."[5]

Cotton Mather cautioned his listeners that premarital or extramarital sex not only would destroy the individual's chances of
salvation, but also would "bloodily Disturb the Frame of our Bodies,
and Exhaust and Poison the Spirits, in our Bodies, until an Incurable
Consumption at last, shall cut us down, Out of Time." Infirmity
and grievous diseases—"Gouts, Cramps, Palseyes, and Scorbetick
Taints"—would thereafter affect the "whole Mass within us." Steril-
ity, weak children, poverty, and "miserable disasters" falling upon
one's offspring could easily result from sexual uncleanness. As if
this were not enough, Mather warned his congregation that they
might contact a "horrible distemper" which would ultimately destroy their bodies and eat away their noses,[6] although venereal
disease was actually rare in seventeenth-century New England.[7]

Ministers recommended various ways to quench "the sparks of
Lusts fire." John Cotton suggested that the assailed might turn his
or her attention to delicate thoughts of God. "The more you set your
heart to consider, how amiable and beautiful, and excellent he is,"
Cotton wrote, "you shall finde he will so satisfie your heart, that you
will finde little content in any other thing besides." The English
Puritan Richard Baxter endorsed eating cold herbs, drinking cold
water, and working to the point of exhaustion to curb lust. Danforth
urged his listeners to keep busy and avoid gluttony, drunkenness,
the company of evil persons, irreligiousness, and profanity. This
minister went so far as to favor castration as the final solution to
male sexual temptation: better to go a cripple into heaven than
to remain "a perfect Epicure to be cast into Hell."[8]

By far the most widely recommended method of avoiding vice's
lure was marriage. William Secker asserted that "a single life is a
prison of unruly desires, which is daily attempted to be broken
open"; those who repudiated married life lay in "the grease of
their own sensuality." Secker reiterated the apostle Paul's dictum: it was better "to be lawfully coupled, than to be lustfully
scorched." The Massachusetts church elders in 1680 agreed that
one of the three functions of marriage was the "preventing of
uncleanness." (The other two were "the mutual help of husband
and wife" and "the increase of mankind with a legitimate issue."[9])
At least one physician advised marriage as a cure for the mysterious penile discharge which, he maintained, many young men

experienced.[10] Lust was an "irresistible instinct," and "the Use of
the Marriage Bed" was, in the opinion of many divines, "founded
in mans Nature" to control that instinct.[11]

Sex and Female Character

Both sexes were subject to this irresistible instinct, but it was
much more serious when a woman acted upon its dictates. Women
had to be particularly careful because even "very proper maidens
. . . of modest behavior" could easily be led astray by solicitous
members of the stronger sex. However, the resistance of the
"weaker sex" was increased by the fact that, if a woman happened to
engage in uncleanness, it would leave an indelible imprint upon her
character. Unless she was of very respectable status, she could, with
one act of intercourse, be transformed from an admirable virgin to a
despicable whore or slut.[12] The male did not face such a total
inversion of his character; whereas the woman was "defiled," "wo-
fully corrupted," or "ruin'd," her partner had merely "committed
folly." A woman who made sexual overtures toward a man was
guilty of "bold whorish carriage," although a male enticer was guilty
only of "lewdness" or "lascivious conduct."[13] Even a woman who
had been raped was in trouble: John Cotton wished the rapist to
marry his victim, if she and her father consented, because "it is
worse to make a whore, than to say one is a whore." Once a woman
had fallen into sin, her return to respectability was nearly impossible. As Cotton Mather declared, "For a Man to be Reclaimed from
the Sin of Vncleanness when once he has been given thereunto is
Rare; but for a Woman to be Snatch'd out of the Unclean Divels
Hands when once he has had any full Possession of her, is more
Extraordinary!"[14] And whoredom was not to be taken lightly, since
it was an extremely venomous typology—perhaps more so then
than now. Nathaniel Ward's simple cobbler of Aggawam, for one,
reported that "surcingled [i.e., tight-waisted] and debauched"
women affected him so profoundly that "I cannot cleanse my phan-
sie of them for a moneth after."[15]

The male was considered the active agent in sexual relations—the
controller, the defiler, or the whoremaster—while the woman was
to respond in passive terms. She "prostituted" herself to him or
allowed a man to "use her body"; in contrast, no woman was ever
described as having had the use of a man's body.[16] Rarely did
Puritans view men as having been defiled, and never was a woman

said to have defiled him. If anything, he defiled both her *and* himself. In many cases of suspected adultery, the authorities prosecuted the presumably more active male for visiting the woman's house. Even though she may have acquiesced, she was assumed to have been less responsible for setting up a liaison. Similarly, in the 1630s Massachusetts magistrates neglected to punish a woman who became pregnant and then married her sexual partner, because he, as the initiator of sex, received the brunt of the blame.

Struggling actively for a feeling of sexual dominance, some Puritan men boasted of the women they had conquered. One even defamed "all the civill & honest wimine in the River of Piscataqua" by saying that "if he pleasd hee could . . . make use of or ly with any whore" there.[17] Because women had not been taught to exercise sexual dominion over men, they needed no such verbal proof of potency. No woman publicly boasted about her sexual conquests, unless she wished to cuckold her husband.

Although some English writers did so, Puritans never discussed sexual activity as a means of communication, as an important bond between two personalities. Instead, they described sexual relations as a matter of the male "using" the female's body (as if she were independent of it). Such a view of the sex act entailed depersonalization of the female, both in the description of the act and in the consideration of its effects. In such illicit intercourse "he" remained "he," although of somewhat more unsavory and corrupted character, while "she" continued to be defined with reference to her body, as one who had allowed her "self" to be defiled. In fact, New Haven Puritans censured one woman who had failed to resist a man's sexual overtures not simply by saying that she had committed a sad offense, but by typing her as "a sad object."[18]

When the woman's behavior was not very feminine, people could easily charge her with whorishness. Hannah Marsh provides a good illustration of this. The New Haven woman was "forward and brawling" after being summoned aboard a ship, and as a result Francis Brewster called her a "Billingsgate slutt." The seamen similarly told her that she had been called on board "to play the slutt." When she complained to the authorities that Brewster had damaged her reputation by his slanderous comments, the magistrates ordered him to confess his wrongdoing but did not sentence him to pay her a specified amount, as was usual in slander cases. Instead, the court reproved Marsh for her "forward disposition," telling her to remember "that meeknes is a choise ornament for weomen" and to take the disparaging remarks to which she had been subjected "as a rebucke from God."[19]

Puritans tied a woman's character to her condition of chastity, and they expected her to protect that chastity with unmitigated zeal. In Cotton Mather's words, "Such is her Purity, that . . . she will not suffer the least Behaviour or Expression to proceed from her, which may Savour of Obscaenity" or permit any "wanton dalliances." She avoided reading seductive romances and blushed at any talk "that shall not sound innocently." "Lightness in Behaviour, sensual lusts, wantonness and impurity, boldness and rudeness, in Look, Word or Gesture," Mather continued, were "scandalous" in her. The lusty woman, in Benjamin Colman's words, committed a great "Rape . . . on the Conscience of Decency, and the Reluctance of native Shame." An inexhaustible reserve of feminine modesty was necessary to "restraineth us from wantonness" and to overcome the men who "Creep (like Serpent, as they are) into Houses, and Lead Captive Silly women . . . away with diverse Lusts."[20] While it was true that the man's crafty, active role made him morally blacker than the "Captive, Silly" woman, once he had actually succeeded, hers became the more damning, irretrievable "fall." Presumably if her "natural" religiosity was once proven too weak to preserve her, a Puritan woman's passivity and lesser reason left her without the means for moral change or renewal.

If a young lass did not verbally resist an enticer "as she ought," she could be whipped for encouraging his lasciviousness. The maiden suspected of having been "deflowered" was often examined by a jury of midwives; if found to possess a ruptured hymen, she was severely whipped for not reporting her "ravisher" to the authorities.[21] Many of these young women may have been convicted when innocent, or acquitted when guilty. As one contemporary sexologist puts it, "a ruptured hymen is certainly not *prima facie* evidence that a girl is not a virgin; and on the other hand, there are those rare cases in which the hymen is so flexible or pliable that coitus can take place repeatedly without rupturing" it. The English Puritan physician Nicholas Culpeper indicated that there was much controversy among anatomists about the hymen, "some holding there is no such thing at all, other that . . . the truth is, most Virgins have it; some hold all [possess it]. I must suspend my own judgment till more yeers brings me more experience; yet this is certain, it may be broken without Copulation, as it may be gnawn asunder by defluxion of sharp humors, especially in yong Virgins, because it is thinnest in them, as also by applying Pessaries to provoke the Terms, and how many waies else God knows."[22]

New World Puritans did not share Culpeper's cautious point of view. Female virginity was extremely important to them. Thomas Dudley described the first woman to die in Massachusetts, in 1631, as "a godly virginne," as if the twin qualities of piety and virginity were quite sufficient to define her character. Sixty-eight years later Ned Ward described the Bostonian's attitude in the following fashion: "A Woman that has lost her Reputation, hath lost her Portion; her Virginity is all her Treasure." William Secker considered virginity "a Pearl of Sparkling lustre," and Benjamin Tompson prepared a poetic eulogy to his deceased daughter which he entitled "The Amiable uirgin memorized." Therein the Roxbury schoolmaster celebrated "heauens fair nunnerye," where "Chast uirgins haue faire entertainment free" and innocently "Enjoy their purest loue in sacred mirth."[23] In the Bay Colony the loss of virginity was such a blemish that a father could sue the man who deflowered his daughter, collecting as much as £15 in damages.[24] (The fine for fornication per se was only £2 to £5.) A Connecticut woman who represented herself as a virgin and was discovered, after her marriage, to have spoken falsely faced the possibility of divorce for having entered into the marriage contract fraudulently. However, there is no evidence that the "fraudulent contract" stipulation could be applied to a man who made the same false claim.[25] The man was, theoretically, supposed to maintain sexual continence, but he was not defined simply in terms of his sexuality, as either a virgin or a whore (and only rarely as a whoremaster).[26] A man had to commit a sin of great seriousness—bestiality, sodomy, incest, or the like —before his personality was branded with the onerousness of his sinful act. Of course, we can probably assume that a pragmatic distinction underlay this double standard: however illicit a man's sexual behavior before or outside his marriage, he could not pass off anyone else's offspring as his wife's.

Despite their belief in the desirability of virginity, particularly for females, Calvinists felt that taking a vow of perpetual virginity, as the Catholics were wont to do, defeated God's purposes. Puritans believed that God had designed the sex organs for propagation, and that, when not ultimately directed toward that end, "such flesh" was "full of imperfection." A vow of perpetual chastity might expose the individual to unnecessary temptations, "unnatural pollutions, and other filthy practices in secret: and too oft . . . horrid Murthers of the fruit of their bodies [i.e., infanticide]." Puritans detested the "Many Fancies" which the Catholic Church "Coyned" upon Christ's being born of a virgin, and considered celibacy "no other than the effort of blind zeal." They took sarcastic swipes at the fascination of the "Whore at Rome" with both celibacy ("Better it were for a Priest to defile himself with many Harlots, than to be married to one Wife") and virginity ("As for their exalting of a Virgin-state, its like him that commended fasting, when he had fill'd his belly"). However, the Puritan attack on such Catholic notions in no way deemphasized their own fascination with premarital virginity. In fact, Cotton Mather suggested that too many persons "doted" on the virginity of maids, and therefore failed to appreciate the virtue of wives.[27]

Although virginity was expected from the unmarried, there was some uncertainty about what constituted proper sexual interest within matrimony. Edward Taylor stated that any withdrawal from sexual relations after marriage "Denies all reliefe in Wedlock vnto Human necessity: and sends it for supply vnto Beastiality when God gives not the gift of Continency." Plymouth Colony authorities affirmed as much when they set Alexander Aimes in the stocks for leaving his family and thus "exposing his wife to the temptacion of being a baud."[28] Yet, despite such pronouncements of the importance of marital union, there was some reluctance to grant a divorce when a wife complained of her husband's impotence, or a husband of his wife's refusal to have intercourse. Katherine Ellenwood clamored about her mate's inability to sustain an erection, saying that "she was very young and would rather die than live with this man," but the Essex County authorities took no action in the case (1682). The Massachusetts Assistants also refused to separate Mary White from her husband, even though Elias White had admitted to neighbors that he could lie with her four or five hours, his penis erect all the while, but then immediately lost his erection whenever he attempted intercourse (1663). The authorities generally assumed that such cases resulted from temporary sexual anxiety and would be resolved in due time. Only the most serious cases (like that of Robert Morris of Wethersfield, Connecticut, who was never able to "perform the Act of Generation" because his "Bowels came down") were terminated in divorce. And if the couple had passed the childbearing years, impotence could not serve as a ground for divorce, since there was no possibility of conception anyway. Thus the Massachusetts Assistants did not see fit to grant fifty-four-year-old Mary Drury a divorce from her new husband, Hugh, even though a permanent injury from "a great peece of timber" had sexually incapacitated him.[29] The magistrates may have believed (as did some English physicians) that men should abstain from relations with women over fifty, because the older woman's inability to expel menstrual blood resulted in its collection "in one whole lumpe, & they are by that means so infectious, that they infect men with their breath, and then cough and other infirmities come" upon their male partners.[30] In any event, Massachusetts and Connecticut authorities granted only four of eight divorce petitions charging a husband with that disorder—whereas 95 percent of all other petitioners received divorces.

If Puritans really believed, as the Connecticut Assistants once put it, that sexual intercourse was "reciprocally due between husband and wife,"[31] they did not always practice what they preached. Indeed, since males identified their penises as the symbolic source of their masculine power, they were reluctant to take impotence seriously. It was altogether too threatening, given the widespread insecurity extant in Calvinist society. Even George Cartwright, one of the King's Commissioners for New England, poked fun at a woman who charged her husband with "insufficiency" in 1665. As Cartwright related, the wife protested to her father, who alerted the church elders, who informed the magistrates. The latter then "sent three several doctors to make inspection [of the husband]; they all have carefully taken the dimensions, and are to be witnesses tomorrow. . . . It will be worth the knowing what or how much is necessary for a holy sister." Nearly two decades later, when Ann Perry was petitioning against her husband for his impotence, John Dunton related that many men believed wives who complained about such matters were "loaded with Impudence." Dunton reminded his Boston contemporaries that women, having "their Natural Inclinations as well as we," ought to protest when their expectations were not fullfilled. Nevertheless, in this case, as in others, the Assistants found "insufficient" cause for divorce.[32]

Puritans felt that unrestrained marital indulgence, like premarital sex, led to sharp fevers, barrenness, disgust, deformity of issue, blindness, dehydration, and death—a fact which, according to one observer, explained why the prolific sparrow lived just three years. Since "Satiaty gluts the Womb, and renders it unfit for its Office," the wife, in particular, ought to curb the delight she derived from kissing and sexually enjoying her husband.[33] Neither party should relish the "pleasures of the flesh" so much that they supplanted, instead of being subordinated to, the "greater glory of God." "[I]m-moderate, intemperate, or excessive lust" could only turn wives into short-lived whores and husbands into deteriorating whoremas-ters. As one anonymous English writer urged, "the Bridegroom should remember that 'tis a Market that lasts all the Year, and be careful that he does not spend his Stock too lavishly." In response to such advice, some Puritans worried about their own overuse of the marriage bed. Michael Wigglesworth would lament to his diary in July, 1655, just two months after his wedding, "Much frothyness, pride, carnal lusts also exceeding[ly] prevailing. *Lord forgive my intemperance in the use of marriage.*" Similarly, when Edward Taylor's wife died, he felt that he himself was being punished for substitut-ing his own "carnal love" for love of God.[34]

In or out of marriage, sexual intercourse was regarded as a serious matter in Puritan New England. That "irresistible instinct" was difficult to harness, and divines repeatedly warned their congrega-tions against sexual "uncleanness" in all its manifold variations. Seventeenth-century magistrates prosecuted well over 2,000 forni-cators. Both sexes could be destroyed by the hot fire of lust, but within the context of a double standard. The assumption that women were less easily reclaimed than men; the explicit affirmation of virginity in women, compared to its more implicit value in men; and the ease with which a woman, but not a man, was converted into a whore all testified to two different standards—not of practice (the man's lust was no less a sin), but of presumed effect. The sinful woman, virgin transformed into whore, became a prototype of the despicable.

Sexually, then, three kinds of female stereotypes existed in Puri-tan New England. (Of course, men were also viewed as types of biblical saints and sinners, but the male typology was more varied.) One was the whore, the woman who did not confine her sexual activities to her husband. The whore had discovered sex and, as a member of the "weaker sex," was lost to its irresistible appeal. Her sexuality, which lacked a condition of emotional dependency on one man and was not centered around the institutional family, was illegitimate, as were the children arising from her liaisons. The antithesis of the whore was the virgin—that pure and innocent woman who waited for a man to sustain and satisfy her in marriage. The third type was the wife, who, while tied to one man for sexual release, remained chaste in outward actions and did not let her desire divert her thoughts from God.

Attitudes Toward Body Exposure

Since sexual activity bore the discomforting stamp of vileness, Puritans viewed any untoward genital exposure as vile. The testimony offered in many trials shows that to "discover another's nakedness" or to expose oneself publicly was considered "lewd and lascivious." In particular, "For a Woman to Expose unto Common View those parts of her Body, which there can be no Good End or use for the Exposing of is for her to Expose her selfe unto the Vengeance of Heaven." That statement by Cotton Mather referred not to the exposing of genitalia, but to the practice of revealing the upper portion of the breasts and the bare back by wearing the latest imported fashions. Such an exposure served a good end only when the woman was to be humiliated thereby, as in a public whipping. If she purposely wore skimpy dresses (by the standards of seventeenth-century New England), her motives had to be immoral. A desire for greater comfort in the heat of summer, or simply the desire to be more fashionable was not a legitimate explanation. A Puritan like Cotton Mather, preoccupied with thoughts of his own "vileness," could only assert that "a Woman by showing a Fair Skin" intended to "Enkindle a Fools Fire in the Male Spectators."[35] However, when men worked bare chested in the New England fields, and when they wore codpieces designed to bring attention to their genitals, they were never accused of alluring women.

Even in marriage there was some reluctance to view the spouse's nakedness. According to pastor John Eliot, all intercourse was to be conducted under night's hiding cloak, for sex was "what nature is ashamed of, either for the sun or any man to see." In 1678 Martha Horcely was sentenced to the most severe penalty for fornication —twenty lashes at each of two different locales—partly because she had intercourse with two men "immediately one after another," but also because she did it by day, "in the sight of each other." Couples apparently did not much investigate one another's bodies, even under the cover of night; when Mary Parsons suspected her husband, Hugh, of witchcraft at Springfield, Massachusetts, in the 1640s, she had to wait until he was asleep before she could search his body for witch's marks, and she was averse to examining his "secret Ptes" at all. When Hugh also wished to search his wife's body for witch's teats, "she resisted for she tould him it was an imodest Thinge."[36]

The extreme value Puritans attached to the male genitalia may explain why women were reluctant to examine their husbands, even when those men faced great physical pain in the region of their "Bowells." "No one that is hurt by bursting [his testicles], or that hathe his priuie membre cut of[f]," it was written in Deuteronomy 23:1, "shall entre into the Congregacion of the Lord." The question of whether one man might legitimately injure the genitals of another in self-defense was left open, but some Puritans did believe that a woman was to do so under no conditions. Charles Chauncy cited Deuteronomy 25:11–12 as proof that any woman who went so far as to injure a man's "secrets," and thereby exclude him from God's community, should have her arm cut off—even if that man were beating her own husband. Though such a woman might argue "that what she did was in trouble and perplexity of her mind, and in her husband's defense," Chauncy in 1642 related, "yet her hand must be cut off for such impurity (*and this is moral, as I conceive*)."[37] There was no similar prohibition against injuring the genitals of a woman.

Procreation and Birth Control

Calvinists thought the Lord had designed the genitals for pur-poses of procreation, and that any use of them which hindered procreation was illegal. Bestiality, as well as anal intercourse with a man or a woman, were therefore capitally punished. Masturbation, which wasted "seed," was also punishable by a severe whipping.[38] Ministers told males that "selfe pollution" would make them "soft, or effeminate"[39] (although the same divines did not warn female mas-turbators that they would become "hard, or masculine"). Sodomy, "which is carnal fellowship of man with man, or of woman with woman," was extremely offensive. John Cotton wished to punish homosexuality by hanging. New Haven Colony did enact such a law, specifying the death penalty "if any woman [or man] change the naturall use, into that which is against nature."[40] It is consistent with the Puritan dislike of wasted seed that in actual practice the only cases of lesbian behavior brought before the courts were not treated as capital offenses. In 1642 Essex County authorities se-verely whipped the servant Elizabeth Johnson and fined her £5 for criticizing her mistress, for being irreligious, and "for un-seemly practices betwixt her and another maid." In 1649 Mrs. Hugh Norman and Mary Hammond, both of Yarmouth, Plymouth Colony, were only admonished for "lewd behavior on a bed."[41]

Confronted with the need to subdue the wilderness, Puritans wanted large families. From the authorities' perspective, birth control was evil because it precluded that end. The woman who encouraged her sexual partner to use *coitus reservatus,* i.e., to "proceed to contact and friction without the emission of semen," was guilty of a crime against nature. Charles Chauncy pointed out that *coitus interruptus* was also a sin of great magnitude; according to this divine, if the man withdrew his penis from the vagina and spilled his seed upon the ground, as the biblical Onan had, that semen was wasted, because from it another human being could have been created. Chauncy reminded his contemporaries that God had killed Onan for so abusing his ejaculate. (Actually, Onan's sin was not the wasting of his seed, but his refusal to obey the levitical law which obligated him, after his brother's death, to supply progeny in his brother's name through intercourse with the widow.[42])

Puritan dames, maidens, and their sexual partners might well have been aware of any number of contraceptive remedies besides *coitus interruptus* and *reservatus.* It is likely that they had some familiarity with the linen sheath (that "armour against enjoyment, and a spider web against danger") and, by the 1690s, with the sheep-gut condom, for the English brothels were rumored to be "veritable arsenals of them."[43] They may also have been aware of the pessary, the suppository, astringents made of comfrey root, a rich variety of oral herbal contraceptives, cold baths (which reduced the possibility of orgasm and dampened desire), and bloodletting, for those were all widely known in England. In New Haven some persons believed that "conserve of Rue will hinder propagacon of children."[44] There is no way of determining how many men and women did consciously practice some form of birth control; since contraception was a heinous sin, they were not likely to report their methods, especially when it "would offend chast ears to hear them related."[45] However, the concern expressed by the divines, the number of infanticides, and the declining birth rate of the 1690s suggest that there was a desire to control the propagation of children.

Of Male and Female Genitalia

Although the sexual organs existed for the important purpose of procreation, Puritans tended to feel that the entire material body was unbelievably odious. Listen to Edward Taylor discourse on "Our Vile Bodies":

> Here is a mudwall tent, where Matters are
>   Dead Elements, which mixt make dirty trade.
>   . . . .
> . . . Guts, Garbage, Rottenness.
> And all its pipes but Sincks of nasty ware
> That foule Earths face, and do defile the aire.
>
> A varnisht pot of putrid excrements,
>   And quickly turns to excrements itselfe,
> By natures Law: . . .

Little else could be expected when human nature was "Corrupt, a nest of Passion, Pride,/ Lust, Worldliness and such like bubs."[46] The genitals naturally partook most vividly of this vileness. In the male, the foreskin represented lust's "Stain"; its removal was designed to prevent "the enmity of his carnal minde" from breaking out upon "any ripening temptacion." God had chosen circumcision as the seal for the covenant of works he made with Abraham because it was a graphic symbol of Abraham's desire to put away "the filth of the flesh"—that "most exquisite feeling" possessed by the unexposed glans. When the male scrutinized his circumcized penis, that external imperfection was to serve as an inspiration for him to circumcize the inward carnality of his own heart.[47]

As the concrete symbol for male sexual identity, the penis itself could hardly be viewed merely as an organ for elimination, procreation, interaction, and pleasure. Instead, it became a diminutive "pricke," an overmagnified "yard," or a punishing "rod."[48] Through such a choice of descriptive terms, men revealed their anxiety about their sexual aggressiveness, their need to control in the sex act, and, ultimately, their own impotence. Had they been less anxious about their sexuality, New England males might have generally used neutral words like "instrument of nature," "pee-er," "phallus," and "penis," for those were commonly used in seventeenth-century England.

The female genitalia were referred to more ambiguously. Puritans generally did not name them at all (with the exception of the womb)—even in those tracts published to prepare pregnant women for their parturition.[49] Although the English Puritan Nicholas Culpeper mentioned the "cleft" and the erectile capacity of the clitoris, New England court records describe the vulva only very generally, as "secret parts," "privates," "her nakedness," or "her body." None of the English colloquialisms like "the pin-box," "the purse," or (that perennial abomination) "cunt" appear in any of the correspondence, medical accounts, or other New England records this researcher has examined; nor do more technical words like "vagina" and "pudendum."[50] Puritans apparently assumed the female genitalia remained best unidentified, and inspected only by the midwife.

However, even midwives sometimes lacked complete awareness of the degree of female genital variation, especially of the many changes attendant upon age. Juries of midwives occasionally mistook the age-loosened folds of the labia majora[51] or a hypertrophied clitoris for a witch's teat. In 1692, when two Connecticut women were accused of witchcraft, one, Elizabeth Clawson, reportedly had a structure growing from within to the outside of the genital lips. It was one and one-half inches long and in the shape of a dog's ear. Clawson's confederate, Mercy Disborough, had "within ye lep of ye same a los pees of skin and when puld it is near an Inch long somewhat in form of ye finger of a glove flattened . . . that lose skin were Judge[d] more than [is] common to women." Only a rare woman would realize that there was nothing abnormal about such structures.[52] The witch-finders did not, however, view a relatively large or wide "yard" as a sign of witchcraft, any more than they considered the loss of testicular tightness in aged men as such a sign.

Had the midwives consulted Nicholas Culpeper's compendium of female genital disorders, they would have read that the clitoris could reach the size of a man's penis in some women, and that this was caused not by witchcraft, but allegedly by "too much nourishment of the part, from the looseness of it by often handling." Culpeper's cure for this "disease" was not hanging, but something at least as excruciating. This physician suggested the application of astringents to dry out the clitoris; then, if the organ failed to diminish in size, "cut it off, or tie it with a ligature of Silk or Horsehair, till it mortifie."[53]

It seems reasonable to assume that the Puritan authorities, highly educated and sometimes trained in medicine, would have shared the attitudes of contemporary European physicians. Those doctors tended to visualize the male genitals as the norm, the reference point against which female genital anatomy and physiology should be described. When "the cleft is so narrow, that it wil not admit of a mans Yard," Culpeper considered the woman "diseased." Culpeper's associates called vaginal lubrication "feminine semen," ligaments in the genital area became "ejaculatory ducts," and one doctor compared a prolapsed uterus to "a Bulls cod [i.e., balls] dangling between her leggs." Not until the latter half of the seventeenth century did the term "ovary" come into use. Before that, and even well into the eighteenth century, physicians believed "spermatic vessels" carried the blood to internal female "testicles," each of which produced about twenty "little Bladders" called eggs. Medical experts continued to designate the ovaries as testicles, even though it was readily recognized that the female organs differed from the male in "Bigness, Temperament, Substance, Form" and "Covering." Like men, maidens reputedly experienced wet dreams. Such descriptions suggested that, genitally speaking, the female was a less complete, more inward version of the male.[54]

Medical authorities assumed that the female sexual organs had a relatively dormant, passive character—the physiological manifestation of the general passivity to which woman was heir "by nature." Many physicians from the time of Aristotle until the seventeenth century believed men had "preeminence and overruling power" in the conceptive process, serving as "the Efficient, or Agent," with the woman as "the Matter, or Patient."[55] *Aristotle's Compleat Masterpiece*, a popular sex manual which went into five English editions by 1700 and at least 26 American ones by 1775, mentioned the "active, injecting Principle" and the "passive, impregnated Principle," attributing the former to man and the latter to woman.[56] Some doctors felt that the fetus developed from a small embryo contained within the male semen and implanted into a vacant egg. Most, however, held that conception occurred by "the exquisite mixture of the Seed of both Sexes," which acted as yeast to stir up a froth out of which the fetus emerged. Descartes likened the entire process to the brewing of beer. In this view, the two seeds did not merely mingle; they wrestled for advantage. Since male semen—"white, clammy, knotty, smelling unto the elder of palme, delectable to bees and sinking downe to the bottome of water [upon] being put into it"—bore more force than the less viscous, cold and moist female semen, the stronger male semen usually overcame the weaker female. The conception of a male fetus (the end result of the male's victory) undoubtedly pleased fathers, but the conception of a female fetus (indicating the superiority of the female seed) quite probably exasperated them. The birth of a girl signaled the father's "effeminacy." [57]

No conception could occur without some love between the partners, which Culpeper maintained was the reason few prostitutes became pregnant.[58] The reason for this was as follows: "Content and Satisfaction of Mind dilate the Heart and Arteries, whereby the vital [semen-nourishing] Blood and Spirits are freely distributed throughout the Body."[59] In 1677 the Dutch optician Anton van Leeuwenhoek discovered wriggling spermatozoa in the nocturnal ejaculate of one man, thereby providing "irrefutable" proof that the male was the decisive force in procreation. Male semen thereafter, more completely than before, became "the original source of life . . . the germ out of which the future generation proceeded."[60]

For Leeuwenhoek, like so many of his associates, the woman served merely as a receptive incubator in the process of generation. Some time earlier, in 1651, the English physician William Harvey had emphatically rejected the prevailing notion that the male was "Master . . . of the original of the Motus and Generation" itself. He pointed out that the male did not "produce" that "which is designed out of the Matter conteined in the Female," since "amongst Animals, some Females do procreate of themselves without a Male . . . but the Male never begetteth any thing without a Female." Both sexes participated in conception with "Efficient" power, but "It is to the uterus that the business of conception is chiefly entrusted; without this structure and its functions conception would be looked for in vain." The woman produced no semen.[61]

However, within thirty years Harvey's ovism would fall before the spermatozooic wayside. Attributing everything to the sperm was ultimately more compatible with a view of woman as the passive, weaker sex. Culture wrote biology: had seventeenth-century observers been inclined to consider the sexes as equal participants in conception, they could have rationally concluded that, since sexual relations did not always result in pregnancy, the uterus either rejected or accepted the invading sperm. Such a position would have conceded the woman a more determining or active role in the conceptive process, and would have served as an important bridge between Harvey and the discoveries of Leeuwenhoek. Although inaccurate by present-day terms, that position would nevertheless have been consistent with the state of seventeenth-century biological knowledge. (As an aside, it ought to be noted that the vagina is far from a completely passive, purely receptive organ. It possesses a finely developed musculature capable of actively clutching the penis, or of, in vaginismus, rejecting it. Relevant here is S. Rado's distinction between male and female sexuality on the basis of the "push and pull" principle. In his terms, the sperm seeks the egg, while the egg attracts the sperm; the penis acts as a pressure pump, while the vagina acts as a suction pump.[62])

A woman might participate energetically in the sexual experience itself, but for purposes of conception her post-intercourse passivity was deemed crucial. According to the medical authorities, the best results occurred when she fell asleep afterward and avoided sneezing, coughing, "or any other Thing that causes a too violent Motion of the body," for such motion might dislodge the fertilized egg. Once the woman became aware that she was pregnant, she had to refrain from much exercise, disturbing passions, filthy smells, and a rich diet—all of which could cause her fragile body to abort the fetus. Miscarriages reportedly occurred because the genital ligaments were "weak, and soon broken."[63]

The assumption that delicate female genitals fell "subject to so many Infirmities" caused men to blame women for continued failure to conceive. Barrenness ostensibly resulted from "stopping of the Menstrus," excessive menstrual flow, flux, uterine retroversion, "Inflammation, Windiness, Heat and Dryness." Women easily angered or those with a quick pulse might render themselves barren; choleric males faced no similar impediment. In fact, as long as a man's penis became erect and he had intercourse with sufficient vigor, he could hardly be viewed as the "inadequate" partner.[64]

Prevailing notions of female weakness-passivity influenced medical interpretations of menstruation as well. Doctors assumed that woman's "weak" internal organs were too fragile to endure much physical stress, especially during the menses. Menstruating women were urged not to enter cold water because their "exposed" uterine blood vessels might freeze. Some Englishwomen played it safe by keeping abed during their "terms," lest the womb's "nourishment" dry up completely and then generate "evil humours." Whether physicians believed that lunar phases, the physiological need to relieve "the assumed plethora of all women," the "natural" desire to rid the body of poisonous substances, or the inability of women to use up all of the rich nourishment borne in the blood best explained the occurrence of menstruation, they all agreed that it was a necessary event, but one too easily obstructed. Any suppression of the menses or irregularity of flow became a symptom of "disease," a sign that the "weak" female genitals were failing to function properly.[65] Such a point of view probably caused women much needless worry, since, as the Boston Women's Health Book Collective has pointed out, "There is no record . . . of a woman with an absolutely regular menstrual cycle," and major changes occur whenever the woman experiences "a great deal of stress." Girls between fourteen (the average age of the menarche) and sixteen would have been particularly irregular.[66] The recommendation for bed rest—based on the assumption that the loss of approximately two ounces of blood was enervating—decreased the immediate quantity of blood lost, but increased the duration of the bleeding, since the bedridden woman could not rely on gravity to assist her. Because bed rest causes the body to lose calcium, as does menstruation itself, the physiological effects of such loss (cramping, headaches, swollenness of the breasts and feet, susceptibility to infection) would have been accentuated by staying in bed.[67] Despite the growing acceptability of a scientific approach to physiology in the late seventeenth century, male doctors apparently did not bother to ask menstruating woman whether they felt better in an upright or a prone position. (Whatever their degree of discomfort, some women may, of course, have considered their bed rest as a needed respite from household duties.)

As might be expected, menstrual regularity became a widespread concern of many women on both sides of the Atlantic. Females took any number of herbal remedies—dittany, mugworth, pennyroyal, savin, and so on—to promote menstrual regularity by giving "an almost incredible motion to the whole nervous system." Some women placed the leaves of mullein in their shoes, a remedy guaranteed to "provoke the Terms (especially in such Virgins as never had them)." Others used lotions, fumes, odors, ointments, and "emplaistration" or let doctors bleed them.[68] Often they considered marrying, so that their husband's lively member might stir their passive bodies into menstrual readiness. Venery, after all, "heats the womb and the parts adjacent, opens and loosens the passages," causing the terms to "better flow to the womb." Had not the French surgeon Ambroise Paré observed that, when a woman experienced intercourse and "on a sudden begins to contain her self, it is verie likely that shee is [thereafter] suffocated by the suppression of the flowers [i.e., menses]"?[69] Some recommended marriage as a cure for both menstrual suppression and irregular flow, showing how deep the image of female dependency ran. Roger Williams and his fifteen-year-old daughter Mary considered that possible way to relieve her irregularity before rejecting it because of her age.[70]

Some of these treatments subjected women to much pain. Mary
Williams took "a flux of rheum" which "much affected her head and
right eye." Pennyroyal and dittany are gentle stimulants, but mugworth and savin are very dangerous. Mugworth can bring about
"trembling, stupor, and later violent epileptiform convulsions, with
involuntary evacuations, unconsciousness, and stertorous breathing, which may or may not end in death." The highly irritating oil of
savin may produce violent inflammation of the mucous membranes
and gastrointestinal injury. An overdose could lead to severe "abdo-
minal pain, bloody vomiting and purging, dimunition or suppression of urine, disordered respiration, unconsciousness, convulsions
and fatal collapse."[71] Bloodletting, one of the treatments Mary Williams received, could also have discomforting as well as humiliating
effects, since horse-leeches were sometimes attached to the neck of
the womb. Despite their popularity, the painful herbal remedies
and bloodletting did little to provoke the menses. Nor did Pare's
cruel treatment for severe cases, in which the physician placed the
afflicted patient on her back, then pulled her pubic hair to shock the
womb out of "strangulation."[72]

Although a symbol of natural female functioning, menstruation
was viewed as unsavory. Seventeenth-century English superstition
held that, if a menstruating woman served wine to guests, it would
turn to vinegar. If a dog tasted her "infectious matter," it would
supposedly run mad within three days.[73] A popular epigram
asserted, "Oh! menstruating woman, thou'rt a fiend,/ From whom
all nature should be closely screened."[74] Some medicinal interest
centered around Pliny's opinion that "Menstrual blood is a fatal
poison, corrupting and decomposing urine, depriving seeds of their
fecundity, destroying insects, blasting garden flowers and grasses,
causing fruits to fall from branches, dulling razors etc."[75] Sexual
intercourse while the woman was menstruating became one of the
most heinous acts a couple could commit. From such a union only
"dull, heavy, sluggish," mentally defective children or even "monsters" could result. To avoid such an eventuality, John Cotton recommended hanging those who had been privy to the "Pollution
of a woman knowne to be in her flowers." When the heretic
Samuel Gorton wished to attack the Massachusetts authorities, his
ultimate abasement was to assert that the Puritans would "bring
nothing but filthy menstruous Clouts [clots] before God, which
stuffe we abhore."[76] Such dislike of menstruation seemed to suggest that the common medieval attitude of woman being "a

temple built over a sewer" was still alive in seventeenth-century England and New England.[77]

Rape: A Cultural Context

In so many ways the Puritan's view of sexuality, like that of their English contemporaries, was male centered. Although Puritans affirmed that the woman ought to enjoy sex, in marital moderation, they valued that sex largely with reference to her dependency on and passivity before the male. The assumption that the male was the seducer, the active force in conception, the insurer of menstrual regularity, and less "ruin'd" by premarital intercourse reinforced male "strength" against female "weakness." Puritans detested sexual license, but their acceptance of the male as initiator, coupled with their belief in explosive sexual "instincts," sometimes brought about the very license they condemned.

It was easy for some men to assume that dependent, passive women existed to fulfill their needs, sexual or otherwise. A man might make advances toward a woman and then justify his "immoral" behavior with the subliminal (if not fully conscious) presumption that he was merely responding to the demand of gonads bursting with unused energy. In fact, the rapist usually defended himself by asserting that the devil or "my own lust overcame me"; he hardly valued the point of view of the "dependent" woman with whom he was attempting to take liberties. Henry Waltham "sett hands" upon or plucked at the bosoms of at least four different goodwives who entered his Weymouth shop (1640). Another man, Mark Meggs of New Haven, visited the wife of Nathaniel Seeley, "came behinde her, and wth his armes clasped her about ye midle, put his hand vnder her aprone (if not worse)," and then "told her he would feele whether ther were a boy ther or not." He forced her to face him and asked her two or three times "whether he should get on her" (1650).[78] Richard Turtall of Plymouth was equally overt: he took hold of Ann Hudson's coats, spoke enticing words to her, and drew out "his instrument of nature that he might prevaile to lye with her in her owne house" (1655). William Collins of New Háven used a somewhat different approach, throwing Mary Pinion upon a bed and saying he had a commission from her husband to lie with her "if she would give her Consent"(1666).[79]

Despite the aggressiveness of their overtures, Turtall, Meggs, and Collins did ask the woman's consent to sexual relations. Other males assumed more literally that women existed to serve *their* needs. In New Hampshire, for example, David Kimball pulled the eighteen-year-old maidservant Ann Snelling into his lap and "asked her to liv with him"; when she struggled, "he said are not woo[men] made for the lives of men" (1670). Similarly, Peter Grant thought the unclaimed single woman should bend before his sexual whim. He flung Edward Wire's servant "down in the streete and got atop hir." A neighbor "caled vppon the fellow to be sivill and not to abuse the mayd, then Edward Wire came forth and ran to the said grant and took hold of him, asking him what he did to his mayd." Grant responded simply by inquiring whether his intended victim was Wire's wife, for he agreed to do nothing to another man's wife. Since she was not in a dependent marital relationship with a man, Peter Grant considered Deborah Hadlock fair game. When Wire prevented him from raping her, Grant threatened to tear down Wire's house.[80]

Grant and at least seventy-one other men appeared before the Puritan authorities in seventeenth-century New England for taking forcible sexual liberties with seventy-eight nonconsenting females. The latter included twenty-six unwed servants, thirty-five wives (including four Indian squaws), nine single women, and eight children between the ages of three and thirteen.[81] In twenty-eight of these cases the woman testified that an actual rape had been completed. Three-fourths of these rapists and would-be rapists made no effort to verbally persuade their victims to consent to sexual relations, relying instead on sheer force.

We cannot now know what caused each man to attempt rape; however, we can look at those cultural tendencies which collectively might predispose him. First was the currency of the belief that women existed to serve men's needs. Second was the Puritan obsession with the explosiveness of "sexual instincts," which meshed with the prevailing notion that no conception could follow a "forced" copulation.[82] A "driven" man who did not want a potential bastardy charge hanging over his head could consider rape a sexual approach preferable to seduction. Third, the very real feeling of powerlessness before God, nature, and the authorities—that same feeling which led Puritans to polarize sex roles into rigid terms of male dominance and female submission—had a sexual reference point. The acceptance of the notion that the "stronger" male was the initiator in sex, in conjunction with the use of words like "prick," "yard," and "impotence" (i.e., without power), indicate that power and control were sexual concerns. The tendency of some men to wear codpieces to accentuate the size of the penis, as if that organ itself were demonstrable proof of masculine potency, further suggests such a preoccupation. The equation of penile size and functioning with personal power may have caused some men to want to test and affirm their masculinity through forcible intercourse. The rapist who told his victim "I will make you yeald to me" certainly revealed his need for a "conquest."[83]

The man rendered "impotent" by Puritan theology and child-rearing practices could easily come to regard the woman not as a person like himself, but as a sexual "type"—an inferior, a receptacle, a virgin, a whore, or a simple answer to his needs. His rape attempt did not necessarily involve any particular hatred of the victim; rather, it displayed his profound inability to acknowledge that women had any basic "rights," including the right to accept or reject his overtures. As a result, the man usually overpowered the woman without using a weapon, and did not brutalize her by sticking foreign objects up her vagina or beating her severely.

At other times, however, the rape attempt might proceed out of a profound sense of misogyny. If a male sensed and struggled against his generalized lack of power, he could easily bring himself to detest a surrogate, someone who was not the cause of his problem. A need for vengeance could follow, making the rape particularly brutal. There are records of two such rapes, both murders. In one instance, the wife of Mr. Willip of Exeter, New Hampshire, was found dead in the Exeter River, "her neck broken, her tongue black and swollen out of her mouth, and the blood settled in her face, the privy parts swollen, etc., as if she had been much abused." The murderer was never apprehended.[84]

Puritans also placed some obstacles in the path of the male who sought a wife. The man who felt that his sexual "instincts" (or, perhaps more accurately, anxieties) needed release could attempt, like Michael Wigglesworth, to find a "help-mate." However, gaining a wife involved an elaborate wooing process, securing her parents' permission, and displaying the ability as well as the willingness to support her. The man who lacked decent prospects or much status in the community might easily be rejected.[85] Delay and urgent desire did not fit well together. Prostitutes did not exist, outside Boston, so seduction was an immediate and (if effective) appeasing answer to the male's dilemma. If his verbal overtures failed, the male might decide to become more forcible; after all, he might reason, wasn't he supposed to be the powerful, activating partner? If his victim went into shock or protested a little, wasn't that because she was simply being a passive female? If she resisted more, wasn't she denying her natural condition to exist for and through a man? Rape might then follow, the result of the bachelor's delusions and egocentricity. Those one-eighth of rapists and attempted rapists who first asked their victim's permission and then rejected their refusals may have been reacting in accordance with this pattern of sex-role conditioning.

The argument that a cultural belief in self-justifying, explosive sexual "instincts" could easily serve as a starting point for rape received some confirmation from the fact that 91 percent of all males who attempted rape were single. This is the reverse of the late twentieth-century situation, where two-thirds of all convicted rapists are married.[86]

Whatever their perceived motives, almost half of all would-be "seducers" stopped using force when the woman called out or objected vociferously. These men may have been troubled by guilt; they may have feared apprehension and punishment; or they may have had more respect for women as persons than those men who did not stop. The tendency not to view sex as a form of interpersonal communication probably made it easier for the rapist to "separate" the woman from her body (if she were a neighbor, for instance) while he momentarily "used" it. Since it was easier for a man to rape an object, a caricature, than for him to accost a human being with rights of her own, the woman who objected strongly may have brought the seducer-rapist to his senses by forcing him to confront her personality.

By promoting the anxieties and illusions which made rape possible, Puritan culture allowed rape to become the instrument through which some men expressed their frustrations, their feelings of inadequacy, and their inability to view women as equals. Yet, even though the culture was implicated in rape, Puritans did not treat that offense lightly. The penalties were severe: New Haven (1656), Plymouth (1671), and New Hampshire (1679) specified capital punishment. Connecticut and Massachusetts authorities made some effort to differentiate between the rape of a single or a married woman, suggesting that some Puritans viewed the offense more as a crime against the man's estate than as a crime against the woman's body. The first Connecticut law code provided capital punishment only for the rape of a woman who was married or contracted to marry (1642). In the same year, the Massachusetts General Court directed that any man who raped a married or espoused woman be hanged, and that all other rapists (if the victim were ten or older) be punished by death or "other grevious" penalty. The rape of children was dealt with separately, though apparently not out of concern for the greater suffering and trauma inflicted. John Winthrop wrote in 1641 that "it should be death for a man to have carnal copulation with a girl so young, as there can be no possibility of generation, for it is against nature as well as sodomy and buggery." The Bay Colony deputies and assistants agreed with the governor and enacted a law capitally punishing any intercourse with a female child of less than ten years, even if the sexual relations were undertaken with her consent (1642). The New Haven General Court also specified the death penalty for any abuse of the "unripe vessel of a Girle" (1656), while New Hampshire enacted a similar statute.[87]

At least six rapists were hanged—five in Massachusetts and the other, a two-time offender, in Connecticut. Two of the seven victims were unwed maidens, one was a child of three, another was a servant, and the remaining three were wives.[88] The authorities convicted two other men, but there are no records of their sentences.[89] One Indian who raped a nine-year-old Indian girl was sold into life-long servitude, a Connecticut offender had an R branded into his cheek,[90] and forty-two men received severe whippings, as well as, in most instances, fines. Only two men escaped with a fine alone: Richard French was sentenced to pay the county £3 and Jane Evans £2 in damages, and John Ashecroft was ordered to make "satisfaction by fine" for raping an Indian woman.[91] The magistrates acquitted eight defendants, and the final disposition of fifteen cases is unknown.

In these seventy-eight cases the magistrates referred to the offense as "rape" or "attempted rape" only about half of the time. Otherwise they used much euphemisms as "ravishing," "carnal knowledge of a female without her consent," "indecent assault," "shameful abuse offered," "indecent actions," or "assault." Such terminology may have reflected "perceived gradations in the enormity of the crime, and a desire to avoid specifying a capital offense,"[92] as Catherine Baker has hypothesized. At any rate, New England penalties were less severe than those in the mother country: English rapists faced hanging, or castration and blinding in both eyes.[93]

Since the usual penalty for forcible rape was death or a severe lashing, the rapist may have attempted to select a victim of low credibility. Servants constituted one-third of the victims but no more than 10 percent of the adult female population; obviously they answered that need, as well as the associated needs of high subservience and availability—especially after 1650, when the social status of the servant plummeted. Identification of the assailant would have been much simpler in seventeenth-century New England than in the populous urban settings of today. Two rapists made sure they would not be identified by killing their victims, and one of these murderers did escape apprehension. Still, homicidal rape was fortunately rare.[94]

The case of William Robinson and Goodwife Fancy at New Haven in 1646 reveals that respectable testimony was a matter of some concern, at least for the intended victim's husband. Robinson reportedly had attempted to have sexual relations with the goodwife in his cellar, in his lot, in a cornfield, in the cowhouse, and in his home while his own wife was asleep. Each time Goody Fancy resisted his overtures and asked her husband to complain to the governor on her behalf. He refused, however, asserting that "his wife haveing bin publicquely punished for theevery, should not be believed." Perhaps he did not believe her himself.[95]

Mr. Fancy's insensitive apprehensiveness was not rooted in a factual understanding of court procedure. Throughout New England the victim's testimony sufficed to convict a man of attempted rape. If an examination by a jury of midwives revealed that a maiden possessed a ruptured hymen or that any woman had lacerations or bruises in the genital area, such findings constituted grounds for conviction on the more serious charge of actual rape. Puritans assumed that rape would immobilize the victim with fear; therefore she was not expected physically to resist a male assault. Since scratching and hitting a man would have opposed her sex-role conditioning, the magistrates did not consider lack of physical resistance as grounds for questioning a victim's testimony, nor did they presume that she was in any way responsible for attracting the assailant. The woman who went into the woods with a man was presumed innocent of any wrongdoing. Contrary to assumptions in more recent times, Puritans thought the woman who chose a male traveling companion was merely protecting herself from danger.

Rape was considered so serious that a woman could not lie about it. Even in the eight cases where the community suspected the woman of inviting an advance, the man who made it received sharp punishment. The case of Susan Clarke v. Ellis Mew, heard before the New Haven town court in 1653, is particularly illustrative. Clarke, a serving maid, complained that Mew forcibly "discouered her nakedness," pulled down his breeches, and would have raped her had she not cried out. Mew gave a different version of the encounter. He explained that Clarke had flirted with him, pulling provocatively on his sleeve; he had placed her on the bed and kissed her until she told him to leave her alone. The town court debated the case for some time because Clarke's veracity was questionable, while Mew had not been known to lie previously. Goodwife Jones testified that "she had taken the girle in some vntruthes," but the court decided "that doth not prove that she tells vntruth in this case; nor is it likely that such a young girle should bee so impudent as to charge such a carriage upon a young man when it was not so." Notwithstanding his unblemished reputation, the selectmen agreed that Mew might lie in an attempted rape case. The townsmen ordered him whipped, to keep children "safe from such temptations and defylement."[96]

Mew was one of but eight rapists or would-be rapists who maintained that their intended victims had enticed them.[97] Most rapists probably never would have thought to make such an argument, for the prevailing belief in female passivity mitigated against it. The male concerned with exercising sexual power and initiative could hardly have granted the female a role in planning the sexual encounter. Describing the female as initiator (and, if resistance followed enticement, as controller) would merely have fed men's anxieties about their own sexuality. Only two men contested the woman's word about whether a sexual attack had occurred. After Mary Clay said Joseph Atkinson had taken up her "Coats and woulde have ravished her," he sued her for defamation of character. However, she received the verdict and was awarded 50s. in damages.[98]

Rape attempts were not simply the spontaneous, thoughtless expressions of a man's uncontrollable desire (or desire to control). They had to be planned in communities so closely knit, and ones where women seldom went far from home by themselves. The scarcity of opportunity, plus the ease with which the rapist could be identified, makes the total of seventy-nine attempts loom larger than it might, at first glance, seem.[99] A potential rapist had to lure a given woman into a secluded spot, or approach a neighbor's house when the adult males were absent, under the pretext of collecting bills or borrowing something. Husbands, sons, brothers, and other women were usually in close enough proximity to make rape impossible. Nevertheless, 20 percent of all rape attempts occurred either in public places or in houses where another person in an adjacent room could conceivably overhear the struggle.

Rape: The Female's Response

New England Puritans lived in small, compact communities, a fact which decreased the chances of a woman meeting a stranger who might rape her. In 85.3 percent of the cases of rape or attempted rape, the victim was a neighbor or even a servant in the same household.[100] The woman's usual familiarity with the man undoubtedly contributed to her willingness to trust him and to journey into the wilderness with him. One-third of the rapes occurred in the forest or other isolated terrain. Since the rapist knew his victim, he may have chosen a woman whom he suspected would not report an assault—a demure, non-assertive woman more inclined to go rigid with fear or to cry than to fight. Most victims did, in fact, respond with shocked disbelief and some verbal objection; only seven actually scratched or bit their assailants. Mary Sholy managed to tear skin off William Schooler's nose before he raped and killed her in 1637, but Mary Davis managed to elude her attacker more effectively by actively resisting. After Jonathan Phillips picked her up and laid her on a bed, she "gott hold of his throat & nipping him hoard gat out of the bed from him & ran away."[101]

Some modern scholars have tried to explain such relative lack of resistance as manifesting the victim's subconscious desire to be forcibly possessed.[102] But it makes more sense to consider that the woman, trained to occupy a passive and dependent position, could not be expected to suddenly transform herself into a fighting, undeferential spirit. Awe and its social product, intimidation, probably helped immobilize women who had already internalized a sense of inferiority. Thus the male assailant's physical advantage was combined with a powerful psychological edge.

If the rapist was a master or master's relative and the victim a servant, his psychological advantage was much increased. In reacting to a sexual overture, the female then had to deal with the inhibiting nature of two conditions of submissiveness: that of female before male, and of servant before master. Both factors suggest that the number of unreported rapes and rape attempts against servants may have been considerable. The fear inspired by such a situation is revealed in the testimony of two maidservants before the Middlesex County Court. After Thomas Hawes, the brother of Sarah Lepingwell's master, pulled her onto his bed one night, she asked him to let her go but did not cry out when he proceeded to have intercourse with her. She later explained, "I was posesed with fear of my master least my master shold think I did it only to bring scandall on his brother and thinking thay wold all beare witness agaynst me." Elizabeth Dickerman more effectively resisted her master, John Harris. He tried to force her "to be naught with him . . . [and] tould her that if she tould her dame: what cariag he did show to her[,] shee had as good be hanged." She replied that she would run away, did so, and then complained to the authorities that "if she should liue ther she shall be in fear of [losing] her life." Harris was ordered soundly whipped.[103]

For an assaulted woman to complain to the authorities required great courage. She had to violate her sex-role conditioning about modesty, undergo the pain attendant upon describing her traumatic experience, and press charges against the "superior" male. And, after all was said and done, she might be regarded as regrettably damaged goods. The community indicated great interest in the details of at least twenty-eight of the seventy-nine rape cases; large numbers of witnesses testified, including fourteen in one trial. Everyone knew who the victim was, which may have prevented many a woman from bringing her rape to the attention of the authorities in the first place. For example, Jane Bond of York, Maine, did not report her rape to the selectmen until Robert Collins had made his third attempt against her in less than a year; he had finally raped her twice in one night, with her six-year-old son looking on.[104] Quite probably the community caused the victim to focus on the fact of her rape long after it had occurred, since she could not attempt to "forget" it when reminders lurked everywhere. The locale where the rape had taken place, the gossip about her case, and the very real possibility of encountering her assailant when she went on her daily rounds could all cause the victim to dwell on her rape for some time. It was with good cause that Elizabeth Pierce told her attacker, "lett mee alone for it will bee both sin and a shame to you *and me* as long as we live."[105]

Modern studies indicate that most women experience severe emotional trauma after they have been raped.[106] Since Puritan recordkeepers paid virtually no attention to the subsequent reactions of rape victims, we cannot know how rape affected their behavior patterns. However, the Puritan belief in rape as contributory to female promiscuity, coupled with the polarization of female sexuality into virginity (or wifely chastity) versus whoredom, undoubtedly caused the woman a good deal of concern. The belief that rape could not lead to pregnancy quite probably caused those who did conceive to wonder if they had somehow consented to their own violation. None of the victims, almost all of whom waited two months to a year before reporting their rapes, became pregnant; those women who did would have faced fornication charges themselves! Moreover, what minimal control the seventeenth-century Puritan woman did exercise was suddenly stripped away in an act of rape, leaving her reduced to the devastated feeling of total helplessness before the onslaught of one man. In a religious society, this concrete deprivation of control could easily be viewed as a perceived threat to the woman's control over her own salvation. Rape had providential relevance: if God let someone rape her, the victim might reason, she *must be* among the literal damned. Jane Bond apparently had such a concern, for she told her assailant, ". . . put your finger but a littell in the fier [and] you will not be able to Induer it, but *I* must suffer eternally."[107]

The woman of independent mind might reject such a Puritan orientation, but those submissive, "ideal" women who were assaulted probably had great difficulty with prevailing expectations. There is a record of at least one female who underwent severe stress. After a frightening encounter with Richard French, Jane Evans was troubled with "very sad fitts, like vnto falling sicknes [i.e., epilepsy]." In these fits she became quite "senceless" and cried out plaintively "Oh this French will kill me."[108]

Even though the magistrates believed the victim's testimony without asking her embarrassing or character-assassinating questions, they did not seem motivated by much humane concern for her. They were, rather, preoccupied with exposing and punishing yet another sinful act. The authorities failed to refer the assaulted female to other sympathetic women or to a clergyman for consolation. Presumably the victim, who had been taught to value her virginity or marital chastity highly and who had been severely frightened (if not actually abused), would be in great need of such consolation. Neither did the magistrates express concern lest a woman's ability to relate to other men, or to herself, should suffer impairment. The authorities allowed damages to the victim in only four cases.[109] If a wife was raped by her husband there were no grounds for even a criminal charge, "for by their mutual matrimonial consent and contract his wife hath given up herself in this kind to her husband, which she cannot retract." Perhaps John Cotton best revealed the ultimate extent of Puritan leaders' insensitivity when he recommended marriage between rapist and victim.[110]

The lack of concern for rape victims and the male-centered character of Puritan sexual attitudes mirrored the general Puritan preoccupation with male control and female dependency in society at large. Rape became a vehicle through which some men expressed the same feelings of inadequacy and anti-egalitarianism that underlay Puritan matrimonial, religious, and political institutions. In bed, as in state and church, the female was the inferior, weaker sex. Whatever benefits women received in terms of their presumed credibility and manifest innocence in rape trials occurred only because Puritans expected female passivity in sexual, as well as other, matters.

1. *Problemes of Aristotle*, pp. E, F4; Hoadly, ed., *Rec. of N. Haven 1638–45*, p. 435; T. Hooker, *Application of Redemption*, p. 234.

2. S. Danforth, *Cry of Sodom*, pp. 16, 18.

3. W. Bradford, *Of Plym. Plant.*, pp. 316–17.

4. In 1659 Mary Clay of Maine was fined 20s. for "her uncivill Carages in suffering James Harmon & his wife to ly in bedd with her" (Libby, Allen, & Moody, eds., *Maine Ct. Rec.*, II, 92).

5. S. Danforth, *Cry of Sodom*, pp. 12–14, 8, 17.

6. C. Mather, *Warnings from Dead*, pp. 46–47, 51, and *Magnalia*, II, 342.

7. For instances of venereal disease, see Winthrop, *Journal*, II, 268; G. Dow, ed., *Essex Ct. Rec.*, VII, 395; L. Hammond, "Diary," p. 170; Petition of George Munnings, Jailer, to the General Court, Oct. 20, 1654, cited in Rutman, *Winthrop's Boston*, pp. 242–43n.

8. John Cotton, *Practical Commentary*, p. 131; R. Baxter, *Reasons of Christian Rel.*, p. 16; S. Danforth, *Cry of Sodom*, pp. 8, 18–19.

9. Secker, *Wedding ring*, n.p.; *Confession of Faith Owned*, p. 53.

10. Dr. Alcock explained that as "a little alum wil caus the mouth to fil with water, so a little acrimony gathering there [in the penis] causeth humours to flow thither amain, which might come away in great quantity, and yet there be plenty of true semen [left] behind." The physician told Michael Wigglesworth that "marriage would take Away the caus of that distemper," which was the reputed natural impulse of his "irresistible instinct." A month later Wigglesworth was wed (Wigglesworth, *Diary*, pp. 404–6).

11. *Ibid*.

12. Libby, Allen, & Moody, eds., *Maine Ct. Rec.*, I, 292–93; Noble & Cronin, eds., *Rec. of Mass. Assts.*, I, 138; II, 137; John Cotton, *Abstract of Lawes*, p. 11; Shurtleff & Pulsifer, eds., *Plym. Rec.*, IV, 106; V, 260; Pulsifer,

trans., "Norfolk Ct. Rec.," I, pt. 1, p. 46; "N. Hamp. Ct. of Quarter Sessions, 1686–99," p. 47.

13. E.g., see Winthrop, *Journal*, II, 138; Noble & Cronin, eds., *Rec. of Mass. Assts.*, II, 87, 91, 93; Hoadly, ed., *Rec. of N. Haven 1653–Union*, p. 138; *Rec. of Suffolk Ct., 1671–1680*, I, 558; Sewall, *Diary*, I, 486.

14. John Cotton, *Abstract of Lawes*, p. 12; C. Mather, *Ornaments for Daughters of Zion*, p. 44.

15. [N. Ward,] *Simple Cobler*, p. 20.

16. Examples appear in Winthrop, *Journal*, II, 318; Noble & Cronin, eds., *Rec. of Mass. Assts.*, I, 70–71; Dexter, ed., *N. Haven Town Rec. 1649–62*, pp. 498, 506.

17. Libby, Allen, & Moody, eds., *Maine Ct. Rec.*, I, 290.

18. Dexter, ed., *N. Haven Town Rec. 1662–84*, pp. 183–84. The anonymously written English sex manual *Aristotle's Compleat Masterpiece*, despite its sometimes moralistic flavor and sexism, provided a generally more positive view of the sexual interaction between man and woman. It not only accented the role of the clitoris in sexual release, but expressed the belief that both human warmth and orgasmic satisfaction were crucial. See 26th American edition (1755), pp. 15, 43, 56.

19. Hoadly, ed., *Rec. of N. Haven 1638–49*, pp. 180–81.

20. C. Mather, *Ornaments for Daughters of Zion*, p. 73.

21. *Ibid.*, p. 48; Colman, *Duty & Honour of Aged Women*, p. 12; Noyes, *Short Catechism*, p. 15; Shurtleff & Pulsifer, eds., *Plym. Rec.*, IV, 22; Noble & Cronin, eds., *Rec. of Mass. Assts.*, II, 121.

22. McCary, *Human Sexuality*, pp. 68–69; *Aristotle's Compleat Masterpiece*, pp. 31–32.

23. Dudley, *Letter to Countess of Lincoln*, p. 13; E. Ward, *Trip to N.-Eng.*, p. 45; Secker, *Wedding ring*, n.p.; Benjamin Thompson, "The Amiable virgin memorized—Elizabeth Tompson, who deceased in Boston, at M^r leggs, august 22, 1712," in Murdock, ed., *Handkerchiefs from Paul*, p. 9; Sewall, *Diary*, I, 171.

24. Pulsifer, trans., "Rec. of Middlesex Ct.," IV, 49.

25. J. Trumbull, ed., *Conn. Rec.*, II, 328; "Conn. Arch. Crimes & Misd.," 1st ser., III, 228–34, 256–58. Edmund Morgan has speculated that "fraudulent contract" referred to "some kind of fraudulent inducement such as misrepresentation of financial resources," but John Rogers and the Connecticut divorce cases make it clear that the reference was to misrepresentation of virginity (Morgan, *Puritan Family*, p. 37; J. Rogers, *Mid-Night-Cry*, pp. 159–60, 165).

26. Interestingly enough, the words "harlot" and "whore" were applied to both sexes in the seventeenth century, and the word "baud" did not become exclusively female until after 1700 (Greer, *Female Eunuch*, p. 260; S. Danforth, *Cry of Sodom*, p. 16).

27. Secker, *Wedding ring*, n.p.; C. Mather, *Ornaments for Daughters of Zion*, pp. 75, 77; Cobbett, *Fruitfull & Usefull Discourse*, p. 174; R. Williams, *George Fox Digg'd*, appendix, p. 61; John Cotton (II), *Meet Help*, p. 15.

28. Edward Taylor, "Commonplace Book," quoted in Morgan, "Puritans & Sex," pp. 592–93; Shurtleff & Pulsifer, eds., *Plym. Rec.*, III, 112.

29. G. Dow, ed., *Essex Ct. Rec.*, VIII, 356; Noble & Cronin, eds., *Rec. of*

Mass. Assts., III, 131–32; Conn. "Ct. of Assts., 1665–77," in "Conn. Rec.," LVI, 36; *Rec. of Suffolk Ct.*, II, 837–39.

30. *Aristotle's Problemes*, p. E4.

31. *Ibid.*; C. Mather, *Warnings from Dead*, p. 47; *Aristotle's Compleat Masterpiece*, p. 43; Perkins, *Oeconomie*, III, 691. See also Jeremy Taylor, quoted in Defoe, *Conjugal Lewdness*, pp. 55–56, and description in Greer, *Female Eunuch*, pp. 208–9.

32. Conn. "Ct. of Assts., 1665–77," in "Conn. Rec.," LVI, 72.

33. "George Carwright to Col. R. Nichols, Jan. 30, 1665," in Sainsbury & Headlam, eds., *Calendar of State Papers*, VI, 272 (no. 921); Dunton, *Letters*, pp. 141–42; Noble & Cronin, eds., *Rec. of Mass. Assts.*, I, 229.

34. Morgan, "Puritans & Sex," p. 594; Cleaver, *A godlie form of govt.*, pp. 155, 177; *Aristotle's Compleat Masterpiece*, p. 39; Wigglesworth, *Diary*, p. 407; T. Davis, "Taylor's 'Occasional Meds.,'" *Early Am. Lit.*, V, 23.

35. C. Mather, *Ornaments for Daughters of Zion*, pp. 52–53.

36. John Eliot, quoted in T. Shepard, *Clear Sun-shine of Gospel*, p. 62; *Rec. of Suffolk Ct.*, II, 915; "Examination of Hugh Parsons, of Springfield, on a Charge of Witchcraft, and the Testimonies given against him, before Mr. William Pynchon, at Springfield, 1651," in Drake, *Annals of Witchcraft*, pp. 240, 244–45, 253–54.

37. "Opinions of Three Ministers on Unnatural Vice, 1642," in W. Bradford, *Of Plym. Plant.*, p. 411.

38. *Rec. of Conn. Part. Ct.*, p. 10; "N. Haven Ct. Rec.," I, 38–39; J. Smith, ed., *Pynchon Ct. Rec.*, p. 224.

39. S. Danforth, *Cry of Sodom*, p. 16.

40. *New-Haven's Settling in New-England and Some Lawes for Government* (London, 1656), in Hoadly, ed., *Rec. of N. Haven 1653–Union*, p. 576.

41. G. Dow, ed., *Essex Ct. Rec.*, I, 44; Shurtleff & Pulsifer, eds., *Plym. Rec.*, II, 137.

42. "Opinions of Three Ministers on Unnatural Vice, 1642," in W. Bradford, *Of Plym. Plant.*, p. 411. Patai, *Sex & Family in Bible*, pp. 93–94, contains a discussion of Onan's sin.

43. Himes, *Medical Hist. of Contraception*, pp. 190–94, and "Note on Early Hist. of Contraception." Himes assumes that Governor Bradford's account of John Lyford's practice of birth control in Ireland was actually a reference to *coitus interruptus*, although there is really no concrete evidence upon which that assumption can be based. See W. Bradford, *Of Plym. Plant.*, p. 168.

44. Mettler & Mettler, *Hist. of Medicine*, p. 955; Schnucker, "Eliz. Birth Control & Puritan Attitudes," pp. 655–67; *Aristotle's Compleat Masterpiece*, p. 33; J. Davenport, "Letter," p. 46.

45. W. Bradford, *Of Plym. Plant.*, p. 168.

46. E. Taylor, "Meds. 2:75, 1:43," in his *Poems*, pp. 209, 70. See also Grabo, *Taylor's Treatise*, p. 46.

47. E. Taylor, "Med. 2:10," in his *Poems*, p. 98; O[xenbridge], *N.-Eng. Freemen Warned*, p. 18; Belcher, *Two Sermons*, p. 10; *Aristotle's Compleat Masterpiece*, p. 12; Defoe, *Conjugal Lewdness*, p. 48.

48. "York Co. Rec.," book B, p. 88; *Rec. of Suffolk Ct., 1671–80*, II, 1061; J. Smith, ed., *Pynchon Ct. Rec.*, p. 224.

49. The author of *Aristotle's Compleat Masterpiece* indicated, however, that Englishmen liked tight vaginas (pp. 33, 73).

50. Culpeper, *Dir. for Midwives, Second Part*, pp. 2–3, 28; Greer, *Female Eunuch*, p. 30; *Aristotle's Compleat Masterpiece*, or any other childbirth guide gives English terms for female genitalia. Rape trials serve as the primary source for Puritan names.

51. Masters & Johnson, *Human Sexual Response*, p. 231, discusses effects of aging on the female.

52. In 1654, after Goody Knapp had been hanged in New Haven, the wife of Thomas Staplies probed the dead body to discover a witch's teat. Goody Staples was surprised to find that the designated structure was "such as she herselfe had, and other women might haue the same." She tugged frantically at the teat and asked other women to affirm what she had discovered. Instead, she met short shrift, one female telling her, "I know not what you have, but for herselfe, if any finde such things about me, I deserved to be hanged as she was" (Hoadly, ed., *Rec. of N. Haven 1653–Union*, pp. 81–82). Clawson's and Disborough's examinations appear in J. Taylor, *Witchcraft Del. in Conn.*, p. 43.

53. Culpeper, *Dir. for Midwives, Second Part*, p. 3.

54. *Ibid.*, pp. 2, 151; Cianfrani, *Short Hist. of Obstet.*, pp. 162, 172, 168, 160; *Aristotle's Compleat Masterpiece*, pp. 19–23.

55. Harvey, *Anatomical Exercitations*, p. 175; Perkins, *Oeconomie*, p. 673.

56. *Aristotle's Compleat Masterpiece*, p. 35.

57. C. Fox, "Pregnancy, Childbirth & Early Infancy in Anglo-Am. Culture," pp. 61–63; Culpeper, *Dir. for Midwives, Second Part*, p. 134; Cianfrani, *Short Hist. of Obstet.*, p. 160.

58. C. Fox, "Pregnancy, Childbirth & Early Infancy in Anglo-Am. Culture," p. 60, quoting Ambroise Paré; Hoadly, ed., *Rec. of N. Haven 1653–Union*, pp. 122–23; *Compleat Midwifes Practice Enlarged*, pp. 284–85, 289; Culpeper, *Dir. for Midwives, Second Part*, pp. 56–57, 84–85.

59. *Aristotle's Compleat Masterpiece*, p. 43.

60. Lewinsohn, *Hist. of Sexual Customs*, pp. 179–84.

61. Harvey, *Anatomical Exercitations*, pp. 159–62, 170, 174–75. Despite his belief in ovism, Harvey too would share the egocentricity of many of his contemporaries, for he considered the male "the more perfect animal." One seventeenth-century German writer actually went so far as to declare the uterus unnecessary for conception and nurturance of the fetus. Count Johann von Keuffstein reputedly created living babies by keeping sperm alive for nine months in a warm, damp place and feeding it on menstrual blood (Hartman, *Life & Teachings of Paracelsus*, pp. 257–58).

62. Rado, "Adaptational View of Sexual Behavior," p. 161. For provocative refutations of the contention that male activity and female passivity in sexuality is an anatomically determined fact, refer to "A Matriarchal Society Writes Biology," in Herschberger, *Adam's Rib*, pp. 79–87, and Rheingold, *Fear of Being a Woman*, pp. 222–26.

63. *Aristotle's Compleat Masterpiece*, pp. 38–39, 44–45.

64. *Ibid.*, pp. 52–53.

65. Riverius, *Practice of Physick*, p. 403; Novak, "Hist. Rev. of Reproductive Physiology," pp. 279–82; Culpeper, *Dir. for Midwives, Second Part*, p. 6.

66. Boston Women's Health Book Coll., *Our Bodies, Ourselves*, pp. 18–19;

Maddux, *Menstruation*, p. 78. *Aristotle's Compleat Masterpiece*, p. 28, states that first menstruation could happen as early as age twelve, but usually occurred at age fourteen. Culpeper, *Dir. for Midwives, Second Part*, p. 86, confirmed *Aristotle's* figure. Today the average incidence is at age 12.5, and sometimes menstruation occurs as early as age nine. Serious menstrual ailments do, of course, occur, including dysmenorrhea (painful menstruation), hypermenorrhea (excessive bleeding), polymenorrhea (bleeding more often than at 24-day intervals), and amenorrhea (failure to menstruate). However, such conditions rarely reach the point where they cause severe problems. See Benson, *Handbook of Obstet.*, pp. 642–54.

67. Adams & Murray, *Minerals*, pp. 57–59; A. Davis, *Let's Get Well*, pp. 246–47.

68. G. Dow, *Every Day Life in Mass.*, pp. 193, 195; W. Lewis, *New Dispensatory*, p. 381; Culpeper, *Dir. for Midwives, Second Part*, pp. 70–90; *Aristotle's Compleat Masterpiece*, p. 50.

69. Culpeper, *Dir. for Midwives, Second Part*, p. 106; Fontanus, *Womans Doctour*, pp. 3–4; Paré quoted in Vieth, *Hysteria*, p. 115.

70. "Roger Williams to John Winthrop, Jr., Dec. 10, 1649," in R. Williams, *Complete Writings*, VI, 189.

71. *Ibid.*, p. 184; Osol & Farrar, *Dispensatory of U.S.A.*, pp. 1474, 1417, 1304, 1576.

72. Vieth, *Hysteria*, pp. 115, 118; Hilda Smith, "Gynec. & Ideology in Eng.," p. 101.

73. Findley, *Priests of Lucina*, p. 146; *Aristotle's Problemes*, p. E4.

74. Quoted in Novak, "Superstition & Folklore of Menstruation," p. 272.

75. Cianfrani, *Short Hist. of Obstet.*, p. 138.

76. *Aristotle's Compleat Masterpiece*, p. 90; John Cotton, *Abstract of Lawes*, p. 11; Gorton, "Letter," p. 13.

77. Roeburt, *Wicked & Banned*, p. 50.

78. A. Forbes, ed., *Winthrop Papers*, IV, 297–98; F. Dexter, ed., *N. Haven Town Rec. 1649–62*, pp. 30–32.

79. Shurtleff & Pulsifer, eds., *Plym. Rec.*, III, 97; F. Dexter, ed., *N. Haven Town Rec.1662–84*, pp. 182–83.

80. N. Hamp. "Ct. Papers," I, pt. 2 (1659–72), p. 423; Middlesex Co. Ct., folio 48, quoted in Morgan, "Puritans & Sex," p. 595.

81. These statistics concern only victims of forcible sexual aggression. I have deleted from consideration four cases of statutory rape in which the female consented to the male's overtures.

A comparison between victims of attempted and actual rapes in seventeenth-century Calvinist New England and victims of forcible rape in modern times yields the following result:

	17th-century N. Eng.		Denver, 1968–69		Philadelphia, 1958, 1960	
	N	%	N	%	N	%
Single	35	44.9	125	62.5	303	47.7
Married	35	44.9	50	25.0	158	25.0
Children under age 15	8	10.3	25	12.5	174	27.4

Source: MacDonald, *Rape*, pp. 77, 111; Amir, *Patterns in Forcible Rape*, pp. 52, 64.

82. *Aristotle's Compleat Masterpiece*, p. 50.

83. Libby, Allen & Moody, eds., *Maine Ct. Rec.*, I, 140.

84. Pulsifer, trans., "Rec. of Middlesex Ct.," I, 62–63; Winthrop, *Journal*, I, 236–37; II, 398.

85. White servants comprised 34.3% ($N=24$) of all would-be rapists, Indian men 11.4% ($N=8$), black servants or slaves 8.6% ($N=6$), yeomen farmers 24.3% ($N=17$), and single members of farm households 11.4% ($N=8$). The records designate just four men as Mr.—the usual title for a gentleman.

86. Medea & Thompson, "How Much Do You Really Know about Rapists?," p. 114.

87. Shurtleff, ed., *Mass.Rec.*, II, 21; *New-Haven's Settling in New-England and Some Lawes for Government* (London, 1656), in Hoadly, ed., *Rec. of N. Haven 1653–Union*, p. 578; Shurtleff & Pulsifer, eds., *Plym. Rec.*, V, 246; VI, 98; Bouton, ed., *Prov. Papers of N. Hamp.*, I, 385; J. Trumbull, ed., *Conn. Rec.*, I, 77; Winthrop, *Journal*, II, 38.

88. Noble & Cronin, eds., *Rec. of Mass. Assts.*, I, 22, 50, 74, 199; II, 69; "Rec., Ct. of Assts. & Superior Ct., 1687–1715," in "Conn. Rec.," LVIII, 21–22; J. Trumbull, ed., *Conn. Rec.*, IV, 132–33.

89. Noble & Cronin, eds., *Rec. of Mass. Assts.*, III, 191, 199.

90. *Ibid.*, III, 216; *Rec. of Conn. Part. Ct.*, p. 3.

91. Pulsifer, trans., "Rec. of Middlesex Ct.," I, 62–63; "Mass. Arch., XXX," 106–7.

92. C. Baker, "Rape in Mass.," p. 2.

93. Francois, "Women's Activities Against the Law, Essex Co., Eng."; Brownmiller, *Against Our Will*, p. 25; Blackstone, *Commentaries on Laws of Eng.*, I, 210–14.

94. Only 2.6% of seventeenth-century victims were killed, a figure equal to that of contemporary times. See MacDonald, *Rape*, pp. 180–91; Hayman, Lanza, Fuentes, & Algor, "Rape in D.C."

95. Hoadly, ed., *Rec. of N. Haven 1638–49*, pp. 233–35.

96. F. Dexter, ed., *N. Haven Town Rec. 1649–62*, pp. 182–83.

97. The available records supply testimony of the male offender in 26 cases. Only eight of these men attempted to argue that the woman was willing, compared to almost all today.

98. The figure of 79 attempts includes the 78 rapists tried, plus the one murderer who was never apprehended.

99. O. Hammond, ed., *N. Hamp. Ct. Rec. 1640–1692*, p. 90.

100. In contemporary America, by comparison, anywhere from 50 to 87% of all forcible rapes are effected by persons unknown to the victim. See Amir, *Patterns in Forcible Rape*, pp. 234, 250; Medea & Thompson, "How Much Do You Really Know about Rapists?," p. 114; Dunham, *Crucial Issues in Treatment of Sex Deviation*, pp. 37–38; MacDonald, *Rape*, p. 77.

101. Winthrop, *Journal*, I, 236–37; Middlesex Co. Ct., folio 40. Sometimes a woman might assert in court, "I resisted as much as I could," but by such a statement she did not usually mean that she attempted to inflict damage upon her assailant. Rather, she was merely indicating that she had protested verbally, pushed, and struggled to break away.

102. For expositions of this point of view, see Deutsch, *Psychology of Women*, I, 283–84; Jenkins, "Making of Sex Offenders"; Murray, *Explorations in Personality*, p. 135; Alexander, *Fund. of Psychoanalysis*, p. 127.

103. Middlesex Ct. Rec., folios 47, 94, quoted in Morgan, "Puritans & Sex," p. 600.

104. Libby, Allen, & Moody, eds., *Maine Ct. Rec.*, I, 140–41.

105. Quoted in Baker, "Rape in Mass.," pp. 7–8.

106. Hayman, Lanza, Fuentes, & Algor, "Rape in D.C.," pp. 95–96; Wood, "Victim in Forcible Rape Case," p. 359.

107. Libby, Allen, & Moody, eds., *Maine Ct. Rec.*, I, 140.

108. Pulsifer, trans., "Rec. of Middlesex Ct.," I, 62–63.

109. The amount granted in damages was usually low, just £2, £5, £5, and 50s. in the four cases cited. In one other case, when the rape was committed against a man's wife, *he* received considerably more—£20. See *ibid.*; Noble & Cronin, eds., *Rec. of Mass. Assts.*, I, 50; II, 106; O. Hammond, ed., *N. Hamp. Ct. Rec. 1640–92*, p. 90.

110. M. Hale, *Hist. of Pleas of Crown*, I, 628; Cotton, *Abstract of Lawes*, p. 12. Cotton's recommendation was quite in accord with biblical teaching. Deuteronomy 22:28–29 directed that the woman, if not betrothed, marry the man who had raped her.

IV

Women in Work and Poverty: The Difficulties of Earning a Living

In defiance of the axiom that he who works, eats, the lady who works has less to eat than the lady who does not. There is no profession open to her which is nearly as lucrative as marriage.

—Emily James Putnam, *The Lady*

FOR SOME TIME NOW, MANY SCHOLARS OF EARLY AMERICAN HISTORY have asserted that the absence of sufficient manpower resulted in extensive economic freedom for the "weaker sex." As Page Smith puts it, "There were, in the early years, very few negative definitions—that this or that activity was unsuitable or inappropriate for a woman to engage in. In consequence colonial women moved freely into most occupations in response to particular needs and opportunities rather than abstract theories of what was proper." Eleanor Flexner has more emphatically concluded, "In a struggling society in which there was a continuous labor shortage, no social taboos could keep a hungry woman idle." Barbara Mayer Wertheimer enthusiastically catalogues many of the jobs held by colonial women, and asserts that the earliest female settlers possessed "power and responsibility such as they had never known in seventeenth-century England or on the European continent . . . [They labored at] many kinds of work outside the home from which they were later barred."[1]

Despite such assertions, there has been no systematic effort to determine the exact occupations available to women, and the extent to which these utilized skills *not* focused strictly around the domesticity and nurturance of the conventional female role.

Moreover, we do not know how many women worked at some occupation other than that of housewife and mother, or how much they earned. Because the characterization of woman as the weaker sex affected Puritan views of sexual behavior, intelligence, and social privilege, we might suspect that it also deterred women from supporting themselves. In fact, as we shall see, economic factors discouraged productive, independent activity on the part of women.

Limitations on Searching Out a Calling

Puritans certainly believed in the efficacy of work. Detesting those who lived "idle like swine," they felt that labor brought "strength to the body, and vigour to the mynde," thereby providing an outlet for energies which could otherwise lead one to sin.[2] The authorities encouraged each person to search out a suitable calling through apprenticeship, self-training, or hiring out. Boys had considerably more options than girls; apprenticeship contracts specified that the latter be taught only housewifely duties like cooking and sewing, while boys could learn the "secrets" of any number of trades, including blacksmithing, husbandry, shop management, milling, carpentry, and seamanship. It is unlikely that those daughters who never served as apprentices learned any of the male occupational "secrets," because limited opportunities for occupational training, as well as denial of access to public schools, put at a disadvantage any "strong-minded" woman who wished to advance in the world of work. Even if she could overcome the limits of her socialization for domesticity, or use that training to hire herself out in a female vocation, a young woman still could not readily accrue the funds necessary to set herself up in a business or trade; besides, she was unable to earn very much at women's jobs.

Moreover, fathers neglected to give their daughters a portion of the family estate as a nest egg, while they did sometimes convey realty to sons. Nor did a daughter inherit anything substantial when her father died. The published probate records of Hartford County, Connecticut, reveal that between 1635 and 1699 daughters received a mean inheritance of £29 3s., while sons got more than twice as much—£61 17s.[3] Just 15.2 percent of all Hartford County daughters inherited more than £60 worth of personal and real estate, whereas 27.7 percent of them received less than £10 and 65.6 percent less than £30. Sons fared much better: two of every five inherited over

£60, just 14.6 percent received under £10, and less than one-third were granted under £30. The firstborn son received at least double what the firstborn daughter did in half of all families having oppo-site sex siblings, and an excess of 50 percent over what she received in 82.4 percent of the total (N = 26 and 42 of 51 families). Nine out of ten fathers gave the eldest son the largest share of their estates, but only 22.6 percent (N = 12 of 53) granted the eldest daughter more than any other daughter. The eldest daughter never received more than the eldest son, even though she had a greater need for it, given her limited options. Nor did fathers tend to give an eldest daughter any more than half of what the second son received. In only 10 percent of all Hartford County families did she obtain more than that, and in just 6 percent of all families with at least one son and one daughter did the children receive equal amounts. The daughter who inherited very much from her father's estate was quite a rarity in seventeenth-century Connecticut; only the daughter of a very wealthy man could actually have taken steps to become economi-cally self-sufficient after her father's demise. Furthermore, daugh-ters tended to receive their share in personalty, not in realty which could be converted into a permanent productive income, whereas for sons the reverse was true. In fact, daughters inherited propor-tionally smaller legacies than had been customary in late medieval England.[4]

The mean and median (£22) values of daughters' inheritances yielded some immediate purchasing power, but did little to increase their occupational possibilities. The average inheritance did not allow a daughter money enough to purchase a home lot near the town's center, which sold for £80 or £100. Nor could she rent a shop and stock it with goods. While the young man could work at a trade and save a tidy sum by his late twenties, the young woman possessed no similar option. Hartford County records indicate that seventeenth-century inheritance patterns made it virtually impos-sible for a maiden, whose access to employment was already lim-ited by her training and lack of education, to become part of the property-holding group which ran New England affairs.

The Single Woman as Servant

While her parents were still alive, or after she inherited too little to buy her own financial independence, a single woman could strive to earn money at only one occupation before 1685. Domestic servitude did little more than insure that the young woman would continue to exist as a member of the submissive, inferior, financially dependent class. Female servants assisted with household duties, child care, and garden maintenance—but always under the supervision of a "mistress" or "master," whose orders had to be obeyed unless they violated criminal law. Servants received meals, clothing, and a place to sleep, but generally earned no financial remuneration in return for their valuable work. The few women who hired themselves out (unlike those invariably single ones who served as apprentices, redemptioners, indentured domestics, and even slaves) enjoyed a small measure of economic reward. Their typical annual salary was just £3 or £4, only 50 to 60 percent of the male hired servant's wage. Even with the addition of a sum for the room and board furnished by the master, the female domestic drew one of the lowest annual incomes of any working person.

Since before 1650 domestic servitude was considered an honorable occupation for a woman, some newly arrived single women sought employment in that capacity. These females, whose mean age was 20.7 years, often lived briefly in Puritan households under conditions of relative equality, and then married into the best families.[5] Still, their actual numbers were few; in addition, male domestics migrating to New England outnumbered females three to one. Only two of the original nineteen Pilgrim servants were women. The ship lists in Charles Edward Banks's *Planters of the Commonwealth* name 3,505 New England arrivals between 1630 and 1639, including only 134 male and 58 female servants.[6] Just 22 female (but 143 male) domestics arrived from the port of Bristol

Chart 4.1
Amount Inherited by Children in Hartford County, Conn., 1635–1699[4]

Amount Received	N Daughters	Total	Mean Value	N Sons	Total	Mean Value
Under £10	62	£ 308 3s. 8d.	£ 4 19s.	24	£ 149 4s.1d.	£ 6 2s.
£10–£29	85	1,602 2. 4.	18 17	28	509 11.5.	18 4
£30–£59	43	1,486 3. 4.	35 8.	46	1,729 13	37 12
£60–£99	14	978 5. 7.	69 17	32	2,430 12. 4.	75 19
£100 and over	20	2,156	107 16	34	5,329 12. 7.	156 15
	224	6,530 14. 11.	29 3	164	10,148 13. 5.	61 17

between 1654 and 1686.[7] Whereas adult females constituted 40 percent of all early immigrants, female domestics comprised barely 25 percent of all incoming servants.[8]

In the first three decades of settlement, then, a handful of women used servitude as a vehicle for marital advancement, although not as a means to accumulate money for future investment. Since such women labored as indentured servants or redemptioners (usually for seven years, in return for the cost of their passage), before 1650 there is no instance of a female hiring out her own time. After that date, however, the image of the servant deteriorated so remarkably that only a severely impoverished single woman would want to become a domestic. Scottish, Irish, Indian, black, and poor English servants soon replaced the earlier "most honourable" English. Many of this later group served against their will: Scottish women accompanied prisoners who were taken in battle and then deported to Massachusetts, and shipmasters kidnapped the "wild Irish" for sale in the New World.[9] When such servants petitioned for their freedom, the Massachusetts and Plymouth authorities usually refused to release them from bondage, even though kidnapping was a capital offense.[10] The respectable Puritan woman would hardly have wished to associate with such alien, potentially rebellious servants in her search for employment opportunities.

Nor would she wish to place herself on the level of the many involuntary servants who were Indian or black. After the defeat of King Philip, hundreds of Indian women and children were forced into servitude; at the same time, New England trading ships brought ever more blacks into Boston, Salem, and Newport. Many of these women found that Puritan racism reduced them to laboring in a different culture for masters not of their own choosing. Although a divine like John Eliot might respond to the Indians as equals, in the sense of having equal access to God, other Puritans called them "beastly minded and mannered creatures," "Lazy Drones," "lying wretches," "savages" unfit for Englishmen to live by, and a group best "rooted out, as being of the cursed race of Ham."[11] New Englanders generally described blacks as savage, barbaric, irrational creatures whose only hope was to pray heartily for assurance of salvation so that they could inherit heaven, where divine fiat would transform them to a lily-white hue.[12] Non-European women must have realized that, notwithstanding Puritan fornication laws, masters sometimes "connived" at breeding slaves to produce offspring who could be profitably sold.[13] Such women probably also observed that masters who abused slaves, even to the point of death, faced only minimal punishment. After Nathaniel Cane of Maine beat his slave Rachel to death, the York County Court of Quarter Sessions fined him only £5; had Rachel been white and free, Cane would have been hanged.[14]

If the single woman of traditional Puritan background was reluctant to join the status of wild Irish, turbulent Scots, beastly Indians, and barbarous blacks, she was also out of place with the likes of poor English servants, including many debtors, prostitutes, and thieves from the English prisons. Calvinists criticized such unpalatable newcomers as disrespectful, intemperate, sullen, saucy, neglectful, rude, sensual, and irreligious. In 1697 Massachusetts officials declined an English offer to send fifty women from Newgate prison over as servants, but by then the Bay Colony already had a large number of "fallen women" and ex-thieves employed at domestic work.[15] The Puritan records reveal that, as the century progressed, increasing numbers of rebellious domestics appeared in court on charges of fornication, theft, or disobedience to the master.[16] The status of servants slipped steadily; no longer "most honorable," by 1700 they were instead called "most profane."

The deterioration of servant status after 1650 made domestic work no longer a realistic option for the "middling" and "better sorts." Because women of those classes no longer became servants, opportunities for them to leave home and hire out their labor decreased. Nor did the poor English, Scottish, Irish, black, and Indian women who became servants and slaves gain even a small measure of control over their own lives. For sustenance, every woman had to rely on a father, master, or husband; marriage became literally basic to survival for many New England women.

As a result, housewifery served as the chief "occupation" for almost all New England women, and it no more facilitated financial independence than had other forms of domestic servitude. Women certainly contributed to the productivity of the family farm. Although they did not often work outdoors planting and harvesting crops, as English farm wives did, many spent a good deal of time cleaning house, spinning flax, dipping candles, canning preserves, roasting meat, caring for children, and performing untold other tasks. Some spun and made stockings, shirts, or breeches, which they sold to neighbors for an occasional shilling. Goodwives also sold poultry, butter, cheese, and garden produce, or bartered such items for desired commodities in the informal village trade networks.[17] However, woman's work in the home was assumed to be less dangerous and time-consuming than men's—a conclusion which may have rankled Puritan women as much as it has irritated housewives in more modern times. Above all else, the wife was not to use her presumed "free time" to exceed her ordained station by taking an interest in commercial activities or any other "outward matters." She could contract for rents and wages, sell goods, and collect debts only when her husband had so authorized.[18] The records from seventeenth-century civil cases reveal that New England husbands granted their wives such privileges in only 6 or 7 percent of all families.[19] The wife's access to experience in "outward matters" which could have provided her with some income in either marriage or widowhood was, therefore, much circumscribed.

The Nurturant Callings of Wet Nurse, Teacher, Doctor, and Midwife

Of course, Puritans did allow married women to labor at activities other than housewifery; but those activities also centered around the female's assumed nurturance, and were unremunerative and part-time. Serving as a wet nurse was one such activity, even though its short-term and low-demand characteristics made it a very insubstantial "occupation." Wet nurses enjoyed some popularity because, despite the strong cultural ideal affirming maternal breast-feeding, Puritan mothers sometimes found it impossible to perform that "duty." Puerperal fever or other serious illnesses incapacitated mothers and, it was believed, could be transmitted through the milk. Sore or inverted nipples, breast inflammations, and scanty milk also necessitated the occasional use of a wet nurse. Fear of the presumed toxic effects of colostrum caused mothers to observe a taboo on suckling infants for three or four days after delivery, which increased possibilities for wet nursing.[20] Still, wet nurses rarely received more than temporary employment, and the payment for that service was probably never very great. In fact, such short-term help may have been freely given, much the way neighboring wives helped out during measles or other epidemics. There is no record of New Englanders "farming out" babies to wet nurses for anywhere from ten to nineteen months, as was common in England.[21] Indeed, Puritan women who wet nursed infants probably did not even think of themselves as being employed at an occupation.

Like wet nurses, teachers maternally provided for the needs of the young. At dame schools, where a wife or "poor patient widow sits/And awes some twenty infants as she knits," the female teacher instructed her neighbor's younger offspring for 10s. to £2 per year, 1/10th to 1/120th of the salary for male teachers in the public schools.[22] As early as 1639 Mistress Jupe taught pupils at the Ipswich dame school; before the century's end, twenty-three or twenty-four other women assisted young scholars in reading, writing, and religion at fourteen different New England locales.[23] These schoolmarms were expected to rely upon their husbands' or ex-husbands' estates for sustenance, not upon any salary for their own work. Moreover, they were barred from working with the upper grades (over age nine or ten), lest the difficulty of the material studied at those levels overtax a woman's "weak" intellectual ability.[24] They constituted only 12.6 percent (25 of 199) of all school-teachers this researcher could locate in the seventeenth-century Puritan records.

The practice of medicine was another nurturant occupational activity open to married women. Many English housewives and their American counterparts learned "chirurgery"—the use of herbs, potions, and poultices to cure any number of maladies. Knowledge of the medicinal properties of wild herbs passed through the female line in some families for generations.[25] Alice Apsley, Lady Fenwick, one of the first women to settle at Ft. Saybrook, Connecticut, distributed homegrown herbs to sick callers at her residence from 1639 until her departure from the colony in 1645. Mistress Field of Salem prepared a green "sympathetic oynment" which purportedly healed sprains, aches, cramps, scaldings, cuts, mange in cattle, stench blood, tumors, the bites of "Venomous Beasts," and "old Rotten Sores." Doctor Margaret Jones of Charlestown, Massachusetts, secured some reputation as a witch because the aniseed, liquors, and small doses of herbs she administered produced "extraordinary violent effects." Hannah Bradford of Windsor, Connecticut, was such a capable physician that she reputedly "taught the first male doctor much of his medical lore."[26] At least three women proved to be able surgeons. Henry Winthrop's widow reportedly "hath very good successe" in her "Surgerye"; Mistress Allyn patched up wounded soldiers as an army surgeon during King Philip's War; and, on Martha's Vineyard, Mistress Blande dispensed "Phisicke and Surgery" to many sick Indians.[27]

Altogether, women comprised 24 percent (N = 42 of 175) of New England's medical practitioners. These female doctors, nurses, and midwives earned the respect of their neighbors, but evidence suggests that they received little income from their services. Medicine in the seventeenth century lacked the financial advantages of ministry, governorship, or commerce; not until the 1690s did physicians begin to achieve some recognition as highly paid, self-conscious professionals. Before that, almost all doctors practiced medicine as a second profession, spending the bulk of their working hours in the ministry, the magistracy, husbandry, or housewifery.[28] This was partly because Puritans expected physicians, particularly chirurgeons, to teach others their trade secrets. The case of one "auncient woman that had good skill in chirigirry and had done many desperate cures" is revealing; Richard Sadler reported that, sometime between 1640 and 1650, this Lynn woman was denied church membership, even though of "a Christian conversation," because she would not share her secrets—those "being the greatest part of her lively whood"—with other, envious women.[29]

Since the husband possessed the legal right to use any income his wife might draw, female doctors who assisted their physician husbands probably could not save up any earnings from their medical labors.[30] Towns also failed to allocate funds to female physicians in compensation for treating the poor, whereas the selectmen sometimes paid male doctors for their services from the town poor rates. Towns did, however, provide money for those "nurses" who cared for "poor people when they are sicke."[31] The amounts went unspecified, so no comparison can be made with the compensation of male physicians. Still, it is suggestive that in 1652 Thomas Lord of Hartford drew from 1s. to 8s. per visit to patient's homes, while Sam Sewall in 1674 paid a nurse who assisted at his wife's lying-in only 2d. (or 1/6 to 1/48th of Lord's sum).[32] Mistress Blande netted only £2 or £5 per year for her "paines and care" of the Indians between 1658 and 1661.[33] For just over a year's work, Mistress Allyn was paid £20; however, she treated wounded soldiers under the stressful conditions of Indian war.[34] Male physicians in civilian life labored fewer hours under less dangerous circumstances, but derived incomes sometimes twice as great as Mistress Allyn's.[35] As the only highly paid female physician of the century, this woman earned only about two-thirds of the average tradesman's wage.[36]

In the 1690s, the professionalization of medicine had severe con-

sequences for female physicians. Men trained through apprenticeship to male doctors began displacing local female chirurgeons.
One can search the colonial records in vain for some mention of
female physicians during that decade. For the first time, particularly
in urban areas, Puritans began distinguishing between male "doctors" and female "nurses," even though such "nurses" assisted
Boston wives in recovering from childbirth, cared for infants' ailments, and treated cases of smallpox.[37] Sam Sewall mentions seven
different male physicians in his diary for the years 1674 to 1699, but
all women who treat illnesses are referred to either as midwives or
as nurses.[38]

Throughout the seventeenth century both sexes dispensed
medical advice, but one realm of expertise, midwifery, remained the
exclusive province of women. (In fact, the York County authorities
fined one man fifty shillings "for presumeing to Act the Part of a
Midwife."[39]) Women learned midwifery from personal experience,
from other midwives, or from standard obstetrical texts like Nicholas Culpeper's *Directory for Midwives* (1651).[40] There were no medical
examinations to pass in New England, nor did a prospective midwife take out a license to practice, as was required in England and
in nearby New Amsterdam.[41]

Midwives occupied a position of some influence. They were given
the important function of examining women accused of premarital
pregnancy, infanticide, or witchcraft;[42] often the guilt or innocence of
the accused rested on the findings of these female juries. In return
for this necessary service, the town selectmen sometimes issued
grants of land to widowed midwives.[43] However, that happened
only in a few instances, and it is significant that this researcher
has found no account book or other record which mentions a
midwife receiving any reward for her services.

Since capable midwives were in such great demand—for example, Widow Wiat of Dorchester assisting in the births of over 1,100
children before her death in 1705 at age 94—these women sometimes received strong support for their occasional outspokenness.[44]
Religious rebel Anne Hutchinson developed an extensive following
in Boston, and, within a decade of her banishment, numerous
Dorchester inhabitants petitioned for the release of Alice Tilly after
she was imprisoned for criticizing the magistrates. Although the
General Court allowed Tilly to practice midwifery by day (as long
as she returned to the prison by dusk), her neighbors and thirteen

Bostonians requested her complete freedom. Miffed, the deputies concluded that there was "as much neede to uphold magistracy in their authoritye as Mrs Tilly in hir midwifery."[45]

Puritans certainly valued midwives' activities, but their approval was far from unqualified. New Englanders realized that their European contemporaries often linked midwifery with witchcraft. Some Calvinists may have worried that unchurched midwives might steal infants' umbilical cords or cauls for use in witch's potions. If the child or the mother died, witchly doings might be suspected.[46] In any event, three of the nineteen midwives this researcher has located in Puritan New England were suspected of practicing witchcraft.[47]

Despite the reputed witchly doings of midwives, in the first century of settlement women could rest secure in the belief that midwifery was one occupation which they could monopolize. Although in England "he-midwives" or "androboethogynists," spouting "long words which convinced patients of their wisdom," were replacing female midwives by the mid-eighteenth century, in America it took much longer for male doctors to force female practitioners out of the field.[48]

Women in Business

Limitations on daughters' inheritances and the lack of remunerative work for single women meant that few could join the property-holding group which controlled capital investment in land. So, too, did the paltry wages of midwives, physicians, teachers, and wet nurses, along with husbandly control over their incomes, prevent working wives from acquiring the economic security which would have enabled them to become property owners. As urbanization increased, especially late in the century, working women were generally unable to accumulate the capital necessary to participate in the Commercial Revolution enveloping New England.

Of course, some women who possessed both money and prestige also maintained small-scale businesses. As early as 1640 Philippa Hammond operated a shop at Boston. So did Widow Howdin (1645), Alice Thomas (before 1672), Ann Carter (1663), Jane Bernard (1672–76), Abigail Johnson (1672–73), Mistress Gutteridge (1690), Elizabeth Connigrave (1672–74), Rebecca Windsor (1672–74), and Mary Castle (1690). Almost all of these women ran coffee or cook shops, thereby utilizing their domestic training.[49] Mary Avery and

Susanna Jacob kept shop between 1685 and 1691, but whether they were owners or merely employees is unknown.[50] Esther Palmer, a merchant, located in the metropolis in 1683, and Florence Mackarta, in partnership with two men, constructed a slaughterhouse on Peck's Wharf in 1693.[51] A 1687 Boston tax list gives the names of forty-eight different women who derived some income from a trade or their estates—11.4 percent of all such persons rated.[52] But businesswomen were rarer than the initial impression suggests. For example, it is not actually specified how many of the women on the 1687 list owned businesses and how many merely drew income from the estates of their deceased husbands. What *is* clear is that fully 85.4 percent of these women were widows.

Businesswomen, whether married or widowed, were few throughout New England. The paucity of early businesswomen can be readily demonstrated by searching through transcriptions of courtroom proceedings, town records, and other sources. Emery Battis's catalogue of early Bostonians, a list based in part on such sources, names 106 tradespeople-merchants, none of whom were women.[53] The 109 businesspeople appearing in Charles Pope's *Pioneers of Maine and New Hampshire, 1623 to 1660,* are all males.[54] In all of New England outside Boston there are records of only nine women who worked at a trade or who ran a business other than innkeeping. By late century Margaret Barton of Salem, a chair frame maker, had accrued a fortune in "ventures at sea." In Hartford County, Elizabeth Gardner, Mary Phelps, and Mary Stanly owned interests in (respectively) an iron mill, a grist mill, and a shop.[55] Jane Stolion appeared in court in 1645–46, accused of charging excessive prices at her New Haven dress and cloth shop. Mistress Jenny came before the Plymouth General Court in 1644 for not keeping the mortars at her mill clean, nor the bags of corn there from spoiling.[56] Elizabeth Cadwell operated her husband's ferry across the Connecticut River at Hartford after his death in 1695. One Maine widow, Elizabeth Rowdan, maintained a blacksmith shop and mill.[57] Other women may have worked in their husbands' bakery, cook, or apparel shops, or may have tailored clothing for sale; but the records observe a rigorous silence on that score, mentioning only one female baker at Salem (1639).[58] Altogether, only 2.3 percent (N = 23 of 988) of all tradespeople-merchants (again excluding innkeepers) were members of the "weaker sex."

An examination of those licensed to keep inns or sell alcoholic beverages indicates that few women supported themselves in this occupation, at least before the 1690s. Since all innkeepers had to secure licenses from the authorities, the records are quite complete. The first female innkeeper does not appear until 1643.[59] Between 1643 and 1689 at least fifty-seven other women operated inns;[60] however, they constituted but 18.9 percent of Boston's innkeepers and only 5 percent of those in the remainder of New England. On Ebenezer Peirce's *Civil, Military, and Professional Lists of Plymouth and Rhode Island Colonies* just three of seventy Plymouth innkeepers are female.[61] In the 1690s, with large numbers of men away fighting in the Maine Indian wars, the New England total increased sharply, to eighty-four women—eight in Maine, twenty-four in New Hampshire, and fifty-two in the Bay Colony. Women then comprised over half of the tavernkeepers in Boston and approximately 20 percent of those in other locales.

Many other women sold alcoholic beverages without taking out a license, or only intermittently procured one. Quite possibly they felt that the £10 license fee, and sometimes a £20 bond for good behavior, were prohibitive. Seven of the twenty-one women licensed to sell liquor at Boston during the 1670s did not choose to renew their licenses for more than two years, but they did attempt to sell spirits surreptitiously, chancing a £2 to £5 fine instead of the £10 to £30 official annual outlay. Elizabeth George, licensed at Dorchester in 1676–77, appeared before the Suffolk County magistrates for unauthorized liquor-selling in three consecutive years before she finally renewed her license in 1681, when she was eighty. Joan Crafts of Kittery, Maine, answered presentments before the York County Court five different times between 1699 and 1709 for the same offense; she had been licensed in 1695, 1697, 1702, and 1705.[62] Another Maine woman, Mary Greenland, hung a tavern sign outside her house and was, as a result, summoned before the magistrates in 1673, 1674, and 1675.[63] The Puritan colonies prosecuted 151 cases of illegal liquor sale by women, or 20.3 percent of all such cases. Maintaining an inn was a costly business, and sometimes defying the law apparently became the only way that a woman felt she could keep herself in food and clothing.

Although innkeeping or some other business may have given the individual woman some measure of personal satisfaction and self-sufficiency, the Boston tax list of 1687 suggests that businesswomen fared less well than businessmen. An occasional woman like the Widow Kellond might derive an annual income as high as £80 from her trade and estates, but she was much the exception. Only nineteen members of the "weaker sex"—39.6 percent of all trades-women—earned £10 or more from their trades and estates, while 74 percent of all tradesmen earned that much. The forty-eight female traders made £580 over the previous year, an average of £12, whereas the 373 male traders made £7,383, or £20 each.[64]

There were several reasons why tradeswomen, when they managed to open shops, earned only 60 percent as much as tradesmen. Since the women possessed little training, their businesses tended to accent service in a way that was compatible with female sex-role stereotyping. Distributing beer, maintaining a cook shop, keeping an inn, and operating a millinery shop utilized talents common to housewives, but ones which returned little profit. Women in such businesses could not easily attract customers on the open market, for they lacked the mobility of carpenters, bricklayers, blacksmiths, and coopers. They could not advertise in newspapers, for none existed. They could not reap the benefits of an international trade, since they lacked ties to the great English trading houses and familiarity with foreign markets. Even credit was a problem. As milliner Hannah Crowell complained in 1696, "being a Woman [I] was not able to ride up and down to get in debts."[65]

Women also lacked the capital necessary to establish large scale businesses. Only after her husband died did the typical woman strike out on her own, with the help of her widow's portion. Of all women who were licensed to sell spirituous liquors, some 71.1 percent were widows.[66] Innkeeping was a ready source of sustenance for any widow whose husband left her their house and little else. Working at a trade became an acceptable means of support for widows of artisans, but even they could only rarely increase the net value of their estates over the amounts they inherited. Age, decreased mobility, and a lack of appropriate training or education each took a toll. Moreover, husbands were often reluctant to provide for their wives by leaving them a full or part interest in their trade tools or their shops. Only two of fifty-seven Hartford County artisans, merchants, and shopkeepers bequeathed their widows interest in their businesses. Another man left a shop at Hartford to his sister.[67]

Even those few widows who enjoyed some occupational independence were expected to restrict their activities to nurturant, housewifely, and comparatively low-status occupations. High-status positions such as public grammar-school teaching, the ministry, and major public offices were limited to men. Elizabeth Jones,

appointed the Boston poundkeeper in 1670, 1676, and 1689, was the
only woman to serve as a public official on even a minor level.[68]

The woman who wished to work "by her own hand," whether
widowed, married, or single, faced still other disadvantages. Before
1647 the Maine General Court forbade any woman from inhabiting
the Isles of Shoales, thereby making it impossible for females to
help out with the fishing or to operate stores at which the fishermen might buy provisions.[69] Perhaps deterred by the sentiment
expressed in Maine law, no woman of record ever fished at sea for
a profit. Nor could women become sailors—when one dressed as
a man and left Massachusetts on a vessel, her fellow seamen, upon
discovering her sex, tarred and feathered her in a nearly fatal maltreatment.[70] The presence of working women on the Atlantic was
so inconceivable to Puritans that when a mysterious "Shallop at Sea
man'd with women" was reported, men attributed the phenomenon to witchcraft.[71]

Wealth and Poverty

The limited, poorly paid, comparatively low status employment
opportunities available to early New England women meant that
they could not really participate in the expanding possibilities
opened by the Commercial Revolution. Despite such disabilities,
some observers might argue that dependent wives were rewarded
in the end, by inheriting sizable properties (although not businesses) from their deceased husbands. Such widows could enjoy
some independence in their later years. The tax lists seem to provide
some evidence for this view; women appear as heads of families
approximately 6 percent of the time, and fare well when their estates
are compared to those of male family heads.[72] The mean estate held
by nine New Haven women in 1643 was worth £357 15s., while the
average male owned an estate valued at £294 12s. In 1680 the
women's margin was even larger—£164 2s. to the men's £97 9s. At
Boston in 1687 and Fairfield, Connecticut, in 1671, the values of
men's and women's estates were almost the same.[73]

Some women were extremely wealthy. The widow of minister
John Davenport of New Haven possessed an estate worth £666 5s.
in 1680; the former wife of merchant Stephen Goodyear owned £666
herself, and the widow of magistrate Thomas Gregson was worth
£500. Widow Kellond ranked in the upper 1.2 percent of Boston's
assessed population (1687) at £120, Widow Maverick in the upper

14.4 percent of suburban Boston (1687) at £88 10s., and Mistress Matthews in the top 5.6 percent of Dover, New Hampshire (1648), at £139 10s.[74] Three Hartford County widows enjoyed the rents and profits deriving from inherited estates valued at £789 6s. 9d., £1000, and £1307 15s. 4d.[75]

Chart 4.2
Values of Estates by Sex (from Tax Lists)

Year	Place	No. Men	Holdings	No. Women	Holdings	Male Avg.	Female Avg.
1643	New Haven, New Haven Colony	112	£32,995	9	£3,220	£294 12s.	£357 15s.
1671	Fairfield, Connecticut	98	15,731 10s.	4	572 11	160 10	143 3
1680	New Haven, Connecticut	187	18,228 19s.	25	4,103 1	97 9	164 2
1687	Muddy River— Rumney Marsh, Massachusetts	94	5,768 4	3	115	61 7	28 15
1687	Boston, Massachusetts	1,136	15,362	88	1,438	13 11	16 7

It would be incorrect to assume, however, that as a group widows in Puritan New England were comparatively well-to-do, for most never appeared on a tax list. Even though these lists include all owners of real estate, plus male laborers, there were no reports on non-propertied widows who lived with children, relatives, friends, or by themselves. The available records mention a good many such women who hired out as domestics and laundresses, or who drew poor relief. Moreover, the properties held by listed women rested in their use, but not under their complete control. Massachusetts and Connecticut widows had to request the permission of specially appointed overseers, county magistrates, or the General Court before disposing of real estate.[76] Furthermore, most of the realty and personalty the widow received was in the form of farmland and cattle—an inheritance which, if she was aged or had small children, could not easily be converted into some kind of income. The widow without grown children could hire help to manage her farm, but that involved a further diminution of her financial resources.

An examination of Hartford County will and inventory allotments illustrates the difficulty widows experienced in securing adequate maintenance after their husbands' deaths. In 45.5 percent of these documents (N = 90 of 198) the widow received all or part of the "use" of her mate's estate, and in another 37.4 percent (N = 74) she gained some or all of his personalty as well. However, the value of all properties left to the widow averaged just £47 5s. 8d., or 26 percent of the husband's median estate (£184 2s. 4d.). Such an estate could probably have returned an annual profit of only about £4. In fact, only 17.9 percent of widows (N = 15 of 84) "controlled" enough property to supply an annual income of £10 or more.[77] Realizing "how hard a thinge it will be for a woman to manage the affaires" of a family when she had lost "a great parte of her livelihood," Henry Smith of Wethersfield granted his wife "full power to dispose of all my estate in howses, Lands, Cattell, and Goods whatsoever"—properties worth £370 18s. 6d. in 1648.[78] Only nine other men conceded their wives such "full power."

Chart 4.3
Value of Property Inherited by Wives in Hartford County,
1633–99

Amount Inherited	No. Women	Total Inheritance	Mean Amount	Mean Probable Income per Annum
£0–£9	5	£23 5s. 6d.	£4 13s.	£ 8s.
£10–£29	22	393 11s.	17 18	1 5s.
£30–£49	16	638 18s.	39 18	3 5s.
£50–£74	11	631 15s.	57 8	4 15s.
£75–£99	11	968 5s. 10d.	88	7 6s.
£100–£199	12	1598 13s. 4d.	133 4	11 1s.
£200–£499	4	1070 10s. 2d.	267 12	22 2s.
£500–£1427	4	4524 2s. 1d.	1131 4	93 17s.
	85	£9850 0s. 11d.	£115 17s.	£9 12s.

Many husbands, well aware that their wives might have difficulty maintaining an estate, specified that their widows live with one or more sons in the family dwelling unit. Such men usually reserved one room, a garden, a cow, and some household goods for their widow's use. In one-tenth of all wills (N = 30 of 282) fathers directed children to maintain their mother with annual supplies or a mone-

tary allotment. The annual maintenance payment rarely amounted
to much, however, averaging £9 13s.; most widows received less
than £7. The meagerness of this allowance is indicated by Nathaniel
Berding's directive that his wife Abigail's £10 yearly sum be paid in
50s. worth of wheat, 50s. in peas, 50s. in Indian corn, and 50s. in
pork.[79] Presumably that was enough to answer her food needs, but
little else. Two men, both very wealthy, gave their wives annual
incomes equal to those of most artisans. In 1655 Thomas Olcott,
worth £1468 8s. 5d., left his wife £28 per year from the rents of his
estate, while twenty years later William Wadsworth, inventoried at
£1677 10s. 9d., gave his wife £20 annually.[80] Such maintenance
allotments by a man's children may have exacerbated family tensions and curbed geographic mobility in the younger generation, as
Alexander Keyssar has suggested for eighteenth-century Woburn,
Massachusetts. If so, the Hartford County records are silent on
that score.[81]

Those widows who had to rely upon their children, either because that was specified by the husband's will or necessitated by the
woman's inability to derive a significant income from inherited
properties, merely exchanged one state of dependency for another.
Keyssar's description of Woburn widows is particularly appropriate: "A widow did not acquire the property rights of the male head
of the household; she was to be cared for, protected, and dependent. According to the terms of most wills and administrations, a
widow's needs were to be met and conveniences provided, but
there was little room for a widow to choose the kind of life she
wanted to lead after her husband's death."[82]

Given the woefully inadequate circumstances most widows
faced, the various colonies gave them special tax exemptions,[83] land
allotments,[84] or positions as innkeepers to help them survive.
Apparently there was a great need for such measures, since the low
£9 12s. average annual income for widows (at least in Hartford
County) applied largely to middle-class women. Kenneth Lockridge
has estimated that only one-fourth or one-third of all New England
men left wills, a figure corroborated by Daniel Scot Smith's study of
eighteenth-century Hingham probate records. If Smith is correct,
the poorer males are geatly underrepresented on the inventory
rolls; therefore the average woman may have derived an annual
income of only £5 or £6.[85]

Although one-sixth or one-fifth of all widows (those of the
middling and better sorts) enjoyed limited affluence, many more

suffered poverty. When George Phillips died at Middletown, Connecticut, leaving a debt-ridden estate of £30 18s., his widow received "a bed and furniture for herselfe and another for her children, which amounted in the Inventory at six pounds; a pot to dress her victuals, & a kettle, & a Tubb to wash her Clothes in & brue her beer, & a dish & spoon to eat her victualls with." There were no land rents or maintenance to sustain her. In 1684 Mary Phelps of Simsbury complained that, since her husband's decease, she had been "in a very helpless Condition; having but £6 allowed In Moveable estate, with the third of the Land for life, which will not yield above 20 Shillings per Annum, which is but a very small matter to maintain me." She petitioned the Hartford County Court for a larger share of her husband's £84 9s. 6d. estate.[86]

Unable to rely on their own labor or their husband's property for maintenance, many impoverished women turned to three sources for poor relief: private beneficence, the church, and the town meeting. Wealthy merchants like Robert Keayne and Henry Webb of Massachusetts left well over £100 to benefit the poor, and almost all Hartford County testators worth over £600 (N = 83 of 681 estates) gave small amounts, usually £5 for the use of the poor. Existing records do not specify whom their monies aided.[87] Church donations supported many needy women; at New Haven, Ellen Bannister relied on the poor box to supply her with necessities through all the more than thirty-five years of her widowhood.[88] New England town meetings periodically levied poor rates; this author has found the names of 118 poor persons mentioned in the records of twenty towns and eleven county courts. Widows were 60 (78%) of the 77 females aided. Another ten were deserted wives, and the final seven were wives whose husbands also received assistance. Since a poor person's name rarely appears in the official records, these 118 men and women constitute only a small portion of the total number aided; however, an examination of their individual cases can tell us a good deal about the problems faced by indigent women in Puritan New England.

The town selectmen or overseers of the poor supplied the indigent with free medical assistance and burials, sometimes placed them out as servants, and gave them essentials like firewood, clothing, food, and lodging. The authorities donated some food or money to 42.9 percent of the women and placed another 20.8 percent of them with male "keepers" who could care for their needs in return for help around the house. One Hartford woman received the right to hire herself out to a master of her own choosing. The amount of aid extended was usually minimal; the median annual grant to keepers of the poor or to indigent women constituted a meager £5. The Boston keeper of Mary Jones, for example, received but twenty-four bushels of corn plus "two blankets and a rug to keepe her warm."[89] Only two women, both widows of ministers, were granted more than £15 per year: Mary Rowlandson, the renowned Indian prisoner and author, could spend £30 annually, a gift from the townsmen of Wethersfield; and in the late 1660s the widow of Hartford pastor Samuel Stone was allotted anywhere from £20 to £60 per annum.[90]

Sometimes the authorities neglected to provide any assistance until the needy women had sunk to the most appalling conditions of poverty. John Davis refused to support his wife at Winter Harbor, Maine, but the York County Court failed to aid her immediately; she was forced to scour the windswept coastline for rockweed, which she could boil and eat to survive. Another woman, the wife of a man who went to sea to relieve their poverty, came to live at Boston "in the straw, very Indigent[ly]" before any relief was forthcoming. The Hampshire County Court refused to assist John Kilum's wife in her "suffering and needy condition" until her apparel was so frayed that she could not dress "in a way sutable and fitting to goe to church."[91] Not without good cause did one poor woman become an early American communist: Mary Boutwell of Lynn underwent a whipping in 1640 because she took away her neighbor's victuals, arguing that those who had ought to supply the essential needs of those who had not, through a general "Comunitie of all things."[92]

If the poor woman was a stranger or not tied to any member of the community by marriage or kinship, she might not receive aid at all. Selectmen sent sharp-tongued, immoral women and potential public charges back to England or unceremoniously warned them out out of town. Between 1671 and 1687 Boston warned out 46 such women (and 178 men).[93] Local authorities sometimes refused to allow a woman to change her place of residence, for fear that she would become a public charge in another town.[94] That practice undoubtedly reduced the woman's ability to search out employment elsewhere. Only Boston put the poor to work in an almshouse.[95]

The appointment of "keepers" for the indigent, or lodging them in the almshouse under a male attendant's supervision, blatantly reinforced female dependence. Such control angered some poor women, and at least two of them entirely rejected the dependence entailed in any form of relief. Mary Webster, a "wretched woman" of Hadley, Massachusetts, protested the efforts of church deacon Philip Smith to mitigate her indigence, expressing herself so sharply "that he declared himself apprehensive of receiving mischief at her hands" (ca. 1684). Jane Bourne of Cambridge refused to accept an allotment from the town for her food and lodging, instead moving out of town to secure employment elsewhere as a servant (1663).[96] A third woman, Abigail Day, was "full of Discontent" and "Impatience under her Afflictions" while at the Boston almshouse. She would "thank neither God nor man" for the objectionable diet there, and she complained that her keeper "had several times made attempts upon her chastity" (1697).[97]

The dissatisfaction of poor women like Abigail Day, Jane Bourne, and Mary Webster is readily understandable, for the paternalism of the Puritan system of poor relief too easily reflected women's difficulties in searching for gainful employment or starting businesses. Wherever they turned, women encountered the fruits of Puritan sexism—in low pay, lack of education and job training, decreased opportunities to secure the funds needed to open a business, and limitations on the kinds of employment available. Like many of their English contemporaries, Puritans believed that women belonged in the home. Innkeeping, coffee shop maintenance, millinery work, wet nursing, keeping a dress shop, schoolteaching, and domestic servitude took place quite literally *within* the home, since shops adjoined living quarters in early New England. Only those women who served as chirurgeons or midwives regularly worked outside their own houses. Ferrykeeper Elizabeth Cadwell, blacksmith-miller Elizabeth Rowdan, and twenty-two female lumber-sawyers and potash-makers imported early to New Hampshire[98] are on record as laboring at typically masculine jobs which required some physical mobility and competence in "outward affairs." Those few exceptions prove the rule that employment opportunities for women centered either around nurturance or on the skills learned in housewifery. Women worked in only a dozen different capacities, while men labored at anywhere from fifty-eight (Battis' Boston lists) to eighty-five (Pope's New Hampshire and Maine genealogy) occupations. The great majority of women in early New England worked under a condition of dependence, whether as servants under the control of masters, poor women under the control of almshouse attendants or other keepers, widows under the relative control of their children, or (in the most common occupation of all) house-wives under the control of their husbands.

The circumstances of life in seventeenth-century Puritan New England hardly had an emancipating effect. New England wives sometimes maintained family businesses in their husband's absence, or occasionally ran shops of their own; but so did English women.[99] In fact, Alice Clark's research indicates that English women, as members of a more urbanized society, labored at many more occupations than did their New England counterparts. A complete comparison cannot be made, because no one has systematically enumerated working Englishwomen and determined what percentage they constituted in each occupation. While all of the information is not yet in, it is striking that 40 percent of New England's adult population comprised just 25 percent of all servants, 24 percent of all medical practitioners (if nurses and midwives are subtracted, the percentage drops to 9.6), 12.6 percent of all schoolteachers, 18 percent of all innkeepers, and 2.3 percent of all tradespeople-merchants. Moreover, these women received much less remuneration than their male counterparts. Although labor shortages were frequent in the first few decades of settlement, such times did not lead to more women on the job market, or to women doing men's work. Inheritance patterns in agrarian locales made it virtually impossible for daughters and wives to exercise much control over capital investment in land. All but a few urban women were similarly unable to acquire real estate or capital which would have enabled them to expand their incomes. The only way for women to experience any upward mobility was to marry well. Seventeenth-century New England was a "Garden of Eden" only for the woman who pursued economic opportunity dependently, as the rib of a (hopefully) prospering and generous Adam.

1. P. Smith, *Daughters of Promised Land*, p. 54; Flexner, *Century of Struggle*, p. 9; Wertheimer, *We Were There*, p. 8.

2. Robinson, *Observations of Knowledge & Virtue*, p. 143; C. Mather, *Christian at His Calling*, pp. 44–45, 48.

3. These figures are based on an examination of 681 men's estates willed or inventoried in the Hartford County records. Enough data exist on 64 of these to determine the amount received by children. See Manwaring, ed., *Digest of Conn. Probate Rec.* Comparisons over a 64-year time span can validly be made because property value assessments changed little. In fact, in New England the values of goods in general were rarely affected by inflation; inventoried assessments per unit item in the 1690s closely paralleled those of the 1640s.

4. Waters, "Family, Inheritance, & Migration," p. 4.

5. Towner, "'Fondness for Freedom,'" pp. 202–4. The mean age comes from a count of the servants listed in Banks, *Planters of Commonwealth*.

6. W. Bradford, *Of Plym. Plant.*, pp. 441–43.

7. Moller, "Sex Composition & Correlated Culture Patterns," p. 118.

8. The total number of adults appearing on the Banks's shiplists is 2,108 males and 1,397 females.

9. Banks, "Scotch Prisoners"; A. Smith, *Colonists in Bondage*, p. 166; Haynes, "Letter," pp. 462–65; G. Dow, ed., *Essex Ct. Rec.*, II, 293–96.

10. Hist. Rec. Survey, *Abstract & Index of Suffolk Ct. Rec. 1680–98*, p. 112; *Rec. of Suffolk Ct. 1671–80*, I, 19–20, 43–44.

11. J. Trumbull, ed., *Conn. Rec.*, I, 576; C. Mather, *Way to Prosperity*, pp. 27–34, and *Magnalia*, II, 344; Hoadly, ed., *Rec. of N. Haven 1653–Union*, p. 352; Winthrop, *Journal*, II, 18–19. See G. Thomas, "Puritans, Indians & Race," and Jennings, *Invasion of Am.*, for treatments of Puritan racism.

12. S. Whiting, *Abraham's Intercession*, p. 220; Josselyn, *Two Voyages to N. Eng.*, p. 187; C. Mather, *Negro Christianized*, p. 4; N. Noyes, "Letter," p. 484; Twombly & Moore, "Black Puritan," pp. 225–26.

13. Josselyn, *Two Voyages to N. Eng.*, p. 28; Sewall, "Selling of Joseph," p. 85.

14. Libby, Allen, & Moody, eds., *Maine Ct. Rec.*, IV, 34–35.

15. Towner, "'Fondness for Freedom,'" p. 209; A. Smith, *Colonists in Bondage*, pp. 104–5.

16. Between 1630 and 1644 just 5.4% of the persons tried by the Massachusetts Court of Assistants were servants. In contrast, fully one-third of the Essex and Suffolk County offenders prosecuted between 1680 and 1699 claimed that occupation.

17. Secker, *Wedding ring*; C. Mather, *Ornaments for Daughters of Zion*; Wigglesworth, "Letter," pp. 140–42; Earle, *Home Life in Col. Days*, pp. 34, 123–52; Abbott, *Women in Ind.*, p. 18; Ulrich, "'Friendly Neighbor.'"

18. C. Mather, *Ornaments for Daughters of Zion*, p. 17; Winthrop, *Journal*, I, 179–80.

19. This figure has been compiled by calculating the percentage of 1,600 civil cases from all Calvinist colonies which list wives as attorneys, or as persons engaging in business matters of some sort.

20. C. Mather, *Eliz. in Holy Retirement*, p. 35; Wadsworth, *Well-Ordered Family*, p. 45; Wickes, "Hist. of Infant Feeding," p. 151.

21. De Mause, "Evolution of Childhood," in his *Hist. of Childhood*, pp. 35–36. For references to wet nursing in New England, see Caulfield, "Infant Feeding in Col. Am.," pp. 675–76; Sewall, *Diary*, I, 40, 166, 228, 442.

22. Widow Sarah Walker was paid 10s. for one year "as the others had" in 1686 and 1692. After paying her taxes, she took home only 1s. 3d. for a three-year teaching stint. The wives of Allen Converse and Joseph Wright split 10s. at Woburn in 1673, while Goodwife Mirick earned 3d. per pupil for each week that she taught. The town of Lyme, Connecticut, in 1681 voted to pay John Waller's wife and another dame school teacher £2 annually. In 1653 the Commissioners of the United Colonies paid William Daniel's wife £6 for instructing Indian children over a three-year period. Various towns paid male teachers £20, £20, £30, £40, £50, £60, and £60 (Cubberly, ed.,

Readings in Hist. of Educ., p. 295; Small, *Early N. Eng. Schools*, pp. 164, 168; J. Burr, ed., *Lyme Rec.*, p. 40; Shurtleff & Pulsifer, eds., *Plym. Rec.*, X. 106; "Town Rec. of Salem," XLII, 41; Seybolt, *Public Schools of Boston*, pp. 78–81).

23. These schoolteachers, as well as members of other occupations, have been culled from secondary accounts, county and town records, letters, and genealogical compilations. Savage's four-volume *Geneal. Dict. of First Settlers of N. Eng.* has proven particularly useful.

24. On intellectual activity overtaxing woman's reputedly frail mind, see ch. 2.

25. C. Mather, *Ornaments for Daughters of Zion*, p. 74; Lawrence, "Cure-alls of Past," p. 35; A. Clark, *Working Life of Eng. Women*, pp. 253–65.

26. Holman, "Story of Early Am. Womanhood," pp. 252–53; Winthrop, *Journal*, II, 345; G. Dow, *Everyday Life in Mass.*, p. 189; Bridenbaugh, "N. Eng. Town," p. 28.

27. Hurd-Mead, *Hist. of Women in Medicine*, p. 413; Shurtleff & Pulsifer, eds., *Plym. Rec.*, X, 205, 247, 261–62.

28. Shryock, *Medical Licensing in Am.*, p. 3; Postell, "Medical Educ. & Medical Schools in Col. Am.," p. 49.

29. Simmons, "Sadler's Account," p. 423.

30. R. Morris, *Studies in Am. Law*, p. 136.

31. Boston Rec. Cmrs., *Rep. Containing Boston Rec. 1660–1701*, p. 187. See also index under paupers or poor persons and *Hartford Town Votes*, I, 108, 225.

32. Packard, *Hist. of Medicine in U.S.*, I, 36; Sewall, *Diary*, I, 3.

33. Shurtleff & Pulsifer, eds., *Plym. Rec.*, X, 205, 247, 261–62.

34. Hurd-Mead, *Hist. of Women in Medicine*, p. 413.

35. In 1628 Plymouth Colony allotted Phineas Pratt £38. 15s., £20, and £20 for three consecutive years of medical service. In 1652 Thomas Lord drew £15 per year from the Connecticut authorities, plus a fee for visits to homes in Hartford and surrounding communities. Lord may have earned over £60 for his annual labors. Most doctors, however, received no town supplement to their income from house calls. See Packard, *Hist. of Medicine in U.S.*, I, 3, 36.

36. Tradesmen's wages appear in Hoadly, ed., *Rec. of N. Haven 1638–49*, p. 36; Shurtleff, ed., *Mass. Rec.*, I, 74, 106, 128; J. Baxter, ed., *Doc. Hist. of Maine*, III, 183–90.

37. Sewall, *Diary*, I, 22–23, 33, 40, 108, 110–11, 113–14, 184, 323, 377, 427.

38. Male doctors appear *ibid.*, I, 21–22, 38, 408, 431, 444.

39. Libby, Allen, & Moody, eds., *Maine Ct. Rec.*, II, 308.

40. For seventeenth-century English childbirth guides, see Mettler & Mettler, *Hist. of Medicine*, p. 950.

41. Packard, *Hist. of Medicine in U.S.*, I, 166–67; Derbyshire, *Medical Licensure in U.S.*, p. 2; T. Forbes, "Regulation of Eng. Midwives."

42. *Rec. of Suffolk Ct. 1671–80*, I, 91, 185–86; Oberholzer, *Delinquent Saints*, p. 133; [H. Norton,] *N.-Eng. Ensigne*, p. 7.

43. Felt, *Annals of Salem*, II, 438; Hurd-Mead, *Hist. of Women in Medicine*, p. 414; F. Dexter, ed., *N. Haven Town Rec. 1649–62*, pp. 67, 80.

44. Committee of Dorchester Hist. & Antiq. Soc., *Hist. of Town of Dorchester*, p. 281.

45. Shurtleff, ed., *Mass. Rec.*, III, 197, 208.

46. T. Forbes, "Midwifery & Witchcraft."

47. These "witches" were Elizabeth Morse, Anne Hutchinson, and Jane Hawkins. See G. Burr, ed., *Narratives of Witchcraft*, pp. 30–31; Koehler, "Amer. Jezebels," p. 74.

48. Goodell, "When & Why Were Male Physicians Employed as Accoucheurs?"; E. Jameson, "18th Cent. Obstet. in U.S."; Mengert, "Origin of Male Midwife"; Spencer, *Hist. of Brit. Midwifery*, pp. 147–49; A. Clark, *Working Life of Eng. Women*, pp. 283–89.

49. Pierce, ed., *Rec. of Boston First Church*, I, 22–25; Boston Rec. Cmrs., *Rep. Containing Boston Town Rec. 1630–59*, p. 83; *Rec. of Suffolk Ct. 1671–80*, I, 339; Boston Rec. Cmrs., *Rep. Containing Boston Town Rec. l660–170l*, pp. 12, 68, 76, 87, 118, 204; Hist. Rec. Survey, *Abstract & Index of Suffolk Ct. Rec. 1680–98*, pp. 45, 65, 73, 98, 100.

50. Abbott, *Women in Ind.*, pp. 23–24.

51. *Ibid.*; Boston Rec. Cmrs., *Rep. Containing Boston Town Rec. 1660–1701*, p. 214.

52. "Tax List and Schedules—1687," in Boston Rec. Cmrs., *First Rep.*, pp. 91–127.

53. In *Saints & Sectaries*, Emery Battis lists occupations for 186 of 361 Bostonians, yet he mentions only two women—midwives Anne Hutchinson and Jane Hawkins.

54. Charles Pope provides the names of 877 adult men, of whom 477 have specific occupations. Fishermen and mariners rank first, with 128 representatives, followed by 109 businessmen and 103 husbandmen. The only working women listed are five servants.

55. Abbott, *Women in Ind.*, p. 15; Manwaring, ed., *Digest of Conn. Probate Rec.*, pp. 305–6, 486, 564.

56. Goodspeed, "Extortion, Capt. Turner, & Widow Stolion"; Shurtleff & Pulsifer, eds., *Plym. Rec.*, II, 76.

57. *Hartford Town Votes*, I, 198; J. Baxter, ed., *Doc. Hist. of Maine*, VI, 268.

58. Felt, *Annals of Salem*, II, 152.

59. Noble & Cronin, eds., *Rec. of Mass. Assts.*, II, 136.

60. This total includes one Connecticut woman, two from Maine, four from New Hampshire, seven from Plymouth, and 45 from Massachusetts.

61. Peirce, *Civil, Mil., & Prof. Lists*, pp. 21, 37, 59.

62. Boston Rec. Cmrs., *Rep. Containing Dorchester Town Rec.*, p. 212; *Rec. of Suffolk Ct. 1671–80*, II, 701, 814, 957, 1015, 1160; Libby, Allen, & Moody, eds., *Maine Ct. Rec.*, IV, 50, 92, 112, 249, 267, 272, 307, 316, 363.

63. Libby, Allen, & Moody, eds., *Maine Ct. Rec.*, II, 252, 284, 307.

64. Nineteen of the 48 tradeswomen were in the £10 or more group, as were 276 of the 373 male traders and estates owners. The actual amount earned may well have been higher than the £12 or £20 mean, because tax assessors sometimes rated property at less than its real value. However, no evidence exists to indicate that women's taxes rated *comparatively* higher or lower than those of their male counterparts.

65. Sewall, *Letter-Book*, p. 167.

66. The marital status of female innkeepers is as follows: widowed, 62; married, 24; unknown, 56.

67. Manwaring, ed., *Digest of Conn. Probate Rec.*, pp. 305–6, 486, 564. Perhaps a fourth woman can be added to this list, since in 1693 Stephen Hosmer allowed his wife the use of land at Hartford, two rooms in the dwelling house, £50 worth of household goods, and a copper still. He directed her to brew outside the house, "especially if she see it bee a snare or temptation to her son Thomas." The will did not specify whether such brewing was for Mistress Hosmore's own use or for sale, but we do know that the still had considerable value (*ibid.*, 472).

68. Boston Rec. Cmrs., *Rep. Containing Boston Town Rec. 1660–1701*, p. 100. Some observers have pointed out that Elizabeth Glover owned the first printing press to arrive in Massachusetts. She did—for a brief period —but the person who actually ran the press (which she inherited from her clergyman husband) was a man, Stephen Daye. When Mistress Glover married Harvard President Henry Dunster, he received the profits of her legacy. Not until the 1770s would women in Puritan New England actually begin to operate presses, even though many other colonies had numbers of such women, and Anne Franklin of Newport printed materials for the Rhode Island government at least as early as 1745. See I. Thomas, *Hist. of Printing in U.S.*, esp. pp. 42–54, 231.

69. Libby, Allen, & Moody, eds., *Maine Ct. Rec.*, I, 119. In one case, however, the Maine authorities did allow John Reynolds's wife to live on the Isles with her husband, so long as "no furder complaynt come against her."

70. Earle, *Curious Punishments*, pp. 126–27.

71. Josselyn, *Two Voyages to N. Eng.*, p. 182.

72. A count of family heads from twenty different tax lists of New England locales between 1633 and 1695 gives 3,058 men and 201 women. New Haven ranked highest, with 11.8% female heads of families in 1680, whereas Dorchester had none in 1641.

73. Hoadly, ed., *Rec. of N. Haven Col. 1638–49*, pp. 91–93; F. Dexter, ed., *N. Haven Town Rec. 1662–84*, pp. 405–10; "Tax List and Schedules—1687," in Boston Rec. Cmrs., *First Rep.*, pp. 91–133; Schenck, *Hist. of Fairfield*, I, 334.

74. F. Dexter, ed., *N. Haven Town Rec. 1662–84*, pp. 405, 409; "Tax List and Schedules—1687," in Boston Rec. Cmrs., *First Rep.*, pp. 94, 132; Scales, *Hist. Memoranda*, I, 235. Personalty is not included in Widow Kellond's and Widow Maverick's totals, but the value of the other women's estates comprise both realty and personalty. The relative difference in assessed valuation may be due to underassessment practices in certain locales.

75. Manwaring, ed., *Digest of Conn. Probate Rec.*, 206, 136, 302. One of these widows, Katharine Harrison, petitioned the county court to settle £470 upon her three daughters—which, of course, decreased her own inheritance by that amount.

76. Keyssar, "Widowhood in 18th-Cent. Mass.," pp. 108–9; J. Trumbull, ed., *Conn. Rec.*, II, 313, 320–21; III, 144, 171, 240; Manwaring, ed., *Digest of Conn. Probate Rec.*, p. 430.

77. The author has calculated the widow's average annual increment by multiplying the inherited value of her property by the rather high figure of 8.3%. Although certainly the increment varied with respect to real estate location and soil fertility, the estates of Joseph Phelps and John Bidwell do

provide us with enough information to allow a suggestive estimate. The estate inherited by Mary Phelps totaled £6 in personalty and approximately £12 in realty, which yielded a profit of less than £1 per annum. In 1681 John Bidwell gave his wife the choice of half interest in "Lands, houseing, Chattells, Cattell, or any other thing whatever"— property worth almost £150—or £8 per annum. Since he did give her that choice, the estate's profits were quite probably roughly equal to the £8, allowing an annual increment of 5.33% (Manwaring, *Digest of Conn. Probate Rec.*, pp. 274, 347).

78. *Ibid.*, p. 35.

79. *Ibid.*, p. 182.

80. *Ibid.*, pp. 138, 246.

81. Keyssar, "Widowhood in 18th-Cent. Mass.," pp. 110–11.

82. *Ibid.*, p. 118. Hartford County widows died worth £60, on the average, but that figure cannot be usefully compared to the male median estate of £205 because the woman's property sometimes included, besides her personalty, the value of realty which she had to grant to her children in accordance with her husband's will. Since such realty is not always included, one cannot determine whether the average widow's holdings declined in value between the time when she received her initial allotment from her husband and the time when she died herself.

83. *Ibid.*, p. 112; Mass. *Acts & Laws, Nov. 20, 1695*, p. 143; Boston Rec. Cmrs., *Rep. Containing Misc. Papers*, pp. 90–110; *Hartford Town Votes*, I, 122, 126, 138.

84. H. Adams, "Allotments of Land in Salem"; J. Trumbull, ed., *Conn. Rec.*, III, 22; *Hartford Town Votes*, I, 157.

85. Lockridge, *Lit. in Col. N. Eng.*, p. 12; D. Smith, "Underregistration & Bias in Probate Rec.," pp. 105–6. The larger figure is probably more accurate, since the widow received a larger portion of her ex-husband's estate when he was poor (Haskins, *Law & Auth. in Early Mass.*, pp. 105–6). In Hartford County the breakdown is as follows:

| | % Left to Widow | | | |
Value of Husband's Estate	0–24	25–49	50–100	N Estates
£0–£99	4	5	14	23
£100–£199	12	8	4	24
£200–£299	7	1	3	11
£300–£499	7	7	1	15
£500–£999	5	1	1	7
£1,000–£3,488	3	0	1	4
	38	22	24	84

86. Manwaring, ed., *Digest of Conn. Probate Rec.*, pp. 496, 347–48.

87. *Ibid.*; Keayne, *Apologia*, pp. 18–20; Boston Rec. Cmrs., *Rep. Containing Boston Town Rec. 1660–1701*, pp. 7, 105.

88. Powers, ed., *N. Haven Town Rec. 1684–1769*, p. 5.

89. *Hartford Town Votes*, I, 235; Noble & Cronin, eds., *Rec. of Mass. Assts.*, II, 102. The Puritan desire to keep poor allotments at a minimum is well illustrated by the case of Sarah Lambert. The Salem selectmen placed Lambert and her child with John Clifford from 1668 through 1671, paying

him £7 per year. Then, in 1672, these officials spoke with Clifford about abating some of the £7, "they thinking it too much for the Towne to Giue." He refused, instead requesting more money "or elce he would not Keep her any longer." The selectmen then placed Lambert with Francis Skerry. They directed him to provide her with food, drink, clothing, and "what Elce is needfull for her" for £5 per annum, but later relented and appropriated an extra £1 for clothing ("Town Records of Salem," pp. 258–59, 265).

90. Peckham, *Captured by Inds.*, p. 16; *Hartford Town Votes*, I, 141, 145, 150.

91. Libby, Allen, & Moody, eds., *Maine Ct. Rec.*, III, 76; C. Mather, *Diary*, II, 46; Hamp. Ct. of "Gen. Sessions & Pleas, no. 1, 1677–1728," p. 169.

92. G. Dow, ed., *Essex Ct. Rec.*, I, 20.

93. Benton, *Warning Out*, pp. 24–25, 55–58, 86; Boston Rec. Cmrs., *Rep. Containing Misc. Papers*, pp. 55–61.

94. "Town Records of Salem," XL, 121; XLII, 89, 259; XLIII, 265–66; LXV, 28.

95. Boston Rec. Cmrs., *Rep. Containing Boston Town Rec. 1660–1701*, pp. 7, 157; "Rec. of Mass. Council Under Dudley," 243–44.

96. C. Mather, *Memorable Prov.*, pp. 54–55; *Rec. of Town of Cambridge*, pp. 145–46.

97. C. Mather, *Diary*, I, 226n.

98. Abbott, *Women in Ind.*, p. 17.

99. A. Clark, *Working Life of Eng. Women.*, pp. 17, 40–41, 54–55, 151–56, 175–78, 202–3, 214, 219, 221, 228–29.

V

Marital Tension in Early New England: When the Ideal Goes Awry

> In describing the husband's authority and the wife's submission it has been necessary again and again to use the word "love."
>
> —Edmund S. Morgan, *The Puritan Family*
>
> Domestic relations were then nearer the cave than now, and the pioneer community was undeniably rougher than the modern one.
>
> —Elwin Lawrence Page,
> *Judicial Beginnings in New Hampshire, 1640–1700*

PURITANS, ACKNOWLEDGING THAT THE FAMILY WAS THE KEY TO THE continuity of the Biblical Commonwealth, took steps to insure that each family member adopted proper role behaviors. The town selectmen oversaw family functions, checking on whether parents catechized their children and children obeyed their parents. Selectmen also observed relations between husbands and wives, in an effort to keep marital tensions at a minimum. Both ministers and magistrates would undoubtedly have been overjoyed if all of their married constituents had adhered rigorously to the marital ideal of obedient, "dutifull, faithful . . . louing" wife and affectionate, protective husband who used his "commanding power" leniently.[1] In the ideal marriage, the husband inspired the proper reverence and submission in his mate by honoring her and responding charitably to her "infirmities." He was not to cast dirt upon her lest she, "the weaker Vessel," be "broken all to pieces." She was better "sweetly drawn" than "sharply driven," so she would come to fear him not with "a slavish Fear, which is nourished with hatred or aversion; but a noble and generous Fear, which proceeds from Love."[2] Under no conditions should a husband punish his wife with "bodily correction or stripes . . . unless it be [given] in his owne defence upon her assalt." The Massachusetts General Court in 1650 specified a fine of up to £10 or a whipping as punishment for any man who struck his wife, or vice versa.[3]

Puritans attempted to keep the behavior of both husbands and wives within God-given bounds. Spokesmen for the several Biblical Commonwealths assumed that the husband would not choose to overextend his authority, or the wife to resist her inferior, dependent status. Yet, in actuality, husbands often took quite literally Puritan directives to wives "that when the husband admonisheth, God admonisheth in him," viewing their authority as virtually limitless.[4] Similarly, wives often stepped out of line by choosing not to behave as submissively as Puritans might wish. Marriage in practice often failed to approximate marriage in theory.

Abusive Husbands

The frustrations and tensions produced by the Puritan *Weltanschauung* (particularly the generalized sense of male powerlessness) and the more idiosyncratic problems caused by the mismatch of "yoke-fellows" often led to marital friction. When John Dunton in 1686 affirmed, "Marriage is the happiest state on this side Heaven," the young Boston spinster Comfort Wilkins disagreed, asking why there were so many "Tears, and Jars, and Discontents, and Jealousies" between spouses. Her daily observations, she admitted, "make more Impression on such Minds as mine, than all that fine Harangue you have made."[5] The various New England courts testify to the accuracy of her conclusions: between 1630 and 1699 at least 128 men and 57 women were tried for abusing their mates.[6]

Men, believing in the dictum that they were to "rule" their wives, wished to be kings in their homes. When John Barrett, a planter of Wells, Maine, was charged with "sleighting & abuseing of his wife" in 1666, he told the York County Court, "What hath any man to do with it, have not I power to correct my owne wife?" Francis Morgan, the doctor at nearby Kittery, in 1667 struck his wife Sarah "to her great Injury, if not the apparent Hazard of her life" because she had spoken to him abusively. Morgan refused to ask the authorities' assistance in his marital distress because he felt "it was below him to

Complayn to Authorities against his wife." Daniel Ela of Haverhill, Massachusetts, screamed at his spouse that she "was nothing to him but a devil in woman's apparel" and ejected her from "his" house. He had refused to denounce her as a scold before the constable, because "it would be a disgrace to him" to have the magistrates whip "his servant and his slave." Eleazer Kingsberry had a similar frame of reference: when reproached for deserting his wife at Wrentham, Massachusetts, in the 1690s, he retorted that "she was a Devilish Jade, and he would never take her more; but when he was settled, and had an House, he would take her as a Servant; and if she would not obey him, he would kick her into the fire." Joseph Beard of Dover, New Hampshire, carried such arrogance still further: Beard threw a stone at his wife,wounding her, and explained to the New Hampshire Inferior Court of Common Pleas in 1692, "I would make no more to kill her than to kill a dog."[7]

Other husbands heaped a variety of abuses upon their wives. Tobias Hill in 1640 asserted his right to dispose of his wife as he saw fit. He told his Essex County neighbors that he had had enough of her for the time being and offered her to any of his fellow townsmen for three or four days. Edward Berry, a Salem weaver, contemptuously ordered his spouse either to fast or to eat meat charred in the coals. He reviled her horribly when she was sick, telling her "he did not care if there were a fire in the south field and she in the middle of it" (1677). The idea that a wife, as her husband's servant, was tied to the home received literal expression from John Tillison in 1656: after throwing a bowl of water on Mistress Tillison one Sabbath day while she was lying sick abed, her husband chained her "by the leg to a plow chain, to keep her within doors."[8]

Many of the male offenders administered physical beatings to their spouses. William Healy of Middlesex County, Massachusetts, beat his wife with a large stick, called her a "lying slutt," bruised her arms, and several times hit her in the face with his fist (1666). Another man, Ephraim Joy of Maine, kicked his mate and bludgeoned her with a club when she refused to feed his pig (1699). Soon after Zachary Dibble of Stamford, Connecticut, received a £40 portion from his wife's father, he took away all her clothing and began beating her "so that he caused the blood to settle in severall places of her body" (1669). One of only three husbands who actually denied assaulting their wives, Dibble claimed his spouse had sucked on her arms to produce the discoloration, attributed her bruised thighs to witchcraft, and told friends she had a witch's teat in her "secret parts."[9] Other men also threatened, or even attempted, to kill their mates. Huburtus Mattoon of Saco, Maine, expressed the wish to poison his wife or to knock her on the head (1681). His neighbor, Francis Herlow, spent an hour in the stocks for swearing he would cut his own mate's throat (1699). Eleazur Parker of Cambridge, "stirred up by strong drink," attempted to stab Mistress Parker, but "a Book in her Bosom" saved her. Joseph Metcalfe of Ipswich made a more premeditated attempt on Rebecca Metcalfe's life, pouring ratsbane into her broth. Fortunately, she did not drink it.[10]

Five men actually did kill their wives. In 1689 an Andover husbandman, Hugh Stone, argued with his wife about selling a piece of land. That argument was brought to a swift conclusion when Stone cut her throat, an action for which he paid the ultimate penalty—the loss of his own life.[11] Peter Abbot was hanged at Stratford, Connecticut, for the same offense; he cut his wife's throat while she was asleep, and attempted the same upon his small child (1667).[12] The remaining wife-murderers were non-white—two Indians and a black.[13] The Connecticut Assistants acquitted one other white male of being "instrumental" in his own wife's death (1682). One Massachusetts woman died under suspicious circumstances: Elias Row's wife, who seldom lay with her husband and was reputedly "given to Drink and quarrelling," died in bed, with "much blood about her, so some think she was choak'd with it." However, a coroner's jury found no sign of violence (1681).[14]

The exact motives of those men who threatened, assaulted, or murdered their wives cannot be adequately determined at this late date. Court records are frustratingly brief, and even when direct testimony is recorded there is usually little account of the dynamics of a specific couple's interaction. Each abusive situation undoubtedly had its own idiosyncratic character, but one common theme stamped virtually every case appearing before the courts: the husbands' belief that they could legitimately punish their wives for obstreperous behavior, whether imagined or real. Abusive husbands apparently felt the need to be "lords of the home." They could easily take refuge in calling their wives gossips, witches, and whores—those negative inversions of proper womanhood —whenever they felt that their own authority or prerogatives needed shoring up. Sometimes the wife's refusal to obey an order, or her criticism of her husband's actions could set him off, but at other times—in fact, about half of the time—she did not even question his "dominion." In such cases the husband may have been focusing upon his spouse the resentments multiplied by life in a repressive society, in his effort to achieve some catharsis and to exercise unquestioned control over something or someone. Because the underlying feeling of helplessness before God, Nature, and the conditioned fears of childhood was so great, a wife's real or imagined insubordination could evoke disproportionate anger and frustration. After a man beat his wife, he could presumably feel that he had "proved" his dominion over her, and thereby experience a more generalized sense of his own power. In any event, the man's weakness gave rise to the need for such proof as it has in other places and at other times. The culture one lives in is strongly implicated in his/her actions, and whenever culturally intensified feelings of powerlessness occur in a social setting that prescribes male dominance, we might expect to find wife abuse fairly common. Although the syndrome is not peculiarly Puritan, Puritan culture created the needs and fears which set the stage for such abuse.

Of course, cultures need not be consistent. Puritan ideology accentuated feelings of powerlessness, which in turn gave rise to wife abuse; yet at the same time the Puritan law code (in Massachusetts, at least) stood as a progressive counterforce to such pressures toward physical aggression against wives. However, such a law was never enforced enthusiastically or effectively. Contributing to this fact may have been the presumption that a degree of physical aggressiveness was a positive attribute for the seventeenth-century New England male, a necessity for one who would cope successfully and skillfully with the demands of the environment, especially in frontier locales. Tolerant courts did not seriously penalize those persons guilty of fighting; fighters and assaulters paid a usual fine of only two to four shillings, an amount less than assessed swearers, Sabbath violators, slanderers, drunkards, card-players, gamblers, and those men who failed to appear for jury duty. Under such circumstances, overly aggressive husbands faced only minimal punishment for abusing their wives. Actual murder merited a hanging, as murder always did, but threats on the life of one's wife were penalized hardly at all.

In Essex County, Massachusetts, the magistrates sentenced only two of twenty-seven wife-abusers to receive lashings, and granted a respite to one of those when he promised to reform. That man had beaten his mate "unmercifully, kicked her about the house and struck her violently upon the head." He had further threatened to slit her throat or to burn her, adding that if she complained to the authorities he would surely kill her. For such indiscretions Thomas Russell ultimately received nothing more than an admonition (1680).[15] Five other men received only admonitions; the remainder were ordered to pay fines of 10s. to £2.

Essex County practice was the rule in Puritan New England. Connecticut offenders were fined £2 or merely placed under the watchful supervision of town-appointed "guardians." Even John Dix, who kicked his pregnant wife, pulled her hair, and neglected to support her, was assessed just 25s. and prevented from selling any part of his estate until he submitted a bond for his family's maintenance.[16] The Plymouth Colony General Court often released similar offenders with admonitions, and Maine practice dictated only that the husband submit a bond of less than £10 to insure his future good behavior. When a wife-abuser received a fine in Maine, he had almost always been guilty of some other offense as well.[17] In New Hampshire erring husbands paid small fines (5s. to £1) and also sometimes had to post bond for good behavior.

The Middlesex, Suffolk, and New Haven County authorities dealt more harshly with abusive husbands. Middlesex offenders paid fines of £2 to £5 or posted an extremely high bond of £10 to £40, while Suffolk and New Haven counties were the only Puritan New England locales where the offending husband received corporal punishment. The Suffolk magistrates ordered ten of the fourteen wife-abusers to be whipped, including twenty lashes for the comparatively minor offense of shutting a wife outdoors (1682).[18] However, the court allowed some of these men to pay a £5 fine in lieu of a whipping. At New Haven three of the four errant husbands received a lashing. Nowhere did an abusive husband ever pay the £10 designated by Massachusetts law.

In most of Puritan New England the magistrates offered wives little security against their husband's disorderly conduct. Even if a wife complained to the authorities, her mate was, more often than not, released after he paid a small fine, or after he was merely admonished to reform his ways. In only a few instances was a wife actually separated from a hostile husband, and in at least a dozen cases the wife complained to the authorities more than once about an abusive mate.

Given such conditions, many women may have resigned themselves to receiving abuse from their husbands, instead of reporting them to the authorities. Beatrice Berry, for one, concealed her

mate's maltreatment because she "was rather willing to groane
under it then to make a publique discovery of his wicked, and
brutish carriage."[19] Sometimes a child or a neighbor, instead of the
wife, would inform local authorities of a husband's wrongdoing.[20]
In any event, a wife could not sue her husband in court for damages,
nor could any woman sue a man who was *not* her husband for
damages resulting from assault and battery. For example, in 1690
the Suffolk County justices abated Christian Herridge's action
against Thomas Bannister in the amount of £10 for his assault on
her, merely because she was a woman![21]

If the husband and wife were separated, the wife could look
forward only to a better "governor," at best, for she was not free to
lead a new, independent life. In 1663, because of "an irreconcilable
distance of Spirit that is in John Betts and his wife in reference to
Coniugall union," the Connecticut Particular Court directed Abigail
Betts's father to take her "vnder his tuition and Gouerment." A year
later the York County justices tried James Harmon for miscarriages
toward his wife and gave Sarah Harmon the liberty to live with her
mother or with some appropriate man. In 1668, after her husband
had refused to support her and had also threatened her physically,
Hannah Browne ran away to her mother-in-law's residence. The
New Haven County Court directed that Mistress Browne could live
with "some good family, under the carefull inspection of ye head or
heads of such family."[22] Husbands, in contrast, were usually free to
live on their own property, unencumbered by any "governor."

Wifely Resistance

As a corollary consistent with the mild treatment of wife-beaters,
even the woman who faced a brutal husband could not legitimately
defend herself against his physical abuse. She was to try to tolerate
her mate's aggression, pray for his reformation, and, as a last resort,
ask the ministers or the town selectmen to intercede on her behalf.
Cotton Mather explained that such a woman "must be directed and
comforted," but was in no way to resist her spouse. Benjamin
Wadsworth taught that a husband who strikes his wife "shames his
profession of Christianity, he breaks the Divine law, [and] he dis-
honours God and him self too, by this ill behavior." However, the
wife who hit her husband was even more reprehensible, even if she
had done so when under assault. She "provokes the glorious God,
tramples his authority under her feet; she not only affronts her

Husband, but also God her Maker, Lawgiver and Judge," Wadsworth warned. While the striking husband's behavior was "ill," the belligerent wife's was absolutely "wicked."[23]

Sometimes it was even assumed that a wife, through her own irresponsibility or willful neglect, had encouraged her husband's violence. If a wife had been more understanding, more dutiful, more deferential—in short, more feminine—her husband would not have felt the need to punish her. The case of Richard and Grace Miller, tried before the York County Court in 1672, illustrates how this attitude could be expressed in the courtroom. Richard Miller was presented before the York associate justices for throwing his pregnant wife out of a floating canoe, for calling her a whore several times, and for once stripping her naked and threatening to pull the child out of her body. The associates fined the offender for drunkenness and swearing, then ordered him to post a bond for good behavior toward his wife. The court also reprimanded Mistress Miller. The justices blamed her lack of industry for bringing out Mr. Miller's "Jelocys" and admonished her to "Attend the care & occasions of her husband & family with more carefullness & diligence."[24]

Despite the sometime practice of blaming the victim, and the many injunctions issued to keep women properly submissive, a large number of wives resisted husbandly dominion and what they felt was an oppressive marital situation. Thirty-two women refused to live with their husbands, establishing alternate residences. Usually such women left swiftly for some locale from which they would not be easily retaken and forced to return. In 1694 Abraham Adams's wife rose in the middle of the night, telling him that she heard their Negro servant about the house. When he got out of bed at 4 A.M. to begin the day's work, he found that his wife, much of the silver plate, the money, and some household articles were gone. At Marblehead, Massachusetts, Susannah Lawrence left her husband to live with William Cock in a secret upper chamber of his house in nearby Beverly. Elizabeth Cooper fled from her Sandwich (Plymouth Colony) home in 1670, seeking refuge and a new husband in Virginia. One Massachusetts wife, Hannah Gross, ran away to Jamaica, where by 1690 she had remarried without benefit of divorce. Elizabeth Colson fled to New Amsterdam to get away from her husband, William Benfield, in Connecticut. She tore up a letter Benfield sent her by way of his lawyer, "sayinge that shee Radder Would laye in prison to Rotte, perpetually, than ever to kome to live

With benfield againe, the Which shee Would not owne to have binne ever a hosband to her, albeit shee hath lived With him." She admitted living in a common-law relationship with another man, claimed "benfield Whas death," and signed a paper acquitting him of any "matrimoniall Engagements" on April 20, 1662.[25] Twelve men filed successful petitions for divorce in Massachusetts, Plymouth, and Connecticut after their wives deserted them.[26]

Running away was a difficult as well as dangerous step for a woman to take. More often than not, the fleeing wife had to find a suitable man with whom to journey through the wilderness, because townsmen often became suspicious of an unattached female, and might check into her background. Travel to Virginia or Jamaica required a sum of £5 or so for transportation, plus enough money to establish herself there—money which, short of theft from her husband, was almost impossible to come by. At least one colony, Plymouth, decided that a woman could be deprived of her dower right if she ran away from her husband or committed "other notorious fact without reconciliation to him in his lifetime" (1685).[27] When the wife did return, she could face criminal charges of adultery or theft, both of which merited severe corporal punishment. Nevertheless, one woman, Ruth Read, "most Impudently" returned to Massachusetts after living for four years in England with a lover, during which time she bore a child. The Assistants sentenced her to stand in the public marketplace on a stool with a paper on her breast inscribed "THVS I STAND FOR MY ADVLTEROVS AND WHORISH CARRIAGE" and to receive thirty lashes (1674).[28]

Some discontented women who continued to live with their husbands may have focused their resentment against property held by their mates, especially since they themselves could own no real estate. In 1667 Edith Crawford was suspected of burning her husband's house, but enough evidence could not be gathered to convict her.[29] Both Alice Clarke of Boston and Bethia Hinckley of Barnstable, Plymouth Colony, gave away their husband's property without consent. In 1672 Clarke "clandestinely" gave over £44 to Widow Bridgham; Hinckley, besides "illegally" granting property, spent much time in "unnecessary visiting," would not explain her frequent absences from home, refused to "revere" her husband or provide for his needs, and treated the Barnstable Church with contempt when it admonished her for her "errors" in 1683.[30] In 1664 Daniel Black, a "pore man . . . that hath nothing to Live by but his Labor" and one cow, lost any profit that the animal might bring him "by his wifes carlesnes." In her defense, Faith Black complained that her husband had called her a bawd and threatened to knock her brains out. She refused to stay at home, to prepare meals for her husband, or to wash his clothes. When a neighbor cleaned Black's clothing while Faith was on one of her many absences, she objected strongly. The Essex County Court finally ordered her to stay at home or be whipped.[31]

The extent to which the actions of Faith Black, Bethia Hinckley, and Alice Clarke grew out of a feeling that they ought to be able to dispose of property as freely as their husbands could, or out of more general discontent with the marital relationship, cannot be determined. Clarke did, however, make some effort to protect her ownership of property inherited from her first husband when she remarried. She and nineteen other women contracted with their prospective husbands to secure the right to own all or part of their inherited realty and, in a few instances, an annual maintenance allotment upon the new husband's decease.[32] Alice MacCoy actually convinced her mate to give his entire estate to her if she outlived him; Hugh MacCoy's Wethersfield properties were inventoried at £100 13s. 6d. in 1683.[33] Signing a premarital contract usually represented little more than a symbolic effort to control possessions, since the Massachusetts magistrates did not consider it legally obligatory. The wife also had to keep such a contract hidden from her husband in Connecticut, where it was considered legal and binding. When Saint Tryon complained in 1689 that her spouse "hath fraudulently conveyed away from her a Writing made between them before marriage," the Hartford County Court decided that her inheritance from her former husband belonged to William Tryon. In this case, the magistrates may have been influenced by the fact that Mistress Tryon produced two witnesses who stated the couple had indeed drawn up such a contract, but that they had not signed it until the morning after their nuptial vows—a time at which she could no longer act as *femme sole*. [34]

Two Connecticut women prepared wills before their husbands had died, thereby behaving as though they were legally capable of independent action. In 1655 Jane Hosford left "her" land to the Windsor Church, her sister, and her sister's children, but only because she was leaving for England to join her husband. Before 1684 Christian Harbert of Wethersfield made a will which her daughter, Elizabeth Blackleach, protested. Christian's husband had conveyed his property to the Blackleachs in return for his wife's maintenance in her old age, but she refused to respect that arrangement. The Connecticut authorities, however, upheld the validity of both women's wills.[35]

While some women made efforts to protect their property rights, others refused to recognize their husbands' "control" over sexuality in marriage. In theory, the husband could "use" his wife's body at any time—provided he did not do so "excessively"—except on Sabbaths, fast days, times of wifely illness, and during menstrual flow. At least eight wives, however, refused relations with their husbands "not only in Some fitt but in a gen[el] way for many yeares."[36] Ann Eaton, the wife of the governor of New Haven Colony, rejected her husband's sexual overtures and moved her bed into another room after he had admonished her for some specific reason (1646). Joan Wade of Connecticut refused intercourse with her spouse for fifteen years, until such time as the General Court divorced them (1657). On her wedding day, Hannah Uffit of New Haven asserted that she had been forced to marry against her will, and she resolved to keep her virginity for one year in protest. Thereafter, she frequently complained "that it is a pittious case that she must live w[t]h one that she did neuer loue," called her husband a fool, and said "she could make him say what she listed [i.e., wished]." In 1657 she was strongly suspected of having had sexual relations with a seaman of loose life—thus trampling upon her husband's sexual prerogative by not only giving herself to another man, but also as if to add insult to injury, selecting one who represented the lowest stratum in society.[37] Sarah Mattoon likewise refused to have intercourse with her mate and lay with other men, protesting that her husband's own adulterous behavior was grounds for divorce. After she left her New Hampshire residence and returned to her onetime home in Saco, Maine, the New Hampshire Councillors granted a separation, but not a divorce (1682).[38]

The Heinous Sin of Adultery

The heavy social pressure on Puritan women to marry at an early age in order to avoid the odious condition of spinsterhood, coupled with their dependent situation once they did marry, often led to bad marital choices and resentful marriages. This, in turn, sometimes caused adulterous impulses. In 1644, for example, eighteen-year-old Mary Latham, after being rejected by one suitor, felt that she would never marry and vowed to wed the next man who asked her. One "ancient" man did ask; she responded affirmatively, entering a marriage that soon became tumultuous. Mistress Latham frequently abused her incompatible husband, "setting a knife to his breast and threatening to kill him, calling him old rogue and cuckold, and . . . [saying] she would make him wear horns as big as a bull." After confessing to adultery with twelve different men, she was ultimately hanged in Boston, along with one of her paramours.[39]

At least two other persons—one from Weymouth, Massachusetts, and the other from New Haven Colony—also were hanged for their extramarital activities, thereby serving as graphic reminders that one must not offend God by violating the sexual exclusiveness implied by the marriage contract.[40] Legislatures devised harsh laws to prevent such violations: Massachusetts, Connecticut, Plymouth, and New Haven Colonies early prescribed the death penalty for adultery committed with either a betrothed or a married woman.[41] Such laws stayed on the books until the 1670s; then, Plymouth substituted one law which punished offenders by two severe whippings and the wearing of an easily recognizable AD sewn on the arm or back of one's garment. New Hampshire adopted the Plymouth statute in the Cutt Code of 1680. Connecticut had,by 1673, liberalized its own adultery law; that colony sentenced adulterers to be whipped, to wear halters around their necks, and to have an A burned in their foreheads. The Bay Colony as early as 1638 allowed severe whipping and banishment instead of the death penalty, but a 1660 enactment capitally punished anyone who refused to leave the colony after conviction. Another law in 1694 removed that penalty and sentenced offenders to spend an hour on the gallows, receive up to forty lashes, and wear a capital A two inches high. Anyone found without his or her letter would receive an additional fifteen lashes.[42]

Whatever the specific law, however, adulterers in all colonies usually received between twenty and thirty-nine lashes. Before 1670 the wearing of an AD was not uncommon in most colonies, but after that date many adulterers were freed upon simply paying a fine of from £10 to £20. The authorities used the death penalty only a few times, all early in New England's history; and Connecticut magistrates did not see fit to brand any offenders.

Puritan law and practice seriously punished both participants in an adultery which involved an espoused or married woman. An unfaithful husband faced a severe penalty only if he committed adultery with a woman who was pledged to another man. He could, if he felt the urge, seek out a single woman to engage sexually; upon apprehension, he then paid the lesser penalty for fornication.[43] The offense of the married woman, however, was always considered adultery, so for her extramarital involvement became a much more serious matter.

Although Puritans considered adultery a breach of wedlock and a transgression against God for either party, they nevertheless viewed the woman's adultery quite differently from the man's. William Gouge wrote, "I denie not but the more inconueniences may follow vpon the womans default then vpon the mans: as, greater infamy before men, worse disturbance of the family, more mistaking of legitimate, or illegitimate children, with the like." William Perkins urged the man not to marry "a woman, as hath beene formerly defloured, or hath and is, or may be convinced of adulterie, and uncleannesse." For Perkins, the male's potential or actual adultery was a less consequential matter. He believed that a man with a concubine was eligible for marriage if he renounced her, but gave such a woman no similar option.[44] Still, despite the sexism of the Puritan viewpoint, adultery reportedly bore "bitter fruit" for either sex, including the perpetual alienation of affection in marital relationships, a general hardening of the heart, and the wastage of family goods through the husband's support of "his harlot" and the adulterous wife's "purloining what she can from her husband." Last but not least, adultery rendered the face "impudent" in appearance.[45] Puritans did subject male and female adulterers to the same severe penalties—a stark contrast to the usual practice of penalizing the "weaker sex" less rigorously.

Even though the authorities punished adulterers and adultresses with equal severity, more than 300 persons allegedly committed that offense or engaged in the somewhat more circumstantial activity of "adulterous carriage," as indicated in Chart #5. Adultery figured as a cause in 51 percent of all divorce cases heard by the authorities (N = 55 of 109).[46] Only one petition alleging infidelity of a mate was *not* granted.

Adultery was one of the most common offenses in Puritan New England, yet most cases probably never came under the surveillance of the authorities. J. W. wrote in 1682 about fornication and adultery in Boston: "Now most certainly if Justice finds out so many Transgressours in this kind, how many must the private ones amount to? I may without being uncharitable think, they include a

Chart 5.1

Persons Convicted of Adultery or Adulterous Carriage, by
Colony and Sex

Colony	Men	Women	Total	% Men	% Women
Massachusetts (excluding Maine & New Hampshire)	81	66	147	55.1	44.9
Maine	30	31	61	49.2	50.8
Connecticut	33	23	56	58.9	41.1
Plymouth	21	13	34	61.8	38.2
New Hampshire	6	1	7	85.7	14.3
New Haven	3	0	3	100.	0.
Totals	174	134	308	56.5	43.5

great part of the Town; for private sins (as these are) seldom fall
under public censure, or at least not so often as more open ones."
The wife of one pastor, J. W. reported, met other men at one of the
taverns. When the watch discovered her activities, he failed to
prosecute, "not willing to make her a publick Example, lest the
wicked should rejoyce, and the uncircumcized triumph at the sweet
downfall of a Daughter of Zion." There were at least eleven other
Boston women, including two with the status of ladies, who, J. W.
asserted, could "tell how to adorn their Husbands Heads with a
Forked Coat of Arms." In 1686 traveler John Dunton described one
well-painted and elaborately clothed woman who every evening
supposedly set aside "her Painting and her Modesty, when she lies
with her own face, tho' some say, not with her own Husband." A
decade later (1699) another traveler, Ned Ward, observed with
sharp sarcasm, "yet, nothwithstanding the Harshness of their Law,
the Women [of Massachusetts] are of such noble souls, and un-
daunted Resolutions, that they will run the hazard of being Hang'd
rather than not be reveng'd on Matrimony."[47]

We can never know exactly how much adultery occurred in
seventeenth-century Puritan New England, for certainly most
offenders took precautions to avoid apprehension. They usually
chose unobtrusive places—the woods at night, the home when the
husband was absent on business, or some other relatively isolated
spot. Of course, pregnancy would not serve as evidence, as it did in
fornication cases, since the wife could attribute any conception to
her actual husband. Often the offense was committed with some-

one who was unlikely to reveal it. Wives sometimes had sexual relations with strangers, transients, Indians, and seamen—men whose residence in a town would likely be brief, and who would therefore be unable to testify against the woman if some suspicion was later aroused. Husbands had no similar option, because un-accompanied, transient women were rare in New England.

We can only speculate as to why so many women chose, despite the heavy onus and penalty, to commit adultery or (in a much smaller number of cases) to behave in an adulterous manner. Some of the offenders may have simply desired relief from boring house-hold tasks. Some may merely have been fascinated by an intriguing taboo experience. Some may have had a "natural" tendency toward promiscuity, for which Puritan society provided no legitimate out-let. Others may have been acting out a frustrated desire for a more egalitarian love. If we are to believe J. W., at least one wife searched for extramarital contacts because her husband, an elderly pastor, "though he has the Gift of Sanctifying in the Spirit, fails much in Satisfying the flesh."[48]

Often the husband's infidelity, maltreatment, or neglect seemed to precipitate the wife's adulterous behavior. Mary Bachelor, wife of the Hampton (New Hampshire) pastor, in 1652 was whipped for her intercourse with another man, although that intercourse oc-curred only after her husband had been punished for soliciting the favors of one of his female churchmembers. After the Mas-sachusetts General Court separated Mistress Bachelor from her mate, without granting her permission to remarry, she once more appeared in court for taking enough liberties with a married man so that he left his own wife. Imprisoned, she stripped herself "almost to the skin," apparently in an effort to entice the jailor to release her.[49] In New London County, Connecticut, the behavior of Elizabeth Gerard's husband was also preliminary to her own mis-conduct. The magistrates decided her crime was mitigated by her husband's "beateing of her & makeing no suitable provision of her maintainance and then in goeing from her & not returneing for some years" (1672). At Stamford, Sarah Dibble went to bed with another man after her husband assaulted her. The case of Stephen Willey and his wife is similar; Willey, a New Hampshire resident, threw his wife down, menaced her with an ax, and threw her out of his house. Later she returned, only to be soon dis-covered in bed with an unknown man who fled, pantless, into the night. Willey then bloodied his wife's head with a chair, swore her would kill her, and began looking for a knife. Fortunately his brother intervened to prevent any further bloodshed.[50]

While wives like Mary Bachelor, Elizabeth Gerard, and Mistress Willey may have wished to cuckold their husbands in retaliation for abusive behavior, few women would berate their husbands with "horrible and abusive speeches" taunting them with their "horned" state, as Jane Halloway of Plymouth Colony did.[51] Since the courts did not punish wife-abusers very heavily, a possible beating from her irate husband deterred the wife from being very open about her extramarital contacts. She had to content herself with the recognition that her adultery was a declarative act—however secret—in a society which allowed women few opportunities to exercise control over their own lives. The woman had to keep in mind that it was also dangerous: even if she observed the utmost care in selecting a paramour and a place to conduct her extramarital liaison, the unexpected could always occur. In 1647 Boston merchant Robert Keayne's son wrote from London that his spouse "has not deserved the name of my wife" because she gave him a venereal disease. Four decades later the Plymouth authorities granted John Glover a divorce after his wife gave him syphilis.[52]

In adultery, many women inverted the proper feminine role by extending sexual overtures to men who were not their mates. Ann Pulman of York kissed Joseph Weare and placed her hand in Thomas Wise's "Cod piss" (1685). Sarah Turner accused her neighbor Roger Tyler of having eaten turnips; when he denied her charge, she playfully responded, " 'Come heth' & let mee kisse thee & then I'le tell yee." She also said that "she would make the folks about the [Lynn iron] works believe the devil was in her before she had done with him" (1650). Grace Mattock of New Haven County made inviting overtures to John Umberfield by pulling up her clothing to expose "her nakedness" to him (1674).[53] Despite the subservient role that women in Calvinist New England were expected to assume, in 60 percent of the cases where adultery was actually committed, the woman served as the "seducer."[54] Such cases suggest that many a woman wished not to be, in Cotton Mather's terms, "a Vertuous Wife"—that helpmate who was so faithful to her husband "that she will not give a Lodging to the least straggling wandring Thought of Disloyalty to his Bed."[55]

Cuckoldry was something women did to men; none of the 174 males tried for adultery or adulterous carriage expressed any desire to make a fool of or retaliate against his wife. There was, in fact, no female equivalent of the cuckold, for the notion that a husband could force his wife "to wear horns" would entail some assumption that the wife also had implicit "control" over her mate's sexuality. Puritans were not willing to go that far. They would not refer to the adulterous husband's "Disloyalty to *her* Bed." Although a wife might consider herself wronged by her mate's "notorious uncleanness,"[56] she would never say that he "has not deserved the name of my husband," for that would suggest that she possessed too much sexual control over him.

Divorce

At least seventy-six Puritan New England women sought divorces or separations by petitioning the appropriate authorities. These women cited eight different offenses which they believed constituted grounds for divorce. Most cited desertion (61.8%) and adultery or bigamy (44.7%). Five other "causes" were less common: impotence (9.2%), failure to provide (3.8%), cruelty (four cases), and incest and heresy (one instance each). Twenty-three women (29.5%) gave more than one reason. In three instances a parent petitioned on behalf of a daughter; two of them specified impotence and desertion as grounds for divorce. The remaining parent, Mary Litchfield, herself a divorcée, requested a divorce for her daughter Mary Straight because the latter's husband "left her almost naked more like an Indian than a Christian swearing most Abominably threatening to split her open," refused to provide "neither for meate, Drinke Cloathing nor Lodging," called her "Dam'd whore," and several times had beaten her.[57] No parent petitioned on behalf of a husband, and only twenty-nine husbands initiated action for divorce. Since men had greater mobility than women, they may have found it easier to move elsewhere and remarry than to go through embarrassing divorce proceedings. After all, a divorce did represent a certain loss of the husband's control over his wife's behavior. Husbands, much more than wives, cited adultery or bigamy as the cause for marital dissolution. Adultery-bigamy was a factor in 79 percent of the cases, desertion in 44.8 percent, cruelty and refusing to have sex in two each, and incest in one other. If the cases in which the charge is unknown are subtracted from the totals, fully 80.8 percent of the husbands but only 48 percent of the wives filed petitions based on their mate's sexual indiscretions.

Petitioning for divorce was an act of great courage, for divorced parties were *persona non grata*, at least in Massachusetts and Plymouth colonies. On one occasion the Plymouth General Court engaged in some semantic juggling to avoid extending an onerous divorce to a petitioner; instead, the deputies allowed the injured party a separation with leave to remarry—a contradiction in terms, but a decision more compatible with public sentiment.[58] Divorce was a dirty word. In Essex County, Massachusetts, divorcée Martha Beale and her new husband complained to the local authorities, "Som persons Take ockacion to abuse us in most reuileing speches," including the accusation of adultery.[59] Only in Connecticut, if we can believe the Puritan traveler Sarah Knight, were divorced men and women much tolerated. Madame Knight reported, concerning the Indians, "they marry many wives and at pleasure put them away, and on ye least dislike or fickle humor, on either side, saying stand away to one another is a sufficient Divorce. And indeed those uncomely Stand aways are too much in Vogue among the English in this Indulgent Colony as their Records plentifully prove." Madame Knight felt that woman, "the foolish sex, have had too large a share" in procuring divorces there.[60] Interestingly enough, the official records bear out this Puritan gentledame's contention. The Connecticut authorities honored at least thirty-six petitions; Massachusetts allowed one-fifth more divorces and separations (N = 43), but that colony had two and one-half times the population of its westerly neighbor.[61] Altogether, women comprised 70.4 percent of petitioners, including 80.8 percent in Massachusetts and 70.5 percent in Connecticut. (Corresponding percentages for New Hampshire, New Haven, and Plymouth were 100, 100, and 22.2.)

Once the General Court, Court of Assistants, or a county court had dissolved a marriage, the guilty party could not refuse to respect that decision or he could be further penalized. Edward Naylor, for one, forfeited his bond for good behavior when his ex-wife complained of his intrusion into her company (1675).[62]

Abusive Wives

Many discontented wives pressed for divorce. Others did not go that far, instead expressing their frustration, desire for independence, or need for personal power by attacking their spouses verbally and physically. The wife of Matthew Giles of Dover frequently cursed at her husband, "saying he had buggered her Servant boy, & Laen with her daughter in Law, & saying her daughter was her husbands hore, & yt she did hope to see her husband hanged ere long." Whatever the truth of her charges, the New Hampshire authorities ordered her whipped twenty lashes and admonished Mr. Giles for his "uncomely & provoking speeches viz in saying that he had taken his daughter as his wife."[63] Daniel Abbot's wife, with "maddness of folly and turbulency of her corrupt will," vowed to destroy her mate, ran away with their children, and plotted to rifle the Abbot house (1683).[64] The wife of Martin Stebbins "offered vyolence to her husband, w^h being divulged, was of such infamy" that she was cast out of the Roxbury Church (1659?).[65] The Plymouth authorities punished Joan Miller of Taunton "for beating and reviling her husband and egging her children to healp her, biding them knock him in the head, and wishing his victuals choake him" (1654).[66] The New Hampshire Council directed Anne Colcord, who had refused sexual communion with her spouse, to "attend her duty" toward him or be whipped. When Edward Colcord then attempted to "use" her body, she scratched his face (1680).[67]

Other wives were even more violent than the scratching Mistress Colcord. Robert Laurence's spouse called him "a bald-pated old rogue and struck him with her fist" (1681). John Davis's wife broke his head open when she hit him with a pot of cider (1680). Elizabeth Fanning took on two men, belting her husband in the face, then knocking out a neighbor with a blow to his head (1682). Hugh Mackie asserted that his wife Alice "hath Cast off the subjection which is due by the marriage Covenant from the wife to the husband, appearing both in her refusing to yeld obedience to my lawfull apointments and in her taking vpon her to rise up against me, fall vpon me and beat me, scratching kicking &c and that without any Cause of provocation." Alice Mackie also spent some unchaperoned time with one man who had a reputation for lewd behavior; she insulted Hugh with the claim that, in his words, "I am no man. That she was still as much a maid as she was before she was married, for all mee. That she had a good haue an old log ly in the bed by her as I. That I am a Steere." Soon after, upon Alice's realizing that she was pregnant, Hugh sardonically commented, "if now she say it is by me, I pray let her tell the Court, how she gat a child by a steere." Alice ultimately deserted her spouse to live with a divorced man, later admitted adultery with yet another male, and was divorced upon her husband's petition.[68]

On occasion an in-law or parent became the object of an irate wife's venom. The Essex County magistrates admonished Mary

Pray for addressing her mother-in-law "old hogge get you whom [home]" and for throwing stones at her. The Plymouth deputies ordered Anna Bessey to pay a £10 fine or be whipped for "choping" her father-in-law in the back (1662).[69] At New Haven, Ann Eaton, the governor's wife, admitted striking her mother on the breast (1640s).[70]

Wives who abused their husbands in word or deed risked a good deal more than husbands who mistreated their wives. The various justices sentenced only 15.9 percent of the guilty men to whippings (some of those were allowed to pay fines instead), but 52.9 percent of the husband-abusers received corporal sentences (and very few of them were given the option of paying a fine). Twice as many husbands as wives escaped with only an admonition—15.9 percent versus 8.3 percent.

One might argue that such inequitable treatment for male and female spouse-abusers arose not out of a desire to punish the offensive wife more severely than the offending husband, but out of the realization that the wife lacked the ability to pay a fine. Since a husband could not be expected to pay the wife's fine for abuse directed at him, a lashing became the only alternative. This position does not, however, stand up under analysis. Certainly the wife generally lacked the income or property necessary to discharge a fine, but the authorities could at least have extended her the opportunity to avoid a whipping through payment of a specified sum. It would have been possible for some women to enlist the help of friends, parents, or sympathizers, as often was the case when the authorities levied fines on Quakers. Instead of ordering a wife whipped, the magistrates could have used less injurious methods of punishment: placement in the public cage, in the stocks, or before the whipping post in public humiliation. Particularly revealing of the Puritan attitude is the fact that magistrates almost insured that even those wives who had been fined would also be whipped, by setting the amount considerably higher than the husbands' fines. Whereas abusive wives paid between £2 and £10, husbands paid only between 10s. and £2 on the average, even though they generally abused their wives in a more threatening and serious manner.

Only at the most extreme level of mate abuse was the punishment actually equal. A woman who killed her husband swung from the gallows, just as did the man who murdered his wife. In 1644 the mayor's court of Gorgeana (later York), Maine, executed a woman who allegedly murdered her husband. This woman, the wife of Mr.

Cornish, confessed to adultery with "divers" men, including the mayor himself, but declared herself innocent of murder. In 1685 Betty Indian killed her mate in Plymouth Colony by throwing a stone at a bottle of liquor and hitting him in the head—though in all likelihood this was a case of manslaughter. Not until 1706 did a clear-cut case of husband murder appear before a New England court: then a Hartford wife was hanged for striking her husband in the head with a pair of scissors.[71]

There were, however, two other instances of attempted murder. In 1641 the Massachusetts Assistants ordered Mary Osborne severely whipped for feeding her spouse quicksilver, and in 1684 the New Haven County Court sentenced the aged widow Sarah Jackson to pay £5 for making an attempt on her late husband's life. The magistrates did not wish to punish her further because she suffered from bodily infirmity, "more than ordinary hurryes; & temptations, & [was] at times crazye in her head." In 1658 the Connecticut Assistants acquitted Katherine Boston of poisoning her husband in New London.[72]

Despite ministerial injunctions urging wives to remain demurely deferential, and a socio-legal system which heavily penalized those who did step out of line, at least 278 wives took action against the persons or the superior positions of their husbands. Probably a good many other seventeenth-century wives failed to appear before the authorities for wrongs done to their husbands. Men did not like to report their wives' disreputable behavior to the magistrates because such an admission reflected badly upon the man's ability to "control" his woman. The husband may also have felt that his wife's abuse was a providential reminder for him to right his own life, and therefore might not seek punishment for her. In such cases the resulting religious introspection undoubtedly diverted interest from the issue of why his marriage was not working out, and which of his wife's needs were not being met.

One Marriage in Turmoil: The Case of the Lawsons

Because the costs were so great, most wives who appeared before the various courts for behavior disruptive to their marriages did so only once; fewer than 10 percent were two-time offenders. Unfortunately, the available records tell us very little about the inner tensions besetting families in Puritan New England; only an occasional case, like that of Elizabeth and Christopher Lawson, reveals a record of long-term marital difficulties. Since it comes from the husband, the report of the Lawsons' problems is probably biased in his favor. But even if it is only partially true, it reveals that Elizabeth Lawson was a very unsubmissive woman.

Elizabeth married Mr. Lawson, a cooper of Exeter, New Hampshire, in the mid-1630s. For ten years thereafter she was "very full of discontent" and frequently expressed a desire to visit friends in England. After her husband consented, she left, but then neglected to return to him. A decade later Lawson had saved up enough money to go to England in search of his wife; he managed to find her, and "hired" her to come home with him.[73] Soon after they boarded a ship for Boston, trouble broke out. In his words, "shee violently laid hands on mee and scratcht mee by the face . . . shee likewise Chalenging mee to trye who was master: upon which I threw her downe on the deck." But that did not end the struggle for dominion, or self-determination, as the case might have been. When they reached the Puritan metropolis, Mistress Lawson hid some of her husband's goods, procured several unspecified warrants against him, and took up residence in another house.

For two years Lawson allowed his wife to live where she wished, but then he once again "hired" her to join him. This reunion was as short as the previous one; ten or twelve weeks after moving to his Maine home, Mistress Lawson "absented her selfe againe and dwelt to and fro at other houses" in town. She later rejoined him for nine months, but when he changed their place of residence she fled to Boston with all his household goods, his clothing, his tools, and his trading material.

Christopher Lawson waited another eight years before he petitioned the Massachusetts magistrates and church elders to send Elizabeth to him. The Bay Colony authorities responded by attempting to convince Mistress Lawson to return to her husband, who was then on the Kennebec frontier. Unsuccessful, they wrote Mr. Lawson that "they seldome met with a woman of her temper." He then came to Boston to retrieve her. She greeted her nominal husband by slamming the door in his face; called him a rogue, a whoremaster, and a syphilitic; then charged him with murder, fornication, and theft. The magistrates required her to submit proof of those charges, but she could not. They took "much paines in perswading her to Liue peaceably" with Mr. Lawson. Her husband described what followed:

she replyed she would rather bee put to death for shee was never lawfully married and I was none of her husband then they told her they would send her to prison: but shee replyed shee cared not for them nor their prison neither: but shee would haue them before the King and be tryed by the Kings lawes: for he [Christopher Lawson] hath broken open my house and stole my goods and hee will not doe mee Justice: Whereupon the magistrates replyed that it was my house and the goods that was in it [were mine]: And forthwith sent the marshal to give mee possession: which he did: And they commanded her to Live peaceably with mee: and the marshal ha[vin]g guien mee possession brought her to mee: but she forthwith fled away and tooke up her ab[od]e elswhere: where shee continues to this day for aught I know: but soon after shee obtained an attachment for my g[o]ods or for want thereof my body.[74]

Elizabeth Lawson had resisted her husband and her marital condition in various ways. She had run away from him several times; she had abused him with words and blows; she had stolen his goods and justified herself by rejecting the common law provision that the woman, upon marriage, gave all her property to her husband. She had harassed Mr. Lawson with criminal and civil warrants, and defied the magistrates who tried to reconcile her to him. Ultimately, after thirty years of struggling, she had successfully taken the right to live by herself. And she was not whipped or otherwise punished by the authorities.[75]

Since her husband seemed unconcerned with them, we know nothing definitive about Elizabeth Lawson's motives for rejecting the marriage that, so far as we know, she had entered upon voluntarily. However, her recurrent economic exploitation of her husband, alternating with her attempts at total physical removal from him, suggests she may have married him for the sole purpose of financial security, in a kind of Moll Flanders response to the female options of the time. She may even have told the truth when she declared he "was none of her husband": she may have been a bigamist with a previous husband in England. On the other hand, she may have brought a good deal to the marriage, and may have felt an equivalent value in goods which remained her due, regardless of the law. In any event, it is clear that her ultimate success in regaining her independence of action (Lawson finally sued for divorce, but the outcome is unknown) depended upon singular persistence, self-assurance, unscrupulousness, and resourcefulness. One would like to know how she supported herself during the years when she lived in England.

As the Massachusetts authorities realized, Elizabeth Lawson was a rare woman—one who continued to assert herself regardless of her husband, the magistrates, and the threat of imprisonment. Few wives could afford to be so assertive over such a long period of time. Many others flared up only occasionally, and only the most serious of these came before the courts. We can never ascertain how many couples snapped at one another in the privacy of their own dwellings, refused to speak to one another at dinner, or fought passively within the confines of the home.

Some scholars might argue that I am painting too bleak a picture of marital life in seventeenth-century Puritan New England—that, indeed, wives like Margaret Winthrop, Margaret Shepard, and Elizabeth Taylor adhered to the ideal weak, modest, faithful, obedient wifely role, and that their husbands were models of kindness and affection. Certainly, such couples bore testimony to the efficacy of Calvinist sex-role stereotyping. If the researcher reads the letters of John and Margaret Winthrop, the autobiographical comments of Thomas Shepard, the poetry of Edward Taylor, and the like, he or she might quite justifiably conclude, as one observer did, that Puritan "married couples were far warmer toward and more companionable with each other than they were to be a century later."[76] But such a conclusion would be too quickly rendered, for the court records and divorce petitions give quite another view

---

Chart 5.2

Total Families Disrupted by Marital Friction in Puritan
New England, 1630–99

Number of families where one spouse abused the other seriously enough to cause the authorities to prosecute	170
Adulteries, adulterous carriage	289
Husbands who refused to maintain or live with spouses, runaway wives	169
Divorce petitions	109
Killing or attempted murder of spouse	10
Refusal to have intercourse	8
Total families	755
Subtracting those families included in more than one category of the above	56
	699

---

of the Puritan marital condition. Marital unhappiness—the "Tears, and Jars, and Discontents, and Jealousies"—abounded, creating innumerable unsatisfactory marriages. Husbands often could not restrain their desires for power over their wives; wives often could not feel comfortable with their subordinate role in this, the most intimate of human relationships. The 699 malfunctional marriages of record should be taken into account before any researcher can hope to generalize about marital conditions in seventeenth-century Puritan New England.

Even those wives who behaved in accordance with the feminine ideal cannot really be used to support the notion that Puritan marriages were particularly warm, for they may have been ideal in outward behavior only. No one knows how many dutiful wives cried alone, in the privacy of their closets, about their husbands' need for "mastery." As Puritanism itself and the anxieties arising out of the English experience thwarted men's need to feel that they could have impact and personal value, so too did marriage, in theory as well as in practice, check woman's need for impact and self-control. For so many couples, marriage became a cauldron of emotional turmoil.

1. Cleaver, *A godlie form of govt.*, p. 81; Gouge, *Of Domesticall Dvties*, pp. 377–78.
2. Secker, *Wedding ring*, n.p.; Willard, *Compleat Body of Divinity*, p. 612.
3. "Coppie of Mass. Liberties," p. 299; Shurtleff, ed., *Mass. Rec.*, III, 212; Hair, ed., *Before the Bawdy Court*, pp. 44, 244.
4. Gataker, *Wife Indeed*, p. 14. See also Cleaver, *A godlie form of govt.*, p. 219.
5. "Letter of Mrs. Sarah Dunton, 1686," in Dunton, *Letters*, p. 266.
6. The breakdown by colony is as follows:

	Husbands	Wives	Total
Massachusetts, 1630–99	59	31	90
Connecticut, 1639–99	18	7	25
New Hampshire, 1640–99	18	6	24
Plymouth, 1633–99	16	6	22
Maine (York Co.), 1636–99	15	4	19
New Haven, 1639–64	2	3	5
Composite	128	57	185

7. Libby, Allen, & Moody, eds., *Maine Ct. Rec.*, I, 264–65, 300; G. Dow, ed., *Essex Ct. Rec.*, VIII, 272; C. Mather, *Warning to Flocks*, p. 20; N. Hamp. "Prov. Ct. Rec.—Ct. of Quarter Sessions: Inferiour Ct. of Common Pleas 1692–1704; Supreme Ct. of Judicature 1694," p. 3.
8. G. Dow, ed., *Essex Ct. Rec.*, I, 17; VI, 297–98; I, 423.

9. "Middlesex Ct. Rec.," folio 42; Libby, Allen, & Moody, eds., *Maine Ct. Rec.*, IV, 247–48; "Conn. Arch. Crimes & Misd.," 1st ser., III, 211–14.

10. Page, *Judicial Beginnings of N. Hamp.*, p. 162; Libby, Allen, & Moody, eds., *Maine Ct. Rec.*, IV, 110; O. Winslow, *Meetinghouse Hill*, p. 186; Essex Co. "Gen. Sessions of Peace, 1692–1769,"n.p.

11. Noble & Cronin, eds., *Rec. of Mass. Assts.*, I, 303; C. Mather, *Magnalia*, II, 357.

12. "Hartford Ct. Rec.," in "Conn. Rec.," LVI, 71; S. Bradstreet, "Journal," p. 43.

13. S. Bradstreet, "Journal," p. 45; Noble & Cronin, eds., *Rec. of Mass. Assts.*, I, 295–96; "Conn. Ct. of Assts., 1669–86, 1696–1701," in "Conn. Rec.," LIII, 19–20.

14. "Conn. Ct. of Assts., 1669–86, 1696–1701," in "Conn. Rec.," LIII, 19–20; Sewall, *Diary*, II, 16.

15. G. Dow, ed., *Essex Ct. Rec.*, VIII, 104–5.

16. Hartford "County Ct. Rec.," in "Hartford Probate Rec.," V, 91. In 1678 two men were appointed by the Connecticut Assistants to supervise the behavior of Martin Moore and his wife because they lived "in a bawling & contentious euill way to the disquietment of their neighbors." In 1682 the Moores were placed under the supervision of the town of Simsbury to insure that they would not abuse one another. In 1695 the Hartford County Court directed that John Baker, Jr., be employed with someone for his family's benefit, since he was reportedly guilty of idleness and unsuitable carriage toward his wife (Conn. "Ct. of Assts., 1669–86, 1696–1701," in "Conn. Rec.," LIII, 25; Hartford "County Ct. Rec." in "Hartford Probate Rec.," IV, 52; V, 87).

17. Charles Bissum, for instance, was fined £5 after he struck and otherwise abused his wife, but he had committed the additional offense of "inordinate drinking" (1686). When Sylvester Stover and his wife spewed foul invective at one another on the Sabbath (1655), he was fined 10s., the usual fine for breach of the Sabbath (Libby, Allen, & Moody, eds., *Maine Ct. Rec.*, III, 225; II, 43).

18. This offender was, however, drunk at the time, and threatened a neighbor who attempted to interfere ("Photostatic Copy of Rec. of Suffolk Ct., 1680–92," pt. 1, p. 109).

19. G. Dow, ed., *Essex Ct. Rec.*, VI, 297–98.

20. *Ibid.*, V, 221.

21. Hist. Rec. Survey, *Abstract & Index of Suffolk Ct. 1680–98*, p. 66.

22. *Rec. of Conn. Particular Ct.*, pp. 267–68; Libby, Allen, & Moody, eds., *Maine Ct. Rec.*, II, 155; "N. Haven Ct. Rec.," I, 18–19.

23. C. Mather, *Diary*, II, 455; Wadsworth, *Well-Ordered Family*, p. 36.

24. Libby, Allen, & Moody, eds., *Maine Ct. Rec.*, II, 460.

25. "Mass. Arch., VIII: Depositions 1662–1766," pp. 26–28; "Essex Ct. Papers," XL, 9; Shurtleff & Pulsifer, eds., *Plym. Rec.*, V, 33; Noble & Cronin, eds., *Rec. of Mass. Assts.*, I, 326; *Wyllys Papers*, pp. 133–34.

26. See Appendix 1.

27. R. Morris, *Studies in Am. Law*, p. 163.

28. Noble & Cronin, eds., *Rec. of Mass. Assts.*, I, 10.

29. *Ibid.*, III, 179.

30. *Rec. of Suffolk Ct. 1671–80*, I, 131–32; Oberholzer, *Delinquent Saints*, pp. 122–23.

31. G. Dow, ed., *Essex Ct. Rec.*, III, 192–93.

32. Manwaring, ed., *Digest of Conn. Probate Rec.*, I, 448, 510; "Ancient Marriage Contract," p. 353.

33. Manwaring, ed., *Digest of Conn. Probate Rec.*, I, 333.

34. *Ibid.*, p. 329.

35. *Ibid.*, pp. 471, 46–47.

36. Cleaver, *A godlie form of govt.*, pp. 176–77; Perkins, *Oeconomie*, p. 689; Gouge, *Of Domesticall Dvties*, pp. 223–24; "Conn. Arch. Crimes & Misd.," 1st ser., III, 235–39.

37. Hoadly, ed., *Rec. of N. Haven Col. 1638–49*, p. 270; J. Trumbull, ed., *Conn. Rec.*, I, 301; Hoadly, ed., *Rec. of N. Haven Col. 1653–Union*, pp. 209–11.

38. Libby, Allen, & Moody, eds., *Maine Ct. Rec.*, III, 87–88; "N. Hamp. Ct. Papers," VI (1681–82), 99–101.

39. Winthrop, *Journal*, II, 161–63.

40. C. Mather, *Magnalia*, II, 348; F. Dexter, ed., *N. Haven Town Rec. 1649–62*, p. 32. At New Haven there was one execution for adultery ca. 1650, but the town records do not make clear whether both parties were hanged for that offense. In late May or early June of the same year another offender was executed at New Haven for unspecific "unnaturall filthynes."

41. Shurtleff, ed., *Mass. Rec.*, I, 92; J. Trumbull, ed., *Conn. Rec.*, I, 77; Shurtleff & Pulsifer, eds., *Plym. Rec.*, XI, 12; Hoadly, ed., *Rec. of N. Haven Col. 1653–Union*, p. 577.

42. *Cols. of N. Hamp. Hist. Soc.*, VIII, 385–86; *Book of Conn. Gen. Laws 1673*, pp. 2–3; Shurtleff, ed., *Mass. Rec.*, I, 301; IV, pt. 1, p. 433; *Acts & Laws, Passed by Mass. Gen. Ct.* (1694), p. 72.

43. Demos, *Little Commonwealth*, p. 97; Noble & Cronin, eds., *Rec. of Mass. Assts.*, I, 342.

44. Gouge, *Of Domesticall Dvties*, p. 219; Perkins, *Oeconomie*, p. 680.

45. Gouge, *Of Domesticall Dvties*, pp. 220–21.

46. The adultery cases include instances of bigamy and incest as well.

47. J. W., *Letter from N.-Eng.*, pp. 4–5; Dunton, *Life & Errors*, I, 115; E. Ward, *Trip to N.-Eng.*, p. 40. Unfortunately, travelers like Ned Ward, John Dunton, and John Josselyn have been unnecessarily maligned. Roger Thompson, as one notable example, feels that none of these wayfarers can be relied upon at all. Following Howard Troyer's criticism of Ward, Thompson dismisses him as "scurrilous and scabrous." Troyer argues that Ward lied about actually coming to Boston because the "traveler" gives neither the exact date nor many details of the voyage itself, because he plagiarized much of his account, and because he did not mention his trip to New England in later books. There is, however, no reason to assume that Ward had to give many details of the voyage across the Atlantic, for that was not his stated intent; nor did he necessarily have to refer to that short journey in later works. Plagiarism was considered no real literary crime in seventeenth-century England, with even established scholars occasionally "borrowing" material. Ward was certainly scatological, but a scatological bent need not preclude depiction of "reality." Reality has its scabrous side, as well as its more refined one. Thompson ignores George Parker Winship's

contrary conclusion, that Ward had "considerable talent for observation and keeness of insight," and his observations were supported by material in the Mathers' sermons.

Thompson's rejections of Dunton and Josselyn are even less well founded. He dismisses Dunton rather hastily because he plagiarized information. Interestingly enough, when Dunton and Ward do, on occasion, borrow material, it often comes from Josselyn—of whom Thompson also disapproves, referring the reader to Fulmer Mood's description of that Englishman's bias. Yet Mood actually states that Josselyn's "tone, by and large, is fair, but scattered through it are to be found some statements that are slyly hostile to the inhabitants of Massachusetts Bay." J. W. and Ned Ward savored any distasteful fact which would reflect unfavorably upon dour Puritans, while Dunton's and Josselyn's prejudices are less readily apparent. Still, if we are to reject any of these men's testimony simply on the basis of their biases, we must in turn reject Puritan narratives—for example, John Winthrop's account of the difficulties caused by Roger Williams and Anne Hutchinson—because of pro-Puritan bias. Travelers' biases need not greatly distort the truth, especially when there is confirmation from the court records and sermons, any more than the Puritans' own biased accounts of their experience need necessarily falsify the facts of the described reality.

The facility with which Thompson brushes aside Josselyn's assertions is perhaps best illustrated in the former's charge that the traveler's suggestion of prostitution in Boston is "unreliable." Thompson questions whether Alice Thomas kept a brothel or house of assignation in 1672, thereby ignoring the Suffolk County Court records of her case and the subsequent legislative enactment against prostitution. Yet he is certainly aware of those court records, because he frequently cites them. Josselyn is clearly vindicated in this matter.

See Thompson, *Women in Stuart Eng. & Am.*, pp. 14, 17, 234, 244; Troyer, *Ned Ward of Grub Str.*, pp. 21–23; Winship, "Introd.," *Boston in 1682 & 1699*, pp. ix–xxviii; Greenough, "Dunton's Letters"; Mood's biography of Josselyn in Malone, ed., *Dict. of Am. Biog.*, X, 219. See also Shurtleff, *Topographical & Hist. Description of Boston*, pp. 51–60, for confirmation of Ward's journey to New England. Paull, *Lit. Ethics*, p. 338, and Lindey, *Plagiarism & Originality*, pp. 72–77, mention the plagiarism of divine Jeremy Taylor, Benjamin Franklin, and William Shakespeare.

48. J. W., *Letter from N.-Eng.*, p. 4.

49. Winthrop, *Journal*, II, 45–46; Libby, Allen, & Moody, eds., *Maine Ct. Rec.*, I, 146, 177; II, 31; A. Forbes, ed., *Winthrop Papers*, IV, 10; Hull, "Memoir & Diaries," p. 192.

50. "New London Ct. Rec.," III, 67; "Conn. Arch. Crimes & Misd.," 1st ser., III, 211–14; "N. Hamp. Ct. Papers," VII (1683): 223, 225.

51. Shurtleff & Pulsifer, eds., *Plym. Rec.*, V, 32

52. *Suffolk Deeds*, I, 84–85; Shurtleff & Pulsifer, eds., *Plym. Rec.*, VI, 190. Benjamin Keayne wrote to John Cotton, "it is a cleare & vnfallible case that no poyson can be receiued from the bodie of a woman, but what shee first has receiued from the infected body of another." Keayne was technically incorrect, for nongonococcal urethritis may result from intercourse with a

partner who has not had previous sexual contact—a virginal wife, for example. However, the fact that Keayne's "Godly frends" daily reported on his wife's indiscrete behavior around men suggests that Keayne was on target with his charge of adultery.

53. Libby, Allen, & Moody, eds., *Maine Ct. Rec.*, III, 129; G. Dow, ed., *Essex Ct. Rec.*, I, 199; "Mass. Arch. IX, Domestic Relations," pp. 132–33; "N. Haven Ct. Rec.," I, 80.

54. I have found 50 cases where the testimony suggests that one party or the other made the initial sexual overture. In 30 of those the woman could be termed the "seducer."

55. C. Mather, *Ornaments for Daughters of Zion*, pp. 83–85. Mather continued: "She is a Dove, that will sooner Dy than leave her Mate, and her Husband is to her, the Covering of her Eyes, at such a rate, that she sees a Desirableness in him, which she will not allow her self to behold or suppose in any other. . . ." He admitted that there were certain situations when this was difficult; e.g., when the husband was beating her with a cudgel. In such situations, the Boston minister perplexedly said, "I know not what further advice to give her," but he did add that the neighbors ought to interfere in an effort to "shame" the fellow.

56. Manwaring, ed., *Digest of Conn. Probate Rec.*, I, 220.

57. Quoted in Morgan, *Puritan Family*, p. 38n.

58. Shurtleff & Pulsifer, eds., *Plym. Rec.*, V, 159.

59. G. Dow, *Essex Ct. Rec.*, III, 269–70.

60. S. Knight, *Private Journal*, pp. 54–55.

61. Greene & Harrington, *Am. Pop. Before Census of 1790*, pp. 14, 48, cite one source which gives a 1701 figure of 80,000 persons in Massachusetts-Maine and 30,000 in Connecticut.

62. Noble & Cronin, eds., *Rec. of Mass. Assts.*, I, 22.

63. O. Hammond, ed., *N. Hamp. Ct. Rec. 1640–92*, pp. 182–83.

64. Calhoun, *Soc. Hist. of Am. Family*, I, 144.

65. Boston Rec. Cmrs., *Rep. Containing Roxbury Rec.*, p. 85.

66. Shurtleff & Pulsifer, eds., *Plym. Rec.*, III, 75.

67. "Rec. of Pres. & Council of N. Hamp.," p. 274; *Cols. of N. Hamp. Hist. Soc.*, VIII, 40.

68. G. Dow, ed., *Essex Ct. Rec.*, VIII, 102–3, 293; "Conn. Arch. Crimes & Misd.," 1st ser., III, 217–21.

69. G. Dow, ed., *Essex Ct. Rec.*, I, 184; Shurtleff & Pulsifer, eds., *Plym. Rec.*, IV, 10.

70. "Trial of Cheever Before N. Haven Church," p. 45.

71. Winthrop, *Journal*, II, 219; Williamson, *Hist. of Maine*, I, 290n; Shurtleff & Pulsifer, eds., *Plym. Rec.*, VI, 153; *Boston News-Letter*, May 20–27, 1706, in Weeks & Bacon, eds., *Hist. Digest of Prov. Press*, p. 328.

72. Noble & Cronin, eds., *Rec. of Mass. Assts.*, II, 108; "N. Haven Ct. Rec.," I, 148; *Rec. of Conn. Part. Ct.*, p. 194.

73. Lawson unfortunately did not explain what he meant by the term "hired." Possibly it refers to a monetary payment or the promise of some material concession in America.

74. Lawson, "Petition."

75. Lawson petitioned twice for divorce, on January 2, 1668/9 and again on October 11, 1670, but there is no record of the Massachusetts authorities granting his request. The fact that he was an agent for the Puritan's opponent Sir Ferdinando Gorges may have contributed to the Assistants' reluctance either to punish his wife or to free him from her (*ibid.*; C. Pope, *Pioneers of Maine & N. Hamp.*, p. 122).

76. Brenton, *Am. Male*, p. 112.

VI

From Self-Punishment to Covert Manipulation: Reactions to Powerlessness

What happens to a dream deferred?

Does it dry up
Like a raisin in the sun?
Or fester like a sore—
And then run?
Does it stink like rotten meat?
Or crust and sugar over—
Like syrupy sweet?

Maybe it just sags
like a heavy load.

Or does it explode?
                    —Langston Hughes, "Dream Deferred"

Expressions of Female Helplessness

THE DIRECT DEFIANCE ENGAGED IN BY SOME PURITAN AND NON-Puritan wives was but one of several types of behavior which indicated that feminine role expectations were a common source of conflict and frustration. Many a woman, reflecting the introspective impress of Puritan conditioning, turned her frustration not outward toward an abusive husband but inward on herself. It was easy for her to blame her sinful self for whatever unholy, insubordinate longings she might have. Converting into guilt the tensions or potential anger she experienced as a result of adhering to a position of relative powerlessness, the woman could then condemn herself for even wishing to be anything but an ideal Calvinist wife. The basic aversion to helplessness (or the need for some sense of freedom and control) could, in the self-castigating world of Puritan thought, be pushed beneath the level of perception, only to surface later in fantasies of destructive aggression. As existential psychologist Rollo May has pointed out, the most docile, unassertive persons often have the most violent dreams.[1]

Elizabeth White is a good case in point. This Puritan woman described herself as outwardly "somewhat more Mild" than her sisters, but with some perceptiveness, realized that she was really "like a Wolf chained up." A very obedient child, she found it difficult to disobey her father's wishes, even when to do so would have facilitated her own salvation. Her repressed self erupted in 1657, when she could not convince a minister that she deserved to enjoy the powerful position of church member. She took at face value her minister's skepticism about whether she had had a conversion experience. For years thereafter White often felt totally helpless, hopelessly sinful, and purposeless before "what GOD hath decreed must be." Her sense of helplessness reached such a profound depth that she could see only one possibility for her redemption: doing "some great Evil," such as committing murder, to shock her into even more abject repentance.[2] That this anguished woman should conceive of murder as a vehicle to salvation is revealing, for that act would be more than a shock to her moral sensibilities; indeed, it would also serve as a protest against her sense of helplessness, as an act of aggression, of control, rather than of proper feminine and Puritan submission.

Elizabeth White fell into a depressed state, during which her feeling of powerlessness became overwhelming. But she did not abandon the struggle for some limited achievement, for some partial assurance of salvation. Other women underwent quite a different experience of depression, involving a total lack of the desire to struggle. Languishing—the sensation of debilitating helplessness —was not uncommon in seventeenth-century New England; there are records of more than a dozen women who languished for long periods, including eleven years in the case of Connecticut pastor John Russell's wife.[3] John Hull's description of Joan Edwards's and Mary Harder's conditions is illustrative. In the 1650s these two Boston women made "doleful" noises, took "no care of or content or pleasure in any thing; can be made to follow no employment; sometimes will hardly receive any food; take notice of nothing that is spoken to them, nor minding their children nor any relations; showing much dislike to any counsel to hear the word [of God] or to labor."[4] Languishing seems to be the extreme extension of female dependency and was a condition apparently limited to the "weaker sex." It manifested the despair that could be produced by woman's relative powerlessness in society. The records show that Puritan men were subject to depressed moods as well, but not to the degree of immobilization involved in languishing. Relevant to this entire discussion is Martin Seligman's observation that people who have experienced helplessness in social settings, and animals in laboratory experiments, reveal the same symptoms as severely depressed persons: social withdrawal, greatly retarded physical activity, loss of appetite, and inability to make decisions—in short, a "complete paralysis of the will."[5]

A few women carried their "weakness" a step further by falling ill with intense, but apparently non-organic, pain. One female, "in a sad destresced condischion," experienced for more than a year an inexplicable prickling which extended from her left side to her face and held her in "such exstremite as she can not rest nigh[t] nor daye." Another, subject to "violent fitts & groaning noise" over a two-year period, thereafter developed severe pains throughout her body, fainting spells, a burning sensation on her left side, frequent coughing, and immobility.[6] The extent to which such women's pains had a physiological basis cannot now be determined, but the kinds of symptoms described are very similar to those observed in patients suffering the psychosomatic effects of conversion hysteria.[7]

A number of women acted eccentric in the way contemporaries called "distracted" or "crazy-brained." Modern observers would describe them as "mentally ill." Little concrete information is available about the behavior of these women (and 83 of the 102 distracted persons of record were women), but what does exist is compatible with Rollo May's assertion that "a common characteristic of all mental patients is their powerlessness, and with it goes a constant anxiety which is both cause and effect of the impotence."[8] "Crazy-brained" women sometimes hallucinated about encounters with fearsome, paralyzingly powerful creatures—demons, witches, and "black things." Isabella Holdridge, for one, between 1655 and 1659 often "fele into a sweat" at her Haverhill home, swooned, "trembled & shooke like a leafe," and dreamed up a veritable menagerie of frightening beasts. A spectral bear ground its teeth and clawed at her. A huge black cat stroked her face at night. A large snake caused her so much terror that she could not speak for an hour after seeing it.[9] Such imaginary creatures not only expressed Holdridge's powerlessness, but also apparently projected her own frustrated anger. Unable to express her own feelings about the conditions, people, or institutions which held her in check, she, like other "distracted" women, invented spectral beings who gave vent to her own "evil" impulses.

The Hysterical Fit

The most common form of "distraction," the hysterical fit, provides us with some opportunity to analyze the kinds of tension which women, particularly young girls, experienced in Puritan New England. Since hysterics complained of pain in various places, barked like dogs, bleated like calves, twisted their necks to the point of breaking, cracked their joints, and extended their tongues out of their mouths to an extraordinary length,[10] the divines prepared elaborate accounts of such outlandish behavior—accounts which can be investigated by the interested researcher.

English physicians attributed these "spasms, paroxysms, palsies, convulsive dancing, stretching, [and] yawning" to an overactive uterus which wandered to and fro as the result of "perturbations of the minde." Some designated "spoilt menstrual blood," "overordinate actions of the body," an idle existence, and sudden bursts of anger, pain, and fear as contributory.[11] New England Puritans utilized several popular English remedies to cure "fits." Treatments included the following: 1) "spiritt of Castar & oile of Amber"; 2) application of "a Suppository, a compound Clyster with Hisigricall Carmanitiue seeds and a stomachical Emplaister"; 3) a mixture of the blood from a he-cat's ear and the milk from a nurse suckling a male child, taken three times; 4) the consumption of filbert-sized pills composed of two drams of castoria, a dram of women's hair, and a little pine tree resin.[12] Perhaps the most exotic remedy, one guaranteed to cure "all deliriums," "frensies," and "manias," was reported by Dr. Kenelme Digby in a letter to John Winthrop, Jr. (1656): "an Elixir made of dew, nothing but dew, purigyed and nipped vp in a glasse, and digested [i.e., dried] 15. months, till all of it was become a gray pouder."[13]

Not all Puritans could accept a completely medical explanation of hysteria, especially when their doctors could not administer

workable cures. Local magistrates often placed afflicted women
under the safekeeping of saintly families, but communities did
not really accept them. When a woman had her inner equilibrium so precipitously, mysteriously, and completely distorted into
a grotesque caricature of "normality," Puritans could easily suspect devilish doings.

Even into the late seventeenth century the bizarre behavior of
hysterics was often viewed as visible proof of bewitchment. New
England Calvinists, so willing to see Satan's hand in any abnormality, suspected at least four "distracted" or "crazy-brained" women
of witchcraft—Mary Parsons, Abigail Soames, Sarah Good, and
Goodwife Glover.[14] In the Salem Village witchcraft epidemic, the
often ambiguous line between mental disequilibrium, physical
disease, and heresy was hopelessly confused and, by mid-1692, for-
gotten altogether. As late as 1719 Cotton Mather could not decide whether diabolical possession or hereditary factors better
explained distraction.[15]

Neither the Puritans nor their English contemporaries dealt with
hysteria as an ailment which had any measure of social causality.
Seventeenth-century physicians focused on the fit as a literal mal-
function of the physical organism, not, as later medical experts
would, on hysteria as a hypochondriacal manifestation of severe
psychological or social disorientation. In the nineteenth century,
the emphasis shifted from the realm of physiology to that of emotional disturbance and repressed sexuality; then the potions of the
seventeenth century gave way to "emotional education," hypnosis,
and psychoanalysis, plus the more barbaric removal of the hysteric's ovaries or clitoris. In more recent times scientists have moved
toward genetic inheritance as an explanation for hysteria, with
some attention being given to the role of repressed aggression. Still,
only one modern observer, the psychiatrist Marc Hollender, has
linked fits to the powerlessness of women in society.[16]

Whether authorities have chosen to explain fits in terms of an
overzealous devil or an overactive clitoris, rarely have they supplied
an analysis of "distracted" women's words, or the context in which
they uttered them. Fits occurred not only in the relative isolation of
the home, but also in very public places. At least three afflicted
Connecticut women were "very often" greatly disturbed while at
Sabbath lectures. When women did experience fits, people came
from miles around to watch them. Neighbors also spent much time
at the homes of the afflicted; in that respect, since recognition and

attention were little extended to the female sex in Puritan New England, the fit provided some temporary compensation. Elizabeth Knapp, for example, did not commence her dog-like barking until she could hear someone approaching her residence. Samuel Willard related that she would "always fall into fits when any strangers go to visit her—and the more go, the more violent are her fits." She wished to be taken to Boston, New England's largest theater, for special presentation to an assemblage of ministers.[17]

Not only did women receive a good deal of attention when they threw fits, but they also had some opportunities to become personally powerful by influencing the authorities' judgments. Between 1662 and 1691 sixteen females, all but two of them under age twenty, accused others of bewitching them. Since the magistrates and ministers listened attentively to denunciations of witches, such hysterics managed to exert unbelievable power—including, in some cases, the power to persuade society's leaders of the legitimacy of their witchcraft claims, and the resulting power of life and death over an undesirable adult. Young witch-accusers did not charge other girls and boys with that offense; rather, they chose to attack their nearer "superiors," adult women (as opposed to adult men, whose power was generally *too* intimidating). Only two girls, Anne Cole and Samuel Debel's daughter, actually went so far as to accuse men.[18] Cole, in fact, designated no fewer than seven, and possibly thirteen, persons as witches in 1662–63.

Besides serving as a means of gaining attention and power, fits also became a vehicle for "legitimately" or covertly abusing the authority of religion and the ministers. Often the afflicted woman had been outwardly noted for "real Piety and Integrity," although she was inwardly troubled by religious conflicts.[19] Through fits, such women temporarily repudiated (probably unconsciously) their anguished search for assurance of salvation by going to the opposite extreme and insulting Puritan religious practice. Resentment of an authoritarian God, a self-abasing faith, and woman's exclusion from participation in the church could easily be hurled at the ideology and institution which so firmly curbed some women's drive for assertion. Since women were officially prohibited from speaking in most churches, three Hartford maidens' disruption of church services with motions and noise had such an impact "that a godly person fainted away under the appearance of it" (1662). Another maiden in Norwich, Connecticut, found herself "violently assaulted and vexed with Diabolical suggestions, in a most blasphemous

maner, especially in the time of religious dueties" (1683), while
Groton's Elizabeth Knapp "belched forthe the most horrid and
nefandous Blasphemies" (1671). The Goodwin children at Boston
expressed their own rejection of religion by refusing to listen to
ministers, roaring to drown out the voices of praying neighbors,
and turning their faces away from the Bible (1688).[20]

In their hysterical fits some women gave vent to a good deal of
repressed aggression. Mary Parsons beat those who attempted to
keep her from tearing her clothing. Martha Goodwin would "fetch
very terrible Blowes with her Fist, and Kicks with her Foot at the
man that prayed." Elizabeth Knapp directed "Railings and Revil-
ings" at pastor Samuel Willard, accused him of "deceiving the
people," and once plotted to murder him. She also considered
killing young children, in effect denying the maternal role at a time
when she, an adolescent, was growing physiologically ready to
fulfill it. Furthermore, she resisted the efforts of as many as six
persons at a time to restrain her, striking them, spitting in their
faces, and then laughing if she had harmed or frightened them.[21]

For thirteen-year-old Martha Goodwin, the fit may have functioned as a sexual outlet. Frequently "her Company" would bring
her an imaginary horse, after which, as Cotton Mather described it,

Settling herself in a Riding-Posture—she would in her Chair be agitated as
one sometimes Ambleing, sometimes Trotting, and sometimes Galloping
very furiously. In these motions we could not perceive that she was stirred
by the stress of her feet, upon the ground, for often she touch't it not; but
she mostly continued in her Chair, though sometimes in her hard Trott we
doubted [i.e., expected] she would have been tossed over the Back of it. . . .
Her Fantastic Journeyes were mostly performed in her Chair without removing from it; but sometimes would she ride from her Chair, and be
carried odly on the Floor, from one part of the Room to another in the
postures of a Riding Woman.[22]

Mather did not realize that this young girl, sitting with legs together
(the posture of a riding woman), feet above the floor, and making
vigorous rocking movements, had probably adopted the thigh-
pressure technique of masturbation.[23]

Fits allowed girls and more mature women to act out any number
of anti-religious behaviors and "unfeminine" impulses without suffering punishment. Idleness, blasphemy, obscenity, castigation of
the authorities, disruption of church services, and masturbation all
became semi-licit when fits served to veil them. The fit was therefore

well suited to the female situation. As psychiatrist Marc Hollender has explained,

Hysteria may be regarded as a special type of behavior which occurs (spontaneously and largely unconsciously) when more direct expressions of feelings are blocked. It is especially likely to erupt when a person who is relatively powerless and dependant cannot cope with one who is powerful and unassailable. . . . In view of the inferior position assigned to women it is hardly surprising that they were more prone than men to react with hysterical behavior, especially if they found it difficult to accept the role assigned to them.

As this psychiatrist points out, the nineteenth-century woman who felt powerless before her husband in their "domestic unhappiness," and the upper-class wife who led an idle, uneventful life were particularly subject to hysterical outbursts. Hollender sums up hysteria as an expression of repressed "sexual, hostile, or other impulses," and also, importantly, as "an outlet, socially sanctioned or at least tolerated, for those who were otherwise trapped by the demands of a rigid, even oppressive, social system."[24] Puritan New England had such a social system.

Before 1692 at least twenty-six New England women took advantage of fits to indulge in the most outrageous behavior. Although such behavior might be rebellious in function, it illustrated at the same time the basic passivity of the feminine role, for the afflicted woman usually did not take wholehearted responsibility for her expressiveness. Some external force distinct from the woman's own personality and will—Satan, a witch, or "induced" madness—overwhelmed her. Thus the witch served as a projection of the afflicted person's own impulses. While discontented men often defended their obstreperous behavior before the authorities, as did many of the proportionately fewer abusive or otherwise criminal females, the fit-prone woman made no effort to justify herself. Perhaps this was because men, primed for more independent, active lives, were likely to possess enough self-confidence to believe in the rightness of their own needs. Women, on the other hand, frequently achieved some rebellious fulfillment through the posited medium of an Other, just as they had been taught to reach their "proper" fulfillment through others—fathers, husbands, and children. Only two adult males of record ever fell into hysterical fits[25] (although twelve male children—those males in a dependent status—did also).

While the fit proceeded out of a condition of passivity and was attributed to an external force, it was strikingly overt. The afflicted woman acted very unfeminine, and the discordance (or cognitive dissonance, to borrow Leon Festinger's term) between that fact and her years of sex-role conditioning often became too much for a woman to handle psychologically or emotionally. Fits were therefore characterized not only by rebellious behavior and a degree of role rejection, but also by self-inflicted suffering. The struggle between the lure of forbidden impulses and the consequent guilt about them precipitated the fit of unfeminine and apparently involuntary behavior; after it had been acted out, the fit itself led to a further need for self-punishment. Blaming devils and witches provided only immediate, temporary relief for the assaulted conscience. Sharp castigation of the self, extreme psychosomatic pain, almost unbearable gloom, and thoughts of suicide accompanied hysterical fits, suggesting the extreme guilt the afflicted women experienced for acting contrary to the religious system and its adjunct, the female role model. Sometimes the punishing agent was Satan himself, or one of his minions. The Goodwin children complained of being placed in a red-hot oven and beaten with great cudgels which left noticeable streaks on their bodies. Martha Goodwin was nearly pulled into the fire by an invisible chain and was choked with an invisible rope until she became black in the face. Elizabeth Knapp was also pulled toward the fire, strangled, scratched on the breast, beaten, and violently thrown down on the floor. Such psychogenic punishment occasionally had a more real physical dimension. Mary Parsons, for example, not only felt psychological pain but "beate herselfe on ye breasts" as well.[26]

The fit lasted as long as the afflicted woman needed to get everything off her chest. Once she returned to God and Puritanism—in effect, when she was again able to read her Bible and pray—her psyche was freed, at least for the moment, of her need to be expressive, denunciatory, and aggressive. Because she had acted out her tensions and animosities, she could resume the role of proper woman. A hysterical fit, one of the very few agencies through which a woman could unload her distress, tended therefore to be cathartic. Anne Cole, for example, underwent a sudden miraculous cure and "continued well for many years, approving herself a serious Christian." One Norwich maiden lived for six months after her fit "in a greater degree of firme composure then before she was thus buffeted."[27] Since the hysterical fit was cathartic and did provide a "harmless" escape valve for socially unacceptable impulses, it actually mitigated against overt efforts to change societal or personal conditions.

Because most fits afforded some purgative release of tension, hysteria was contagious. Epidemics broke out at least four times in Puritan New England. In 1662–63, three women followed Anne Cole's example at Hartford. Six years later, five girls and a boy in Essex County, Massachusetts, accused Goodwife Burt of bewitching them. At Boston in 1688 the afflictions of the Goodwin children (two girls, two boys) precipitated fits in two other lads outside the family.[28] The most notable epidemic took place in Salem Village and surrounding areas in 1692: no fewer than thirty-six females and six males experienced hysterical symptoms.[29]

It seems unlikely that many of these persons consciously feigned hysterical seizures.[30] The enterprising woman or child might have done so in a deliberate effort to achieve notoriety and attention, but the degree of emotional and physical pain experienced by most of the afflicted makes duplicity a doubtful charge. Hysterics at least appeared sincere. In one case, however, the possibility of conscious connivance becomes somewhat apparent: in 1664 Hannah Cheney was summoned before the Essex County magistrates to answer a fornication charge, but, "being subject to sore fits (*especially upon such occasions as this*)," she pleaded for clemency.[31]

While the fit apparently represented an attempt to gain attention, to strike out aggressively at Puritanism, and to punish the self for having or acting out such inclinations, this is not to suggest that the patient constraint and submissive non-assertiveness expected of dependent persons in Puritan New England was the only precipitating factor. More purely idiosyncratic factors (e.g., a high-stress situation like a fornication charge) or actual physiological illness may also have been contributory, at least in some cases. In general, however, the peculiar dynamics of the hysterical fit clearly bear out Marc Hollender's contention that society is implicated in the women's mental disturbances.

A Context for Suicide

The fit represented an effective coping device, a vehicle for violating some prescriptions of the ideal female role. Although fits involved extensive self-punishment, they became at the same time ways to avoid giving up altogether. Not all anguished women fell into purgative hysteria; in fact, some viewed suicide as the only solution to their personal turmoil.

At least seven of the twenty-one women who committed suicide in New England between 1620 and 1709 grew up in very pious homes.[32] These seven were "in good and very commendable repute for Christianity as well as family and neighborly civility" before they took their own lives, and Puritans could incredulously blame only "the Violence of Satans Temptations" for such acts.[33] Two other women could not become assured of their value in God's scheme of things. In 1645 a goodwife of Saco, Maine, drowned because she believed herself an unredeemable "reprobate." In 1692 Florence Whitteridge of Ipswich, Massachusetts, became conscience striken; urged to consult her Bible, she turned its pages for an hour or so, clapped it shut, said she would never look at it again, and that evening drowned in "a little puddle of water not sufficient to cover all her face."[34]

None of the female suicides behaved in outwardly rebellious ways, lived heretical lifestyles, or abused their husbands. Indeed, their behavior seemed quite the opposite. This pious pre-suicidal behavior is very much in accord with one 1949 psychoanalytic study's finding that suicidal patients were less aggressive than non-suicides.[35]

Why this should be so is a complex question. Surely one aspect concerns the extent to which these women took Puritanism seriously. The uncertainties arising out of the search for assurance of salvation, the tendency to introject frustration, and the predisposition toward self-hatred established both by theology and by the less distinctly Puritan belief in female inferiority could easily have given rise to suicidal impulses. One scholar, S. E. Sprott, argues that times of repression and times of libertinism lead to an increase in suicides; he has asserted that self-executions spread as Puritanism became a more potent force in England during the 1640s and 1650s, then decreased with the Restoration. Although Sprott's statistical conclusions are questionable, Englishmen during the Civil War did seem to feel that "gross self-murthers" were growing out of bounds. John Donne pointed out in *Biathanatos* (1646) that the popular belief in predestination caused some people to feel hopelessly damned despite their good works. Outraged Puritans rejoined that suicide was an inexcusable sin against "God, man, the church, the state, relatives, friends, the victim himself, his body, his entire person." As the suicide rate increased, Calvinist instructor Anthony Tuckney said he knew of one man who actually killed himself as a result of reading *Biathanatos*.[36]

Sprott's thesis cannot be adequately tested in the New World (by comparing suicide rates in Puritan New England with those in less repressive locales, for example) because the official records mention suicides rarely. Only twenty-five of the fifty-six New England suicides described in Appendix #3 appeared in official town, county, or colony records. Another twenty-one are known only from diaries, and the remainder have been gathered from letters, general histories, newspapers, and multiple sources. It therefore seems reasonable to assume that many more suicides were committed than were recorded.

There is no reason to doubt Sprott's fundamental assumption that an individual's motives for suicide may well be related to the religio-social system in which that individual finds himself or herself living. As sociologist Austin L. Porterfield has pointed out, "The social system must be implicated in suicide because it furnishes, or does not furnish, satisfying roles and statuses, or value systems, that yield satisfaction to its people. Some who do not have satisfying roles and statuses destroy themselves and some destroy others." Jack Gibbs and Walter Martin have theorized that more suicides occur in societies where the "individuals in the population occupy incompatible statuses" and "are confronted with role conflicts." Durkheim, the father of the study of suicide, asserted that suicides are common in societies with low degrees of social regulation, as well as in societies at the other extreme—where people's futures "become pitilessly blocked and passions violently choked by oppressive discipline."[37]

Equally relevant to the examination of suicide (especially female suicide) in Puritan society is the link perceived by some modern theorists between suicidal behavior and individual autonomy. Calista Leonard believes that a child's inability to develop a sense of identity separate from his or her parents may create a tendency toward suicide in later years. Robert White and M. L. Farber have emphasized the suicide's lack of a "sense of competence"; that is, of "the feeling of being able to control the world, and, by implication, of being sure that the world will satisfy one's needs." Some empirical evidence supports this point of view.[38]

Dissatisfaction over social status, the lack of an individual identity, blocked hopes, and feelings of little competence were recurrent afflictions of women in Puritan New England and may help to explain why some women chose to kill themselves. We cannot know the extent to which suicide was a response to the dependency and limitations of the ideal female role, since no suicide left a detailed diary. Still, some evidence strongly suggests that at least two women attempted to escape a specifically female condition. Abigail Claghorne of Yarmouth, Plymouth, had nineteen children and was pregnant with her twentieth when she hanged herself in 1677.[39] A second woman responded to her "oppressive" situation as an unattached female. The widowed Martha Coghan, "discontented that she had no suitors," encouraged the only available man, her "meane" hired farm-helper, "to make a motion to her for marriage." The man responded positively and she, guilt-ridden over what she had done, "grew discontented, despaired, and took a great quantity of ratts bane, and so died" in 1660.[40]

Unlike "distracted" behavior in general and the hysterical fit in particular, suicide did not have more relevance to women than to men. More males than females have caused their own deaths, in whatever locale and over whatever time span scholars have chosen to study. Durkheim's statistics on suicides in seven nineteenth-century European countries reveal that between 17.9 percent (Austria, 1873–77) and 26.7 percent (England, 1863–67) of the victims were women.[41] A 1968 United Nations report on suicide in seventeen countries gave a range of 20.5 percent (Finland, 1961–63) to 41.5 percent (Japan, 1961–63) for females. In comparison with these more recent figures, the percentage in Puritan New England was high: there 38.9 percent of all suicides were women (or 41.1 percent, if possible suicides are included), a figure greater than any country in Durkheim's study and exceeded by only one country in the 1968 report. By comparison, in the New England of 1967 women comprised 30 percent of all suicides.[42]

Perhaps it is surprising that even two-fifths of all suicides in Puritan New England were women, when innumerable factors in the female's environment mitigated against her taking her own life. By lifelong training she had been prepared for a passive, rather than an active, decisive existence. (Here it should be noted that although suicide may in one sense be less aggressive than murder, it is still an aggressive act, denying stoical acceptance of what is.) Dependent upon her father, husband, and minister for guidance, the woman was not expected to possess much will or self-direction and was unable to easily justify what she wanted to do. Since men were socialized to act more decisively and to be less dependent upon others for guidance, it was probably easier for them to commit the act of self-annihilation. This observation may help us to understand why women now "fail" at suicide[43] more often than do men (although we cannot know whether that was true in seventeenth-century New England). Elizabeth Janeway explains, "When we are told that women are, by nature, bad at making decisions, we might reflect that they have usually had little practice at choosing consciously to initiate overt action."[44]

Male and female suicide methods varied. In Puritan New England nineteen women used seven different techniques (in another two cases the method went unspecified), and twenty-seven men used a total of six different ways (six additional cases were not specified). Women favored drowning as a means of self-annihilation; 47 percent of the women drowned themselves, and 21 percent hanged themselves. For men those preferences were reversed—18.5 percent for drowning and 59.3 percent for hanging. Drowning is, of course, a less abrupt form of self-execution; the fact that so many more women chose this method lends credence to the argument that women felt somehow more inhibited and less decisive about suicide.[45] The behavior of one Dorchester woman testifies to that female uncertainty: in 1692 she "skipt into a well" in an attempted suicide, "but finding the water cold she bethought herself and came out."[46]

Drowning may have appealed to women more than to men because it is a relatively passive mode of suicide. Drowning involves yielding to a stronger independent force, whereas hanging is more completely the product of the victim's effort. As the woman yielded to the power of her husband and father in life, so she yielded to the power of the water in death. A total of eleven women died by passive means: nine drowned, one poisoned herself, and another starved herself to death. Not all women, however, chose passive modes: four hanged themselves, one choked herself with a neckcloth before jumping into the water, and two others cut their throats. In 1702 Mary Bowtel of Cambridge devised perhaps the ultimate technique in terms of inflicting pain, setting fire to her right arm, left hand, and genitals.[47]

The fact that over half of all women suicides chose a passive mode of death reveals that the female socialization process left its impress even on the way women chose to die. (Fifty-eight percent of the women but only 22.2 percent of the men died passively.[48]) The socialization process also led women to inhibit their rage, a fact which had some bearing on the act of suicide. The white heat of outward anger did not accord with social conditioning which taught the woman to be demure and deferential, sometimes leading her to deflect anger inward against her own unfeminine self. As Gene and David Lester have observed, the suicidal woman often feels not depressed but "burned up or boiling inside." Her inhibited rage at last explodes, and the resultant "violence to herself could fulfill both a need for expression of that rage and a need to punish herself for her 'unfeminine' violence."[49] Ultimately she remained a woman, denying her ability to "control" the external world and feeling guilty about her natural needs. The seven saintly women who killed themselves may have been experiencing such tensions.

Female suicide patterns did not remain the same throughout the seventeenth century, instead reflecting changes in conditions women faced. Only one of seven female suicides hanged herself before 1675, whereas after King Philip's War seven of twelve women used the more active methods. As Chapters XII through XIV will indicate, the latter period was a time of great change in the quality of life for both men and women, with a declarative, relatively nonfeminine style becoming more possible for the "weaker sex." Since women were increasingly thinking and acting in defiance of the ideal role, their suicide methods revealed greater conviction and aggressiveness.

Abigail Claghorne's twenty pregnancies, Martha Coghan's inability to exist without a man, and the inward tortures of the seven women who were ideal Calvinist ladies in external appearance all illustrate the kinds of frustrations to which a woman could be heir. In that respect, suicide seemed a further, more extreme form of the hysterical fit. The fit was both self-punitive and purgative; after it had run its course, inner equilibrium could be restored. Suicide, in contrast, carried the inner distress to the ultimate form of escape and/or self-punishment. For the suicide, desperation became so profound that there was no possibility of purgation—only the compelling need to destroy a self which society had in part created and thrown into conflict. The suicide punished herself without acting out her anger in hysterical style. No catharsis occurred.

It was not that suicidal women had failed to discover the fit's cathartic effect, but that the catharsis lacked permanency or completeness. At least three of the twenty-one female suicides were subject to long term distraction.[50] If we had more information about seventeenth-century suicides, we might find evidence to corroborate recent studies which discovered that 22 percent of attempted female suicides suffer from hysteria (13 of 60 women in one study) and that 20 percent of hysteria patients make suicide attempts (19 of 95 patients in another study).[51]

Suicide may even have seemed less a means of self-punishment than a way to assert the validity of frustrated needs or impulses. Abigail Claghorne, for instance, may simply have seen suicide as the only way to protest and terminate her perpetual child-bearing.

The weak and dependent in old New England—those who, in their frustration, often turned their aggression back upon themselves or felt the need for an escape—became particularly subject to fits and suicidal inclinations. Twelve of fourteen males who experienced fits of hysteria were dependents; so, too, did at least three-tenths of the male suicides occupy an obviously dependent or "unfree" status. These relatively powerless men included one prisoner at the Boston jail, four servants, one possible slave, and four Indians who killed themselves after the defeat of King Philip had broken Indian resistance in much of New England. In an interesting instance of sex-role reversal, one other dependent male hanged himself after his wife died; ostensibly he felt that "his Wives discretion and industry had long been the support of his Family," and he worried that "he should now come to want before he dyed."[52]

Using the Feminine Role to Advantage

Of course, not all women found their personal situations equally onerous, or reacted to them with fits or suicide. In fact, many seemed content with the ideal feminine role. Some undoubtedly found that behaving in accordance with the ideal gained them certain advantages, including protection and support, as well as a measure of social respect. A number of women found that the orthodox female role allowed them some latitude for covert manipulation of men, or even for expression of very un-Puritan desires.

Comfort Wilkins, a young Boston lass, is one case in point. In behavior she was the picture of modesty and obedience. As John Dunton observed in 1686, these "two great vertues essential to the Virgin-State" were "as remarkable in her, as if she was made of nothing Else. . . . Her looks, her Speech, her whole behaviour are so very chaste, that but once going to kiss her [in greeting], I thought she'd ha' blush'd to Death." But Wilkins's blushes were more calculating than Dunton was willing to admit. She affected a coy demeanor whenever sex and marriage were under discussion, yet obviously relished such conversations. Furthermore, she was capable of carefully phrased seductive comments herself.[53]

When the happily wed Dunton wished to lavish platonic affection on Wilkins, this "modest" lass expressed the desire for a more physical relationship with him. Journeying on horseback with Dunton outside of Boston, she told her traveling partner, "I think 'tis strange to hear a married man commend Platonick Love, since by his Marriage he has overthrown the Notion." She proposed an idea about love quite the contrary of Dunton's, explaining, "whene'er I love, I will propose some End in doing it; for that which has no End, appears to me but the Chimera of a Distempered Brain: And what end can there be in love of Different Sexes, but Enjoyment? And yet Enjoyment quite spoils the Notion of Platonick Love." Wilkins told Dunton, with never a reference to his wife, that he was the one man in 10,000 she could live with, concluding her remarks on sexual love with the comment, "[I] declare myself against it, and oppose real Fruition, in your Platonick Notion."[54]

Almost any other woman who spoke with such élan would have been fined by the Puritan authorities for lascivious speech, but, since Wilkins was modest in her general behavior, Dunton failed to take her overture at face value. He considered the conversation purely intellectual, thereby ignoring the fact that they were in isolated countryside and that his companion was praising both him *and* sexual love. Yet Dunton recognized that a modest appearance could serve as a cover for immodest sexual desires. He described Mistress A—l's "strange affected kind of Coyness; which yet differs from Modesty as much as Hemlock from Parsley." "She will part with all or none," he explained, "and it is easier to obtain from her the last favour in private, than a kiss in Public."[55]

Joseph Beacher, one of Dunton's contemporaries, complained in 1688 that too many women affected "sighs & blushes, faint resistance & exclamations" to hide their own "despicable lechery." This Bostonian felt that such women assumed a modest demeanor as a way to secure the best marriage partner. "By pretending to be w^t they have not they inhance the price of their purchase [i.e., their dowry]," Beacon wrote, "whereas should they seem to be w^t they are indeed, they would probably be paid with kick & curses."[56]

A falsely deferential posture could lead to substantial gains, but women were likely to fare better when they did not push too hard in pursuit of their ends. Consider the twenty-year-old lass "of rare Witt and sense" who mailed solicitous letters to Cotton Mather after his wife's death in 1702. As that Boston minister described it, the woman confessed "herself charmed with my Person, to such a Degree that I should make her mine; and that the highest Consideration she had in it was her eternal Salvation, for if she were mine, she could not but hope the Effect of it would be, that she should also be Christ's." Such words were designed to warm the cockles of a vain minister's heart, but when they failed to have that immediate effect, this woman proved she was capable of working behind Mather's back for her own ends. She visited the minister's father, brought "her good Mother with her," and succeeded in charming "the Neighbours into her Interests." When Mather did not ask her to marry him, she then circulated unspecified rumors about him among "a foolish People," so that community pressure could be brought to bear upon him. Her suit ultimately failed, but she had demonstrated that a seemingly proper Puritan woman could use underhanded means in pursuit of her purposes.[57]

Within marriage, a bountiful presence of "sweet allurements" allowed the ideal wife to be quite assertive. The elder Lucy Downing's manner of expressing her opinion about coming to the New World indicates how deference and assertiveness could be linked for better effect. Downing did not wish to live in America, since she feared that many people and few commodities would endanger continued existence there. Furthermore, she explained to her husband that the trip across the Atlantic, with its many "hazards" and "our litell ones shrikinge about vs," was not a welcome adventure. She wrote to her brother John Winthrop in 1636, "now you may saye I take to[o] much upon me, I am but a wife, and therefore it is sufficient for me to follow my husban. for that let me answeer you, that what I say to you, by way of caueat I haue obiected to him." She declared it her duty to object to her husband's projected residence in New England unless he or Winthrop supplied her with a sufficient rationale. Then, she said, "I will be with you as sone as I maye."[58]

Such remarks were far from submissive; indeed, they affirmed Lucy Downing's ability to think independently, rationally. Yet they were phrased in a submissive way—a way to which her male associates were most likely to respond positively. She carefully pointed out that her woman's weakness would not allow her to face New

World "exstremities": "I haue litell confidence in my self in such cases." She admitted that women were more "fainted harted" than men and explained that she was never *"peremptory"* against her husband's departure. Winthrop or Emmanuel Downing may have assuaged Lucy's fears with reasonable arguments, for she soon came to Massachusetts. Although Mistress Downing had been unable to convince her male associates to allow her to stay in England, she had, by accentuating her weakness as woman, presented her wishes in a way that at least insured they would be listened to.[59]

Other wives more successfully maintained their point of view by appealing to their husbands' feelings of superiority. As early as 1623 the women of Plymouth Colony objected strongly to the established practice of communal labor, calling the performance of such communal services as dressing meat and washing clothing "a kind of slavery." (Presumably doing equally menial tasks for their own husbands, whom they had to some degree chosen and through association with whom they had probably gained some personal status, provided more support to their sense of individual worth.) Yet the "enslaved" women did not respond very aggressively or emphatically; rather, they assumed a demeanor of delicacy, alleging that women were too weak to labor under such conditions. Their objections fed their husbands' own feelings of discontent with the communal lifestyle, while the wives' method of protest diminished the possibility of sharp conflict. With both husbands and wives upset, private property soon replaced communal property, and contented wives "went willingly into the field."[60] Change had occurred partly because the women had objected, but there is no evidence that Pilgrim men viewed those objections as a dangerous declaration of independence. Nevertheless, word did reach England that the sexes had achieved more equality than was tolerable in the motherland. Governor Bradford wrote a letter home explaining that it was *not* true that women could vote at Plymouth.[61]

Being modest, deferential, and weak—in short, living up to the Puritan ideal—insured that women could occasionally have impact upon their male overlords. Some of those who sought concessions may have felt that they were simply acting as proper women ought; others quite probably were conscious of manipulative intent, as well as content. Those who gave birth out of wedlock and then accused an innocent but eligible young man of fathering the child certainly fell into the latter group. Since Puritans assumed that a pregnant woman could not, at the moment of delivery, lie about the father's identity, witnesses then kept a ready ear open for the name of the man she accused. Such a means of determining paternity was designed to protect the community from paying child support, but in practice it was easy for mothers to misuse the court's belief in their female weakness and good faith. Instead of naming the real father, a woman sometimes accused the most desirable of her male associates, who could most adequately supply the child's wants. Elizabeth Due, a Salem servant, first named the prominent Zerobabell Endicott as the father of her unborn child; later she changed her story and married a fellow servant, Cornelius Hulett (1654). In Maine, Alice Metherill accused two different neighbors of fathering her child, but at parturition "it appeared that a Negroe was the father of it" (1695). After the Massachusetts General Court passed its bastardy law of 1668, one Middlesex County maidservant reportedly said "that If shee should bee with Child shee would bee sure to lay it vn to won who was rich enough [and] abell to mayntayne it wheather it wear his or no." When she later conceived, this woman, Elizabeth Wells, laid her child to her master's son instead of to the purported father, another servant.[62]

One woman indicated the lengths to which a pregnant female could go in falsifying fatherhood. She wrote a letter to her boyfriend which found its way into the files of the Middlesex County Court. It reads as follows: "der loue i remember my loue to you hoping your welfar and i hop to imbras the[e] but now i rit to you to let you nowe that i am a child by you and i wil ether kil it or lay it to an other and you shal have no blame at al for I haue had many children and none have none of them" (i.e., none of their actual fathers is supporting any of them).[63]

Modest wives who tried to convince their husbands of a particular course of action, maidens who attempted to increase their value on the marriage market by affecting naiveté, and pregnant women who lied for their children's benefit all found ways to utilize the ideal feminine role to good advantage. Manipulation of males became one survival device adopted by some seventeenth-century New England women. Manipulative behavior could bring the woman privileges she could not otherwise accrue: a measure of sexual freedom as the subtle enticer, a degree of influence over her husband's decision-making prerogative, and a desirable maintenance for her children. Manipulative behavior was, for the woman who used it successfully, a step toward the external, toward dealing with her frustrations on some practical outward level, instead of internalizing them in self-blaming, self-destructive ways. Although such behavior occasionally involved the victimizing of others, at the same time it became a vehicle for transcending the paralyzing limitations of women's prescribed destiny—beyond the inwardly focused stress of languishing, "crazy-brained" actions, hysterical fits, and suicide.

1. May, *Power & Innocence*, pp. 24–26.
2. E. White, *God's gracious Dealing*, pp. 3–13.
3. Sibley, *Biog. Sketches of Harvard Grads.*, I, 117.
4. Hull, "Memoir & Diaries," p. 181.
5. Seligman, *Helplessness*, pp. 75–106.
6. Underhill, "Letter," p. 188; Haynes, "Letters," pp. 452–62.
7. Hansen, *Witchcraft at Salem*, pp. 36–52; Ziegler, "Hysterical Conversion Reactions"; Chodoff & Lyons, "Hysteria, Hysterical Pers., & 'Hysterical' Conversion"; Friedman, "Conversion Symptoms in Adolescents."
8. May, *Power & Innocence*, p. 25.
9. G. Dow, ed., *Essex Ct. Rec.*, I, 388; II, 158–59.
10. Hansen, *Witchcraft at Salem*, pp. 36–52, contains an excellent description of the hysterical fit.
11. Vieth, *Hysteria*, passim, esp. pp. 21, 30, 122–23, 126–27, 132–33, 143; Greer, *Female Eunuch*, pp. 38–40.
12. G. Dow, *Everyday Life in Mass.*, pp. 183–84; Josselyn, *Two Voyages to N. Eng.*, p. 93.
13. Digby, "Letter," p. 17.
14. J. Trumbull, *Hist. of Northampton*, I, 49; Shurtleff, ed., *Mass. Rec.*, I, 160; G. Dow, ed., *Essex Ct. Rec.*, VIII, 237; Drake, *Annals of Witchcraft*, p. 181.
15. C. Mather, *Diary*, II, 583–84.
16. Vieth, *Hysteria*, pp. 201, 203, 210–11, 240, 253–54, 261, 265–67; Sperling, "Conversion Hysteria & Conversion Symptoms"; Chodoff, "Re-exam. of Aspects of Hysteria"; Marmor, "Orality in Hysterical Pers."; Silverman, "Role of Aggressive Drives in Conversion"; Gershon, Dunner, & Goodwin, "Toward a Biology of Affective Disorders" (contains a good bibliography of works on the genetic approach to hysteria); Hollender, "Conversion Hysteria."
17. J. Whiting, "Letter"; Willard, "A briefe Account of Eliz. Knap," pp. 11, 18–19.
18. J. Whiting, "Letter"; Wyllys, "Wyllys Col. Suppl. Witchcraft in Conn. 1662–93," pp. 37–43.
19. J. Whiting, "Letter," pp. 466–68; C. Mather, *Memorable Prov.*, p. 2; Caulfield, "Ped. Aspects of Salem Witchcraft," p. 799.
20. J. Whiting, "Letter," pp. 466–68; Fitch, "Letter," p. 475; Willard, "A briefe Account of Eliz. Knap," pp. 11, 16; C. Mather, *Memorable Prov.*, pp. 16–23, 34–37, 43, 51.
21. J. Trumbull, *Hist. of Northampton*, I, 49; C. Mather, *Memorable Prov.*, pp. 34–35; Willard, "A briefe Account of Eliz. Knap," pp. 9, 17.
22. C. Mather, *Memorable Prov.*, p. 25–26. For discussion of the horse as an erotic symbol for teenaged girls, refer to D. Morris, *Naked Ape*, pp. 185, 189–90.

23. This technique is described in Katchadourian & Lunde, *Fund. of Human Sexuality*, pp. 221–22.

24. Hollender, "Conversion Hysteria."

25. Benjamin Gold, age 23, and John Indian fell into fits in the Salem Village witchcraft proceedings ("Salem Witchcraft—1692," n.p.). Interestingly enough, Charles F. Malmquist has found that boys subject to hysteria have "feminine interests or girlish traits" ("Hysteria in Childhood," p. 116).

26. C. Mather, *Memorable Prov.*, pp. 12–13, 21–22, 31–32; Willard, "A briefe Account of Eliz. Knap," pp. 7, 13; J. Trumbull, *Hist. of Northampton*, I, 49.

27. I. Mather, *Essay for Recording Illus. Prov.*, p. 140; Fitch, "Letter," p. 475.

28. J. Whiting, "Letter"; Woodward, ed., *Rec. of Salem Witchcraft*, II, 262–65; C. Mather, *Memorable Prov.*, p. 75.

29. Hysteria epidemics are a fairly common phenomenon. See Benam, Horder, & Anderson, "Hysterical Epidemic in Classroom"; Taylor & Hunter, "Observation of Hysterical Epidemic in Hospital Ward"; Schuler & Parenton, "Recent Epidemic of Hysteria in La. High School"; McEvedy, Griffith, & T. Hall, "Two School Epidemics"; Friedman & Sulianti, "Epidemic Hysteria."

30. At least one seventeenth-century male, however, viewed fits as the products of female duplicity. See Cyrano de Bergerac, "Lettre contre sorciers, 1654," pp. 211–18.

31. G. Dow, ed., *Essex Ct. Rec.*, III, 151. Italics mine.

32. If the number of possible suicides is included, the figures increase to eight of 24 women.

33. "Salem Witchcraft—1692," I, n.p. (case of Christian Trask); Marshall, "Diary, 1697–1709," p. 17 (Mary Wilder); Marshall, "Diary, 1697–1711," p. 155 (Mary Fuller); Hull, "Memoir & Diaries," pp. 195–96 (Goodwife Dwight), 214 (Elizabeth Bishop); *Boston News-Letter*, Aug. 6–13, 1705, in Weeks & Bacon, eds., *Hist. Digest of Prov. Press*, p. 232 (Susanna Griffin).

34. "Thomas Jenner to John Winthrop, Mar. 28, 1645," in A. Forbes, ed., *Winthrop Papers*, V, 14; W. & E. Adams, "Memoir," pp. 17–18.

35. Hertz, "Further Study of Suicidal Configurations in Rorschach Rec.," p. 68, Table 4.

36. Sprott, *Eng. Debate on Suicide*, passim; Sprott, "Puritan Problem of Suicide." Donne's *Biathanatos* was completed in 1607 but did not appear before the English public until his son published it in 1646.

37. Porterfield, "Problem of Suicide," p. 53; Gibbs & Martin, *Status Integration & Suicide*, p. 297; B. Johnson, "Durkheim's One Cause of Suicide," 875–76.

38. Leonard, *Understanding & Preventing Suicide*; White & Farber, "Motivation Reconsidered"; Lesters, *Suicide*, pp. 44–45.

39. Shurtleff & Pulsifer, eds., *Plym. Rec.*, V, 249–50; L. Hammond, "Diary," p. 169.

40. J. Davenport, "Letter," p. 45.

41. Durkheim, *Suicide*, p. 71, Table 4.

42. World Health Organization Public Health Paper no. 35, Table 2, in Stengel, *Suicide & Attempted Suicide*, p. 22. The 1967 New England statistics are from U.S. Dept. of Health, Educ., & Welfare, *Vital Stats. of U.S.*, II Mortality, Pt. A, Table 1–26.

43. Shneidman & Farberow, "Stat. Comparisons between Attempted & Committed Suicide," pp. 19–47; Parkin, "Suicide & Culture in Fairbanks," Table I.

44. Janeway, *Man's World, Woman's Place*, p. 86. Here I must add that the quality or wisdom of the decision is not at issue.

45. Hirsch, "Methods & Fashions of Suicide"; Segal & Humphrey, "Comparison of Suicide Victims & Attempters in N. Hamp.," p. 834; Stengel, *Suicide & Attempted Suicide*, p. 40.

46. Russell, "Diary," p. 56.

47. Sewall, *Diary*, II, 52.

48. "Active" methods of suicide included hanging ($N = 16$), cutting one's throat (2), stabbing oneself (1), and shooting oneself (2). Six men killed themselves more passively, five by drowning and one by starvation.

49. Lesters, *Suicide*, p. 47.

50. "Salem Witchcraft—1692," I, n.p. (case of Christian Trask); Sewall, *Diary*, I, 208–9 (Hannah Marion); *Boston News-Letter*, July 16–23, 1705, in Weeks & Bacon, eds., *Hist. Digest of Prov. Press*, p. 224 (Lydia Potter).

51. Schmidt, O'Neal, & Robins, "Evaluation of Suicide Attempts as Guide to Therapy," p. 552; Bibb & Guze, "Hysteria in a Psychiatric Hospital," p. 226.

52. *Publick Occurences Both Forreign and Domestick*, Sept. 25, 1690, in Weeks & Bacon, eds., *Hist. Digest of Prov. Press*, p. 29.

53. Dunton, "Letter to Mrs. Sarah Dunton, 1686," in his *Letters*, pp. 265, 271.

54. *Ibid.*, pp. 271, 275; Dunton, "Letter to George Larkin, 1686," *ibid.*, p. 99.

55. Dunton, "Letter to George Larkin, 1686," *ibid.*, p. 113.

56. Beacon, "Solitary Meds.," p. 217 (no. 171).

57. C. Mather, *Diary*, I, 457–58, 476–77, 484.

58. "Lucy Downing to John Winthrop, ca July 1636," in A. Forbes, ed., *Winthrop Papers*, III, 278–80.

59. *Ibid.*

60. Bradford, *Of Plym. Plant.*, pp. 120–21.

61. Bradford & Allerton, "Letter," p. 299.

62. G. Dow, ed., *Essex Ct. Rec.*, I, 361; Libby, Allen, & Moody, eds., *Maine Ct. Rec.*, IV, 47–49; Middlesex Ct. Files, folio 52 (latter case cited in Morgan, "Puritans & Sex,"pp. 601–2).

63. Middlesex Ct. Files, folio 30, cited in Morgan, "Puritans & Sex," p. 602.

VII

Unwomanly Women: A Variety of Non-Ideal Behaviors

[I]t . . . appears that when we plot the distribution of behaviors in a situation where individuals are said generally to conform, we find the following condition: Rarely, if ever, do we find that all the individuals conform completely.

—Allport, "J-Curve Hypothesis"

Licit and Illicit Forms of Non-Ideal Behavior

PURITANS FIRMLY BELIEVED THAT THE TWO SEXES HAD DIFFERENT DESTINIES, constructing a society which institutionalized male superiority-dominance and female inferiority-submission. Despite the role rigidity enforced by Puritan culture, not all men or women behaved as their social roles dictated. Social psychologist Gordon W. Allport explains, "The danger with the role concept is that the personal nexus *containing* the role-habits is likely to be overlooked. . . . each culture has a type of personality that corresponds to its cultural pattern . . . [but] no single individual reflects all these traits and outlooks, and . . . some individuals may reflect virtually none of them."[1] Floyd Allport points out that individuals conform in varying degrees around a posited norm. New England women grew up in a number of different family situations, possessed different genetic makeups, and were born under different astrological signs. Some had high-spirited mothers, or fathers of "weak parts." Some matured in cities, some on farms, and others in frontier settings. Therefore we might expect a rather broad range of female behaviors.

The available records indicate as much. While many women did not object to the limitations imposed on them by adherence to a subordinate social role, some attempted to use the feminine role to manipulative advantage as the preceding chapter indicates. A woman could legitimately take certain "strong-minded" steps. One Hatfield girl, for example, attempted to get more education than was allowed for females by sitting outside near the schoolhouse door so she could hear the boys recite their lessons.[2] Lady Moody left the comfort of her village home to lead a party of colonists into the wilderness; in 1643 she went against the advice of her friends by removing from Lynn to Dutch-claimed territory on Long Island. Considered a "dangerous woeman" by the Bay Colony authorities because of her endorsement of the heresy of Anabaptism, she played a prominent political role in Gravesend's village affairs thereafter.[3] Another woman, a forty-eight-year-old spinster named Elizabeth Pole, in 1637 purchased the lands at Tetiquet, Plymouth Colony, from the Indians, reportedly for only a jackknife and a peck of beans. She then moved her cattle from Dorchester, excavated some stalls from the Tetiquet hills, and became the first settler of what would become Taunton. After the discovery of iron ore on the banks of Two-Mile River, Pole also became a prominent stockholder in the Taunton ironworks. The city fathers honored her on the Taunton seal adopted on January 1, 1865, with the words *Dux femina facti* ("A woman the leader of the enterprise").[4]

Elizabeth Pole and Deborah Moody received a good deal of respect for their "active" behavior. However, most women who did things which were considered "masculine," or who acted non-deferentially, ended up facing censure instead of acclaim. At least 2,954 women were charged with 3,276 offenses in the several county and colony courts. More than one-fifth of these offenses can be viewed as severe violations of the female sex role. The authorities prosecuted 393 female offenders for refusing to be passive and deferential—248 for hurling verbal invective or physically abusing their husbands or neighbors, 105 for heaping contempt upon the colony authorities, and 40 for committing manslaughter or murder. Another 83 became outspoken advocates of Quakerism or other religious "heresies," thereby assuming the right to guide their own religious destinies. At least 61 women who had some reputation as ill-behaved, outspoken community reprobates faced prosecution on witchcraft charges.[5] Thirty-eight women took God's name in vain, while 135 adulteresses rejected their husbands' implicit sovereignty over their sexual beings.

Another 38 percent of all female offenders appeared reluctant to respect the prevailing value of premarital virginity. At least 1,233 women let themselves be "defiled" in fornication, or behaved in unfeminine, lewd, and lascivious ways. These sexual "rebels" violated the orthodox feminine role, but not as actively as the 710 "severe" violators did. Some fornicators, considering themselves the "weaker sex," may have succumbed to the amorous overtures of "stronger" men. Other "lewd" women had a more than passive interest in sexuality: after sitting for some time under an apple tree with a man of bad reputation, Sarah Chapman of New London County, Connecticut, said "shee would lett him Com to her house in spight of all the world" (1671). In Essex County, Massachusetts, Sergeant Jeret Hoyt's daughter rejected monogamy, acquiring some notoriety as a woman who "would never love any man more than a fortnight" (1674).[6] At New Haven, Mary Hitchcock enticed a young man to have sexual relations with her by telling him "he looked like a wenching fellow" and then saying "come, shall we goe to Bedd" (1661). A second New Haven lass, Grace Todd, did not report the Indian who reached underneath her coats and handled her genitals; instead, she spoke about it in a jesting manner (1664).[7] Several other women had more than one illegitimate child, suggesting that their sexual inclinations were stronger than their fear of censure and hardship.

At least one maiden asserted a measure of personal independence by behaving "immodestly" in the presence of her neighbors. The case began after Jacob Murline seized Sarah Tuttle's gloves at New Haven and demanded the medieval forfeit, a kiss, "whereupon they sate downe together, his arme being about her, & her arme vpon his shoulder or about his neck, & he kissed her & shee him, or they kissed one another, continuing in this posture about half an houre." Although her mother told Sarah "not to keep company wth him," Sarah disobeyed that directive. Her father claimed Murline had inveigled her, but the young woman denied that charge. The New Haven governor then fined Jacob for his "corrupt & sinfull" carriage, and Sarah for her lack of discretion. In 1660 a "bold" kiss could get a girl into trouble.[8]

A third category of female offender was charged with crimes which required activity considered more extraordinary for a woman than for a man, and which therefore entailed some violation of the female sex role. Theft often involved planning, danger, and on occasion some aggressiveness. However, most female thieves rather easily stole bits of food or clothing from the families with whom they lived. Those women tried for keeping disorderly houses, where the alcohol flowed freely and dancing was common, "actively" provided opportunities for sinful behavior, instead of attempting, in feminine fashion, to prevent such wrongdoings. Female arsonists gave vent, surreptitiously, to a great deal of personal antagonism, while drunken women were often a little too outspoken for their own good (although that was not an implicit characteristic of drunkenness itself). The female servant who ran away from her master demonstrated an unwillingness to abide by his rule. Running away, an implicit rejection of the expected subservience, was not, however, as blatantly unfeminine as was confronting the master directly.

Seven percent of the female criminals were tried for offenses involving behavior not particularly in violation of the female sex role—selling alcohol without a license, lying, nightwalking after the 9 P.M. curfew, playing cards, and marrying "contrary to law." Twice that many committed offenses rather appropriate to the condition of female passivity; these women were absent from Sabbath meetings, idle, or did not appear when summoned to court.

To rank female criminals in terms of severity of their sex-role violations is somewhat arbitrary, since the same crime may be committed in a quite different spirit by different women. Therefore, to draw a more concrete picture of the way in which such offenders violated the sex-role expectations of their society, it is necessary to examine in greater detail the activities of these "rebels." Many of the offenders in this chart are mentioned elsewhere in this work, but others seem singularly appropriate for treatment here, in a discussion of the most unfeminine, aggressive criminal protest. A consideration of three kinds of female criminals—disobedient servants, abusive women, and infanticidal mothers—illustrates the scope and force of female assertion.

Disobedient Servants

A maidservant could behave quite obstreperously if she set her mind to it. As early as January, 1636, the wife of Massachusetts Deputy Governor Thomas Dudley complained to Margaret Winthrop about the antics of a once dutiful serving maid who suddenly "hath got such a head and is growen soe insolent, that her carriage towards vs, especially myselfe is vnsufferable." Whenever Mary

Dudley ordered the maid to perform a task, she "will bid me doe it my selfe, and she sayes how shee can give content as well as any servant but shee will not." The deputy governor entreated the recalcitrant servant to stop directing "reviling speeches and filthie

Chart 7.1

Female "Criminals" in Seventeenth-Century Calvinist
New England

Severe Violators of the Passive, Deferential Female Sex Role	710	(21.7%)
Abusive behavior	248	
Adultery; adulterous carriage	135	
Contempt of the authorities	105	
Quaker; "heresy" violations	83	
Witchcraft (obstreperous "witches" only)	61	
Swearing	38	
Manslaughter, murder	40	
Fornication	1,233	(37.6%)
Moderate Violators of the Female Sex Role	292	(8.9%)
Theft	180	
Drunkenness	55	
Keeping a disorderly house	36	
Runaway servants	14	
Arson	7	
Offenses Involving Little or No Sex Role–Related Behavior	226	(6.9%)
Operating tavern illegally	146	
Lying	52	
Nightwalking	11	
Marrying contrary to law	10	
Card-playing	7	
Offenses Appropriate to the Passive Female Sex Role	465	(14.2%)
Sabbath absence/ Sabbath violations	431	
Non-appearance in court	26	
Idleness	8	
Other (Miscellaneous, Unspecified)	350	(10.7%)

language" at her mistress, but the lass responded by professing "that her heart and her nature will not suffer her to confesse faults." She was clearly not the kind of woman who could remain content with the deferential role which was her heritage both as a female and as a servant. Yet she avoided any serious punishment for her misdeeds, because the Dudleys did not bring her before the county magistrates.[9]

Other maidservants responded similarly. In the Maine wilderness, which had no functioning court system as early as the 1630s, John Winter had much trouble with his servant Priscilla Bickford. She objected to working for the Winters and twice hid herself away in the woods on Richmond's Island. Winter's wife had to watch her carefully while the maid did her daily chores; Winter further related, "We Cann hardly keep her within doores after we ar gonn to beed, except we Carry the kay of the doore to bed with vs." Mistress Winter finally beat the girl. Her husband approved of the treatment, since Bickford had not been hurt by his wife's chastisement.[10] The Connecticut magistrates ordered another serving maid, Susan Coles, kept on a coarse diet at hard labor in the House of Correction and had her whipped weekly for "rebellious cariedge towards her mistress" (1645).[11]

Nearly a hundred maidservants stole some money or goods from their masters or mistresses, surreptitiously providing themselves with rewards for their labors while working under indenture. (Servants, it must be remembered, had no incomes of their own if they were either redemptioners or indentured.) The case of Mary Johnson indicates how theft could conceivably be linked to resentment of servitude. In 1646 the Connecticut Assistants whipped Johnson twice for thievery; thereafter, instead of humbling herself before the hand of God, she began dabbling in witchcraft. Disliking her own servile condition, she turned her attention to Satan, who offered "her the best service *he* could do for *her*." She claimed that the Devil helped her perform her daily chores, not to mention leading her into the joys of sexual intercourse (and, as an unfortunate consequence, the pain of infanticide). He became her good friend, not merely another "master" to order her around.[12]

Only fourteen female servants of record appeared before the various magistrates on charges of running away from the masters, but this small number is not really surprising. Flight was difficult in Puritan New England, especially for women. Calvinist communities tended to view strangers, particularly unaccompanied females, with suspicion; moreover, a woman had virtually no opportunities for remunerative employment in any new locale. Therefore, it was imperative that a runaway maidservant find a male protector, as did Mary Punnell of Dorchester in 1674, or at least that she ride away dressed in men's apparell, as Sarah Phillips of Boston did in 1679.[13]

Several black women—either indentured servants or slaves —also reacted in non-deferential and un-Puritan ways. In 1702 Betty Negro struck a white man, called his mother half a witch, and received ten lashes.[14] The magistrates prosecuted fourteen black women for taking an unfeminine (but, contemporaries would have said, distinctly African) interest in sex; two of these were convicted thrice of fornication and another four were two-time offenders. On the other hand, in 1639 one black "Queen" refused to obey her master's directive to fornicate with a black male whom he had selected for breeding purposes.[15] Maria, a Roxbury slave, set her master's and a neighbor's houses on fire, killing a baby girl in the process. The authorities responded by sentencing Maria to perhaps the most horrible execution of the seventeenth century: she burned to death on the Boston Common in July, 1681, the only instance in the entire century where an offender of either race or sex faced that punishment. Her execution had such a profound impact upon one sixteen-year-old apprentice that he refused thereafter to eat pork because "its odor brought back to him a sickening whiff of wind from the woman he had seen burned alive."[16] The public example of such unprecedented punishment, along with the frequent whippings given to black offenders, presumably curbed the amount of discontent overtly expressed by black women; but at the same time it probably heightened the frustration they experienced in a condition of servitude.

Black women, particularly those newly arrived from Africa or Barbados, had little opportunity to internalize Puritan notions of femininity. When they exhibited aggressive, active, sensual behavior, they may merely have been responding in accord with the socialization patterns of their native cultures. Only those black women who were raised in New England homes can be seen as "rebels" against the confinement of the Puritan sex role. Yet Calvinists considered all such behavior unfeminine, since they believed that the Bible drew no cultural distinctions in matters of sex-role conditioning.

Abusive Women

Many women who were neither servants nor slaves appeared in court because they spoke their minds too freely and castigated the most prestigious males in Puritan society. Attacks on ministers and magistrates constituted anti-social behavior for both sexes; but the women's aspersions had a double impropriety, since the feminine role prohibited overt criticism of lesser male figures. Women often hurled sharp criticism at ministers in particular. In 1652 an Essex County grand jury presented Holgrave's wife before the court for saying "if it were not for the law, shee should never com to the [Sabbath] meetings, the teacher [William Perkins] was soe dead." Mistress Holgrave felt Perkins was "fitter to be a ladyes chamberman" than a preacher, thereby taking potshots at his ministerial *and* his male authority[17]—what could be more insulting for a Puritan man than to be a woman's servant? Two years later, Elizabeth Legg confessed to slighting William Walton, the Marblehead pastor, by claiming she "could have a boy from the Colledg that would preach better than Mr. Walton for half ye wages." In 1682 Widow Mary Hammond was admonished for "speaking reproachful words against the worship of God in saying that going to hear the minister preach is the way to hell," as well as for refusing to allow her daughter to attend the Gloucester meeting.[18]

Women also expressed some dislike for the local and colonial public officials. At least two Maine women made serious attacks upon the family of Governor Edward Godfrey in 1649. Goody Mendum called Godfrey "a dissembling man," while Elinor Raynes charged Godfrey's wife with "being a liar." Godfrey reacted by having his court pass an order that punished any woman who abused her husband *or other persons* with "opprobrious language." Such women were to be placed in the stocks for two hours and afterwards whipped if "incorrigible."[19] Another woman, Mary Rann, did not wish to keep her head submissively covered when she appeared in court after her arrest for scorning the authorities. Instead, she threatened to "pull off her head clothes, and come in her hair to them, like a parcel of pitiful beggarly curs as they were."[20]

Some female "rebels" threw invective at the members of Puritan New England's focal social institution, the church. The Reading Church suspended Elizabeth Hart in 1655 for maintaining, among other things, that the church was composed of old fools lacking in wit (i.e., enjoyment of life). Thomas Trusler's wife in 1644 paid twenty marks for expressing the opinion that "there was no love in the church and that they were biters and devourers." She further asserted that Salem pastor Edward Norris taught the people lies, objected to making Norris and Governor John Endicott the foundation stones of the church, and went so far as to question the legitimacy of the Massachusetts government. In the same year Elizabeth Gyles was sentenced to be whipped or to pay a £1 fine for speaking "revyling words against some of the members of the Church of Christ in Dover," New Hampshire.[21]

Still other women vented anti-religious feelings in a more nonverbal way. Elizabeth Johnson of Essex County covered her ears with her hands whenever the Bible was read (1642). Many females, instead of listening diligently to their minister's Sabbath lectures, fell asleep in the meetinghouses. Their enormous bonnets shielded them from public view, causing Samuel Willard to complain that "hee doth seeme to be preaching to stacks of straw with men among them."[22] Such women could not be prosecuted in court, as was true for their more outspoken neighbors. Still, women who slept during services indicated that they took the Puritan brand of religion less seriously than might be expected.

Most of those women who did speak abusively threw disparaging remarks not at ministers, magistrates, or church members as a group, but at their neighbors. Women frequently appeared before the authorities for "unnecessary talking," "bearing tales from house to house," and setting out differences between members of the community.[23] Others more directly and pointedly called their female associates names like "whore," "strumpet," "witch," or "thief," and described males whom they disliked as "rascals," "rogues," and "liars." One woman, Mary Towsley of Southfield, Massachusetts, was whipped twice in 1684 for "wicked lying slandering cursing wretched Scolding murderous threatening & dangerous Languages," and for breaking her impounded livestock out of their sequestration. At Springfield, Priscilla Hunter was gagged and placed for half an hour in a public street after neighbors declared her "upon every occasion to be exorbitant with her Toung" (1673). Goodwife Hitchcock called Goody Andrewes "a liar & a backbiter." At another time Hitchcock told Richard Beckly "that his nose was in his wiues brich [i.e., ass] & her self a hammer to drive it in." Such remarks led the New Haven town court to conclude in 1659 that the "poyson of asps" was under her lips. That body sentenced her to pay a £2 fine to the town and £10 in damages to Beckly.[24]

Many an acid-tongued woman proved that she could hold her own in confrontation sessions with other men and women. Less apparently, the gossip who told tales outside her victims' hearing was also expressing some "power"—on the principle that making another look bad made oneself look good. Gossiping became a way not only to pat oneself on the back, but also to get at persons whom one hated or envied (i.e., those who possessed more "power" —status, possessions, personal impact, etc.—than the gossip). Whatever the functions of "scoldings" and gossip, women who practiced the same encountered frequent censure and punishment. The Massachusetts General Court enacted a law which ordered scolds to be gagged, set in a ducking stool, and submerged in the water (1672). Even deceased gossips could not escape community rancor, as one gravestone in Pownall, Vermont, testifies:

> Here lies in silent clay
> Miss Arabella Young
> Who in the twenty-first of May
> Began to hold her tongue.[25]

From Physical Blows to Murder

Some women did not rely merely on words to express their aggressiveness. Mary Tucker of Marblehead belted a man who heaped "scurrilous" language upon her, grabbed him by the hair, pulled him down upon the stones paving her yard, and pounded his head against those stones (1681). Rebecca Morgan of New Hampshire threw down Goodman Jones and beat him with a stick (1687), while Ann Belding of Hadley, Massachusetts, was guilty of the "most shameful & odious Murtherous purposes & practices agt the body & life" of Mary Webster (1680).[26] Mary Loggia of Essex County awoke one night to find an Indian in her bed. She took the redman by the hair and beat him with her fist until he fled pell-mell out the window (1677). In 1691 maidservant Bridget Denmark fought with laborer Rice Griffin in the mud along the Boston docks and succeeded in drowning him. Perhaps the most outrageously assaultive females were Mary Coultman and Abigail Betts of Hartford County, Connecticut. These two women took hold of Edward Hall, pulled down his breeches, pinned his shirt over his shoulders, and clapped him with their hands on "the Naked Back & on the naked Belly." They then stripped off John Lattimore's breeches and drawers, dragged him about the room by his shirt, clapped him as well, and threatened to do the same to a third man.[27]

On occasion women committed murder—with purpose and vengeance. The best-known instance of unmitigated female rage was Hannah Dustin's slaying of ten Indians. Captured in a raid on Haverhill, Massachusetts, in 1697, she had watched as the red warriors murdered her week-old babe. Soon after, with the assistance of a nurse and a young boy, Dustin tomahawked their ten captors to death under cover of night, scalping the victims and later collecting £50 in scalp-bounty money.[28] Other women reacted to the Indians with a great deal of "active" bitterness. On July 15, 1677, when fishermen brought two captive red men to Marblehead, the females there, having suffered much from King Philip's depradations, "in a boisterous rage" seized the Indians, beat them to death with stones and billets of wood, cut off their heads, and pulled their flesh from the bones.[29]

Although Puritans tolerated such displays of female animosity toward the Indians, they subjected females who slew whites to the most severe legal penalties—a sharp lashing or, in most instances, a hanging. The magistrates tried 40 women for killing or attempting to kill 43 different persons. Ninety percent of their victims were members of their own families, whereas only 11 of the 112 male "murderers" were accused of directing violence at a family member. Seven males and five females attempted to kill their mates. Two men beat their servants to death, while the remaining 36 family victims were young children. *Only* women snuffed out their offspring's lives, and 88 percent of all women's victims were children. (Two mothers and two fathers were tried for helping their daughters dispose of illegitimate babies.)

Four of the child victims were more than a year old. As early as 1637 Anne Hett, the wife of a Hingham cooper, "having been long in a sad melancholy distemper, near to frenzy," unsuccessfully tried to drown her child. Five years later she threw another child far out into a creek, but a wayfarer saved it. John Winthrop recorded, "She would give no other reason for it, but that she did it to save it from misery . . . and that she would not repent of any sin."[30] Dorothy Talby, whose husband expressed "much pride and unnaturalness" toward her, plotted to kill him and her children by him. She broke the neck of her three-year-old daughter, suggestively named Dif-

ficult (presumably in reference to the difficulty of her delivery), and
was on December 6, 1638, executed by the Massachusetts authorities. Like Anne Hett, Dorothy Talby refused to be penitent. In
Connecticut a third woman, Mercy Brown, spent some time in a
"distracted condition" before she killed her own son with an ax and
was hanged for her deed (1690).[31]

Thirty-two of the child-victims were newborn babes. Sixteen
mothers were hanged for the offense of infanticide—ten in Massachusetts, three in Connecticut, two in Plymouth, and one in
Maine. The magistrates found five other women "negligent" in their
infants' deaths and sentenced them to twenty or thirty lashes. Since
mothers often bore their children in secret, neglected to take any
postnatal steps to insure their survival, and, upon discovery of a
dead baby's body, swore it died of "natural" causes, infanticide
convictions were difficult to secure. Charges could not be proven
against ten suspects, and no record of the court's final disposition
remains for another four cases.[32]

Puritans became increasingly upset about the numbers of infanticides as the century progressed. In 1677, when a dead child was
found at the Boston dock, the magistrates ordered a "search of all
the Women of the Town, to see if thereby they could find out the
Murdress." Investigating midwives failed to reveal the guilty
mother's identity, but their search did unexpectedly determine that
several maidens were pregnant.[33] Eight years later, a male infant
was found pinned up in a "sorry cloth" after a nighttime snowfall.
Again, the search failed to discover the mother. Sam Sewall sorrow-
fully reported, "So far as I hear this is the first Child that ever was in
such a manner exposed in Boston."[34] At the turn of the century,
the Massachusetts (1692), Connecticut (1699), and New Hampshire
(1714) legislatures considered negligent infanticide such a serious
matter that they passed laws providing that the accused woman
must prove her innocence, instead of the colony proving her guilt.
All three laws specified that women who secretly buried or
drowned their infants and then claimed, when the child's remains
were discovered, that it had died of natural causes would hang as
murderers, unless they supplied the corroborative testimony of at
least one other witness who had been present at the child's birth.[35]

Nineteen of the thirty-two women accused of infanticide were
single maidens who did not or could not marry their babies' fathers,
and who did not wish to care for illegitimate children. Ten others
were wives who did not relish bearing and rearing any more chil-

dren. Another was a widow. The marital status of two women is unknown. Single women usually hid their pregnancies under billowing skirts, then gave birth in isolation and killed the child through an act either of omission (e.g., refusal to clear the infant's air passage, to clothe it in cool weather, or to suckle it) or of commission (e.g., smothering or drowning it). Married women also gave birth secretly, although keeping a pregnancy secret became more difficult. Even if no one else did, the woman's husband would most assuredly know of her physical state. Such a woman might tell her mate that the child had been born dead; but, if so, one wonders how she managed to convince him not to report the death to the town selectmen. Some women may have had the complicity of their husbands, parents, and even neighbors. In at least one case the Massachusetts authorities forced Salem's Dr. Emery and the mother of an accused maiden to sit on the gallows with ropes around their necks while the maiden was hanged, since those two had been "assessories" to her child's murder. The consequences were even more severe for John and Ester Andrews of Lakenham, Massachusetts. They were hanged for concealing their daughter Susanna's murder of her twins and her secret burial of the infants.[36]

Mothers who chose infanticide acted out of strong conviction. They had up to nine months to come to their decision and to grapple with the moral consequences of their act. Once their crime was exposed, such mothers rarely expressed much penitence. One went so far as to deposit her newborn offspring—perhaps symbolically— in the pond behind the Newbury meetinghouse (1700).[37] On her day of execution Sarah Smith of Deerfield, Massachusetts, "slept both at the prayer and the sermon. . . . And seem'd the most unconcern'd of any in the assembly." Before her hanging she did warn other women not to follow her example, admitting she "had sinned away great convictions and awakenings," but she expressed virtually no demonstrable sorrow for the specific act of murder (1698). Sarah Threenedles, a laborer's daughter, showed even less concern for her afterlife and no guilt over causing her infant's death. In fact, while in prison awaiting her execution, she proceeded to have sexual relations with another prisoner (1698).[38]

By Calvinist standards, the child-murderer sinned against much of what a woman was supposed to be. Through infanticide, the mother denied that for which God had reputedly made her—the conception, bearing, and care of children. She was not simply killing another person, but actually nullifying her own existence as a woman. In the words of one European physucian, she then became totally "worthless."[39]

Killing one's child was a serious and unfortunate business, one which begs for analysis of the individual mothers' motives. Unfortunately, we possess only a smattering of information about infanticidal mothers. Yet the desire *not* to bear a child appears quite widespread in Western culture. From medieval days through the late nineteenth century, many a mother either caused her own infant's death or left it with a foundling hospital.[40] Twentieth-century psychoanalysts have found that their female clients, particularly the severely depressed ones, often express either the wish to kill their infants or the fear that they might stab, decapitate, or strangle them. Sometimes such murderous thoughts are expanded to include husbands, neighboring children, and close relatives as well.[41] Most recently, in a 1976 poll Ann Landers asked her readers, "If you had it to do over again, would you have children?" A surprising 70 percent of the respondents answered negatively.[42]

Of course, regret at having raised children need not necessarily lead to a desire to kill them. For example, there is no evidence that a woman like Deacon Samuel Fletcher's wife, who called her children "by the name of rogue, rascal, hellhound" and said "the devil will take them," literally wanted to kill them (1668).[43] Still, regret can easily be transformed into resentment, and that into overt hostility, especially in women frustrated by the requirements of the Puritan ideal. A. K. Chapman has found that twelve of twenty mothers with murderous impulses toward their infants were "very passive women, who had little capacity for expression of anger or self-assertive feelings." Dominated by associates, relatives, or husbands, they experienced intense guilt about expressing hostility or assertiveness. Their passive facades covered an inner turbulence, often manifested in a desire to annihilate the dominating persons or a child surrogate. Deprived of effective control over their own lives, infanticidal mothers wished, in compensation, for the symbolically absolute power of life and death over someone—be it their offspring or the real oppressor.[44] Since the exercise of control over women was a Puritan norm, many of New England's infanticidal mothers, especially the married ones, may have been acting out this same need for influence and retaliation. We know that at least one woman, Dorothy Talby, wanted to kill both her husband and her children. Mistress Talby may have wanted to get back at her husband by killing the children who would carry on *his* name, and whom he valued dearly. Joseph Rheingold has pointed out that often the infanticidal mother wishes to destroy a child as a way of punishing her husband.[45]

Some New England mothers who killed their newborn babies may have viewed the child, on some level, as the oppressor. Rheingold writes, "Many women hate the unborn baby because they feel it has maliciously trapped them in an insufferable situation."[46] Indeed, it was easy for the New England mother to associate the reproductive function with death, for childbirth quite dramatically "killed" the mother's relative freedom to enjoy her own time. Being a housewife was considerably less hectic than being a housewife *and* a mother. In a strange turnabout, infanticidal "liberation" from motherhood could preserve the mother's own appreciation for life itself. Yet the mother might resent the child for quite another reason, deriving from the pain experienced in childbirth. New England women delivered in a prone position, which caused the uterus to press on the inferior vena cava and aorta, thereby cutting off the flow of oxygenated blood to the uterus and producing shock-like symptoms in the mother. Women also prolonged the agony of delivery by failing to use the beneficial effects of gravity to facilitate the child's exit.[47] Mothers quite probably associated the intense physical pain of childbirth with death, since many of them died in childbed. Instead of viewing her pain as a reminder to cleanse her soul, the new mother could blame the innocent child for nearly killing her, and then express her anger toward it by destroying it.

The single women who practiced infanticide might have chosen to violate one component of their female role (the maternal) in order to preserve another (the semblance of feminine virtue). Few men would want to marry a woman with an illegitimate child; nor did community censure—not to mention a fine or a whipping for fornication—prove a very heartening prospect. If a woman chose to enjoy sexual activity with a man who neglected to use a birth control device, she often paid the price. Unwillingly pregnant, she could not get rid of the child by leaving it on the steps of a foundling home, for New England had no foundling homes. She could not leave it at the meetinghouse or a neighbor's home, for the authorities might order a search of all the women in the town and her parturition would be discovered. Sometimes infanticide seemed a woman's only tolerable alternative to public reproach, diminution of her marriage chances, and tying herself to a child whom she did not want for five or six years (until it reached an apprenticeable age).

Given such undesirable options, Elizabeth Emerson and Elizabeth Clements each killed two infants. Clements gave birth to no fewer than three illegitimate children before her execution in 1691. Sarah Threenedles had one bastard before she killed her second child.[48]

Fertility could become a serious problem, to married as well as single women. Within a single year Mary Parsons of Springfield bore not one, but two babies and fell ill (apparently psychosomatically) while carrying the second child. After that infant's birth on October 26, 1650, Parsons deprived it of care until it died four months later. Nursing and diapering two children less than a year old appealed little to this frontier woman, who was hanged for her offense in mid-1651.[49] Pregnancy caused another woman such serious problems that she simply chose to ignore its reality before her death in childbirth in 1705.[50]

Oddly enough, some women may have killed their children not out of any need to preserve their own lives or to destroy their infants, but out of a profound sense of nurturance. A woman like Anne Hett may actually have believed the world was so cruel that her children were better off dead. The three black women tried for infanticide may not have wished to subject their offspring to lifetimes of slavery.[51] Whatever their motives, only one woman expressed any guilt over what she had done, a fact which is quite consistent with Rheingold's finding that some mothers kill their children without experiencing either guilt or anxiety.[52] Perhaps some of them effectively blocked out whatever positive feelings they had for the child. Some probably never accepted the fact of the child's humanity; others may have felt no guilt because they blamed the child for causing them great pain and bringing about a potentially bleak future. Since "doing away with the child means escape from anxiety," as Rheingold puts it, that relief may have counterbalanced any feelings of remorse. (These explanations are, of course, not mutually exclusive.) In almost all instances, infanticide represented a search for power—whether it be the power to exercise vengeance against the child for causing the mother pain in childbirth or more long-lasting pain in her future life, the power to destroy someone the husband valued, or the power to control the conditions under which a woman would bear children. Unfortunate though their acts of infanticide might be, these mothers were implicitly rejecting one central characteristic of the feminine ideal. Whether self-consciously or not, they were rebels.

If a woman chose not to undergo the pain of childbirth or decided to deliver her offspring secretly and then kill it, why did she not take steps to abort it instead? Some women did. Early in the century the future wife of Henry Lake of Dorchester, while single, had used "means to destroy the fruit of her body" but could not "effect it." Later, accused of witchcraft, she confessed to the attempted murder of her fetal child as an explanation for her ill luck. Nevertheless, she was hanged as a witch between 1648 and 1656.[53] In 1667 Ruth Briggs of New Haven took savory in an effort to abort, and then killed the child after its birth. Apprehended, she was hanged for that crime. A third woman, Sarah Smith, made a similar unsuccessful attempt, then smothered the baby at its birth. When her neighbors found out what she had done, she "made the usual pretence, That the Child was born dead," and was also hanged.[54]

The woman who wished to abort may have tried any number of different techniques. Since physicians warned that "Running, Leaping, Lifting, immoderate Exercise," eating putrefied meat, starving oneself, emotional distress, riding in coaches, hot and cold baths, bleeding, strong purges, and vomits could produce a miscarriage, a woman might subject herself to all of these prohibitions in an effort to bring about a spontaneous abortion. Or she could keep herself in an emotionally frenzied state, as the experts held that fretting, hearty laughing, chiding, and even excessive joy could dislodge the fetus by drawing heat away from the womb.[55] Yet none of these methods were (or are) very effective. Furthermore, the pregnant woman had to deal with physicians' reminders that fevers, vomiting, convulsions, ulcerations, and hemorrhages accompanied abortions. In Gerard Van Swieten's words, "Abortions are far more hazardous and painful than mature and natural deliveries; because the embryo cannot be destroyed without great violence, whether it is done by medicaments, particular meats and drinks, fumigations, or any thing else whatsoever."[56]

The lack of effectiveness of seventeenth-century abortion techniques, coupled with warnings about their danger,[57] quite probably increased the feasibility of infanticide. In any event, the legal penalties were the same. Charles Chauncy wrote that the Bible contained "no express law against destroying conception in the womb by potions, yet by analogy . . . we may reason that life is to be given for life."[58]

It appears, then, that despite the patency of Puritan sex-role conditioning, New England women participated in any number of unfeminine activities. They killed their own offspring. They heaped contempt upon the authority of magistrates, ministers, and husbands. They fought, slandered, swore. They drank liquor until they could not walk in a straight line. They fornicated and sang wanton ditties. They defiled the Lord's Day by working. They picked pockets, burglarized dwellings, and escaped from prison.[59] Several of these "unfeminine" women had long histories of disorderly conduct. Their styles, geographic locales and social classes varied, as examinations of the lives of four such women will illustrate. But all were reacting, in very unfeminine fashion, to the exigencies of life in Calvinist New England.

Anne Hibbins, Wealthy Witch

Anne Hibbins, the wife of one Massachusetts Assistant, was a woman with a will of her own. In 1640, after one joiner charged her £13 for some work he had originally said would cost £2, she accused him and several other joiners of engaging in a conspiracy to set prices. Ten "neutral" arbiters were chosen to decide the case, including some of the Boston joiners. Mistress Hibbins objected that their decision could not be fair, since they were in "confederacy"; she suggested that truly neutral arbiters be chosen from joiners outside Boston. She then consulted one Salem joiner and some other persons, who informed her that the work in question was not worth half of what had been charged.[60]

Ignoring Mistress Hibbins's complaints of a carpenters' conspiracy, the Boston First Church elders denounced her for "great pride of spirit" and summoned her before the church, first for an admonition and then for excommunication. In these proceedings it soon became clear that Mistress Hibbins's primary offense was unsubmissive behavior. Sergeant Savage accused her of "transgressing the rule of the Apostle [Paul] in usurping authority over him whom God hath made her head and husband, and in taking the power and authority which God hath given to him out of his hands. And when he is satisfied and sits down contented, she is unsatisfied and will not be content, but will stir in it—as if she were able to manage it better than her husband, which is a plain breach of the rule of Christ." Other church members agreed that she made "a wisp" of her husband. John Cotton attacked her for thinking herself "more upright" than all the church, and for "exalting yourself against your guide and head—your husband I mean—when you should have submitted yourself." "You have scorned council and refused instruction,"

Cotton continued, "and have like a filthy swine trampled those pearls under your feet."[61]

In their zeal to reprimand a woman who was assuming too much independence, the church elders conveniently forgot one important fact: William Hibbins had given his wife "leave to order and carry on this business to her own satisfaction." Although admonished by the church, she did not let that body silence her. Instead, she carried on a public defense of herself, which led the elders to initiate excommunication proceedings. As Cotton phrased it, "with a restless and discontented spirit you have gone from person to person, from house to house, and from place to place, not only in this town but to other towns and persons out of this congregation; and [you] have vented your slanders and evil reports."[62]

The Boston church members disliked Anne Hibbins's outspokenness; they also found her lack of modesty (or, rather, abundance of self-possession) reprehensible. Over a decade and a half, enough public resentment mounted against her that she fell under suspicion of practicing witchcraft. Among other things, her habit of dressing very elaborately (even haughtily, in diamond rings, a black satin doublet, and "taffety" cloak) caused "*Vox populi*" to go "sore against her." A jury found her guilty of witchcraft, but the magistrates refused to consent to their verdict. The case was referred to the General Court, where, in 1656, the deputies agreed to hang her.[63]

Alice Thomas, Middle-Class Madam

Alice Thomas may have been in the audience on the day when Anne Hibbins was hanged. Thomas, a member of the "middling sort," did not have Anne Hibbins's money, but she did have some of that alleged witch's independent spirit. In 1662 Evan Thomas died, leaving a brewhouse, warehouse, wharf, and lands to his widow. Although he owed Thomas Clarke £38 for the land, Alice Thomas managed to pay Clarke that sum, along with a £3 12s. annual rental fee, within a year.[64] Since there is no evidence that she possessed any income separate from her husband's estate, and her brewhouse could not have returned a profit of £40 in one year, one wonders how she managed to discharge her deceased husband's obligation to Clarke. As later events revealed, she derived some income from assorted illegal activities.

A report of male laughter in Alice Thomas's brewhouse after the nine o'clock curfew led to an investigation by the authorities and her subsequent prosecution before the Suffolk County Court. That investigation disclosed that Thomas had knowingly purchased stolen goods, sold liquors without a license, profaned the Sabbath by dispensing alcohol, and "entertained" idle persons, youths, and servants. Moreover, it substantiated rumors that she was "a common Baud."' Indeed, Alice Thomas ran New England's first assignation house (i.e., a place where couples can come to engage in sexual activity).[65]

In January, 1672, the Suffolk County justices sentenced Thomas to pay £67 10s. 11d. to the owners of stolen goods found at her place of business, to pay a £50 fine to the county, to stand for an hour in public humiliation at the gallows with a rope around her neck, to be stripped to the waist at her gate and to be whipped there. That whipping was to be followed by the administration of not less than thirty-nine lashes as she walked from the gates of her home to the gates of the prison. The magistrates did not specify a time of imprisonment, instead leaving her term to the court's pleasure. At the same court, four men were punished for burglarizing warehouses, ketches, and cellars, Mary More and several other persons were also sentenced for fornication. Bostonians suspected some of the latter of "re-iterated whoredom," and we know that at least one suspect, More, frequented Alice Thomas's bawdy house. More had been observed there with Edward Naylor, a notorious adulterer.[66]

Less than a year after the sentencing of these sexual "rebels," the General Court in its October session enacted a law which directed that every "Baud, whore, or vile person" be whipped thirty lashes "as the cart's tail"' and kept at "hard fare and hard labour" for an indefinite term in the House of Correction. Once a week such incarcerated fornicators had to don hair frocks and blue caps and pull the city's offal cart down to the seaside for dumping.[67]

Alice Thomas spent three months in prison, and for six months thereafter she could travel abroad by day as long as she spent the hours between 6 P.M. and 8 A.M. safely locked up. Finally, in the same month when the General Court enacted its anti-prostitution measure, the deputies granted her liberty from any further restraint, but only if she "inhabit not in Boston." A different residence in Suffolk County did not, however, render her completely a law-abiding citizen. In 1673 the county magistrates ordered her to post £100 bond for selling alcohol to an Indian.[68]

For the next three years Thomas's behavior was tolerable, so the magistrates permitted her to return to Boston in 1676. Although she never appeared in court again on a criminal charge, she had not lost her unorthodox spirit. Between 1679 and 1695 she became Boston's most litigious woman initiating five different suits against various persons and winning all of them, collecting £176 15s. plus some good acreage.[69] Such suits undoubtedly helped her restore the losses incurred in her huge fine and restitution costs—losses which may have contributed to her taking out a £150 mortgage on her property in 1680.[70] Although troubled by lameness in her later years, Mistress Thomas managed to conduct a thriving business. In 1687 her income from real estate and trade amounted to £12, the average figure for a tradeswoman.[71]

Rachel Webster and Joan Andrews, Troublesome Women to the North

A third disorderly woman, Rachel Webster, never experienced the severe punishment that Alice Thomas and Anne Hibbins underwent. Yet, for two decades after her husband's death she continued to be a pesky, unfeminine thorn in the side of the Portsmouth, New Hampshire, authorities. Opening her ex-husband's inn to all sorts of unsavory people, she thrice faced prosecution for running a disorderly house (1663, 1669, 1670). She also appeared in court for profaning the Sabbath (1663), refusing to attend church on that day (1669), and being "naught[y] & unseemly" with a man (1670). She also fell under suspicion of fornication (1671). Since fines and admonitions failed to deter Rachel Webster from criminal activity, the New Hampshire authorities at last ordered the Portsmouth selectmen to "dispose of her into some good house of Government to Serviss & to worke & Labor." Placement with an overseer apparently had some impact, at least from the authorities' point of view. Webster only appeared in court once more, on a charge of drunkenness.[72]

Rachel Webster was a small-time "criminal" who only moderately violated her sex role. While Anne Hibbins was hanged, Alice Thomas faced the lash's sting, and Webster had her activities supervised by an overseer, the Maine woman who became perhaps the most continually contentious female of the century suffered very little punishment. For sheer number and variety of offenses committed, no one exceeded Joan Andrews of Kittery. Andrews was four times summoned before the local justices for heaping abuse upon individual men and women (1652, 1657, 1659, 1666);[73] nor were the authorities themselves safe from her spirited tongue. She disparaged a grand jury with threatening and reviling speeches (1653), attacked the governor (1651), and renounced the authority of one justice of the peace with the assertion that "shee Cared not a Toard [i.e., turd] for [Edward] Rishworth nor any Magestrate in the world" (1657).[74] Andrews cursed (1654, 1657), lied (1654), drank too much (1660), created contentions among her neighbors (1652), and stole goods from them (1654, 1657). Suspected of adultery on two occasions, she was also not above outright mischief (or fraud?), once selling an unsuspecting neighbor a firkin of butter in which she had placed two large stones.[75]

Joan Andrews's contemporaries might well have considered her little better than a witch. She herself once swore that she would sign an oath of fidelity to the Devil, become a witch, and take vengeance upon the community.[76] Maine, however, was not Massachusetts. Whereas Anne Hibbins paid the ultimate price for her disorderly conduct, the Kittery authorities left Joan Andrews relatively free to behave as she wished. Only three times did they sentence her to a whipping, and three other times penalize her with an admonition. The liberal frontier air of Maine allowed the bawdy Andrews to experience a measure of freedom which the more proper, semi-respectable Hibbins could not.

Female Criminals in Perspective

In 1831 Elizabeth Sanford explained, "There is something unfeminine in independence. It is contrary to Nature and so it offends."[77] Although she wrote two centuries after the arrival of the first Puritans in Massachusetts, she succinctly summed up their basic reaction to female criminal behavior. Such an assumption underpinned a rigidified process of sex-role conditioning and quite probably helped to keep female offenses down to only one-fifth of the total crimes.[78] Crime often involved a degree of aggressive, declarative, and controlling behavior, for which their conditioning little suited women. Still, many of the nearly 3,000 offenders indicated that the feminine ideal became a deadweight to their own predispositions and desires. On some level, women like Anne Hibbins, Alice Thomas, Rachel Webster, and Joan Andrews found being an ideal very "unnatural." Behaviorally, such women made constant declarations of independence—independence from Puritan law, magistracy, the church, sexual repression, modesty, passivity, maternity, and sex-role deference. Instead of internalizing their frus-

tration and becoming depressed, hysterical, or suicidal, these
women unleashed their alienation upon society and the persons
they chose to confront.

This is not to suggest that many female criminals or other unconventional women were overt rebels against the Puritan female ideal.
Many were reacting intuitively, spontaneously, in accord with
deeply felt personal needs, rather than as rebels who understood
the full implications of their protest. As psychologists have long
known, people often do not wish to grasp that which is painful to
them. Given the patency of their lifelong sex-role conditioning,
many women may therefore have attempted to rationalize or sub-
jectively deny the "unfemininity" of their own role violations. Lacking diaries or other accounts of their innermost thoughts, we cannot
now determine to what extent rebellious women understood the
social implications of their behavior.

However, at the same time we cannot simply assume that the
dissonance between belief and behavior lacked all cognitive impact,
especially when the authorities pointed specifically to that incongruity. In fact, the deviant women we know about certainly exhibited varying degrees of sex-role awareness. Anne Hibbins could
hardly have avoided viewing her own actions as out of tune with the
posited female norm, for the divines verbally assailed her with that
disharmony. Notwithstanding such "exposure," Hibbins refused to
alter her behavior, suggesting some level of cognitive, as well as
behavioral, independence. Six young women of Scotland, Connecticut, also apparently disapproved of the prevailing male superior–
female inferior polarity. These women mischievously, but in a
pointedly symbolic manner, constructed their pew in the meetinghouse higher than the men's pew—against the orders of the Scotland town fathers. The selectmen gave the maidens one month to
lower or forfeit the pew.[79] In yet another case, Boston women
rejected the equation of feminine modesty with female character.
After one man in 1707 told his mate that "a woman that had lost her
Modesty, was like Salt that had lost its savor; good for nothing but to
be cast to the Dunghill," seven or eight women called the man out of
bed at night, asking him to show them the way in the dark. With the
help of a Negro youth, they then "tore off his Cloaths and whip'd
him with Rods." The women soon after fled south to Rehoboth, but
the authorities managed to apprehend one of their number. This
rebel they sentenced to a whipping.[80]

It might be expected that women would sometimes protest not as rebels against their submissive condition, but as humane, nurturant individuals against the cruelty of an insensitive world. And protest they did. In 1676, for example, when a man was being hanged, one "mad woman" rushed out of the crowd and snatched away the rope. Her effort proved futile (the constable soon secured a new rope), but the woman had at least declared her feelings. In 1690 "sundry women of quality" expended much time and energy on behalf of the condemned pirate Tom Pounds, finally managing to secure a pardon for him. In 1704 Sam Sewall reported that, at one mass hanging of six persons in Boston, "there was such a Screech of the Women that my wife heard it sitting in our Entry next the Orchard, and was much surprised at it [s volume]."[81]

Thus, large numbers of women did express their discontent (whether sex-role related or not) in a variety of comparatively overt ways. Some literally exploded—abusing and killing, either symbolically or actually, colonial authority figures, husbands, neighbors, and their own unwanted offspring. Others disobeyed the orders of their masters, ran away, fornicated, stole, cheated, lied, committed adultery, and protested Puritan executions. Usually such rebels appear to have reacted personally, not ideologically, to the world in which they lived. We cannot now know how, or even if, they justified their behavior to themselves. We only know that the repressive force of Puritanism could not hold them totally in check.

1. G. Allport, *Pers. & Social Encounter*, p. 22.

2. Earle, *Child-Life in Col. Days*, p. 96.

3. James, James, & Boyer, eds., *Notable Am. Women*, II, 569–70.

4. Seaver, "Two Settlements of Taunton"; Morison, *Story of the "Old Colony*," p. 207.

5. The various authorities also prosecuted 44 other "witches" who did not, as far as we can tell, have contentious or otherwise unsavory reputations. See Appendix 5 for a complete list of New England "witches."

6. "N. London Ct. Rec.," *III*, 38; G. Dow, ed., *Essex Ct. Rec.*, V, 402–3.

7. F. Dexter, ed., *N. Haven Town Rec. 1649–62*, pp. 497–99; Hoadly, ed., *Rec. of N. Haven Col. 1653–Union*, p. 543.

8. F. Dexter, ed., *N. Haven Town Rec. 1649–62*, pp. 450–52.

9. "Mary Dudley to Margaret Winthrop, ca. Jan. 1635/6," in A. Forbes, ed., *Winthrop Papers*, III, 221.

10. "John Winter to Robert Trelawny, July 10, 1639," in J. Baxter, ed., *Doc. Hist. of Maine*, III, 166–68.

11. *Rec. of Conn. Particular Ct.*, p. 33.

12. *Ibid.*, pp. 43, 56; C. Mather, *Memorable Prov.*, pp. 61–63; J. Hale, *Modest Inquiry*, pp. 19–20.

13. *Rec. of Suffolk Ct. 1671–80*, I, 484; II, 1063.

14. J. Smith, ed., *Pynchon Ct. Rec.*, p. 375.

15. Josselyn, *Two Voyages to N. Eng.*, p. 28.

16. Noble, "Case of Maria"; C. Mather, *Magnalia*, II, 351; Green, "Slavery at Groton," p. 193.

17. G. Dow, ed., *Essex Ct. Rec.*, I, 275.

18. *Ibid.*, I, 378; VIII, 367.

19. Bourne, *Hist. of Wells & Kennebunk*, pp. 16–17.

20. Belknap, *Hist. of N. Hamp.*, I, 225.

21. Oberholzer, *Delinquent Saints*, p. 64; G. Dow, ed., *Essex Ct. Rec.*, I, 68; O. Hammond, ed., *N. Hamp. Ct. Rec. 1640–92*, p. 16.

22. Quotes from Shurtleff & Pulsifer, eds., *Plym. Rec.*, III, 159; Libby, Allen, & Moody, eds., *Maine Ct. Rec.*, I, 333.

23. Hamp. Ct. of "Gen. Sessions & Common Pleas, no. I, 1677–1728," p. 81; J. Smith, ed., *Pynchon Ct. Rec.*, p. 278; F. Dexter, ed., *N. Haven Town Rec. 1649–62*, I, 413–16.

24. G. Dow, ed., *Essex Ct. Rec.*, I, 44; Willard quoted in Earle, *Sabbath in N. Eng.*, p. 71.

25. Whitmore, ed., *Col. Laws of Mass.*, p. 206; "Pownall Epitaphs."

26. G. Dow, ed., *Essex Ct. Rec.*, VIII, 327; "N. Hamp. Ct. Papers," IX (1685–87): 313; Hamp. Ct. of "Gen. Sessions & Common Pleas, no. 1, 1677–1728," p. 42.

27. G. Dow, ed., *Essex Ct. Rec.*, VI, 295; Noble & Cronin, eds., *Rec. of Mass. Assts.*, I, 358; "Hartford Ct. Rec.," in "Conn. Rec.," LVI, 95.

28. C. Mather, *Decennium Luctuosum*, pp. 138–43.

29. I. Mather, "Diary," p. 405; Axtell, "Vengeful Women of Marblehead."

30. Hubbard, *Gen. Hist. of N. Eng.*, VI, 422; Winthrop, *Journal*, II, 60–61; Noble & Cronin, eds., *Rec. of Mass. Assts.*, II, 126.

31. G. Dow, ed., *Essex Ct. Rec.*, I, 6, 9; Noble & Cronin, eds., *Rec. of Mass. Assts.*, II, 78; Winthrop, *Journal*, I, 282–83; Bentley, "Description & Hist. of Salem," p. 252; Perley, *Hist. of Salem*, II, 52; "Rec. Ct. of Assts. & Superior Ct. 1687–1715," in "Conn. Rec." LVIII, 11–12, 19.

32. See Appendix 4.

33. Dunton, "Letter to George Larkin, Mar. 25, 1686," in Dunton, *Letters*, p. 72; L. Hammond, "Diary," p. 169.

34. Sewall, *Diary*, I, 103.

35. *Acts & Laws, Passed by Mass. Gen. Ct.* (1692), p. 23; J. Trumbull, ed., *Conn. Rec.*, IV, 285; *Acts & Laws, Passed by N. Hamp. Gen. Ct.*, p. 42.

36. S. Bradstreet, "Journal," p. 44; Mass. "Superiour Ct. of Judicature, 1686–1700," pp. 49–50.

37. Pike, "Journal," p. 134.

38. C. Mather, *Magnalia*, II, 363–65; Marshall, "Diary," p. 153. An occasional woman did, of course, experience great remorse and penitence for her deed. See *Magnalia*, II, 348, 363–64.

39. Van Swieten, *Commentaries*, XII, 452.

40. Langer, "Infanticide," pp. 55–67; Ryan, *Infanticide*.

41. Bloch, "Feelings That Kill"; Asch, "Depression," pp. 166–69; Chapman, "Obsessions of Infanticide"; Rheingold, *Fear of Being a Woman*, passim.

42. *Hist. of Educ. Quart.*, III, 462.

43. Fiske, *Notebook*, p. 207.

44. Chapman, "Obsessions of Infanticide."

45. Rheingold, *Fear of Being a Woman*, p. 37.

46. Rheingold, *Mother, Anxiety, & Death*, p. 126.

47. All of the many English childbirth guides mention the mother's position for delivery. For some discussion of the negative aspects of the prone position, see Boston Women's Health Book Coll., *Our Bodies, Our Selves*, pp. 277–78.

48. Sewall, *Diary*, I, 349, 379; Noble & Cronin, eds., *Rec. Mass. Assts.*, I, 357; C. Mather, *Magnalia*, II, 364.

49. Drake, *Annals of Witchcraft*, pp. 66–67, 226–27. In her second pregnancy Mary Parsons complained of a pain like "the pricking of Knives" in her neck, on her left shoulder, under her left breast, and about her heart. She experienced such "lamentable Torment" that a neighbor feared for Mary's life, saying, "I never saw a Woman in such a Condition in Child Bed, for she could not lie downe in her Bed, neather doe I aperhend that she had any other Kind of Sicknesse, but that prickling Paine." A prickling pain is one of the symptoms frequently seen in women suffering conversion hysteria reactions.

50. *Boston News-Letter*, Jan. 15–22, 1705, in Weeks & Bacon, eds., *Hist. Digest of Prov. Press*, p. 160.

51. "Ct. Files—Suffolk Co.," V (1663), no. 605; Noble & Cronin, eds., *Rec. of Mass. Assts.*, I, 29; "Mass. Arch., LX: Maritime Affairs," p. 279; C. Mather, *Magnalia*, II, 362.

52. Rheingold, *Mother, Anxiety, & Death*, pp. 128–29.

53. J. Hale, *Modest Inquiry*, pp. 17–18.

54. "Conn. Arch.: Crimes & Misd.," 1st ser., I, 32–33; C. Mather, *Magnalia*, II, 364–65.

55. Culpeper, *Dir. for Midwives*, p. 146; Guillemeau, *Child-Birth*, pp. 22–23; *Problemes of Aristotle*, pp. F3–4.

56. Van Swieten, *Commentaries*, XII, 454.

57. Indeed, many of these potions—the same ones used for menstrual irregularity—were dangerous. See ch. 3.

58. "Opinions of Three Ministers on Unnatural Vice, 1642," in Bradford, *Of Plym. Plant.*, p. 411.

59. Sarah Hales broke out of the Boston prison in 1641, and Mary Saywood ran away from a private place of internment in Maine in 1683 (Noble & Cronin, eds., *Rec. of Mass. Assts.*, II, 109; Libby, Allen, & Moody, eds., *Maine Ct. Rec.*, III, 176).

60. "Proc. of Excommunication against A. Hibbins," in Demos, ed., *Remarkable Prov.*, pp. 221–39.

61. *Ibid.*

62. *Ibid.*

63. Weeden, *Econ. & Social Hist. of N. Eng.*, I, 229; Hubbard, *Gen. Hist. of N. Eng.*, V, 174.

64. *Suffolk Deeds*, V, 374, 480.

65. The Suffolk County Court's charge that Alice Thomas was guilty "of giving frequent secret and vnseasonable Entertainmᵗ in her house to Lewd Lascivious & notorious persons of both Sexes, giving them oppertunity to

commit carnal wickedness" more strongly suggests that she was maintaining a house of assignation than a brothel. See *Rec. of Suffolk Ct. 1671–80*, I, 82–83.

66. *Ibid.*, pp. 83–85, 87–88; Hull, "Memoir & Diaries," p. 232; Noble & Cronin, eds., *Rec. of Mass. Assts.*, III, 226.

67. Shurtleff, ed., *Mass. Rec.*, IV, pt. 2, p. 513.

68. *Rec. of Suffolk Ct. 1671–80*, I, 126, 266.

69. *Ibid.*, II, 721, 1071; Hist. Rec. Survey, *Abstract & Index of Suffolk Ct. 1680–98*, pp. 48, 51, 80, 90.

70. *Suffolk Deeds*, XI, 326–28.

71. *Rec. of Suffolk Ct. 1671–80*, I, 339; "Tax List & Schedules—1687," in Boston Rec. Cmrs., *First Rep.*, p. 100.

72. O. Hammond, ed., *N. Hamp. Ct. Rec. 1640–92*, pp. 184, 253, 259, 269, 289; "N. Hamp. Ct. Papers," I, pt. 1 (1659–72), p. 279.

73. Libby, Allen, & Moody, eds., *Maine Ct. Rec.*, II, 52, 82, 176, 264.

74. *Ibid.*, I, 164; II, 12, 52.

75. *Ibid.*, I, 165, 176; II, 22, 27, 31, 52, 55, 92–93.

76. *Ibid.*, II, 52.

77. Sanford, *Woman*, p. 13.

78. This proportion is based on a total of 12,149 male and 3,276 female offenses.

79. Earle, *Sabbath in N. Eng.*, pp. 53–54.

80. Sewall, *Diary*, II, 194.

81. I. Mather, "Diary," p. 404; Bullivant, "Journal," p. 104; Sewall, *Diary*, II, 110.

VIII

The Weaker Sex as Religious Rebel:
From Williams through Hutchinson

Long before the emergence of a feminist "movement,"
there had always been some women who felt the need for
greater intellectual activity than was required by their
domestic tasks.

—Aileen S. Kraditor, ed., *Up from the Pedestal*

AS MIGHT BE EXPECTED IN A PARTICULARLY RELIGIOUS CENTURY, MANY
women's searches for power—for control over their own lives and
for impact upon others—had important religious components. Like
their Puritan contemporaries, the Antinomians, Gortonists, Anabaptists, and Quakers tied themselves to the absolute power of God
and interpreted the Bible in accordance with their own needs. Both
Puritans and heretics used religion to order their realities in some
coherent, comprehensive way. The relatively powerless Calvinists
of Old England and the heretics of New England tied themselves to
theologies which became sounding boards for grievances about
society. Religion justified unorthodox behavior. It offered the powerless a link with God, the incarnation of power; it solidified conviction and provided the security of knowing that one's deeply felt
needs were permissible.

Women, in particular, were susceptible to the lure of heresy.
Cotton Mather related, "It is the mark of [religious] seducers that
they lead captive silly women" into sin because the "'weaker sex' is
more easily gained by the devil." "Indeed," he wrote, "a poyson
does never insinuate so quickly, nor operate so strongly, as when
women's milk is the vehicle wherein 'tis given."[1] Female weakness

served as an easy explanation of why there were so many woman heretics, and Mather did not (*could* not) look at some of the broader reasons for their participation in the century's various religious "movements." However, the modern researcher, unfettered by seventeenth-century expectations, can do so.

From Williams to Hutchinson

New England's first influential religious rebel was Roger Williams, the Salem minister who infuriated Massachusetts authorities by preaching that the civil magistrate ought to stay out of church affairs, that Indians were the rightful owners of the New World land, that more humility was needed in Puritan churches, that forced worship "stinks in God's nostrils," and that each person ought to be allowed the liberty to believe as conscience dictated.[2] Williams developed some following at Salem, especially among the devout, church-going women, several of whom separated from the church there. Jane Verin, Mary Oliver, Margery Reeves, and maidservant Margery Holliman refused to worship with the congregation from 1635 to 1638, and the latter two women denied that the churches of the Bay Colony were true churches.[3]

Why these women adopted Williams's theology is a matter for speculation, since none of his female followers left records explaining his appeal, and Williams himself felt that women were by nature unfit for preaching, governing, or other "Manly Actions and Employments."[4] However, we can infer that this theology offered women certain privileges and compensations. Williams's belief that Puritans ought to humble themselves before God in sackcloth and ashes had, theoretically, special meaning for women. An emphasis on humility celebrated and raised to a position of some "power" that which was the female sex's "natural" condition. Reducing men to such a level of visually apparent humility eased the power gap between men and women; furthermore, it served as practical testimony of the equality of the sexes before God. Women could also interpret Williams's constant defense of liberty of conscience to mean that choice of a belief system was their individual prerogative—an act of intellectual and spiritual freedom. In a world where female freedom was carefully curbed, where women were to ask their husbands and fathers for religious guidance, liberty of conscience had revolutionary implications. To be free to believe was the first step in becoming free to do as one wished.

Williams did not really grasp the full implications of his religious pronouncements; nor apparently did his female followers, at least on a conscious intellectual level. No female leader emerged to channel the energies of the Salem women against the authority of Puritan society. On the contrary, Williams's female followers contented themselves with such minimal protest that the Salem authorities did not even see fit to punish them. At the time of Williams's abrupt departure in January, 1636, the Bay Colony women had not expressed any discontent about Puritanism or their stereotyped sex-role conditioning. That situation soon changed, however, and with the marked increase of Antinomian sentiment in Boston and Anne Hutchinson's powerful example of resistance, the distressed females of Massachusetts discovered how to channel their deeply felt frustrations into a viable theological form and to rebel openly against the spiritual and secular status quo. Since they had only a rudimentary consciousness of what they were doing, Antinomian women could embrace a belief system which actually minimized the importance of individual action, for Antinomians felt that salvation could be demonstrated only by the individual experiencing God's grace within.[5]

The issue of the relative importance of good works (i.e., individual effort) and grace (i.e., God's effort) in preparing man for salvation nagged English Calvinists from their earliest origins and engendered a sizable amount of theological debate. In New England, John Cotton, the teacher of the Boston Church, opened a Pandora's box when "he warned his listeners away from the specious comfort of preparation [through good works] and reemphasized the covenant of grace as something in which God acted alone and unassisted."[6] When Cotton directed his congregation "not to be afraid of the word Revelation," the elders of the Bay Colony feared that "Revelation" might be dangerously construed to invalidate biblical law.[7]

The elders' fears were justified in that respect, because Bostonians of every rank, age, and sex enthusiastically supported the notion of personal revelation and solicited converts to an emerging, loosely knit ideology which the divines pejoratively called Antinomianism, Opinionism, or Familism.[8] The authorities were shocked to hear Antinomian principles defended at military trainings, in town meetings, and before the various courts. They complained that all of society's institutions—church, state, and family —were being "turned upside down among us."[9] That such turmoil should result from a turning to revelation was only natural, for many individuals and groups were hungry for power in Puritan New England. It was easy for each potential rebel to perceive the operation of God's grace upon his or her own soul, and to use that perception to consecrate a personal rebellion against contemporary authorities and institutions. Women in particular used a feeling of the inward-dwelling Holy Spirit to castigate various authorities: magistrates as guardians of the state, ministers as guardians of the church, and their husbands as guardians of the home. As the most outspoken of these female rebels, Anne Hutchinson spread her opinions among all social classes through contacts made in the course of her midwifery, and in biweekly teaching sessions at her home. Thomas Weld believed her lectures responsible for distributing "the venome of these [Antinomian] opinions into the very veines and vitalls of the People in the Country." Indeed, she was soon called "the leader" and "the prime seducer of the whole faction."[10]

A Women's Rebellion

Many women identified with Anne Hutchinson's rebellious intellectual stance and aggressive spirit. Edward Johnson wrote that "the weaker sex" set her up as "a Priest" and "thronged" after her. Soon after his arrival in late 1636, Johnson met "a little nimble tongued Woman" who "said she could bring me acquainted with one of her own Sex that would shew me a way, if I could attaine it, even Revelations, full of such ravishing joy that I should never have cause to be sorry for sinne, so long as I live, and as for her part shee had attained it already." John Underhill reported he daily heard a "clamor" that "New England men usurp over their wives, and keep them in servile subjection." Governor Winthrop blamed Hutchinson for causing "divisions between husband and wife . . . till the weaker give place to the stronger, otherwise it turnes to open contention," and Weld charged the Antinomians with using the yielding, flexible, and tender women as "an Eve, to catch their husbands also." One anonymous English pamphleteer found in Antinomianism a movement "somewhat like the Trojan horse for rarity" because "it was covered with womens aprons, and bolstered out with the judgement and deep discerning of the godly and reverent."[11]

From late 1636 to early 1637 the expression of female discontent ascended to a higher pitch in the Boston church. At one point, when pastor John Wilson rose to preach, Hutchinson left the congregation; many women followed her out of the meetinghouse. Because these women "pretended many excuses for their going out," it was impossible for the authorities to convict them of contempt for Wilson. Other rebels did, however, challenge the pastor's words as he spoke them, causing Weld to comment, "Now the faithfull Ministers of Christ must have dung cast on their faces and be no better than Legall Preachers, Baals Priests, Popish Factors, Scribes, Pharisees, and Opposers of Christ himselfe."[12]

Included among these church rebels were two particularly active women, Jane Hawkins and Mary Dyer, both of whom Winthrop found obnoxious. The governor considered the youthful wife of William Dyer to be "of a very proud spirit," "much addicted to revelations," and "notoriously infected with Mrs. Hutchinson's errors."[13] The other was no more agreeable: Winthrop denounced Hawkins as being "notorious for familiarity with the devill" because, in her capacity as a midwife, she dispensed fertility potions to barren women and occasionally fell into a trancelike state in which she spoke Latin. The General Court, sharing the governor's apprehension, on March 12, 1638, forbade Hawkins to question "matters of religion" or "to meddle" in "surgery, or phisick, drinks, plaisters or oyles." She apparently disobeyed that order, for three years later the deputies banished her from the colony under the penalty of a severe whipping or such other punishment as the judges thought fit.[14]

Other women, both rich and poor, involved themselves in the Antinomian struggle. William Coddington's spouse, like her merchant husband, was "taken with the familistical opinions." Mary Dummer, wife of the wealthy landowner and Assistant Richard Dummer, convinced her husband to move from Newbury to Boston so that she might be closer to Hutchinson.[15] Mary Oliver, a poor Salem calenderer's wife, and onetime supporter of Williams, reportedly exceeded Anne "for ability of speech, and appearance of zeal and devotion." According to Winthrop, Mary Oliver might "have done hurt, but that she was poor and had little acquaintance [with theology]." This Salem rebel held the "dangerous" opinions that the church was managed by the "heads of the people, both magistrates and ministers, met together," instead of by the people themselves, and that anyone professing faith in Christ ought to be admitted to the church and the sacraments. Between 1638 and 1650 she appeared before the magistrates six times for making remarks contemptuous of ministerial and magisterial authority; for these offenses she experienced the stocks, the lash, the placement of a cleft stick on her tongue, and imprisonment. One Salem magistrate became so frustrated with Oliver's refusal to respect his authority that he put her in the stocks without a trial. She sued him for false arrest, collecting a minimal ten shillings in damages. Her victory was short lived, however, and before she left the Bay Colony in 1650 she had managed to secure herself some reputation as a witch.[16]

Mary Oliver and the other female rebels could easily identify with the Antinomian ideology, because its theological emphasis on the individual's inability to achieve salvation echoed women's inability to achieve recognition on a socio-political level. As a woman realized that she could receive wealth, power, and status only through a man—her father or her husband—so the Antinomian realized that he or she could receive grace only through God's beneficence. However, Antinomianism's accentuated condition of dependency was also its great appeal, because in the "new" theology *both* men and women were relegated, vis-á-vis God, to the status that women occupied in Puritan society vis-á-vis men: that is, to the status of malleable inferiors in the hands of a higher being. All power emanated from God, respecting no sex, rather than from male authority figures striving to interpret the Divine Word. Fortified by a consciousness of the Holy Spirit's inward dwelling, the Antinomians could rest secure and self-confident in the belief that they were mystically experiencing the transcendent power of the Almighty, a power far beyond anything mere magistrates and ministers could muster. Antinomianism could not secure for women such practical earthly items as sizable estates, professional success, and participation in the church and civil government, but it provided compensation by reducing the significance of these powers for men. Viewed from this perspective, Antinomianism accomplished what Williams's theology had strongly hinted at, extending the feminine experience of humility to both sexes (although not through the vehicle of sackcloth and ashes). That, in turn, paradoxically created the possibility of feminine pride, as Anne Hutchinson's dynamic example amply demonstrates.

One Woman before the Judges

Anne Hutchinson's example caused the divines much frustration. They were chagrined to find that she was not content simply to repeat to the "simple Weomen"[17] the sermons of John Wilson;

rather, she chose to interpret and even question the content of those sermons. When she charged that the Bay Colony ministers did not teach a covenant of grace as "clearly" as Cotton and her brother-in-law John Wheelwright, she was summoned in 1636 to appear before a convocation of the clergy. At this convocation, and in succeeding examinations, the ministers found particularly galling her implicit assertion that she was intellectually able to judge the biblical truth of their theology. Such an assertion threatened their collective self-image as the community's intellectual leaders and as the spokesmen for a male-dominated society. The ministers and magistrates therefore sharply criticized Anne for not fulfilling her ordained womanly role. In September, 1637, a synod of elders resolved that women might meet "to pray and edify one another"; however, when one woman "in a prophetical way" resolved questions of doctrine and expounded Scripture, the meeting was "disorderly." At Anne's examination on November 7 and 8, Winthrop began by charging that she criticized the ministers and maintained a "meeting and an assembly in your house that hath been condemned by the general assembly as a thing not tolerable nor comely in the sight of God nor fitting for your sex." Later in the interrogation Winthrop accused her of disobeying her "parents," the magistrates, in violation of the Fifth Commandment, and paternalistically told her, "We do not mean to discourse with those of your sex." Hugh Peter, the Salem Pastor, also indicated that Anne was not fulfilling the properly submissive, non-intellectual feminine role. He ridiculed her choice of a female preacher of the Isle of Ely as a model for her own behavior and told her to consider "that you have stept out of your place, *you have rather bine a Husband than a Wife and a preacher than a Hearer; and a Magistrate than a Subject.*"[18]

When attacked for behavior inappropriate to her sex, Anne Hutchinson demonstrated (sometimes coyly, sometimes pointedly) that she was the intellectual equal of her accusers. She tried to trap Winthrop when he charged her with dishonoring her "parents": "But put the case Sir that I do fear the Lord and my parents, may not I entertain them that fear the Lord because my parents will not give me leave?" To provide a biblical justification for her teaching activities, she cited Titus' rule (2:3-4) "that the elder women should instruct the younger." Winthrop ordered her to take that rule "in the sense that elder women must instruct the younger about their [women's] business, and to love their husbands." But Anne disagreed with this interpretation, saying, "I do not conceive but that it is meant for some publick times." Winthrop rejoined, "We must. . . . restrain you from maintaining this course," and she qualified, "If you have a rule for it from God's word you may." Her resistance infuriated the governor, who exclaimed, "We are your judges, and not you ours." When Winthrop tried to lure her into admitting that she taught men, in violation of Paul's proscription (I Timothy 2:11-2),[19] Anne replied that she thought herself justified in teaching a man who asked her for instruction, and added sarcastically, "Do you think it not lawful for me to teach women . . . [then] why do you call me to teach the court?"[20]

Hutchinson soon realized that sarcastic remarks would not persuade the court of the legitimacy of her theological claims. Alternatively, therefore, she affected a modest style to cozen the authorities. But, at the same time, she expressed a kind of primitive feminism through double-entendre statements, and by attacking the legitimacy of Paul's idea of the nonspeaking, non-intellectual female churchmember. When the court charged her with "prophesying," Anne responded, "The men of Berea are commended for examining *Pauls* Doctrine; wee do no more [in our meetings] but read the notes of our teachers Sermons, and then reason of them by searching the Scriptures."[21] Such a statement was, on one level, an "innocent" plea to the divines that the women were only following biblical prescription. On another level it was an attack on the ministers for presuming to have the final word on biblical interpretation. On yet a third level, since she focused on "Paul's Doctrine" and reminded "men" that they should take another look at that teaching, her statement suggested that ministerial attitudes toward the "place" of women ought to be reexamined.

At another point, Anne responded to Winthrop's criticism with another statement which had meaning on three levels. The governor had accused her of traducing the ministers and magistrates and, when summoned to answer this charge, of saying that "the fear of man was a snare and therefore she would not be affeared of them." She replied, "They say I said the fear of man is a snare, why should I be afraid. When I came unto them, they urging many things unto me and I being backward to answer at first, at length this scripture came into my mind 29th Prov. 15. The fear of man bringeth a snare, but who putteth his trust in the Lord shall be safe."[22] Again her response was phrased as an "innocent" plea to God to assuage her fears, while at the same time it implied that God was on her side, in opposition to the ministers and magistrates. Her statement also assured women that, if they trusted in God and relied on his grace for support, they need not fear men, for such fear trapped them into being "backward" about reacting in confrontations with men.

Although she was aware of the "backwardness" of women as a group, Anne did not view intensified group activity as a remedy for woman's downtrodden status. Her feminism consisted essentially of the recognition of her own strength and gifts, and the apparent belief that other women could come to the same recognition. A strong, heroic example of female self-assertiveness was necessary for one to develop this recognition of her own personal strength; as Anne was a strong example for the other discontented women of Massachusetts, so she had chosen a woman preacher on the Isle of Ely as her own particular heroic model. She did, Hugh Peter chided, "exceedingly magnifie" that preacher "to be a Womane of 1000 hardly any like to her." Anne could thus dissociate herself from the "divers worthy and godly Weomen" of the Bay Colony and confidently deride them as being no better than "soe many Jewes," unconverted by the light of Christ.[23] Other Massachusetts women who wished to reach beyond the conventional, stereotypic behavior of "worthy and godly Weomen" attached themselves to the emphatic example of Anne, and to God's ultimate power, in order to resist the constraints which they felt as Puritan women.

Fearful that other women might imitate Hutchinson, the divines wished to catch her in a major theological error and subject her to public punishment. Their efforts were not immediately successful. Throughout her 1637 examination Anne managed to parry the verbal thrusts of the ministers and magistrates by replying to their many questions with queries of her own, forcing them to justify their positions from the Bible, pointing out their logical inconsistencies, and using innuendo to cast aspersions upon their authoritarianism. With crucial assistance from the sympathetic John Cotton, she left the ministers with no charge to level against her. Female intellectuality was not a prosecutable offense, and she was winning the debate when, in an apparently incautious moment, she gave the authorities the kind of declaration for which they had been hoping. Raising herself to the position of judge over her accusers, she asserted, "I know that for this you goe about to doe to me, God will ruine you and your posterity, and this whole State." Asked how she knew this, she explained, "By an immediate revelation."[24] That was too much for the ministers. They were convinced of her heresy and took steps to expose her in excommunication proceedings before the Boston church, hoping thereby to expel a heretic from their midst, to reestablish support for the Puritan way, to prevent unrest in the state and the family, and, in the process, to shore up their own anxious egos.

The ministers' predisposition to defame Hutchinson before the congregation caused them to ignore what she was actually saying in her excommunication trial. Although she did describe a relationship with Christ which was closer than anything Cotton had envisioned, she did not believe she had experienced Christ's Second Coming in her own life. Such a claim would have denied the resurrection of the body at the Last Judgment, and would have clearly stamped her as a Familist.[25] Anne's accusers, ignoring Thomas Leverett's reminder that she had expressed belief in the resurrection, argued that, if the resurrection did not exist, biblical law would have no validity and the marriage covenant would lack all legal or utilitarian value. The result would be a kind of world which no Puritan could tolerate, a world where the basest desires would be fulfilled and "foule, groce, filthye and abominable" sexual promiscuity would run rampant. Cotton, smarting from a psychological slap Anne had given him earlier in the excommunication proceedings[26] and in danger of losing the respect of the other ministers, admonished her with these words: "though I have not herd, nayther do I thinke, you have bine unfaythfull to your Husband in his Marriage Covenant, *yet that will follow upon it*." By referring to "his" marriage covenant, Cotton did not even accord Anne equal participation in the making of that covenant. The Boston teacher concluded his admonition with a criticism of Anne's pride: "I have often feared the highth of your Spirit and being puft up with your owne parts."[27]

Cotton believed the woman who thought for herself would not choose to respect her husband's power over her, or his right to the exclusive use of her body. Many women used adultery as a way to get back at their husbands; so Cotton apparently feared that indiscriminate sexual relations would be the necessary consequence of the extension of freedom to the female sex. Such an imputation in all likelihood shocked Anne Hutchinson, who enjoyed a close relationship with her own husband, William, and had borne fifteen children by him.

The introduction of the sexual issue into the trial, and Cotton's denunciation of Hutchinson, must have curbed dissent from the congregation. Few Puritans would want to defend Anne in public when such a defense could be construed as supporting promiscuity and adultery. Since Cotton had earlier been sympathetic to the Antinomian cause, and had tried to save Anne at her 1637 examination, his vigorous condemnation of her probably confused her followers. Cotton even went so far as to exempt male Antinomians from any real blame for the controversy when he characterized Antinomianism as a women's delusion. He urged that women be watched, like children; he reproved Hutchinson's sons for not controlling her theological ventures; and he called those sons "Vipers . . . [who] Eate through the very Bowells of your Mother, to her Ruine." Cotton warned the Boston women "to looke to your selves and to take heed that you reaceve nothinge for Truth which hath not the stamp of the Word of God [as interpreted by the ministers] . . . for you see she [Anne] is but a Woman and many unsound and dayngerous principles are held by her." Thomas Shepard, the Cambridge minister, agreed that intellectual activity did not suit women and warned the congregation that Anne was likely "to seduce and draw away many, Espetially simple Weomen of her owne sex."[28]

Because of Paul's injunction against women speaking in church, the female church members, who would have had good reason to resent the clergy's castigation of Hutchinson and themselves, could not legitimately object to the excommunication proceedings. They had been spoken to as if they were children, but, lacking a clearly defined feminist consciousness and filled with "backward" fear, the women could not ignore that injunction. Their heroic model had been presented by the clergy as the epitome of despicableness, a woman of simple intellect and a liar, puffed up with pride and verging on sexual promiscuity. Although five men rose to defend Anne, their objections were dismissed as arising out of self-interest or misguided affection for her.[29]

In Anne's excommunication proceedings the ministers demonstrated that they had found the means to deal effectively with a rebellious woman and a somewhat hostile congregation. At her examination and her excommunication trial, Anne attempted to place the ministers on the defensive by questioning them and forcing them to justify their positions, while she herself explained little. She achieved some success in the 1637 trial, but before her fellow church members a few months later she found it difficult to counteract the misrepresentation of her beliefs and the attack on her character. Perhaps fearing the banishment which had been so quickly imposed on her associate, John Wheelwright, she recanted, but even then she did not totally compromise her position. She expressed sorrow for her errors of expression, but admitted no errors in judgment and assumed no appearance of humiliation. When Wilson commanded her "as a Leper to withdraw your selfe out of the Congregation," Anne rose, walked to the meetinghouse door, accepted Mary Dyer's offered hand, and turned to impugn her accusers' power: "The Lord judgeth not as man judgeth, better to be cast out of the Church then [sic] to deny Christ."[30]

Aftermath

In the years following Hutchinson's excommunication and banishment, the Massachusetts ministers and magistrates prosecuted several other women who had been infected by her rebellious spirit. In April, 1638, soon after Anne left for the wilderness of Rhode Island, the Boston church cast out Judith Smith, the maidservant of William Hutchinson's brother Edward, for her "obstinate persisting" in "sundry Errors." On October 10 of the same year, the Assistants ordered Katherine Finch to be whipped for "speaking against the magistrates, against the Churches, and against the Elders." Less than a year later Finch again appeared before the Assistants, this time for not carrying herself "dutifully to her husband," and was released upon promise of reformation. In September, 1639, the Boston church excommunicated Phillip(a?) Hammond "as a Slaunderer and revyler both of the Church and the Common Weale." After her husband's death she had resumed her maiden name, operated a business in Boston, and argued in her shop and at public meetings "that Mrs. Hutchinson neyther deserved the Censure which was putt upon her in the Church, nor in the Common Weale." The Boston church also excommunicated the outspoken Anne Hibbins, largely because she was allegedly not behaving as a submissive wife (1641), and expelled from membership two other women who partially imitated Anne Hutchinson's example: Sarah Keayne was found guilty in 1646 of "irregular prophesying in mixed assemblies," and Joan Hogg nine years later was punished for "her disorderly singing and her idleness, and for saying she is commanded of Christ so to do."[31]

The Salem authorities followed Boston's example in dealing with overly assertive women. In late 1638 the Salem church excommunicated the four female followers of Roger Williams who had separated themselves from the congregation there.[32] In October, 1637, the Essex County Court ordered Dorothy Talby of Salem chained to a post "for frequent laying hands on her husband to the danger of his life, and contemning the authority of the court"; later it ordered her whipped for "misdemeanors against her husband." In mid-1638 Talby claimed a "revelation from heaven" instructed her to kill her husband and children; she did kill one child, and was hanged for it. Hugh Peter prevented Antinomianism from having much impact upon Salem by arguing that Talby's adoption of Anne Hutchinson's claim of "immediate revelation" demonstrated the error and the sinful character of that theology.[33]

It is difficult to know how many of these female rebels were primitive feminists, that is, women who consciously recognized that sexual inequities existed in society, found those inequities objectionable, and protested against them by design. A woman like Phillipa Hammond, who resumed her maiden name and defended Anne Hutchinson, can be seen as a primitive feminist. Those women who violated the sexual norms of Puritan society by abusing their husbands, speaking out in church, arguing abstruse points of theology, and attacking the authority of the ministers and the magistrates probably realized that their own behavior was incongruous with their sex-role conditioning, especially when the authorities reminded them of it in church and court. The cognitive dissonance which resulted from such realizations led the discontented women to clamor that their husbands kept them in " servile subjection." However, venting of frustrations could in many cases have been totally unreflective, for unfeminine behavior need not always lead to feminism. Rather, the explosion of powerful, alienated feeling may simply have occurred at a time when Antinomian agitation had established a mood for the expression of that feeling. At those times when feminism—primitive or otherwise—is a matter of some public concern, that fact tends to stimulate female rebellion. (In more contemporary times there seems to be a connection between the popularity of the women's movement and the sharp increase in the number of female criminals, although those offenders would not likely see themselves as liberationists.[34])

An examination of the criminals appearing before the General Court and the Court of Assistants suggests that the activity of the Antinomian women did increase the number of female defendants who appeared before those courts. This increase is probably the result of two factors: a greater rebelliousness in women, and a hardened magisterial attitude. Between 1630 and 1634 only two of the 115 offenders were female; both were prosecuted for sexual indiscretions. During the heyday of Antinomianism, the number of female offenders was significantly higher—22 women (7.2% of the criminals) in 1635–39. Since the female percentage of the population remained stable,[35] this increase suggests that by 1640 the magistrates could no longer afford to dismiss with verbal chastisement those females who were guilty of drunkenness, cursing, or premarital fornication. For example, between 1630 and 1639 only two women were punished for fornication or enticement to the same. Because the male was considered the active, initiatory agent and the female the passive, yielding participant, women who became pregnant and then married their children's fathers did not experience the whippings or fines which their husbands received. After the assertiveness of many women in the Antinomian and post-Antinomian days proved to the authorities that the weaker sex was too often refusing to play the submissive role, magistrates apparently came to believe that women had to be held accountable for their actions, especially regarding sex. Haunted by the specter of "foule, groce, filthye and abominable" promiscuity, the authorities began prosecuting and punishing both parties to premarital sexual liaisons. From 1640 through 1644, 21 men and 12 women were so punished, increasing the percentage of female offenders to 9 percent of the total.

Not only did the number and percentage of female offenders increase, but the crimes they committed were sometimes quite serious. Six women were tried for contempt of the religious or civil authorities between 1635 and 1644, and three attempted to kill their children or husbands. Four females proved their lack of feminine modesty by swearing; six abused their husband's sexual prerogative through adultery or behaving in an adulterous way; one was guilty of abusive carriage; seven were punished for thievery; one broke out of jail; yet another ran away from a master whom she disliked.

It is difficult to assess the impact of Antinomianism on life in the Bay Colony because the early records of the Suffolk County Court (where most Antinomians would have been tried) no longer exist, and female Antinomians were not usually summoned before the court justices. Of the sixteen females described in this book as Antinomians or women in some way directly affected by Antinomianism, only five appeared before the General Court or the Court of Assistants between 1636 and 1644. Eight were punished only by the church, and another three—Dummer, Dyer, and Coddington —received no punishment at all.[36]

The Massachusetts ministers and magistrates did, however, take special care to ensure that Antinomianism would be rooted out of the Bay Colony. The threat of a humiliating courtroom appearance and a possible whipping was designed to keep Antinomians quiet. When Anne Hutchinson's son-in-law William Collins and son Francis reviled the churches and the ministers while on a journey to Boston in 1641, they were assessed record fines, a fact which helped clamp the lid on dissent.[37] New ministers were carefully scrutinized, lest they deliver "some points savoring of familism,"[38] and several publications were prepared to justify the emergent orthodox position. Of these publications, which were directed at audiences in both New and old England, Cotton's *Singing of Psalmes a Gospel-Ordinance* most significantly asserted the need for women to behave submissively. Apparently keeping Anne Hutchinson in mind, the Boston teacher told his readers that "the woman is more subject to error than a man." Cotton continued, "It is not permitted to a woman to speak in the Church by way of propounding questions though under pretence of desire to learn for her own satisfaction; but rather it is required she should ask her husband at home. For under pretence of questioning for learning sake, she might so propound her question as to teach her teachers; or if not so, yet to open a door to some of her own weak and erroneous apprehensions, or at least soon exceed the bounds of womanly modesty." A woman could speak in church only when she wished to confess a sin or participate in hymn-singing.[39]

Other Bay Colony leaders popularized the idea that the intellectual woman was influenced by Satan and therefore could not perform the necessary functions of womanhood. Weld described Mary Dyer's abortive birth as "a woman child, a fish, a beast, and a fowle, all woven together in one, and without an head," and wrote of Hutchinson's probable hydatiform mole[40] as "30. monstrous births . . . none at all of them (as farre as I could ever learne) of humane shape."[41] According to Winthrop's even more garish account of the Dyer child, the stillborn baby had a face and ears growing upon the shoulders, a breast and back full of sharp prickles, female sex organs on the rear and buttocks in front, three clawed feet, no forehead, four horns above the eyes, and two great holes upon the back.[42]

John Wheelwright wrote from his new home in Exeter, New Hampshire, to attack the governor's farfetched description of these births. He called Winthrop's portrayal "a monstrous conception of his brain, a spurious issue of his intellect," and told the governor that he ought to know better "then to delude the world with untruths. [For] I question not his learning, etc. but I admire his certainty or rather impudence: did the man obtestricate [obstetricate]?" Wheelwright further attacked the governor for his views of Jane Hawkins and Mary Dyer. The Exeter pastor felt that the governor was too "rigid in his opinion" of Hawkins, and that he was "pregnant" with "a spirit of censure and malice" when he considered Dyer's unfortunate birth.[43]

Wheelwright's criticism of Winthrop was not accompanied by a total affirmation of the Antinomian women, for he, like so many other divines, felt that women ought not to attempt intellectual "impossibilities." He agreed that Hutchinson had "good judgment" in civil matters, but he also found his sister-in-law given to "the power of suggestion and immediate dictates, by reason of which she had many strange fancies, and erroneous tenents possest her." Although he defended Mary Dyer against Winthrop, he believed that her "disordered" birth proceeded out of a "disordered" mind, or vice-versa! Wheelwright's patronizing attitude toward the Antinomian women was shared by John Underhill, another man who was prosecuted for his Antinomian sympathies. Underhill advised his associates not to despise the advice and counsel of their wives, though they be "but women," and directed them to honor their mates as the "weaker vessel." "Yet mistake not," he warned, "I say not that they [men] are bound to call their wives in council, though they are bound to take their private advice (*so far as they see it make for their advantage and their good*)."[44] In family affairs the husband was to have the final decision-making power, and he could reject his wife's wishes if they were not to his advantage.

Underhill and Wheelwright may have been reacting to gossip which asserted that Antinomian men were ruled by their wives' whims. Although William Hutchinson had been a prosperous landowner, a merchant, a deputy to the General Court, and a Boston selectman, Winthrop described him as a "man of very mild temper and weak parts, and wholly guided by his wife." Roger Clap also felt that William Hutchinson and the other Antinomian men were deficient in intellect and judgment. He expressed surprise that any of the men in the movement had "strong parts."[45]

Charges of the Antinomian women's lack of feminity and the Antinomian men's lack of masculinity were, in the public mind, added to Cotton's allegation of their "inevitable" promiscuity. Some Massachusetts residents viewed the unfortunate births of Anne Hutchinson and Mary Dyer as the products of the women's "mis-

hapen opinions" as well as of their supposed adulterous inclinations. Clap and Edward Johnson lamented the "phantasticall
madnesse" of those who would hold "silly women laden with their
lusts" in higher esteem than "those honoured of Christ, indued
with power and authority from him to Preach." A rumor reached
England that the Antinomian Henry Vane had crossed the Atlantic
in 1637 with Mistresses Dyer and Hutchinson; during the voyage he
"debauched both, and both were delivered of monsters."[46] It was
also widely rumored that three of the rebellious women, Hutchinson, Hawkins, and Mary Oliver, had sold their souls to Satan and
become witches. Anne in particular "gave cause of suspicion of
witchcraft" after she easily converted to Antinomianism one new
male arrival on Rhode Island.[47]

While Massachusetts gossip focused on disordered Antinomian
births, weak Antinomian men, and lusty Antinomian women,
Winthrop and Cotton tried to convince their English and New
England readers that public opinion had been solidly behind Hutchinson's excommunication. Winthrop contended that "diverse
women" objected to this rebel's example and would have borne
witness against her "if their modesty had not restrained them."
Cotton supported the governor's claims by construing the relative
silence at Anne's church trial to mean that the "whole body of the
Church (except her own son) consented with one accord, to the
publick censure of her, by admonition first, and excommunication
after." By asserting this falsehood and ignoring Leverett's admission that many church members wished to stay Anne's excommunication, Cotton made it appear that any person who complained
about her censure was contradicting the nearly unanimous opinion
of the silent majority.[48]

The effort to discredit the Antinomians and Antinomian sentiment in the Bay Colony was ultimately quite successful. By the
mid-1640s Antinomianism was no longer threatening in a practical
sense. The ministers had been returned to a position of public
respect, and fewer people dared to challenge the authority of the
magistrates. A number of sermons and publications had reaffirmed
the appropriateness of female submission. But women seemed no
more contented in 1644 than they had in 1637. They no longer had a
theological movement with which to identify and through which to
express their discontent, so their dissatisfaction was less organized
and more individual. Unlike the Antinomian woman of 1637, the
woman of 1644 may well have felt that she was alone in the world,

that her struggle was a solitary one. Women who, between 1640 and 1644, condemned the authorities, attempted child-murder, abused a neighbor, committed adultery, and petitioned for divorce could not focus their intuitive resentments through a self-justificatory theology. In 1642, Anne Hett could not justify her attempt to drown her child with the same spirit that Dorothy Talby, fortified by "immediate revelation," had used four years earlier in plotting her own daughter's death. Whereas "immediate revelations" had previously been used to justify the entire gamut of rebellious behaviors, by the mid-1640s the grace versus good works issue was, for all practical purposes, dead in Massachusetts.

Although she would have lamented the way in which Talby construed "immediate revelation," Anne Hutchinson had set in motion the expression of discontent over women's assigned social role. Anne had violated the conventional, non-intellectual female role in a profound way, and she was attacked by the authorities for so doing. Stirred by a primitive feminism, she was not (as the ministers might have wished) a submissive, quiet dove, content to labor simply in the kitchen and the childbed. She was witty and aggressive, as well as intellectual. She had no qualms about publicly castigating the men who occupied the most authoritative positions. She claimed the right to define rational, theological matters for herself, and by her example she spurred other women to express similar demands. Far from bewildered, as historian Emery Battis would have her,[49] she thwarted her accusers with her intellectual ability.

Perceiving Anne as a threat to the family, state, religion, and status hierarchy, Puritan authorities directed their antagonism against her character and her sex. They chided her for choosing the female preacher as a role model, and they refused to attribute any merit to her sometimes subtle, sometimes caustic intellectual expressiveness. They could see the work of Satan in Anne's aggressiveness, but they could not discern the more human desire for equal opportunity and treatment which this rebel never hesitated to assert by her own example in intellectual skirmishes. The oppression of female life in a male-dominated society, combined with biological bondage to her own amazing fertility, could not destroy her self-respect. The Puritan authorities found ways to deal with Anne, and thereby managed to salve the psychological wounds inflicted by one who trod so sharply upon their male status and their ministerial and magisterial authority. To them she was an upstart who could easily fall into promiscuity and witchcraft—for their paternalism, religion, and male egos would let them view her as nothing else.

1. C. Mather, *Magnalia*, II, 446.

2. Polishook, ed., *Williams, Cotton, & Rel. Freedom*, pp. 1–35.

3. Winthrop, *Journal*, I, 162, 168; Felt, *Annals of Salem*, II, 573, 576; C. Pope, *Pioneers of Maine & N. Hamp.*, p. 382.

4. R. Williams, *Geo. Fox Digg'd*, p. 16; appendix, pp. 26–27.

5. Much of the information throughout the rest of this chapter closely parallels or duplicates that appearing in Koehler, "Case of Am. Jezebels," and in "Letter."

6. E. Morgan, *Puritan Dilemma*, p. 137. Michael McGiffert's introduction to Thomas Shepard's autobiography and journal contains a discussion of the Puritans' problems with assurance of salvation. See [T. Shepard,] *God's Plot*. Puritan attitudes toward the preparation process are treated comprehensively and perceptively in Pettit, *Heart Prepared*.

7. John Cotton, *Treatise of Covenant of Grace*, p. 177. Cotton's subsequent debate with the other ministers appears in Hall, ed., *Antinomian Controversy*, pp. 24–151.

8. The Familists or Family of Love, a sect which originated in Holland about 1540 and spread to England, gained a largely undeserved reputation for practicing promiscuity. Antinomianism was associated in the Puritan mind with the licentious orgies that accompanied the enthusiasm of John Agricola in sixteenth-century Germany. "Opinionism" was a term often used for any theology that the divines disliked (Hastings, ed., *Encyc. of Rel. & Ethics*, I, 581–82; V, 319; IX, 102).

9. Winthrop, *Short Story of Rise of Antinomians*, pp. 203, 208–9, 253.

10. *Ibid.*, pp. 207, 262; C. Mather, *Magnalia*, II, 446.

11. E. Johnson, *Wonder-Working Prov.*, p. 132; Underhill, *Newes from Am.*, p. 5; Winthrop, *Short Story of Rise of Antinomians*, pp. 205–6, 253; *Good News from N. Eng.*, p. 206.

12. John Cotton, *Way of Cong. Churches Cleared*, pt. 1, p. 61; Winthrop, *Short Story of Rise of Antinomians*, p. 209.

13. Winthrop, *Journal*, I, 266; *Short Story of Rise of Antinomians*, p. 281.

14. E. Johnson, *Wonder-Working Prov.*, pp. 132, 134; Winthrop, *Short Story of Rise of Antinomians*, p. 281; Shurtleff, ed., *Mass. Rec.*, I, 224, 329.

15. Winthrop, *Journal*, I, 270; "The Rev. John Eliot's Record of the Church Members, Roxbury, Massachusetts," in Boston Rec. Cmrs., *Rep. Containing Roxbury Rec.*, p. 77.

16. Winthrop, *Journal*, I, 285–86; G. Dow, ed., *Essex Ct. Rec.*, I, 12, 138, 180, 182–83, 186; Noble & Cronin, eds., *Rec. of Mass. Assts.*, II, 80; Perley, *Hist. of Salem*, II, 50; T. Hutchinson, *Witchcraft Delusion*, p. 6.

17. "Rep. of Trial of A. Hutchinson before Boston Church," p. 365.

18. Winthrop, *Journal*, I, 234; "Examination of A. Hutchinson at Newton Ct.," pp. 312–14, 318; "Rep. of Trial of A. Hutchinson before Boston Church," pp. 380, 382–83.

19. Paul ⌐ld woman that she was to hold her tongue in church and

be careful not "to teach, nor usurp authority over the man, but to be in silence."

20. "Examination of A. Hutchinson at Newtown Ct.," pp. 313–16.

21. Winthrop, *Short Story of Rise of Antinomians*, p. 268.

22. "Examination of A. Hutchinson at Newtown Ct.," p. 330.

23. "Rep. of Trial of A. Hutchinson before Boston Church," p. 380. That Anne chose a woman preacher as a model for her own rebellious behavior, instead of selecting the more popular "Spirit-mystic" and "apostle of Ely" William Sedgwick, indicated her level of feminist self-awareness and suggested that she was not greatly in need of that male guidance which the historian Emery Battis has maintained she really desired. (See Battis, *Saints & Sectaries*, pp. 51–52.) Cotton expressed the view that she was far from satisfied with his guidance: "Mistris Hutchinson seldome resorted to mee, and when she did come to me, it was seldome or never (that I can tell of) that she tarried long. I rather think, she was loath to resort much to me, or, to conferre long with me, lest she might seeme to learne somewhat from me" (Cotton, *Way of Cong. Churches Cleared*, pt. 1, p. 89). Of course, Cotton's testimony may not be completely accurate, since he was writing to wash the Antinomian stain off his own hands.

Little is known about Anne Hutchinson's role model, the woman of Ely. Thomas Edwards, an English Puritan divine, remarked "that there are also some women preachers in our times, who keep constant lectures, preaching weekly to many men and women. In Lincolnshire, in Holland and those parts [i.e., the parts about Holland in Lincolnshire] there is a woman preacher who preaches (it's certain), and its reported also she baptizeth, but that's not so certain. *In the Isle of Ely (that land of errors and sectaries) is a woman preacher also*" (Edwards, *Gangraena* . . . [London, 1646], pt. 2, p. 29, quoted in Battis, *Saints & Sectaries*, p. 43n).

24. Winthrop, *Short Story of Rise of Antinomians*, p. 273; "Examination of A. Hutchinson at Newtown Court," p. 337.

25. A good discussion of the theological issues surrounding resurrection is provided in Rosenmeier, "N. Eng.'s Perfection." Rosenmeier, however, describes Hutchinson too explicitly as a Familist, without supplying sufficient evidence of the same.

26. Anne had responded to an argument of Cotton's with the rejoinder, "I desire to hear God speak this and not man" ("Rep. of Trial of A. Hutchinson before Boston Church," pp. 358, 362, 355).

27. *Ibid.*, p. 372.

28. *Ibid.*, pp. 369–70, 365.

29. *Ibid.*, 385–87, 366–68.

30. *Ibid.*, pp. 378, 388; Winthrop, *Short Story of Rise of Antinomians*, p. 307.

31. Pierce, ed., *Rec. of Boston First Church*, I, 22, 25; Noble & Cronin, eds., *Rec. of Mass. Assts.*, II, 78, 82; Oberholzer, *Delinquent Saints*, p. 85; Hull, "Memoir & Diaries," p. 192n; "Proc. of Excommunication against A. Hibbins," in Demos, ed., *Remarkable Prov.*, pp. 221–39.

32. Felt, *Annals of Salem*, II, 573, 576.

33. G. Dow, ed., *Essex Ct. Rec.*, I, 6, 9; Noble & Cronin, eds., *Rec. of Mass. Assts.*, II, 78; Bentley, "Description & Hist. of Salem," p. 252.

34. Criminologist Dorothy Gates has argued that the women's liberation

movement opened up numerous opportunities for women, including opportunities in crime (*Chicago Tribune*, July 3, 1972, sec. 2, p. 3). Between 1960 and 1972 serious crimes were up 80.7% for men but 256.2% for women, according to the FBI Uniform Crime Reports. Violent crimes for males under eighteen increased 203.2%, while for young females the increase was a staggering 388.3% (*Cincinnati Enquirer*, June 23, 1974, p. 4–H).

35. If Charles E. Banks's enumeration of 3,505 passengers from ship lists is representative of the more than 20,000 persons who came to Massachusetts between 1630 and 1639, it can be assumed that the percentage of women in the total population remained stable. Banks's ship lists reveal that 829 males and 542 females came to the Bay Colony between 1630 and 1634, a number which increased in the next five years to 1,279 males and 855 females. (Banks, *Planters of the Commonwealth*). The percentage of females in the total population rose only 0.6%, from 39.5% between 1630 and 1634 to 40.1% between 1635 and 1639. Therefore, although the number of female offenders may not seem significant at first glance, a z-score comparison of the 1630–34 and 1635–39 populations yields a result statistically significant at the 5% level. A comparison of the 1630–34 and 1640–44 populations yields an even more astounding result, significant at the 1% level. That is to say, there is only a 1% statistical probability that the increase in female offenders from 1630 to 1644 is due to chance alone.

36. Mary Dyer and the excommunicated Anne Hibbins were later to appear before the Assistants. They were hanged as an unrepentant Quaker and a witch, respectively.

37. William Collins was sentenced to pay £100 for charging the Massachusetts churches and ministers with being anti-Christian and calling the king of England the king of Babylon. Francis Hutchinson objected to the popular rumor that he would not sit at the same table with his excommunicated mother; feeling that the Boston Church was to blame, he called that body "a strumpet"—a statement for which he was fined £40. The Assistants fined only one man, Captain John Stone, an amount equal to that assessed Collins. Stone had assaulted Assistant Roger Ludlow and called him a "just ass." Only one other man was fined more than young Hutchinson; Robert Anderson was penalized with a £50 fine for "contempt" (Noble & Cronin, eds., *Rec. of Mass. Assts.*, II, 35, 66, 109; Winthrop, *Journal*, II, 38–40; John Cotton, "Letter,"p. 186).

38. In 1639 the authorities criticized the Reverend Hanserd Knowles for holding "some of Mrs. Hutchinson's opinions," and two years later they forced the Reverend Jonathan Burr to renounce certain errors which, wrote Winthrop, "savor[ed] of familism"' (Winthrop, *Journal*, I, 295; II, 22–23).

39. John Cotton, "Psalm-Singing a Godly Exercise," p. 266.

40. Dr. Paul A. Younge has diagnosed Hutchinson's "30. monstrous births" as a hydatiform mole, a uterine growth which frequently accompanies menopause (Battis, *Saints & Sectaries*, p. 346).

41. Winthrop, *Short Story of Rise of Antinomians*, p. 214.

42. *Ibid.*, pp. 280–81.

43. Wheelwright, *Writings*, pp. 195–96, 198.

44. *Ibid.*, pp. 197–98; Underhill, *Newes from Am.*, pp. 5–6.

45. Winthrop, *Journal*, I, 299; Clap, "Memoirs," p. 360.

46. Winthrop, *Short Story of Rise of Antinomians*, p. 214; E. Johnson, *Wonder-Working Prov.*, p. 28; Clap, "Memoirs," p. 360; Scott, "From Majr. Scott's Mouth," p. 132. John Josselyn wrote that he was surprised, on his first visit to Massachusetts in 1639, to find "a grave and sober person" who told him about Mary Dyer's "monster" (*Two Voyages to N.-Eng.*, pp. 27–28).

47. Winthrop, *Journal*, II, 8.

48. Winthrop, *Short Story of Rise of Antinomians*, p. 307; John Cotton, *Way of Cong. Churches Cleared*, pt. 1, pp. 58–59.

49. Battis, *Saints & Sectaries*, pp. 9, 50–56.

IX

The Weaker Sex as Religious Rebel:
Gortonists, Anabaptists, and Quakers

Sir, a woman preaching is like a dog's walking on hinder legs! It is not done well; but you are amazed to find it done at all.

—Samuel Johnson

The Gortonists' Brief Episode

ALTHOUGH BY THE 1640S PURITANISM HAD TRIUMPHED OVER Antinomianism in Massachusetts, that colony's factionalism continued. Deputies and assistants intensified a struggle for political supremacy which had begun in the previous decade. Popular pressure mounted for the establishment of a uniform law code to prevent magistrates from exercising discretionary justice. Discontent flared over the church elders' strong position in defining governmental matters, and nonmembers were restless because they could not legally vote. Massachusetts expansion into New Hampshire and Shawomet (Warwick, Rhode Island) agitated many local inhabitants in those areas.[1] During this new period of turmoil, the specter of female assertiveness recurred, again in a religious context, but this time it offered little possibility for fusing self-affirmation with religious deviance. The prevailing heresies of the 1640s, Gortonism and Anabaptism, had only brief or germinal appeal for the weaker sex.

Samuel Gorton was the first heretic after Anne Hutchinson to thoroughly arouse the ire of the Puritan authorities. He and his meager following sharply reproved the Puritans for their silly rituals, their ministerial arrogance, and their land greed. Partly to gain control over Gorton's home territory of Shawomet and partly to attack the censorious Gortonists, the Massachusetts General Court dispatched Captain George Cook with forty soldiers to bring these heretics to Boston in late 1643. After a long siege Cook returned with nine male prisoners, seven of whom were ordered to be separated, "dispersed into seven several towns, and there kept to work for their living, and wear irons upon one leg." The court directed them not to maintain, either by word or in writing, "any of their blasphemous or wicked errors upon pain of death."[2]

No punishment the General Court might visit upon the Gortonists could cause them to stay their tongues. Despite their shackles and forced labor, the Gortonists found time to explain their theology to ready listeners—a fact which caused Governor Winthrop to comment, "we found that they did corrupt some of our people, especially the women, by their heresies." When one male church member had reproached the Gortonists prior to their sentencing, his wife had responded, "Husband . . . pray do not boast before the victory be known, it may be the battle is not yet ended."[3] The authorities actually arraigned only one woman, Lucy Pease of Salem, for embracing Gorton's ideas;[4] but, perhaps fearing (among other things) another outbreak of female assertiveness, they took steps to prevent further expansion of Gorton's heresy. In March, 1644, they banished the Shawomet captives from Massachusetts.[5]

Considering the Gortonists' brief and restricted stay in the Bay Colony under the supervision of Puritan masters, it is rather astounding that they amassed any following at all. Still, some women may have appreciated Gorton's belief that a woman could define her own religious destiny without seeking her husband's guidance. They may have sympathized with the sentiment expressed in one letter from eleven Gortonists to the General Court, which charged the Massachusetts authorities with claiming Rhode Island territory in order to hide their own sins, just as Adam had blamed Eve for his. Puritan women may also have known that Plymouth Colony had once expelled Gorton for defending a female servant who had smiled in church, and for wooing the Plymouth pastor's wife away from her husband's religious overlordship.[6] However, such interest could be no more than incipient, as the Gortonists did not stay long enough to have a profound impact.

The Anabaptist Heresy

The second heresy of the 1640s, Anabaptism, had a bit more influence. However, that theology never managed to stir women quite as forcefully as Anne Hutchinson's Antinomianism had, even though it too had a female leader of high standing. Lady Deborah Moody, the daughter of an active champion of popular liberty in Parliament and a cousin of onetime Antinomian Governor Henry Vane (1636), had arrived in Boston about 1639 and soon after purchased an extensive farm in Lynn. She began criticizing the Lynn church members for their "high conceite," their petty squabbling (which "did eate out Christian society and starve common humanity"), their self-imposed estrangement from nonmembers, and their ingratitude toward Mother England. Accounting her "a dangerous woman," the Lynn selectmen presented her, with Mistress King and John Tilton's wife, before the Essex County Court on December 14, 1642, "for houldinge that the baptizing of Infants is noe ordinance of God." She was ordered to repent or be banished.[7]

The baptism of infants became a central issue for Lady Moody and other Anabaptists. These heretics denied the Puritan doctrine of hereditary election, the idea "that sainthood flowed through the loins of the saint." They argued that even the infants of saints should not be baptized until they had the opportunity to become assured, through God's "further light," that they were indeed among His elect. Lady Moody's followers supported passive resistance to authority, "denied all magistracy among Christians," disavowed the importance of an educated ministry in favor of lay clergymen, and allowed congregations to choose ministers entirely on their own, without counsel from church elders or General Court—all of which helped to stamp them as heretics in the Puritan view. The Anabaptist claim of "further light" also sounded suspiciously like Anne Hutchinson's belief in God's self-justifying grace. Indeed, Hutchinson herself had endorsed Anabaptism before her death in 1643.[8]

Although Massachusetts Anabaptists were apparently few, Puritans felt that the sect's actual numbers would tempt God to destroy the entire Biblical Commonwealth. News from England exacerbated this concern. By 1645 John Winthrop was complaining of the "many books coming out of England, some in defence of anabaptism and other errors, and for liberty of conscience as a shelter for their toleration, etc., others in maintenance of the

Presbyterial government . . . against the congregational way."[9]
The turbulence produced by the English Civil War had unleased
sundry such "errors," including the following phenomena described by historian Keith Thomas:[10]

the lively discussion of polygamy and marriage within the forbidden
degrees; the unusual part played by women in war, litigation, pamphle-
teering and politics; the appearance in English of continental feminist
writings; and the attacks, sometimes by women themselves, on their limited educational opportunities, their confinement to domestic activity,
their subjection to their husbands and the injustices of the commercial
marriage market.

As many incoming books probably testified, English society
appeared on the verge of religious disaster, with church government in disarray, social status being undermined,[11] people ad-
vocating nudity and free love,[12] and the ideal female sex role
facing dissolution.

Ministers and magistrates wished to prevent such ideas from
getting a foothold in New England. Four divines prepared refutations of the various heresies, while John Cotton in *The Bloudy Tenent,
Washed, and Made White* launched a full-scale intellectual attack upon
the "liberty of conscience" argument.[13] The General Court enacted
two repressive laws, one banishing all Anabaptists (1644) and
another sentencing all contemners of the Congregational Church or
its ministers to a £5 fine or to a humiliating two-hour stand atop a
stool in public (1646). The latter penalty would ostensibly "shame"
others of like mind.[14]

To a large extent, the Puritan authorities' fears seemed over-
blown, since in 1643 Lady Moody and many other Lynn dissenters
removed to the Dutch-controlled locale of Gravesend, Long Island.
There Lady Moody continued to expound her Anabaptist ideas,
achieving a position of great respect. According to one biographer,
the Gravesend town patent was "remarkable as being probably the
only one of its kind where a woman heads the list of patentees."[15]
After her departure from Lynn, few Anabaptists remained in that
town or elsewhere in Massachusetts. In Essex County between 1643
and 1649 only twelve males and six females underwent prosecution
for denying infant baptism,[16] and no Anabaptists appeared before
the General Court or the Court of Assistants until much later.

Moreover, the "rebels" who did appear before the Essex County justices were not particularly aggressive; most of them had merely withheld their own children from baptism.

The Massachusetts authorities nevertheless worried about the growth of Anabaptism at home and in neighboring colonies. The ghost of Anne Hutchinson still haunted them; they also expressed concern over Lady Moody's close cooperation with the Dutch. (She lent money to Governor Peter Stuyvesant, who reciprocated by giving her the power to nominate the Gravesend magistrates.) The Dutch claimed the Puritan colony of New Haven, where Lady Moody had developed some following among the colony's most prominent women. One of this Anabaptist leader's correspondents, Ann Eaton, the wife of New Haven's governor, was nearly banished in 1646 for her unorthodox baptismal beliefs. A confederate of Mistress Eaton, Lucy Brewster, reportedly said that she was "sermon sicke" and told her son to convert into wastepaper some notes taken on John Davenport's sermons. Lucy Brewster wished to complain before the New Haven General Court that Ann Eaton had seduced her, so that the two of them could be banished together and then go to tolerant Rhode Island. Another New Haven rebel, Mistress Moore, attacked the "divine" institution of Puritan ministry. She alleged that Christ had once appointed ministers, but "now pastors & teachers are but the inventions of man." Her daughter Miriam explained that sometimes she herself had a mind to join the Puritan church, but did not act because she found so many untruths there.[17]

If New Haven Colony was in danger of falling to the Anabaptists and the Dutch, Plymouth was in little better condition. At Secunk (now Rehoboth) thirteen or fourteen persons were rebaptized in 1649. Soon after that, eleven persons formed the first Anabaptist church in Puritan New England there. The Plymouth authorities, never having had an Antinomian controversy and possessing more lenient dispositions than their counterparts in the Bay Colony, did not choose to persecute these Anabaptists, despite reports that "divers" of them neglected "all Churches and Ordinances" and that one woman had been rebaptized in the nude.[18]

The Massachusetts deputies and assistants were much appalled at such activities. When Lady Moody requested permission to return to Lynn so that she might look after her property, they refused to allow it, "vnless shee will acknowledge her euill in opposing the Churches, and leaue her opinions behinde her." This Lady Moody could not do and she spent the remaining years of her life on her sixty-acre farm at Gravesend, dying there in 1659.[19]

When the Massachusetts magistrates heard about the Secunk baptisms, they wrote to the Plymouth authorities and threatened to use "overtures" if the Anabaptists were not punished. Perhaps as a pacificatory gesture, the Plymouth General Court in June, 1650, passed a law penalizing anyone who slandered a minister or a church, and providing a ten-shilling fine or a whipping for those who profaned the Sabbath. In 1651 another enactment required, for the first time, that all persons attend Congregational Sabbath services. Between 1651 and 1654 the deputies punished ten men and seven women, most of whom were Anabaptists, for Sabbath absences.[20]

Non-Theological Female Rebellion in Heretical Times

Despite widespread Puritan fears, Anabaptism did not offer much solace to potential rebels in Calvinist New England. Although its emphasis on nonviolent resistance may have given women who wished to protest the authority of fathers or husbands an opportunity to do so, in a way consistent with their female training, the theology did not (except on Rhode Island) extend lay preaching to the female sex. In that sense, it lacked the implicitly democratic appeal of Antinomianism. Since infant baptism became the only theological issue around which much discussion revolved, this new heresy could not provide (as Antinomianism had) an elastic theology which could be construed in a self-justificatory way. The departure of the leading female Anabaptist, Lady Moody, before she had an opportunity to develop a following in Massachusetts further discouraged women from adopting that theology.

Nevertheless, there were some indications that women's freedom was a concern in the 1640s. John Brock lamented in 1644, "Sisters are not so prudent in their [religious] meetings," and he was distressed to find his own sister "not so humble & heavenly as is desired." When Dr. Robert Child and six other men petitioned for extension of the franchise to Anglicans, Presbyterians, and other non-Congregationalists in 1646, their position was very popular among women who also wished to be included among the enfranchised.[21] One anonymous English tract published in 1648 concluded that in New England "divers, who love the preheminence of both sexes" had "taken a trick to preach to advance themselves."[22]

That anonymous pamphleteer could have been speaking of Gortonists, Anabaptists, or Child supporters. Yet the phenomenon described was widespread enough to affect, although in a comparatively "private" way, some of the most prominent gentledames. Ann Eaton was one case in point, but the most articulate of all such women was one who had no fascination for either Anabaptists or Gortonists: she was not a religious theorist, but a poet. Before 1650 Anne Bradstreet, the wife of a Massachusetts assistant, prepared a poem in honor of Queen Elizabeth, arguing that Good Queen Bess "hath wiped off th' aspersion of her sex,/ That wisdom women lack to play the rex." Bradstreet eulogized this powerful ruler in crisp verse:

> Was ever people better ruled than hers?
> Was ever land more happy freed from stirs?
> Did ever wealth in England more abound?
> Her victories in foreign coasts resound;
>
>   . . . .
>
> Now say, have women worth? or have they none?
> Or had they some, but with our Queen is't gone?
> Nay Masculines, you have thus taxt us long,
> But she, though dead, will vindicate our wrong.
> Let such as say our Sex is void of Reason,
> Know tis a Slander now, but once was Treason.[23]

Anne Bradstreet had not chosen a female heretic for her role model; rather, she had selected the Queen of England. Even Puritans had to respect the glory that was Elizabeth's. Bradstreet not only celebrated the unfeminine accomplishments of the famous queen, but she warned men to watch what idealized limitations they placed on women. She made no effort to preach (like Anne Hutchinson), or to criticize the church ordinances (like Lady Moody). Instead, she stayed in her Ipswich home, cared for her children, loved her husband, and wrote private verses. Her brother-in-law John Woodbridge described her as "a woman, honoured, and esteemed where she lives, for her gracious demeanour, her eminent parts, her pious conversation, her courteous disposition, her exact diligence in her place, and discrete managing of her family occasions."[24] She was not what the authorities would call "a dangerous woman," so they ignored the substance of her writing.

Anne Bradstreet had a great deal to say, for she was frustrated by her own inability to win recognition in a male-dominated field. Once she lashed out

> I am obnoxious to each carping tongue
> Who says my hand a needle better fits,
> A poets pen all scorn I should thus wrong,
> For such despite they cast on Female wits:
> If what I do prove well, it won't advance
> They'll say it's stol'n. or else it was by chance.[25]

There may have been other women like Anne Bradstreet, who adopted the conventional sex role but hungered for more recognition in an unfeminine field. If so, they left no record of their thoughts and turmoils. Few women could release their tensions through poetry; many could, however, express their frustrations through illegal activity. In Essex County alone between 1636 and 1644 women (excluding Anabaptists) committed just 24 offenses—9 percent of all offenses during that period. During the Anabaptist years of 1645 to 1654, the number of such offenses increased to 93, and the percentage to 16.8. In Norfolk County (New Hampshire) and York County (Maine), after the Massachusetts magistrates assumed control over those areas, the percentage of female offenders roughly doubled, from 6.1 to 13.8 percent in the former and 17.6 to 30.7 percent in the latter.[26]

Of the other colonies in Puritan New England, only Plymouth had more than 15 percent female offenders, although the proportion increased in all colonies during the Anabaptist decade. In Plymouth, females comprised 6.3 percent of all convicts before 1645; that figure jumped to 17.7 percent between 1645 and 1654. In New Haven between 1639 and 1644, 11 percent of the offenders were women, and that percentage edged upward to 12.4 in the next decade. Corresponding percentages for Connecticut were 5.9 and 13.7.

Women seemed to become more rebellious in the late 1640s to mid-1650s. In areas where there was an Anabaptist element, or the fear of one, increasing numbers of non-Anabaptist women were convicted for severe violations of the female sex role.[27] In Essex County the severe sex-role violations comprised 29.2 percent of all female offenses before 1644, but 31.8 percent of those in the next ten years. In Maine, the percentages were utterly astounding—66.7 percent before the Massachusetts takeover and 74.1 percent after. In

New Haven such violators increased from 16.7 to 23.5 percent of the total.[28] Connecticut experienced an increase from 0 to 36.4 percent, whereas tolerant Plymouth was the only colony with a decrease, from 33.3 to 11.1 percent.[29] Even when the women who were absent from Sabbath services are deleted from these calculations (since their offense was not prosecutable before the 1650s), Plymouth still had a decrease in severe violations, from 33.3 to 20 percent.

Puritans Respond to Quaker Invasion

The female discontent which surfaced in the Antinomian years and festered in the Anabaptist years virtually exploded at midcentury. Between 1656 and 1664 a large number of female Quakers traveled throughout Calvinist New England from their headquarters in Rhode Island–Providence Plantations, vocally condemning the Calvinist way and inspiring other women to become more assertive.

The first Quakers entered Massachusetts on July 11, 1656. Two women, Ann Austin and Mary Fisher, brought a hundred heretical books to Boston from Barbados, intending to propagate their faith in New England. Austin was a middle-aged mother of five, and Fisher a twenty-two-year-old Yorkshire maidservant. Bay Colony authorities, fearing that these women intended "to oppose the ministry, and also to breed in people a contempt of magistracy," lodged them in Salem prison for five weeks until they could be sent home. In the meantime, the women were searched for witch's teats, and their books were burned in the Boston marketplace.[30]

Austin and Fisher were still in prison when the second group of Quakers arrived in Boston on August 7. The magistrates imprisoned those four men and four women until they, too, could be returned to England. One of them, Mary Prince, expressed her disapproval by yelling through the jail windows at Governor John Endicott, "Woe unto thee, thou art an oppressor." She also wrote a protest to Endicott, which caused the governor to bring her into his house twice to confer with him and a couple of ministers. They attempted to convince her of her errors, but Prince, unmoved by their Ramian logic, reproached them as "hirelings, deceivers of the people, Baal's priests, the seed of the serpent, of the brood of Ishmael, and the like."[31]

Endicott and the ministers could not shake Mary Prince's faith or curb her sharp tongue, any more than Puritan authorities from New

Hampshire through New Haven could prevent other such obdurate heretics from speaking out in public during the next decade. Between 1656 and 1661 every colony enacted laws to root out this new heresy, whether or not many Quakers appeared within its boundaries. These laws fined persons who brought in or entertained Friends and anyone who distributed their books. Massachusetts and New Haven made whippings mandatory for "vagabond missionaries"; a returning Quaker would receive an ear-cropping, boring through the tongue, or branding with an H (for heretic) or an R (for renegade)—depending upon the number of times he returned. Both colonies exempted the "weaker sex" from ear-croppings and brandings, but not from tongue-borings. In Massachusetts, four-time violators of either sex received the death penalty. Although tolerant Plymouth and uninvaded Connecticut penalized offenders with more modest fines, no bodily mutilations, and less severe whippings, the authorities there had no love for Quakers, either.[32]

The Puritan authorities wished to prevent outspoken Quakers from polluting "the fayth," since the Friends' rancor for the authorities was exceeded only by their zeal.[33] And the women were as zealous as the men. Katherine Scott, Anne Hutchinson's sister, came from Providence to Boston in 1658 and told the assistants, "you take too much upon you, you Magistrates, more than ever God gave you." She raised herself to a position of judge over her accusers, as her sister had done twenty years before. In the process she expressed a belief in the inherent equality of all people: "Art not thou my fellow-creature? Did not that God that made thee, make me? And hath he not given me as good right to breath in his air, and tread upon his Earth, as any of you?" Governor Endicott could not tolerate her lack of respect for his authority, any more than his predecessor Winthrop had been able to tolerate her sister's attack. Endicott "cryed out," along with the other magistrates, that "She had too much tongue," and then sentenced her to ten lashes at the whipping post.[34]

Katherine Scott's confederate, the onetime Antinomian Mary Dyer, made three trips to Boston. Each time she heaped abuse upon the Massachusetts authorities. In the words of one Dutch writer, Dyer was a "person of no mean extract and parentage, of an estate pretty plentiful, of a comely stature and countenance, of a piercing knowledge in many things, of a wonderful sweet and pleasant discourse, so fit for great affairs, that she wanted [i.e., lacked] nothing that was manly, except only the name and the sex." She had

Chart 9.1

Increase in Number of Criminal Offenses Committed by Females in the Anabaptist and Quaker Decades

(With Anabaptists and Quakers in Parentheses)

Locale	Pre-1645					Anabaptist Years (1645–54)					Quaker Years (1655–64)				
	Males	Females	% Females	SVFSR*	%@	Males	Females	% Females	SVFSR	%	Males	Females	% Females	SVFSR	%
Massachusetts															
Essex County	250(6)	28(4)	10.1(40)	11(4)	39.3(100)	470(10)	95(2)	16.8(16.7)	32(2)	33.7(100)	528(150)	246(148)	31.8(49.7)	65(31)	26.4(20.9)
Middlesex Cty.	XXX	XX	XXXX	XX	XXXX	34(2)	12(0)	26.1	3(0)	25.0	170(7)	33(2)	16.3(22.2)	12(2)	36.4(100)
York County	XXX	XX	XXXX	XX	XXXX	61(0)	27(0)	30.7	20(0)	74.1	213(0)	42(0)	16.5	19(0)	45.2
Maine^c	28(0)	6(0)	17.6	4(0)	66.7	22(0)	0(0)	0	0(0)	0	XXX	XXX	XXXX	XX	XXXX
New Hampshire^&	31(0)	2(0)	6.1	1(0)	50.0	125(2)	20(0)	13.8	8(0)	40.0	205(20)	34(11)	14.2(25.5)	10(1)	29.4(9.9)
Plymouth	182(0)	12(0)	6.2	4(0)	33.3	132(7)	27(0)	17.0	3(0)	11.1	328(122)	46(9)	12.3(6.9)	24(9)	52.2(100)
New Haven	97(0)	12(0)	11.0	2(0)	16.7	149(1)	21(0)	12.4	8(0)	38.1	133(4)	37(0)	21.8	14(0)	37.8
Connecticut															
Assistants	32(0)	2(0)	5.9	0(0)	0	139(0)	22(0)	13.7	8(0)	36.4	118(0)	14(1)	10.6(100)	4(1)	28.6(100)
New London Cmrs.	XXX	XX	XXXX	XX	XXXX	XXX	XX	XXXX	XX	XXXX	17(0)	10(0)	37.0	2(0)	20.0

* Severe Violations of the Female Sex Role

@ Percentage of Total Female Cases Involving Severe Violations of the Female Sex Role

^c Statistics for Maine during the Time Span When that Locale Was Not under Massachusetts Rule. For cases when that locale was under the governance of the Bay Colony refer to York County Statistics.

^& Norfolk County, Massachusetts, after 1643

Chart 9.2

Increase in Number of Criminal Offenses Committed by Females in the Anabaptist and Quaker Decades
(Excluding Offenses Committed by Anabaptists and Quakers from the Totals)

Locale	Pre-1645					Anabaptist Years (1645–54)					Quaker Years (1655–64)				
	Males	Females	% Females	SVFSR*	%	Males	Females	% Females	SVFSR	%	Males	Females	% Females	SVFSR	%
Massachusetts															
Essex County	244	24	9.0	7	29.2	460	93	16.8	29	31.8	378	98	20.5	34	34.6
Middlesex Cty.	XXX	XX	XXXX	XX	XXXX	32	12	27.3	3	25.0	163	31	16.0	10	32.3
York County	XXX	XX	XXXX	XX	XXXX	61	27	30.7	20	74.1	213	42	16.5	19	45.2
Maine	28	6	17.6	4	66.7	22	0	0	0	0	XXX	XX	XXXX	XX	XXXX
New Hampshire	31	2	6.1	1	50.0	123	20	13.8	8	40.0	185	23	11.1	9	39.1
Plymouth	182	12	6.2	4	33.3	125	27	17.7	3	11.1	206	37	15.2	15	40.5
New Haven	97	12	11.0	2	16.7	148	21	12.4	4	23.5	129	37	22.3	14	37.8
Connecticut															
Assistants	32	2	5.9	0	0	139	22	13.7	8	36.4	118	13	9.9	3	23.1
New London Cmrs.	XXX	XX	XXXX	XX	XXXX	XXX	XX	XXXX	XX	XXXX	17	10	37.0	2	20.0

* Severe Violations of the Female Sex Role

converted to Quakerism while living in England between 1652 and
1657. While returning home to Newport, Rhode Island, she stopped
over at Boston, where she was quickly imprisoned for contemptuous remarks. On this and subsequent visits she attacked the
superior airs affected by the ministers, explaining that she wished
for the prayers of all the people of God—but not for those of the
church elders, because few people of God existed among them. She
valued the prayers of "a child, then a young man, then a strong [i.e.,
adult] man, before an elder in Christ Jesus." In an eloquent speech
she requested the General Court to accept her "counsel" and to
repeal all laws against the Quakers. She asked the deputies and
assistants to "search with the Light of Christ in ye, and it will shew
you whom, as it hath done me and many more, who have been
disobedient [to God] and deceived, as now you are; which Light as
you come into, and obeying what is made manifest to you therein,
you will not repent, that you are kept from shedding Blood, though
it were from a woman." This "Comely Grave" matron had phrased
her appeal in a feminine way, emphasizing her own unimportance
as a member of the "weaker sex"; but she had also courageously told
the authorities that she possessed a truth which they lacked.[35]

The Bay Colony magistrates ordered Mary Dyer whipped, twice
banished, and ultimately hanged. In late October, 1659, her two
Quaker confederates, Marmaduke Stevenson and William Robinson, were hanged; Dyer received a reprieve as she stood atop the
ladder. Unwilling to accept it, she asserted that "She was there
willing to suffer, as her Brethren did, unless they would null their
wicked Law." The people then cried for the marshal to pull her
down and return her to prison. The next day she again expressed a
desire to die, but the authorities instead carried her fifteen miles
toward Rhode Island. A year later she returned, once more to
charge the authorities with sinful carriage. This time the General
Court was not lenient: on June 1, 1660, Mary Dyer became the
only woman ever executed for contempt of the Puritan authorities and religion.[36]

Puritan magistrates did not like to hang "silly women" led "by
the Spirit of the Devil to run about the Country and wandring,
like Whores and Rogues." But neither whippings nor the fear of
hanging seemed to deter these strong-minded women. Female
Quakers flooded Massachusetts and defended their missionary
activity against both ministers and magistrates. Mary Miles justified
such behavior as follows: "The Earth is the Lord's and the Fulnes

thereof; and he can command his Servants to go wheresoever he pleaseth to send them; and none can hinder his Power, for it is unlimited."[37] Almost all of these female missionaries warned the Puritans of God's impending vengeance for their "Blood-thirst" and denounced society's leaders to their faces, in church and in court. Margaret Smith's 1659 statement to the magistrates and ministers, "ye are given to a Spirit of Error, and Hardness of Heart, and Blindness of Mind," was repeated all too frequently by Quakers. Female Friends found any number of ways to agitate the authorities. While Quaker Wenlock Christianson was on trial for his life, Katherine Chatham walked the streets of Boston dressed in a sackcloth, in an effort to call the magistrates away from arrogance to humility (1661). Sarah Gibbons and Dorothy Waugh also used symbolism to cast aspersions upon the authorities: each broke a bottle at the Salem meetinghouse as a testament to the emptiness of pastor John Norton's sermons (1658).[38] Anne Coddington, another onetime Antinomian who turned to the Society of Friends, wrote from Newport to remind the Massachusetts leaders of the incongruity of their actions. In 1660 she accused them of using "Whips, Knive, and Halters" because they were not "armed with spiritual Weapons, as good soldiers of Christ Jesus," continuing as follows:

Would you not have thought it hard Measure, if any of you had been used so by the Bishops [in England]? Nay, did you not so think, tho. they did less than you yourselves have done? Is this following the Command of Christ, who said, "Whatsoever ye would that Men should do unto you, that do unto them." But you will say, "They break your Laws." Well, consider which of you hath not broke the Law of God; Have you not had other Gods beside Him?[39]

Quaker women did and said all kinds of embarrassing, eccentric things, but most shocking of all was the behavior of Deborah Wilson and Lydia Wardwell. In 1662 Wilson walked naked through "some part" of Salem. When apprehended, she explained that her behavior accentuated the cruelty and immodesty of stripping Quaker women to the waist and then whipping them in public. Unconvinced, the Essex County magistrates decided she should once again walk the streets of Salem, this time tied to a garbage cart, with only the upper half of her body exposed. A whip-laden constable followed her, periodically administering a severe lashing. Between 1661 and 1667 Deborah Wilson was fined thirteen times for Sabbath absences; and in 1669 she was dismissed from further prosecution for that offense because, in the words of her judges, "she is distempered in her head."[40]

Lydia Wardwell of Hampton responded dramatically when the church elders several times requested her to appear before them to explain why she had not been coming to Sunday meetings. In 1663 she finally did show up for a Sabbath lecture—but, like Deborah Wilson, she was stark naked. Later she told the court she had wished to wake up church members who were "blinded with Ignorance and Persecution." If nothing else, she had managed to do that; but for her unclad performance she received between twenty and thirty lashes at the whipping post. Her husband also received fifteen lashes for defending his wife's right to appear nude in public.[41]

Quaker women of all ages and conditions traveled about New England. Their numbers included sixty-year-old Elizabeth Hooton from England, eleven-year-old Patience Scott from Rhode Island, the crippled Anne Coleman, Horod Gardner with her suckling babe, and many others.[42] These women and their male compatriots proved effective proselytizers. By 1663 sizable Quaker communities had developed at Salem, in Sandwich, and along the Piscatauqua River dividing Maine from New Hampshire.[43] If we can believe the claims of the Dutch historian Gerard Croese, Lady Moody and many of her followers at Gravesend, Long Island, "turned Quaker."[44] In all of these communities female Friends played outspoken roles. At Salem, 29 local women appeared before the Essex County justices a total of 149 times for contempt of the authorities, Sabbath absence, or heresy. Nicholas Phelps's wife expressed the opinion that Salem minister John Higginson "sent abroad his wolves and his bloodhounds amongst sheep and lambs, and that the priests were deceivers of the people," and Elizabeth Legg warned the church members that they "would all go to hell" if they followed the Puritan ministers.[45] At least nine Sandwich women faced prosecution before the Plymouth General Court. The Mills sisters of Maine actively proselytized, aided by the usual tolerance of York County authorities.[46]

Lowering the Boom on Assertive Women

Female Friends affected many Puritan women by their assertive example and by bringing attention to the authorities' cruelty.

Women were in the crowd which demanded Mary Dyer's release upon her reprieve in 1659, and they often listened to Quaker missionaries without informing the local selectmen. When the Hampton constable directed one Puritan woman to strip Quakers Anne Coleman, Mary Tompkins, and Alice Ambrose to the waist so that he might whip them, she refused. The irate constable then stripped the three Quakers himself.[47] Goodwife Crabb of Greenwich, New Haven Colony, was so impressed by the Friends' innocence that she secured some Quaker books, studied them, fell away from church attendance (where she was afraid she might cast her soul to the Devil), and began attacking the magistrates for being "shedders of bloud, ye bloud of the saints of God."[48]

Other Puritan women were less certain about how to react to these female missionaries. John Hull described the confusion of one: "Sometimes she would hate Quakers, sometimes plead for them: sometime, weeping tears, she could out of herself, speak not a word to any; sometime [she would] weary others with much speaking" (ca. 1658). Ultimately, Mistress Knapp was lodged in prison for railing speeches and for "being troublesome."[49] Five other women, perhaps equally confused, fell into violent fits.[50]

Strong, vocal Quaker women created disequilibrium in the minds of some Puritans. What *was* one to believe, the proper Puritan female might ask, when again and again these obstreperous women from Rhode Island, England, and New York kept entering Puritan locales and speaking out, despite threats of whippings and death? The Quakers seemed unbelievably courageous, profoundly unable to be intimidated. They were not passive, submissive, or modest, and castigated the authorities to their faces. They made over two dozen converts to their faith in Salem alone, and they received a great deal of attention from all sectors of society.

Quaker women helped weaken the force of traditional Puritanism at particularly distressing times, when divisive agitation had already flared up over the Half-Way Covenant, and when the Crown's interference with Puritan franchise requirements was causing resentment. By demonstrating a more assertive alternative, female Friends spurred Puritan women to action. The number of non-Quaker women appearing before the several courts did not increase, relative to men, over the Anabaptist years, but the percentage of women who severely violated the female sex role did. Such violations increased drastically in New Haven, Plymouth, and Middlesex County, Massachusetts; remained stable in New Hampshire and Essex County; and decreased in Maine and Connecticut. The percentage of female offenders remained relatively stable or even decreased slightly in three courts, decreased sharply in two (Middlesex and York Counties), and increased in two others (New Haven and Essex County). However, in absolute terms, the number of female offenders increased in *all* Puritan courts, with the single exception of the Connecticut General Court–Court of Assistants. (Connecticut was the colony least affected by Quakerism.[51])

The Quaker example may have indirectly encouraged still other forms of female action. In Massachusetts between 1656 and 1664 seven women petitioned for divorce, compared to eight during the previous twenty-six years and only three in the following decade. In Plymouth one of only two women to request divorces throughout the entire seventeenth century did so in 1661. However, in unproselytized Connecticut, the number of female divorce petitioners did not greatly increase until the subsequent decade.[52] Particularly in Boston, women appealed to town and county courts for the right to become innkeepers. Between 1661 and 1663 Widow Upshaw, the notorious Alice Thomas, Martha Beamsley, and Joanna Courser were all granted licenses to sell alcoholic beverages—the first women allowed to do so since 1647. Female innkeepers appeared in New Hampshire, Maine, and Plymouth colonies for the first time.[53] Also in these turbulent times, women more decisively carried through the steps necessary for self-destruction. Between 1660 and 1664 four Bay Colony women and one from Plymouth killed themselves—a record for any five-year interval in the seventeenth century.[54]

Of course, not all women acted decisively, or wished to. For many, the Quaker invasion probably brought home the dangers of unrestrained will. Good Puritan women then turned increasingly to their own faith as a reaffirmation of certainty in a troubled decade. At least one outraged female considered the Quakers extremely dangerous; she volunteered the services of her own husband to hang Stevenson, Robinson, Dyer, and William Leddra, for want of anyone else to perform that task.[55]

New England women could hardly ignore the female Quakers —the incongruity between Quaker behavior and their own social conditioning was too great. Some Puritan women repudiated a large measure of their sex-role sterotyping and became Quakers themselves; some were confused; some denounced the Quakers as devil-driven witches and sexual perverts.[56] Others responded on a less cognitive level, simply by giving free reign to an inner desire to act and to reject at least part of the Puritan feminine ideal.

As in Antinomian days, things were once again "turned upside down"—not only in Boston and Salem, but this time in much of the remainder of New England. Some women and many men expressed much distress over the antics of these sharp-tongued women who broke bottles and ran about nude. Men in particular felt it necessary to "prove" their power over such women by beating them into submission. In 1662 Hampton constable William Fifield told the "Vagabond Quakers" Anne Coleman, Mary Tompkins, and Alice Ambrose, "I profess you must not think to make Fools of Men"; he then stripped them to the waist and administered ten lashes to each. The next year another constable lashed Coleman with particular virulence. She collapsed in agony when one of the whip's knots split open her nipple, creating wounds from which some observers thought she might die.[57] John Hill of Oyster River, New Hampshire, boasted that he could overcome Mary Tompkins with logic; upon finding her wit too sharp, he retaliated by striking her in the stomach and pulling her down from where she had been preaching. Joseph Hull, a minister, reportedly assisted by "pinching" Tompkins. On another occasion Norfolk County magistrate Thomas Wiggins struck Tompkins when she would not obey his order to stop preaching. At Great Island this missionary faced even more male cruelty: a group of men threw her headfirst down a flight of stairs.[58] Many Quaker women were whipped harshly, including the aged Elizabeth Hooton, who within six months was imprisoned at Hampton and Cambridge, stocked at Dover, and lashed a total of eighty times in six different Massachusetts towns.[59]

Male Quakers were also beaten severely. Thirty lashes served as the usual punishment, although the Boston jailer struck William Brend until his flesh was black "and as into a Gelly, and under his Arms the bruised Flesh and Blood hung down, clodded as it were in Baggs." Three Quaker men had ears cut off in Massachusetts, while Christopher Holder was branded on the hand in New Haven.[60] However, unlike these male rebels, female Quakers endured severe punishment partly because they had stepped outside their sexual bounds.

Harsh punishments suited the abrasive Quaker character, Puritans felt, for Satan led these heretics into innumerable excesses. Although the Friends assailed lust and promiscuity,[61] Puritans often viewed them as sexually unrestrained individuals in the Familist

tradition. Boston Calvinists suspected Ann Austin and Mary Fisher
of having had sexual relations with the devil and accused the second
group of incoming Friends of sexual uncleanness. One man called
Elizabeth Kitchin "a quaking slut,"[62] while others asserted, with
Quakers in mind, "That All the Armies on Earth cannot subdue one
Lust in Man and Woman."[63] Margaret Smith was rumored to have
kissed a fellow Friend in front of the audience at her whipping in
1660.[64] Since Quakers could not curb their tongues, Puritans felt
that it made complete sense to generalize that lack of restraint to all
forms of behavior. Puritans, brimming over with sexual anxieties,
could view Quaker women as nothing but sluts.

To prevent Quaker women from heaping contempt upon Puritan
authorities or the church, and from turning to witchcraft or lustful
activities, the magistrates directed husbands to restrain their rebellious wives. However, as William Hutchinson had earlier told three
Boston missionaries, "He was more nearly tied to his wife than to
the church"; so too did many Quaker men defend their wives.
Anthony Needham told the Essex County authorities that, if his
wife wished to preach, that was her business; he was not, as Calvinist theory dictated, her supervisor. Eliakim Wardwell defended his
wife's right to appear nude in public, while Richard Crabb, not a
Quaker himself, told the New Haven authorities that his wife's
religion was as good as their own. John Smith's letter to Governor
Endicott on behalf of his wife affirmed his love for her, spoke
sympathetically of her need to define her own religious destiny, and
asked the governor, "where is it written [in Scripture], That they did
banish any for Conscience-sake."[65]

What Quakerism Offered Women

Supportive mates made it easier for wives to be self-assertive. Yet
encouraging husbands alone cannot explain why so many women
were willing to put up with public beatings, severe whippings,
vicious rumors, and even the possibility of death. The women
who adopted Quakerism found an unbelievable source of inner
strength in that theology. Somehow it gave them the courage not to
cower before the male authorities of Calvinist New England, or to
fear their awesome punishments.

By emphasizing an extremely close relationship with Christ,
Quakers gave the individual a sense of her or his own ability to
transcend the status relationships of Puritan society. The only

valued power proceeded out of the highly personal and compelling union of man (or woman) and God. The Quaker God was a benign force, capable of occasional vengeance, but with liberal quantities of kindness. Such a God established no elect body, but offered the joy of salvation to everyone who would open his or her heart. Nor did the Quaker God respect social ranks of superior or inferior, saved or unsaved. For the Friend, God served as a justifier of deeply felt egalitarian needs. The Puritans created a harsh, vengeful God in accordance with their own needs; so, too, did the Quaker make God in his or her own image. Identification with a benevolent God gave the Quaker greater security in emphasizing love over hate, self-assertion over obsequiousness, peaceful persuasion over forced belief. If the Friends demonstrated a tinge of masochism, or a bit of a martyrdom complex, that need arose out of a desire to be supremely close to God by imitating Christ's life and death.

There was much in Quaker theology to appeal to discontented women. The Quaker founder, George Fox, and other theorists accentuated the important fact that Christ was as strong in the woman as the man, and asserted that God preferred some women before thousands of men. Fox argued that the biblical example of female preachers—women like Miriam, Huldah, Philip's four daughters, and Mary Magdalen—could be repeated in contemporary times. After all, he urged, "Moses and Aaron and the seventy elders did not say to those assemblies of women: 'we can do our work ourselves and you are more fitted to be at home to wash the dishes' or such like expressions, but they did encourage them in the work and service of God."[66] The disciple Paul's injunction against women speaking in church assemblies was directed only at the "ignorant women" of the Corinthians, since it was specified, "If they learn anything, that is, if they be farther instructed concerning some points of doctrine, Let them ask their husbands at home." Obviously a woman must be ignorant if she had to ask her husband for advice, whereas the woman who experienced Christ's inner light could edify.[67] The Friends further believed that God might occasionally choose a woman to rule, as He had in the cases of the biblical Deborah and, more recently, Queen Elizabeth. Fox suggested that women might occupy the traditionally male positions of mayor, sheriff, justice, and even general if God's light so directed them. The extension of equal education to girls and boys made such possibilities more feasible.[68]

The Quaker view of marriage had many un-Puritan features.

More than the Puritans, Friends stressed that emotional closeness between husband and wife which reflected a "Union of Souls." Like Calvinists, Quakers celebrated the importance of love in marriage; but, unlike the former, the latter considered love a necessary precondition for marriage—not merely a "duty" or "Christian charity" imposed on it afterward. Friends disapproved of marriage for financial gain, largely because such a union lacked love. While Puritans warned that too much love of one's spouse could detract from the love due God, Quakers felt that closeness between husband and wife was emblematic of the closeness between the individual and God. When Quakers wed, both spouses agreed simply to be "loving and Faithful"; there was no mention of the wife obeying her husband.[69]

Quakerism did not, however, offer women complete equality with men. Like so many of their contemporaries, Quaker males considered woman "the weaker sex," rarely chosen by God to rule.[70] Valuing female modesty, they instituted separate men's and women's meetings in Rhode Island, Salem, and Piscatauqua to preserve it. Women were directed to keep their heads covered, even while preaching, a sign of their modesty.[71] Women's meetings usually exercised power only over nurturant, female matters—the instruction of inexperienced wives and mothers in child-rearing, the management of servants, the allocation of poor relief, and the approval of expressed intentions to marry.[72] In all nonreligious matters Quakers expected women to be subject to their husbands.[73]

Despite these aspects of sex-role inequality, Quakerism offered women a great deal. It provided them the opportunity to occupy one of the most prestigious positions in seventeenth-century society—that of preacher. It incited women to argue with men on an intellectual level, to speak declaratively, and to exercise dominion over their own religious lives. It removed women from the strict confines of the home, opening most of New England as an arena for very unfeminine missionary activity. Quaker theology allowed women to deflect or avoid the kinds of tensions and frustrations they might experience as members of the "weaker sex."

Quakerism could sometimes accomplish miracles in freeing women from despondency. Goodwife Horndall of Newport was subject to frequent fits of depression in which she cried out, "I am that bloody whore, and the blood is spilt upon the earth, and there is no salvation for me." Neighboring Quaker women, learning of her depression, offered support. Initially she greeted their overtures with foolish laughter, but in time her self-concept altered dramatically, she became a Friend, and her fits of depression vanished.[74]

Not all women could be "healed" of their depression and frustration by adopting a nontraditional belief system and finding friends among supportive heretics. However, each religious heresy of the century—Antinomianism, Gortonism, Anabaptism, and Quakerism—at least offered women the chance to protest the limits imposed by Puritan society upon their own achievements. Fortified by the egalitarianism of Gorton, the prestigious example of Lady Moody, the grace of Antinomianism, and the inner light of Quakerism, women railed at ministers and assailed magistrates. They attacked the practical symbols of power (political and religious authority figures) as well as the more abstract symbol of authoritarianism—the Puritan way. Not always aware of the causes of their rebelliousness, they had no social formula for restructuring the world in which they lived. As women hungry for freedom but restricted by seventeenth-century awarenesses, they could do little more than adapt their religious beliefs into a vehicle for protest.

Because these strong women were able to endure frequent assaults upon their theology, their character, and their physical bodies, they influenced other women in Puritan New England. As a result, the female heretics converted, inspired, and made Puritan women aware of another realm of behavior. They planted the twin germs of action and protest in so many female minds that the courts had to deal with more offenses by women, offenses which, in most Puritan courts, violated the orthodox sex-role with increasing severity.

1. J. Adams, *Founding of N. Eng.*, I, 209–14; Winthrop, *Journal*, I, 151, 302; II, 3, 36–37, 46–52, 64–66, 117–20, 170–71, 176, 211–18, 229–32, 235–40, 271, 289–313; [J. Norton,] "Negative Vote"; "John Winthrop's Defense of the Negative Vote, June 5, 1643," in A. Forbes, ed., *Winthrop Papers*, IV, 384–88.

2. E. Winslow, *Hypocrisie Unmasked*; Gorton, *Simplicities Defence*; Hubbard, *Gen. Hist. of N. Eng.*, V, 402–6; Winthrop, *Journal*, II, 116–25, 143, 147–49.

3. Winthrop, *Journal*, II, 149; Gorton, *Simplicities Defence*, p. 122n.

4. Shurtleff, ed., *Mass. Rec.*, I, 50; Felt, *Annals of Salem*, II, 578. Lucy Pease recanted, and her case was dismissed.

5. Hubbard, *Gen. Hist. of N. Eng.*, VI, 407.

6. Gorton, *Incorruptible Key*, pt. 1, pp. 41, 83; pt. 2, pp. 89–90, and *Simplicities Defence*, p. 61, and *Letter to Morton*, pp. 6–7; Shurtleff & Pulsifer, eds., *Plym. Rec.*, I, 100, 105.

7. Lechford, *Plain Dealing*, p. 97; Mrs. Edwards, "Lady Deborah Moody,"

pp. 96–99, 101–2; Savage, *Geneal. Dict. of First Settlers of N. Eng.*, III, 225; Simmons, "Sadler's Account of Mass. Churches," p. 416.

8. McLaughlin & Davidson, eds., "Baptist Debate of 1668," pp. 101–33; Winthrop, *Journal*, II, 39.

9. Winthrop, *Journal*, II, 257.

10. K. Thomas, "Women & Civil War Sects," p. 55. See also Hill, *World Turned Upside Down*, pp. 163, 250–51.

11. The Diggers fostered the development of egalitarian rural communities, while the Levellers wished to reduce the influence of their social betters (Hill, *World Turned Upside Down*).

12. *Ibid.*, pp. 174, 192, 184, 250–56.

13. Hubbard, *Gen. Hist. of N. Eng.*, VI, 415; John Cotton, *Bloudy Tenent*, pp. 26–27, 66–69.

14. Shurtleff, ed., *Mass. Rec.*, II, 85, 149.

15. Mrs. Edwards, "Lady Deborah Moody," p. 101.

16. G. Dow, ed., *Essex Ct. Rec.*, I, 52, 70, 81, 92, 98–99, 101, 178.

17. Lewis & Newhall, *Hist. of Lynn*, p. 188; Hoadly, ed., *Rec. of N. Haven Col. 1638–49*, pp. 243, 246, 254.

18. "Roger Williams to John Winthrop, Jr., Nov. 10, 1649," in A. Forbes, ed., *Winthrop Papers*, V, 376; Langdon, *Pilgrim Col.*, pp. 65–66, 81–82; J. Clark, *Ill Newes from N. Eng.*, p. 55. The Anabaptist missionary Obadiah Holmes was accused of adultery, witchcraft, blasphemy, and the rebaptism of Goodwife Bowdish in the nude. He wrote to Governor Endicott in his own defense, asserting that the goodwife in question "had comly garments from the Crown of her head to the sole of her foot, many being present with [i.e., including] her husband can testifie."

19. "John Endicott to John Winthrop, April 22, 1644," in A. Forbes, ed., *Winthrop Papers*, IV, 456; Mrs. Edwards, "Lady Deborah Moody," pp. 101–2.

20. Shurtleff, ed., *Mass. Rec.*, IV, 174; Shurtleff & Pulsifer, eds., *Plym. Rec.*, II, 57–58; III, 80–81; IX, 20.

21. Brock, "Autobiographical Memoranda," p. 100; "Samuel Symonds to John Winthrop, Jan. 6, 1646/7," in A. Forbes, ed., *Winthrop Papers*, V, 125.

22. *Good News from N. Eng.*, p. 213.

23. A. Bradstreet, "In Honour of That High and Mighty Princess Queen Elizabeth of Happy Memory," in her *Works*, pp. 196–98.

24. John Woodbridge, "Epistle to the Reader," in A. Bradstreet, *Works*, p. 4.

25. A. Bradstreet, "Prologue," in her *Works*, p. 16.

26. Some of this increase may have been due to the fact that proportionately more women were coming into underpopulated Maine and New Hampshire, but it is highly unlikely that twice as many women as men entered those areas in the Anabaptist decade (or in one five-year span, as was the case in Maine).

27. Severe violations of the female sex role, as specified in ch. 6, include abusive behavior, adultery, contempt of the authorities, blasphemy, swearing, murder, servant disobedience, and witchcraft.

28. The number of offenders in New Haven Colony does not include the many men who were prosecuted for watch violations or for having defec-

tive arms at militia trainings. Such "crimes" were prosecuted by the deputies and assistants only in that colony, and their sheer numbers ($N = 310$) would seriously distort the comparative results.

29. A decrease also occurred in New Hampshire, by 10%, but the sample is so small before 1645 ($N = 2$) that legitimate comparisons cannot be made. The same holds true for Connecticut.

30. Bishop, *N.-Eng. Judged*, pp. 4–10; [H. Norton,] *N.-Eng. Ensigne*, pp. 5–7; Hull, "Memoir & Diaries," p. 178. A note on sources: throughout this treatment of the Quakers, I have relied heavily upon accounts by Quakers themselves. While one might expect such reports to be factually biased, the Quaker descriptions in almost all instances parallel the information appearing in court records.

31. T. Hutchinson, *Hist. of Mass.*, I, 168.

32. Shurtleff, ed., *Mass. Rec.*, III, 415–16; IV, pt. 1, pp. 308–9, 345; IV, pt. 2, pp. 2–3, 165–66; Hoadly, ed., *Rec. of N. Haven Col. 1653–Union*, pp. 239–41; J. Trumbull, ed., *Conn. Rec.*, I, 283, 308, 324; Shurtleff & Pulsifer, eds., *Plym. Rec.*, XI, 68, 100–101; III, 196, 206; IV, 7, 10.

33. Shurtleff, ed., *Mass. Rec.*, III, 416.

34. [H. Norton,] *N.-Eng. Ensigne*, pp. 96–97; Bishop *N.-Eng. Judged*, p. 95.

35. Bacon, *Quiet Rebels*, pp. 29–33; Bishop, *N.-Eng. Judged*, p. 114; [Burrough,] *Declaration of Persecution of Quakers*, pp. 25–27; H. Rogers, "Mary Dyer Did Hang," pp. 168–75.

36. H. Rogers, "Mary Dyer Did Hang," pp. 168–75; [Burrough,] *Declaration of Persecution of Quakers*, pp. 24–25; Bishop, *N.-Eng. Judged*, pp. 134–35; Shurtleff, ed., *Mass. Rec.*, IV, pt. 1, pp. 349, 366–67, 383–84, 419.

37. Besse, *Col. of Quaker Sufferings*, II, 264.

38. *Ibid.*, p. 184.

39. "Anne Coddington to the Gov., Deputy Gov., and Assts., July 8, 1660" *ibid.*, pp. 207–8.

40. Bishop, *N.-Eng. Judged*, p. 383; G. Dow, ed., *Essex Ct. Rec.*, III, 17, 88.

41. Bishop, *N.-Eng. Judged*, pp. 374–78; G. Dow, ed., *Essex Ct. Rec.*, III, 64, 100.

42. Besse, *Col. of Quaker Sufferings*, II, 229–30, 224; Bishop, *N.-Eng. Judged*, pp. 430, 60.

43. Cudworth, "Letter," pp. 268, 271; Burnyeat, *Truth Exalted*, p. 51. In Salem at least 54 local adults appeared before the Essex County Court for Quaker offenses. Most inhabitants of Sandwich became Quakers, and the Piscatauqua Friends had a large enough group to hold separate men's and women's meetings.

44. Croese, *Gen. Hist. of Quakers*, pp. 156–57. Other historians have contested Croese's claim; see sources cited in James, James, & Boyer, eds., *Notable Am. Women*, II, 570.

45. G. Dow, ed., *Essex Ct. Rec.*, II, 314, 190.

46. Libby, Allen, & Moody, eds., *Maine Ct. Rec.*, II, 225; *Rec. of Suffolk Ct. 1671–80*, II, 843; Sewall, *Diary*, I, 43.

47. Bishop, *N.-Eng. Judged*, pp. 367–68, 440.

48. Hoadly, ed., *Rec. of N. Haven Col. 1653–Union*, pp. 242–47.

49. Hull, "Memoir & Diaries," p. 192.

50. These women included Joan Edwards and Mary Harder of Boston,

Sarah Miller and Mary Parsons of Northampton, and Isabella Holdridge of Haverhill. See *ibid.*, III, 181; Drake, *Annals of Witchcraft*, pp. 251–52; J. Trumbull, *Hist. of Northampton*, I, 49; G. Dow, ed., *Essex Ct. Rec.*, I, 388; II, 158–59.

51. During the Quaker years compared to the Anabaptist years, the increases in non-Quaker (and non-Anabaptist) female offenses are as follows:

Locale	Female Offenses			Severe Violations of Female Sex Role		
	1645–54	1655–64	% Incr.	1645–54	1655–64	% Incr.
Massachusetts						
Essex Co.	93	98	5.4	29	34	17.2
Middlesex Co.	12	31	158.3	3	10	233.3
Maine	27	42	55.6	20	19	−5.0
Plymouth	27	37	37.0	3	15	400.0
New Haven	21	37	76.2	4	14	250.0
Connecticut	22	13	−40.9	8	3	−62.5
New Hampshire	20	23	15.0	8	9	12.3

52. See Appendix 1.

53. See Appendix 2.

54. See Appendix 3.

55. Maule, *Truth Held Forth*, p. 217.

56. See ch. 10 for a discussion of Quakers as witches.

57. Bishop, *N.-Eng. Judged*, pp. 367–68, 430.

58. *Ibid.*, pp. 386, 373, 394.

59. Besse, *Col. of Quaker Sufferings*, II, 229–31.

60. *Ibid.*, p. 186; Bishop, *N.-Eng. Judged*, pp. 65–66, 78, 91–92; Hoadly, ed., *Rec. of N. Haven Col. 1653–Union*, pp. 233–34.

61. Lloyd, *Quaker Social Hist.*, p. 9; Besse, *Col. of Quaker Sufferings*, II, 215.

62. [H. Norton,] *N.-Eng. Ensigne*, pp. 7, 12; G. Dow, ed., *Essex Ct. Rec.*, II, 219. The Essex County magistrates admonished Edmond Baker for calling Kitchin that name, but had the Quaker woman been a proper Calvinist, her detractor would also have paid restitution for slandering her.

63. Bishop, *N.-Eng. Judged*, p. 446; "John Smith of Salem to Endicott about Smith's wife Margaret, 1660," in Besse, *Col. of Quaker Sufferings*, II, 209.

64. Bishop, *N.-Eng. Judged*, p. 448.

65. "Proc. of Boston Church against the Exiles," pp. 391–92; Bishop, *N.-Eng. Judged*, p. 382; G. Dow, ed., *Essex Ct. Rec.*, III, 100; "John Smith of Salem to Endicott about Smith's wife Margaret, 1660," in Besse, *Col. of Quaker Sufferings*, II, 208–10.

66. G. Fox, *N.-Eng. Fire-Brand Quenched*, pt. 2, pp. 58–59; Maule, *Truth Held Forth*, pp. 123–24; G. Fox, *A Collection of Many Christian Epistles*, quoted in O'Faolain & Martines, eds., *Not in God's Image*, pp. 265–66; Fox, *Epistles*, MS I, folio 36, quoted in Lloyd, *Quaker Social Hist.*, p. 107.

67. Sewel, *Hist. of Rise of Quakers*, II, 636.

68. G. Fox, *N.-Eng. Fire-Brand Quenched*, pt. 2, p. 60; Brinton, *Friends for 300 Yrs.*, p. 150.

69. Frost, *Quaker Family*, pp. 152, 162, 167, 174.
70. G. Fox, *N.-Eng. Fire-Brand Quenched*, pt. 2, p. 58.
71. Burnyeat, *Truth Exalted*, pp. 47, 51–52; Maule, *Truth Held Forth*, p. 124.
72. Lloyd, *Quaker Social Hist.*, pp. 110–11; "Rec. of Monthly Meeting of Women Friends for R.I.," n.p.
73. Sewel, *Hist. of Rise of Quakers*, II, 636.
74. [H. Norton,] *N.-Eng. Ensigne*, pp. 110–16.

X

The Heresy of Witchcraft: Anxiety and the Supernatural in Calvinist New England

There is no law under which you can denounce a person for being personally distasteful to you, but you can denounce him on grounds of witchcraft. The witch idea then is a device that enables people to dress up their animosities in an actionable guise—in the guise of an offense committed against themselves.

—Philip Mayer, "Witches"

ONE CANNOT ADEQUATELY DISCUSS SEVENTEENTH-CENTURY WOMEN —or, for that matter, seventeenth-century New England religion —without extensive reference to the arch-heresy of witchcraft. Perhaps Perry Miller is right when he asserts that "the intellectual history of New England can be written as though no such thing [as the 1692 Salem Village hysteria] ever happened,"[1] but Miller and other scholars have failed to realize the significant impact of witches and the occult upon the emotional life of Puritans. There has been a great tendency to consider Puritan witchcraft in a vacuum, as if that phenomenon were a purely incidental concern before 1692, and as if the Salem Village outbreak were an "immediate" product of popular ignorance, charter tensions, the duplicity of adolescent hellions, neighborhood antagonism, and sexual repression. Such social factors were not limited to one time and place, however, and the more than one hundred accused witches who existed in New England before 1692 deserve their fair share of attention.

Anthropologists have long described the particular functions of witchcraft accusations in various primitive cultures, but historians have usually construed New England witchcraft as an expression of the seventeenth century's intellectual outlook. Only within the last decade have scholars like Paul Boyer, Stephen Nissenbaum, John Demos, and Chadwick Hansen attempted to provide a broad based social and psychological assessment of New England witchcraft.[2] My own approach is synthetic and will attempt to describe the complexity of seventeenth-century witchcraft from several frames of reference: the impact of the occult in Calvinist cosmology, the characteristics of those persons regarded as witches, the reasons why witchcraft was often associated with the female sex, and the particular functions which the concern over witchcraft served for the Puritan community.

Sinister Happenings in Old New England

From the perspective of the Calvinists, a constant struggle raged between the Biblical Commonwealth and the forces of evil.[3] Conflicts with the Quakers, Anabaptists, Gortonists, and Antinomians represented one form of that struggle. Puritans also believed that Satan ravaged the countryside like "a roaring lion," assaulting the conscience, the spirit, and the material person of man, woman, and child. Melancholy persons were considered especially subject to his allure; their problems were "the devils bath, wherein he delights to be stirring." Satan precipitated thunderstorms, created illusions and delusions, and bewitched people into "unreasonable Phrensies." Ministers and magistrates frequently reminded the populace from church and court to lead proper lives and to fear God's providential punishments.[4]

Demons, ghosts, unnatural phenomena—the ominous creations of God and Satan—saturated the Puritan vision of reality. Some people felt that the Lord's supernatural confederates honored them with heavenly visits. In 1686 Cotton Mather wrote of the appearance of a glistening angel who bore Christ's message in answer to a prayer. The message directed Mather to publish many books at home and abroad, and to do "great works" for Christ's Church "in the revolutions that are now at hand." In 1693 Mistress Carver of Salem, like Mather, revealed a need to plug into the power of God—to enhance her own ego in the process. She reported being visited by the "shining spirits" of "good Angels," who supplied her with the knowledge that "a new storm of Witchcraft" would soon chastise the iniquity of New England.[5]

Other spectral encounters were less benign. Large numbers of

people watched wide eyed while a strange scythe-shaped light
appeared in the Massachusetts sky (1681), a ghost ship allegedly
floated atop the water near New Haven (1647), and a spectral spear
pointed westward in the heavens over the Bay Colony (1667).[6]
Seafaring New Englanders told the English traveler John Josselyn
of a phantom "shallop at Sea Man'd with women."[7] A local spirit
supposedly appeared regularly at Cavendish, Vermont, between
1680 and 1790; legend had it that Marblehead, Massachusetts, was
annually assailed by the eerie screams of a girl who had been
murdered by pirates.[8]

In the 1680s three homes—George Walton's at Great Island, New
Hampshire; William Morse's at Newbury, Massachusetts; and
Nicholas Disborough's of Hartford, Connecticut—were assailed by
stones, sticks, and chairs thrown by an invisible hand. The stone-
throwing was accompanied by snorting and whistling on Great
Island, while the Newbury poltergeist nearly tore Morse's cap off his
head and threw a cat at his wife.[9] The Disborough demon flung
stones, corn cobs, and pieces of earth through doors and windows,
down the chimney, and up from the floor of the chamber.[10]

Many individuals sought help from the assaults of devils and
witches. Some used herbs, plants, and fumes to preserve themselves from the malicious designs of Satan's minions. Some placed
"sweet bays" under their door stoops to prevent witches from
entering. Others sought cures for the toothache, the ague, and
many physical ailments by saying magical words or wearing a paper
upon which such words were written. "White Whitches, which do
only Good-Turns for their Neighbors," did a flourishing business,
advising their associates on how to ward off various physical and
psychological illnesses.[11]

The occult provided innumerable methods whereby individuals
could predict the future and define the present. New Englanders
used many "wicked charms" to find out secrets. A sieve or a key
could disclose how lost goods had been disposed of. Glasses and
basins could reveal whether and whom a person would marry.
Some Massachusetts residents used their Bibles in a "way of
sorcery" by letting God's book fall open and then reading the first
word as a revelation of the state of the reader's soul.[12] Edward
Peggy found that special powders could win the affections of
young maidens.[13]

Astrologers who predicted the future did a thriving business,
which caused Cotton Mather to lament that the "Energy of Devils"

lurked in their "impulsive" judgments. Yet while Mather considered astrological advice not worth a hundredth part of what the enquirer paid for it, and viewed astrology as "a sort of" witchcraft, poet Anne Bradstreet mentioned astrology favorably in several of her poems, and almanac-makers relied on the periodic movements of the planets when making their annual predictions.[14] Mr. Stafford of Tiverton carried his calculations so far that he could predict "what day, hour and minute was fortunate for vessels to sail."[15] In another instance, Caleb Powell, a ship's mate, turned to the stars in an effort to "find out whether or no there were diabolicall means used" in the mysterious assault of flying things upon the Morse house. Powell vindicated Elizabeth Morse of any guilt in the matter (1679), but the Massachusetts Court of Assistants found her guilty of witchcraft (1680) and suspected Powell of the same.[16]

New England inhabitants "greedily sought after and quickly bought up" books on fortune-telling and sorcery, volumes like *The Compleat History of Magick, Sorcery & Witchcraft*, and *Saducismus Triumphatus*. Josiah Cotton complained, "If there come forth a Pamphlett Entitled 'Strange News, or a Dreadfull Discourse of ye Dispossessing of One from a Devil in the Likeness of a headless Bear' or any other Idle Tale worth some such Pompous Title, it is exceedingly taken & gains the formost assent."[17] By the turn of the century Cotton Mather was lamenting that too many people "had been led away with little sorceries, wherein they . . . would often cure hurts with spells, and practice detestable conjurations with sieves, and keys, and pease, and nails, and horseshoes, and other implements." Magic books, white witches, charms, astrologers, and fortune-tellers abounded, despite warnings that such mocked God's power of foreordination and brought down His wrath.[18] Lovesick lasses, pregnant women, apprehensive farmers, and other superstitious individuals would not be denied their interest in magic.

The divines charged that charms and potions were the work of the devil, and the person who dabbled in any magic, black or white, could fall under suspicion of dealing in witchcraft. For example, Mistress D—, a sharp-tongued Bostonian, placed nine sticks upon the ground, mumbled a few words over them to make them stand on end, and thereafter had "the Report of a Witch." Some of her neighbors gossiped that she had signed a covenant with the devil, giving him her soul in return for superhuman powers.[19]

Witches could bring injury and even death to their enemies, or to anyone else they wanted to assault. They possessed the power to plunge children into fits simulating a hysterical condition, to move objects without touching them, and to transport themselves through the air on broomsticks or devil-steeds.[20] The latter conveyances carried witches to weekly night-time esbats or the quarterly sabbats, where they reportedly met with the devil in a celebration of evil, defying God and subjecting themselves to the defilements of wine, the dance, and sexual revels.[21]

The troubles witches caused were legion. They allegedly pinched at women's breasts, and threatened to make their opponents "as bare as a birds taile."[22] They traveled to and fro disguised as cats, bears, and other spectral creatures, killing pigs, cattle, children, and an occasional adult. They tipped off loads of hay and put them back on wagons. They soured butter. They forced persons to scald themselves and to become temporarily deaf, dumb, or blind.[23] They caused afflictions by placing pins in a rag puppet which represented the victim.[24]

Such manifestations of *maleficium* (i.e., the ability to injure humans and property through supernatural means) were frequent recurrences in seventeenth-century New England. Anything magical or mysterious fascinated the public. One early eighteenth-century rationalist wrote that the "Common People" of Massachusetts "suck[ed] in the Wildest Errors" and imbibed the "grossest notions" concerning occult phenomena.[25] The divines held themselves apart from a credulous public, arguing that black magic must be approached "rationally," legalistically. Each accused witch had to receive a trial at which all the evidence was heard, and her mental state had to be examined by qualified physicians to make sure that she (or he) was neither "crazy-brained" nor "distracted."[26] At the same time, the ministers believed that every effort should be made to root out witches, wizards (male witches), magicians, fortune-tellers, and panderers of charms, because "plain Scripture, undoubted History, and personal Experience" all testified to the reality of black magic. The Bible was filled with disapproving references to the occult—in Isaiah, Leviticus, Deuteronomy, II Kings, I Samuel, Galatians, Revelation, and Exodus.[27] Exodus 22:18 stated simply, "Thou shalt not suffer a Witch to Live"; accordingly, the colonies of New Plymouth (1636), Massachusetts (1641), Connecticut (1642), New Haven (1656), and New Hampshire (1680) enacted laws capitally punishing any "Solemn Compaction or conversing with the Divell by way of Witchcraft, Conjuration or the like."[28]

How to Catch a Witch

A watchful populace used any number of ways to "catch" suspected witches. One popular notion was that heating the urine of a witch, or of those bewitched, would soon bring the witch running.[29] A similar method of detection involved burning part of the body of a bewitched creature, or the carcass of an animal which had allegedly died by witchcraft.[30] That technique, too, would supposedly make the witch appear. Yet another method involved tying an accused witch hand and foot and tossing her into a pond. If the accused sank to the bottom—thereby facing probable death by drowning—his or her innocence was confirmed. If the bound witch floated, guilt was proven: in one Connectut magistrate's words, "ye witch having made a covenant with ye devill she hath renounced her bapt[is]m & hence ye antipathy between her & water."[31]

Magistrates and ministers rejected such popular tests. Connecticut divines considered the water test "unlawful and sinful," while Bay Colony authorities asserted that the "Urinary Experiment" was "an unwarrantable way to find out Witches."[32] Rather, civil and religious leaders wished to rely upon the Bible and "rational" proof. William Jones summed up such proofs in his "Grounds for Examination of a Witch." First he cited "notorious defamacon by ye common report of the people." Then, in rapid succession, he mentioned other legitimate evidences of guilt: cursing or threatening someone, after which death or mischief ensued; contradictory answers in court; the inability to read religious books, mention the Lord's name, or say the Lord's prayer without stumbling; suspicious behavior by old friends, spouses, servants, children, and companions of previously convicted witches; voluntary confessions; the testimony of two witnesses to an act of witchcraft; the use of enchantments; the appearance of the spectral form of a dead person at the accused witch's request; and the sight of a witch's familiar in any form, "mouse cat or other visible creature."[33]

Every witch had a familiar—that manifestation of Satan which regularly accompanied and daily suckled each of his covenated minions. To accommodate the familiars, Satan equipped his witches with one or two special teats, located in unobtrusive places—inside the mouth, underneath the shoulder, or (most commonly) within the genitalia.[34] Searchers carefully examined the breasts of accused witches to determine if they had an extra nipple.[35] Often an examining jury of several women, usually midwives, and an occasional male physician subjected accused females to humiliating and painfully thorough examinations. The women appointed to search Quaker Ann Austin treated her so roughly that Austin, who had borne five children, said "That she had not suffered so much in the birth of them all, as she had done under their barbarous and cruel hands."[36]

It was also believed that the devil might symbolically mark the body of a covenanted witch. Any area dark in color and insensitive to the touch was held to be proof of Satan's presence. Often this mark was found in the genitals. King James VI of Scotland had announced in 1597 that the Devil, in order to produce his mark on witches, "Doth lick them with his tongue in some privy part of their body." Other sources maintained that Satan gave his initiates "a sharp nip on some part of the body" to produce the mark.[37]

Even in the late seventeenth and early eighteenth centuries some observers began to question the reality of witch's marks and teats. John Hale wrote, "I have been informed by a skillful midwife that hath known vertuous Women that had those Piles . . . [which] are without sense of feeling . . . and after cold, handling etc. are apt to draw up into the Body," therefore disappearing. Francis Hutchinson explained that some teats were withered parts of the body, hollow spaces between the muscles, scurvy spots, piles, hanging warts "which in Old Age may grow large and fistulous," moles, scars, or "Marks [made] in the Womb, from the Mother's Imagination."[38] In more recent times, psychiatrist Thomas Szasz has written as follows:

Witch's marks were supernumerary nipples, a common anatomical variation, slightly more frequent in men than women, or any kind of skin lesion, such as a birthmark, mole, scar, or hemangioma [i.e., a congenital localized lesion of the skin and subcutaneous tissues resulting from an excessive concentration of blood or lymph vessels]. The mark was thought to indicate the spot on which the possession was branded by the devil, like an animal by its owner, and constituted proof of a pact between that person and Satan. This made it easy enough to diagnose almost anyone as a witch.[39]

Sex and Witchcraft

While many people were curious about the abnormality of witches' genitalia, others demonstrated concern about their erotic behavior. The devil was not content merely to brand witches with his mark, or to equip them with an extra teat; often he wished to violate their chastity. Descriptions of witches' activities at nocturnal orgies, and of initiation rites in which a new witch kissed the devil's ass, intrigued many European theologians. Some observers, both Catholic and Protestant, argued that copulation with a demon gave superb sexual pleasure to a witch, partly because the demon took a form consistent with the witch's ideal of beauty, and also because devils came equipped with superb sexual organs. Other theologians disagreed, arguing that intercourse with devils was only pleasurable when performed on holy days; at other times it was excruciatingly painful. Confessed witches could by no means resolve the pleasure-pain controversy; some claimed to have found demonic intercourse exquisitely pleasant, and others complained of the pain.[40]

New England ministers did not wholeheartedly approve of such erotic tales. When Increase Mather heard of Mary Johnson's description of her "Uncleanness with Men and Devils" (1650)[41] or of Rebecca Greensmith's admission of Satan's "frequent use of her body with much seeming (but indeed horrible, hellish) delight to her" (1662),[42] the Boston clergyman felt that both women were hallucinating. "The World is full of Fabulous Stories concerning some kind of Familiarities with the Devil," he explained, "and things done by his help, which are beyond the power of creatures to accomplish. What Fables are there concerning Incubi and Succubae, and of Men begotten by Daemons? No doubt the Devil may delude the fancy that one of his Vassals shall think . . . that he had carnal and cursed Communion with them, beyond what is real."[43]

Mather's progressive belief that witches hallucinated about sexual relations with devils may have been accurate. Self-proclaimed New England witches who held meetings in the wilderness may have imbibed (as did their European counterparts) concoctions of belladonna, hemlock, aconite, and thorn-apple, in order to induce a dreamlike state which placed them in a "world of fantasy and emotion."[44] In drugged delirium, these witches may well have imagined some form of intimate contact with Satan, including a sexual experience of supreme intensity.

Increase Mather did not believe in incubi and succubi, but many of his associates linked witchcraft with sexual excess. The popular books on magic and witchcraft described coital relations between witches and devils. The *Saducismus Triumphatus*, while maintaining that devils could not themselves commit "Venereal Acts" and bring forth toad or serpent offspring, asserted that Satan could "either

animate dead bodies, and by the help of them commit those Villanies, which modesty bids us to conceal; or some other way compound, and thicken Atomes into what shape he pleases."[45] Josiah
Cotton asserted that one of the "grossest notions" which the common people "sucked" in was the idea that humans copulated with
demon lovers.[46]

Often the words "base old baud and spiteful old witch" were
shouted slanderously at neighbors, all in one passionate breath.[47]
At least one man, Edward Sanders of Great Bay, New Hampshire,
equated female sexual assertiveness with witchcraft. He accused
Sarah Lynne of attempting to entice him into her bed, and then,
when he failed to respond, with coming into his bed, placing her
hand in his codpiece, and opening her shift, "soe he hath discerned
a secrett marke in her body in such parte as were very immodest"
(1645).[48] Given the existence of attitudes like Sanders's, it is not
surprising that many young men testified to the nocturnal activities
of witches who crawled through keyholes, climbed atop or pressed
hard against the sleeping men's bodies, and almost suffocated
them.[49] After all, hadn't two women actually confessed to intercourse with devils? And hadn't a third admitted attempting to pull
out a young boy's bowels?[50] Many witchcraft accusations reflected
Puritans' sexual anxieties.

Any unconventionality in a woman's sexual attitudes or behavior
was liable to arouse suspicions of witchcraft. In New Haven (1654)
Eleanor Bayley fell suspect because she was guilty of "impudent and
notorious lying; endeauoring to make discord among her neighbors; and filthy & vncleane speeches."' Her natural attitude toward
sexuality made her particularly suspect. Once, when the Bayley dog
attempted to copulate with a sow in heat, a neighbor told her
husband to kill the dog; but Mistress Bayley had responded, "what
would you haue the poor creature doe, if he had not a bitch, he must
haue some thing." Another time, upon hearing that George Larri-
more had "miscaried wth many persons in a filthy way," she had
said, "alass, what would you haue the man doe, if his owne wife was
weake, he must haue some body." After making such statements,
Mistress Bayley "was told that in these things she hath acted as one
possessed wth the very deuill, who is a malitious, lying, vncleane
spirit." Elizabeth Godman, a neighbor of the Bayleys, was herself
accused of witchcraft, in part because she was observed going
through the motions of being suckled and was thereafter heard to
mutter to herself "as if some body had laine wth her." Ann Finer of

Connecticut escaped prosecution as a witch, although she had a sexual rationale which witches might have found appealing: according to her, God was despicable because He "made poor Creatures on purpose to damme them." She said the devil was a thousand times more merry than the Puritan God and wished herself "in ye darkest nook in hell." After supplying this justification, Finer admitted adultery and infanticidal neglect of her child[51]—the kind of behavior witches relished.

Some Real Witches

Satan offered a variety of enticements to those who would leave their souls in his hands: sexual excitement of a purely lustful sort generally suppressed in Calvinist society, as well as more respectable lures that appealed particularly to "have nots" (servants, the poor, and women). Prospects of money, fine clothing, freedom from labor, a view of the world's sights, personal power, and control over the destinies of others were especially tempting to persons with little status in Calvinist society, those "insignificant people in their normal environment, who wanted to be far superior to, and very different from, what they really were." In H. Debrunner's terms, these people suffered from a "suppressed power impulse," and society had not "provided sufficient outlets for [their] self assertion."[52] Women, defined by their submission and deference to men, suffered particularly from such suppression. As Elizabeth Janeway has written, "the witch role permits the woman to imagine that she can exercise some sort of power, even if it is evil power."[53]

At least three observers have recognized that persons could construe the workings of their imaginations in such a way as to believe they actually were witches, although historians of the 1692 Salem Village outbreak generally do not assert that self-proclaimed witches were running about old New England. Barrett Wendell has hypothesized that some of the Salem accused could not feel sure of their membership among God's elect; in moments of religious despair and frustration, they toyed with the occult. They then unconsciously hypnotized several women and girls into having fits, much as Wendell felt that well-meaning and honest mediums in his own time unwittingly hypnotized themselves to speak in trances. Chadwick Hansen has argued that many of the accused, before and during 1692, practiced witchcraft in a state of hysterical anxiety, the causes of which he does not speculate upon. In his short story "Young Goodman Brown" Nathaniel Hawthorne has demonstrated how one man, struggling with his own inclination toward evil, could actually perceive himself as being tempted to witchcraft by a flesh-and-blood devil.[54]

Three accused witches had, in fact, suspicious fascinations with the occult. In 1678 a few girls found "a babie [witch's puppet] with a piece of lace on it" in Anis Hoar's house at Beverly. When Hoar's friend Margaret Lord was caught dancing on the Sabbath, she threatened one intruding servant by saying that "Shee had a book in which she could read and call the diuell to kill" and burn that servant.[55] In the 1650s Elizabeth Godman of New Haven could often be found, according to her neighbors, "speaking aboutt witches and rather justifye them then condemne them." Knowing that her contemporaries suspected witchcraft when people fell strangely and unexpectedly ill, she often said, when asked about such cases, "what, doe you thinke I haue bewitched her." Godman also saw "strange appearitions, and lights aboute her bed, and strange sights w[ch] affrighted her." She was thrice brought before the authorities on suspicion of witchcraft, but was ultimately released "wth respect to her health" in 1655.[56]

Seven persons actually admitted that they had practiced witchcraft. Mary Johnson of Wethersfield, Connecticut, was found guilty of consorting with Satan, based on her own confession that he had offered her sexual excitement and freedom from her labors. She became very penitent before her execution in 1648.[57] Mary Parsons of Springfield was acquitted of witchcraft but convicted of infanticide by the Massachusetts General Court on May 7, 1651. Sentenced to be hanged for the murder of her child, she confessed, sometime between May 7 and May 27, that she had indeed practiced witchcraft. On May 29 she was executed.[58] In 1653 Goodwife Knapp of Fairfield, New Haven Colony, admitted that she was a witch; her teats were discovered upon a search, and she too hanged.[59] Rebecca Greensmith, a "lewd, ignorant, considerably aged woman" of Hartford, after listening to an accusatory transcription taken from Anne Cole, "forthwith and freely confessed those things to be true" and admitted her own carnal relations with Satan. She was executed in January, 1663.[60]

Two decades later, James Fuller of Springfield confessed to familiarity with the devil but later retracted that admission. The authorities then convicted him of lying and ordered him to receive thirty lashes, a £5 fine, and to be disposed of as a servant if he could not pay that amount.[61] Another man, John Redman of the Isles of Shoals in Maine, was presented before the York County Court in 1661 for saying he "belonged to the Divill & if the Divill had his due hee had him seaven yeares agoe." There is no record of his further prosecution.[62]

Goody Glover was the last person to admit her own witchcraft prior to the 1692 outbreak. Accused of afflicting the Goodwin children at Boston in 1688, and confronted with irrefutable evidence of her own wrongdoing, she agreed that she was guilty of bewitchment. As Cotton Mather has related,

Order was given to search the old womans house, from whence there were brought into the Court several small Images, or Puppets, or Babies, made of Raggs, and stuff't with Goat's hair, and other such Ingredients. When these were produced the vile Woman acknowledged, that her way to torment the Objects of her malice, was by wetting her Finger with her Spittle and stroking of those little Images. The abused Children were then present, and the Woman still kept stooping and shrinking as one that was almost presst to Death with a mighty Weight upon her. But one of the Images being brought to her, immediately she started up after an odd manner, and took it into her hand; but she had no sooner taken it, than one of the Children fell into sad Fits, before the whole Assembly. This the Judges had their just Apprehensions at: and carefully causing the Repetition of the Experiment, found again the same event of it. They asked her Whether she had any [character wittnesses] to stand by her: She replied, She had; and looking very pertly in the Air, she added, No, He's gone. And she then confessed, that she had One, who was her Prince [of Darkness], with whom she maintain'd, I know not what Communion. For which cause, the night after, she was heard expostulating with a Devil, for his thus deserting her; telling Him that Because He had served her so basely and falsly, she had confessed all.

Goody Glover also admitted going to a meeting where Satan and four others were present, but she would not give Mather complete answers to his questions because her "Spirits" would not give her leave. She predicted that the children's fits would continue after her own execution, since other witches had a hand in afflicting them. After she was hanged the afflictions did, in fact, continue.[63]

None of the seven witches just discussed underwent any duress to force their confessions, in marked contrast to the subsequent prosecutions of the Salem Village witches in 1692. Furthermore, both Goody Glover and Rebecca Greensmith claimed that many of their confederates were also active witches. The truth of those charges cannot be ascertained, for few people would openly admit to occult interests when they could be hanged for such confessions. If witches used puppets, they kept them hidden. Evidence of charms and incantations was easily erased. Witches held their esbats and sabbats deep in the forest on moonless nights, when all "normal" persons were supposedly home abed. Elizabeth Godman aroused suspicion when she was discovered walking downstairs late at night. Her explanation sounded very suspect: she wished to "looke for two grapes she had lost in the flore" because she "feared the mice would play wth them in the night and disturb ye family."[64] But she escaped conviction, for it was hard to catch a witch practicing her craft.

Why Women Were Witches and Witches Were Women

Most of those who covenanted with Satan and most of the accused witches were women, usually elderly women. Five of the seven self-confessed witches were females, and four of those were over the age of fifty. In New England before 1692, women comprised 76.7 percent of the 103 persons who acquired some reputation as witches or who faced prosecution for practicing witchcraft. This figure is comparable to the relative number of women accused from 1692 to 1697; in those six years 72.7 percent of the 216 "witches" were females, and 40.8 percent of those were over fifty.

Why so many of the accused happened to be (older) women is a complex question. Some would argue that their accusation resulted from a deep-rooted misogyny, perhaps with primeval origins. Others might assert that Puritans envied female biological creativity and lashed out desperately at those fruitful women who most aroused such jealousy. John Demos explains that witchcraft accusations "strongly suggest that [projected] aggression and orality [produced by the trauma of early weaning] were more or less constant themes in the pathology of the period."[65]

At best, all analyses of causation are speculative, since we have no live Puritans before us—Puritans whose mentalities we can probe in elaborate detail. Yet, from this author's own point of view, certain basic cultural themes helped suggest that women would be witches. One of these themes was the presumed susceptibility of the "innately weaker sex" to devilish temptation, particularly when a given woman suffered from fits of melancholy. Witchcraft accusations may have permitted displaced aggression toward undesirable women, if not toward women in general, for more than one Puritan observed that the weaker sex had qualities which predisposed it to the devil's designs: impatience, superstitiousness, a desire to command, malice, and vengefulness.[66] Many Puritans had good cause to feel hostile toward those women who used attention-getting and expressive devices—hysterical fits, making faces at neighbors, various "distractions"—which, although disapproved of by some, could not be prosecuted as crimes in court. If someone (particularly an unassertive female) had any animosity toward an eccentric member of the weaker sex, she could actuate that animosity through a witchcraft accusation. Men might resent the behavior of such eccentrics because the latter accentuated the former's own feelings of powerlessness. Women who drew community attention toward themselves could arouse male envy. Women who failed to behave like proper ladies could cause men to fear the dissolution of the social system, depriving males of what little security they could derive from their superior position. People could bring men to court for using more direct forms of expression, such as abusive speech, swearing, and fighting, but neither men nor women could bring an obnoxious or eccentric woman to her knees by prosecuting her.

Puritan sexual anxieties also helped brand women as witches. Needing to constrain lust's irresistible lure, the male often escaped a sometimes exasperating dilemma by projecting his own sexual impulses onto a blatantly sexual Other—a woman, whose sexual appeal was, at least in part, the source of his tension. The male's contradictory impulses (sex as materially good but spiritually evil) created the kind of self-punishing fear which led men to hallucinate about being suffocated while asleep, or having their bowels pulled out. In contrast, the woman's sexual anxieties were not so easily projected onto the opposite sex. The widespread belief in female sexual passivity, the "innate" modesty of women, and the usual reluctance of proper wives and daughters to accuse a "superior" male all served to diminish the likelihood of allegations against men. When an accusing female gave vent to her own sexual desires, for example by complaining of pain in her bowels, she charged either a witch (another female) or Satan (a "safe" male Other).

Sexual repression, the presumed susceptibility of the weaker sex to satanic allure, and displaced aggression were all aspects of the

tendency to accuse female witches. One other factor accentuated
that tendency, this one bearing on the relatively expendable status
of the elderly woman. No longer raising children and often without
even her husband to care for, she faced a condition of comparative
idleness. Since Puritans believed that idle persons were particularly
vulnerable to devilish assaults, the woman who lived by herself fell
automatically under suspicion—unless she was well known for
public service, as a deaconess, for example. Furthermore, widows
were often a drain on the community's resources, for the largest
portion of poor relief went to them. Although we tend to think of the
nuclear family as a fairly recent development, as Demos has shown
in *A Little Commonwealth*, it was the rule in colonial New England;
the extent of outward migration among the young, surely a factor
contributing to the impoverishment and isolation of older women,
had been documented by Linda Bissell.[67] By their mid-fifties, many
women were expendable. Not surprisingly, these women were
usually the ones whom afflicted persons accused. Not that the
accusers were concerned with expendability as such; rather, they
knew which adults were least respected.

Some women may have responded to what they perceived as
satanic overtures because they had internalized the notion that
women were weak, and therefore easily tempted. If so, that belief in
female frailty may have helped them absolve themselves of responsibility for practicing witchcraft. If Satan tempted a woman and she
responded positively, she could view herself as being led into witchcraft, instead of "deciding" to become a witch. Although the result
was the same, her guilt (especially if she had been raised a proper
Puritan) would be less. At the same time, the fact that she would
manage to retain a measure of her valued feminity made the
strength gained by her witchly power more psychologically tolerable. Certainly witchcraft was, on some level, appropriate to the
feminine condition: it involved subterfuge, indirect affliction, and
the casting of spells, rather than overt verbal or physical castigation.

Other women may have become witches because they wanted to
possess the more direct power Satan offered them. Satan offered
witches greater control over the destinies of other persons and over
nature itself than God could ever practically promise, even to men.
The Devil gave the witch the power to afflict, to suspend natural
laws, to cause fits, illness, injury, and death. Some women may
have (as Barrett Wendell has asserted) grown sour on their own
impotent search for assurance of membership among God's elect.

One could never become *absolutely* certain of one's status with God; in contrast, the control witches exercised had an active, ongoing, readily observable materiality. Participation in the Lord's power was altogether too abstract, whereas participation in Satan's was perceptibly concrete.

Many aged widows, having lost their twin value-referents of husband and children, quite probably had a special need to affirm their own importance and worth on some practical level.[68] Witchcraft became a way to accomplish this, a "new" proof of the female potency which women could hardly enjoy or assert in Calvinism. The discontented woman demonstrated such potency by denying the centers of the ideal woman's existence: submission before the husband, and childbearing. Disqualifying herself from the restraints of the feminine role, and in fact inverting it, the witch began life anew.

The testimony of confessed witches indicates that they were far from loving toward their husbands and children. Even before being herself accused, Mary Parsons was one of the foremost accusers of her own husband. She explained that Hugh Parsons had bewitched their child, made a strange "gablinge Noyse" when he slept, and at times, when he did not come home until midnight and then in a "distempered Frame," had pulled the bedcovers off her. Moreover, she testified, "he hath thrown Pease about ye Howse and made me pick them up." Rebecca Greensmith also accused her husband of witchcraft, stating that he had a fox as a familiar. Hugh Parsons and Nathaniel Greensmith both maintained their innocence; while the court acquitted the former, the latter was hanged with his wife on January 25, 1663.[69]

Marital friction also helped bring attention to a woman who was already under suspicion for witchcraft. A lack of wifely deference, coupled with cantankerousness, confirmed people's belief in a woman's guilt. Susanna Martin, whom a jury found guilty of witchcraft in 1669, had a long-standing contention with her mate, and at one point appeared in court for assaulting him. Bridget Oliver (later Bishop), accused in 1680 and executed in 1692 for too great a familiarity with Satan, had an unsatisfactory relationship with her second husband. In 1669 the Essex County magistrates fined the Olivers for fighting, and in 1677 ordered them to stand gagged back to back in the meetinghouse because they called one another opprobrious names. Goody Glover's husband "sometimes complained of her, that she was undoubedly a Witch, and that whenever his Head was laid [to rest], she would quickly arrive unto the punishments due to such a one."[70] He did not explain whether he felt she practiced *maleficium* upon him, but implied that.

The fact that confessed witches focused most of their *maleficium* against children undoubtedly fueled the popular belief that a witch was combatting the proper maternal role.[71] Mary Parsons was hanged for killing one of her own children. Mary Johnson confessed to murdering a child through black magic. Rebecca Greensmith testified to having bewitched a young girl. Goody Glover admitted using puppets to afflict the Goodwin children, and the suspected witch Elizabeth Godman delighted in frightening the youngsters at the house where she resided.[72] In fact, none of the confessed witches admitted attempting to kill or afflict any adults.

At least 40.5 percent of the 79 females suspected of witchcraft before 1692 were accused either of bewitching (24) or killing (8) children, whereas only 16.7 percent (4 of 24) of the male witches were so accused.[73] Any incomprehensible interference with the normal processes of birth and infant nurturance, or the birth of a deformed child, immediately raised suspicions that a witch was to blame. One accused wizard supposedly caused a child to withdraw into its mother's womb at parturition, before its final, painful expulsion (1667).[74] When John Chase's wife was "sorely troubled with sore breasts, that she hath lost both, and one of them rotted away," the local witch, Elizabeth Morse, was blamed (1680).[75] A year later, a rat bit Roger Brown's wife on the breast; her milk became "knotty" and the nipple turned so sore that her infant could not suckle it, all of which caused her to believe she had been bewitched.[76]

Midwifery, that nurturant female profession so intimately associated with childbirth, was especially suspect, particularly if, as Roger Forbes has pointed out, a "delivery had an unhappy outcome or if the non-obstetrical patients whom some midwives attempted to treat did not recover."[77] The fact that many obstetricians dabbled in mysterious potions also increased suspicions of wrongdoing. Using "herbs and common sense, garnished with charms" to "cure disease, to defeat spells, detect thieves or find stolen goods and to protect . . . neighbors from every kind of evil," these sometime "white" witches had a great deal of popular respect.[78] Newport's Granny Morgan, for one, accustomed herself "on occasion to a hocus pocus, & making cakes of flour and her own Urine and sticking them full of pins and divining by them." Jane Hawkins, the Boston midwife who became an ardent supporter of Anne Hutchinson, was considered too familiar with the Devil because she fell into trances and gave fertility potions to barren women.[79] The Newbury neighbors of Elizabeth Morse, another midwife, suspected her of *maleficium* for several years.[80]

Female herb doctors who were not midwives also came under suspicion. Margaret Jones of Charleston was accused of a satanic alliance because her medicines had violent effects, and because she had told those patients who would not take her physic that they would never be healed. Goodwife Burt, a "potion doctress," fell under suspicion in 1669 after she told two girls that they would be cured of their fits only if they believed in her god (presumably Satan).[81]

Who the Witches Were

"Witches" came from all social classes. Anne Hutchinson, the daughter of an English minister, had married a prominent merchant. Anne Hibbins's husband was extremely wealthy and occupied the important position of assistant. She herself was probably the daughter of Governor Thomas Dudley.[82] Nathaniel Greensmith owned properties in Hartford valued at a sizable £137. 14s. 1d.[83] Several witches were middle-class tradesmen or their wives. Jane Walford was the wife of a Dover blacksmith, John Redman a smithy on the Isle of Shoals, John Carrington a Wethersfield carpenter, and Hugh Parsons a Springfield bricklayer-sawyer.[84]

In most instances, however, the accused witch was a person of low social status. Five were either current or recent servants: Nicholas and Margaret Jennings (Saybrook, Connecticut, 1661), Mary Johnson, Elizabeth Garlick (Easthampton, Long Island, 1658), and Margaret Lord (Beverly, Massachusetts, 1678).[85] Mary Webster (Hadley, 1683) was at one time a lowly hog reeve,[86] Mary Wright (Boston, 1660) was reportedly "a poor and ignorant woman,"[87] and Eunice Cole (Hampton, New Hampshire, 1656–80) became a town pauper after her husband's death.[88] Thomas Turpin of Strawberry Bank, New Hampshire, a fisherman, owned property valued at only £28 upon his death in 1650. Witch Margaret Gifford's husband served as a laborer at the Lynn ironworks.[89] More than half of all accused witches had indeterminate social status, suggesting that they were probably poor, since court records usually mention the occupation of those tradesmen or people of "the better sort" who faced trial or submitted testimony.

Whatever their social origins or status, witches had one thing in common: they were eccentric or contentious, or had records of prior criminal activity. They were misfits in the kind of society the Puritans wished to build and foster.[90] Persons of litigious or slanderous dispositions and those who generally "showed a froward discontented frame of spirit"[91] often fell under suspicion, as did those who gave their neighbors "a fierce look" or went "in an offensive way to folkes houses in a rayling manner."[92] Any slightly unconventional behavior—muttering to oneself, hallucinating about sexual intercourse with demons, working too proficiently[93]—and any community rebellion might be viewed as a manifestation of witchcraft at work. As Cotton Mather explained it, rebellion against God's authority and His divinely appointed ministers "has very much like to Witchcraft in it" because in rebellion men and women cast off God, refused the salvation of Christ, and served the Devil's interests.[94]

Anne Hutchinson caused the ministers and magistrates a great deal of trouble in the Antinomian years by demanding a position of relative equality with them (at least as an interpreter of divine writ). Anne Hibbins dressed too lavishly and behaved too aggressively for stolid Puritan tastes.[95] A sharply outspoken Katherine Harrison told one magistrate that his soul "was damned long ago."[96] Eunice Cole posted bond for her good behavior after slandering two women in 1645; she was presented before the Norfolk County Court for unspecified offenses in 1648 and 1653, paid a half-crown fine for "misdemeanors" in 1651, and was later whipped as a Quaker.[97] Nathaniel Greensmith appeared in court for setting his barn on common land without leave, for lying, for fighting, and twice for stealing.[98] Nicholas and Margaret Jennings ran away from their master, stole various items, and committed fornication.[99] Altogether, eight witches were either convicted or strongly suspected of stealing.[100]

Elizabeth Seager of Hartford obstreperously committed several improprieties. She was convicted of adultery in 1663 and accused of blasphemy then and in 1665. After one hysterical girl called Seager a witch in 1662, she retorted that the Wethersfield minister, Joseph Haynes, "had writ a great deal of hodge podge" about the matter. She also said that she would send Satan to tell the magistrates that she was *not* a witch![101]

Contentious, thieving, fighting, rebellious persons simply did not demonstrate the kind of behavior which proper Puritans could tolerate. Since occult phenomena constituted very real manifestations of God's providential warnings and Satan's insidious designs, it was easy for Calvinists to link them (in the latter capacity) to social deviance. Anyone who was a bit too unorthodox, too eccentric, or too rebellious moved outside the pale of God-given "normality," and therefore fell within Satan's sphere. In Puritan terms, one became either a member of God's elect or an inhabitant of hell —either a proper lady, struggling to live up to a stereotyped ideal; or a whore or witch, undermining modesty and the reputed joys of submissive maternity.

Why the Number of Witchcraft Accusations Fluctuated

At least 103 persons were accused of familiarity with the Devil between 1638 and 1691. These persons came from 35 different locales in Massachusetts (where the 48 alleged witches included 8 Quaker missionaries), Connecticut (32), New Hampshire (16), Maine (2), Plymouth (2), Long Island (2), and Rhode Island (1).[102] Hartford ranked first, with eleven witches, and Hampton second with nine. The facts that the population was inclined to believe, intellectually and emotionally, in witchcraft, and that some persons did confess to practicing it, are both central to understanding the authorities' tendency to prosecute accused witches. It does not explain, however, why the authorities and the populace pursued witches more zealously at one time than at another. Why, for example, were no witches accused before 1638? And why did the number prosecuted fluctuate, by decade and by colony, between that date and 1692? Why did only two accusations (both resulting in acquittals) occur in Plymouth, but thirty-three in Connecticut, where twelve people were hanged and only four received outright acquittals, especially since both colonies had roughly parallel populations?[103]

To learn why witchcraft accusations fluctuated, one must examine how Puritans reacted to anxiety. Puritans "knew" that the world was abysmally evil and, as Edmund S. Morgan has so clearly indicated, they were continually faced with the dilemma of how to do good in such a world. They had to repress many of their own impulses toward the enjoyment of material things—e.g., fine clothing, sexual excitement, dancing—and substitute a guilt-ridden introspection, a constant search for some assurance of their own membership among God's elect. The Biblical Commonwealth, initiated to stamp out all tendencies toward sin, could continue only if everyone exercised the utmost watchfulness. Enemies assailed the "City upon a Hill" from all sides. Externally there were Quaker missionaries, Rhode Island heretics, French Catholics, pagan Indians, and Anglican officials to guard against; within their own ranks Puritans could find persons contemptuous of the authorities, disobedient children, blasphemers, swearers, thieves, fornicators, murderers, and women who would not behave as proper females. All of these required censure and punishment.

When the Biblical Commonwealth appeared shaky, Puritans feared they had fallen from God's favor. They searched for some means of purification, some way to return to God's confidence by expunging evil from the Commonwealth. At such times, especially if too few threatening heretics seemed to need punishment, Puritans searched for a scapegoat upon whom all of the threatening evil

Chart 10.1
Witchcraft Accusations in Seventeenth-Century New England*

Interval	Massachusetts[†]	Connecticut (Inc. New Haven)[#]	New Hampshire	Maine	Plymouth
1607–38	0	0	0	0	0
1638–44	2	0	0	0	0
1645–49	6	2	0	0	0
1650–54	12	7	1	0	0
1655–59	8	5	4	1	0
1660–64	8	15	4	1	1
1665–69	5	5	2	0	0
1670–74	5	0	2	0	0
1675–79	4	0	1	0	1
1680–84	11	1	9	0	0
1685–89	5	0	0	0	0
1690–91	1	0	0	0	0
Total:	49	33	16	2	2

*In cases like that of Eunice Cole, who had the general reputation as a witch between 1656 and 1680, I have entered one accusation per five-year interval during that time span.
†Includes Anne Hutchinson of Rhode Island, since she was accused of witchcraft by Governor John Winthrop and not by her own neighbors, and the case of Lydia Wright of Long Island, because her trial was held in Massachusetts (1640, 1660).
#Includes Elizabeth Garlick of Long Island because she was tried by the Hartford Court of Magistrates in 1658.

could be cathartically focused. Scapegoats expressed those nasty impulses which each proper Calvinist was struggling to restrain within him or herself. Dancing, sexual intercourse, disobedience to the authority of parents and magistrates, outspokenness, female rebellion, and even witchcraft itself were all too alluring to people hungry for independence, excitement, and a measure of self-declaration. Scapegoating permitted the Calvinist to reject evil desires by projecting them onto another, who could then be punished for having such sinful, destructive characteristics. The annihilation of the scapegoat annihilated the evil (at least temporarily) in his or her accuser, and thus maintained the delicate balance within the individual, the religion, and the society. Calvinists had a special proclivity for scapegoating, since, as psychoanalysts F. Kraupl Tayler and J. H. Rey have pointed out, "The need for scapegoat victims seems to arise particularly in individuals who are predisposed by an inclination to adopt extra-punitive attitudes to others and who are disturbed by an unacknowledged sense of guilt and self-dissatisfaction."[104]

Still, the earliest Puritans had less need for scapegoats than many of their descendants did. Moving to the New World in compact, tightly knit groups, the initial settlers possessed a feeling of communal unity, a common belief in their own divine mission. Since everyone knew virtually everyone else, it was easy to oversee the behavior of one's neighbors. There were no settlements deep in the wilderness (along the Connecticut River or in Rhode Island, for example) which could undermine the perception of solidarity and optimism. The Indians were few and initially friendly.[105] The French Catholics and English Anglicans were far away. No Quakers or Rhode Island heretics existed. Criminals could be easily apprehended and punished, and servant rebelliousness was easily constrained by a sharp whipping. Roger Williams ruffled Massachusetts's feathers for a time, and Antinomians seriously disrupted the colony's unity between 1636 and 1638; but Puritans could rest secure in the belief that banishment of such heretics maintained the Bay Colony's purity.

The controversies centering around Williams and the Antinomians were local affairs, limited to Salem and Boston. However, they did have profound and far-reaching implications about the lack of religious unity in the Biblical Commonwealth. It was difficult to call one's intimate associates totally evil in some quick, offhand manner. Only when the danger Anne Hutchinson posed had been graphically and relentlessly demonstrated over a two-year period did she become the arch-heretic. In time, three Antinomian women secured reputations as witches, but no one was hanged for that offense. In fact, the Antinomian heretics usually escaped with only minor sentences.[106]

Puritan anxieties increased during the Anabaptist decade (1645–54), as internal conflicts erupted between assistants and deputies, freemen and nonfreemen, officials of church and state. Indian warfare seemed imminent. Pained over the loss of respect for their authority, magistrates searched for scapegoats; although Samuel Gorton posed no practical threat to the Bay Colony, the Cooke expedition against him and his following at Warwick served that purpose. However, the prosecution of the nine Warwick captives in 1643 and of a few Anabaptists before 1650 only momentarily allayed tensions. The Gortonists soon returned to Warwick, too many Anabaptists proved saintly in behavior, and the Puritans needed some new, more totally evil scapegoat upon whom they could foist their own fears and disillusionment. The existence of such inner anxieties and the increasing numbers of unfeminine women—first with the Antinomian crusade, then with Lady Moody's following, and finally with the upsurge in female crime—made the times ripe for witchcraft.

Meanwhile, in the midst of Civil War, British witchcraft prosecutions had also skyrocketed. Between 1600 and 1642 it had been common practice, particularly in Royalist circles, to maintain that witches drugged themselves with "soporiferous medicines" and suffered more from self-delusion than from any relationship with Satan. Many Puritans objected, and, in the areas where they managed to secure power during the 1640s, the authorities executed witches with alarming rapidity. In Essex County, for instance, only twenty-five witches faced indictments between 1620 and 1639, but in the single year of 1645 a total of thirty-six women endured prosecution; nineteen of them were hanged, and another nine died of jail fever. Such English activities served as dangerous precedents for a New England which had its own fears to confront.[107]

L. Berkowitz and J. A. Green have observed that visibility and a sense of another person's or group's strangeness are important elements in the scapegoating process.[108]. Calvinists of the late 1640s tended to focus their emergent witchhunting zeal against those whose eccentric behavior made them both visible to and different from the rest of the community. Such eccentrics became witches in the public eye, even though there was no tangible proof of their actual witchcraft. Between 1645 and 1649 six persons were accused of afflicting children, knowing events before they happened, cutting pudding with an invisible knife, reading magic books, assuming a cat's likeness, cursing a neighbor's garden, and causing a ship to rock mysteriously.[109] That number of witches doubled during the next five-year interval.

Three of these accused witches were hanged. In 1648 the assistants directed that Margaret Jones of Charlestown, a "very intemperate, lying . . . and railing" woman, be executed for her "malignant touch," her knowledge of "secret speeches," and the presence of "an apparent teat in her secret parts as fresh as if it had been newly sucked." In 1650 the wife of a Dorchester inhabitant named Henry Lake was hanged; she had been known for her sexual indiscretions. A year later a Watertown woman, Mistress Kendall, followed her to the gallows, accused of causing a small child's death by occult means. After Kendall's death it was revealed that the major witness against her, a nurse, had kept the child out in the cold for a long time. That circumstance—not witchcraft—had caused the youngster to "mysteriously" change color and die.[110]

Connecticut authorities wished to make certain that the troubles afflicting Massachusetts did not reach them. Disturbed by threats of an Indian-Dutch conspiracy, the infertility of the soil, the apparent demise of the fur trade, and the friction developing between church members and nonmembers,[111] as well as by internal church disputes over the power assumed by ministers,[112] Connecticut Puritans had anxieties of their own to expunge. There were no Anabaptists, Gortonists, or other heretics upon whom convenient blame could be placed. In an effort to purify Connecticut, the authorities hanged five witches—Alse Young on May 26, 1647, the first witch ever hanged in New England;[113] Mary Johnson on December 7, 1648;[114] John and Joan Carrington after March 6, 1651;[115] and Lydia Gilbert in 1654.[116] Three of the five lived in Wethersfield, a locale in which serious "ecclesiastical and economic problems had turned neighbor against neighbor," causing a substantial portion of the population to migrate elsewhere.[117]

In the 1650s New Haven, the most stringent New England colony, faced the threat of an antagonistic Indian-Dutch union. Moreover, the merchants and wealthy tradesmen who had founded New Haven in the 1630s became disillusioned with the unproductivity of the terrain and the failure of their own commercial interests in Delaware and New Jersey.[118] The fact that witches were being executed in both Massachusetts and Connecticut made some impact upon the New Haven settlers, who themselves had plenty of frustrations but no heretics (only a few Anabaptists among the colony's prominent women) upon whom they could be projected. Between 1651 and 1660 accusations were frequently lodged against Elizabeth Godman of New Haven town. Still, despite her eccentric behavior, the authorities acquitted her of any witchly wrongdoing.[119] Nicholas and Eleanor Bayley, also of New Haven, were acquitted of witchcraft but advised to leave the colony.[120] Goody Knapp fared less well; she was hanged in 1654.[121]

Between 1647 and 1654 ten women and one man were hanged as witches in three colonies; eleven women and four men had fallen under suspicion of practicing witchcraft. Such executions did little to allay tensions, however. Although the establishment of the New England Confederation offered Puritans some security, fears of Indian warfare continued through the late 1650s. The qualifications of church membership and the acceptability of the Halfway Covenant came under fire.[122]

An onslaught of Quaker missionaries who refused to kowtow before the authorities exacerbated the religious friction. Quakers were the personification of the anti-Christ. Utterly contemptuous and despicably eccentric, they emphasized irrationality over reason and attacked university learning. Some of them even walked naked in public. Consequently, Quakerism and witchcraft were often linked. A jury of aged women stripped the first two Quaker women to arrive in Boston and searched them for the Devil's marks. Elizabeth Kitchin was accused of "powwowing," like the pagan Indian sorcerers.[123] Mary Wright, a missionary from Long Island, answered a presentment for witchcraft before the Massachusetts General Court in 1660. That body acquitted her of practicing *maleficium* but banished her from the colony because she was a Quaker.[124] Deputy Governor Bellingham denounced Dorothy Waugh as a witch when he sentenced her to a whipping for attempting to speak at Sabbath services. Governor Endicott called the elderly missionaries Elizabeth Hooten and Joan Brokesup witches, and he explained to Wenlock Christianson in 1661, "Thou art come in among us in Rebellion, which is as the Sin of Witchcraft, and ought to be punished"[125] There were frequent complaints that Quaker Eunice Cole, a testy woman who once bit a constable, used *maleficium* between 1656 and 1680.[126]

In New Hampshire and Plymouth colonies, some Quakers were suspected of confederacy with Satan. When the Great Island men threw Mary Tompkins head first down a flight of stairs, they said her survival was proof of her witchcraft: had she not been a witch, her neck would have been broken. Alice Walton, the Quaker wife of a prosperous inhabitant of the same place, was also "acounted a witch." When the Plymouth authorities took four cows and some calves from Barnstable Friend Ralph Jones for the Pilgrim minister's maintenance and the minister's daughter died after eating some of their meat, the clergyman charged Quakers with bewitching her. John Josselyn visited New England in 1663 and reported that Puritans found too many witches, especially "bottle-bellied witches amongst the Quakers."[127] Neither the Puritan populace nor the authorities took note of George Fox's denunciation of witchcraft or of Quaker opposition to fortune-telling.[128] The extraordinary assertiveness of Quaker women had helped to create a Puritan state of mind which inextricably linked Quakerism with witchcraft.

In 1656, just before the initial Quaker arrival in Massachusetts, the authorities had acquitted two witches and hanged another after an extensive conflict between the assistants and deputies. Anne Hibbins, the executed witch, was, ironically, the widow of William Hibbins, who had sat on the same Court of Assistants that sentenced witch Margaret Jones to hang.[129] By hanging Mistress Hibbins, the deputies managed to assert their own power over that of the assistants, who had overturned a jury verdict convicting her. After the Quakers began entering Plymouth, Massachusetts, New Hampshire, and Maine, they monopolized subsequent witchcraft accusations. Eleven of the twenty-two accusations made in those colonies between 1656 and 1664 were directed at Quakers. Even those not accused of witchcraft could be smartly lashed and banished, as other rebels had been. If a banished Quaker returned several times, he or she could be mutilated or hanged. The visibility and strangeness of the Quakers made them particularly suitable scapegoats, with the result that no witches were hanged in Massachusetts or in Puritan-controlled New Hampshire.

Because fewer Quakers reached Connecticut, things there were different. Witchcraft accusations, prosecutions, and executions continued with new intensity. One witch was exonerated of any wrongdoing, and two others were released after a jury could not agree on its verdict.[130] But in 1662 Hartford residents, sharply divided by ecclesiastical controversy,[131] became literally obsessed with the belief that extraordinary numbers of witches were threatening their security. That scare officially began when a hysterical Anne Cole accused several persons of afflicting her. One of the accused, Rebecca Greensmith, after admitting her own guilt, corroborated Cole's testimony by testifying against many other suspected witches. By January 1663 the two Greensmiths, Mary Sanford, and Mary Barnes had been executed. Two others had been convicted but then released. William Ayres, his wife, and James Wakeley escaped prison and fled to Rhode Island. At least three others may have fled to escape hanging; only one of these, the wife of Peter Grant, was known to have any Quaker sympathies.[132]

Few witchcraft accusations surfaced in Maine, Plymouth, and New Haven. One minister at Black Point, Maine, accused Eleanor Bayley, who had settled there after her prosecution in New Haven Colony, of bewitching his cow (1659). Two years later John Redman admitted his alliance with Satan.[133] Neither of these persons faced a court trial for witchcraft, for Maine's inhabitants were a materially minded people, usually possessing Anglican sentiments if they claimed any religion at all. They had no Biblical Commonwealth in mind when they settled in the colony, and they did not try to repress their material joys. A heavy theme of individualism saturated Maine culture, even after the Massachusetts Puritans took ineffective control over that area in the 1650s. Actual enemies abounded there—French, pirates, Bay Colony authorities, other fishermen brimming for a fight—and any resentments felt by Maine people could be aggressively hurled against any number of them. No witches were needed.

Plymouth law specified the death penalty for witchcraft, but in practice the authorities were more moderate than Massachusetts' leaders in controlling and punishing offenders. Lacking the zeal of the Bay Colony magistrates, Plymouth Separatists handled dissent without grave confrontations.[134] They were relatively tolerant of Anabaptists and Quakers. Instead of friction over the franchise, political apathy was the order of the day.[135] Plymouth did suffer from somewhat poor crop yields, but its residents were less bothered by the Indian problem than were the Puritans of Connecticut, New Haven, and Massachusetts. The frustration, tension, and insecurity which generally assailed the Puritan consciousness was considerably weaker in this, the oldest New England colony. Moreover, the Dutch, with whom the Pilgrims lived for a decade and a half before coming to America, were skeptical about witchcraft proceedings. No witchcraft trials occurred in Holland after

1610, and three Dutch scholars, Johann Grevius, Balthasar Bekker, and Johann Weyer, published early books attacking the "mythology" of witchcraft.[136]

Given such conditions, the first witchcraft case in Plymouth afforded more humor than anything else. When in 1660 Dinah Sylvester of Scituate accused William Holmes's wife of assuming the shape of a spectral bear in order to afflict her, disbelieving magistrates asked the maiden "what Manner of Tayle the Bear had." Of course, bears have no tails; but Sylvester responded as if hers might have had one, giving the logical answer that she could not tell "because the bear's head was towards her." The justices then ordered her to make public acknowledgement of her slander of Mistress Holmes or be whipped.[137]

New Haven Colony is a more difficult case to explain. There, although conditions during the Quaker decade were seemingly optimal for witchcraft accusations, only one witch was actually tried, and he was acquitted (1657).[138] Between 1643 and 1660 New Haven's merchants underwent an economic crisis of severe dimensions; trade was obstructed, commodities scarce, estates declining, and "great discouragements upon the most, if not all."[139] No flexible medium of exchange existed, and the tide of immigration beginning about 1660 brought many new faces but little capital into the colony. Many nonfreemen demanded the extension of the franchise to those who were not church members, and some attempted to vote at the General Court of Elections, which was held each spring to choose colonial officals.[140]

Internal dissention threatened to tear the colony apart. Some of the inhabitants of Stamford, Southold, and Milford participated in one insurrection against the rule of New Haven church members in 1645. Connecticut made efforts to annex the colony as early as 1661 and, perhaps lured by the appeal of the northerly colony's liberal franchise requirements, Southold, Guilford, Stamford, and Greenwich inhabitants voted to join Connecticut in 1662. Two years later Milford also broke away from New Haven Colony. Mother England was also disatisfied with New Haven; Restoration authorities were outraged that the colony's officials had hidden the fleeing Edward Whalley and William Goffe, the two "executioners" of Charles II who had been exempted from a parliamentary act of amnesty. Reports of New Haven's disobedience of the navigation acts brought down royal disapproval. In 1664 the King's Commissioners for New England ordered that colony to submit to Connecticut rule, and what remained of New Haven Colony reluctantly acquiesced on January 5, 1665.[141]

Yet the severely disrupted affairs of New Haven did *not* culminate in an upsurge of witchcraft accusations. The reason: witches can be prosecuted only where a viable, respected government can provide legitimacy for such prosecution. Early New Haven authorities possessed such legitimacy and gave careful attention to proper legal process, trying all criminals in orderly fashion. However, by the mid-1650s the New Haven government could hardly function. In 1653, when some men of Stamford charged that the townsmen there "were made asses of" by New Haven and that it was "time for them to look to themselves and to throw their burden of [taxation off]," the colony authorities could apprehend the major offenders and prosecute them.[142] Two years later Southold, "in an unsetled frame" over rates, refused to send deputies to sit in the New Haven General Court; this act caused the legislature to send two magistrates there to try offenders and to choose town officials for the upcoming year.[143] In both cases the colony authorities acted effectively. In the midst of these struggles, the witch as scapegoat became a usable motif. Two witches were ordered to leave the colony in 1655, and a third was suspected of *maleficium* (1653, 1655). As tensions continued, however, the New Haven authorities became increasingly impotent in the face widespread resistance, so that soon no "legitimate" authority remained to prosecute suspected witches. The town of Greenwich refused to cooperate with New Haven officials.[144] Colony magistrates could not force several Southold men to take an oath of fidelity to the colony.[145] The same magistrates could only watch in helpless frustration as four towns joined Connecticut in 1662. The General Court and the Court of Magistrates were able to try only the most serious and obvious offenders—fornicators, arsonists, disobedient servants, and Quakers—who almost everyone agreed ought to be prosecuted. Between 1660 and 1664 New Haven public officials tried only seventeen cases of criminal activity, a decline of twenty-four from the previous five-year interval.

Why, then, didn't the New Haven authorities prosecute witch-scapegoats within the village of New Haven itself, where their control was viable and respected? For one thing, New Haven itself did not need a purge; the "evil" was occurring elsewhere, in areas which rejected the cohesion the colony offered. If any witches existed, they most certainly resided in Greenwich, Southold, or

Stamford, not in New Haven. Inhabitants of the former areas could not be convinced that witches lived among them—that would have destroyed their own sense of independent solidarity, of unity. Secondly, the colony officials wished to win the alienated towns-men back into the New Haven fold, not to alienate them further, which witchcraft proceedings might do. Given the special situation of governmental decay in New Haven, there was no possibility of scapegoating there throughout the early 1660s, nor were there many religious heretics upon whose shoulders blame could be placed.

By the 1660s New England society was no longer as unified and compact as it had once been, with Puritan communities spread from the Connecticut River Valley to the borders of New York to the far reaches of Cape Cod. Limited contact between these different areas caused Calvinists some anxiety. Distances, immigrants who lacked religious zeal, and the irresistible novelty of the wilderness di-minished watchfulness and made central control an impossibility. Even if a community preserved its own relative purity, its members could not be convinced that more distant neighbors were equally careful. Heresy could easily become rooted anywhere in the New England wilderness—wasn't Rhode Island an awful example of that?—and when tensions erupted, crops failed, and Quakers in-vaded, anxiety also increased. Since Puritan theology admitted the reality of maleficent witches and contemporary England suffered an upsurge of prosecutions during the Civil War, fearful Puritans be-came quite willing to perceive society's eccentrics as witches. The great migration of the 1630s and 1640s had brought many potential scapegoats to the New World. As a result of Puritan insecurity, the prevailing cosmology, the English example, the availability of un-womanly women, and the special situation of each colony, fifteen witches were hanged (four in Massachusetts, ten in Connecticut, and one in New Haven) between 1647 and 1662.

There *were* self-avowed witches in old New England. Those women detested their ordained feminine roles of submission and maternity, and they inspired a great deal of fear. However, their practice was not as extensive as Puritan contemporaries would have us believe. Many women and a few men faced prosecution despite little, if any, concrete evidence of actual guilt. In fact, guilt become largely irrelevant, because witchcraft accusations filled a necessary function in an anxiety-ridden, repressive society which viewed independent-minded women with suspicion and alarm. In the words of F. Kraupl Tayler and J. H. Rey, "The scapegoat, whether guilty or innocent, whether fully or partially culpable, may be punished with a ferocious severity which fits the enormity of the projected guilt."[146] The frustration experienced by the individual in Puritan New England needed some outlet, and the intangible quality of the witch's offense made the "abnormal" female the handiest target. Had there been no witches, the Puritans would have invented some. Lewis Coser has written that "groups engaged in continued struggle with the outside tend to the intolerant within. . . . Their social cohesion depends upon total sharing on all aspects of group life and is reinforced by the assertion of group unity against the dissenter." Moreover, "the evocation of an outer enemy or the invention of such an enemy strengthens social cohesion that is threatened from within."[147] The witch, although living within the community, was defined as such an "outside enemy."

Witchcraft fulfilled many functions in seventeenth-century society. It became a way to explain events which negatively affected an individual's life. It served as a societal purgative, and as a vehicle for the expression of neighborhood resentment and repressed sexuality. Not least important, it was an avenue for female resistance and for the assertion of female power—as well as, paradoxically, a way to keep offensive women in line.

1. Miller, *N. Eng. Mind: From Col. to Prov.*, p. 191.

2. Boyer & Nissenbaum, *Salem Possessed*; Demos, "Underlying Themes in Witchcraft of N. Eng."; Hansen, *Witchcraft in Salem*.

3. In Calvin's home base of Geneva, Switzerland, the authorities prosecuted at least 273 "witches," banished 172, and executed 48 between 1537 and 1662. See Monter, "Witchcraft in Geneva."

4. C. Mather, *Memorable Prov.*, pp. 12, 22; I. Mather, *Essay for Recording Illus. Prov.*, p. 99.

5. C. Mather, *Diary*, I, 86–87, 172.

6. E. Taylor, "Letter," pp. 629–31; Winthrop, *Journal*, II, 346; Josselyn, *Two Voyages to N. Eng.*, p. 275.

7. Josselyn, *Two Voyages to N. Eng.*, p. 182.

8. Nye, *Unembarrassed Muse*, p. 11.

9. C[hamberlain], *Lithobolia*, pp. 58–77.

10. I. Mather, *Essay for Recording Illus. Prov.*, pp. 142–55.

11. *Ibid.*, pp. 248–49, 252, 268; C. Mather, *Wonders of Invisible World*, pt. 3, pp. 5–6; Bouton, ed., *Prov. Papers of N. Hamp.*, I, 417.

12. C. Mather, *Wonders of Invisible World*, pp. 26–27; Brattle, "Letter," p. 181.

13. *Rec. of Suffolk Ct. 1671–80*, I, 486. In 1674 Peggy paid a £10 fine for fathering an illegitimate child.

14. C. Mather, *Diary*, I, 600; A. Bradstreet, *Works*, p. 226; Holwell, *Predictions*; [T. Shepard,] *Almanack for 1656*.

15. F. Dexter, ed., *Literary Diary of E. Stiles*, I, 385–86.

16. Coffin, *Sketch of Newbury*, pp. 123–27.

17. Josiah Cotton, "Some Observations—Concerning Witches," n.p. Joseph Glanvill's *Saducismus Triumphatus* was a large (597 pp.) compilation of philosophical and evidentiary essays dealing with witches, haunted houses, and other occult happenings. Published at a time when the English authorities were skeptical about witchcraft (1689), it constituted an effort to restore belief in the reality of witches.

18. C. Mather, *Magnalia*, II, 186; Oberholzer, *Delinquent Saints*, p. 75; Libby, Allen, & Moody, eds., *Maine Ct. Rec.*, III, 49; Dunton, *Life & Errors*, I, 138; C. Mather, *Wonders of Invisible World*, pt. 3, p. 27.

19. Dunton, *Life & Errors*, p. 114.

20. See selections in Robbins, *Encyc. of Witchcraft & Demon.*

21. *Ibid.*, pp. 414–24.

22. J. Taylor, *Witchcraft Del. in Col. Conn.*, pp. 67, 111–12.

23. See cases cited in Drake, *Annals of Witchcraft*.

24. Puppets were, however, not a necessary prerequisite to affliction, for "some Witches make their own bodyes to be their Poppet's" (C. Mather, "Letter to Richards, May 31, 1692," p. 395).

25. Josiah Cotton, "Some Observations—Concerning Witches," n.p.

26. According to Sanford J. Fox, "there was a substantial amount of science involved in the [witch] trials, in contradiction to the widely held belief that the whole matter was almost entirely an exercise in superstition, with a little psychopathology and backbiting thrown in" (Fox, *Science & Justice*, p. 2).

27. C. Mather, "Letter to Robert Calef, 1694," in W. Ford, "Mather-Calef Paper on Witchcraft," pp. 245, 254–57.

28. Drake, *Annals of Witchcraft*, p. 56; John Cotton, *Abstract of N. Eng. Laws*, p. 10; J. Trumbull, ed., *Conn. Rec.*, I, 77; *New-Haven's Settling in New-England and Some Lawes for Government* (London, 1656), in Hoadly, ed., *Rec. of N. Haven Col. 1653–Union*, p. 576; Bouton, ed., *Prov. Papers of N. Hamp.*, I, 384.

29. Bouton, ed., *Prov. Papers of N. Hamp.*, I, 415–16; C. Mather, *Memorable Prov.*, p. 59; I. Mather, *Essay for Recording Illus. Prov.*, p. 266; "Danvers Church Rec.," p. 133.

30. J. Hale, *Modest Inquiry into Witchcraft*, p. 21; "Witchcraft in Maine," p. 195; Hoadly, ed., *Rec. of N. Haven Col. 1653–Union*, p. 224.

31. Quoted in J. Taylor, *Witchcraft Del. in Col. Conn.*, p. 41.

32. *Ibid.*, pp. 41, 73, 75; I. Mather, *Essay for Recording Illus. Prov.*, pp. 266, 281; "Danvers Church Rec.," p. 133; C. Mather, *Memorable Prov.*, p. 59.

33. J. Taylor, *Witchcraft Del. in Col. Conn.*, p. 40. Much uncertainty existed, however, as to the legitimacy of specter evidence as proof of witchcraft. Some believed Satan might delude by causing affliction in the specter likeness of an innocent, while other authorities felt God would never allow that to occur. See Miller, *N. Eng. Mind: From Col. to Prov.*, pp. 193–94, 198–99, 201, 250–52.

34. G. Dow, ed., *Essex Ct. Rec.*, II, 159; Upham, *Salem Witchcraft*, II, 274; "Salem Witchcraft—1692," I, n.p.

35. "Ct. Files—Suffolk Co.," XIII (1673), no. 1228.

36. [H. Norton,] *N.-Eng. Ensigne*, p. 7.

37. James VI quoted in Cartland, *Woman the Enigma*, p. 96; Hole, *Witchcraft in Eng.*, p. 36.

38. Hale, *Modest Inquiry*, pp. 71–73; F. Hutchinson, *Hist. Essay Concerning Witchcraft*, p. 176.

39. Szasz, *Manufacture of Madness*, p. 32.

40. R. Masters, *Eros & Evil*, p. 60; Robbins, *Encyc. of Witchcraft & Demon.*, p. 254; Sprenger & Kramer, *Malleus Maleficarum*, p. 113; Hole, *Witchcraft in Eng.*, p. 37.

41. C. Mather, *Memorable Prov.*, p. 62.

42. Whiting, "Letter," p. 468.

43. I. Mather, *Essay for Recording Illus. Prov.*, pp. 175–77.

44. Belladonna produces "excitement, which might pass to delirium," while hemlock and aconite "would produce mental confusion, impaired movement, irregular action of the heart, dizziness and shortness of breath" (Hughes, *Witchcraft*, pp. 128–29). Aconite and thorn apple grew wild in seventeenth-century America. New England witches may have imported hemlock and belladonna from Europe. The latter two plants have since flourished in the climate of the northeast (Osol & Farrar, *New Dispensatory of U.S.A.*, pp. 120, 1117, 1410).

45. Glanvill, *Saducismus Triumphatus*, pp. 271, 572, 596–97.

46. Josiah Cotton, "Some Observations—Concerning Witches,"n.p.

47. Libby, Allen, & Moody, eds., *Maine Ct. Rec.*, IV, 49; G. Dow, ed., *Essex Ct. Rec.*, VI, 387.

48. Libby, Allen, & Moody, eds., *Maine Ct. Rec.*, I, 85–86.

49. Fogg, "Witchcraft in N. Hamp.," p. 39; G. Dow, ed., *Essex Ct. Rec.*, III, 413; VI, 207–9; Boyer & Nissenbaum, eds., *Salem-Village Witchcraft*, pp. 41–45; "Ct. Files—Suffolk Co.," II (1654–60), no. 256a.

50. The bowel-pulling witch was Goody Glover. See C. Mather, *Memorable Prov.*, p. 10.

51. F. Dexter, ed., *N. Haven Town Rec. 1649–62*, pp. 245–46; Hoadly, ed., *Rec. of N. Haven Col. 1653–Union*, p. 34; "Conn. Arch. Crimes & Misd.," 1st ser., I, 6–9.

52. Baroja, *World of the Witches*, p. 256; Debrunner, *Witchcraft in Ghana*, pp. 84–85. Some anthropologists have observed that witchcraft-sorcery is an expression of individuality and personal power, as well as an economic leveling device. See Evans-Pritchard, *Witchcraft among the Azande*, p. 100; Beidelman, "Witchcraft in Ukaguru," p. 93.

53. E. Janeway, *Man's World, Woman's Place*, p. 129. This scholar argues that witch beliefs arise out of the mother's magical ability to fulfill her child's wants, and the child's realization that sometimes his or her wants are *not* taken care of, e.g., when he or she is left wailing (pp. 126–27).

54. Wendell, "Were the Salem Witches Guiltless?"; Hansen, *Witchcraft at Salem*, pp. 34–54; Hawthorne, "Young Goodman Brown," pp. 1033–42.

55. G. Dow, ed., *Essex Ct. Rec.*, VII, 43–45, 49–50.

56. Hoadly, ed., *Rec. of N. Haven Col. 1653–Union*, pp. 29–34; F. Dexter, ed., *N. Haven Town Rec. 1649–62*, p. 249.

57. C. Mather, *Memorable Prov.*, pp. 61–63.

58. Shurtleff, ed., *Mass. Rec.*, IV, pt. 1, pp. 47, 73; III, 229.

59. Hoadly, ed., *Rec of N. Haven Col. 1653–Union*, p. 81.

60. Whiting, "Letter."

61. Noble & Cronin, eds., *Rec. of Mass. Assts.*, I, 228–29.

62. Libby, Allen, & Moody, eds., *Maine Ct. Rec.*, II, 106.

63. C. Mather, *Memorable Prov.*, pp. 7–13.

64. F. Dexter, ed., *N. Haven Town Rec. 1649–62*, pp. 249–52.

65. Demos, "Underlying Themes in Witchcraft of N. Eng.," pp. 1325–26.

66. Steadman, "Eve's Dream & Witchcraft Conventions"; Richard Bernard, *Guide to Grand Jurymen with Respect to Witches* (London, 1627), quoted in Davies, *Four Centuries of Witch-Beliefs*, pp. 98–99.

67. Demos, *Little Commonwealth*, pp. 62–64; Bissell, "From One Generation to Another."

68. A comparison of New England witches with those in other cultures testifies to the thesis that witchcraft was a way for women whose social value was low to achieve some semblance of personal value. See Kluckhohn, *Navaho Witchcraft*, p. 59; Godwin, "Scandal of Witch-Doctor"; Linton, *Effects of Culture on Mental & Emotional Processes*, pp. 303–4; Wilson, *Reaction to Conquest*, p. 316.

69. Drake, *Annals of Witchcraft*, pp. 233–35, 239–40; Whiting, "Letter."

70. G. Dow, ed., *Essex Ct. Rec.*, IV, 133, 90, VI, 386–87; C. Mather, *Memorable Prov.*, pp. 2–3. The magistrates disagreed with the jury's conviction of Susanna Martin and released her.

71. Alan MacFarlane reports that in Essex County, England, 291 "witches" were accused of bewitching 341 victims, including 92 children (*Witchcraft in Tudor & Stuart Eng.*, p. 162). In New England the proportion of child victims was considerably higher; of 88 total victims, 53 had not reached their twentieth birthday.

For the pattern of unfeminine women being charged with witchcraft in other cultures, see Beidelman, "Witchcraft in Ukaguru," p. 74; Nadel, *Nupe Rel.*, p. 187; Midelfort, *Witch Hunting in Southwestern Germ.*, p. 196.

72. Shurtleff, ed., *Mass. Rec.*, III, 229; IV, pt. 1, pp. 47, 73; C. Mather, *Memorable Prov.*, pp. 61–63, 1–15; Whiting, "Letter," p. 466; F. Dexter, ed., *N. Haven Town Rec. 1649–62*, p. 252.

73. The available records do not make clear the specific charges against 38 female and 12 male witches. If we consider only those against whom a substantive charge was levied, one-third of the men and 78% of the women were accused of afflicting or murdering children.

74. Wyllys, "Wyllys Col. Suppl. Witchcraft in Conn. 1662–93," p. 39.

75. Drake, *Annals of Witchcraft*, p. 280.

76. "Ct. Files—Suffolk Co.," XXIII (1680–81), no. 1958.

77. T. Forbes, *Midwife & Witch*, pp. 126–27, and "Midwifery & Witchcraft"; Hole, *Witchcraft in Eng.*, p. 54.

78. Hole, *Witchcraft in Eng.*, pp. 129–30.

79. F. Dexter, ed., *Literary Diary of E. Stiles*, I, 385–86; E. Johnson, *Wonder-Working Prov.*, p. 132; Winthrop, *Short Story of Rise of Antinomians*, p. 281; Shurtleff, ed., *Mass. Rec.*, I, 224.

80. G. Burr, ed., *Narratives of Witchcraft*, p. 31n.

81. Winthrop, *Journal*, II, 344–45; Woodward, ed., *Rec. of Salem Witchcraft* II, 262–67.

82. Drake, *Annals of Witchcraft*, pp. 98–99.

83. J. Taylor, *Witchcraft Del. in Col. Conn.*, p. 96.

84. G. Burr, ed., *Narratives of Witchcraft*, p. 61n; Libby, Allen, & Moody, eds., *Maine Ct. Rec.*, II, 106; *Rec. of Conn. Part. Ct.*, p. 93; Drake, *Annals of Witchcraft*, p. 66.

85. F. Morgan et al., *Conn. as Col. & State*, I, 219–20; C. Mather, *Memorable Prov.*, pp. 61–63; "Witchcraft on L.I."; G. Dow, ed., *Essex Ct. Rec.*, VII, 43–45.

86. Drake, *Annals of Witchcraft*, p. 117.

87. Todd, "Witchcraft in N. Eng.," p. 174; Noble & Cronin, eds., *Rec. of Mass. Assts.*, I, 233.

88. Drake, *Annals of Witchcraft*, pp. 100–101.

89. *Ibid.*, p. 107; J. Baxter, *Pioneers of Maine & N. Hamp.*, p. 212; Savage, *Geneal. Dict. of First Settlers of N. Eng.*, II, 249.

90. Many observers have reported that witchcraft accusations are a device to insure conformity to social role expectations, as well as to express expectations of proper conduct. See Evans-Pritchard, *Witchcraft among the Azande*, p. 112; Marwick, *Sorcery in Social Setting*, p. 239; MacFarlane, *Witchcraft in Tudor & Stuart Eng.*, pp. 158–59; Nadel, *Nupe Rel.*, p. 171; La Fontaine, "Witchcraft in Bugisi," p. 217; Buxton, "Mandari Witchcraft," p. 104; Omoyajowo, *Witches?*, p. 25; Kluckhohn, *Navaho Witchcraft*, p. 35. John Demos has pointed out that New England "witches" had "some kind of personal eccentricity, some deviant or even criminal behavior that had long since marked them out as suspect" (Demos, "Underlying Themes in Witchcraft of N. Eng.," p. 1317).

91. Hoadly, ed., *Rec. of N. Haven Col. 1653–Union*, p. 29.

92. *Ibid.*, pp. 30–32; C. Mather, *Memorable Prov.*, p. 26; Todd, "Witchcraft in N. Eng.," p. 174; Demos, "Underlying Themes in Witchcraft of N. Eng.," pp. 1317–19.

93. Katherine Harrison of Wethersfield fell under suspicion because, among other things, she could spin unusually large skeins of yarn (J. Taylor, *Witchcraft Del. in Conn.*, p. 56).

94. C. Mather, *Wonders of Invisible World*, pt. 3, pp. 10–12.

95. See ch. 7.

96. J. Taylor, *Witchcraft Del. In Conn.*, p. 59.

97. G. Dow, ed., *Essex Ct. Rec.*, I, 88, 143, 238, 313.

98. *Hartford Town Votes*, I, 135; *Rec. of Conn. Part. Ct.*, pp. 81, 86, 107.

99. J. Trumbull, ed., *Conn. Rec.*, I, 338; F. Morgan et al., *Conn. as Col. & State*, I, 219–20.

100. These thieves included N. Greensmith, the Jennings, Mary Johnson, Anis Hoar, and Margaret Lord. Suspicion also fell on Elizabeth Morse and Jane James. See J. Taylor, *Witchcraft Del. in Conn.*, p. 96; F. Morgan et al., *Conn. as Col. & State*, I, 219–20; *Rec. of Conn. Part Ct.*, p. 43; G. Dow, ed., *Essex Ct. Rec.*, VI, 52; VII, 43–45; I, 200, 11.

101. Wyllys, "Wyllys Col. Suppl. Witchcraft in Conn. 1662–93," pp. 45, 56–60; J. Taylor, *Witchcraft Del. in Conn.*, p. 81; Conn. "Ct. of Assts. 1665–77," in "Conn. Rec.," LVI, 52.

102. The Connecticut figure includes five witches from New Haven Colony.

103. In 1665, for example, 8–9,000 people lived in Connecticut, 13,080 in

Plymouth, and 25,000 in Massachusetts (Greene & Harrington, *Am. Pop. before Fed. Census of 1790*, pp. 11, 13, 47).

104. Taylor & Rey, "Scapegoat Motif in Soc.," p. 253.

105. A few years before the Pilgrims arrived at Plymouth Rock, a smallpox epidemic had wiped out most of the Indians along the eastern seaboard--a fact which decreased the possibility of Indian unrest.

106. Ronald A. Cohen ("Church & State in Mass.") persuasively argues that early Puritans had "a substantial degree of cohesiveness" which Antinomianism, with its "inherent individualism," threatened. Yet, Cohen points out, after the controversy the church and the state wished "to forgive and forget," since both had a sense of the community's continued vitality and solidarity.

107. Davies, *Four Cent. of Witch-Beliefs*, pp. 61–109, 147–61; MacFarlane, *Witchcraft in Tudor & Stuart Eng.*, pp. 28, 135; Ross, "Calvinism & Witchcraft in Eng."; Teall, "Witchcraft & Calvinism in Eliz. Eng."

108. Berkowitz & Green, "Stimulus Qualities of the Scapegoat"; Berkowitz & Holmes, "Generaliz. of Hostility to Disliked Objects."

109. E. Johnson, *Wonder-Working Prov.*, p. 237; Shurtleff, ed., *Mass. Rec.*, III, 229, 273–74; IV, pt. 1, pp. 47, 73, 96; G. Dow, ed., *Essex Ct. Rec.*, I, 108, 199, 204, 229, 276, 301, 325, 348.

110. Winthrop, *Journal*, II, 345–46; N. Mather, "Letter, 1684," pp. 58–59; T. Hutchinson, *Witchcraft Delusion of 1692*, pp. 7–8n; J. Hale, *Modest Inquiry*, pp. 17–19.

111. Non-church members expressed "bitterness over their lack of a voice in hiring and firing the ministers whose maintenance they helped pay, as well as over their inability to participate either in the wordly business or the spiritual blessings of the church." For a discussion of this friction, see Lucas, "Church v. Town," and *Valley of Discord*, pp. 41–78.

112. Lucas, *Valley of Discord*, pp. 50, 61–63.

113. Winthrop, *Journal*, II, 323; J. Taylor, *Witchcraft Del. in Conn.*, pp. 35, 145–47, 156.

114. J. Taylor, *Witchcraft Del. in Conn.*, p. 144; J. Trumbull, ed., *Conn. Rec.*, I, 171; *Rec. of Conn. Part. Ct.*, p. 56; C. Mather, *Memorable Prov.*, pp. 61–63.

115. J. Taylor, *Witchcraft Del. in Conn.*, pp. 38, 147; *Rec. of Conn. Part. Ct.*, p. 93.

116. J. Taylor, *Witchcraft Del. in Conn.*, pp. 148–49; J. Trumbull, ed., *Conn. Rec.*, I, 220.

117. Lucas, *Valley of Discord*, pp. 41–42, 50–51.

118. Andrews, *Col. Period of Am. Hist.*, II, 174n.

119. Hoadly, ed., *Rec. of N. Haven Col. 1653–Union*, pp. 29–36; F. Dexter, ed., *N. Haven Town Rec. 1649–62*, pp. 249–52, 256; J. Taylor, *Witchcraft Del. in Conn.*, pp. 85–96.

120. J. Taylor, *Witchcraft Del. in Conn.*, p. 149; F. Dexter, ed., *N. Haven Town Rec. 1649–62*, pp. 244–46, 256–58.

121. Hoadly, ed., *Rec. of N. Haven Col. 1653–Union*, pp. 77, 80–81.

122. B. Trumbull, *Complete Hist. of Conn.*, I, 301–3, 461; Stiles, *Hist. & Geneal. of Ancient Windsor*, I, 202–3; R. Pope, *Half-Way Covenant*, pp. 198–233; Beales, "Half-Way Covenant & Rel. Scrupulosity."

123. [H. Norton,] *N.-Eng. Ensigne*, p. 7; G. Dow, ed., *Essex Ct. Rec.*, II, 219.

124. Rubincam, "Lydia Wright & Her Sister," p. 108.

125. [H. Norton,] *N.-Eng. Ensigne*, p. 69; Bishop, *N.-Eng. Judged*, pp. 403–5; Besse, *Col. of Quaker Sufferings*, II, 222.

126. Drake, *Annals of Witchcraft*, pp. 99–103; Noble & Cronin, eds., *Rec. of Mass. Assts.*, III, 253; "Mass. Arch.," CXXXV, 2–15; Bouton, ed., *Prov. Papers of N. Hamp.*, I, 241–42.

127. Bishop, *N.-Eng. Judged*, pp. 394, 466–67, 492; Josselyn, *Two Voyages to N. Eng.*, p. 182.

128. Gummere, *Witchcraft & Quakerism*, pp. 20, 28.

129. Hubbard, "Gen. Hist. of N. Eng.," VI, p. 174.

130. J. Trumbull, ed., *Conn. Rec.*, I, 338, 572.

131. That controversy would last for twenty years, setting a seventeenth-century record for continued ecclesiastical contention. Wethersfield, New London, and Middleton also experienced a good deal of friction in their respective churches between 1656 and 1662. In the latter year, the ministerial leadership in Connecticut was so demoralized by the affirmation of the Half-Way Covenant in Massachusetts that no Connecticut clergyman or layman bothered to attend meetings of the Boston synod. See Lucas, *Valley of Discord*, pp. 52–54, and "Church v. Town," pp. 4–11, 25; see also "Papers Relating to Controversy in Hartford Church."

132. I. Mather, *Essay for Recording Illus. Prov.*, pp. 135–37; C. Mather, *Magnalia*, II, 448; Whiting, "Letter"'; J. Taylor, *Witchcraft Del. in Conn.*, pp. 96–100; Wyllys, "Wyllys Col. Suppl. Witchcraft in Conn. 1662–93," pp. 44–60.

133. "Witchcraft in Maine," p. 195; Libby, Allen, & Moody, eds., *Maine Ct. Rec.*, II, 106.

134. H. Ward, *Statism in Plym.*

135. Langdon, "Franchise & Pol. Demo. in Plym.," pp. 518–21, argues that few Plymouth residents wanted the privilege of freemanship, and that the number of landowners who sought enfrachisement declined throughout the century. Those eligible to vote simply did not take the necessary oath of fidelity.

136. Robbins, *Encyc. of Witchcraft & Demon.*, pp. 45, 538–40, 353.

137. Drake, *Annals of Witchcraft*, pp. 116–17.

138. J. Taylor, *Witchcraft Del. in Conn.*, p. 149; Hoadly, ed., *Rec. of N. Haven Col. 1653–Union*, p. 224.

139. Quoted in Andrews, *Col. Period in Am. Hist.*, II, 173.

140. *Ibid.*, II, 173–93; Hoadly, ed., *Rec. of N. Haven Col. 1653–Union*, p. 177.

141. Andrews, *Col. Period of Am. Hist.*, II, 173–93.

142. Hoadly, ed., *Rec. of N. Haven Col. 1653–Union*, pp. 48–49, 55–66.

143. *Ibid.*, p. 143.

144. *Ibid.*, p. 285.

145. *Ibid.*, p. 144.

146. Taylor & Rey, "Scapegoat Motif," p. 254.

147. Lewis Coser, *Functions of Social Conflict*, pp. 103, 110, as quoted in Cohen, "Church & State in Mass.," pp. 488–89.

XI

The Rhode Island Alternative

... the God of Peace, the God of Order ... hath of one
Bloud, made all Mankinde, to dwell upon the face of the
Earth, [but] all [are] confounded and destroyed in their Civill
Beings and Subsistences, by mutuall flames of warre from
their severall respective Religions and Consciences.
—Roger Williams, *The Bloudy Tenant Yet More Bloody*

Rhode Island is a chaos of all religions and like *materia prima*
susceptive of all forms.
—Raymond P. Stearns, ed., "Correspondence
of Woodbridge & Baxter"

IN SEVENTEENTH-CENTURY NEW ENGLAND THE IDEAL FEMININE ROLE
encountered more than one kind of stress. On the one hand, dissatisfied women reacted in a variety of ways (as witch, abusive
wife, hysteric, heretic) to the static role expectations posited and
reinforced by early Calvinist society. At the same time, those role
expectations were tested—not only on an individual level, but
over time and space as well. In the various colonies controlled by
Calvinists, different external and internal factors helped to mod-
ify the practical import of the ideal female role over the century's
course. And in Rhode Island–Providence Plantations, that colony
with a singularly un-Puritan cast of mind, both expectations and
possibilities for women were quite unlike anything the Puritans
had visualized.

The "Land of Errors"

A uniquely tolerant colony, Rhode Island was, in Puritan terms, an area populated by religious heretics and social riffraff. Calvinists generally called it "Rogue Island" or "nothing else than the sewer of New England," an area where "All the cranks of New England retire," creating a "colluvies of Antinomians, Familists, Anabaptists, Antisabbatarians, Socinians, Quakers, Ranters, and every thing in the world but Roman Catholicks, and real Christians."[1] Roger Williams's rebels at Providence, Anne Hutchinson's followers at Portsmouth and Newport, the thoroughly outrageous Gortonists at Warwick, and Quakers throughout the Narragansett Bay area[2] worried Puritan leaders who were struggling to maintain their respective Biblical Commonwealths.

Criminals indicted in Puritan colonies often fled to Rhode Island.[3] "Witches" Elizabeth Seager, James Wakeley, and Judith and William Ayres, indicted in Connecticut, found Rhode Island attitudes more tolerable.[4] Fugitive adulterers could live there without much fear of apprehension, and unwed pregnant women sought refuge in this "land of errors"—if only long enough to deliver the child and leave it with a willing Rhode Island family.[5]

"Criminals" and religious heretics did not value social institutions with the same rigorous intensity as the Calvinists; nor did they celebrate the necessity of regulating each individual's behavior in minute detail. Before King Philip's War, those watchdogs of propriety, the selectmen and tithingmen, did not exist in this land where people believed in the essential right of the individual to behave in accordance with his or her conscience. Rhode Island preachers paid little attention to the doctrine of original sin and man's despicableness, talking instead about the ability of every person to reach heaven. There seemed to be almost no fear of impending providential justice or social chaos or rampant immorality. No public school system taught youngsters that an authoritarian God might sentence them to a horrifying hellfire. Quaker meetings and colony authorities occasionally urged poor people to place their children out as apprentices, but never because those parents were guilty of moral turpitude.

A Freer Life for Children

Roger Williams, a man of basically Calvinist temperament, worried about the moral state of his Rhode Island contemporaries and blamed the Quakers, in particular, for causing disarray. In his famous 1672 debates with English Friends at Newport and Providence, he charged the Quakers with teaching inferiors to disrespect their superiors. Some members of the audience at those debates reported that they had heard Quaker children accuse their own parents of lying. While he was not present there himself, George Fox subsequently justified such children's actions in a post-debate commentary by arguing that if parents called Christ but "a fancy," their children could then become "uncivil and irreverent." Friends allowed young men and women to prophesy, "if they were of clean lives, and what they had to say, [had been] approved [at a Quaker meeting]."[6] Since God had not limited his "inner light" to adults, the child, in some spiritual sense, had the power to judge the religious orientation of his or her ostensible superiors. Many younger people found Quakerism appealing, in part undoubtedly because it respected their ability to exercise judgment on religious matters. Quakerism also gave youngsters, and women, a great feeling of self-confidence through mystical participation in the omnipotence of God.

Young Quaker missionaries, including many girls, spoke as censoriously as adults. Katherine Scott's eleven-year-old daughter Patience accompanied her mother to Boston and there spent some time in prison for her spirited defense of Quaker principles. The Massachusetts authorities finally released the child, reasoning that she was too young to have a complete understanding of religion.[7] In 1664 fifteen-year-old Hannah Wright of Long Island came to Boston to give a "warning in the name of the Lord"; three years earlier the Bay Colony magistrates had lodged her in prison for Quaker activities.[8] Calvinists, much concerned about the corruptibility of their own children, imprisoned or sold as servants the sons and daughters of arrested Friends.[9] Apparently Calvinist fears had some basis in fact, for the Quaker missionary Samuel Hooten in 1666 reported, "the younger sort of people [at Cambridge] had a great love to me," while many of the adults were "envious and bitter against me."[10]

Calvinists disliked the Quaker style of childrearing. Friends, like their Calvinist contemporaries, denounced any delighting in "folly and pranks," music, dancing, card playing, games, and sports by children; but, unlike the Puritans, they believed that all children were innocent of sin until they had reached an age where they could determine right from wrong. Although the early Quakers assumed that children were to obey parents in daily matters and to respect their parents' desires to educate them for adulthood, they did not find unquestioning reverence for parental authority and fear as important as the Calvinists did. When a Quaker child erred, the parents' first approach was to appeal to his or her understanding. A rebuke or "timely restraint" was felt to have more impact than the use of the rod, for the latter might fill a child with anger and make him or her more stubborn. One traveler described children of a Quaker household on Nantucket as follows: "They are corrected with tenderness, nursed with the most affectionate care, [and] clad with that decent plainness, from which they observe their parents never to depart: in short, by the force of example, which is superior even to the strongest instinct of nature, more than by precepts, they learn to follow the steps of their parents."[11] Many personal journals cited examples of "indulged children who dominated the household."[12] Often Friends did not even force their children to attend meeting with them. In 1683 some Quaker parents lamented that children too frequently came together "at inconvenient places & at unreasonable times, spending their time to ye Dishonour of truth."[13] Even so, in such cases the most extreme action taken was to publish "such papers of instruction . . . that all [parents] may be stirred up," relying on persuasion rather than the Puritan style of legal enforcement or the rod.[14]

The Gortonists were like the Quakers in accepting the civil "magistracy" of parents over their children, while arguing against discipline enforced by fear: "We profess right unto all men, and do no violence at all, as your prescripts threaten to do to us," they wrote to the Massachusetts Puritans, *"for we have learned how to discipline our children or servants without offering violence unto them."*[15] The Gortonists were the first seventeenth-century New England group to assert outright that sparing the rod did *not* spoil the child.

Furthermore, Gorton himself would chastise those who failed to recognize that each person, child or adult, male or female, was an individual, deserving respect and capable of shaping his or her own spiritual destiny. He disagreed with Calvinists' theory that the sins of the father were visited upon his children "unto the thirds and fourths of them that hate the Lord" (Exodus 20:5), and that an unruly child was a providential reminder of God's discontent with a given parent. In Gorton's terms, the Calvinist concept of election was too aristocratic a notion; a propensity for salvation simply could not flow through the loins of the saints. Instead, he argued, the "word generacion is not in the Hebrew text"; the relevant passage referred only to the unity of haters of God in the four corners of the earth.[16] Gorton attacked those of his associates who "cannot give like dignity unto the Son as to the father at all times and in all things," particularly in acknowledging the son's right freely to dispose of his inherited property without facing serious litigation.[17]

Gorton and his followers may have been responsible for the omission of a provision for capital punishment of rebellious children from the law code of 1647. Instead, the child who "shall rise vp or rebell against his superiour" spent half a year in the house of correction, provided he or she did *not* humble him or herself before the parents. Rhode Island laws made no provision even for whipping such offenders before 1663, when the assemblymen enacted a law directing that rebellious children receive up to ten lashes and a prison term until they humbled themselves.[18] In practice, however, the authorities did not prosecute violators of either the 1647 or the 1663 law.[19]

Boys and girls who wished to think for themselves did not face much punishment, or even reproof, from the church, the state, or the educational system. Rhode Islanders considered a public school system unnecessary before 1670,[20] leaving each child's training to the individual family.[21] Learning the three R's had some importance, but, respect for children notwithstanding, Rhode Islanders felt that too much education could corrupt their egalitarian lifestyle. As Samuel Baily asserted in his poem "The Colledges ferula," Harvard-trained Puritans were too "academic" to value good humor, spoke ambiguously in words "of double sence," and assumed a demeanor of grave sophistry. Such "educated" youths thought themselves better than their "aged fathers," considering themselves above the practical arts of ploughing, carting, and caring for livestock.[22]

In Rhode Island–Providence Planatations, widespread leniency, toleration, and the lack of rigidifying social institutions, particularly the school, facilitated creative development in children. Youngsters who grew up in this freer atmosphere tended to exercise, as adults, a measure of independence unknown in Puritan New England. Lacking most fears and anxieties of Puritan children, Rhode Island youngsters did not live in a world where Satan continually grasped at their souls and witches periodically assailed them.

Even though boys and girls could become missionaries in Rhode Island, their relative equality in that respect had no economic significance. Missionaries could claim no financial compensation for

their efforts, and the apprenticeship system failed to teach girls to be
self-supporting, although it did so for boys. Male apprentices, like
their Puritan counterparts, received instruction in reading, writing,
and a trade; girls learned housewifery, cooking, and sewing. Their
apprenticeship training destined them only for the future role of
wife.[23] Probably few children were apprenticed—as reflected by the
scarcity of existing apprenticeship records, the colony's predomi-
nantly agrarian character, and the lack of any fear of expressing
affection toward children—but certainly it seems likely that sex-role
differences commonly prevailed in the instruction children received
at home.

Differing Views on the Female Sex

Rhode Islanders, like so many of their contemporaries, believed
that males and females were suited for separate roles in society. Yet
there were qualitative differences in how the Quakers, Samuel
Gorton, and Roger Williams defined maleness and femaleness.
Williams, the Calvinist, expressed a strange blend of the sentimen-
tal and the arrogant. Once, while visiting the Indians, he sent "an
handfull of flowers make up in a little Posey" to his "dear wife" and
their "dear children, to look and smell on, when I as the grasse of the
field shall be gone, and withered." Such tokens, Williams wrote to
his wife, "I know will be sweeter to thee than the Honey and the
Honey-combe, and stronger refreshment then the strongest wines
or waters, and of more value than if every line or letter [of my note]
were thousands of gold and silver."[24]

The founder of Providence valued female "softness" and sensitiv-
ity, but he did not appreciate female independence. He pointed out
that the Bible consigned woman to a subordinate role: even "though
the Holy Scripture were silent, yet Reason and Experience tell us,
that the Woman is the weaker Vessel, that she is more fitted to keep
and order the House and Children, & c." This divine argued "that
the Lord hath given a covering of longer Hair to Women as a sign or
teacher of covering Modesty and Bashfulness, Silence and Retiredness; and therefore [women are] not so fitted for Manly Actions
and Employments."[25] For ladies to preach in public assemblies
represented "open violence" to God's way, "a business all sober and
modest Humanity abhor to think of." For the weaker sex to become
"Lord Majors and Bailiffs, and Sheriffs, and Justices and Constables, Captains, Colonels, Generals, and Commanders by Sea

and Land" became a notion even too ridiculous to attack. When, in Williams's 1672 debate with the Quakers, Rhode Island Governor Nicholas Easton's wife rose to protest the Providence divine's charge that Scripture barred female preachers, he refused to respond. "If a man had so alleadged," the Calvinist later wrote, "I would have answered him: But I would not Countenance so much the violation of Gods Order in making a Reply to a Woman in Publick." Williams did not, however, object to a woman speaking publicly in his defense at the same debate.[26]

Valuing female modesty so strongly, Williams was utterly shocked to find out that two female Quakers in Massachusetts had the "Impudency (which stinks to Heaven and cries for vengeance)" to appear naked in public. This minister held the female body in some distaste—to him the bringing forth of children had "the filthiness and stinks of Nature"[27]—and he continually attacked Quaker men for allowing their women to appear naked "under a pretence of being stirred up by God as a Service or Worship unto God." Friend John Stubbs, in defense of the women, referred Williams to Isaiah 20, in which Isaiah "was commanded to goe naked for a sign to the Egyptians and Ethyopians, to prophesie and denounce that they also should go naked with their buttocks uncovered as the [Bible's] words are." The outraged minister answered that the day of signs was over. Furthermore, he maintained, a great difference existed between the nakedness of men and of women: "The Sex of Women is more fitted and framed by God for a Covering, for Retiredness and keeping at home and for Modesty and Bashfulness." Even the "naked Barbarians," he pointed out, allowed their male children to run about nude until age seven, while they covered their female infants' genitals from birth.[28]

Williams felt that too many Rhode Island women failed to seek salvation in a properly feminine fashion. "I must (and O that I had not cause) grieve," he lamented, "because so many of Zion's daughters see not and grieve not for their souls defilements."[29] An awful destiny might await the outspoken, dissatisfied woman, he warned, using the case of Joshua Windsor's wife as an example. The discontented Mistress Windsor had, Williams wrote, "made a passionate wish that God would part them & take away him or her. It pleased his Jealousie to heare her, & to take away a Childe in her wombe allso, of which she could not be deliuered."[30] Contented Christian women like Phoebe, Priscilla, Mary, and Persis in Romans 16 more appropriately illustrated the kind of feminine behavior

Williams valued. Even though they became "eminently noted for helping forward the work of Christ Jesus, to wit, the glorifying of God in the saving of the poor sons of men," their missionary work was conducted with a submissive, modest, family-centered spirit.[31]

Roger Williams had fixed ideas about woman's place. By comparison, his radical Warwick neighbor, Samuel Gorton, had a much more difficult time resolving the tension between his own egalitarianism and his belief in the desirability of female dependence. Gorton vigorously attacked all forms of status arrogance—titles like "Sir" and "Lord," reserving the "uppermost seats in the assemblies and synagogues" for high-ranking persons, and wealthy university-trained ministers who attempted "to set up particular men in temporary authority, to praise the able and worthy and to press the poorer sort with burdens of sins and such abundance of servile obedience, as to make them slaves to themselves and others."[32]

Religion did not, in Gorton's terms, focus around a vengeful God, the heavenly aristocracy of God's Elect, or Satan's prowling the countryside like a hungry lion.[33] Rather, it manifested humankind's desire for betterment, perfection, and unity with Christ and other Christ-like persons "as one mystical and spiritual body." Anyone could potentially become a part of that mystical body. Gorton argued that a Christlike spirit could not develop out of transitory titles and wealth, out of the need to separate oneself from others —rich from poor, male from female, titled from untitled. Instead, it developed when one joined oneself with others as "co-partners or companions," "brothers and sisters," in Christ's kindly excellence. Being an "apostle of Christ" opened up each person's humane potential and freed the individual from the self-seeking, purely material world with all its "intanglements of national Priviledges, natural Genealogies, Families, Tribes, and Ceremonial Injunctions."[34]

For Gorton, in some limited sense, woman embodied frailty and man strength. He did not believe, however, that such qualities should be ranked on a hierarchical continuum. Because he did not view the world in Calvinist terms of opposing, inclusive dichotomies, he felt man possessed some frailty and woman held some strength, "in such sort as the Man is not without the Woman; nor the Woman without the Man in the Lord."[35] This egalitarian Rhode Islander wished to blend all qualities, all realities—humility with exaltation, rationality in theological matters with the emotive power of grace, the abstract with the concrete, weakness with strength, male with female. Concerned with the essential synthesis, the unity, of divinely created existence, he thereby rejected the Calvinistic emphasis on separation (of man from God, flesh from spirit, man from woman), on the inner conflict between things. No dualist, he felt that the Puritans' consciousness of divisions in the world curbed true understanding and produced unsavory actualities like competition, self-aggrandizement, brutality, and war. Closeness to God could not, in his view, result from denying the senses, fasting, afflicting the flesh, or indulging in introspective anguish; rather, it could be achieved by opening oneself up to a mystical union with Christ.[36]

In the Gortonian synthesis, even God possessed traditionally male *and* female qualities—the protective tendency of man, the nurturant force of woman. Indeed, at one point Gorton described Christ as a mother hen nesting her faithful offspring under her wings, nourishing and giving them her warmth.[37] True, he had said that the man was the "head" of the woman, as Paul specified in I Corinthians, but he also pointed out that rulership did not equal superiority, nor submission obedience. Man's headship meant he must protect, cherish, and guide his wife in certain matters. He must furthermore defend her "in all suits that come against her, or challenge [s] that can be made of her."[38] But the wife had her own realm of governance, and therefore an "equal authority" with her husband. She had absolute control over domestic matters: "The woman can order and dispose of *all* things in the family: yea, clothe her husband and houshold in scarlet," if she wished.[39] She did not exist merely to serve man, but to exercise dominion in her own right.

Gorton indicated that the biblical story of Deborah illustrated the wife's individual importance through a celebration of her creative power. Deborah, a judge who did not hesitate to give the Hebrews military advice, had submitted herself to Solomon, as a wife ought; but the resultant children were described as hers alone, and her name was to "be remembered in all generations." Gorton explained, "it is she that constitutes her sons as princes in all lands, Psalme 45. as though no husband were concerned in any of them."[40] This Warwick tailor-turned-theologian did not argue for the creation of a matrilineal society in Rhode Island, but he used Deborah's example to stress female independence within customary relationships.

Samuel Gorton confined women to the home and a maternal existence,[41] but his sexism was qualitatively different from that of

Roger Williams and the more orthodox Calvinists. He made some effort to see that the achievements of women were recognized as of equal value to those of men. He conceded women the right to preach and found nothing objectionable in the fact that one of his female followers considered Anne Hutchinson a prophetess.[42] He believed women possessed intellectual ability. Indeed, Eve had convinced Adam to eat the forbidden fruit through her *"arguments* and *reasonings"* [italics].[43]

Gorton sharply criticized those who would merely subject woman to man and give the male sex all the honor. Such persons, he maintained, "know not how to make the husband and wife of equal authority." Although he felt that the husband possessed some degree of headship over the wife, that did not give him the right to instruct her in religious matters; she could work out theological controversies on her own, if she wished. Like the Calvinists, Gorton considered "that conjugall tie betwixt man and wife, for the propagation of mankind on the earth" as fixed as "the Sun, Moon, and Stars in the firmament"; however, he apparently thought divorce allowable under a wide variety of circumstances. One of his English critics, Robert Baylie, reported in 1645 that Gorton, his followers, and Anne Hutchinson "do maintaine, that it is lawfull for every woman to desert her husband when he is not willing to follow her in her Church way, and to take her selfe for a widow."[44] Certainly this Rhode Island rebel would not have wished any woman to force her husband to abide by her religion, any more than he expected the husband to impose his own religion upon his wife. Nevertheless, divorce by reason of religious incompatibility was by no means an outlandish idea to the man who considered religious oppression a detestably Calvinist trait.

The Quakers had yet another definition of what was properly male and female. Like almost all seventeenth-century peoples, they considered woman the weaker sex, urged female subjection at home, and celebrated feminine modesty. Like the Calvinists, they opposed material "filthyness" in man or woman,[45] but, unlike their Puritan neighbors, the Friends defended with great zeal the right of women to preach publicly.[46] Quakers construed the apostle Paul's proscription on female preaching as applicable only to ignorant women and "tatlers."[47] Although they much approved of female modesty, the men were not as shocked as Roger Williams to learn of the two Quaker women who went nude in public. John Burnyeat explained that Friends abhorred "Impurity and Uncleanness and the Appearance of it . . . yet nevertheless if it should please the Lord God to stir up any of his Daughters so to appear as a Sign and Testimony against the Nakedness of others [before God], they durst not condemn it." William Edmundson agreed, adding that "he believed it to be a great Cross to a Modest womans Spirit, but the Lord must be obeyed."[48]

The sexes were considered equal on a spiritual plane, and God's "inner light" could be used to justify all sorts of eccentric behavior. Quaker men and women did hold separate meetings, though, and the Rhode Island men's monthly meeting of March 23, 1682, considered whether that practice violated the religious equality of the sexes. Ann Bull, one of two women in attendance, "Justified the separate meeting & said she had Consolation in it & comfort." Her companion, Ann Hunt, wished the men and women to meet together, then changed her mind after speaking to the men. The Quaker males nevertheless decided that separate meetings did reproach "the truth" and brought "griefe to the harts of all the faithfull"; they therefore denied the plea of two women who felt intimidated by the allegedly stronger sex.[49] Although no record exists of the women's monthly meetings before 1690, it can be surmised that the women vetoed the male enactment, since separate meetings continued after that date.

Old Images and New Privileges in a Different Land

The Quakers, Roger Williams, and Gorton represented three streams of thought in this "heretical" land, where different perspectives were an intrinsic component of the contemporary lifestyle. Despite the relatively egalitarian thrust of Gorton and the Quakers, many non-Calvinists in Rhode Island borrowed liberally from the sexist matrix of many parts of England and other Puritan locales. The Newport merchant William Richardson, for one, wrote in his account book a poem in which he urged men, "Give not thy Strength to women/ Nor thy ways to that which destroyeth/ Kings[.] Nither lett pation overcom the/ but let Virtue guid thee in all thy ways." For Richardson, conceding women the right and opportunity to be strong was not virtuous. John Saffin, a poet as well as a political figure, made woman's supposed curiosity the butt of a joke: "There was a Gentlewoman came into a Painters room & turn'd a Picture," he wrote, "and [she] behold the Genitiles of a man at which Shee blusht & was laugh't into Shame."[50] The

Rhode Island General Assembly in 1671 held a chiding reference to the governor as "Your honorable wife" to be extremely contemptous, sentencing Francis Usselton to fifteen lashes for that and other scornful statements.[51]

Sharing in some of the sex-role prejudices so common in Calvinist New England and the mother country, the men of Rhode Island did not allow women to vote or to hold positions of political power. They took no steps to help females become self-supporting, beyond allowing them to learn the domestic arts as servants or apprentices.[52] They permitted the husband to administer the financial affairs of a couple's estate in accordance with common law; when he was absent for some time, the wife had no power to use the estate for her own benefit, unless he had specifically granted her that power. Not until 1712 did the General Assembly allow wives to receive the "Debts, Rents and Profits" of such estates, as a measure to prevent their impoverishment. However, even then the mates of absent "Merchants and Mariners" were granted administrative power only after the husband had been away for three consecutive years.[53]

Nevertheless, an examination of sources reveals that the Rhode Island authorities extended women more rights and privileges than did the Calvinists. While the latter were divided on whether a wife's agreement was necessary before a husband could sell realty, the former recognized the right of wives to veto their spouses' real estate transferals.[54] While the Massachusetts Assistants declared pre-nuptial contracts of no effect, in Rhode Island (and Connecticut) such contracts were binding.[55]

Rhode Island was the only colony to enact an early law granting widows the right, in intestate cases, to administer their deceased husbands' estates (1663).[56] Whether or not a man had made a will in which he conveyed the right of executorship, in 80 percent of the cases his widow became the sole or co-administrator of the surviving estate.[57] By comparison, in Maine and in Suffolk County, Massachusetts, the widow received the right of administration only half of the time, while Connecticut practice resembled that of Rhode Island. When a widow in Puritan New England remarried, her new husband assumed the executorship, but Rhode Islanders did not follow that example. Rhode Island authorities expected female administrators to keep their ex-husbands' estates functioning adequately, a requirement which may have led some women to refuse to serve. Mary Mowry, for example, in 1669 "denied to owne" her executorship because her ex-husband's property "would not discharge just debts, and pay legacies, &c."[58] When a woman "wasted the estate and not so improved it as it ought to be," she could be deprived of her administration, although Rhode Islanders hardly construed such an action as any reflection on woman's ability. Husbands who similarly neglected or wasted their estates forfeited some, if not all, of their realty for their families' use.[59] Unlike some of their Puritan neighbors, the Rhode Island assemblymen allowed widows to manage their new property without supervision by male overseers.

Notwithstanding the easy accessibility of widows to their husbands' properties, some women faced severe poverty. The various towns aided at least thirteen "desolate" women, including three wives who became impoverished while their husbands remained absent from the colony, three who suffered from "distemper" or "distraction," and one facing blindness in her old age.[60] Two women received employment as a result of petitioning for assistance, and not as servants. After Andrew Edmonds's death in the Maine Indian wars, the General Assembly, which had previously ordered the town of Providence to maintain his wife for five years, granted Mary Edmonds the right to derive an income from maintaining the ferry between Providence and Rehoboth.[61] The other woman, Mary Pray, received permission to operate a "house of entertainment" at Providence (1681–84) as a means of supporting herself after her separation from her husband. Since she could not pay the annual £1 license fee, she offered her inn for the town's use (for meetings, etc.) in lieu of that sum.[62]

Usually poor relief consisted of a sizable allotment. When Grace Lawton requested help in her husband's absence, the Assembly in 1676 ordered her paid 6s. per week in silver (£15 12s. per year) during her life or until Thomas Lawton returned to care for her.[63] Only two women received less than £10 per annum. Such allotments would have shocked the Puritans, who granted impoverished women only the bare minimum—shelter, a couple of dozen bushels of corn and two blankets, some clothing, or a grant of 50s. to £10. Only four of seventy-two women aided in Calvinist colonies received over £10. The average Rhode Island allotment was *twice* as high as the average Puritan one.[64]

Rhode Island women usually fared better than other New England women, not only in terms of the privileges wives and widows enjoyed and in the sums allotted for poor relief, but also when they

Chart 11.1

Executorship in Seventeenth-Century New England, in Cases Where
There Was a Surviving Widow

Designated Executor	Rhode Island, 1636–99		Maine, 1655–79		Suffolk County, 1680–91		Connecticut, 1639–99	
	N	%	N	%	N	%	N	%
Wife alone	47	64	25	39	14	44	162	57
Wife and others	11	15	7	11	2	6	67	24
Son or sons	8	11	8	13	3	9	23	8
Daughters	1	1	0	0	0	0	0	0
Relatives	4	6	5	8	1	3	7	3
Others	1	1	19	30	12	38	25	9
	73		64		32		284	

appeared in court to answer criminal presentments. Calvinists often
punished female offenders corporally, without giving them the
benefit of remission through payment of a fine. As Chart 11.2
illustrates, anywhere from 23 to 57 percent of all female convicts in
Calvinist New England received lashings, brandings, or death
sentences. By contrast, only 13 percent of Rhode Island's female
offenders were so punished. Although there is no significant difference in the relative numbers of crimes committed, or the relative degree of seriousness, between male and female offenders,
Calvinist authorities more often penalized women corporally, sentencing only 12.8 to 30 percent of all male convicts to corporal or
capital punishment. In each court cited, with the exception of Rhode
Island, there is a significant gap in the percentages of males and
females so sentenced. Women in Rhode Island (as in the rest of New
England) lacked money and sometimes faced lashings when they
were unable to pay fines; but in Rhode Island they at least had the
opportunity to enlist financial help from a husband or benefactor.
Women in Calvinist locales rarely had such an option.

Equal Punishment for Sexual Offenders

In their treatment of sexual offenders the Rhode Island authorities
revealed a usually tolerant attitude, one which prompted the Puritans to describe the "licentious republic" as "too sluttish to be
handled."[65] Puritans were appalled that early Rhode Islanders
made no effort to punish fornicators until reports of the "whore-

Chart 11.2

Corporal and Capital Punishment in Seventeenth-Century
New England

Locale/Court	Male Offenders			Female Offenders		
	N	Capitally & Corporally Punished	%	N	Capitally & Corporally Punished	%
Massachusetts Court of Assts.-Gen. Ct., 1630–44	444	133	30	49	28	57.1
Suffolk Co. Ct., Mass., 1680–98	477	100	21	134	38	28.4
Conn. Ct. of Assts-Gen. Ct., Hartford Co. Ct., 1636–99	742	95	12.8	133	43	32.3
Plym. Gen. Ct., Bristol & Plym. Co. Cts., 1636–99	841	109	13	147	34	23.1
Rhode Island Cts., 1638–99	322	42	13	84	12	14.3

dom" there had reached the ears of Oliver Cromwell.[66] Fearing this Puritan Protector's intervention, the Rhode Island legislature enacted laws against adultery (1655), masters who tolerated their charges' "Licentious courses" (1656), and fornication (1657).[67] Compared to Calvinist enactments, the adultery and fornication laws were quite liberal. Adulterers did not hang or face up to forty lashes at a time, as was true in the rest of New England; instead they received fifteen lashes at two different locales (with enough time in between so that their wounds could heal) and a £10 fine.

Edward Richmond and Abigail Davis, a couple who lived together without benefit of marriage, became in 1658 the first persons penalized for fornication in Rhode Island's twenty-three year history.[68] Between then and 1699, 57 other men and 68 other women appeared in court on fornication indictments. Eleven of these persons (four women, seven men) received acquittals, including one woman who actually pled guilty![69] The convicted fornicators paid £2 fines (or, in a few cases, bore the smart of the lash) during the 1660s and 1670s, but by the early 1680s the usual fine had decreased to £1 6s. 8d., and by the 1690s to £1 (or ten lashes). On certain occasions the fine was even lower: Howlong Harris of Providence paid a mere 5s. in 1682, because the Newport Court of Trials accepted her argument that "she was soe surprissed by drink" she could not resist the temptation to have sexual relations with Thomas Deney. Although the law specified a double penalty for two-time offenders, Ruth Bayly of New Shorum, "haveing had sundry Bastards," was ordered to pay only £1. 6s. 8d. or receive fifteen lashes (1682).[70] Whatever the penalty assessed, the authorities administered it equally to both parties.

Calvinist colonies, by contrast, allotted different punishments to male and female fornicators. From Maine through Connecticut, before 1680, the county and colony magistrates generally sentenced male fornicators to a fine of £5 and/or a whipping of twenty lashes; females received fifteen lashes. In the century's last two decades that fine decreased to 50s. or £2, and the number of lashes to fifteen for men and ten for women. Unlike the Rhode Island authorities, who penalized all offenders equally, Calvinists considered sex between engaged couples less reprehensible and fined them a smaller amount—£3 for the male and £2 for the female violator before 1680, and 30s. thereafter. Thus the fines for premarital sexual activity were 33 to 167 percent higher in Calvinist locales. The number of lashes administered was often five more than in Rhode Island, particularly when the offender was a man. No offender in Calvinist New England escaped with a fine of less than 20s. (or ten lashes). When an offending Puritan woman did receive a lashing, the usual number of strokes was equal to the Rhode Island penalty. Nevertheless, the fact that Rhode Island authorities sentenced her partner to no more lashes than the woman received for the offense more clearly reflected a notion of her equal moral responsibility, her capacity for giving as well as receiving in a given sexual liaison.

Rhode Islanders did not prosecute persons who indulged in lascivious speech or gestures, or who attempted to entice members of the opposite sex into bed. Only the case of John Deane and Joan Cowdall, a couple caught in a highly suspicious situation, qualifies as an uneffected yet prosecuted enticement. The constable apprehended Deane, a seaman, when he was lying in bed with the widow Cowdall in 1672. Deane fled from his indicters; the widow was stripped to the waist, bound to the great gun at Newport, and forced to stand there for fifteen minutes—not a very painful punishment, from either a physical or a financial standpoint.[71] A couple caught in such a situation in Calvinist New England would have faced the full penalty for fornication. No Calvinist offenses such as lewd conduct, adulterous carriage, or swearing existed in Rhode Island, whereas in Puritan locales persons who swore paid a 10s. fine. Puritan men and women who made obscene gestures could expect up to fifteen lashes. The man and the married woman who kissed one another received ten lashes each, and those guilty of "lascivious Gross & foule Actions tending to Adultery" faced thirty stripes "well laid on."[72]

Rhode Island magistrates punished male and female adulterers less harshly than their Calvinist counterparts, and in accordance with the 1655 law. Sometimes half that sentence (fifteen lashes and £5) was remitted if the offender confessed his or her wrongdoing,[73] and in three instances the adultery was treated as a case of fornication.[74] In yet another case, the magistrates suspended an adulteress's sentence completely on the condition that she leave the colony and return to her husband.[75]

At midcentury elsewhere in New England, extramarital intercourse was a capital crime. A few violators were hanged for that offense, but later male offenders faced a £10 to £20 fine and/or thirty or forty lashes; adulteresses paid £10 fines and/or received twenty lashes.[76] Rhode Island women did receive more lashes—thirty—but no more than fifteen at any one time, and they were to be "moderately," not "well laid on." Furthermore, Rhode Island justices halved or suspended the sentences of one-fourth (5/20) of all adulterers brought before them, whereas the Calvinists remitted a penalty only 4.3 percent (10/230 cases) of the time. Furthermore, those Calvinist remissions were quite small, consisting of only a few lashes or a few pounds. No one in Calvinist New England ever received a suspended sentence in favor of leaving the colony.

While the Rhode Island penalties for adultery deserve to be called impartial, the legislature's description of the offense in the first law code differs from the Calvinist standard only relatively. Adultery was still "declared to be a vile affection, whereby men do turn aside from ye naturall use of their wives, and do burn in their lusts towards strange flesh."[77] The statement did not exclude from prosecution as did Calvinist practice married men who had intercourse with single women, but it did strongly imply that males initiated adulterous liaisons. Nevertheless, when Mary Ridgly attempted to argue that she had been induced into adultery several times by "the over perswassion" of John Andrews, the Newport Court of Trials in no way felt that his "strong" enticement mitigated her guilt, and sentenced her to the maximum punishment.[78] As in Puritan locales, the notion of feminine passivity was not seen as diminishing moral responsibility or participation, but as calling for (presumably) passive resistance.

In only one area of sexual offenses did the Rhode Island authorities respond more severely than their Calvinist neighbors. Rapists received short shrift. In 1679 Peter Pylat, a black servant, was hanged for "Assaulting, Battering, & Ravishing" his master's daughter. In another case an Indian was hanged for attempted rape, a crime which was not capital in Calvinist locales.[79] Some racism may have been involved in the harsh sentences, although Rhode Islanders tended to treat the Indians more fairly than did Calvinists. In any event, these two men were the only ones to come before the authorities in connection with rape.

Sex and sin were less intimately connected in Rhode Island than in Calvinist New England. Ministers did not warn their listeners of the constant need to harness the foul expression of lust's "irresistible instinct." Flirtatious behavior, overt enticing gestures, and profane language were tolerated. The obscene speech of one captain's wife so shocked the Dutch Calvinist Jasper Danckaerts that he would write, on a trip to Rhode Island in 1680, "I have never in my whole life witnessed a worse, more foul, profane, or abandoned creature."[80] The inhabitants there called fornication and adultery "unnatural" instead of abominably sinful, and made no sexual distinction in punishment. Nowhere is there a record of sexual intercourse being referred to as a man's "defiling" or "using" a woman's body. One searches the available records in vain for any mention of the idea that a single act of intercourse could convert a woman into a whore, or that in sexual relations a woman "prostituted her body" to a man. In fact, to call an unmarried woman a whore was specifically actionable under a Rhode Island slander statute, although no other New England colony had such a provision.[81] Indeed, no references to "godly virgins" emerge from the letters, poetry, or other records of the Rhode Islanders. Only Roger Williams celebrated "Virgin Love," and he was among the most Calvinist of early settlers.[82]

Common Law Marriage, Divorce, and Instances of Marital Stress

While apparently not as fascinated by virginity as their Calvinist neighbors, Rhode Islanders did link sex with marriage—as their prosecution of fornicators suggests. When Rachel Andrew went to bed with a neighbor, the Newport county clerk reported that "she tooke Clement Weaver to be her husband" (1678).[83] But many colony residents did not regard marriage as legitimate only within an institutional context. As one historian has written, persons taken with "the Rhode Island idea" held "that marriages are made in heaven, and regarded the fees to the officials for publishment, license and marriage as an unthrifty expence."[84] There are records of at least five couples who lived together without actually marrying. One, Horod Long and George Gardiner, stayed together for eighteen or twenty years (ca. 1644–64) and had at least one child. Another, Henry Gardiner and Abigail Remington, had two children before 1694; after his own wife's death, Gardiner recognized his mistress as his wife, but without benefit of actual marriage, and mentioned her thus in his will.[85]

Colony officials attempted to prevent marriages by agreement only. The law code of 1647 stated that banns must be published at two town meetings, and the marriage be registered with the town clerk; the "head officer of the town" was given responsibility for solemnizing all marriages. Rhode Islanders who did not follow these steps paid a £5 fine. After the Long-Gardiner case came to the authorities' attention in 1663, the General Assembly directed that the 1647 act be "punctually observed," stipulating that there would be a further penalty inflicted upon common law couples: "That is to say, they shall be proceeded against and punished for fornication." In the same year "An Act for preventing Clandestine Marriages" extended the right to perform the marriage service to assistants, justices of the peace, and town wardens; it also legitimized all common law relationships entered into before 1665. A later act, in 1702, extended recognition to Quaker and Anglican ceremonies.[86] By the 1680s, virtually any male could procure a license to perform the marriage ceremony.[87]

Rhode Island was the only New England colony where there seemed to be much concern about common law relationships. Common law marriage, except in secret (for example, when a woman pretended to be a man's sister), could not exist in Puritan New England, but the number and context of the Rhode Island laws suggests that many couples lived in illicit relationships. Others, especially those who had eloped to Rhode Island in order to marry without parental consent, neglected to publish themselves for fourteen days before they wed. Couples also failed to register their marriages with the town clerks, which caused the General

Assembly to lament in 1698 that many children in the colony were officially bastards.[88]

Although no one can know how many of the arraigned fornicators had actually taken up residence together, 92 percent of them were officially unmarried at the time of their prosecution. In Calvinist New England, by comparison, only 60.9 percent of such offenders were single. Such a difference—assuming that all cases of pre-seventh-month births brought before the authorities were in fact tried— suggests that Rhode Island couples more often failed to marry, at least officially, even when the woman realized she was pregnant.[89]

Calvinists did not like common law relationships either, but they made the entire marriage procedure more difficult. A notice of intent had to be published not twice but three times prior to the ceremony. Before 1686 only a colony magistrate could legally solemnize a marriage, and after that date the privilege was extended only to ministers and justices of the peace.[90] "Unordained" ministers and Quakers could not marry couples in seventeenth-century Calvinist New England.[91]

A couple could also more easily obtain a separation, and possibly a divorce, in Rhode Island. An act of 1650, intended to make Rhode Island laws agree with English enactments, allowed for divorce only in cases of adultery; in practice, however, the authorities granted divorces for desertion and impotence as well. On at least one occasion a local magistrate assumed the power to divorce petitioners, creating the possibility that couples need not rely on the General Assembly to dissolve their marriages. John Lewis and his wife believed that a signed paper of dismissal which granted Mr. Lewis "libertie to marrie another woman" sufficed to terminate their own marriage (1675).[92] The Lewises had good precedent. Twenty-one years before, John Coggeshall had given his wife Elizabeth a divorce; for some time she had "neglected and utterly refused to Performe the Marriage Covent" and continually requested the dissolution of their marriage. At last her husband drew up the appropriate agreement, and the Court of Commissioners rubber-stamped it.[93] Mistress Beggarly did not even bother to get a divorce from her husband before she married John Greene, and the justices did not interfere. In yet another case of relative leniency, the magistrates separated Henry and Elizabeth Stevens after the Court of Trials had ordered Henry to supply a £20 bond for threatening his wife's life.[94] Threatening a mate or refusing to be "a meete help"' were not sufficient grounds for a separation in Calvinist areas; furthermore, the Rhode Island assemblymen may have granted divorce on grounds of physical abuse, grounds not accepted in the rest of New England. When Ann Warner complained against her husband, Warwick Assistant John Warner, for "laying violent hands on her," the Assembly separated them and postponed an "absolute finall divorce, until the fact [of his assault] hath been tried at the Court of Tryalls." That court, finding Warner guilty, ordered him to supply a £50 bond for good behavior (1683); unfortunately, no subsequent record of Assembly action on Ann Warner's petition remains.[95]

Not all marital friction ended in divorce or separation, although those options seemed readily available in Rhode Island. Sixteen of the 24 discontented couples whom this researcher has found requested a divorce or separation upon petition of one or both partners, compared with 109 of 699 such couples in Calvinist locales. (It is likely that a seventeenth case led to a divorce petition, for that was usual when one party ran away and remarried.[96]) Whether or not the authorities granted a divorce or separation in a given instance, they penalized abusive husbands more severely than abusive wives, reversing the practice in Puritan locales. Rhode Island magistrates ordered all three abusive husbands to post very high bonds (£10, £20, and £50) for their continued good behavior, compared to a bond of less than £10 or a small fine in Puritan areas.[97] On the other hand, when one Rhode Island wife threatened to destroy her spouse "Root and Branch," to set his house afire, and to take all his goods while he was away from home, the magistrates did not penalize her at all. Had she lived in Puritan New England, Margaret Abbot would have received a smart lashing; in Rhode Island, her husband's only recourse was to post written warnings that he would not pay any debts she contracted or allow her to sell any of their estate (1683)[98] Of course, not all penalties differed in the two areas. When a husband killed his wife, (as did the Indian Oldman in 1674), he was hanged (the jury was half Indian), as he would have been elsewhere in New England.[99]

To be sure, long-term marital discontent did exist in Rhode Island, and over the same issues that plagued Calvinist marriages. One case reveals how a woman's desire for independence from institutional marriage, through which she was deprived of her name and her property, could conflict with her need for financial maintenance. Horod Long, married in England to John Hicks when she was thirteen or fourteen, moved with him first to Weymouth,

Massachusetts, and then Newport about 1640. The young couple
soon fell to fighting. Hicks accused her of adultery, and on December 12, 1643, he wrote to John Coggeshall as follows: "if ther be any
way to bee used to untie that Knott, wch was at the first by man tyed
that so the world may be satisfied I am willing ther unto, for the
Knot of affection on her part have been untied long since, and her
whordome have freed my conscience. . . ." Soon after, Hicks was
ordered to post £10 bond for beating his wife, and she was directed
to present evidence at the next Aquidneck Quarter Court.[100] No
direct record proves that she appeared, but later evidence reveals
that the justices separated her from her husband and guaranteed
her the right to use the estate she had received from her mother. An
angry John Hicks then stole her personalty and ran away to the
Dutch. Mistress Long, resuming her maiden name, soon entered
into a common law relationship with George Gardiner which lasted
approximately twenty years. Hicks at one point (1655) brought
charges against Gardiner for keeping her as his wife, but the jury
ruled that the plaintiff had not made good his charge.[101]

By 1665 Horod Long was experiencing a great deal of trouble with
Gardiner. She described her difficulties to the King's Commissioners for New England as follows:

I was drawne by George Gardener to consent to him soe fare as I did, for my
mayntainance. Yett with much oppression of spiritt, judging him not to be
my husband, never being married to him according to the law of the place:
alsoe I told him of my oppression, and desiered him, seeing that hee had
that little that I had, and all my labour, that hee would allow mee some
maintainance, either to live apart from him, or else not to meddle with mee;
but hee has always refused. Therefore, my humble petition to your honours
is, that of that estate and labour hee has had of mine, hee may allow it mee;
and that house vpon my land I may enjoy without molestation, and that he
may alow mee my child to bring vp with maintainance for her, and that hee
may be restrained from ever meddling with me, or trobleing mee more.

The commissioners referred her petition to the Rhode Island General Assembly, which fined the couple £20 each for their continuing fornication and directed "that from henceforth they presume
not to lead soe scandolose a life, lest they feel the extreamest penalty
that is or shall be provided in such cases."[102]

The Rhode Island authorities had separated Horod Long from
two "husbands," the only time that ever occurred in seventeenth-

century New England. However, her legal problems did not end after her separation from George Gardiner. In 1667 she appeared before the Court of Trials to answer a presentment for fornication with John Porter; a jury cleared her of the charge, but she soon married Porter.[103] Two juries thus acquitted her of wrongdoing with two different men, even though it was apparent that she and Gardiner lived together as man and wife. Rhode Islanders apparently lacked the zeal to penalize *all* fornicators, irrespective of their common law status. Legal practice does not always harmonize with legal enactments when people have comparatively tolerant attitudes.

Individualism and the Relative Lack of Sex-Role Rigidity

Rhode Islanders little valued rock-ribbed orthodoxy, in either a religious or a social realm. Individualism became an important cultural value, and even a Calvinist like Roger Williams, a man who detested the Quaker theology, believed that members of the Society of Friends could be free to practice their "erroneous" beliefs. Many Rhode Island marriages were religiously mixed, and the children of such couples sometimes claimed no religion at all.[104] Only a few Quakers censured the expression of pride in personal appearance or in personal accomplishment, and the colony's assemblymen, unlike their Puritan counterparts, took no action to restrict elaborate styles of dress to a certain class of citizens.[105] Men and women could wear whatever they wished. No laws prevented them from donning the apparel of the opposite sex, or forbade men to wear their hair long.

While Puritans worried about the effeminating effects of long hair on men, many Rhode Island "heretics" had shaggy locks. A surviving portrait of the Anabaptist leader, Doctor John Clarke, shows him in patriarchal beard and long hair. In England, George Fox received much criticism because of his hair length, and one of his followers observed disapprovingly that Puritans "made it a kind of holiness to wear short hair."[106] Two New England Quakers, Edward Wharton of Salem and Thomas Harris of Providence, possessed hair long enough to infuriate the Massachusetts authorities. Deputy Governor Richard Bellingham requested a pair of scissors so that he might personally cut off Harris's offending locks.[107] Another outraged Plymouth magistrate proposed that a law be enacted providing for the shaving of every male Quaker's head. "It would have been the best remedy for them," he argued, because "it would have both sham'd and cur'd them."[108]

When one Quaker missionary, Mr. Thurston, arrived in Providence "with extraordinary long hair hanging over his shoulders," an aged woman there "demanded of him why he ware it so long since Nature itself did teach it to be a shame for a man to wear long Hair, as the holy Scripture afirmed?" Thurston responded in a style which many Rhode Islanders could appreciate: "when that God bid me wear it, bids me cut it off, then will I cut it off."[109] While not all Rhode Islanders found long hair tolerable on men, full locks were enough in evidence to suggest that many inhabitants were not preoccupied with their alleged effeminating tendency.

Just as men could wear long hair in Rhode Island, women could behave in ways verging on the masculine. They could swear, with gusto and without fear of prosecution. They could do "male" work; Jane Power, for example, demonstrated some ability in "outward matters" by constructing her own cellar, while Widow Smith ran her husband's grist mill after he died.[110] In Quaker meetings women could exercise a measure of control over the Society's dispersal of funds.[111] Most important, women could and did wield great influence as religious preachers and, to a lesser extent, as political spokespersons.

The Woman as Religious and Political Force

After Anne Hutchinson's arrival at Portsmouth in 1638, the Puritan Edward Johnson wrote that "there were some of the female sexe who (deeming the Apostle Paul to be too strict in not permitting a room [for women] to preach in the publique Congreagation) taught notwithstanding . . . having their call to this office from an ardent desire of being famous." According to Johnson, Hutchinson, "the grand Mistress of them all . . . ordinarily prated every Sabbath day, till others, who thirsted after honour in the same way with her selfe, drew away her Auditors."[112] Although the particular theology of these new female preachers is unknown, many of them may have been Anabaptists; Anne herself turned to that religion for solace after her husband's death. Her sister Katherine Scott became a particularly active Anabaptist missionary who (if John Winthrop can be believed) numbered Roger Williams among her converts.[113]

Quaker as well as Anabaptist and Antinomian women thrived in

Rhode Island. Hutchinson's close confederate, Mary Dyer, had been one of the first persons to foster Quakerism in Rhode Island. Many of Dyer's female contemporaries, moved by their own "inner light," became Quaker preachers, a practice which caused Williams to lament that the "weaker sex" were "too much inclin'd" toward Quakerism.[114] "Women Ministers, Women Apostles, Women Embassadors to all Nations" moved readily about the colony and into neighboring locales, preaching to all comers. Quaker husbands supported their wives; Margaret Smith even converted her husband to her faith.[115] Other Rhode Islanders supported the right of women to be religiously active, just as they had earlier supported Anne Hutchinson's "unfeminine" activities. At his death in 1678 Governor Benedict Arnold, himself a Quaker, left his gray horse to the Friends for the specific use of female missionaries who wished to visit points in New England or New York.[116] The climate was such that when Williams refused to discuss theology with Mistress Eaton in 1672, John Nichols rose to reprove him, saying, "In Christ Jesus [there is] neither male or female."[117]

From the earliest years, Rhode Island men listened to the wishes of women and protected their "liberty" to preach and to attend services of their choosing. When Joshua Verin, one of the original settlers at Providence, restrained his wife, Jane, from attending religious services at Roger Williams's house, a town meeting took up the matter. John Greene, a Gortonist, argued that if men were allowed to restrain their wives, "all the women in the country would cry out." The more conservative William Arnold rejoined that God had ordered the wife to be subject to her husband; such a commandment should not be broken merely to please women. The townsmen agreed with Green, however, and disfranchised Verin as long as he refused to respect his wife's "libertie of conscience." Verin returned to Salem—after this censure but not before he had "trodden" Jane "under foot tyranically and brutishly," endangering her life. Williams wrote to John Winthrop in 1638, urging the governor to prevent this "boisterous and desperate" young man from hauling "his wife with ropes to Salem, where she must needs be troubled and troublesome."[118]

Rhode Islanders valued acting as conscience dictated, establishing the kind of social climate in which women could determine their own religious destinies. In "the land of errors" wives did not have to ask their husbands for clarification of abstract or concrete religious issues; instead, they could think for themselves. And religion was not the only sphere where Rhode Island women exercised a great deal of influence. Some also expressed strong opinions on political subjects. Not long after her arrival on the island, Anne Hutchinson entered into an alliance with Samuel Gorton and the poorer inhabitants of Portsmouth against the leadership of Governor William Coddington. The rebels found Coddington's autocratic rule, his preferential land allotment policy, and his fascination with Puritanism objectionable. Hutchinson provided the theological rationale for their resistance by attacking the legitimacy of *any* magistracy. She and Gorton were the primary instigators of the rebellion of April 28, 1639, in which the poorer Portsmouth residents formed a new body politic and expelled Coddington from power.[119] Although Anne later moved to Coddington's headquarters at Newport, she could not totally reconcile herself to the quality of life there, or to the fact that Coddington had some support among Bay Colony authorities. Disgruntled and fearing that Massachusetts would seize Newport and Portsmouth, she sought refuge in New Netherland in 1642, still remaining outspoken. When Thomas Leverett, in a letter dated March 1643, called her a railer, a reviler, and a "Haughty Jezebel," Anne wrote him that she could not be guilty of "Railing or Reviling" as long as God's Truth shone within her. Furthermore, she prophesied, Massachusetts, having lost that Truth, would fall. This rebel did not live to witness that fall: a few months later raiding Indians annihilated her, along with much of her family.[120]

While the Massachusetts ministers and magistrates rejoiced at Anne Hutchinson's death, her "seduced followers" reminded those authorities that she had had a significant impact upon Rhode Island. Her sister considered her no less than a "saint," and her onetime Portsmouth neighbor, Randall Holden, implicitly asserted that she was responsible for creating the kind of mood in which the "great and terrible word magistrate . . . hath no great lustre in our ordinary acceptation."[121]

Like Anne Hutchinson, Quaker women protested against contemporary political arrangements. They objected to the "cruelty and oppression" of the Puritan magistrates and sharply criticized the Calvinist authorities' fascination with titles like "Sir," "your Honor," and "Your Grace." Male and female Friends affirmed the right of the poor to rank among the honorable, the politically powerful, and the holy.[122] Still, neither Anne Hutchinson nor the Quaker women appealed for the further extension of political power to the weaker sex. One Providence widow did, however, assert that taxation of women without representation was unfair. In a carefully worded, properly deferential letter to the Providence town meeting, Abigail Dexter objected to paying both the house tax and the rate levied to pay the salary of the sergeant who warned all male inhabitants to attend town meetings. Dexter's letter, dated June 6, 1681, reads as follows:

Honrd Gentelmen, if the poor and low Condition, of a poor widow have no Influence upon the hearts of your rate makers, but to rate me where there is no justice for it before God nor man, that they should rate me to sergeant's wages, and House rent, I cannot see just Cause, for these reasons, first the sergeant hath neither power, nor occasion to warn me to your meetings, knowing I am not allowed any vote there. Secondly all my lands and meadows and orchard lies Common to your Benefit, and not to mine nor the orphans of my Deceased Husbands. Thirdly if I should have Come to have Voted to day in your Election, perhaps it would have been said what had I to do there: and If I have not to do to Vote and make use thereof, I leave to your wisdoms to Judge of: praying your Consideration of it, and your Determination of the same,

Your poor widow and friend

Abigail Dexter[123]

Unlike the women of Puritan New England, Abigail Dexter, living in a more egalitarian society, was uncertain about her political rights. She knew that women did not vote in town meetings, but felt that it might be allowable: "*perhaps* it would have been said what had I to do there." She therefore requested a measure of justice and, in a roundabout way, received it: the town inhabitants failed to extend her the franchise, but they did decide that thereafter "no widows shall be rated to House rent nor Sargeant's wages."[124]

Abigail Dexter may have been aware of Mary Starbuck's important role in town affairs on the nearby island of Nantucket. After Starbuck's removal from Massachusetts to Nantucket in the 1660s, she became an important preacher there. Adhering to no particular sect, she persuaded the townsmen not to pay maintenance for any preacher on the island. Townsmen consulted Starbuck on all matters of public importance because they considered her judgment superior. She also participated actively in the town meetings. Her husband "appeared not a Man of mean Parts," but, according to one Quaker observer, "she so far exceeded him in Soundness of Judg-

ment, Clearness of Understanding and an elegant way of expressing herself, and that not in an affected Strain . . . that it tended to
lessen the Qualifications of her Husband." Esteemed as a "Judge"
among the islanders, "little of moment was done without her."[125]
On an isolated island like Nantucket, one frequently visited by
Rhode Island Quakers, a talented woman could apparently create
her own opportunities.

In Rhode Island–Providence Plantations, women asserted themselves in religious and political realms, but not in the economic
world. Although widows usually administered their deceased husbands' estates, they often remarried shortly after receiving the
power of executorship. Only 5.9 percent of the landowners appearing on one 1688 rate list were females, a percentage comparable to
that in other New England locales.[126] Women did not live alone,
nor were many self-supporting. Some worked as servants, Mary
Pray and Mary Sanford maintained inns, Widow Smith operated a
mill, Mary Edmonds became a ferrykeeper, and Sarah Reape
owned at least one ship. But these women were the exceptions,
rather than the rule.[127] George Keith claimed that Friends put
"many poor Mechanicks, servants, and women that have no good
way of living . . . into such ways of Trade and business, whereby
to live plentifully by which means, many who had nothing are become rich." Unfortunately, the available Rhode Island records
are insufficient to bear Keith out.[128] Even the usual nurturant professions of midwifery, medicine, and dame school teaching (after
1670) involved few females, for Rhode Islanders disliked public
education, available matrons usually served as midwives,[129] and
only one female physician has come to this author's attention. Upon
the death of Doctor Mary Hazard, at Newport, in her hundredth
year (1739), the *New York Gazette* reported that "she was accounted a
very useful gentlewoman, both to rich and poor on many accounts,
and particularly amongst sick persons for her skill and judgment,
which she did gratis."[130]

Sex Roles in This More Open Society

Seventeenth-century Rhode Island society was comparatively
open, and women helped to keep it open. In this land where
institutional constraints were disliked, the power of ministers and
magistrates devalued, and equality affirmed in court, women
achieved more rights and privileges than in Calvinist locales. These
included the right to preach and debate theology, a greater recog-

nition of widows' executorship privileges, the guarantee of a relatively comfortable existence for poor women, and the comparative ease with which separations could be effected. Only in Rhode Island could Anne Hutchinson carry on her protest against political and religious inequality with maximum effectiveness. Only there could Katherine Scott actively convert many of her neighbors, male and female, to Anabaptism. Only there could Abigail Dexter feel motivated to make a plea for no taxation without representation. Perhaps Mary Brattle best demonstrated the kind of spirit a woman could have in Rhode Island. When she entered Thomas Clarke's pewter shop on a 1684 journey to Boston and demanded the key to a house of office, he refused, adding that she was "a prating hussy." Uncowed, she retorted that he was a "Beggars Brat and Cheate" and that at home she "kept a better man to wipe her shoes."[131]

Although Rhode Islanders of both sexes established a tradition of individualistic protest in this most heretical of colonies, life there was no utopia for women. The wife's economic dependence upon her husband prevented any radical alteration of the contemporary marriage style. Marital distress and at least one attempted abortion came to the attention of authorities.[132] Despondent and distracted women existed,[133] and adultery occurred. However, available records indicate that infanticide, suicide, and hysterical fits were not common, suggesting that the degree and prevalence of women's stress was reduced. Sex roles certainly existed in Rhode Island, but they were less rigidly structured. In Calvinist areas the images of the virgin, the dutiful wife, the spinster, the whore, and the witch conveyed character and anti-character, good and evil, while in Rhode Island a woman was considerably more than a "condition" of virginity or whoredom, of marriage or spinsterhood. The all-inclusive value definitions of whore, virgin, and spinster, those imperative reminders of proper and improper female status, occur rarely—if ever—in Rhode Island records.

Rhode Islanders, who were not inclined to define women as character types, did not, in times of stress, search for witches as ultimate personifications of evil upon whom they could foist their own guilt. Rather, they protested when Massachusetts executed three witches between 1648 and 1651. In the latter year William Arnold wrote to the Bay Colony, "Some of them of Shawomet [the Gortonist settlement] . . . cryeth out much against them which putteth people to death for witches, for say they there be no witches upon earth nor devils, but your own pastors and ministers and such as they are, &c."[134] The 1647 law code did specify capital punishment for witchcraft, and the Calvinistic Williams on at least one occasion accused the Quakers of consorting with evil spirits,[135] but the authorities prosecuted not a single "witch" throughout the century. Only one witchcraft accusation came before the courts, and the accuser had been drunk when he had spoken so sharply to his neighbor.[136] In many ways, Rhode Island was the alternative society in seventeenth-century New England.

1. Bridenbaugh, *Fat Mutton & Liberty of Conscience*, p. 3; C. Mather, *Magnalia*, II, 450.

2. Nicholas and Sarah Davis, for example moved to Newport after their house was searched for Quaker writings. Christopher Holder (the Quaker who lost an ear for his "heresy"), John Chamberlain (whipped no less than nine times as a Quaker), and the missionary Catherine Chatham all resettled in Newport. Jane and Joseph Nicholson left Salem for Portsmouth, and Robert Hodgson, who had been beaten and chained at New York for his faith, also located there. See Austin, *Geneal. Dict. of R.I.*, pp. 63, 102, 40, 139, 100.

3. C. Mather, *Magnalia*, II, 450.

4. Savage, *Geneal. Dict. of First Settlers of N. Eng.*, IV, 44, 387; *R.I. Ct. Rec.*, II, 6, 73.

5. "William Arnold to the Massachusetts Governor, August 1, 1651," in Bartlett, ed., *R.I. Col. Rec.*, I, 235; *R.I. Ct. Rec.*, II, 6; Winthrop, *Journal*, I, 287; Pierce, ed., *Rec. of Boston First Church*, I, 55; Boston Rec. Cmrs., *Rep. Containing Roxbury Rec.*, p. 93; Rogers & Field, eds., *Early Prov. Rec.*, X, 2–6, 10.

6. G. Fox, *N.-Eng. Fire-Brand Quenched*, pt. 1, p. 157; J. Richardson, *An Account*, p. 81.

7. T. Hutchinson, *Hist. of Mass.*, I, 170; Bishop, *N.-Eng. Judged*, p. 114.

8. Besse, *Col. of Quaker Sufferings*, II, 224; Bishop, *N.-Eng. Judged*, pp. 461–62.

9. Bishop, *N.-Eng. Judged*, pp. 57, 107, 112; Besse, *Col. of Quaker Sufferings*, II, 97, 224.

10. Hooten quoted in Cadbury, "Early Quakers at Cambridge," p. 81.

11. Lloyd, *Quaker Social Hist.*, pp. 2, 167–68; Frost, *Quaker Family*, pp. 32, 66–67, 77–78; traveler quoted in Cohen, *Family in Col. Am.*, p. 6.

12. Lloyd, *Quaker Social Hist.*, pp. 2, 167–68.

13. "Rec. of Quarterly Meetings of R.I.," p. 5.

14. "Minutes of Sandwich Men's Monthly Meetings," p. 35.

15. E. Winslow, *Hypocrisie Unmasked*, pp. 5, 22.

16. Gorton, *Antidote Against Common Plague*, pp. 140–41.

17. *Ibid.*, p. 81. Of course, Gorton was here referring not merely to the sons of men, but also to the tendency of many to honor the Old Testament God the Father over His redeeming son, Christ.

18. Bartlett, ed., *R.I. Col. Rec.*, I, 162–63; *Acts & Laws of R.I.*, p. 4.

19. Throughout the century, Rhode Island authorities punished only one

child for abusing his parents; in 1673 they hanged Thomas Cornell after his mother burned up in a suspicious fire. His sister, Sarah, was acquitted of abetting the murder ("Gen. Ct. of Trials. Newport Co.," pp. 11, 24).

20. In 1640 Robert Lenthall had been "by vote called to keep a public school for the learning of youth" at Newport, but that school functioned for only a year and a half before disbanding. No further record of any publicly supported education exists before 1663, when the town sold or leased the school lands to secure revenues for training poor children. Apparently the educational fund assisted *only* children of the poor, those least likely to know the 3 R's. Another school operated at Warwick for a brief time in the 1650s. No general system of public education came into being until 1670. See Higginson, *Hist. of R.I. Public School System*, pp. 1–11; Bridenbaugh, *Cities in the Wilderness*, p. 125; Chapin, ed., *Early Rec. of Warwick*, p. 75.

21. For provisions for the teaching of children in apprenticeship contracts, see Chapin, ed., *Early Rec. of Warwick*, pp. 235–36, 265–67, 273–74, 289–90, 317–19, 333–34.

22. Baily, "The Colledge ferula."

23. As in Puritan New England, apprenticeship contracts specified that boys would learn English and a trade, while girls were to be instructed in housewifery, needlework, and meat preparation.

24. "Roger Williams to his wife, ca 1650," in R. Williams, *Complete Writings*, VII, 42.

25. R. Williams, *George Fox Digg'd*, appendix, p. 26.

26. *Ibid.*, pp. 12, 16, 19–20; appendix pp. 27, 140.

27. *Ibid.*, p. 86; R. Williams, *Complete Writings*, V, 418–19.

28. R. Williams, *George Fox Digg'd*, pp. 28, 38–40, 86.

29. "R. Williams to John Winthrop, Oct. 24, 1636," in Williams, *Complete Writings*, VII, 10.

30. Cited in Oberholzer, *Delinquent Saints*, p. 121.

31. R. Williams, *Complete Writings*, VII, 92.

32. Gorton, *Saltmarsh Returned*, pp. 5, 23, and *Antidote Against Common Plague*, pp. 33, E3, H.

33. In his *Antidote Against Common Plague*, a religious treatise of more than 300 pages, Gorton mentions the Devil less than a dozen times. In many Puritan tracts Satan is mentioned that often on a single page.

34. *Ibid.*, passim, esp. pp. A2, B3, E3, G2–4.

35. Gorton, *Incorruptible Key*, pt. 1, p. 83.

36. See esp. *ibid.*, pp. 84–88; pt. 2, p. 14.

37. Gorton, *Antidote Against Common Plague*, pp. 249–51.

38. *Ibid.*, pp. 10–11.

39. *Ibid.*, p. 82.

40. *Ibid.*

41. Gorton argued that the widow was disadvantaged for several reasons, one of them being that she had no way to perform her essential female function, i.e. "to multiply and increase the family" (*ibid.*, p. 11).

42. E. Johnson, *Wonder-Working Prov.*, p. 129.

43. Gorton, *Incorruptible Key*, pt. 1, p. 83.

44. Gorton, *Antidote Against Common Plague*, epistle dedicatory; Baylie, *Dissuasive*, p. 16.

45. "Minutes of Sandwich Men's Monthly Meetings," p. 21.

46. Men determined what sum would be allotted the women's meetings, but the ladies decided how to spend that money. See "Rec. of Monthly Meeting of Women Friends," n.p.; "Minutes of Men's R.I. Monthly Meeting," n.p.

47. R. Williams, *George Fox Digg'd*, appendix, p. 26.

48. *Ibid.*, pp. 38–41, 202–3.

49. "Minutes of Men's R.I. Monthly Meetings," n.p.

50. W. Richardson, "Newport Account Book," p. 25; Saffin, "Painters Premonition," p. 93.

51. Bartlett, ed., *R.I. Col. Rec.*, II, 392.

52. For a rare example of female indenture, see Brigham, ed., *Early Portsmouth Rec.*, pp. 409–10.

53. *Acts & Laws of R.I.*, pp. 67–68.

54. Austin, *Geneal. Dict. of R.I.*, pp. 207, 316.

55. *Ibid.*, p. 308; Rogers & Field, eds., *Early Prov. Rec.*, IV, 83; XVII, 13–14 (nos. 551–52). Widow Rose Grinnell of Newport made a prenuptial agreement with Anthony Paine; so did Ephraim and Hannah Pierce, before their marriage.

56. *Acts & Laws of R.I.*, p. 14.

57. See Chart 11.1, compiled from the 73 cases cited in Austin, *Geneal. Dict. of R.I.*, where the husband, through his will, or the town council appointed a widow or someone else as executor. The corresponding cases from Maine, Suffolk County, and Hartford County have been taken from the "Ct. Files—Suffolk Co."; Libby, Allen, & Moody, eds., *Maine Ct. Rec.*; and Manwaring, ed., *Digest of Conn. Probate Rec.*

58. Bartlett, ed., *R.I. Col. Rec.*, II, 244–45.

59. *Ibid.*, II, 126; III, 103; Austin, *Geneal. Dict. of R.I.*, p. 76.

60. Rogers & Field, eds., *Early Prov. Rec.*, XI, 7; II, 104; XV, 39 (no. 43); XVII, 65 (no. 463); Bartlett, ed., *R.I. Col. Rec.*, III, 280.

61. Bartlett, ed., *R.I., Col. Rec.*, III, 280, 313.

62. Austin, *Geneal. Dict. of R.I.*, p. 358. Some years earlier, in 1655, Mary Pray had gotten into trouble with the authorities because she neglected to register her wine and liquors with them. See Rogers & Field, eds., *Early Prov. Rec.*, II, 84.

63. Bartlett, ed., *R.I., Col. Rec.*, II, 544–45.

64. Cf. ch. 4. Of course, neither Rhode Island nor Puritan authorities aided all petitioners for assistance. Women who were strangers or who appeared with a child were, at least in Providence by the 1690s, directed to supply a bond for their continued maintenance. If they lacked the necessary funds, the local authorities warned them out of town. Male strangers and men with children were similarly treated. In Providence, warning out became a way to prevent pregnant maidens from delivering their children in the town and then abandoning them. See Rogers & Field, eds., *Early Prov. Rec.*, X, 2–7, 10–14, 26–28, 34–35, 37, 41.

65. Lovejoy, *Glorious Rev. in Am.*, p. 204; Stearns, ed., "Correspondence of Woodbridge & Baxter," p. 573. Joseph Muzye in 1650 indicated the low esteem in which young female "heretics" were held when he told his Essex County neighbors that John Bradstreet "had dealings with the maids at

Road Island, set them on their heads, took them by the gingoes," and fathered three or four bastards there. (The gingko is a Japanese tree cultivated for its ornamental foliage and known also by the name of maidenhair tree. "Taking maids by the gingoes" is a double entendre, meaning in one sense "having intercourse with maids by the trees," and in another "taking them by the pubic hair.") Massachusetts authorities attacked the egalitarian Gortonists for failing to respect the marriage tie and for instead maintaining "licentious lust like sauage brute beasts." Gregory Dexter, the Providence town clerk, in 1654 expressed his fear that "a sweete cup hath rendered many of us wanton and too active." The Suffolk County justices agreed with that view, in 1674 banishing one adulteress, after punishment, *to* Rhode Island. See G. Dow, ed., *Essex Ct. Rec.*, I, 210–12; Deane, "Notice of Gorton," pp. 215–16; "Apologetical Reply," p. 235; "Letter of Gregory Dexter to Sir Harry Vane, Aug. 27, 1654," in Bartlett, ed., *R.I. Col. Rec.*, I, 288; "Ct. Files—Suffolk Co.," XIV (1673–74), no. 1325.

66. Bartlett, ed., *R.I. Col. Rec.*, I, 173, 311–12.

67. *Ibid.*, I, 311–12, 332, 355.

68. *R.I. Ct. Rec.*, I, 45.

69. This woman, Mary Read, in 1660 admitted her guilt and was bound over to the next court. In March 1661 those justices acquitted her after she had paid court costs (*ibid.*, I, 65, 72).

70. "Ct. of Trials. Newport Co.," p. 62.

71. *Ibid.*, pp. 8–9.

72. Noble & Cronin, eds., *Recs. of Mass. Assts.*, I, 234, 240, 252–53; Pulsifer, trans., "Rec. of Middlesex Co. Ct." I, 158; *Rec. of Suffolk Co. Ct., 1671–80*, I, 185.

73. *R.I. Ct. Rec.*, II, 82, 85.

74. *Ibid.*, II, 71; "Ct. of Trials. Newport Co.," p. 21. The case of Sarah Gregory illustrates the kind of situation which the colony authorities considered more properly punished as fornication. Although Gregory was married, her husband, described as a "filthy man," had abandoned her (1673). Puritans drew no such distinctions.

75. Bartlett, ed., *R.I. Col. Rec.*, II, 293–94.

76. These figures refer to the modal adulterer. Some women were sentenced to thirty and, at least in five cases, to forty lashes. Since adultery was considered such a heinous offense, males and females received the same sentence in many cases.

77. Bartlett, ed., *R.I. Col. Rec.*, I, 173.

78. "Ct. of Trials. Newport Co., '" p. 44.

79. *Ibid.*, pp. 49, 3.

80. Danckaerts, *Journal*, p. 252.

81. Bartlett, ed., *R.I. Col. Rec.*, I, 184. The Calvinist colonies allowed civil prosecutions when a woman was called a whore, but no law existed to guarantee them. Because in all such prosecutions the accused woman was married, the insult against her also became an insult against her husband. Only Rhode Island protected the single maiden from such slanderous charges.

82. R. Williams, *George Fox Digg'd*, p. 80.

83. "Gen. Ct. of Trials. Newport Co.," pp. 30, 32.

84. Libby, Allen, & Moody, eds., *Maine Ct. Rec.*, II, 217n. When Thomas Monsall of Providence, one man taken with "the Rhode Island idea," was summoned into court (1675) for living with Lidia Way without benefit of marriage, he pleaded that he was guilty but only "accordinge to the *Law of Man*" ("Gen. Ct. of Trials. Newport Co.," p. 24).

85. Bartlett, ed., *R.I., Col. Rec.*, I, 102; Austin, *Geneal. Dict. of R.I.*, p. 81. Edward Richmond and Abigail Davis (1658), William Long and Ann Brownell (1666), and Monsall and Way (1675) comprised the remaining three common law couples (*R.I. Ct. Rec.*, I, 45; II, 48; "Gen. Ct. of Trials. Newport Co.," p. 24).

86. Bartlett, ed., *R. I. Col. Rec.*, I, 148; II, 102, 105; *Acts & Laws of R.I.*, pp. 12, 47–48.

87. As one example, in 1685 Richard Speare, "affirming himselfe Batchelor of Arte," had only to promise that he would procure a license after he was prosecuted for assuming the authority to marry without one ("Gen. Ct. of Trials. Newport Co.," p. 73).

88. Bartlett, ed., *R.I. Col. Rec.*, III, 361, 435–36.

89. Of Rhode Island fornicators, ten were married (8%) at the time of their prosecution and ten others were living in common law relationships; the corresponding percentages were 37.3 and 2.7 in Calvinist locales. Of course, it is possible that the liberal Rhode Island authorities did not prosecute all offenders who later married, but, if this was so, the court records in no way indicate it. Any contention that the prosecutions had a selective character must deal with the fact the son of a prominent merchant like John Coggeshall was included in the few premarital prosecutions, along with the sons and daughters of the very poor.

90. Howard, *Hist. of Matrimonial Institutions*, II, 134–47.

91. Calvinists particularly objected to the Quaker marriage practice of couples merely promising each other love, fidelity, and life-long companionship, without the intervention of minister *or* magistrate (Sewel, *Hist. of Rise of Quakers*, II, 631).

92. Bartlett, ed., *R.I. Co. Rec.*, I, 231, 312; II, 188–89, 479; *Muddy River & Brookline Rec.*, p. 69. Warwick Assistant John Greene divorced Richard and Mary Pray when the General Assembly would agree only to separate them. The Assembly reproved Greene for his interference, but the townsmen of Warwick continued to recognize the Prays' divorce.

93. Klyberg, ed., *R.I. Land Evidences*, I, 89.

94. Hubbard, "Gen. Hist. of N. Eng.," VI, p. 337; Bartlett, ed., *R.I. Col. Rec.*, II, 251; *R.I. Ct. Rec.*, II, 74.

95. Bartlett, ed., *R.I. Col. Rec.*, III, 124; "Gen. Ct. of Trials. Newport Co.," p. 67.

96. In 1648 Elizabeth Feake had left her husband and "pretends marriadge" to William Hallet in New Netherlands (Eaton, "Letter," pp. 349–50; Haynes, "Letter," p. 360).

97. "Aquidneck Quarter Ct. Rec.," II, 151; *R.I. Ct. Rec.*, II, 74; "Gen. Ct. of Trials. Newport Co.," p. 67.

98. Rogers & Field, eds., *Early Prov. Rec.*, XVII, 37–38 (no. 431).

99. "Gen. Ct. of Trials. Newport Co.," p. 20. There is no record of a Rhode Island wife attempting to murder her husband.

100. Aquidneck was the Indian name for Rhode Island.

101. "Aquidneck Quarter Ct. Rec.," II, 151–52; Bartlett, ed., *R.I. Col. Rec.*, II, 99–100; *R.I. Ct. Rec.*, I, 13.

102. Bartlett, ed., *R.I. Col. Rec.*, II, 101–3.

103. *R.I. Ct. Rec.*, II, 61, 65, 70.

104. C. Mather, *Magnalia*, II, 450.

105. Massachusetts enacted two early sumptuary laws in 1634 and 1636, ostensibly to prevent the growth of pride. These laws penalized anyone who wore gold, silver, silk laces or girdles, hatbands, beaver hats, ruffs, embroidered needlework caps and bands, cutworks, and sleeves with more than two slashes. Later sumptuary laws in the Bay Colony (1651) and Connecticut (1641) had quite a different intention. These were designed to keep "men and women of meane condition educations & callings" from taking "uppon them the garbe of gentlemen, by the wearing of gold and silver lace, or buttons or poynt at their knees, . . . [or] great bootes." The law prohibited women of mean rank from wearing "silk or tiffany hoods, or scarfs, which though allowable to persons of greater estates or more liberal education" were "intolerable" attire for their social inferiors. See Shurtleff, ed., *Mass. Rec.*, I, 126, 183; IV, pt. 1, p. 243; J. Trumbull, ed., *Conn. Rec.*, I, 64; II, 283.

106. Plate 44 in G. Dow, *Every Day Life in Mass.*; Sewel, *Hist. of Rise of Quakers*, I, 235, 297; Bacon, *Quiet Rebels*, p. 10.

107. Bishop, *N.-Eng. Judged*, p. 324; [H. Norton,] *N.-Eng. Ensigne*, p. 73.

108. C. Mather, *Magnalia*, II, 453.

109. R. Williams, *George Fox Digg'd*, p. 32.

110. Austin, *Geneal. Dict. of R.I.*, p. 358; Rogers & Field, eds., *Early Prov. Rec.*, II, 41, 48.

111. "Rec. of R.I. Women's Monthly Meetings," n.p.; "Minutes of R.I. Men's Monthly Meeting," n.p.

112. E. Johnson, *Wonder-Working Prov.*, p. 186.

113. Winthrop, *Journal*, I, 297.

114. R. Williams, *George Fox Digg'd*, pp. 12, 138, 160.

115. Besse, *Col. of Quaker Sufferings*, II, 206.

116. Weeden, *Econ. Hist. of N. Eng.*, II, 544.

117. R. Williams, *George Fox Digg'd*, p. 12.

118. Winthrop, *Journal*, I, 286–87; Bartlett, ed., *R.I. Col. Rec.*, I, 16; "R. Williams to J. Winthrop, May 22, 1638 and October, 1638," in R. Williams, *Complete Writings*, VI, 95–96, 124.

119. E. Winslow, *Hypocrisie Unmasked*, pp. 44, 54–55, 67; Winthrop, *Journal*, I, 297, 299; Chapin, *Doc. Hist. of R.I.*, II, 56–57; "William Coddington to John Winthrop, Dec. 9, 1639," in A. Forbes, ed., *Winthrop Papers*, IV, 160–61; Baylie, *Dissuasive*, p. 150.

120. Groome, *Glass for People of N.-Eng.*, pp. 13–15; Holden, "Letter," p. 13; Niles, "Summary Narrative," p. 201. That same party of Indians killed 13 other persons and burned up several cows before they passed over to Long Island; there they assaulted the residence of another "heretic," Lady Moody. Enough settlers lived at Gravesend to repel the attackers, however (O'Callaghan, *Hist. of N. Neth.*, p. 287).

121. K. Scott, "Letter"; Holden, "Letter," pp. 13–15.

122. Brinton, *Friends for 300 Yrs.*, pp. 126–43; Gray, *Contributions of Quakers*, p. 29.

123. Rogers & Field, eds., *Early Prov. Rec.*, XV, 230–31 (no. 343).

124. *Ibid.*, XV, 231 (no. 343).

125. A. Coffin, *Life of Tristam Coffyn*, pp. 56–57; Hinchman, *Early Nantucket Settlers*, pp. 123–27; J. Richardson, *An Account*, pp. 86–90; Chalkley, *Journal*, pp. 19–21; Story, *Journal*, p. 350.

126. The percentage of female "heads of families" in 19 locales ranged from 0 to 11.8. Providence ranked fifth-highest in percentage of such women. See Rogers & Field, eds., *Early Prov. Rec.*, XVII, 122–26.

127. Bartlett, ed., *R.I. Col. Rec.*, II, 241, 280, 313; Rogers & Field, eds., *Early Prov. Rec.*, II, 41, 48, 84; Bridenbaugh, *Fat Mutton & Liberty of Conscience*, p. 119.

128. George Keith in *Prot. Episcopal Hist. Cols.*, I, xx.

129. Austin, *Geneal. Dict. of R.I.*, p. 330.

130. New York *Gazette*, March 13, 1739, quoted in Dexter, *Col. Women of Affairs*, pp. 58–59.

131. Rogers & Field, eds., *Early Prov. Rec.*, XVII, 53 (no. 443).

132. In 1683 the Newport Court of Trials sentenced Deborah Allen of Dartmouth to receive 15 lashes for "indeavoringe the distruction of the Child in her womb" ("Gen. Ct. of Trials. Newport Co.," p. 67).

133. E.g., see "R. Williams to Robert Williams & Thomas Harris, Feb. 22, 1651," in R. Williams, *Complete Writings*, VI, 208; Rogers & Field, eds., *Early Prov. Rec.*, II, 56, 89, 104.

134. "William Arnold to the Massachusetts Governor, Aug. 1, 1651," in Bartlett, ed., *R.I. Col. Rec.*, I, 235.

135. Bartlett, ed., *R.I. Col. Rec.*, I , 173; R. Williams, *George Fox Digg'd*, pp. 22, 172.

136. In 1672 a well-lubricated Stephen Sabeere called Henry Palmer's wife a witch; Palmer retaliated by calling him "French dog, French rogue." The matter was then placed before two arbiters, who directed both parties to acknowledge their errors (Austin, *Geneal. Dict. of R.I.*, p. 143).

XII

Storm and Stress: Calvinist Colonies in Changing Times, 1665–89

It can be argued that after 1660 New England ascended, threw off the shackles of a narrow theology and a restrictive society, and became a more open, tolerant community.
—A. Vaughan, ed., *Puritan Tradition in America*

Surely this day New-England is sick, the Country is a sickly Country, this Country is full of healthful Bodies, but sick souls.

—Thomas Walley, *Balm in Gilead*

THROUGHOUT THE SEVENTEENTH CENTURY, NEW ENGLAND PURI-tans coped with an awesome and sinful reality by accentuating moral rectitude and sex-role rigidity. They struggled to achieve the ideals of the Biblical Commonwealth, so that they might avoid Rhode Island's "sluttish," hellish example. But Puritan behavior and attitudes did not remain consistent throughout the century, for the events gradually created unique conditions in each Calvinist-controlled colony. The personal declarativeness which emerged by the 1690s had an important impact upon sex roles and female behavior.

A General Turmoil

In most of New England, the years following the Quaker invasion of 1656 to 1664 were a time of great physical and psychological stress, as well as of great change in the focus and quality of life. King Philip's War took a heavy toll in human lives and property damage.

Relations with England worsened during the 1670s and 1680s, as royal authorities increasingly complained about the "New England disease" of avowed independence.[1] Violations of the Navigation Acts, the illegal coinage of money, the Puritan refusal to allow religious toleration, and the limitation of the franchise to Puritan church members ultimately resulted in the forfeiture of all charters previously issued for New England. The appointment of Sir Edmund Andros as royal governor of the Dominion of New England caused widespread distress, for Andros eliminated the colonial assemblies, cast doubt upon the legitimacy of local government and land titles, levied taxes as he saw fit, and used "packt and pickt" juries in the courts he established between 1687 and 1689. The governor refused to allow more than one town meeting at a time and his retinue, that "crew of abject persons," "squeezed . . . extraordinary and intolerable" probate fees from New England's inhabitants. Feeling deprived of any possibility of self-government and traditional bases of power, the Pilgrim descendants and their brethren in Massachusetts and Connecticut resented his rule. Governor Andros had very effectively invalidated any notion that the laws of England did "not reach Amerrica."[2]

The New England colonies faced economic as well as political stress. Indian war increased the tax rate to hitherto unheard of amounts. Beginning in the 1660s, worms periodically decreased the pea yield, blasts and mildews assailed the grain crop, and drought had a potent impact in what were already financially troubled times.[3] Pirates often preyed on New England vessels.[4] No fewer than ten destructive fires broke out in Boston alone, including one in 1679 which destroyed three hundred households.[5] Outbreaks of "malignant fevers" and smallpox kept large numbers of people enervated and unproductive for lengthy periods of time.[6] Refugees from the Maine Indian wars flooded the Massachusetts seacoast cities, establishing pockets of poverty.

These and other sources of tension caused many men and women to reevaluate themselves and their relationship to Puritan society. Assailed too often by the twin specters of Poverty and Death, proper Puritans sharply castigated themselves for deviating from God's holy way or for not watching their neighbors' behavior diligently enough. Others, less inclined toward self-blame, related to a tense reality by abandoning old expectations, old forms—by beginning to believe, feel, and act differently. These individuals—notwithstanding the potent social conditioning of their childhood—managed to help create a new social order. To most observers, the cracks in the Puritan armor grew more visible with each passing decade, as repressed desires for merriment, self-achievement, personal pride, and freedom found release in changed circumstances. The New England of the 1690s, the result of great economic, political, ideological, and behavioral change, would have shocked the rigidly authoritarian Puritans of the century's early decades. An atmosphere of contention and fragmentation had replaced the earlier belief in the coherency and purposiveness of the Biblical Commonwealth. By 1700, "the Splintering of Society" suggested that people had found new avenues to personal truth, new lifestyles for a new reality.[7] The varying causes and nature of this splintering, so particularly relevant to both men and women, deserve fuller treatment.

Massachusetts in Decline

Between 1665 and 1689, Massachusetts experienced a seventeenth-century population explosion. The 15,000 inhabitants of 1643 became 23,467 by 1665, 42,000 by 1680, and almost 50,000 by 1690,[8] in the largest population upsurge of any New England colony. Boston, with approximately 5,088 inhabitants in 1690, had 25 percent more people than any other city in the English mainland colonies:[9] the little metropolis comprised about one-tenth of Massachusetts's total population at that time. From the 1660s to the mid-1680s an active, flourishing commerce brought goods and persons from far-off places into Boston, Salem, and other seacoast centers, helping to create a cosmopolitan atmosphere. Richly dressed merchants, poor fishermen, French Huguenots, black slaves, Scottish servants, English travelers, and "Jack Tars" added color and variety to the Puritan landscape. In many shops, entrepreneurs sold imported English finery, the latest fashions, books, toys for children, dice, and cards, besides the "essentials." Hetty Shepard, a sixteen-year-old maiden from rural Plymouth, wrote in her diary on March 2, 1676/7, "Through all my life have I never seen such an array of fashion and splendor as I have seen here in Boston. Silken hoods, scarlet petticoats, with silver lace, white sarconett plaited gowns, bone lace and silken scarfs. The men with periwigs, ruffles and ribbons."[10] Low-necked dresses, a pride in material things, and increased forms of recreation—those products of an extensive trade—gradually eroded the rigidity and moral strictness of Puritanism. Taverns proliferated much more rapidly at Boston than in other locales; on an annual average, seven were functioning in the 1660s, 15 in the 1670s, 31 in the early 1680s, and 51 in 1690.[11]

In a very general way, Bernard Bailyn has admirably described the impact of this commercial expansion upon the Puritan way of life:

> . . . the business community represented the spirit of a new age. Its guiding principles were not social stability, order, and the discipline of the senses, but mobility, growth, and the enjoyment of life. Citizens of an international trading world as well as of New England colonies, the merchants took the pattern for their conduct not from the Bible or from parental teachings but from the picture of life in Restoration England. To the watchmen of the holy citadel nothing could have been more insidious.[12]

New people, new material goods, and new modes of perception came to Massachusetts, creating along the eastern seaboard a dynamic, outward focus. That reality, in turn, created new problems (or old problems, in a radically altered cast) for the Puritan population. Law enforcement became difficult. Rebellious young men, unwilling to give the authorities unremitting respect, stole the constables' staffs of office and threatened to "beat out" their "Braines."[13] Carousers often met, invisible to the watchmen's eyes in the darkness of night, to gamble, speak obscenely, plot mischief, and drink past the 9 P.M. curfew. Under Governor Andros's rule, the Massachusetts courts barely functioned. His Courts of General Sessions tried many fewer persons than had the Puritan justices.

The loss of viable Puritan control and the spread of a cosmopolitan, materialistic way of life spurred into action those men, women, and children who felt much frustration and discontent. Ministers complained that the Bay Colony's inhabitants neglected their religious duties, fell asleep during Sabbath services, and turned "their Backs upon the publick Worship before it be finished."[14] Congregations argued over the acceptability of the Halfway Covenant,[15] the respective powers of the minister and church members,[16] and the proper form for Calvinism. By 1671 there existed "three forms of disciplinarians . . . rigid Independents [Congregationalists], moderate ones, and those that are Presbyterianly addicted, though their numbers are few and their horns kept short."[17] Church members frequently fell into disunity, with "evil surmisings, uncharitable and unrighteous censures, backbitings," and tale-bearings.[18] By 1677, in the midst of such fractiousness, Solomon Stoddard, the

Northampton pastor who became "Pope of the Connecticut Valley," had launched a full-scale controversy with the eastern churches over the issue of broadening membership but constricting local control of churches.[19]

Even "heretical" churches came into being. In 1674, over bitter protests, Quakers constructed the first brick house of worship in Boston. Anabaptists opened a meetinghouse in 1679; that structure survived despite a successful effort to nail shut its doors.[20] Governor Andros outraged Puritans by disallowing the rate levied to pay the minister's salary, by celebrating the "pagan, papist" holiday of Christmas, by holding Anglican services in Congregationalist meetinghouses, and by establishing an Anglican church in Boston. Irate Puritans broke the windows of this King's Chapel, tore the minister's service book, smeared crosses of human excrement upon the chapel doors, and then stuffed keyholes full of the same.[21]

All authority fell into great disrepute. The Puritans hardly respected Andros's rule. Impressments to supply sailors and soldiers for the watch, the militia, or the English navy met with popular disapproval. At least fifty men refused to serve, and more than half that many deserted once they had been impressed. Two dozen others broke into the various town pounds where constables had lodged their confiscated livestock. Inhabitants hurled censorious epithets at ministers, magistrates, and local officials, including such choice descriptions as "Rogues and Rascalls," "Drunkards and Whoremasters," "devil," "old blue beard," "pitiful fellow," and "arse-kisser."[22] Such opprobrium exceeded even the invective of the earlier Quakers. It was for good reason that the Reverend Charles Chauncy snapped, "The rewards of a painful ministry are not regarded by covetous earthworms."[2]

Faced with religious fragmentation and a declining respect for the authorities, ministers drew further away from their congregations. During the 1680s "the ministers began to suggest that they themselves constituted a peculiarly holy group of men—as if in a society gone wrong they alone embodied the religious life of the community." Their sermons reflected their own anxiety about declining prestige, sounding more like whining supplications than stern, scolding rebukes from patriarchal figures.[24] The new class of merchant-magistrates emerging in the 1670s and 1680s also tended to view themselves as a people apart, adopting the periwigs and foppish dress of the wealthy English. These public officials tolerated un-Puritan behavior to a large extent. When they did bring offenders into court, the penalties were often much less than they had been before 1665. (For example, the average punishment for fornication decreased by half.) While the ministers and magistrates effectually isolated themselves from semi-egalitarian contact with most inhabitants, the townsmen took advantage of the difficulties imposed by a deteriorating relationship with the mother country, almost effortlessly stripping the selectmen of extensive local supervisory control.[25] Furthermore, after 1670 townsmen increasingly neglected to maintain grammar schools, those nurseries of Puritanism.[26] Despite the pretentiousness of "moderates" (merchant-magistrates) and ministers, the individualizing, equalizing trend of the times loosened the rigidity of social roles. Puritans had, of course, always been individualists, in a limited spiritual sense (*i.e.*, in the struggle for assurance of election); but that individualism now assumed a broader social and ideological character. Poor people occupied the meetinghouse pews reserved for their social betters. Servants and others of the "meaner sort" appeared abroad "in their Silks and Bravery as if they were the best in the Land."[27] Parents acted so "sinfully indulgent" that children ceased to be "kept in due subjection." Parent-child role differences became less sharp and were less closely supervised, a fact which prompted one young man to charge "that they dealt with children here as the people with their young shoates in Virginia, to take them up and marke them and turne them into the woods."[28] Many communities appointed special youth wardens, each equipped with a hefty "wand," to keep youngsters from "Laughing and Jutting others that sat" near them in church, "spitting in one another's faces, jousting boys off their seats, heaving things into the other gallery among the girls who sat there and breaking the glass windows" of the meetinghouse.[29] Youth wardens might force youngsters to assume the proper outward behavior in church, but outside, in the unsupervised isolation of their own homes and the secretive darkness of night, boys and girls could meet with "Corrupt Company," play pranks, talk obscenely, and do many things proper Puritans detested.[30]

By the 1690s the evaporation of rigid social roles, the strained political conditions, economic hardship, booming materialism, and religious disunity testified to the erosion of any compact, carefully regulated community. For the first four decades of settlement New England ministers had reminded their constituents that disrespect of the Puritan authorities, sensuality, drunkenness, contentiousness, inexorable lust after land titles,[31] and the practice of usury[32] all merited sharp punishment. After 1665, as such sinful behavior became more common, the divines rushed to the attack, preparing a large number of hortatory sermons which bewailed New England's loss of godliness. These jeremiads echoed the same theme: "repent, New England, for you have strayed from God's path and from the high achievements of the founding fathers. God will not long tolerate such a profligate people."[33]

Before King Philip's War, few Puritans seemed to listen very self-consciously to the ominous jeremiads. The earlier Quaker prosecutions had, in the view of many, purged Massachusetts of its ills. The decade from 1665 to 1674 became a time of peace, commercial expansion, and prosperity. In such benign times there was no need for scapegoating. Witchcraft accusations dropped to eight, a record low for any decade after 1645, and the authorities acquitted, released outright, or neglected to prosecute all of them.

The Indian War of 1675–76 changed all that. A war which left six hundred dead and two thousand destitute lent particular credence to the jeremiads.[34] Increase Mather graphically described the way in which King Philip's braves undermined Puritan security. "Is it nothing," he lamented, "that so many have been cut off by a bloddy and barbarous Sword? Is it nothing that Widdows and the Fatherless have been multiplyed among us? that in a small Plantation we have heard of eight widows, and twenty fatherless children in one day? And in another of the Villages of our Judah, of seven Widows and about thirty fatherless children, all at once?"[35] God clearly *was* angry.

The desperation, shock, and guilt engendered by King Philip's activities produced an upsurge in witchcraft accusations. The total number of witches accused between 1675 and 1684 (14) was exceeded only in 1645–64, and in the 1692 outbreak at Salem Village. However, none of these witches faced hanging, for worsening relations with England deflected public attention to more concrete "oppressors"—customs collector Edward Randolph, Governor Andros, and one's opponents in the partisan political life of Massachusetts after 1676.[36] Furthermore, English Anglicans heartily disapproved of witch hunts.[37]

Governor Andros, in particular, served as an admirable witch-substitute. Virtually everything he did angered both the Puritans and the many non-Calvinist inhabitants of Massachusetts. Vicious rumors began circulating about him—that he was a secret papist, a French collaborator, and a covert encourager of Indian hostility. No one actually suggested that he practiced *maleficium* (they could have been hanged as traitors for such an accusation), but the governor clearly personified evil nevertheless. The "non-elected" Andros exacerbated Puritan feelings of powerlessness at the same time that he fed the colonists' already angry spirits. Their intense feelings were expressed through refusals to observe a designated fast day, one "riotous" militia muster, and protests against the governor's taxation policy. Andros speedily clapped his critics in prison, and packed juries sentenced them to exorbitant fines of up to £50. Such quick suppression of discontent did indeed "terrify others," thereby producing a need to find alternative outlets for frustration.[38]

The execution of Goody Glover for witchcraft—the first witch hanging in thirty-three years—provided one momentary, but ominous, expression of Puritan frustration before irate Bostonians removed Andros from power on April 18, 1689. After the rebels took the governor into custody, some wished to kill both him and Edward Randolph. Cooler heads prevailed, however, and Andros was shipped off to England.[39] Yet, after this little Glorious Revolution, Puritans who looked back upon their recent history had to conclude, in the sociologist Kai Erikson's words, "that the trajectory of the past pointed in quite a different direction that the one they now found themselves taking: they were no longer participants in a great adventure, no longer residents of a 'city upon a hill,' no longer members of that special revolutionary elite who were destined to bend the course of history according to God's own word. They were only themselves, living alone in a remote corner of the world."[40]

While some were drifting away from the church and the Puritan way, others, following the example held forth by the ministers, grasped at traditional forms to ease their growing sense of disorientation. Anxious about the changes which daily confronted them, they joined the Church, seeking solace and security there. For their own part, the churches, faced with the profound need to shore up the Biblical Commonwealth against Satan's assaults, relaxed their own strict membership requirements. Previous argument over the acceptability of the Halfway Covenant ceased, as churches anxiously wished to make sure that "virtually no member of the rising generation would be excluded from the benefits of both church discipline and the preaching of the gospel."[41] Ironically, in thus relaxing their own standards, Puritans participated in the very process of societal liberalization which they hoped to combat.

Church members new and old realized that crime was reaching

great proportions, and that much of it was hidden from public view.[42] The often secret character of criminal deviance reflected the Biblical Commonwealth's slippage, the blatant erosion of its accepted norms of conduct.[43] So, too, did the large number of sinful strangers entering Massachusetts towns; between 1671 and 1687 the Boston authorities alone rejected 224 persons who wished to establish residence there.[44]

The social atmosphere legitimating and intensifying norm slippage in the Bay Colony propelled discontented people into acting upon their own thwarted needs. In earlier days these malcontents had complied outwardly with the Puritan way, hiding any contrary feelings from the watchful eyes of their righteous neighbors. But as alternative modes of behavior became more common, particularly along the urban seacoast, such "rebels" felt freer to vent their frustration. The Calvinist faith bore within itself the seeds of its own destruction, for the ability of rebels to act freely in innumerable back alleys or seaside haunts, in the cloaking isolation of the forest, and often even in public places became an impelling example to other repressed persons. Crime often became an important way to affirm the self—to act on the perceived integrity of impulse. Wearing clothing beyone one's social rank, attacking Governor Andros, rejecting military service, and chiding the authorities all constituted attempts to declare one's self-importance, have an effect on others, and exert personal influence. Spitting in the face of the oppressor, metaphorically as well as literally, served as a way to exercise independent will—what Puritans would denounce as pride. Women, in particular, were guilty of such pride.

Bay Colony Women Become More Individually Assertive

Commercial expansion, urbanization, and the resulting opportunities for contact with other, different people tugged at the underpinnings of Puritan society. Puritans recognized the urban scene was a dangerous environment which could easily corrupt the naive country girl. The English Calvinist Alexander Niccholes warned: "enter her into that school of vanity, set but example before her eyes, shee shall in time become a new creature, and such strong mutation shall so strangely possesse her, that she shall haue new thoughts, new purposes, and resolutions, and in the end so shoulder out her modesty, that shee shall not blush to do that unlawfully, which before shee was bashfull to thinke on lawfully." In the city

"embroidered haire, embared breasts, virmillioned cheekes, alluring lookes, fashion gates, and Artfull countenances" threatened
to stimulate "that boyling damned putrefaction of the bloud,"
lust.[45] Puritans especially deplored Englishwomen who wore "the
long white brest . . . so low . . . as the world call them kodpeece
breasts," exposing naked bosoms like meat in a shop, and inviting
flesh-flies to savor their "full spread paps."[46]

The many ships visiting Boston and Salem added to Puritan
concerns, not only because they brought in trade goods, new people, and new ideas, but also because visitors related the latest
information about changes occurring in England. New Englanders
may well have heard about expanding educational opportunities for
Englishwomen, about the appearance of female scientists and dra-
matists, and about the patriarchal father's diminishing control over
his daughter's marital destiny.[47] In the 1680s Boston booksellers
stocked volumes like *Wonders of the Female World, or A general History
of Women . . . To which is added a Discourse of Female Pre-eminence,*and
*Her and His, the Feminine Gender more worthy than the Masculine, Being
a Vindication of that ingenious and innocent Sex from the biting Sarcasms
. . . of malevolent Men.*[48]

Female criminal offenses were definitely on the upsurge. Nowhere in Massachusetts did women commit as many as 15 percent
of the total crimes before 1644. By the 1665–74 decade, after the
Quaker invasion had made female rebellion more fashionable, the
percentage of women criminals exceeded that figure in Essex, Middlesex, and Suffolk counties. In all of Massachusetts, the number
and percentage of female crimes increased from 498 (18.3%) between 1630 and 1664 to 1,039 (22.8%) in 1665–89. Only in the
more isolated, static frontier settlements along the Upper Connecticut River (Hampshire County) did the percentage of male and
female offenders remain constant.

The number of offenses committed by women in Massachusetts
increased at almost twice the men's rate. In 1665–89 males faced
prosecution for 58.3 percent more crimes than they did in 1630–64,
while female criminals increased by 108.6 percent. Only in Hampshire County did the margin of male increase exceed that for
females. A female crime wave was quite literally in progress, for the
substantial difference between the male and female increases cannot be attributed to a surplus female population. In the 1630s
women comprised about 40 percent of the adult population, a figure
which may have approached 50 percent by midcentury. There is no

Chart 12.1
Number and Percentage of Female Offenses in Puritan New England

Court	1630–1664			1665–1689			1690–1699		
	No. Female Offenses	Total Offenses	% Women	No. Female Offenses	Total Offenses	% Women	No. Female Offenses	Total Offenses	% Women
Massachusetts	498	2,725	18.3	1,039	4,564	22.8	325	1,111	29.3
General Ct.-Ct. of Assistants	73	792	9.2	32	209	15.3	19	141	13.5
Essex County Ct.	369	1,617	22.8	517	2,114	24.5	117	433	27.0
Middlesex Co. Ct.	45	249	18.1	142	661	21.5	75	220	34.1
Suffolk Co. Ct.	—	—	—	310	1,353	23.0	96	235	40.9
Hampshire Co. Ct.	11	67	16.4	37	227	16.4	18	82	22.0
Maine (York Co. Ct.)	75	399	18.8	188	869	21.6	65	216	30.1
New Hampshire	56	417	13.4	134	659	20.3	61	218	28.0
Connecticut	118	803	14.7	250	1,407	17.8	97	461	21.0
Plymouth	85	721	11.8	68	536	12.7	47	161	29.2
Martha's Vineyard	—	—	—	4	54	7.4	8	36	22.2

Chart 12.2

Relative Comparison of Male and Female Rates of Increase, Criminal Offenders, in Seventeenth-Century Puritan New England

Court	No. Male 1630–64	Offenses 1665–89	% Increase	No. Female 1630–64	Offenses 1665–89	% Increase	Difference, Female over Male, 1630–64 & 1665–89	No. Male Offenses 1690–99	No. Female Offenses 1690–99
Massachusetts	2227	3525	58.3	498	1039	108.6	+50.3	768	325
Gen. Ct.-Ct. of Assistants	719	177	−75.4	73	32	−56.2	+19.2	109	19
Essex County Ct.	1248	1597	28.0	369	517	40.1	+12.1	316	117
Middlesex Co. Ct.	204	519	154.4	45	142	215.6	+61.2	145	75
Suffolk Co. Ct.	—	1042	—	—	311	—	—	139	96
Hampshire Co. Ct.	56	190	260.7	11	37	236.4	−24.3	59	18
Maine (York Co. Ct.)	324	681	110.2	75	188	150.7	+40.5	151	65
New Hampshire	361	525	45.4	56	134	139.3	+93.9	157	61
Connecticut	685	1157	68.9	118	250	111.9	+43.0	364	97
Plymouth	633	468	−26.1	85	68	−20.0	+6.1	114	47
Martha's Vineyard	—	50	—	—	4	—	—	28	8

These tables are based on all available seventeenth-century court records, plus additional cases which appear in diaries, letters, or contemporary published accounts. Unfortunately, a large portion of the records are no longer extant; these include the Plymouth court records before 1633 and after 1690, the Suffolk County records before 1670, and the Fairfield County (Connecticut) records. Partially missing are the Middlesex County records in the 1660s, the Hampshire County records before 1677, the Suffolk County records in the 1680s and 1690s, the records of the Massachusetts Court of Assistants after 1644, the Essex County records in the 1690s, and the New Hampshire records during 1682–86. Massachusetts totals for the 1690s do not include the special witchcraft courts of 1692.

reason to suspect that women ever constituted more than half of the adult population.[49] Perhaps as many as 5 percent of the adult males died in King Philip's War, but many women also perished in that conflict. The large number of seamen, merchants, fishermen, pleasure seekers, and Anglicans who visited the Bay Colony's developing urban centers were almost entirely male and ought to have more than made up for the casualties inflicted by King Philip's braves. Many women, widowed by Indian warfare, chose Boston as the most appropriate locale for resettlement; their numbers did not necessarily distort the city's male-female ratio, however, since Boston was also the locale to which the many travelers most frequently came—if only temporarily.[50] To attribute the increased percentage of female criminal offenders to an increased proportion of women in the population would only be justifiable if, comparing the pre-1644 figures to the 1665–89 ones, women exceeded 90 percent of the adult population in the latter period[51]—an obvious impossibility. When we compare the pre-1664 years (including large numbers of female Quaker missionaries) with 1665–89, the natural-increase hypothesis would appear correct only against a projected female figure of 56.1 percent of the population over the latter time span. (Here I am estimating the percentage of women in the population prior to 1665 as 45 percent.) This too is very unlikely, since in 1765, when everyone admitted there was a surplus female population, adult women constituted but 54.6 percent of the total adult population.[52]

As the number of female offenses increased, so did their variety. In 1630–64 the courts tried women for thirty-one different types of crimes; by 1665–89 that number had grown to forty-three. New offenses included casting dice, playing shuffleboard, nightwalking (being abroad after the 9 P.M. curfew), and forgery. By 1690 women were committing almost all types of offenses (with the exception of a few specifically male crimes, such as neglect of public office and rape).

Only a handful of the old female rebels, the Anabaptists and Quakers, appeared before the authorities after 1665, but the few who did continued to abuse the Puritan magistrates in sharp terms. For example, Margaret Brewster arrived in Boston from Barbados in 1677 and entered the meetinghouse with "her hair dishevelled and flying loosely about her shoulders, ashes upon her head, her face blackened, sackcloth upon her upper garments, and her feet bare." Magistrate Simon Bradstreet placed her and her "party"—a group composed of Lydia Wright of Long Island, Sarah Mills of Maine,

Elizabeth Bowen of Cambridge, and John Easton, Jr., of Rhode Island—in prison for "making an horrible disturbance, and affrighting the People, . . . whereby several Women . . . are in great danger of miscarrying." This cosmopolitian group soundly chastized the Bay Colony authorities in court.[53]

At least twenty-one other women adopted the Quaker's censorious style, slashing at the unequal power possessed by ministers and magistrates. One such woman flew into a rage and charged a Boston minister with lying when he reproved her for drunkenness. Another lady maligned a Northampton minister's character by accusing him of lascivious carriage and speech (1685).[54] Such outright defamation, the product of freer times, would have appalled the sensitive Anne Hutchinson. Other women, approximately one hundred in number, refused to attend church services. When two Salem tithingmen awoke one such woman and asked the reason for her nonappearance, Mary Meds angrily responded that they "had more neede to look after Rude boys." Furthermore, she asserted self-confidently, if not haughtily, that "she cold not nor wold not goe to meeting for none of them all" (1679).[55] Recalcitrant women who did come to church often misbehaved there, most notably by "hunching" neighboring women with their elbows.[56]

Some female "criminals" dressed too proudly and provocatively for stolid Puritan tastes. In the 1670s and 1680s divines complained that New England women were exposing portions of their own breasts in low-cut dresses, immodestly "laying out their hair," wearing laces and whalebone corsets which physicians believed hindered conception, and adopting other "whorish Fashions." Increase Mather wrote, with some chagrin, that a "proud Fashion no sooner comes into the Country" than haughty women take it up, "and thereby the whole land is at last infected." Mather viewed the Indian practice of taking many women captive as a providential reminder to women that they, too, were contributing to the Biblical Commonwealth's decline, since Indians often shocked their female captives' "innate" sense of modesty by stripping them "naked as in the day that they were born." This divine warned that God was using the "burning heat of the sun" to singe away the women's pride, because, by tanning the captives' skins, God caused them to lose their naturally white beauty.[57]

Other women dressed in fine and alluring clothing to participate in illegal "Gynecandrical" or "Promiscuous" dances (i.e., all dances with the opposite sex). Widespread "Promiscuous" dancing, that

Chart 12.3

Extent of Fornication Increase in Seventeenth-Century Puritan New England

Court	No. Fornications		% Increase	No. Forn.	% Total Offenses		
	1630–64	1665–89		1690–99	1630–64	1665–89	1690s
Massachusetts Gen. Ct.-Ct. of Assistants	242	780	222.3	344	8.9	17.1	31.0
	53	3	–94.3	0	6.8	1.6	.0
Essex County Ct.	127	378	197.6	145	7.9	17.9	33.5
Middlesex Co. Ct.	53	161	203.8	121	21.3	24.4	55.
Suffolk Co. Ct.	—	201	—	65	—	14.9	27.7
Hampshire Co. Ct.	9	37	311.1	13	17.9	16.3	15.9
Maine (York Co. Ct.)	7	103	1,371.4	59	1.8	11.9	27.3
New Hampshire	27	105	288.9	84	6.5	16.2	38.5
Connecticut	80	217	171.3	124	10.0	15.4	26.9
Plymouth	70	92	28.6	72	9.8	17.2	44.7
Martha's Vineyard	—	0	—	1	—	.0	5.6

Chart 12.4

Fornications as Percentage of Total Female Offenses, 1630–99

Court	1630–64			1665–89			1690–99		
	No. Female Forn.	No. Female Offenses	%	No. Female Forn.	No. Female Offenses	%	No. Female Forn.	No. Female Offenses	%
Massachusetts Gen. Ct.-Ct. of Assistants	100	498	20.1	413	1,039	39.7	193	325	59.4
Essex County Ct.	15	72	20.8	1	32	3.1	0	19	.0
Middlesex Co. Ct.	56	369	15.2	205	517	40.0	78	117	66.7
Suffolk Co. Ct.	25	45	55.6	79	142	55.6	62	75	82.7
Hampshire Co. Ct.	—	—	—	114	311	36.	46	96	47.9
Maine (York Co. Ct.)	4	11	36.3	14	37	37.8	7	18	38.9
New Hampshire	4	75	5.3	54	188	28.7	33	65	50.8
Connecticut	13	56	23.2	59	134	44.0	51	61	85.0
Plymouth	34	118	28.8	107	250	42.8	63	97	64.9
Martha's Vineyard	27	85	31.7	43	68	63.2	38	47	80.9
	—	0	—	0	4	0.0	1	8	12.5

Chart 12.5

Comparison of Female and Male Increase in Offenses Other Than Fornication

Court	Females			Males			No. Female Offenses 1690–99	No. Male Offenses 1690–99
	No. Offenses 1630–64	No. Offenses 1665–89	% Increase	No. Offenses 1630–64	No. Offenses 1665–89	% Increase		
Massachusetts Gen. Ct.-Ct. of Assistants	398	626	57.3	2,085	3,155	51.3	132	635
Essex Co. Ct.	58	31	−46.6	681	172	−74.7	19	122
Middlesex Co. Ct.	313	312	−.3	1,177	1,424	21.0	39	249
Suffolk Co. Ct.	20	60	200.0	176	437	148.3	13	86
Hampshire Co. Ct.	—	224	—	—	955	—	50	120
Maine (York Co. Ct.)	7	23	228.6	51	167	227.5	11	54
New Hampshire	71	134	88.7	321	632	96.9	32	125
Connecticut	40	76	90.0	347	479	38.0	10	124
Plymouth	84	143	70.2	639	1,047	63.8	34	303
Martha's Vineyard	58	25	56.9	593	419	−29.3	9	80
	—	4	—	—	50	—	8	28

"mad" amusement where "unchast Touches and Gesticulations" had "a palpable tendency to that which is evil," appalled the ministers. Cotton Mather admonished such female dancers:

> Because the daughters of Zion are haughty,
> and walk with outstretched necks,
>   glancing wantonly with their eyes,
> Mincing along as they go,
> tinkling with their feet;
> The Lord will smite with a scab
>   the heads of the daughters of Zion,
>   and the Lord will lay bare their private parts.[58]

As the court records testify, many women did, of their own volition, frequently "lay bare their private parts." In 1665 the General Court complained of many persons' unwillingness to save their virginity until marriage. Three years later the deputies passed a bastardy law to relieve towns from supporting the illegitimate fruit of fornication. In 1686 John Dunton wrote, "There hardly pases a Court Day, but some are convened for Fornication; and Convictions of this nature are very frequent."[59] Dunton did not exaggerate: in Essex, Middlesex, and Hampshire Counties the absolute number of fornicators was increasing about twice as fast as the population. Between 1630 and 1664 fornicators comprised 8.9 percent of all criminal offenders, but from 1665 to 1689 they constituted fully 17.1 percent of the total. The number of fornicators, relative to the total number of offenders, rose in all county courts except that of inland Hampshire County.

Female fornicators comprised about two-fifths of all female offenders during 1665–89, an increase of 20 percent over the previous thirty-five years. However, it cannot be argued that more women were committing only that crime. If fornications are subtracted from all offenses, the female crime rate still increased slightly faster than the male, 57.3 versus 51.3 percent.

No longer did the women of Massachusetts remain as demure and virginal as the divines might like. Modesty lost much of its restraining influence, as indiscreet servants, lusty fishermen, and lewd-talking sailors spoke with women on the streets of Boston and Salem. Even prostitution—from the Puritan perspective, that most despicable of professions—had made its appearance in Boston by 1672.[60] Nudity, too, was losing its shameful character, as is indicated by J. W.'s humorous anecdote (1682):

A Vintner in Boston put up a new Sign called *The Rose and Crown*, with two naked Boys being Supporters, and their Nudities Pendent: the sight disturbed one Justice S—r, who commanded it down; and away were the Boys sent to the Carvers to be dismembered: but the unlucky Dog of a Carver sent them back again two chopping Girles with Merkins [i.e., pubic hair] exposed. This enraged the Justice more, and the Sign was summoned before the wise Court, where they gravely determined (to keep the Girles from blushing) they should have Roses clapt upon their Merkins; which is the original of our new Proverb, Vnder the Rose a Merkin.[61]

Before the 1670s no one would have attempted such a joke at the expense of the magistrates.

In the bustle and anonymity of city life, women could drink with the opposite sex, sit on men's laps in taverns, and, bit by bit, discard their earlier inhibitions. They developed a sense of pride in their personal appearance, wore enticing "love-locks," and virtually exposed their breasts in public. One woman, Mary Leonard, went so far as to bring her chair down to the Ipswich River so that she could watch the naked male swimmers and shout out bawdy comments at them. Another woman, placed on the Boston gallows for "impudence," had the further impudence to laugh at her state there, instead of demonstrating the expected humiliation.[62] A quick look at some of the forty-six women whom the Boston selectmen warned out of town between 1671 and 1687 reveals the kinds of independence exercised by members of the "weaker sex." Three of them arrived in the metropolis unmarried but "big with child." Martha Smallage was a bigamist, and another woman was an adulterer. Ann Tilige refused to return to her husband, and Mary Oxnahaon had left her Newfoundland home without her husband's consent. Elizabeth Ford, who came from Rhode Island, delivered a child in Boston and claimed to have a husband in New York; however, "accordinge to a certificate herewith [she is] a very bad woman."[63] Since very few persons were warned out of town before 1660, and such people rarely appeared in court for their offenses after that date, the actual number of female "criminals" was much larger than the court records suggest.[64]

Women were becoming more assertive not only in court, but also in the occupational world. When sons and husbands of Massachusetts women were away, fighting King Philip's warriors or on commercial ventures, wives and daughters performed many "masculine" tasks—sowing, reaping, cutting firewood, and single-handedly maintaining businesses. At one point in the Indian war it was feared that even Boston might be invaded. Many women left their samplers, spinning wheels, "pastry-crust and tarts" to labor, sweat, complain, and faint while building a wall about the city. As the women furled their "undulating silks" and worked awkwardly at their chosen tasks, some of the available men came forward to help, and together they constructed "sturdy bulwarks" of "mud and turfe" across Boston neck. Benjamin Tompson, though amused by the women's effort, realized that they were consciously seeking personal achievement in an other-than-womanly realm. He called their effort "A Grand attempt some Amazonian Dames/contrive whereby to glorify their names."[65]

The Boston women were not the only ones to do men's work during stressful times. When the town of Chebacco wished to build its own meetinghouse in 1680 and the mother town of Ipswich would not approve, Chebacco women, with the assistance of a hired hand and some men from Gloucester and Manchester, erected the meetinghouse while their husbands were arguing with the Ipswich inhabitants. Ipswich issued warrants against all those who aided the mutinous women, but the General Court resolved the issue by allowing Chebacco to have its own church.[66]

More women began to argue civil cases before the courts. The *Aspinwall Notarial Records* list five women and 192 men who received appointments as attorneys between 1644 and 1650 in Suffolk County.[67] Between 1671 and 1674, 5.8 percent of all Suffolk County civil cases involved a woman as plaintiff, defendant, or both; that percentage almost doubled in the next five years.[68] In 55.9 percent of the cases involving women between 1671 and 1689, the female was the plaintiff. Not all of these women argued their cases without assistance, however: 36 percent of the plaintiffs (N = 22/65) and 31 percent of the defendants (N = 15/48) in the 1670s had the help of a husband, estate co-executor, or male attorney. Only one-eighth of the males used an attorney, but in eight cases that attorney was a wife. Not until 1676 did the authorities call both a husband and wife to court in cases to which the wife was a party; previously the husband alone had appeared. The case of Edward and Mistress Smith v. Widow Ann Bromhall [69] served as a precedent for later suits arising out of a wife's administration of an inherited estate, debts owed her, or slander. The continuation of the practice of equal citation in cases previously reserved to the husband indicated that Puritans no longer felt so strongly about the husband's "rights" to his wife's inheritances, debts, or protection of her good name.

The number of businesswomen shot upward. At least nine women conducted shops in Boston between 1672 and 1689; there had been only three before 1672. The percentage of female innkeepers exploded from none before 1659 to 19 percent between 1660 and 1682 and 45 percent in 1690. The number of female tavern operators increased from 1.4 per year in the 1660s to 2.8 in the 1670s, 6 annually from 1680 to 1682, and 23 in 1690.[70]

Dame school teachers also increased rapidly, from only two before 1673 to seven in 1680. As women proved their competence at law, innkeeping, and teaching, a few towns opened their public schools to the "weaker sex."[71] The private school, a new development in Massachusetts, welcomed girls. At least nine such schools were founded in Boston between 1665 and 1689.[72]

In the cosmopolitan, tradition-rending world of late seventeenth century Massachusetts, the spirit of the times and the desire of many women for a measure of self-direction, declarativeness, and personal freedom had begun eroding the passive, submissive feminine ideal of earlier days. Those women who insulted the authorities, abused their husbands, argued vigorously with their neighbors, committed fornication, participated in the excitement of "Promiscuous" dancing, and adorned their bodies had started to rely upon the legitimacy of their own feelings in these individualizing years. Before 1665 most female rebels[73] justified their unfemi-

---

Chart 12.6

Female and Male Lawyers in Suffolk County, Massachusetts

ears	Total Cases	Cases w/Female Pl. or Def.		As Pl.	As Def.	Women with Assistance of Husband or Co-executor	Women Using Male Attorneys
671–74	433	25	5.8%	15	11	1–1	2–0
675–79	702	81	11.5%	46	37	10–13	9–0
680–84	876	101	11.5%	58	51	19–3	—
685–89	269	26	9.7%	18	8	—	—
690–94	608	73	12.0%	36	41	—	—
695–99	508	71	14.0%	49	32	—	—
	3396	377	11.1%	222	180		

nine activities by placing them within some grand theological context—Antinomianism, Anabaptism, or Quakerism. After that date,
rebellion needed no further justification than that it was in accord
with a woman's own wishes. Between 1665 and 1689 only 19 percent
(5/26) of those women who abused the authorities relied upon the
compensatory external power offered by a heretical theology,
whereas before 1665 93 percent (27/29) of the contemptuous women
had relied on such a theology. Not without good cause did orthodox
Puritans protest "the unmortified Pride which is in the hearts of the
sons *and* daughters of men," that pride (or, rather, self-assertion)
encouraging "disobedience in Inferiors toward Superiors, in Families, in Churches, and in the Commonwealth."[74]

Despite the popularity of so many forms of rebellious and sinful
activity, there remained vestiges of the earlier rigidifying, punitive
Puritanism. Ministers continued to reiterate the virtues of Calvinism to large audiences—with some effect. Magistrates continued to
prosecute offenders of the Puritan laws, albeit with less diligence.
Goody Glover's hanging in 1688 served as a graphic reminder that
witchcraft was still a capital offense. Even in times when perhaps
one out of every eight women was known to have committed the
crime of premarital fornication,[75] most women probably preserved
their virginity until marriage. Perhaps three-fourths of the women
were never charged with a crime in any county or colonial court. The
great majority of females did not become innkeepers, shopowners,
or school dames. Many Puritan maidens and mothers attended
church services regularly, observed the orthodox moral standards,
and remained submissive, dependent, and modest. Stunned by the
irreligious behavior of so many other women, they tied themselves
to the certainty and security offered by the church.[76] Whatever
unholy longings these good women might have harbored, the
church, at least, conveyed purpose and continuity, an anchor in
times when order and tradition seemed to have been cast adrift.

Yet all these changes did affect even the most proper Puritan
ladies. Hetty Shepard wrote in 1676: "Mother has counseled Father
about many things, and when Father said that women knew naught
about such matters she told him how Capt. Underhill's wife saved
him in his expedition against the Block Islanders, in 1636, when our
country had more straits to pass through than even now when
Philip is breathing out threatenings and slaughter." Shepard's wife
was a very pious woman, but she claimed the right to give advice to
her husband. To justify that claim she cited a heretic, John Under-

hill, who had participated in the Antinomian conflict. (Underhill had credited his wife with saving his life by convincing him to wear a helmet during the Pequot wars.) Although Hetty Shepard held that too much merriment was sinful, she seemed intrigued by the fine apparel she observed at Boston.[77] Perhaps other Puritan women also felt the need to stretch the absolutism of their faith late in the century.

Connecticut's Modest Variation on the Massachusetts Example

Connecticut's inhabitants reacted similarly to many of the changes occurring in seventeenth-century life. Like their brethren in the Bay Colony, Connecticut Puritans considered themselves "A Citty set on a Hill,"[78] a reservoir of moral uprightness against the world's iniquity. They also became concerned, as the century progressed, over the weakening sense of unity and purposefulness in the colony's life.

This westerly colony certainly had its share of problems. Its eastern inhabitants quarrelled, sometimes violently, with Rhode Island claimants to disputed boundary lands.[79] King Philip's War cost Connecticut £30,000 and a number of lives.[80] Wheat blasts, mildews, and pea worms, all common for years, added to the colony's economic woes.[81] In the 1680s there was a great fear that the Crown would halve Connecticut, giving the eastern portion to Massachusetts and the western to New York.[82] As in the Bay Colony, Connecticut's inhabitants chafed under Governor Andros's rule, objecting to his dissolution of the General Court, his encouragement of the Anglican faith, and his directive that all parties must travel the long distance to Boston before they could settle any probate matters.[83]

By the 1660s, a spirit of contentiousness had developed, fostered by the relative isolation of the twenty-two Connecticut towns. In this land of plantations too remote for "Convenient Assembling," the maintenance of a unified approach to church problems became well nigh impossible. In 1671 the Reverend John Woodbridge, Jr., complained, "[O] ur great wound and disease is a spirit of Separation, which so many are drencht with and so few without tincture of." Even the ministers voiced significantly different points of view on basic theological issues, some endorsing the Congregational approach, others preferring Presbyterianism. The town churchgoers listened reluctantly to the divines' pretenses of theological leadership, a fact which caused Woodbridge to lament, "the people are growne so rude, Insolent, and Coltish (Independency has so fatted them) that the Ministers that have most Authority have not enough [power] to stamp a Judgement and sentence of good mettall [mettle] to make it current with them."[84]

Much holiness existed in Connecticut, "yet Censuring, ground-lesse Derogations, and unchristian Bickerings" disrupted many congregations. Passionate arguments over the acceptability of the Halfway Covenant, the merits of Presbyterianism versus Congrega-tionalism, and the power of church members relative to that of the ministers afflicted virtually every town during the 1660s. In 1670 alone, three churches—at Hartford, Windsor, and Stratford—di-vided into six.[85] Ministers complained that citizens neglected their religious duties, attended Sabbath lectures in a "flighty and sleepy manner," and failed to catechize their children.[86] Often the secular and spiritual authorities came under abuse. Men and women faced trial for refusing to pay the minister's rate,[87] fomenting open rebel-lion,[88] and threatening the lives of authorities.[89] One individual told the governor and assistants that "he cared not a turd for them & would show them no more Respect than he would to an Indian."[90]

After the terror of King Philip's War subsided, the Connecticut magistrates asked the ministers to consider "fully the Provocations of which the People of God had been guilty." The resulting Council of Ministers (1683) protested religious abuses, sensual lusts, exces-sive drinking, love of money, fraudulent bargainings, and fancy apparel.[91] A few of these ministers began using jeremiads to shore up the colony's religiosity.[92] Only "when the Lord is the Glory in the midst of a People," James Fitch warned, will there be a protective "Wall of Fire around about them." John Whiting argued for a greater degree of magisterial and community watchfulness: "The lusts of men will easily run wild, if there be no restraint laid upon them: Some men (and not a few neither) will without fail do shamefully, if there be none to put them to shame for what is done. They that have not conscience enough, must have somewhat else to curb them."[93]

Like their Massachusetts counterparts, the Connecticut ministers attacked the tendency of many to disobey their "Superiors"—chil-dren their parents, servants their masters, wives their husbands. Others dressed as if they were of a higher social rank, thereby indicating "that parity is pleasing to their Pride." Role rigidity was vanishing, as the neglectful inhabitants no longer felt any "band upon their hearts and Consciences in [proper] relation to others."[94]

Between 1665 and 1689 Connecticut women increasingly stepped outside their sphere. From 1639 to 1664 the Connecticut and New Haven authorities tried 118 women for 15 different offenses; over the next twenty-five year period those authorities charged 250 women with 30 crimes. Female offenders increased much faster than males (111.9% versus 68.9%). As in Massachusetts, approximately 40 percent of these 1665–89 offenders committed the sin of fornication; if fornications are removed from the total, the rate of increase in female criminals exceeds the male rate by only 70.2 percent to 63.8 percent.

In Connecticut a desire for "parity" did threaten the social roles, but not as seriously as in the Bay Colony. Female fornications shot upward by 214.7 percent in Connecticut, but a shocking 313 percent in Massachusetts. The variety of offenses committed by women increased by one-third in the Bay Colony, but by only one-fifth in Connecticut. Moreover, women did not commit as great a percentage of the total crimes in Connecticut (17.8%, compared to Massachusetts's 23% in 1665–89). The Connecticut percentage of female offenders roughly equaled the figure for nearby Hampshire County (16.4%). Nor did many women secure employment as innkeepers, businesswomen, or school dames; only one female teacher (New Haven, 1651) and one innkeeper (Mistress Guilbert, Hartford, 1688) appear in the Connecticut records.[95]

The individualizing trend appeared weaker in Connecticut. While in Massachusetts only about one-fifth of the women found guilty of contempt of the authorities or religion belonged to heretical groups, in Connecticut four of seven such offenders did—and all four were New London Antisabbatarians. Often called Rogerene Baptists or Rogerene Quakers, members of this sect considered all days equally sanctified and regarded "a steeple, a pulpit, a cushion, a church, and a salaried minister in a black suit of clothes, as utter abominations."[96] John Rogers, the group's founder, believed in the inferiority, dependency, and modesty of women, but female Antisabbatarians proved quite capable of unfeminine behavior. New London magistrates found Bashoba Smith guilty of "much pride and obstinacy" (1682). Johanna Way received fifteen lashes for coming several times into New London to rebaptize persons, there "so Affrighting & amazeing" the people that several women reportedly "swouned & fainted away" (1685). Mary Ransford and James Rogers's wife threw scalding water on constables who attempted to distrain their property for delinquent payment of the minister's rate.[97] The rebellious behavior of these Antisabbatarians either affected or reflected the relative independence of New London women, for that area's female offender rate was the highest of any Connecticut county.

Nineteen Connecticut wives petitioned successfully for divorces and another received a separation.[98] Christian Herbert made a will, with her husband's approval, and even though King Henry VIII had specified that a married women—a *femme couvert*—lacked the legal power to bequeath property, the Connecticut Court of Assistants accepted her testament in 1684. Herbert's daughter, Elizabeth Blackleach, who apparently was given only a small inheritance by her mother, objected to the will's "illegality" in a sophisticated legal argument. Her petition to the Assistants asserted that Henry VIII's directive nullified her mother's action, and maintained that her father had had no authority to grant his wife that privilege. Blackleach asserted that

the whole estate of a feme Covert (while so) is her husbands right, is as undeniable a principle as any in law, and the sole and one ground of the Husbands enjoying what comes in his wives right; nor can any man lift his wife out of the Coverture the Law puts her under, and the consequents of it, for the Law is above all in those things, so that she being no person in law to take the right, but that still remaining by law in her husband, she cannot will what in Law shee can have no right personally and seperately in.

A husband could *not* convey legal personhood upon his spouse. Furthermore, their daughter pointed out, Benjamin Herbert had implicitly overruled his wife's action by nullifying an early will, one "wch gave all the strength to his wives will," and preparing a new testament. Even if Mr. Herbert did possess the power to allow his wife's will, he had followed an illegal procedure— for, Blackleach argued, he had served as a witness to that will, and a witness could not be a testator or a party to a will.[99] (Here the daughter was assuming, quite logically, that in making a will, as in any other legal action, the wife served only as her husband's representative; therefore, Benjamin Herbert could not, as *de facto* testator, witness the will. Mr. Herbert apparently assumed, contrarily, that he and his wife were independent persons.) Although Elizabeth Blackleach had constructed a sensible argument (judged by the standards of the times) in an effort to receive compensation for the years her parents had spent with her in their old age, there is no record that the Assistants acted on her petition. The highest court in the colony had recognized that a husband could give his wife a measure of independence from himself, which the law must respect.

Despite the important decision of the Court of Assistants and the activities of some women, Connecticut lagged behind Massachusetts in the overall degree of change. So, too, did it differ in other ways. Connecticut divines, like their Massachusetts counterparts, struggled to understand the contention rising or continuing in many churches, and to discern the providential meaning of King Philip's War. However, the explicatory jeremiads they adopted lacked the harsh, condemnatory character of so many Massachusetts sermons.[100] Social decay existed in Connecticut, to be sure, but it lacked the overt dimensions of the Bay Colony's. No women wore bosom-revealing dresses, no nude carvings existed to shock moral sensibilities, few outspoken heretics solicited the inhabitants, and no lewdspeaking foreigners haunted the wharfs and back alleys of Connecticut's villages. The heavy weight of Puritan repressiveness produced only occasional cracks in this Biblical Commonwealth's armor.

Connecticut appeared to be changing, but not as radically as the Bay Colony. Although the population of both jumped between 1665 and 1690, Connecticut's growth was more diffuse. No major metropolitan center emerged in the western wilderness; in fact, by 1690 Boston had almost as many inhabitants as the four leading Connecticut villages combined.[101] The colony did produce wheat, cattle, and other agricultural produce, conducting a lively local trade with more specialized fishing and lumbering communities in Massachusetts, but almost no international trade. One 1680 report to the Lords of Trade maintained that only about "20 petty merchants" lived in the colony. Foreign merchants, large numbers of fishermen and seamen, and people of various nationalities did not come to Connecticut. The same 1680 report claimed that only one or two families of English, Scottish, and Irish immigrants settled in the colony each year. Few servants and not more than thirty black slaves existed there,[102] and almost no Quakers, Anabaptists, or Anglicans were located in Connecticut.[103] Under such conditions, people had little opportunity to develop a cosmopolitan point of view—to meet others of varying appearances, beliefs, and lifestyles. Instead, each Connecticut locale remained relatively isolated in space and time, and followed its own evolutionary course.

Several jeremiads warned the people of the need to reform their ways, but also conveyed the notion that Connecticut was *still* protected by God's "Wall of Fire." The people listened, some attentively, some not, and then continued to perform the same day-to-day tasks they had worked at for years—for no minister had enough power "to stamp a Judgment" upon them. Between 1665 and 1676 problems erupted with the New Amsterdam Dutch, the English officials at New York,[104] and the Indians, but the Biblical Commonwealth weathered them all. During those somewhat troubled years the authorities arrested five witches, but thereafter only one person was suspected of practicing witchcraft.[105] Not quite so alienated, desperate, solitary, insecure, and suffering in conscience as many of their Massachusetts neighbors, isolated Connecticut residents had less need for witches. Only the rule of Governor Andros profoundly shattered their belief in their own independent destiny and unique accomplishments.

Subdued Plymouth

Of all the New England colonies, Plymouth had the most unchanging lifestyle. While the Massachusetts population increased by 111.2 percent and that of Connecticut by 92 percent, the descendants of the Pilgrims increased by only 50 percent. Boston alone had, in 1690, nearly 70 percent of the entire colony's population. Having "neither good river, nor good harbor," Plymouth developed trade on a very small scale, exporting some whale oil, fish, and horses to Boston in return for imported goods.[106] The inhabitants had little contact with people of different racial or national origins. The spirit of religious conviction which had moved the first Pilgrims to come to America had not died, since almost all adults still became church members. Plymouth churches uniformly rejected the Halfway Covenant, viewed synods with great suspicion, and endorsed the autonomy of local churches.[107] No crime wave inundated the colony; in fact, the actual number of offenses *decreased* by a full 25 percent between 1630 and 1664, making Plymouth the only New England colony to experience such an absolute decrease during the seventeenth century.

Notwithstanding the relatively static quality of life in the poorest and most rural of colonies, disastrous events occurred with startling frequency after 1675. King Philip's War wrought unbelievable havoc—with the actual burning of three of the fourteen towns, extensive damage in three others, raids on two more, the loss of from 5 to 8 percent of the colony's adult males, and the expenditure of £11,743 on that war.[108] Yet the colony took such losses in stride, and returned to what Governor Thomas Hinckley called "a very happy condition." The Andros regime brought new strain, undercutting the civil security that the colony's residents had enjoyed for over sixty years. The new governor's high taxes, excessive probate fees, disestablishment of Congregationalism, removal of the colony's records to Boston, and interference with the whale oil trade angered the settlers.[109] When Taunton, Plymouth's most populous town, refused to raise the requested tax money, the governor clapped the town clerk in prison for three months.[110]

Political and financial turmoil did not have an ideational component. Very few persons complained about the little commonwealth's declining religious vitality. In early 1642 William Bradford had lamented "the breaking out of sundry notorious sins," and in 1669 Thomas Walley, the Barnstable minister, denounced his associates for their contentiousness, lethargy, covetousness, pride, and profanity. Few people seemed to be listening, however. Not until King Philip's War did church members respond to warnings of God's providential chastisement; then many churches renewed their original covenants. Apparently that was enough, for, as John Cotton related, "God turned his hand against our Heathen-enemies and subdued them wonderfully."[111]

After 1676, Plymouth ministers made no systematic effort to convince church members that they had strayed dangerously far from the Calvinist Way; nor did the political authorities. Reflecting the relative tolerance which had always existed in this small colony, Plymouth magistrates placed no obstacles in the way of Quakers, who opened a meetinghouse at Scituate, or Anabaptists, who founded a congregation at Swansea.[112] When some townsmen neglected to support their Congregationalist ministers, the authorities did not force anyone to pay the minister's rates. Instead of fining such offenders, Rehoboth townsmen in 1677 voted to send the church deacons from house to house in an effort to "persuade" men to contribute the delinquent amount.[113]

No significant internal stresses existed in Plymouth between 1650 and 1687. Occasionally someone hurled abuse at ministers or magistrates, but their speech lacked the sharp-tongued emphasis of the Massachusetts-Connecticut examples. Taverns did not abound. Even the number of fornications increased by only 28.6 percent, making Plymouth the only area where the rate of fornication increased more slowly than the population. Despite a good deal of tension caused by external sources, in the economically, politically, and socially static enviroment of Plymouth Colony it was difficult to become convinced of the colony's declining state. From 1665 to 1687 colonists continued living much as they had for decades, adhering to an Independent Congregationalism, "woven with some of the finer and more spiritual threads of Anabaptism."[114] Society and conscience needed no purgative, no witch-scapegoat who could epitomize and, in death, carry away the pervasive stain of sin. Only one "witch," Mary Ingham, faced prosecution—significantly enough, during the last year of King Philip's War. Accused by Mehittable Woodworth of causing her much pain "in the Way of Witchcraft or Sorcery," Ingham requested a trial and was easily acquitted.[115]

Throughout the seventeenth century women continued properly submissive, essentially occupying the same rigid social roles that the Pilgrims had brought with them in 1620. Between 1630 and 1664 women committed 11.8 percent of all crimes, a percentage almost equivalent to the 1665–89 figure (12.7%). In both intervals the Plymouth percentage of female crime was the lowest of any Puritan colony. The number of female fornicators did rise from 27 to 43 (from 32 to 63 % of all female offenders), but the number of other female offenses decreased by 56.9 percent, much larger than the male decrease of 29.3 percent. The variety of crimes committed by women also declined, from twenty in 1630–64 to fifteen in 1665–89.

Plymouth women did not actively seek employment opportunities. Domestic servants, male or female, were few, and only five businesswomen dispensed their wares or services between 1663 and 1690. (In the latter year alone, Boston had 23 female innkeepers.) Nor did Plymouth women attempt to free themselves from onerous marriage relationships. Between 1665 and 1689 only one wife (but five husbands) filed petitions for divorce; another petition was filed by a father on behalf of his daughter. By contrast, Massachusetts and Connecticut wives (N = 24 and 22, respectively) comprised 80 percent of the petitioners for divorce.

The "norm slippage" occurring in the Bay Colony and, to a lesser extent, in Connecticut failed to affect the Pilgrim Colony. There the quality of life, deadened by rural isolation and Calvinist stringency, presumably created repressed women but provided no cathartic outlet for that repression. No dynamic spirit of change led Pilgrim malcontents to seek a freer, fuller reality. Locked into the dependent roles of submissive wife and dutiful mother, women little resisted the passivity of their orthodox sex role. They attended church regularly, rarely used abusive words or gestures, and preserved their virginity until marriage. However, their needs for excitement, sexual pleasure, declarativeness, and power simmered underneath the placid surface, occasionally bubbling up and out in riotous form. The Quakers managed to activate some of the latent tensions experienced by Plymouth women, and the behavior catalyzed by Singing Quaker Jonathan Dunen was particularly revealing.

The Singing Quakers, a group originating on Long Island, sang, danced, professed "extraordinary raptures of joy," and at times fell into raving fits of frenetic ecstasy as a part of their religious ritual. In the summer of 1683 or 1684, Dunen, one of this group, arrived in Plymouth Colony and convinced the wife of a Marshfield resident to accompany him. A second woman, Mary Ross, joined them and became utterly possessed by Dunen's religion. At one point Ross stripped herself naked, burned all her clothing, and declared that she was Jesus Christ. After designating Dunen her Apostle Peter, she asserted that she would lie dead for three days before being resurrected. Within a few hours this female savior revived, and then ordered Dunen to sacrifice a dog. The Singing Quaker did her bidding and afterward danced with the two women. By that time all three had seen fit to wear only shirts as an expression of their nakedness before the Lord.[116]

Through such outlandish "religious" behavior, Mary Ross had claimed personal power equal to that of Christ, had asserted her control over a man (Dunen later declared that he simply could not resist her), and had had some fun in the process. Although the Marshfield woman claimed no special power of her own, she did, through her nearly nude dance, effectually repudiate Puritan standards of feminine modesty, as had Ross. Both women, starved for excitement and self-expression, had given vent to the frustrations which many other women may have experienced in Plymouth, where conditions for women had not changed since the earliest years.

The Fractious Inhabitants of Maine and New Hampshire

Although the northerly colonies of Maine and New Hampshire were controlled by Massachusetts for much of the century, their residents were far different from those of Calvinist locales. Few in numbers (perhaps no more than 7,000 by 1690), they had no sense of community solidarity or of their elected role in God's scheme of things. Puritans existed in both areas, but the religiously diverse population also included Antinomians, Anabaptists, Anglicans, Quakers, and others who, in the words of one historian, "cared little about theological dogma and church reform." For these sailors, adventurers, fishermen, English gentlemen, small landowners, rich merchants, and their wives, "religion was second in importance to the struggle for a living because they took for granted the form of religion taught them in childhood and were willing to let others follow their own course."[117] Not so fearful of the material joys of life as their Puritan neighbors, these northerly inhabitants earned a bad reputation in Calvinist areas because they spent so much time "drinking, dancing, [and] singing scurrulous songes."[118]

The farther Maine and New Hampshire people lived from Massachusetts, the more inclined they were to depart from orthodox religions and forms of behavior. The residents of Hampton, the settlement nearest Massachusetts, had strong Puritan leanings, whereas Dover, in the north, was heavily Quaker. The fishermen who annually visited the Maine seacoast, in Cotton Mather's view, "aimed no higher than the advancement of some Wordly Interests."[119] In the backcountry along the Kennebec and Sheepscot Rivers, enough debtor refugees from the Puritan courts had gathered to found three small plantations within an eight- to ten-mile radius. Until 1672 these plantations, "inhabited by the worst of men," functioned without a government, depending on the sea for sustenance and sharing their goods, boats, and wives.[120]

Political and domestic factionalism divided the inhabitants of these northern areas. Some supported the land claims made by more than a dozen English proprietors, including, most notably, Sir Ferdinando Gorges and Captain John Mason. Under a charter secured in 1629, Gorges and Mason claimed, respectively, all of southern Maine and New Hampshire. The Massachusetts Puritans, who had had designs upon these territories from the earliest years, resisted the Gorges-Mason claims, as did many of the independent-minded inhabitants who would have fallen under their purview. Between 1641 and 1679, Bay Colony magistrates assumed jurisdiction over New Hampshire, converting the area surrounding Dover, Portsmouth, Exeter, and Hampton into Norfolk County. After 1653 those magistrates began also to supervise the affairs of Maine, creating York County. Roughly half of New Hampshire's adult males refused to submit to Massachusetts rule,[121] and protests continued in both "counties" until 1679. From 1653 to 1664 the York County justices prosecuted approximately one out of every ten men in Maine on contempt of authority citations.[122] Between 1655 and 1689 those justices forced Maine settlers to answer 140 present-ments for contemptuous behavior—a higher number than were presented in Connecticut (N = 133), and almost half the Massachu-setts totals (N = 281). (Comparatively, Maine had approximately one-fourth the population of Connecticut, and one-tenth that of Massachusetts.) Norfolk and York County inhabitants petitioned the English Crown, objecting to Bay Colony rule, the Gorges-Mason claims, and the speculative ventures of land-hungry New Hamp-shire and Massachusetts merchants.[123]

In King Philip's War, the northern Indians killed or captured about 260 Maine residents, reduced five settlements to ashes, cost the inhabitants £8,000, and precipitated the flight of entire commu-nities to more benign locales. Those remaining after peace returned in 1677 initially objected to the reimposition of Massachusetts rule, but then submitted, fearing "the Indians would speedily fall upon them & begin a new war." Shortly after that, 115 residents of Kittery, Wells, and York protested the high taxes imposed by the Bay Colony and asked the King "to allow them to have a govern-ment of their own, according to the laws and constitutions of the Province." Charles II did not grant their request. Thus, despite fear of Indians, the Maine protests continued throughout the early 1680s.[124]

In New Hampshire, the neutral Pennacook Indians had served as a buffer to King Philip's braves and the Maine hostilities. Suffering minimally from Indian incursions, the settlers there had little fear of the red men and continued to protest vigorously against whatever government happened to be officiating. Many inhabitants ex-pressed their discontent with the pro-Puritan Cutt Councillors whom the King had commissioned to govern New Hampshire in 1679. These merchant-councillors favored close connections with Massachusetts. Perhaps because the Councillors intended to ex-ploit the timber trade of the colony's interior, "the people in gen-eral . . . expected an invasion of their property soon to follow." Some refused to pay the taxes assessed by the Councillors for Puritan ministers' salaries, "alleging that they ought to have liberty of conscience."[125]

The arbitrary actions taken by New Hampshire's first royal gov-

ernor, Edward Cranfield, between 1682 and 1685 further antagonized the inhabitants. Whereas the Cutt Councillors had attempted
to foster Puritanism, Cranfield, an Anglican, detested it. The new
governor tried to destroy the power of Puritan ministers (even
imprisoning one of them), established a Court of Pleas without
legislative authorization, appointed justices of the peace to supervise town affairs, dissolved the Assembly, and assisted Robert
Mason in collecting the quit-rents guaranteed him by the Crown on
the basis of his grandfather's claim. One assemblyman, Edward
Gove, made an effort to raise and arm a colony-wide faction against
Cranfield. After Gove was apprehended, a special court ordered
him to be hanged, disembowelled, beheaded, and quartered.[126]
Town officials hid their tax records from Cranfield's collectors. (In
1684 the governor reported the names of 422 delinquent taxpayers
to the Crown.) Men shook clubs at marshals, chased them with
swords, assaulted them, and told them to use their warrants for
toilet paper. After an argument with Robert Mason, one man tossed
both the proprietor and the deputy governor into a fire.[127] In response to such widespread opposition, the Crown finally recalled
Cranfield in 1685.

From the 1640s through the 1680s, Maine and New Hampshire
festered with political contention. However, with the creation of the
Dominion of New England and Governor Andros's arrival, protests
decreased amazingly.[128] Though his enactments sometimes disadvantaged the northerly settlers, the new royal governor did leave
them essentially free to run their own affairs. Moreover, Andros
removed the odious ministers' rates imposed by Massachusetts,
and he disapproved of the economic pretensions of the wealthy
land speculators who had "cutt themselves out large dividends and
disinherited many who were in possession upon antient titles before the Indian warr." The governor also took steps to protect the
inhabitants from the French and Indians by stationing 566 men in
eleven forts constructed between Pemaquid and Wells, Maine.
Oddly enough, he whom the Puritans called a tyrant thus brought
relative peace to northern New England.[129]

The individualistically minded residents of Maine and New
Hampshire had no particular need to spend long hours in religious
introspection, to respect authority as God given, or to develop a
sense of their grand participation in a holy community. Tough and
aggressive, they found that conflict was a pervasive reality—but
that conflict focused upon who should rule, and in what context,

rather than upon witches, sinful behaviors, or Evil. In all, ten persons received some reputation as witches—eight of them in the Puritan stronghold of Hampton—but none were convicted. All social and religious extremes were represented in this small, poly-glot culture of Anglicans, Puritans, and heretics; of wealthy mer-chants and very poor fishermen; of Eleutherian refugees and English gentlemen; of moralists and free lovers. Each group, iso-lated from others, could easily devise its own standards, its own view of reality in these frontier communities which neglected even to construct or maintain sufficient public highways.[130] A rich variety of people, living at some distance from one another (espe-cially in Maine) and having little attachment to any specific gov-ernment, evolved quite differently from the populations in Puritan locales. Except for the Puritans among them these people had no sense that their society was decaying,[131] for they had only a limited sense of participation in a "society" in the first place.

The female sex role lacked rigidity in these northerly reaches, especially in Maine. When men sailed away to fish or marched away to fight Indians, women planted corn, gathered thatch, filled orders for planks and staves, traded with red men, and served as their husbands' attorneys in court.[132] John Mason early used twenty-two women as lumber sawyers and potash makers at Piscatauqua. Al-though businesswomen were few in Maine, at least one widow, Elizabeth Rowdan, maintained a blacksmith shop and a mill.[133] Another, Mistress Houlatt of New Hampshire, became so success-ful in the poultry business that she loaned her husband money; Ensign Houlat affirmed his wife's right to do so, rejecting the Puritan argument that a wife's income automatically belonged to her husband.[134] Nine other Maine women petitioned Governor Andros for confirmation of land claims; among them was Widow Bridgett Phillips, who requested 1,200 acres on the south side of the Saco River.[135] Unlike the Massachusetts divines, northern min-isters did not prepare sermons celebrating a dependent, modest role for women.

Lacking books and schooling, frontier women had little chance or need to internalize Puritan definitions of proper female behavior. Modesty and total submission did not suit those in areas where aggressiveness was the norm. As a result, they little hesitated to abuse the authorities not only verbally, but physically. In 1668 Mary Fulsham of Exeter snatched a warrant out of the marshal's hands and tore it up. During the Cranfield unrest, Seabank Hodge called the "governor and the rest of the gentlemen . . . a parcel of beg-

garly curs . . . come to undo us both body and soul." The wives of
John Gilman, Sr., and Moses Gilman kept kettles of water boiling
at their Exeter homes, intending to scald the marshal if he came to
demand tax payment. At Strawberry Bank, the wives of William
Cotten and Nehemiah Partridge threatened the same, further denouncing the constable as "a rogue and a rascal." The sheriff tried
to apprehend tax rioters at Dover one Sabbath day, but was frustrated by strong opposition from both men and women. Indeed,
one young maiden knocked down one of Cranfield's officers with
her Bible.[136] In Maine another woman, appropriately named Sarah
Anger, received ten lashes for "casting severall ref[1]ecting
speeches upon the Reverend Mr. Dummer," and Mary Frost was
given lashes for treating Andros's sheriff to "Scurrilous, Opprobrious and abusive Languages and threatenings" (1685, 1688).[137]

Before 1689 the women of Maine and New Hampshire appeared
frequently in court, not only for condemning the authorities but also
for hurling invective and blows at their neighbors. (Or for more
mischievously taking a man's cap off his head, then "pulling him
from his seat backward."[138]) Fourteen "contemptuous" women
came before the magistrates in New Hampshire, and thirteen in
Maine—a combined number which exceeded the totals for Plymouth and Connecticut together, and which totaled almost half of
all such Massachusetts offenses. A comparison of "abusive" women
yields the same result. In fact, 24.2 and 18.3 percent of all women
to commit a crime in New Hampshire and Maine, respectively,
appeared in court for the very unfeminine offenses of condemning,
abusing, or hitting someone. If a woman came before the New
Hampshire authorities, she was twice as likely to be a fighter as was
her counterpart in any distinctly Puritan colony. Moreover, not all
fighting women came before the magistrates, because political disorder often made it impossible to apprehend them.

Like women in Puritan locales, those on the frontier frequently
fornicated. The first New Hampshire compilation of laws, the
Cutt Code, called that crime "this prevailing sin"[139] in 1680. Altogether, fornications comprised 44 percent of all female offenses in
New Hampshire and 28.7 percent in Maine (1665–89). The New
Hampshire rate of increase—330.8 percent, if we compare 1630–64
with 1665–89—paralleled that of Massachusetts; the Maine rate far
exceeded that of any other New England locale, due to the fact that
Maine authorities had been reluctant to prosecute fornicators before
the Massachusetts takeover.

Those women who had come to New Hampshire from Puritan

locales or elsewhere managed to leave much of the stereotypical sex role behind them. In the uninhibited atmosphere of the seacoast and interior settlements, women could feel free to behave spontaneously, assertively. They had no need to rely on heretical faith to justify their rebelliousness; they simply acted, and the relative number of female offenders shot upward. In New Hampshire, the number of female criminals increased nearly twice as fast as the number of males! Even with fornicators removed from the totals, women offenders still increased 52 percent faster, comprising 13.4 percent of all criminals before 1664 but 20.3 percent in 1665–89.

The number of Maine women appearing in court expanded, relative to the number of males, by 40.5 percent although that difference vanishes if fornicators are subtracted from the total. The instability of the population makes any conclusions dubious, for the proportion of soldiers, transient fishermen, and English travelers caused marked fluctuations. Since seventeenth-century women were less mobile than men, the sex ratio changed from season to season and year to year. Notwithstanding Maine's usual male surplus, however, women comprised fully 18.8 percent of all offenders in 1630–64 and 21.6 percent in 1665–89. Indeed, Massachusetts, with a considerably higher proportion of women, had almost the same percentage of female offenders as did Maine.

The "free aire" of New Hampshire and Maine allowed women to express their tensions more easily. A quick word or a nasty fight was cathartic; perhaps because women had that aggressive outlet, they did not feel moved to seek independent employment. Few women requested licenses to maintain inns, or attempted to open shops in

Chart 12.7

Contemptuous and Abusive Females as Percentage of Total Offenders
Before 1690

Locale	N Contemptuous Women	N Abusive Women	N Female Offenses	% Contemptuous Women	% Abusive Women	Combined %
New Hampshire	14	32	190	7.4	16.8	24.2
Maine	13	35	263	4.9	13.4	18.3
Connecticut	13	33	368	3.5	9.0	12.5
Massachusetts	55	122	1,537	3.6	8.0	11.5
Plymouth	5	10	153	3.3	6.5	9.8

areas where ship-building, fishing, and farming constituted virtually all of the economic enterprises. Neither Maine nor New Hampshire in all the years before 1690 had as many female innkeepers as Boston had in that one year. Sex roles underwent transformation in these northern lands but, unlike in Massachusetts, the changes were in a few very specific directions.

Women and Witches in a Changing World

Each New England locale, then, had its own particular set of causative circumstances, its own peculiar character—commercially explosive, religiously declining, cosmopolitan Massachusetts; isolated, agrarian, slow-changing Connecticut; static, subdued Plymouth; turbulent, materialistic Maine and New Hampshire. The conditions each colony experienced affected the way women looked at themselves and their possibilities. In Massachusetts the ideal sex role was influenced by forces which threatened to tear the colony apart; the opening of occupational opportunities and the expanding crime rate both reflected and catalyzed the loosening of that ideal role. In Connecticut, where norm slippage was less extensive, the female role underwent more gradual, but nevertheless important, change. Plymouth Colony lacked the environmental stimulus necessary to actualize female frustration and discontent, whereas Maine and New Hampshire, less affected by Puritan standards, did provide atmospheres in which women could at least become assertive.

All of these societies, experiencing new stresses and old, needed some in-depth purgative as the 1690s approached. Throughout the 1670s and 1680s, as tension built up, a witch hunt might have seemed the most likely vehicle for release. Yet Puritans accused only 41 witches and hanged but one between 1665 and 1689 (compared to 68 accusations and 15 executions between 1638 and 1664). Several conditions produced this diminished interest in witchcraft proceedings. First, the fact that Puritans had any number of concrete enemies—Indians, English officials, religious and political opponents—deflected people's interests from witches. Second, the jeremiads reiterated the theme that Puritans themselves were to blame for the decay enveloping the Biblical Commonwealths. Third, the skeptical attitude of the English authorities toward witchcraft helped to create a more tolerant Puritan worldview; soon English rationalists would open fire on witchcraft proceedings as ignorant and superstitious events. Already in the 1670s and 1680s New England ministers had begun searching for natural explanations of such "supernatural" events as comets, solar eclipses, and earthquakes.[140] Fourth, the sexual expressiveness revealed by increasing numbers of fornication cases may have undercut the sexual repression which so often played a role in witchcraft accusations. Finally, the numbers of secular women were increasing so gradually, and within such an individualized (often at least partially legitimate) context, that Puritans apparently did not assume that all female "rebels" must be witches.

Gone was the graphic example of Quaker and Antinomian times, when women spoke against ministers and magistrates in church and court. The "new" secular, nontraditional woman did not attach herself to heretical religions or argue theological matters with the authorities. Relying on her own individualistic judgments, she was certainly eccentric, but hardly as uniformly vocal or as blatantly corrupting as earlier heretics. She did not usually attack the authorities directly (or, like Quaker women, search them out to chastize them), thereby minimizing the extent to which the authorities felt personally threatened by any individual woman. Rather, the nontraditional woman wore fine clothing, made herself attractive, danced "promiscuously," and had sexual as well as social intercourse with men. No longer an inhibited Virgin or an undeclarative Wife, she was not quite a Whore or a Witch. Indeed, more than ever before, she had become her own person, her own source of power.

1. Sainsbury & Headlam, eds., *Cal. of State Papers*, IX, 153 (no. 403).

2. J. Adams, *Founding of N. Eng.*, pp. 364–430; Lovejoy, *Glorious Rev. in Am.*, pp. 122–219; Byfield, *Account of Late Rev.*, pp. 10–17.

3. C. Mather, *Magnalia*, II, 270; J. Trumbull, ed., *Conn. Rec.*, III, 297; H. Dow, "Journal," I, 578; S. Danforth, "Rec. of Roxbury First Church," pp. 162–63, 165, 360; Morton, *N.-Eng. Memorial*, pp. 172, 177.

4. G. Dow, *Pirates of N. Eng. Coast*, pp. 25–31, 44–53.

5. C. Mather, *Magnalia*, II, 270; Westgate, "Letter to I. Mather," p. 578; N. Mather, "Letter to I. Mather," p. 22; Bridenbaugh, *Cities in Wilderness*, pp. 58–60.

6. Bridenbaugh, *Cities in Wilderness*, pp. 86–87; Moody, "Letter to Samuel Nowell," p. 372; C. Mather, "Letter to J. Cotton" and "to John Richards, Sept. 5, 1693," pp. 383–84, 401–2; "Secretary John Allen to Simon Bradstreet, Aug. 9, 1689," in J. Trumbull, ed., *Conn. Rec.*, IV, 1; Belknap, *Hist. of N. Hamp.*, I, 241; I. Mather, "Diary," pp. 355, 357, 402, 406–7. For mention of six serious epidemics, see S. Danforth, "Rec. of Roxbury First Church," pp. 85–86, 298, 300; S. Bradstreet, "Journal," pp. 43–45; Duffy, *Epidemics in Col. Am.*, pp. 43–48, 115, 215–16.

7. For discussions of late century changes, see Breen & Foster, "Puritans' Greatest Achievement," p. 20; Youngs, "Cong. Clericalism," p. 487; Miller, *N. Eng. Mind: From Col. to Prov.*, p. 305.

8. These and succeeding population figures are based largely upon estimates appearing in Greene & Harrington, *Am. Pop. Before Census of 1790*, pp. 4, 11–14, 19–21, 47–48, 70. Such compilations are rough, for the estimates vary, but I have attempted to choose those which seem most accurate and present a consistent pattern of growth. At times I have multiplied the number of militiamen (almost all men between the ages of 16 and 60) by 5 1/3 to produce an estimate of the total population. See note *ibid.*, p. xxxiii, and comparison of militiamen to total population in Rhode Island census, p. 65.

9. See list of urban populations in Bridenbaugh, *Cities in the Wilderness*, p. 6n.

10. [H. Shepard,] "Puritan Maiden's Diary," p. 24.

11. The number of taverns per capita increased from one for every 428 persons in 1660 to 1:145 in 1680 and 1:99 in 1690.

12. Bailyn, *N. Eng. Merchants*, p. 139.

13. G. Dow, ed., *Essex Ct. Rec.*, VII, 248, 251.

14. I. Mather, *Practical Truths*, pp. 209–10, and *Necessity of Reformation*, pp. 3–5; Maule, *Truth Held Forth*, p. 215; Whitmore, ed., *Col. Laws of Mass.*, p. 234.

15. Morgan, *Visible Saints*, pp. 130–38; Pope, *Half-Way Covenant*, pp. 132–85.

16. G. Dow, ed., *Essex Ct. Rec.*, IV, 350–66; Flynt, "Manuscript."

17. Stearns, ed., "Correspondence of Woodbridge & Baxter," p. 574.

18. [I. Mather,] *Necessity of Reformation*, p. 5.

19. Morgan, *Visible Saints*, pp. 146–49; Stoddard, *Doctrine of Instituted Churches*, passim.

20. Wertenbacker, *Puritan Oligarchy*, p. 242; Benedict, *Gen. Hist. of Baptist Denomination*, pp. 391–94.

21. Maule, *N.-Eng. Persecutors Mauled*, p. 51; C. D., *N. Eng. Faction Discovered*, II, 10.

22. "Rec. of Middlesex Co. Ct." V, 99, 76; G. Dow, ed., *Essex Ct. Rec.*, VII, 2; *Rec. of Suffolk Co. Ct. 1671–80*, I, 554; Hist. Rec. Survey, *Abstract & Index of Suffolk Co. Ct. 1680–98*, p. 132; "Essex Ct. Papers," XXXIII (1683), 9.

23. Quoted in O. Winslow, *Meetinghouse Hill*, p. 116.

24. Youngs, "Cong. Clericalism"; Breen, *Character of Good Ruler*, pp. 100, 210.

25. Lockridge & Kreider, "Evolution of Mass. Town Govt."

26. Traford, "Transformation of Mass. Educ.," p. 290.

27. I. Mather, *Earnest Exhortation*, p. 7.

28. [I. Mather,] *Necessity of Reformation*, p. 5; Stearns, ed., "Correspondence of Woodbridge & Baxter," p. 575.

29. *Rec. of Suffolk Co. Ct. 1671–80*, I, 305–6; J. Smith, ed., *Pynchon Ct. Rec.*, p. 275; G. Dow, ed., *Essex Ct. Rec.*, V, 311–12; Wertenbacker, *Puritan Oligarchy*, p. 177.

30. Whitmore, ed., *Col. Laws of Mass.*, p. 236.

31. Miller, *N. Eng. Mind: From Col. to Prov.*, pp. 36–37.

32. Winship, "Introduction" to *Boston in 1682 & 1699*, p. xvi.

33. A. Vaughan, ed., *Puritan Trad. in Am.*, p. 305. Miller's *N. Eng. Mind: From Col. to Prov.*, pp. 25–52, contains an excellent description of the form, content, and psychology of the jeremiad.

34. "Edward Randolph's Narrative, Sept. 20 and Oct. 12, 1676," in T. Hutchinson, ed., *Col. of Original Papers*, p. 493; Craven, *Colonies in Transition*, p. 123.

35. I. Mather, *Earnest Exhortation*, p. 2.

36. Massachusetts in the 1680s had almost innumerable political factions, based on church affiliation (Anglican vs. Puritan), economic interests (urban merchants vs. rural traditionalists), ideology (preference for democracy vs. preference for a more aristocratic, English form of government), power struggles between the branches of government (deputies vs. magistrates), and family connections. See Miller, *N. Eng. Mind: From Col. to Prov.*, pp. 137–46; Breen, *Character of a Good Ruler*, pp. 123–33; Bailyn, *N. Eng. Merchants*, pp. 154–67.

37. Although witchcraft died hard in England, persecutions did decline after the Restoration of Charles II. Between 1658 and 1667 various judges tried 23 witches and hanged but one; from 1668 to 1677 those numbers dropped to 12 and zero. Royalist judges matter-of-factly took steps to secure acquittals in all witchcraft cases (Davies, *Four Centuries of Witch-Beliefs*, pp. 181–203).

38. Breen, *Character of a Good Ruler*, pp. 134–51; *Newes from N.-Eng.*, p. 1; Lovejoy, *Glorious Rev. in Am.*, pp. 182–86.

39. Lovejoy, *Glorious Rev. in Am.*, pp. 182–86.

40. K. Erikson, *Wayward Puritans*, p. 156.

41. R. Pope, *Half-Way Covenant*, pp. 185–286; Beales, "Half-Way Covenant & Rel. Scrupulosity."

42. See, e.g., I. Mather, *Earnest Exhortation*, p. 3.

43. For a fuller explanation of crime as an index of norm slippage, see Reckless, *Am. Criminology*, pp. 3–5; Reckless & Shoham, "Norm Containment Theory," *Excerpta Criminologica*, III, 637–44.

44. Boston Rec. Cmrs., *Rep. Containing Misc. Papers*, pp. 55–61.

45. Niccholes, *Discourse on Marriage & Wiving*, pp. 20–22.

46. Morgan, *Visible Saints*, pp. 48–51; "On a Puritan" in *Facetiae*, II, 136.

47. Adburgham, *Women in Print*, pp. 19–25; Gagen, *New Women*, passim; Pinchbeck & Hewitt, *Children in Eng. Soc.*, I, 55.

48. Elliott, *Power & Pulpit in Puritan N. Eng.*, p. 57.

49. Thompson, "17th-Cent. Eng. & Col. Sex Ratios," p. 158; S. Norton, "Pop. Growth in Col. Am.," pp. 445–46; Greven, *Four Generations*, p. 122.

50. Because no decent census data exist prior to 1765, the percentage of women in the adult population is a highly speculative matter. Too many observers, relying on evidence of increasing numbers of widows and spinsters, have concluded that there must have been a surplus of females by the 1690s. Such an interpretation ignores two factors: 1) in those freer times, fewer widows may have wanted to remarry, and increased economic opportunities may have led maidens to postpone the age at first marriage; 2) men also may have wished to postpone marriage because of the constant necessity of military preparedness in the wartorn 1690s.

51. If, for example, we set 8.86 (%of female offenders before 1644)/

40 (minimal estimate of % of females in adult population before 1644) equal to 22.8 (% of female offenders, 1665–89)/X (% of women in adult population, 1665–89), X would be an impossible figure of 102.5%. The relative increase in female criminals therefore far exceeded the increased number of women generally.

52. Benton, *Early Census Making in Massachusetts*, appendix.

53. Besse, *Col. of Quaker Sufferings*, II, 260–64; Rubincam, "Lydia Wright & Her Sisters."

54. Oberholzer, *Delinquent Saints*, pp. 67–68; Hampshire Co. "Ct. of Gen. Sessions & Common Pleas, no. 1, 1677–1728," p. 88.

55. G. Dow, ed., *Essex Ct. Rec.*, VII, 248.

56. *Rec. of Suffolk Co. Ct. 1671–80*, I, 305–6; "Salem Witchcraft—1692," I, n.p.

57. Shurtleff, ed., *Mass. Rec.*, V, 59; I. Mather, *Earnest Exhortation*, p. 7.

58. I. Mather, *Account Against Profane Dancing*, pp. 2–3, 19; C. Mather, quoted in W. Bliss, *Side Glimpses*, pp. 134–35.

59. Shurtleff, ed., *Mass. Rec.*, IV, pt. 2, pp. 143, 393–94; Dunton, *Letters*, p. 72.

60. In 1672 the authorities discovered and closed Alice Thomas's bawdy house (see ch. 7); in the same year they bound Thomas Moxen to his good behavior after he was accused of offering Elizabeth Langbury half a crown if he could" be naught[y] wth her" (*Rec. of Suffolk Co. Ct. 671–80*, I, 82–83, 94).

61. J. W., *Letter from N.-Eng.*, p. 9.

62. G. Dow, ed., *Essex Ct. Rec.*, V, 351–55; Sewall, *Diary*, I, 21.

63. The available records specify no offense for three-quarters of these women (Boston Rec. Cmrs., *Rep. Containing Misc. Papers*, pp. 55–61).

64. Benton, *Warning Out in N. Eng.*, passim.

65. Thompson, "On a Fortification," pp. 235–36.

66. Starkey, *Cong. Way*, p. 120.

67. Female attorneys appear on pp. 120, 250, 273, 322–23, and 355 of Aspinwall, *Vol. Relating to Early Hist. of Boston*.

68. King Philip's War did not lead to an increased number of female attorneys, as might be expected. Eight women argued cases in 1675, the same number as in 1674. Not until 1677—after the war had ended—did women exceed 10% of all plaintiffs and defendants.

69. *Rec. of Suffolk Co. Ct. 1671–80*, I, 692.

70. Innkeepers appear in Boston Rec. Cmrs., *Reports Containing Boston Town Rec. 1634–60 & 1660–1701*.

71. Northampton and Hatfield allowed girls to enter the public schools, and the increased number of women who could sign their names in Massachusetts suggests that other towns also opened their schoolhouse doors to the "weaker sex" (Small, "Girls in Col. Schools," pp. 532–34; J. Trumbull, *Hist. of Northampton*, I, 222).

72. Seybolt, *Private Schools of Boston*, pp. 3–9.

73. Although all criminal behavior is, in a broad sense, rebellious—"social order" theorists prefer the word "maladaptive"—not all such behavior can or should be viewed as benign. The woman who kills her newborn child, for example, takes an unfortunate step. Certainly, the child's death saddens us; but in reacting to the nonmaternal mother, we should not lose sight of her

turmoil, or of her action's larger meaning. Infanticide constitutes a rebellion against nature (for the lack of a foolproof means of birth control) and against society (for providing no means by which the child might be removed from her care, and for stigmatizing her as a fornicator or even a whore).

74. I. Mather, quoted in Winship, "Introduction," *Boston in 1682 and 1699*, pp. xv-xvi.

75. Anyone wishing to examine a more complete breakdown of premarital pregnacy by various Massachusetts seacoast locales should consult the numerous tables in Smith & Hindus, "Premarital Pregnancy in Am.," pp. 554, 560–65.

76. As Robert G. Pope has pointed out, women between 1660 and 1689 comprised from 55.2% (Dorchester) to 67.1% (Charlestown) of all new church members (Pope, *Half-Way Covenant*, pp. 213–14, 217–18, 225, 279–86).

77. [H. Shepard,] "Puritan Maiden's Diary," pp. 21, 24.

78. Bulkely, *People's Rt. to Election*, II, 93.

79. Richman, *R.I.*, II, 232–68; J. Trumbull, ed., *Conn. Rec.*, III, 265–90; Bartlett, ed., *R.I. Col. Rec.*, II, 32–34, 45–48, 439–42.

80. J. Trumbull, ed., *Conn. Rec.*, III, 301. Connecticut's losses were light, in comparison with the rest of New England's, largely because the Connecticut Indians tended to befriend the settlers.

81. *Ibid.*, III, 297, 301.

82. The Duke of York actually claimed the western half of Connecticut in a proprietory grant, but the colony adamantly refused to recognize the claim (Lovejoy, *Glorious Rev. in Am.*, p. 99).

83. *Ibid.*, pp. 203–8; J.Trumbull, ed., *Conn. Rec.*, III, 355–60.

84. Stearns, ed., "Correspondence of Woodbridge & Baxter," pp. 576–77.

85. *Ibid.*, pp. 564–65, 577–78; B. Trumbull, *Complete Hist. of Conn.*, I, 301–3, 307, 309, 460–64; J. Trumbull, ed., *Conn. Rec.*, II, 76–77, 85–86, 99, 113–14; R. Pope, *Half-Way Covenant*, pp. 75–131; Lucas, "Church v. Town," pp. 12–18.

86. Fitch, *Explanation of Solemn Advice*, pp. 10–14, 19.

87. "Rec., Ct. of Assts., 1687–1715," in "Conn. Rec.," LVIII, 9.

88. Conn. "Assts. Rec., 1669–86," in "Conn. Rec.," LIII, 9.

89. *Ibid.*, pp. 17, 33.

90. "N. London Ct. Rec.," V, 156.

91. Fitch, *Explanation of Solemn Advice*, pp. 1–2, 10–23, 38–39, 42–43, 45. For other ministers' criticisms, see "Ministers of Connecticut to the Churches of Connecticut, 1676," in *Wyllys Papers*, pp. 234–39; Lucas, *Valley of Discord*, pp. 87–102.

92. E.g., see Fitch, *Holy Connexion*, and *First Principles of Christ's Doctrine*; S. Hooker, *Righteousness Rained from Heaven*; J. Whiting, *Way of Israel's Welfare*.

93. Fitch, *Holy Connexion*, p. 1; J. Whiting, *Way of Israel's Welfare*, p. 27.

94. Fitch, *Explanation of Solemn Advice*, pp. 33, 43.

95. F. Dexter, ed., *N. Haven Town Rec. 1649–62*, p. 88; A.T[rumbull], *Recs. of Conn. Part. Ct. During Administration of Andros*, p. 3.

96. Caulkins, *Hist. of N. London*, p. 205.

97. J. Rogers, *Mid-Night-Cry*, pp. 140, 147, 164–65; "N. London Ct. Rec.," II, 25; V, 99–101; Caulkins, *Hist. of N. London*, pp. 211, 216.

98. See Appendix 1.

99. Manwaring, ed., *Digest of Conn. Probate Rec.*, I, 46–47.

100. R. Bliss, "Secular Revival," p. 130.

101. The population of the various New England colonies increased as follows:

Year	Mass.	Conn.	Plymouth	N. Hamp.	Maine
1643	15,000	5,500	3,312	1,000 (1639)	1,400 (1636)
1665	23,467	8–9,000	—	—	—
1671	—	10,933	5,333	—	3,000
1680	42,000	12,535	6,400	2,400	3,000
1690	49,554	16,324	7,423	4,021	2,000

(Williamson, *Hist. of Maine*, I, 265–67; Greene & Harrington, *Am. Pop. Before 1790 Census*.)

102. "In answer to a query by the Lords of Trade, 1680," in J. Trumbull, ed., *Conn. Rec.*, III, 296–98; "Sir Edmond Andros to the Earl of Sunderland, March 30, 1687" in Bartlett, ed., *R.I. Col. Rec.*, III, 223–24; Sainsbury & Headlam, eds., *Calendar of State Papers*, XII, 329 (no. 1160); R. Bliss, "Secular Revival," pp. 134–35.

103. "In Answer to a query by the Lords of Trade, 1680," in J. Trumbull, ed., *Conn. Rec.*, III, p. 299.

104. Dunn, *Puritans & Yankees*, pp. 170–86.

105. J. Taylor, *Witchcraft Del. In Conn.*, pp. 47–61, 153; Wyllys, "Wyllys Col. Suppl. Witchcraft in Conn. 1662–93," pp. 37–43.

106. Sainsbury & Headlam, eds., *Calendar of State Papers*, XII, 300 (no. 1000), 344 (1103); Langdon, *Pilgrim Col.*, p. 143.

107. Langdon, *Pilgrim Col.*, pp. 132–34. Only the Scituate Church actually accepted the Half-Way Covenant.

108. *Ibid.*, pp. 181–83.

109. *Ibid.*, pp. 216–22.

110. Inhabitants of Boston, *Rev. in N.-Eng. Justified*, pp. 82–83.

111. W. Bradford, *Of Plym. Plant.*, p. 316; Langdon, *Pilgrim Col.*, pp. 69–78; Walley, *Balm in Gilead*, p. 8. Cotton quoted in Langdon, p. 185.

112. Langdon, *Pilgrim Col.*, p. 131; C. Mather, *Magnalia*, II, 459.

113. Langdon, *Pilgrim Col.*, p. 121.

114. Stearns, ed., "Correspondence of Woodbridge & Baxter," p. 573.

115. Shurtleff & Pulsifer, eds., *Plym. Rec.*, V, 223–24.

116. I. Mather, *Essay for Recording Illus. Prov.*, pp. 341–46.

117. Andrews, *Col. Period in Am. Hist.*, I, 438; Ernst, *N. Eng. Miniature*, p. 128.

118. Jenness, *Isles of Shoals*, p. 172; "Thomas Gorges to John Winthrop, Feb. 23, 1640/1," in A. Forbes, ed., *Winthrop Papers*, IV, 322–23.

119. Quoted in De Normandie, "Manners, Morals & Laws of Piscataqua Col.," p. 169.

120. J. Baxter, ed., *Doc. Hist. of State of Maine*, IV, 201, 262.

121. At Dover 25 men agreed to submit to Massachusetts rule in 1641, but less than four months earlier 41 men had signed a "Combination" to establish a government. Sixteen adult males had therefore neglected to sign the articles of submission. Of the 22 who submitted at Exeter—not over 44% of the total adult male population—only four of them had signed an earlier "Combination" in 1639. Originally, Antinomian refugees from Massachusetts had founded Exeter, but no Antinomian agreed to submit to Bay Colony rule. Some of these relocated in Wells, Maine, after Massachusetts assumed control over New Hampshire. See Bouton, ed., *Prov. Papers of N. Hamp.*, I, 126–28; Bell, *Hist. of Exeter*, pp. 17–18, 45–46.

122. Seventy-three men appeared before the York County justices. The number of militiamen, according to one estimate, was 700 in 1672 (Sainsbury & Headlam, eds., *Calendar of State Papers*, VII, 332 [no. 762]).

123. *Ibid.*, VI, 347 (no. 1103), 311–12 (1021); IX, 455 (1037); Bouton, ed., *Prov. Papers of N. Hamp.*, I, 253, 279, 284–86.

124. Williamson, *Hist. of Maine*, I, 553–61; R. Moody, "Introduction" to Libby, Allen, & Moody, eds., *Maine Ct. Rec.*, III, xiii.

125. Belknap, *Hist. of N. Hamp.*, I, 177; Sainsbury & Headlam, eds., *Calendar of State Papers*, XI, 50 (no. 106); Bouton, ed., *Prov. Papers of N. Hamp.*, I, 430.

126. Page, *Judicial Beginnings of N. Hamp.*, pp. 168–71; Bouton, ed., *Prov. Papers of N. Hamp.*, I, 433–44, 458–61, 494–96; Sainsbury & Headlam, eds., *Calendar of State Papers*, XI, 522 (no. 316), 577 (1508), 373 (906), 388 (952).

127. Page, *Judicial Beginnings of N. Hamp.*, pp. 208–11, 216–17, 222–28; Belknap, *Hist. of N. Hamp.*, I, 198–99, 211; Bouton, ed., *Prov. Papers of N. Hamp.*, I, 549–54; Sainsbury & Headlam, eds., *Calendar of State Papers*, XI, 678 (no. 1845).

128. E.g. in York County the number of protests against the local and colonial authorities, both spiritual and secular, decreased from 14 in mid-1685 through mid-1687 to just four in the next two-year interval.

129. R. Moody, "Introduction" to Libby, Allen, & Moody, eds., *Maine Ct. Rec.*, III, xxx-xxxii, xlvi-xlviii; Williamson, *Hist. of Maine*, I, 599–600.

130. Libby, Allen, & Moody, eds., *Maine Ct. Rec.*, II & III, indexes, and G. Dow, ed., *Essex Ct. Rec.*, II, 376, contain information on the poor road upkeep in New Hampshire and Maine.

131. The pro-Puritan Cutt Council in March, 1681, did call a fast, upon "serious consideration of the manifold sinful provocations among us, as of the sundry tokens of divine displeasure evident to us" but that was an unusual action (Bouton, ed., *Prov. Papers of N. Hamp.*, I, 429).

132. "Norfolk Ct. Rec.," in G. Dow, ed., *Essex Ct. Rec.*, VII, 275; "Ct. Files—Essex Co.," II, 295–97, 407–9, 442; VI, 412; Libby, Allen, & Moody, eds., *Maine Ct. Rec.*, III, 24, 250; "N. Hamp. Ct. Papers," VII, 23.

133. J. Baxter, ed., *Doc. Hist. of State of Maine*, VI, 268.

134. "Ct. Files—Essex Co.," VIII, 10.

135. J. Baxter, ed., *Doc. Hist. of State of Maine*, VI, 231, 260, 274–75, 278, 315, 350–51, 385.

136. "Norfolk Ct. Rec.," in G. Dow, ed., *Essex Ct. Rec.*, IV, 24; Bouton, ed., *Prov. Papers of N. Hamp.*, I, 508–9, 551; *Col. of N.-Hamp. Hist. Soc.*, VIII, 179; Belknap, *Hist. of N. Hamp.*, I, 215, 223–24.

137. Libby, Allen, & Moody, eds., *Maine Ct. Rec.*, III, 225, 272.

138. This woman, Mary Colby, in 1665 paid a fine for such "bold and uncivil carriage" ("Norfolk Ct. Rec.," in G. Dow, ed., *Essex Ct. Rec.*, III, 251).

139. Bouton, ed., *Prov. Papers of N. Hamp.*, I, 386.

140. Wertenbacker, *Puritan Oligarchy*, pp. 252–68; Savelle, *Seeds of Liberty*, pp. 85–90.

XIII

The Salem Village Cataclysm: Origins and Impact of a Witch Hunt, 1689–92

. . . what confronted Salem Village, as seems clear in retrospect . . . was a group of people who were on the advancing edge of profound historical change.

—Paul Boyer and Stephen Nissenbaum,
Salem Possessed

[The afflicted Salem Village] girls seem to have no power of consolidating a female identification, for they avoided any ritual that required of them a womanly compliance or they modified it until it gave them opportunity for male activity.

—Merell Middlemore,
"Treatment of Bewitchment in Puritan Community"

THE TENSIONS WHICH HAD BEEN ACCUMULATING BETWEEN 1665 AND 1689 intensified during the next three years. In Essex County, Massachusetts, they culminated in a search for scapegoats—a witch hunt which reflected many of the multiplying concerns of a disoriented populace, including concerns about the behavior of "new women." Among other things, the Essex County accusations cast in the scapegoat role those perceived inferior yet now very threatening citizens of the Biblical Commonwealth, those nontraditional women believed to be covetous of unnatural power. Yet, as we shall see, the nontraditional woman left her mark even on those proceedings designed, in part, to ferret her out.

General Background: The Fearful Post-Andros Years

Between 1689 and 1692 a large number of political, economic, and religious frustrations raised the already high anxiety level of Calvinist New England. The governments established in Massachusetts, Connecticut, Plymouth, and New Hampshire after Andros's expulsion suffered from a general inability to reassert political or religious order. Even though the King approved of these transitional governments, Puritans realized that they no longer determined their own futures. The Crown's reluctance to restore the old charter privileges soon convinced all but a few skeptics that the independence and relative isolation of earlier years had almost vanished. Many who believed the charters were New World Magna Cartas—valued symbols of the Biblical Commonwealths' continued viability—felt stripped of self-government, law, and religious purpose, not to mention humiliated and helpless before royal whim. After Connecticut and Massachusetts had dispatched agents to petition King William for the restoration of old privileges, a pamphlet war ensued, revealing Puritan fears that Andros's "arbitrary" government would return to destroy "all our Good things" and exalt "ye Vilest men." Prone to see conspiracies everywhere, Calvinists worried about the disruptive effects of a "monstrous" Catholic plot involving Andros, James II, the Canadian French, and the Indians.[1]

Distressed by the political factionalism of the 1680s, many Massachusetts Puritans expressed great concern over the nature, as well as the legitimacy, of the government installed after the little Glorious Revolution. That coalition, composed of moderate Dominion officials, old-style Puritans from the pre-1686 charter government, and Boston merchants without previous experience in public office, was united only by a common fear of counterrevolution. The new governor, Simon Bradstreet, served ineffectually and sometimes suffered sharp attacks from an angry populace. The rural-based General Court, wishing to revive the charter and a sense of holy mission, opposed those merchants and non-freemen who desired changes, including a new franchise law and more extensive guarantees of property. In fact, "Liberty and Property" became the clarion call of the 1690s.[2] Anglicans (about 5% of the population) also pressed for liberty, because they feared a resumption of the charter would force them to move to New York, northern New Hampshire, or Maine.[3]

Other sources of stress undermined Massachusetts's stability.

Pirates, particularly French ones, roamed the New England coast-line.[4] The wheat blast continued to destroy a major portion of the annual grain crop.[5] Smallpox, "burning and spotted Fevers, shaking Agues, dry Belly Acks, plagues of the Guts, and divers other sore distempers" killed more than 150 persons between February and June, 1690.[6] Trade fell to a point where it was insufficient to sustain the colony's economy, debts came due without payment, and the poor, according to one observer, seemed "ready to eat up one another, or turn Levellers." Severe taxation, levied to cover the costs of Indian warfare, left the colony deep in debt,[7] and an inflated paper currency forced farmers to receive payment for their scanty crops in money worth only 60 to 70 percent of its stated value.[8] The outbreak of warfare with the French and Abnaki Indians caused the colonists to fear the disastrous effects of another bloody, financially debilitating conflict.

In such impoverishing times, a growing sense of materialism treatened the spiritual basis of the Bay Colony. Cotton Mather angrily stated in 1691, ". . . might I hold out a Turf of earth; and say, Here is the God of many a poor New-England man! A beelzebub indeed! a fine God, made of Dung!"[9] Governor Bradstreet and the General Court proclaimed that laws, having "too much lost their edg" through Andros's non-enforcement, had fallen into widespread disrespect, as people sinned in "Blasphemy, Cursing, Profane Swearing, Lying, Unlawful Gaming, Sabbath-breaking, Idleness, Drunkenness, Uncleanness, and all the Enticements and Nurseries of such Impieties."[10] Magistrates often hesitated to prosecute such offenders, or gave them very minor punishments.

The abuse of old moral values, property contention, illness, war, poor crop yields, pirates, and political disarray testified to the disruption of virtually all aspects of Puritan life. "In imminent danger of perishing" and feeling completely powerless before a God whose "Ax is laid to the Root of the trees," many Puritans reportedly imagined that the colony had been reduced to a Hobbesian state of nature, where only the strong would survive. The once-proud Commonwealth had become a chaotic "labyrinth of Miserys."[11] Indeed, life's problems pressed in so profoundly that a tendency toward "self-murder" lay "fierce upon some unhappy people," threatening a veritable "epidemic" of suicide.[12]

Like Massachusetts, Connecticut faced, after Andros's expulsion, a general political confusion. Three factions—the "moderates," ex-deputy James Fitch's democrats, and Gershom Bulkeley's royalists—vied for ascendancy; although Fitch's group emerged temporarily victorious, tensions remained high. People were apprehensive about the King's hesitation in responding to three petitions for the restoration of charter privileges.[13] Many feared that William might divide the colony between New York, with its Catholic governor, and Massachusetts.[14] Still, Connecticut citizens possessed a good deal of independent spirit. As three prominent men wrote to the English monarchs on September 16, 1692: "This is a hard country wherein we cannot long subsist under your oppressions and abuses. An house divided agst itself cannot stand. There is no living without justice. It is hard for us to bequeath and entaile certaine slavery & vassalage to our posterity. It is impossible for us to serve two masters, your royall Majesties & this soveraigne corporation, if we serve the one we must forsake the other."[15] Such strong words revealed an amazing degree of self-confidence.

Connecticut did have its share of troubles, however. Expenditures on the French and Indian war, including the financing of an abortive three-pronged invasion of Canada in 1690, helped precipitate much grumbling about "intolerable taxes."[16] An extensive drought, followed by a damaging flood in 1689, created economic turmoil, as did the enervating effects of epidemic illness. One epidemic placed two-thirds of Connecticut's inhabitants in bed for long intervals. Secretary John Allen related on August 6, 1689, "It is feared some suffer for want of tendrance and many are dead among us." Two very sickly years followed, including a severe outbreak of smallpox, fluxes, and fevers in the militia ranks (1690). Illness so debilitated the inhabitants that the General Assembly could not even meet between 1689 and 1691.[17]

While Connecticut faced illness, economic distress, and political "discontents and murmurings," Puritans there did not feel quite the same degree of confusion as prevailed in Massachusetts; nor did they berate themselves with quite the same intensity. None of the Connecticut authorities would protest quite as bitterly as the Massachusetts Governor and Council, who in 1690 exclaimed, ". . . shall our Father spit in our faces and we not be ashamed!"[18]

In usually stolid Plymouth Colony, difficulties also multiplied between 1689 and 1692, with new, impoverishing rates to pay for another Indian war, apprehension about the French threat, concern lest the Crown annex New Plymouth to New York, and general fear that the colony's significance would be "squeezed into an atom."[19]

Plymouth faced utter bankruptcy, for between October 1689 and December 1690 the General Court levied £6,270 in taxes on estates rated at £35,900—a figure of 17.5 percent! Four towns refused to collect any of the assessed taxes. In addition, the colony could raise only one-third of the amount necessary to pay an agent to represent Plymouth's interests before the English monarchs. Beset by such problems, many residents rejoiced when the King included New Plymouth within the Massachusetts charter of 1691, because the Bay Colony had a much larger tax base, and the government would then still be in the hands of saints.[20]

While Massachusetts, Connecticut, and Plymouth struggled to avert disasters in one form or another, the settlers of Maine and New Hampshire had to confront the daily possibility of Indian warfare. Massachusetts leaders recalled Andros's troops from the northerly forts in 1689. Soon afterward, Indians overran two hundred miles of coastline from the St. Croix to the Piscatauqua rivers, destroying seven forts and the towns of Pemaquid, New Harbor, New Dartmouth, Sagadehoc, North Yarmouth, Richmond's Island, and Saco. Warriors killed or captured over three hundred persons and caused property damage totalling £60,000 in 1689–90. Commercial fishing and the mast trade all but ceased. Some Maine residents stayed on, begging England for help; others moved to Salem and Boston, where they often received allotments of poor relief.[21] In 1691, partly to provide for the protection of Maine, the Crown included that "province" with the Massachusetts charter.

Between 1689 and 1691 the Indians also caused much damage in raids upon Cochecho, Salmon Falls, and Exeter, New Hampshire. The several town commissioners, loosely federated after Andros's expulsion, could not muster enough men or militia provisions to prevent such incursions. With no other alternative available, the towns in 1690 petitioned Massachusetts for protective assistance. Bay Colony authorities extended some military aid, but, preoccupied with their own internal problems, they could not assume civil control over their northerly neighbors. From the time of Andros's removal until the reinstatement of a governor by the Crown in 1692, New Hampshire existed in an "unsettled state," with no central government.[22]

While each New England colony (with the possible exception of Rhode Island) underwent severe distress between 1689 and 1692, the diverse sources of tension did not affect all geographical areas in similar or equally intense ways. Residents of Hampshire County, for example, had little sense of the turmoil enveloping much of eastern Massachusetts. Many Maine settlers, on the other hand, could become profoundly concerned only about the stinging effects of total warfare.

Disorganization on a Local Level: The Case of Salem Village

The sources of tension which the inhabitants of Essex County, Massachusetts, shared with Puritans elsewhere were numerous and somewhat diffuse, but nevertheless hard felt. Salem, the only "really significant merchantile center in the colony" other than Boston, had become cosmopolitan and wealthy—much to the chagrin of people in the more tradition-oriented, financially declining inland areas. The diminishing availability of land at communities like Andover, Topsfield, Ipswich, Wenham, and Salem Village often led to sharp conflict over land boundaries.[23] Rural Puritans with decreasing acreages envied the material prosperity of Salem merchants with their "great houses," although that was not the only factor disconcerting many inland settlers. The Salem merchants, like their Boston counterparts, ignored the old laws against usury and excessive profit-taking. Agriculturalists, once protected by fair-price and fixed-wage laws, now were at the mercy of the international market. Moreover, the material products of trade, so readily apparent in the many Salem shops, threatened to push more spiritual concerns into oblivion. A flourishing commerce brought newcomers, novelty, and a spirit of individualism—Paul Boyer and Stephen Nissenbaum call it "private will"—into an area desperate for stability and unity. Taverns, those symbols of the moral decay which so many Puritans felt was becoming altogether too common, proliferated, especially along roads connecting town centers to Salem.[24]

Salem Villagers, in particular, experienced great political, economic and social strain. With no real power for the church, town government (Salem Village did not have official town status), or selectmen, all institutional authority had broken down by 1692.[25] Lacking viable channels for the expression of their grievances, especially in these times of colony-wide political insecurity, the inhabitants had fallen into "uncomfortable divisions and contentions." According to one contemporary, "brother is against brother and neighbors against neighbors, all quarrelling and smiting one another." Villagers addressed their ministers in "scoffing" and "contemptuous tones." By 1689–90, 20 percent of all rated persons refused to pay the minister's salary, and that figure increased to 29 percent the following year. Many inhabitants of the eastern and southern portions of Salem Village had large landholdings and connections with Salem's merchant community, thereby cutting off possibilities for real estate expansion and reducing the influence of prominent village families like the Putnams.[26]

The many problems confronting Salem Villagers in 1692 "encompassed some of the central issues of New England society in the late seventeenth century," as Boyer and Nissenbaum have demonstrated. Sources of tension included "the resistance of back-country farmers to the pressures of commercial capitalism and the social style that accompanied it; the breaking away of outlying areas from parent towns; difficulties between ministers and their congregations; the crowding of third-generation sons from family land; the shifting locus of authority within individual communities and society as a whole; the very quality of life in an unsettled age." Salem Villagers sought security, a place which "could offer shelter against sweeping social change and provide a setting where the Puritan social vision might yet be realized."[27] In early 1692, quite suddenly, everything exploded.

An Epidemic of Witchcraft

The Salem Village witch mania began easily enough, when several young girls experimented with fortune-telling and read occult works. In late January 1692, these girls began creeping under chairs and into holes, uttering "foolish, ridiculous speeches," assuming odd postures, and, on occasion, writhing in agony. Their antics soon became full-fledged hysterical fits. Their tongues extended out to "a fearful length," like those of hanged persons; their necks cracked; blood "gushed plentifully out of their Mouths." A local physician named William Griggs, unable to explain the girls' behavior in medical terms, warned that it must be due to an "Evil hand." The fits quickly spread to other youngsters ranging in age from twelve to nineteen, as well as to married women like Ann Pope, Sarah Bibber, Ann Putnam, and "an Ancient Woman, named Goodall."[28]

The afflicted girls initially charged Sarah Good, Sarah Osborne, and the minister's Indian slave Tituba with practicing *maleficium* upon them. Local magistrates served warrants on these designated witches, who faced a courtroom examination on March 1. Twenty

days later, Deodat Lawson, an ex-Salem Village pastor visiting from
Boston, delivered a rousing anti-witchcraft sermon after observing
the convulsive fits of Mary Walcott and Abigail Williams.[29] A week
later, Samuel Parris called his congregation to search out the many
devils in the church.[30] Parris was an old-line Puritan—a man anxious about his declining ministerial power, intensely suspicious of
his neighbors, obsessed with thoughts of his own filthiness, and
fearing the subversion of the Biblical Commonwealth.[31]

The half-dozen afflicted girls had accused only three witches in
February and four in March, but after the ministers' warnings no
fewer than fifteen girls and women of Salem Village accused
witches—at least twenty-five additional during April, and fifty-
one in May. "Witch" Martha Corey warned the authorities in
March, "We must not believe all these distracted children say," but
prosecutions continued.[32] More persons from areas outside Salem
Village were added to the list of accused witches—thirteen from
Topsfield, most of whom had previously quarrelled with the Putnam family over land boundaries;[33] twelve others from Gloucester;
thirteen from the port of Salem; and fifty-five from Andover, a locale torn by land stress.[34] Twenty-eight different persons, including four Andover women, fell subject to hysterical attacks in five
outlying towns. Altogether, these ostensibly betwitched persons
denounced almost all of the 56 men and 148 women accused of practicing witchcraft in 1692–93. Not only were three-quarters of the
accused persons females, but of the 56 men half were singled out
only after a close female relative or a wife had been accused—a
sort of guilt by association. The reverse pattern holds true for only
one, or possibly three, of the remaining male witches. Thus the traditional notion of the witch as a specifically female type held true
for most Essex County accusations—even during times of severe
stress, when virtually anyone might suffice as a scapegoat.

Estimates of the actual number of witches at large ranged from 307
(by confessed witch William Barker) to 500 (Susannah Post, Thomas
Maule).[35] Sir William Phips, the newly appointed royal governor
who arrived in May, soon established a Special Court of Oyer and
Terminer to try the many recently imprisoned witches. This court
included Salem magistrate John Hathorne, Sam Sewall, the strin-
gent chief justice William Stoughton, Dorchester merchant John
Richards, Salem physician Bartholomew Gedney, Cavalier Waitstill
Winthrop, the wealthy Peter Sargent, and Nathaniel Saltonstall of
Haverhill—all members of the coalition government, who, in Roger

Thompson's words, "were very much on trial themselves."[36] Al-though Saltonstall soon disapproved of the proceedings, resigned, and was replaced by Salem magistrate Jonathan Corwin, the justices listened to testimony against witch after witch, usually presuming that the accused was guilty before the trial began.[37] In court, the afflicted girls pointed to imaginary specters, and officials flailed away at such witches until the floor was "all covered" with

Chart 13.1
Witchcraft Accusations Made in Massachusetts, by Locale, 1692–3

Locale	Males	Females	Total
Andover	18	37	55
Salem Village	11	20	31
Salem	1	14	15
Topsfield	5	8	13
Gloucester	0	12	12
Haverhill	2	8	10
Boston	3	6	9
Beverly	1	6	7
Reading	0	7	7
Billerica	2	4	6
Lynn	2	4	6
Rowley	3	2	5
Boxford	2	2	4
Woburn	0	3	3
Malden	0	3	3
Charlestown	0	2	2
Ipswich	0	2	2
Manchester	2	0	2
Marblehead	0	2	2
Rumney Marsh	1	0	1
Salisbury	0	1	1
Amesbury	0	1	1
Chelmsford	0	1	1
Wenham	0	1	1
Milton	0	1	1
Great Island, N.H.	1	0	1
Wells, Maine	1	0	1
Hartford, Conn.	1	0	1
Unknown	0	1	1
	56	148	204

invisible blood.[38] As the frenzy escalated, ten persons broke out of prison to hide in other locales, and eight or ten more fled "upon rumor of being apprehended." One of these, sixteen-year-old Elizabeth Colson, outraced the Reading constable and his dog in a wild chase through thick bushes, while Philip English escaped a group of searchers by hiding behind a bag of clothing.[39]

The Court of Oyer and Terminer sentenced Bridget Bishop to be hanged on June 10. Five more women followed her to the gallows on July 19, four men and a woman on August 19, and seven women and a man on September 22. On September 16 the authorities ordered Giles Corey pressed to death under a pile of stones when he refused to plead.[40] All these witches, Cotton Mather related, faced execution "impudently demanding of God, a Miraculous Vindicacion of their Innocency."[41]

Faced with the awful possibility of their own deaths, other accused witches began propitiously confessing their wrongdoings. After the July 19 hangings, five accused Andover witches "made a most ample, surprising, amazing Confession, of all their Villanies and declared the Five newly Executed to have been of their Company." Such "witches" may have observed the immediate leniency extended to self-confessed offenders like Tituba and Sarah Churchill. In August and September fifty-five other "witches" confessed —many, if not all of them, under extreme duress.[42]

Accused witches clogged the prisons of eastern Massachusetts, where they suffered from the biting cold of winter and sometimes from a lack of sufficient food. Often jailors held them in irons for long periods, to prevent them from afflicting their accusers by moving their bodies.[43] The Salem jailor tied each of three boys neck and heels together "till the blood was ready to come out of their Noses" (and did, in fact, gush out of William Proctor's).[44] Thirteen or fourteen accused witches at Ipswich prison petitioned the General Court for release on bail as winter approached, asserting they were "all most destroyed with soe long an imprisonment."[45] By October six "witches," including Sarah Osborne, had died in jail. Two, Abigail Faulkner and Elizabeth Proctor, gave birth under such atrocious conditions.[46]

Witchcraft accusations diminished during the summer (eight in June, seven in July), but after a council of eight ministers at Cambridge affirmed the reality of specter evidence on August 1, charges again boomed—twenty-five in August and twenty-seven in September, mostly from Andover.[47] Throughout 1692 people intently scrutinized their neighbors' behavior, being especially watchful of those against whom they had some personal grievance. In court, "it was usual to hear evidence of matter foreign, and of perhaps Twenty or Thirty years standing, about over-setting Carts, the death of Cattle, unkindness to Relations, or unexpected Accidents befalling after some quarrel." The accusatory tone established in the trials helped activate animosities existing within families as well, with many parents therefore "believing their Children to be Witches, and many Husbands their Wives, etc."[48]

The Accusers

For many people who were already struggling against spiritual, political, and economic deprivation, and against the force of late seventeenth century changes, making a witchcraft accusation expressed their anxiety while it reasserted a sense of their own potency. Sociologist Dodd Bogart's conclusion that demon or witch charges are attempts to restore "self worth, social recognition, social acceptance, social status, and other related social rewards" is pertinent to the Salem Village situation.[49] Accusations allowed the angry, the helpless, and sometimes the sensitive to fight the imagined malign powers that frustrated them by scapegoating suitable incarnations of evil. By testifying against a witch, they not only exposed but also conquered their own feelings of powerlessness in a changing world. By blaming witches, men and women attempted to reestablish some feeling of order, of control, when confronted by the discomforting effects of threats both external (e.g., Indians, political anarchy, urban materialism) and internal (e.g., the inability to achieve assurance of justification before God, or to understand, if assured, why God had chosen to "providentially" destroy a given animal or person).

The sixty-three men and twenty-one women who testified as corroborating witnesses against accused witches had much in common with the six males and thirty-seven females whose hysterical fits initiated proceedings. In specifically sex-role-defined ways, members of each sex responded to an apparent condition of helplessness. Men primarily appeared before the magistrates and, in typically straightforward fashion, gave accounts of the witches' *maleficium*; women usually made their accusations more circuitously, behind the cover of a fit. Men revealed their feelings of fear and impotence by describing how witches had pressed them

into rigid immobility; bewitched women demonstrated dramatically, before the very eyes of the justices, how that—and far worse
—could happen.[50]

Women, particularly those adolescents who experienced fits,
used the witchcraft accusation as a viable form of self-expression in
1692–93. Burdened by the restrictive contingencies of the ideal feminine role, with its dictum (reinforced in church and school) that
good girls must control their longings for material joy and submit to
stronger adult authority figures, many young females probably felt
a great deal of frustration as they searched for gaiety, attention,
accomplishment, and individual autonomy. This was especially
true considering the recent fits of the Goodwin children in Boston
(1688), the occupational assertiveness of female innkeepers and
school dames, and the patent examples of so many women who
violated Puritan laws—all of which had an impact upon the con-
sciousnesses of developing adolescents.

Chart 13.2

Persons Experiencing Hysterical Accusatory Fits in
Massachusetts, 1692–93

Marital Status	M	F	Total	Age	M	F	Total
Single	4	27	31	9–10	1	1	2
Married	2	10	12	11–15	1	8	9
	6	37	43	16–20	1	14	15
				21–25	1	1	2
				26–30	0	1	1
				Over 30	1	7	8
				Unknown	1	5	6

After studying spirit possession and shamanism in primitive
societies, I. M. Lewis concluded that accusatory fits are "thinly
disguised protest movements directed against the dominant sex.
They thus play a significant part in the sex-war in traditional
societies and cultures where women lack more obvious and direct
means of forwarding their aims. To a considerable extent, they
protect women from the exactions of men and offer an effective
vehicle for manipulating husbands and male relatives."[51] Lewis's
conclusion is equally applicable to Salem Village. There, in the
paranoid atmosphere of 1692, girls used the fit—although not
necessarily consciously—as a vehicle to invert the traditional social

status hierarcy. Similarly, adult women, those perpetual children, expressed, through the fit, a need for excitement and dominion. For females, such assertion entailed, symbolically and on occasion literally, the elimination of the immediate oppressing force—the adult, the husband, or, in Mercy Short's case, the Indians. The bewitched parties, through their accusations, did help to eliminate authority figures—if not actual parents or husbands, whose destruction would be *too* discomforting or would deprive them of necessary support, then surely "representative" substitutions. A female figure suggestive of parental authority by her mature years, or one closely associated with a male of high position, was frequently chosen as a safer but still satisfactory surrogate.[52] Later, as the afflicted girls achieved more self-confidence, they actually attacked men, including at least two ministers.

All of the afflicted women, most particularly the Salem Village girls, exercised fantastic power. The public watched spellbound while the girls contorted their bodies into unbelievable shapes. Magistrates hung on their every word, believing them even when the girls were caught in outright lies.[53] At least one justice changed his opinion of a prominent friend after that man came under accusation.[54] Accused witches hardly knew what to say, save to maintain their innocence, when confronted by the awesome spectacle of girls throwing themselves about the courtroom, pulling four-inch-long pins and broken knife blades out of their own flesh. Some accused witches even became confused as to their own complicity in such goings on.[55] Anyone who criticized the court proceedings or the afflicted quickly fell under accusation as another witch, including even defecting members of the girls' own group.[56]

As early as March 20 the afflicted proved they could also, on occasion, assume a more self-consciously assertive stance. When Deodat Lawson prepared to give a Sabbath lecture, eleven-year-old Abigail Williams shouted out, "Now stand up, and Name your Text." In the beginning of his sermon Goodwife Ann Pope told him, "Now there is enough of that," and after it was finished, Williams asserted, "It is a long Text." Twelve-year-old Anne Putnam shouted out that an invisible yellow bird, a witch's familiar, sat on Lawson's hat as it hung on a pin. In the afternoon sermon Williams again spoke up: "I know no Doctrine you had," she informed the minister, "If you did name one, I have forgot it."[57] Such outspokenness dumbfounded the congregation. Here three females had violated the biblical injunction against women speaking in church; furthermore, a little girl had criticized the minister. Obviously witches were to blame!

Not only had such females assumed the power to speak in church, and to designate men and women as witches; they also claimed the ability to vanquish supernatural creatures. They asserted that they could see and talk to the Devil, yet emerge unscathed from those encounters. Tituba, powerless both as servant and as woman, told imaginative tales of her own fearless contact with frightening spectral creatures—hairy upright men and great black dogs.[58] Another "very sober and pious woman," uncowed by a malign specter's appearance, disputed with it about a scriptural text.[59] Mercy Short, a fifteen-year-old Boston girl who two years before had watched while Indians cut down her frontier family, in her fits dared the Devil (interestingly enough, a man "of Tawny, or an Indian colour") to kill her: "Is my Life in Your Hands? No, if it had, You had killed me long before this Time!—What's that?—So you can!—Do it then if You can.—Poor Fool! . . . . What? Will you Burn all Boston and shall I bee Burnt in that Fire?—No, tis not in Your Power." Although "Satan" was able to cause her much physical pain, she ultimately emerged victorious in their confrontations by relying upon the transcendent power of God. Always assertive while in her fits (although she did not blame witches for them), Mercy Short hardly hesitated to call one onlooker a fool when that person objected to singing a psalm which Mercy had requested.[60]

Power and influence were not the only deep-seated impulses revealed by the fit. Filled with what Marion Starkey has called "repressed vitality, with all manner of cravings and urges for which village life afforded no outlet," the bewitched girls of Salem Village danced and sang for several hours at Job Tyler's house. Ephraim Foster's wife also danced at her home, and Martha Sprague sang for nearly an hour—both ostensibly under the influence of witchcraft.[61] Mercy Short's torments sometimes "turned into Frolicks; and she became as extravagant as a Wild-Cat." Margaret Rule laughed much and would drink nothing but rum in her fits. When Sarah Ingersoll accused one girl of lying about Goody Proctor's witchcraft, that girl placed this need for joy on an overtly conscious level by declaring simply, "they must have some sport."[62]

Repressed sexuality also emerged as a theme in the behavior of some of the afflicted, in the charges levied, and in the confessions of "witches." In her fits Ann Pope suffered a "grievous torment in her

Bowels as if they were torn out,"[63] which may have been a manifestation of her sexual fears, since the bowels were considered the seat of passion. Mary Warren, age twenty, believed that a spectral nineteen-year-old male witch sat on her stomach, and she sometimes crossed her legs together so tightly that "it was impossible for the strongest man ther to [uncross] them, without Breaking her Leggs."[64] Such behavior is frequently observed in sexually repressed hysterical women. Margaret Rule reacted with obvious sensual appreciation when Cotton Mather rubbed her stomach to calm her, but she greeted a similar well-meaning effort by a female attendant with the words "don't you meddle with me." In her fits she loved being "brush'd" or "rub'd," as long as it was "in the right place." Sometimes she wished only men to view her afflictions; once "haveing hold of the hand of a Young-man, said to have been her Sweet-heart formerly, who was withdrawing; She pull'd him again into his Seat, saying he should not go to Night."[65]

At times the sexual theme was even more explicit, although not as much as it often was in European witchcraft proceedings. One girl cried out that witch John Alden "sells powder and shot to the Indians and lies with Indian squaws and has Indian papooses."[66] Two "witches," Bridget Bishop and Elizabeth Proctor, reportedly afflicted while dressed only in their shifts—by Puritan standards, a most seductive approach.[67] "Witch" Rebecca Eames admitted giving the Devil her "soul & body"; then, in "horror of Conscience," she took a rope to hang herself and a razor to cut her throat "by Reason of her great sin in committing adultery." Mercy Wardwell, daughter of the hanged "witch" Samuel Wardwell, confessed to having sexual relations with Satan after "people told her yt she should Neuer hath such a Young Man who loved her." Abigail Hobbs also admitted giving herself "body and soul to the Old Boy."[68]

In the increasingly secular world of the 1690s, Satan reputedly offered alluring temptations to Puritan women—"Carnal and Sensual Lusts," wine, "pretty handsome apparell," a horse to facilitate physical mobility, "a piece of money," "a pair of French fall shoes," "gold and many fine things." When asked how Satan had approached them, many confessed "witches" explained that they were "Discontent at their mean Condition in the World" and wished to sample the many joys he offered. They asserted that feasting, dancing, and jollity were the rule at witch meetings.[69] Witches indulged in all those pleasures that good Puritans detested—the

same pleasures that had gained so many adherents in these changing times. Regardless of whether they were sincere or merely
prompted by the desire to escape execution, such confessions
helped fuel both the spreading panic of the general community and
the fervor of the most active accusers—not only because they *were*
confessions, but also because their details echoed the same forbidden impulses with which their accusers, as well as many of the
courtroom spectators, were grievously "afflicted."

The nine ringleaders of the Salem Village accusations included
the daughter and niece of the minister, the daughter of a church
deacon, and the wife and daughter of the parish clerk. Since material luxuries, expressions of vitality, and power impulses were not
completely acceptable, especially to women who had grown
up in very religious families, the psychosomatic pain experienced
in fits, and the afflicted's obsession with imagining "Coffins, and
bodies in shrowds" calling out for vengeance against their witch-
murderers,[70] manifested the accusing women's guilt at the unac-
ceptability of their own disowned impulses. Caught between their
training and their desires, there was no resolution, save in laying
the blame for the latter on someone who by definition epitomized,
in a fully malign way, those same impulses. Condemning the witch
purged the self. Projecting the self into accusations of witchcraft
helped religious women and envious adolescents to deal with the
change in the female sex role which began occurring gradually after
1665. They were able to resist such change, while on another level
giving explosive expression to it behind the fit's veil.

The choice of victims, many of them eccentrics, suggests that the
bewitched females were most discomforted by those women who
had acted upon their own inner needs to ignore or defy the ideal
feminine sex role; i.e., those women who best illustrated the projected desires of the afflicted. Unable to be similarly assertive, the
accusers turned instead to equally unfeminine, but disguised and
purely destructive, aggression in punishing those nontraditional
women. The psychoanalyst Merell Middlemore appears correct
when he writes that the Salem Village girls could not "consolidate a
female identification"—but only if his remark is qualified to read
Puritan, or perhaps seventeenth-century, female identification.[71]

Scapegoating witches did not always work for the individual
accuser, as the shocking inhumanity of sending people to the gallows sometimes became too much for the afflicted girls to handle.
Some initial accusers ceased to have fits or to denounce witches long
before the frenzy abated. Mary Warren, after actively accusing a

number of witches, suddenly began to charge that the "afflicted children did but dissemble." Immediately she was cried out upon as a witch, but in prison she continued to speak out against the proceedings, asserting several times that the magistrates "might as well examine Keysar's daughter that had been distracted many years." She explained, "when I was afflicted, I thought I saw the apparitions of a hundred persons," but then added that her head had been "distempered." In court, however, the other girls, Ann Pope, and John Indian attributed their violent fits to her, and under stringent cross-examination Mary Warren fell once again into fits. Imprisoned for a month, she finally retracted her criticism, admitted her own witchcraft, and once more began accusing others.[72] Similarly, when Deliverance Hobbs wavered from her accusatory afflictions, the bewitched girls denounced her. She, like Mary Warren, denied signing the Devil's book, but then, under the magistrates' relentless questioning, also admitted her witchcraft.[73] Another of the girls, Sarah Churchill, fell under suspicion of practicing witchcraft, probably for the same reason. After her examination she cried and appeared "much troubled in spirit." She explained to Sarah Ingersoll that she had confessed her *maleficium* only "because they threatened her, and told her they would put her into the dungeon."[74]

The line between witch and bewitched was dangerously thin, both on the psychological level and in terms of the social distribution of power which an accuser manipulated. Once a woman began having fits in which she declared herself afflicted by agents of Satan, she could afford no second thoughts, however sane and humane. Once she had "sold her soul"—that is, disavowed responsibility for her own deepest impulses—she could not recover it without sharing the fate of her accused victims, without becoming as powerless as they in the grip of the larger Puritan community.

The Accused: Innocent Victims of Circumstance

Many of the alleged witches fell under suspicion not for any personal deviance, but because friction existed between families who contended over land. When some failed to secure satisfaction from the county courts or town meetings, they themselves, or women in their families, could easily accuse opponents of witchcraft in order to get even. In this respect, the 1692 outbreak represented a new departure in the history of seventeenth-century New England witchcraft. Previous witch-scapegoat accusations had been hurled at community eccentrics; in Essex County, however, because of the extreme level of anxiety prevailing, the witch's character in many instances became irrelevant. The Salem Village bewitched included at least three females who would have been privy to the antagonisms between the Putnams and their neighbors. As Boyer and Nissenbaum have pointed out, the Putnams, a fairly well-to-do family with old roots, envied the prosperity of the *nouveau riche* Porters, who had close ties to Salem mercantile interests. Accusations followed, not of patriarch Israel Porter—perhaps because he was related by marriage to Judge John Hathorne—but of persons more distantly connected to the family. The bewitched girls charged Daniel Andrews, who was the husband of Sarah Porter, a schoolmaster, an ex-deputy to the General Court, the owner of a Salem apothecary shop, and one of the four wealthiest men in Salem Village.[75] Another "witch," Philip English, a confederate of the Porters, owned an imposing house in Salem, fourteen town lots, and twenty sailing vessels. He fled with his wife, Mary, rather than appear before the Court of Oyer and Terminer.[76] Andrews's brother-in-law George Jacobs, Jr., and Jacobs's wife and daughter faced prosecution, as did Andrews's tenant Peter Cloyse, his wife, and the wife of a servant in John Porter's household.[77] Francis Nurse, the brother-in-law of Cloyse, had long antagonized the Putnams, by living on land which Nathaniel Putnam claimed and by his ties to Salem, where he had served as constable. Despite her reputation as a holy and God-fearing person, Nurse's wife, Rebecca, was hanged for practicing *maleficium*.[78] Altogether, twelve of fourteen accused Salem Village witches lived in the eastern part of the village, near Salem, as did twenty-four of twenty-nine witch defenders, whereas thirty of thirty-two accusers lived in the west.[79] Chart 13.3 indicates the connections between twenty-three "witches" at Salem Village.

Because the Putnams had also become involved in land disputes with some inhabitants of Topsfield, the afflicted girls and the Putnams accused the most economically and politically important persons at Topsfield—those most able to injure the Putnam cause. Charges were filed against Isaac Easty, who was a selectman, tithingman, surveyor of highways, and member of many different town committees, as well as against his wife, Mary. The latter was hanged on September 22, two months after her sister Rebecca Nurse. Sarah Wilds, mother of the Topsfield town constable, was also hanged, on July 19.[80]

Antagonism over land existed on a more local level in Topsfield as well. The Hows and Perleys had argued over property boundaries; ten-year-old Hannah Perley accused the entire How family of afflicting her, and on July 19 Elizabeth How was hanged. Mistress How's brother and her nephew were also accused.[81] Similar antagonisms affected the Wild and Gould families. After John Wild's first wife, Rebecca Gould, died, inheritance problems arose between the two families, both of whom were in the wealthiest one-fifth of Topsfield's taxpayers. John Wild testified against John Gould in a treason case in 1686; subsequently Gould's sister too began spreading witchcraft stories about Sarah Wild. These tales stopped when Wild threatened to sue Gould for slander. In 1692 such charges resurfaced, along with accusations against Wild's daughter and son-in-law, Sarah and Edward Bishop. The Goulds were aided in their accusations by the Putnams, to whom they were related by marriage. John Gould had earlier become co-owner, with Nathaniel Putnam, of the Rowley ironworks.[82]

Local friction also erupted at Andover, where no fewer than fifty-five "witches" faced accusations. Philip Greven has reported a heightened concern over Andover land titles after 1662, the result of first-generation monopolization of community land. In the 1660s the townsmen reduced the amount of realty available to those newcomers who wished to take up estates. Notwithstanding this, "outsiders" purchased 67.8 percent of all lots offered for sale between 1668 and 1686; still, they never enjoyed much status in the community. Joseph Ballard, one of these "outsiders," brought the Salem Village girls into Andover to point out his ill wife's afflicters. The resultant accusations soon came to reflect the "great Controversie in ye towne, about giving out land," as charges were levied against nine of Andover's thirteen wealthiest families (in terms of land allotted before 1662). Twenty-nine of the fifty-five accused witches were either nuclear family members, descendants, or related by marriage to these nine, who belonged to the Bradstreet, Osgood, Parker, Fryer, Stevens, Barker, Dane, Faulkner, and Tyler families.[83] Chart 13.4 shows the family connections between these "witches."

The Accused: Nontraditional Women

While many witches served as scapegoat-victims of various men's land greed, others more clearly fitted the image of social deviants. Women who did not toe the ideal feminine line offered the afflicted

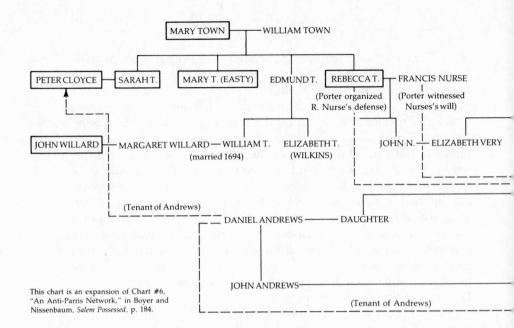

Chart 13.3
Connections Between Various "Witches" at Salem Village

This chart is an expansion of Chart #6, "An Anti-Parris Network," in Boyer and Nissenbaum, *Salem Possessed*, p. 184.

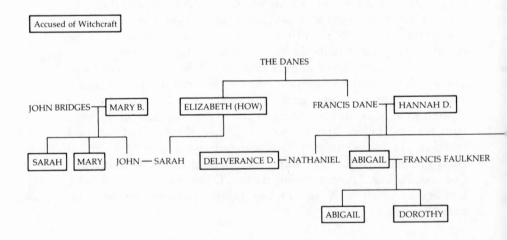

Chart 13.4
Connections Between Various "Witches" at Andover

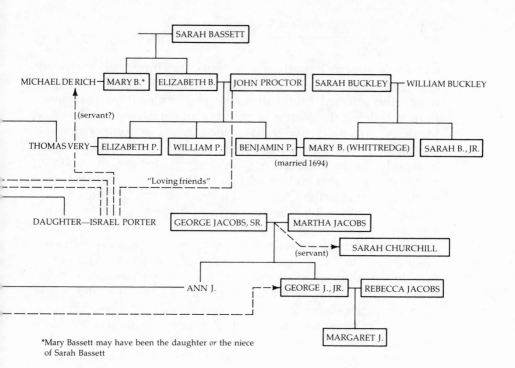

SARAH BASSETT

MICHAEL DE RICH — MARY B.* — ELIZABETH B. — JOHN PROCTOR   SARAH BUCKLEY — WILLIAM BUCKLEY

| (servant?)

THOMAS VERY — ELIZABETH P.   WILLIAM P.   BENJAMIN P. — MARY B. (WHITTREDGE)   SARAH B., JR.

(married 1694)

"Loving friends"

DAUGHTER—ISRAEL PORTER   GEORGE JACOBS, SR. — MARTHA JACOBS

(servant)   SARAH CHURCHILL

ANN J.   GEORGE J., JR. — REBECCA JACOBS

MARGARET J.

*Mary Bassett may have been the daughter *or* the niece
of Sarah Bassett

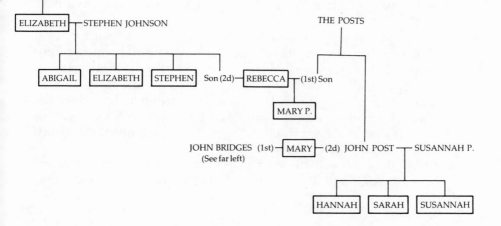

ELIZABETH — STEPHEN JOHNSON   THE POSTS

ABIGAIL   ELIZABETH   STEPHEN   Son (2d) — REBECCA — (1st) Son

MARY P.

JOHN BRIDGES (1st) — MARY — (2d) JOHN POST — SUSANNAH P.
(See far left)

HANNAH   SARAH   SUSANNAH

females a superb opportunity to work out their own projected aggressions and needs for dominion—those unacceptable urges which the afflicted found desirable yet incompatible with their Puritan training. In what was probably an overstatement, Thomas Maule estimated that two-thirds of the accused were either guilty of rebellion against their parents (who included, in Puritan terms, husbands and magistrates) or of adultery.[84] One, Sarah Osborne, had lived in a common law relationship with her "wild" Irish servant; another, Martha Corey, had given birth to a mulatto child.[85] "Witch" Susannah Roots had earned a reputation as a "bad woman" who entertained company late at night.[86]

Those women who had openly flouted the ideal role in the changing world of the late century received quick convictions. One of the first three persons accused, Sarah Good, was such a woman. Born into a wealthy family, she had been cheated out of her inheritance after her father's suicide in 1672. She married twice, both times to men who became debt ridden. By 1689 her second husband, William Good, had lost all of his land and seventeen head of cattle to his creditors. Too poor to own a house, he lived with Sarah and their infant daughter in neighbors' houses, barns, and sometimes open ditches. Turbulent and vitriolic, Sarah Good often scolded and "fell to muttering" when people extended charity to her. When one neighbor refused her lodging, she was not above setting his cattle loose. In court she answered the magistrates "in a very wicked spiteful manner, reflecting and retorting against the authorities with base and abusive words." After the minister Nicholas Noyes urged her to confess, since "she knew she was a witch," Sarah pulled no punches in lashing out, "you are a liar; I am no more a Witch than you are a Wizard; and if you take away my Life, God will give you Blood to drink." She died on July 19, protesting to the end.[87]

Bridget Bishop, the first "witch" hanged, would not be dominated by her three husbands. She operated an unlicensed tavern where visitors congregated late at night to play the illegal game of shuffleboard, and she dressed provocatively—some of her contemporaries might say whorishly—in a red paragon bodice. Once she had driven an accusatory stranger off her porch with a spade. Like so many other alleged witches, she protested her innocence, asserting, "I know not what a witch is."[88]

Martha Carrier, accused of no less than thirteen witchly murders at Andover, had actively disputed with neighbors over land, physically shaken up one twelve-year-old girl in church, and threatened a male opponent by saying that "She would hold his Nose close to the Grindstone as ever it was held since his Name was Abbot." Her interrogator asked at the witch trials, "What black man did you see?" She retorted, "I saw no black man but your own presence." She charged the magistrates with not listening to what she said, while they "shamefully" paid attention to every little utterance of the bewitched girls. Cotton Mather, detesting her outspokenness, termed her "this rampant hag."[89]

Many other witches revealed their deviance both in and out of court. Abigail Hobbs expressed no fear of lying out in the woods at night, explaining that "she was not afraid of any thing." Disobedient to her parents, she had once sprinkled water in her mother's face, saying she "baptised hir in the name of the Father Son and Holy Ghost."[90] Susannah Martin of Amesbury, long accounted a witch, spoke harshly to neighbors, accused the girls of "dealing in the Black Art," and pointed out (to the magistrates' chagrin) that the Old Testament described Satan's appearance in the shape of an innocent, one "glorified Saint."[91] Mary Parker had once shocked her associates by coming to the tavern after her husband and there "railing" at him.[92] Ann Pudeator possessed a long-standing reputation as "an ill-carriaged woman," while Mary Obinson several times abused Thomas Hill, calling him "cuckold & old foole." Mammy Read had the gall to tell Mistress Symmes, after an argument, that she wished her antagonist "might never piss, nor shit, if she did not goe [i. e., leave]."[93] Read, Pudeator, Martin, Carrier, and Bishop all swung from the gallows, but Hobbs received a reprieve after her conviction. No further record exists of Obinson's case. Whether any of these women actually practiced witchcraft cannot now be determined, but it is unlikely.[94] The fact that women in 1692 had more freedom than ever before—a reality produced in part by the lack of witchcraft prosecutions after 1665—would presumably have decreased the need for "rebels" against the feminine ideal to assume the totally malign inversion of the proper role. The clarity and force of the earlier typologies of Witch and Whore, as well as Virgin and Wife, had considerably weakened by the 1690s, only to dramatically resurface in 1692.

Despite their realizations that they faced a death sentence, most of the accused women refused to insure their own releases by concocting confessions. Instead, they "would neither in time of Examination, nor Trial, Confess any thing of what was laid to their

Charge; some would not admit of any Minister to Pray with them, others refused to pray for themselves."[95] Nineteen women died protesting their innocence, including five in prison. One of the hanged "witches," Mary Easty, knowing that she could not save her own life, wished to save those "that are going the same way with myself." She urged the Salem Court to examine carefully all confessing witches who accused others, for, she explained, they "have belyed themselves and others."[96]

Those women who walked bravely to the gallows may have summoned strength from their religious faith, or from recognition of the integrity of their own personhood. Other women signed petitions supporting accused witches, even though such petitioners should have been aware that the afflicted girls quickly accused their critics. Two Putnam opponents, Israel and Elizabeth Porter, headed a petition signed by sixteen other women and twenty-one men on behalf of Rebecca Nurse. Another thirteen men and seven of their wives requested leniency for the Proctors. At Salisbury fifty-eight women and fifty-seven men, neighbors of "witch"' Mary Bradbury, asserted they had never heard that Bradbury "ever had any difference or falleing oute wth any of her neighbors man woman or childe but was always, readie and willing to doe for them wt laye in her power night and day, though wth hazard of her health or other danger more." Twelve women and forty-one men of Andover also petitioned for the release of their accused neighbors.[97] No one, however, argued on behalf of the nontraditional women accused.

During the trials, from time to time an occasional unaccused woman went so far as to attack the character of one or more of the afflicted. For example, Lydia Porter charged Goody Bibber with mischief-making and lying.[98] Mary Phips, the wife of the governor, expressed her own disagreement by pardoning one convicted witch in the governor's absence, although she had no legal power to do so.[99] Lady Phips, Lydia Porter, and the almost one hundred female petitioners, as well as many of the "witches," were acting assertively in varying degrees, reflecting and contributing to the style of the nontraditional woman.

An End to Witchcraft

As witchcraft accusations increased in number, protests also mounted, from men as well as from women. Husbands spoke up in defense of their wives.[100] Ex-deputy Robert Pike told Justice Corwin that "diabolical visions, apparitions or representations" were "more commonly false and delusive then real," also pointing out that the afflicted women raised the dead, like the Witch of Endor in biblical times.[101] A Salem Quaker named Thomas Maule anonymously blasted the Puritans for murdering one another under the Devil's influence, and as early as June the Anabaptist William Milbourne protested to the General Court against the use of "bare specter testimonie" to convict "persons of good fame and of unspotted reputations."[102] A Boston merchant by the name of Thomas Brattle, in an October letter, penned a scathing criticism of the Salem proceedings.[103] At about the same time Samuel Willard published a disapproving analysis of the arguments used against witches, in *Some Miscellany Observations on our Present Debates Respecting Witchcraft, In a Dialogue between S[alem] and B[oston]*. Cotton Mather had begun to doubt the reality of specter evidence, while other ministers, including Joshua Moody, John Hale, John Wise, Francis Dane, James Allen, and John Baily, raised objections to the proceedings. Willard and Moody took occasion to preach the text, "they that are persecuted in one city, let them flee to another," and then counselled four "witches" to escape from prison.[104]

The afflicted girls ultimately insured that the witchcraft proceedings would halt—by accusing the most prestigious members of Puritan society. The girls had first charged contentious, penniless Sarah Good, disreputable Sarah Osborne, and the exotic Barbadian Indian slave Tituba. Sensing their own power in the court's response, they subsequently broadened their attack by clamoring not only against low-status eccentrics, but also against virtuous women like Rebecca Nurse, and even against men. On May 31 attorney Thomas Newton would assert that they "spare no person of what quality so ever."[105] By November the bewitched had charged the wives of critics Moody, Hale, and Dane, as well as several members of Boston's ruling elite. However, the authorities were reluctant to prosecute. Margaret Thatcher, the widow of Boston's wealthiest merchant and mother-in-law of Judge Jonathan Corwin, who presided at witchcraft trials, escaped apprehension, even though she was much complained about by the afflicted. So did Mary Phips, Samuel Willard, and Mistress Moody. The magistrates did issue a warrant for the arrest of a prominent merchant named Hezekiah Usher, but he received lodging in a private house and then was permitted to leave the colony.[106]

Bostonians had less respect for the orders of the Salem Court than

did the citizenry of any other area; their constables ignored warrants. Accused witches broke out of prison altogether too easily,
suggesting complicity on the part of the jailor. In fact, the keeper
had no apparent hesitancy about releasing one "witch" upon receipt
of Lady Phips's pardon.[107] Other Bostonians hid "witches" who had
escaped from prison or fled apprehension.

The Salem Village girls who accused proper Bostonians quite
possibly exploited the resentment of many rural Salem Villagers for
those alien yet very powerful urbanites who often valued capital
over land, commerce over husbandry, ornamentation over simplic-
ity, and new ideas over old. The Putnams, in particular, facing
diminishing land resources and declining status, had a good deal to
resent; they listened with open ears while the girls accused nine
prominent Bostonians and denounced Nathaniel Saltonstall, the
Haverhill Councillor who had resigned his seat on the witch
court.[108] Those with Boston connections also faced prosecution. In
Andover, for example, three prominent Bradstreets—a family with
close marital and political ties to Boston's ruling elite—fled prosecution.[109] Before the witchcraft frenzy had abated, even the secretary
of Connecticut had been denounced.[110]

Perhaps nothing better illustrates many people's dislike for the
merchant class than the destruction wrought against the property of
the wealthy French Huguenot, Philip English. (There was undoubtedly some anti-French feeling involved in English's case as
well.) After English and his "aristocratic" wife, Mary, escaped from
Salem prison, an irate group of citizens sacked their "great house" at
Salem, destroying or carrying away various old family portraits and
furniture and robbing storehouses of goods valued at £2,683. When
English later returned, he found a single servant's bed the only
furniture remaining in the house.[111]

The colony's economic and political leaders objected to the accusations levied against so many of their friends and wives. Quite
probably their objections were crucial in bringing the frenzy to a
halt. Robert Calef credited one prominent Bostonian with stopping
proceedings at Andover by threatening to sue his accusers there in a
£1,000 defamation action.[112] Governor William Phips initially left all
witchcraft affairs to the Court of Oyer and Terminer, but after
returning to Boston from an expedition against the Maine Indians
he found "many persons in a strange ferment of disatisfaction."
Soon the royal governor forbade the issuance of any new literature
on the subject, asked the Crown for counsel, and dissolved the

Court of Oyer and Terminer. In the winter of 1692–93 Phips pardoned some convicted witches, caused some to be let out on bail, and "put the Judges upon considering a way to relieve others and prevent them from perishing in prison." The General Court on December 16, 1692, directed the newly created Superior Court to try the "witches" still in custody within Essex County. The Superior Court, meeting on January 3, 1692/3, acquitted forty-nine "witches" and convicted three. Deputy Governor Stoughton, the chief justice, ordered the execution of those three, as he had of other "witches," but Phips pardoned these and five other convicted persons.[113] Stoughton, enraged, refused to sit on the bench of the next court at Charlestown. That body released all the accused persons tried before it.[114]

Before the Superior Court met at Salem, the bewitched girls had ceased their afflictions. Perhaps by then they had realized that their reach exceeded their grasp. Perhaps they felt guilty over precipitating the deaths of twenty-five persons. Perhaps their power impulses had been satiated. (After all, for some time people as far away as Boston, Andover, and Gloucester had sought their advice in pointing out witches.) Perhaps they were drained by the physical and emotional strain which attended fits. Perhaps they felt purged, for a time, of their own unfeminine longings. For whatever reasons, they *had* had their day; now it seemed only appropriate that they return to their status as unobtrusive members of the Puritan community. Only in Boston did two girls, Mary Watkins and Margaret Rule, continue to have fits during 1693.[115]

More than forty Massachusetts residents had suffered from hysterical fits in 1692 and 1693, accusing over two hundred persons of witchcraft. While Massachusetts was not the only colony to experience such an outbreak, the events in Connecticut, where for the first time in three decades the courts also began trying several "witches," ultimately produced a very different outcome. In late 1692 and early 1693, a seventeen-year-old French maidservant at Fairfield assumed the hysterical fit pattern of the Bay Colony's afflicted persons. Catherine Branch sometimes acted as one struck dumb, "put out her tong to a great extent," and experienced "a pinching & pricking at her breast." Like many at Salem Village, she sought the joys of "Singing, Laughing, Eating, [and] Rideing" in her fits. As she threw herself convulsively about, she complained of six different witches afflicting her.[116] The accused included among their small numbers both the virtuous and the unholy.

Mercy Disborough, the only one of these "witches" to receive the
death sentence, had the worst reputation; she had tossed harsh
words at many men in the community and had earned a
general reputation as a witch before 1692.[117] Elizabeth Clawson, on
the other hand, never spoke threatening words. Believing in the
motto "we must liue in pease," she often served as a mediator
whenever her neighbors argued.[118]

Unlike many Essex County inhabitants, those in Fairfield County
had a more skeptical attitude about witchcraft. Some thought
Catherine Branch "desembled." Abigail Wescott, her mistress, said
none of the girl's accusations held any validity; she reportedly
claimed that Branch "was such a Lying girl that not any boddy
Could belieue one word what she said." Sarah Betts wished to treat
the young woman's bewitchment through medicinal bloodletting,
while Sarah Ketcham expressed disbelief that any witches at all
existed in Fairfield.[119] Men also objected to Branch's charges, and
the special Court of Oyer and Terminer held at Fairfield on September 15, 1692, freed all the accused save Mercy Disborough; she
received a death sentence, but later (in May 1693) the Connecticut
General Assembly granted her a reprieve. On October 17, 1692, a
meeting of Connecticut ministers held the water test to be "unlaw-
full and sinfull," rejected special evidence, considered "unusuall
excrescencies" or teats no proof of witchcraft, dismissed strange
accidents as no evidence whatsoever, and expressed the view that
Catherine Branch was deluded by the Devil.[120] Two successive trials
of "witches" resulted in acquittals. Like the Salem Village girls,
Branch had made a play for power, but she could not convince her
associates of the legitimacy of her claims.

Connecticut was not ripe for a witch hunt. A progressive ministry
helped to undercut any accusatory zeal there. Although the colony's residents certainly experienced much tension between 1689
and 1692, their general anxiety level did not equal that of their Bay
Colony neighbors. Political affairs were volatile, but the relative
isolation and independence of towns defused the political turmoil.
Land antagonisms, although emergent, had not reached serious
proportions.[121] The conflict between rural and urban lifestyles, so
clear at Salem Village, was insignificant in this almost completely
agrarian colony. The concern over moral decay was somewhat less
extreme than in Massachusetts. Connecticut did not have to suffer
the frightening effects of a witch hunt; instead, residents could cope
with stress through less harsh actions, such as voting to catechize all

"Bachelors and boys from eight years ould and upwards . . . once a fortnight on the Lords Daye in Ye meeting house."[122]

The inhabitants of Maine, New Hampshire, and Plymouth had no concern about witches. In Maine, the Indian problem diverted attention from any occult concerns, while both the "red devils" and political factionalism had the same effect in New Hampshire. In both areas real enemies abounded, and neither had a history of witchcraft accusations. In Plymouth, the basic problem—a high tax rate—was alleviated through incorporation into the Bay Colony.

Only in eastern Massachusetts, with its intense and numerous frustrations, could a sustained witch hunt be mounted. There the reality of the nontraditional woman loomed larger, helping to pre-cipitate fits in powerless adolescents and religious Puritan wives, as well as aggravating the already established tendency to view unfeminine behavior as witchlike. Those independent-spirited women who faced prosecution as witches were the victims of other, more conservative women's unconscious search for power.

1. Lovejoy, *Glorious Revolution in Am.*, pp. 277–93, 325–28, 331–33, 340–42.

2. Dunn, *Puritans and Yankees*, p. 259; Lovejoy, *Glorious Revolution in Am.*, pp. 167–80, 243–45, 350.

3. Sainsbury & Headlam, eds., *Cal. of State Papers*, XIII, 40 (no. 129). In 1689 Increase Mather estimated that one in twenty adults was an Anglican (*Vindication of N. Eng.*, II, 42).

4. G. Dow, *Pirates of N. Eng. Coast*, pp. 31–43, 54–83.

5. Sainsbury & Headlam, eds., *Calendar of State Papers*, XIII, 255 (no. 862).

6. "Gov. Simon Bradstreet and Council to the Agents, Nov. 29, 1690," in Whitmore, ed., *Andros Tracts*, III, 53–54; Scottow, *Old Men's Tears*, p. 15.

7. Lovejoy, *Glorious Revolution in Am.*, pp. 350–51.

8. Miller, *N. Eng. Mind: From Col. to Prov.*, p. 162; Breen, *Character of the Good Ruler*, p. 173.

9. C. Mather, *Fair Weather*, p. 25.

10. *By Gov. & Gen. Ct. of Mass., March 13, 1689/90*, p. 1.

11. *Ibid.,*; Mather quoted in Miller, *N. Eng. Mind: From Col. to Prov.*, p. 162; Palmer, *Impartial Account of N. Eng.*, p. 27.

12. C. Mather, *Memorable Prov.*, p. 22.

13. Sainsbury & Headlam, eds., *Calendar of State Papers*, XIII, 400 (no. 1374); Lovejoy, *Glorious Revolution in Am.*, pp. 248–50; Dunn, *Puritans & Yankees*, pp. 286–302; Bulkeley, *Will & Doom*, pp. 69–269.

14. Bulkeley, *Will & Doom*, pp. 76, 133; Sainsbury & Headlam, eds., *Calendar of State Papers*, XIII, 400 (no. 1374), 521 (no. 1691), 585 (no. 1987), 644 (no. 2247).

15. *Hoadly Memorial*, p. 51.

16. Sainsbury & Headlam, eds., *Calendar of State Papers*, XIII, 267 (no. 886), 400 (no. 1374), 474 (no. 1585), 759 (no. 2763), 760 (no. 2766).

17. Bulkeley, *Will & Doom*, p. 216; C. Mather, *Wonders of Invisible World*, p. 22; "Council of Conn. to Council of Mass., May 28, 1690," in *Wyllys Papers*, p. 320.

18. S. Bradstreet & Council, "Letter to Agents," in Whitmore, ed., *Andros Tracts*, III, 53.

19. Lovejoy, *Glorious Revolution in Am.*, pp. 245–46; Langdon, *Pilgrim Colony*, pp. 238–42; C. Mather, *Letters*, p. 21.

20. Bowen, "1690 Tax Revolt of Plym. Col. Towns"; Langdon, *Pilgrim Colony*, pp. 233–34, 238–40.

21. Sainsbury & Headlam, eds., *Calendar of State Papers*, XIII, 140–41 (no. 407), 212 (no. 740), 528 (no. 1726); Lovejoy, *Glorious Revolution in Am.*, pp. 351–52.

22. Bouton, ed., *Prov. Papers of N. Hamp.*, II, 30–56; Belknap, *Hist. of N. Hamp.*, I, 237–50.

23. Boyer & Nissenbaum, *Salem Possessed*, pp. 86–91; Towne & Clark, "Topsfield in the Witchcraft Delusion," pp. 24–26. While the value of the average Salem Village estate grew by one-third between 1661 and 1681, the size of the average landholding decreased by half—from almost 250 acres in the 1660s to 124 acres in 1690.

24. Boyer & Nissenbaum, *Salem Possessed*, p. 109.

25. Boyer and Nissenbaum give an excellent description of the very real powerlessness existing at Salem Village; *ibid.*, pp. 30–79, 107–8.

26. *Ibid.*, pp. 45, 163, 66, 86, 94: "Jeremiah Watts to George Burroughs, April 11, 1682," in Boyer & Nissenbaum, eds., *Salem-Village Witchcraft*, pp. 170–71.

27. Boyer & Nissenbaum, *Salem Possessed*, pp. 180, 106. Several other observers have explained the Salem Village witch hunt with reference to the effect of stress and religio-political-social change, including Bednarski, "Salem Witch-Scare Viewed Sociologically," pp. 151–63; Miller, *N. Eng. Mind: From Col. to Prov.*, pp. 19–208; and Ziff, *Puritanism in Am.*, pp. 242–50.

28. Lawson, *Brief & True Narrative*, pp. 153–55: Calef, *More Wonders of Invisible World*, p. 342.

29. Lawson, *Brief & True Narrative*, pp. 151–54.

30. Samuel Parris, "Christ Knows How Many Devils There Are," in Boyer & Nissenbaum, eds., *Salem-Village Witchcraft*, pp. 129–31.

31. For a good description of Parris's character, see Boyer & Nissenbaum, *Salem Possessed*, pp. 153–78.

32. Corey quoted in Upham, *Salem Witchcraft*, II, 45.

33. Towne & Clark, "Topsfield in the Witchcraft Delusion."

34. Lockridge, "Land, Population & Evolution," supplies general information on the declining size of estates throughout Massachusetts.

35. Barker in "Salem Witchcraft—1692," I, n.p.; Post in "Ct. Files—Suffolk Co.," XXXII (1692–93), no. 2705; [Maule,] *N. Eng. Persecutors Mauled*, p. 181.

36. Thompson, "Review Article: Salem Revisited," p. 322.

37. Whether the judges presumed a witch guilty before examining him or her depended, to a large extent, on the witch's respectability. Hathorne and Corwin asked the low-status Sarah Good such questions as "Why do you hurt these children?" "Sarah Good, do you not see now what you have

done?" "Why do you not tell us the truth?" However, with saintly Rebecca Nurse, the tone was much more tentative: "You see these accuse you. Is it true?" "Are you an innocent person, relating to this witchcraft?" "You would do well, if you are guilty, to confess." Cf. examinations in Boyer & Nissenbaum, eds., *Salem-Village Witchcraft*, pp. 5–6, 23–25.

38. Calef, *More Wonders of Invisible World*, p. 355.

39. Foxcroft, "Letter"; Noble, "Doc. Fragments Touching Witchcraft Episode of 1692," pp. 15, 19; Upham, *Salem Witchcraft*, II, 457.

40. Corey refused to enter a plea, apparently to avoid the confiscation of his property upon being found guilty.

41. C. Mather, *Diary*, I, 142.

42. Brattle, "Letter," p. 189. Later, many "witches" repudiated their confessions, explaining that their own fear of execution and the urging of their friends had convinced them to admit to untrue charges. Tituba testified "her master did beat her and other-ways abuse her to make her confess and accuse (such as he called) her sister-witches, and that whatever she said by way of confessing or accusing others was the effect of such usage; her master refused to pay her fees unless she would stand to what she had said." Even before the trials had ended, Sarah Ingersoll, "crying and wringing her hands," repudiated the earlier confession she had made for fear of being tossed into the "dungeon" (Calef, *More Wonders of Invisible World*, pp. 374–75; Upham, *Salem Witchcraft*, II, 169–70).

43. Fowler, "Biog. Sketches of Green, Clark, & Wadsworth," p. 58; Foxcroft, "Letter," p. 80.

44. Calef, *More Wonders of the Invisible World*, p. 363.

45. "Salem Witchcraft—1692," III, n.p.

46. Starkey, *Devil in Mass.*, p. 239.

47. The Cambridge Council stated that Satan "may sometimes have a Permission to Represent an Innocent Person as Tormenting such as are under Diabolical Molestations. But such things are rare and extraordinary, especially when such Matters come before Civil Judicatures." See I. Mather, *Cases of Conscience*, pp. 32, 63.

48. Calef, *More Wonders of Invisible World*, pp. 372–74.

49. Bogart, "Demonism as Function of Status Certainty Loss," pp. 41–42.

50. See ch. 6 for a full treatment of the hysterical fits' psychological dynamics.

51. I. Lewis, *Ecstatic Rel.*, p. 31, also pp. 66–99.

52. John Demos writes that "it is quite probable that adolescent girls in early New England were particularly subject to the control of older women, and this may well have given rise to a powerful underlying resentment. By contrast, the situation must have been less difficult for boys, since their work often took them out of the household and their behavior generally was less restricted." This historian stresses the importance of the defense mechanism of projection in that process, but connects the resentment to severe breast-weaning trauma and not explicitly enough to the position of women in Puritan society. After all, if weaning occurred early, boys and girls would presumably be similarly affected. See Demos, "Underlying Themes in Witchcraft of N. Eng.," pp. 1318–19, 1322–26.

53. Robert Moulton pointed out discrepancies in Susannah Sheldon's stories, asserting that whereas she had once told him that witches had hauled her upon her belly through the yard and over a stone wall, later she contradicted herself by saying she came over the wall through her own power. However, the magistrates ignored Mouton's evidence, as they earlier had ignored the more convincing testimony presented by a young man at Sarah Good's trial. One of the afflicted girls had pulled out half of a knife blade, which she claimed Good had been using to stab her; but the young man produced the remainder of the knife and said the girl had been present when he had thrown away the other half. The Court bade him "not to tell lyes." The judges also swept aside the skepticism of some male jurors and failed to note that most persons who criticized the proceedings were all too readily designated witches (Woodward, ed., *Rec. of Salem Witchcraft*, II, 208; Calef, *More Wonders of Invisible World*, pp. 357–58).

54. Calef, *More Wonders of Invisible World*, pp. 353–54.

55. Sarah Wilson stated "that the afflicted persons crying out of her as afflicting them made her fearfull of herself" and caused her to feel "in the dark as to the matter of her being a witch." Mary Bridges was "told that she certainly was a witch and so made to believe it, though she had no other grounds so to believe" ("Recantation of Confessors of Witchcraft").

56. See pp. 398–99.

57. Lawson, *Brief & True Narrative*, p. 154.

58. Woodward, ed., *Rec. of Salem Witchcraft*, I, 45–47.

59. *Ibid.*, I, 105.

60. C. Mather, *Brand Pluck'd Out of Burning*, pp. 261, 269, 275.

61. Starkey, *Devil in Mass.*, p. 13; "Salem Witchcraft—1692," II, n.p.

62. C. Mather, *Brand Pluck't Out of Burning*, p. 271; Calef, *More Wonders of Invisible World*, p. 327; Woodward, ed., *Rec. of Salem Witchcraft*, I, 115.

63. Lawson, *Brief & True Narrative*, p. 156.

64. Woodward, ed., *Rec. of Salem Witchcraft*, I, 105–6; "Salem Witchcraft —1692," II, III, n.p.

65. Calef, *More Wonders of Invisible World*, pp. 325, 327.

66. *Ibid.*, p. 353.

67. "Salem Witchcraft—1692," I, n.p.; Nevins, *Witchcraft in Salem Village*, p. 170.

68. "Salem Witchcraft—1692," II, III, n.p.; Upham, *Salem Witchcraft*, II, 128–29.

69. Lawson, *Christ's Fidelity the Only Shield*, pp. 116–18; Boyer & Nissenbaum, *Salem Possessed*, p. 210.

70. I. Mather, *Further Account of Tryals*, p. 10.

71. Middlemore unfortunately brings in the "cause" of allegedly deepseated, subconscious "castration anxiety" in the girls to explain a complex phenomenon in a chauvinistic way. Another psychoanalyst's observation that witch hunters become inquisitors to avoid probing their own painful inner assumptions and desires appears more accurate. See Middlemore, "Treatment of Bewitchment in a Puritan Community," p. 57; Rosenman, "Witch Hunter."

72. Upham, *Salem Witchcraft*, II, 114–20.

73. Woodward, ed., *Rec. of Salem Witchcraft*, II, 188.

74. Upham, *Salem Witchcraft*, II, 169–70.

75. Boyer & Nissenbaum, *Salem Possessed*, pp. 120–22, 130–31.

76. *Ibid.*, pp. 131–32.

77. *Ibid.*, p. 182. In 1674 Nathaniel Putnam complained to the magistrates that George Jacobs had driven Putnam's horses into the Ipswich River, threatening to "drown them if he could." Jacobs argued that the horses had trespassed on his property. The justices directed only that Jacobs pay court costs (G. Dow, ed., *Essex Ct. Rec.*, IV, 428).

78. Boyer & Nissenbaum, eds., *Salem-Village Witchcraft*, pp. 48–54; G. Dow, ed., *Essex Ct. Rec.*, V, 117; VI, 8.

79. Boyer & Nissenbaum, *Salem Possessed*, p. 35.

80. Towne & Clark, "Topsfield in the Witchcraft Delusion," pp. 34–36.

81. *Ibid.*

82. W. Davis, "Wildes Family."

83. For description of interfamilial friction at Andover, see Greven, *Four Generations*, pp. 41–65.

84. [Maule,] *N. Eng. Persecutors Mauled*, p. 184.

85. G. Dow, ed., *Essex Ct. Rec.*, III, 5, 402; VI, 374–75; IV, 237; Boyer & Nissenbaum, *Salem Possessed*, pp. 193–94, 146.

86. Woodward, ed., *Rec. of Salem Witchcraft*, II, 52–3.

87. *Ibid.*, I, 12–29; Calef, *More Wonders of Invisible World*, pp. 357–58; Boyer & Nissenbaum, *Salem Possessed*, pp. 203–5.

88. Boyer & Nissenbaum, eds., *Salem-Village Witchcraft*, pp. 155–62.

89. Woodward, ed., *Rec. of Salem Witchcraft*, II, 56–66; "Salem Witchcraft—1692," n.p.; C. Mather, *Wonders of Invisible World*, pp. 125–28.

90. Woodward, ed., *Rec. of Salem Witchcraft*, II, 177–78.

91. C. Mather, *Wonders of Invisible World*, pp. 113–20.

92. *Ibid.*, p. 156.

93. Woodward, ed., *Rec. of Salem Witchcraft*, II, 15–16; "Photostatic Copy of Suffolk Ct. Rec., 1680–92," pt. 1, p. 192; "Salem Witchcraft—1692," III, n.p.

94. All evidence of actual witchcraft being practiced in Essex County in 1692 is dubious, at best. Those women who confessed did so only under great psychological, if not physical, duress. Chadwick Hansen makes much of John and William Bly's testimony that they once found "several puppets made up of rags and hogs' bristles, with headless pins in them" upon tearing down the wall of Bridget Bishop's house, but such evidence is worthless. In the hallucinatory climate of mid-1692, the Blys may have misconstrued their earlier find, converting harmless dolls into pin-laden puppets. If not, then we are left wondering why John Bly had not reported such awesome evidence to the authorities. (Obviously William Bly could not, because he was only eight years old.) At a time when so many persons were imagining specters and strange beasts, it is difficult to accept the Bly testimony and other accounts at face value. (See Hansen, *Witchcraft at Salem*, pp. 95–96.)

95. Lawson, *Christ's Fidelity the Only Shield*, p. 112.

96. Calef, *More Wonders of Invisible World*, p. 368.

97. Upham, *Salem Witchcraft*, II, 272, 307; T. Hutchinson, *Hist. of Mass.*, II, 32–33; Woodward, ed., *Rec. of Salem Witchcraft*, I, 115; II, 172–74.

98. Woodward, ed., *Rec. of Salem Witchcraft*, II, 203–4.

99. T. Hutchinson, *Hist. of Mass.*, II, 46n.

100. Other husbands, however, such as Giles Corey, William Good, and Edward Bishop, testified against their wives.

101. "Robert Pike to Jonathan Corwin, August 9, 1692," in Pike, *New Puritan*, pp. 149–57.

102. [Maule,] *N. Eng. Persecutors Mauled*, p. 56; G. Burr, ed., *Narratives of Witchcraft*, pp. 196–97n.

103. Brattle, "Letter," pp. 169–90.

104. Drake, *Witchcraft Delusion in N. Eng.*, pp. 179–81; Woodward, ed., *Rec. of Salem Witchcraft*, II, 66–68; Upham, "Salem Witchcraft & C. Mather," p. 212, and *Salem Witchcraft*, p. 364; G. Burr, ed., *Narratives of Witchcraft*, p. 187n.

105. Quoted in Boyer & Nissenbaum, *Salem Possessed*, p. 32.

106. Brattle, "Letter," pp. 177–78.

107. T. Hutchinson, *Hist. of Mass.*, II, 46n.

108. Sewall, *Diary*, I, 373.

109. Dudley Bradstreet, the son of Massachusetts Governor Simon Bradstreet (1679, 1689–92) and an ex-Councillor, imprisoned 40 "witches" at Andover, then refused to sit in judgment on any more, and fled the colony to avoid apprehension himself. His brother John with his own wife, Ann, ran away to New Hampshire. The afflicted girls thereafter accused the Bradstreets of assailing dogs in spectral form, and two such dogs were executed. Amazingly enough, the family patriarch was not accused even though he had criticized the witchcraft proceedings and had weathered sharp criticism himself as an ineffectual governor. See Calef, *More Wonders of Invisible World*, p. 372; Brattle, "Letter," p. 184; Breen, *Character of the Good Ruler*, pp. 171–72.

110. T. Hutchinson, *Witchcraft Delusion of 1692*, p. 41n; Woodward, ed., *Rec. of Salem Witchcraft*, II, 53.

111. Clever, "Sketch of P. English," I, 160–61. English, after his return, reportedly constructed a secret room in the garret of his house which might serve as a place of temporary concealment in the event of another witchcraft frenzy.

112. Calef, *More Wonders of Invisible World*, pp. 372–73.

113. Phips, "Letters," pp. 196–202. Phips meant well by his pardons, but one "witch" so freed indicated that even a pardon could not restore her good name. Abigail Faulkner, of Andover, complained in 1700; "The pardon so far had its effect so that I am as yet suffered to live, but this only as a malefactor, convicted upon record of ye most heinious crimes, that mankind can be suffered to be guilty, which, besides its utter Ruining and Defaming my Reputation, will certainly expose myself to Iminent Danger by new accusations, which will thereby be ye more readily believed, and will remain a perpetual brand of Infamy upon my family." She requested that the General Court "order the Defacing of ye record against me." See Fowler, "Biog. Sketches of Green, Clark, & Wadsworth," p. 59.

114. Calef, *More Wonders of Invisible World*, pp. 382–83.

115. Mary Watkins, once a servant to Dame Swift at Salem and often reportedly "distracted," denounced her ex-mistress, but was threatened with punishment if she persisted in such accusations. Then, "falling into Melancholly humours she was found strangling her self . . . and immediately accused her self of being a Witch." The Superior Court, however, acquitted her on April 25, and she was thereafter sold into servitude in Pennsylvania. The other girl, Margaret Rule of Boston, after an argument with one woman "who had frequently Cured very painfull Hurts by muttering ouer them certain Charms," fell into fits in which her joints became "strangely distorted," mysterious black and blue marks appeared on her body, pins were stuck in her back and neck, blisters raised on her skin, and she experienced "exorbitant Convulsions." See *ibid.*, pp. 308–23, 383–84; Watkins, "Discolored Hist. of Witchcraft."

116. Wyllys, "Wyllys Col. Suppl. Witchcraft in Conn. 1662–93," pp. 7–8; J. Taylor, *Witchcraft Del. in Conn.*, pp. 109–12.

117. J. Taylor, *Witchcraft Del. in Conn.*, pp. 63–71. John Barlow testified that, in one argument with Mercy Disborough, the alleged witch had sworn "if shee had but the strength shee would tear me in peses." She threatened to make Thomas Benit "as bare as a birds taile" and spoke harsh words to others. Often neighbors accused her of afflicting their cattle, and Thomas Benit, Jr., told her to "unbewitch" his uncle's child "or else he would beat her hart out."

118. Wyllys, "Wyllys Papers. Depositions on Witchcraft," pp. 19–21.

119. *Ibid.*, p. 32; J. Taylor, *Witchcraft Del. in Conn.*, pp. 102–5.

120. J. Taylor, *Witchcraft Del. in Conn.*, pp. 73, 75; J. Trumbull, ed., *Conn. Rec.*, IV, 76–77.

121. A treatment of the gradual development of Connecticut land difficulties appears in Bushman, *From Puritan to Yankee*.

122. J. Burr, ed., *Lyme Rec.*, p. 20.

XIV

Women and Society in the Secular Nineties

There is historical evidence that by this time culture, amenities, fine furnishings, and even handsome women were to be found in Boston houses. . . . Here the conscientious analyst found himself indeed bogged down in an ethical quagmire to which ancient rules seemed every year less and less applicable.

—Perry Miller, *The New England Mind*

THE TERMINATION OF THE MASSACHUSETTS AND CONNECTICUT witch prosecutions in 1693 all but ended such proceedings in colonial New England.[1] Many individuals who desired vengeance for presumed wrongs may have derived some satisfaction from the trials of their opponents, and the afflicted persons may have fulfilled their own needs for personal power. Yet, as Puritans struggled with their guilt over allowing so many now obviously innocent persons to face imprisonment, deprivation, and death, they lost much of a sense of society's decay, of its moral debasement by malign forces, and of their own participation in a closely knit Puritan community; for it was this sense that had created such destructive paranoia and self-righteousness in the first place. Witchcraft accusations had served as a last-ditch effort to restore the stability of the purely logical,"given," authoritarian force of Old Puritanism by wiping out evil elements in the community, including non-ideal women. Such women could not, however, be so easily eradicated. The world of the 1690s was clearly not the world of the 1630s.

A Gradual Easing of Tensions

In the last decade of the century numerous problems, particularly political ones, continued to upset New Englanders, even though these lacked the intensity and alienating impact they had had in earlier times. The royal charter of 1691 had deprived Massachusetts citizens of their right to choose the governor, his excellency's twenty-eight-man Council, or members of the judiciary. These citizens looked increasingly to the General Court and town meetings as institutions which could protect their "liberties." The charter also disturbed some old-line Puritans because it guaranteed freedom of conscience. But, despite the charter's discomforting aspects, it created a beneficial system of checks and balances and restored a tone of legitimacy to Massachusetts affairs. Controversy soon cooled, and the years from 1694 to 1702 became, politically, a "Short era of good feelings."[2]

Political concerns in Plymouth Colony—never very polarized—ended with the charter, since that document included Plymouth, Nantucket, Martha's Vineyard, Maine, and Nova Scotia under Bay Colony rule. Many of Plymouth's leaders had campaigned for just such a union before 1691. In Connecticut, on the other hand, political antagonism persisted throughout much of the decade, as royalist Gershom Bulkeley, democrat James Fitch, and moderate Fitz-John Winthrop attempted to establish order in "the mire of popular confusion." Furthermore, local friction flared up between town proprietors and new inhabitants over land allotments, and between persons living at the town center and on the outskirts over the creation of new parishes.[3] Perhaps because of such contention, the Connecticut authorities continued to prosecute (although not to convict) witches until 1697. Yet stabilizing factors did exist. Fitz-John Winthrop managed to secure a restoration of the old charter of 1662, a feat Increase Mather had failed to achieve for Massachusetts. Voters participated in the annual elections of the governor, councillors, and assemblymen. The judiciary functioned as it had before Andros. Internal dissension, maintained within a comparatively stable context, did not produce the sense of political "Anarchi" somewhat in evidence between 1689 and 1692.[4]

In "Anarchi" existed anywhere in New England, it was in Maine, and perhaps New Hampshire. Between 1689 and 1697 the French and Abnaki Indians almost completely disrupted Maine affairs, laying waste most of the settled portions of that province. Nearly

1,000 persons died in these northerly reaches, and many others fled
to New Hampshire and the Massachusetts seacoast ports. When
peace returned, some observers suggested that depopulated Maine
"be garrisoned with 1,000 soldiers and peopled with poor families
sent over from England, who could quickly produce sufficient quantities of rozin, pitch, tar, and hemp."[5]

New Hampshire too suffered from Indian raids, but the Abnaki
never devastated that colony as severely. Still, its settlers were not
otherwise content, for they resisted control by English proprietors
as much as they resisted Indians. After Samuel Allen had purchased
the Mason interest in the colony and sent his son-in-law, John
Usher, to order his affairs there, Usher found little support. People blamed him for the English impressment practices, the General
Assembly refused to vote him any money, and upstarts shot his
horses to demonstrate their contempt.[6] Some inhabitants apparently desired self-rule even with the Indian problem, believing that
"New Hampshire men were better woodmen [i.e., forest fighters]
than the Massachusetts men, and that it would be of no advantage
for the province to be united to Massachusetts." Others favored a
loosely federated union with the Bay Colony. In January 1697 some
of the latter formed themselves into a Council and removed Usher's
officials. When Usher dispatched militia warrants ordering officers
to call up their troops in retaliation, the prospective soldiers "turned
their backs contemptuously upon him and refused to stay and hear
the warrant." The new councillors, however, had no trouble summoning the militia for use *against* Usher. Dispirited, he fled into the
Bay Colony.[7]

While Usher sent his complaints to the Crown, Samuel Partridge,
who had received a lieutenant governor's commission in 1696,
assumed control of the government at Council's request. Partridge
cooperated fully with the rebels, even to the extent of removing
Usher's few supporters from positions of influence. When pro-
prietor-governor Allen arrived in 1698, he managed to reassert
some control over the colony's affairs. He appointed a few judges,
militia captains, and naval officers, dismissed the recalcitrant Assembly, reinstated Usher on his Council, and considered using
English soldiers to restore discipline. However, the next year Lord
Bellomont, the newly appointed royal governor of Nova Scotia,
Massachusetts, and New Hampshire, restored peace by removing Allen's appointed officials and letting New Hampshire locals
largely govern themselves.[8]

By the 1690s, people not only in New Hampshire but throughout New England had lost a great deal of respect for the religious and political authorities, be they English, colonial, or local. In 1698, after his return to Connecticut from English negotiations, Fitz-John Winthrop asserted, "I have observed in the kings Court a most Extraordinary reverence payde to the judge and all ministers of justice . . . but in this wilderness (eyther from principles of too fond familiarity or not remembring the rules abroad) they are wanting to introduce such fitting formes and customes as should support the honor of the Courts and give them a reputation and character abroad in other parts of the world."[9] Cotton Mather put it more bluntly: "It is true every Publick Servant must carry two Handkerchiefs about him, one to wipe off Sweat, of Travail, another to wipe off the Spit of Reproach."[10]

Ministers and magistrates came under attack. The royal governor, Sir William Phips, received reproof for his "mean mechanical" background; some asserted that he had only "learned to write since he was married and cannot yet read a letter."[11] Cotton Mather frequently complained of the disrespect Bostonians showed him, while at least one man maintained that New Hampshire's prominent Joshua Moody "made it his busness to cheat men."[12] At New London, Connecticut, John Rogers defied the governor and councillors in Christ's name and accused all ministers of "devil worship." His following fell under suspicion of burning down the local meetinghouse. Bathsua Fox, one Rogerene Quaker, actually placed witches' puppets in that building (1694).[13]

Other New Englanders failed to maintain the once proper respect for their "superiors." Men resisted military officers who attempted to impress them,[14] refused to heed the tax collector,[15] and ignored warrants.[16] One man threw a county magistrate over a barrel, and another threatened to decapitate a constable. Militia lieutenant William Furbur refused to obey John Usher's directives, then "turned his britch upon the Lt. Governr & pist in his presence, and lett a fart."[17] Others, engaged in the fishing trade or employed on merchant ships, objected when the English navy forced them into military service for the Crown.[18]

Churches themselves participated in the disruptive processes. By 1700 Solomon Stoddard had organized the churches of the upper Connecticut Valley into a federation which substituted associational approval for owning the church covenant as the core of church governance. At Westfield, a locale not in Stoddard's federation,

Edward Taylor emphasized mysticism to an extent well beyond the old Puritan standard. Boston's Brattle Street Church, with its "genteel" merchant congregation, liberalized previous policy by allowing baptism to the children of "any professed Christian" and opening the Lord's Supper to all persons of "visible sanctity."[19] Ministers in the Boston area met regularly, less as an expression of church unity than as a reflection of the professionalization of the ministry.

The people themselves seemed reluctant to participate in church affairs. Joshua Scottow complained in 1694 that "brethren of low degree" neglected to serve as elders, giving several excuses: "they know not the way of the Lord, they are men of mean estates, and low capacities, their counsel will not meet with acceptance." As Larzer Ziff has argued, no longer did New Englanders link education to religious discovery; Harvard students were increasingly considering religious training to be merely a matter of process (i.e., becoming a minister). As churches developed privileged interests and a ministerial class desirous of protecting them, the professing believers themselves became, in Nathaniel Mather's words, "no truth, no body, having no compaction amongst themselves any more than the loose stones in the highways in Ireland and in France and in New England are an house or body of stones."[20] The number of persons admitted to full membership in the various churches did not keep pace with the general population growth in the 1690s.[21] Paul R. Lucas estimates that, in six Connecticut communities, only about one-third of the people were full or halfway church members.[22]

The individualizing trend of three decades or more had, by 1700, hit Puritan New England full force. Many men and women "pretended" importance beyond their station and means. On the wharves in particular "Noys and Strutt pass[ed] for Whitt."[23] "Liberty and Property" became two of the most frequently reiterated words of the 1690s. Even an old-line Puritan like Cotton Mather would assert, "A Man ha's a Right unto his Life, his Estate, his Liberty, and his Family, altho' he should not come up to these and those Blessed Institutions of Our Lord."[24]

A flourishing international commerce helped stamp life with a material quality unknown in previous New England history. By 1698 Massachusetts had a fleet of 171 seagoing vessels, excluding fishing ships engaged only in local coastal trade. The tonnage of Boston's 124-ship fleet outranked that of all English ports save London and Bristol.[25] Four years later Massachusetts had 200 vessels, 20 of them over 100 tons burden, plus more bottoms above the size of herring boats than Scotland and Ireland combined. Connecticut, rapidly developing its own trade, had another 30 vessels.[26] Ships also frequently visited New Hampshire to tap that colony's mast trade. Despite French raids on New England bottoms, and a loss of some portion of the Maine–New Hampshire commerce in masts due to Indian warfare, extensive trade with the West Indies in woodwork, horses, and slaves brought great prosperity to many Puritans.[27]

English obstacles to a free trade—indeed, English attempts to govern in general—had little effect. Despite the Navigation Act of 1696, with its establishment of vice-admiralty courts to handle smuggling cases, New England merchants conducted an active, although illegal, trade with Scotland, Holland, and France.[28] Connecticut tried all maritime cases within its own court system.[29] Edward Randolph repeatedly protested New England violations of the navigation acts, but England, preoccupied between 1689 and 1697 with King William's War, made little attempt to interfere in colonial affairs. Massachusetts legislators submitted all of their laws and proceedings to the Crown for approval, but often avoided a royal veto by passing temporary measures and then reenacting them the next year.[30] The assemblymen warmly welcomed Lord Bellomont upon his arrival at Boston in 1699, but neglected to pay him a permanent salary; instead, they voted him an annual monetary "present," perhaps as a regulatory check on his activities. Bellomont lacked Andros's zeal for controlling colonial affairs, and left both New Hampshire and Massachusetts much to their own devices.[31]

Relatively benign relations with the Crown were also due, in part, to the fact that postrevolutionary New England had lost a sense of its self-possessed, independent-minded, communitarian identity. The large number of Maine refugees, the replacement of white servants by black slaves, and the prevalence of members of the merchant marine English soldiers and seamen helped diversify the quality of life in the seaport centers, sending the population on an upward spiral. Massachusetts inhabitants (including those in Plymouth Colony) increased from 56,977 in 1690 to 70,000 in 1701. Connecticut nearly doubled its number of inhabitants over the same time span, from 16,324 to 30,000, and the number of New Hampshire residents, notwithstanding the ravages of Indian warfare, shot upward still faster, from 4,021 to 10,000.[32]

In this "half-provincial and half-independent, half-English and half-American" society, [33] materialism of every variety flourished. People sometimes painted, in un-Puritan fashion, "Abominable Beasts & creeping things" on their buildings.[34] Dozens of unlicensed taverns dispensed beer and ale.[35] Even legitimate ordinaries hung out suggestive signs featuring women's painted faces, advertising "to Strangers that they shall find Entertainment there."[36] Sailors—a daily sight on Salem and Boston streets—drank heartily, fornicated, and were notorious for "Filthy Speaking, Bawdy Speaking, Uncleane and Obscene Ribaldry"—practices which caused Cotton Mather to call the sea "a School of Vice."[37] Although the law prohibited card-playing, some discontented gamesters scattered a pack of cards over magistrate Sewall's lawn to "mock" him (1699).[38] Young adults filled "the Joy of Harvest . . . with Folly and Lewdness." Ned Ward reported that lecture days were by some called "Whore-Fairs."[39] The relative numbers of fornicators doubled throughout New England—from 17.1 percent of the total criminal offenders in Massachusetts (1665–89) to 31 percent (1690–99, excluding Plymouth and Maine), from 17.2 to 44.7 percent in Plymouth, from 11.9 to 27.3 percent in Maine, from 16.2 to 38.5 percent in New Hampshire, and from 15.4 to 26.9 percent in Connecticut.[40] Of all county courts, only inland Hampshire County had a relative decrease in the percentage of fornication cases. Even though the numbers of fornicators jumped from 15 (1665–89) to 29 per year (1690s) in Essex County, from 10 to 22 in Middlesex County, and from 10 to 16 in Suffolk County, by the late 1690s magistrates were so tolerant of fornication that they halved the penalty for that offense. In 1699 the New Haven whipper actually refused to flog one woman convicted of such wrongdoing.[41]

As the magistrates lost some of the persecuting zeal of earlier times, punishment ceased for minor offenses like swearing, gaming, and dressing in fashions beyond one's station. One source commented, "It is the general complaint, that Connecticut Government is *too* Mild."[42] Massachusetts magistrates no longer served as watchdogs for the Biblical Commonwealth. Only a rare justice, like John Foster, could be accounted sufficiently pious by the standards of earlier days.[43] The old union between church and state had passed, as even the ministers began burying the jeremiad as a literary form after 1693.[44] Moral decay—now so widespread—simply had ceased to be as frightening as in the days of the Commonwealth. In fact, Increase Mather, one minister who still believed in reminding his contemporaries of God's impending judgment, lamented in 1699 that so many New Englanders—"Fools," he called them—derided even the concept of sin itself. "They mock at sin," he wailed, "Their own and other mens sins are more a matter of mirth than any thing else. . . . Sin is the least thing that troubleth them." John Williams indicated that many persons, when reproved from the pulpit, would simply assert that they were "not of the minister's mind." Such "rebels" sometimes told him that their material prosperity proved that God supported their actions.[45] "Private will" had won the day.

The patriarchal family, once the cornerstone of Puritan social theory, had also lost its force. "Sundry" inhabitants complained that sons and servants neglected to demonstrate proper obedience to their master's will. Many such "inferiors" absented themselves without leave or absconded on one of the many ships visiting New England ports.[46] The school failed to have its previous impact, as town support for education decreased throughout the 1690s. In 1693 Deodat Lawson lamented that many adolescent boys could "read little and understand less of the Holy Scripture."[47] Children also exercised more independence in the selection of their marital partners. Fitz-John Winthrop wrote in 1707, "it has been the custome of the country for young folkes to choose [their spouses], and where there is noe visible exception everybody approves it." Forty-six years before, Winthrop had professed his willingness to subordinate his "owne will and desires" in marital matters to his parents' "pleasure and intensions concerning me."[48] By the 1690s "inveigling" a young maiden without parental consent had ceased to be a prosecutable offense.

Some felt that the current childrearing style was simply too permissive. Williams complained about parents who watched their children and servants "wantonly toying & dallying with one another, foolishly sporting on beds before their eyes, unreproved." Cotton Mather believed that New Englanders often raised their youngsters in the "abominably indulgent" fashion of the pagan Indians.[49]

Many New Englanders no longer relished discipline and authority. In a changed society, people were more free to pursue their own ends, instead of seeking the ends of a community of saints. Unencumbered by many of the legal restrictions, religious inhibitions, and anxieties of the Puritan founders, these people had less need to observe the clearly defined rules and roles of earlier times. In the process, they contributed to the "Indianization" of Puritan strongholds, having adopted innumerable habits more common, in Cotton Mather's belief, to red "rattle-snakes" than to God-fearing people.[50]

Such a metaphorical Indianizing of New England life had particular impact upon women. Those who had felt confined by the subordinate and narrow possibilities of the role allotted them in the now decaying Biblical Commonwealth readily took advantage of the widespread social disorientaion. Mather stigmatized them as succumbing to the pagan lure of the encroaching wilderness; he was not speaking strictly in metaphorical terms, for approximately a thousand persons spent varying amounts of time in Indian captivity during the 1690s. Hundreds of women and children vanished into the wilderness, were adopted into Indian tribes, forgot their catechisms and often their language, then returned to Puritan society "half-Indianized or Romanized" by the French. Sometimes married to a "Canadian half-breed" or an "Indian slut," such returned captives helped to alter Puritan values.[51] They too played a role, however small, in the secularization of the late seventeenth century life.

Women, the Indians, and the French

In captivity, women and girls, who comprised approximately 56 percent of those taken prisoner by the Indians between 1677 and 1699, had to grapple with the many disconcerting realities of wilderness life, with physical exhaustion on the forced march, sometimes with Indian cruelty and impulsiveness, with the horrifying death of loved ones, and often with residence among the alien, Catholic French. For some, it was a time of great religious testing. Alone, feeling totally abandoned and uprooted in the almost surrealistic experience of captivity, such women became absolutely dependent upon God for support against the so obviously precarious nature of their human condition. God was all that remained of their civilized life. Captives like Mary Rowlandson, Hannah Swarton, and Grace Higiman could only pray, again and again, to be physically and psychologically freed from devilish Frenchmen and satanic Indians.[52] They felt the repellent touch of sin in the ferocious songs, wild dances, open sexuality, and blasphemies of those whom they considered red "Wolves." It is not entirely surprising that the wife of the Reverend Shubael Dummer reportedly "died of grief."[53]

Captivity sometimes gave women the opportunity to defend their faith in the "masculine" manner made popular by the Quakers. When one Frenchman at Montreal boasted of his rosary beads to a captive Deerfield woman, "she knocked them out of his hands on the floor; for which she was beaten, and threatened with death, and for some days imprisoned." Another young woman, given the choice of wearing a cross or being whipped, chose the latter. A third female had her ears boxed by a nun, her hands struck by a rod, and her arms pinched black and blue after she refused to cross herself.[54]

Ransomed or recaptured women sometimes experienced a "captivity neurosis" upon returning to Puritan civilization. Mary Rowlandson suffered from insomnia, became perpetually watchful, and found herself alienated from her unconverted neighbors. Mercy Short hallucinated "Tawney" specter-devils who bit her and slashed her skin. Subject not only to traumatic memories of suffering but to guilts and torments for having possibly eaten human flesh to avoid starvation, or having even found savage temptations enjoyable, many women may well have felt thoroughly distanced from their fellow Puritans, especially when neighbors cast about innuendoes concerning their "unchastity" with "beastly savages."[55]

Not all females reacted antagonistically to life with the Indians or French, however. Robert Vail has observed, "One strange feature of this captivity business is the surprisingly large number of prisoners who refused to return to their old homes when they had the chance."[56] Although Puritans frequently raised money to redeem captives, and the French were willing to release them, almost half of those taken failed to return. One-third of the total apparently chose to remain in New France. At least forty percent of these females converted to Catholicism and married Frenchmen; five others became nuns. Fifteen percent of the captives vanished completely.

The fact that so many women became Catholics may have indicated some degree of dissatisfaction with Puritanism or Anglicanism, or simply a desire to gain French husbands and adapt to their new setting. The relative scarcity of women in New France may have led some to consider staying there. At least one observer has argued that "the retiring role assigned to the women in New England was in striking contrast to the prominent part played by the few women in the French colony."[57] The Reverend Joseph Allen reported that Rebecca Clark, taken from Falmouth in 1690, lived so contentedly among the French "that when money was sent for her ransom she refused to leave; sending word that the money sent was

Chart 14.1

A Selection of Indian Captives Taken in New England, 1677–99*

Colony	Returned, Redeemed, Rescued		Escaped		Died or Killed after Capture		Remained in Canada		Took French Spouse		Took Religious Orders		Unknown		Total	
	M	F	M	F	M	F	M	F	M	F	M	F	M	F	M	F
Maine	28	38	4	1	6	2	11	17	5	8	0	1	7	5	56	63
N.H.	4	18	2	2	2	2	8	10	4	8	0	1	1	2	17	32
Mass.	11	9	5	2	0	3	6	5	1	2	0	1	10	14	32	33
Unknown	0	0	0	0	0	0	7	13	0	0	0	2	0	0	7	13
	43	65	11	5	8	5	32	45	10	18	0	5	18	21	112	141

*Based on names appearing in Emma Coleman, *New England Captives Carried to Canada*.

not sufficient to supply her table for a single day."[58] Another woman, Abigail Willey, found at Quebec personal relief from a husband who had beaten her and threatened her life, and from whom she had run away before; after his death, she remarried in New France.[59] One young girl found Catholicism more appealing than life with her family in Dover. Sarah Gerrish, age eight, burst into tears when told that she must return to New Hampshire after spending sixteen months with the Indians and French. When her brother attempted to steal a crucifix which had been given to her, the young girl hid it in her armpit. The year following her return she sent a gold piece to the Mother Superior of the convent Hotel Dieu, where she had resided while in Quebec.[60]

Some women, particularly the young, were adopted into Indian communities, often to return later to their old way of life. When they did so, "corrupted" by the Indians' freedom of impulse, action, and sexual expressiveness, such women helped to undermine the force of Puritanism. Many others never returned to white-inhabited locales; these, Thomas Hutchinson reported, "mingled with Indians and contributed to a succession of savages to exercise cruelties upon the English frontiers in future wars, and perhaps upon some of their own relations."[61]

Indian warfare worked against the orthodox Puritan sex role by virtually requiring women to assume a rather "masculine" energy and spirit. Forced to endure long marches while summoning up every ounce of courage, captive women sometimes held themselves ready to flee into the unfamiliar wilderness if a suitable opportunity arose. At least five women escaped from their captors and returned home over some distance. Others reacted aggressively against the Indians. Elizabeth Tozier of Salmon Falls reportedly foiled red attackers by throwing boiling soap on them. She stood guard, dressed in male clothing, while men worked fields nearby, and was captured possibly three times between 1675 and 1690.[62] Cotton Mather reported that, after the Indians attacked Wells in 1691, "the women in the garrison on this occasion took up the Amazonian stroke, and not only brought ammunition to the men, but also with a manly resolution fired several times upon the enemy."[63] A better-known example of masculine spirit is Hannah Dustin's slaying of several of her Indian captors.[64] Women who had gone through such experiences could hardly have found it easy to be deferential, passive wives.

Although the actual numbers of women spending much time

with the Indians and French constituted less than 1 percent of the total female population, in quite another way the so-called red "rattle-snakes" had a profound effect upon the quality of life for women in seacoast Massachusetts. Throughout the 1690s large numbers of Maine inhabitants, including many widows and orphans, fled to the Bay Colony's calmer urban shores, bringing with them their peculiar set of attitudes and expectations. These often non-Puritan female refugees were more joy-loving, more assertive, and quicker to abuse the authorities than were their Massachusetts counterparts. Through the refugees' personal example and their zealous search for employment, they too helped to accelerate the process of change, particularly sex-role change, in places like Boston, Charlestown, and Salem.

Nontraditional Women Ascendant

As the contingencies of Indian warfare made women like Hannah Dustin and Elizabeth Tozier more aggressive than they might otherwise have been, so the changed realities of provincial life accentuated female deviance. At one time those women who possessed the audacity to dress in alluring fashion had received reproof from the Boston authorities, but in the 1690s "Fantastick Attire and Ornaments, monstrous Head-Towers," bracelets, bare backs, partially exposed breasts, and "changeable suits of Apparell" became the rule, rather than the exception. In more rural Connecticut even the daughters of poor farm folk found gay clothing "dreadful pretty."[65] Well-dressed women, by their obviously materialistic appearance calculated to win attention, helped undermine the desirability of the grave, humble, spiritual female ideal. (Of course, in the process, these new women also reinforced the tendency of many men to view them as types—as beautiful bodies or mere parrots of fashion—instead of complex personalities in their own right.)

Women deviated from old patterns in sometimes opposite directions. A leisure class of women had emerged, the wives of bewigged merchants and public officials. Unwilling to respect Puritan injunctions against the evils of idleness, these women not only dressed well, but often amused themselves with card games instead of those "cards which fit the Wooll for the Wheel."[66] Others, the young as well as the elderly, were either unwilling or unable to experience a leisurely lifestyle but, of necessity, worked in a self-supportive capacity. In 1693 Florence Mackarta of Boston became the first New

England woman to build a slaughterhouse (in conjunction with two men), while Margaret Barton "alias Mrs. Peggey" served a full apprenticeship in "chair frame making," then found her fortune in international trade. She lived in Boston with at least one black servant before the selectmen warned her out of town in 1709 as a person of "Ill-Fame." No tax lists from the 1690s specify the number of women who operated businesses, but in 1695 the Massachusetts General Court gave single women "that live at their own hand" a tax break, indicating numbers of such women in the colony.[67]

The number of female innkeepers shot upward, both relatively and absolutely. The eight female innkeepers in Maine, 24 in New Hampshire, and 52 in Massachusetts exceeded the totals of such women for 1630 to 1690 combined ($N = 2$, 4, and 43). In New Hampshire, women comprised almost half of all liquor-sellers in the 1690s. In Maine the proportion of lady innkeepers zoomed, from 40 men and three women between 1660 and 1687 to 25 men and 8 women over the next dozen years. In Essex County eight of the 40 dispensers of alcoholic beverages were women in 1692, a jump from two out of 15 in 1682. At Boston, females comprised a stable 20 percent of the innkeeping population from 1660 to 1682, but in 1690 their percentage shot up to 45.1, and a year later to 57.5. Such women had become so common in provincial New England that when Madame Knight made a journey to New York in 1704, she stopped at inns maintained by "landladies" at Dedham (Massachusetts), Westerly (Rhode Island), New London, the Niantic River crossing, Saybrook ferry, and Norwalk (all in Connecticut).[68]

Educational opportunities for middle-class girls expanded during the 1690s, with at least three matrons and three men opening coeducational private schools in Boston.[69] One study of wills revealed that the percentage of women signing their names on such documents (instead of merely making a mark) increased from 42 percent of the total in 1653–56 to 62 percent in 1689–97. Another study corroborated these results. Kenneth A. Lockridge's examination of 175 women's wills has revealed that 30 percent of the women were "literate" in 1650–70, a figure which increased to 42 percent in 1705–15.[70] We have no direct information about an increased number of girls in the public schools, but, if the Hatfield situation is indicative, it probably shot upward. In Hatfield in 1700 four girls —out of 46 students—appeared on the schoolmaster's class list; nine years later, 16 girls attended classes, comprising one-fourth of the students.[71] Certainly, opening the schools to girls could have

Chart 14.2
Liquor Licenses at Boston, 1642–1691*

Years	N. Licenses	To Males	To Females	% to Females
1642–59	14	14	0	.0
1660–69	68	54	14	20.6
1670–79	154	126	28	18.2
1680–82	93	75	18	19.4
1690	51	28	23	45.1
1691	40	17	23	57.5

*Based on licenses recorded in "Boston Town Records," *Second* and *Seventh Reports of the Boston Record Commissioners* (Boston, 1877, 1881).

served a conservative purpose (i.e., as an indoctrination device to create "Daughters of Zion"), but it also gave them an opportunity to develop skills usable in the search for employment.

Women made other gains. In New Hampshire, Elizabeth Harvey became the first New England woman of record to serve as post-mistress.[72] Women increasingly demonstrated their legal ability, arguing as plaintiffs or defendants in 12 percent of all civil cases heard before the Suffolk County Court in 1690–94 and 14 percent of those decided in the next five-year interval. (The comparative percentages for 1675–84 and 1685–89 were, respectively, 11.5 and 9.7) Lady lawyers won 72.1 percent of their cases as plaintiffs and 17.4 percent as defendants. The former figure compares favorably with the male plaintiff's 71.4 percent victory rate, but the latter falls somewhat short of the male's 29 percent.[73] Before the Court of Assistants, women won a higher percentage of their cases as both plaintiffs and defendants: 66.7 and 71.4 versus men's 41.5 and 57 percent in the 1690s. Women argued in 6.1 percent of all high court civil cases between 1673 and 1686 ($N = 42$ of 683) and 14.9 percent of those between 1689 and 1693 ($N = 13$ of 87). In two-thirds of the former and 84.6 percent of the latter, they acted without the assistance of co-executor or husband.[74] In 1711 Sam Sewall, after more than two decades of experience with female attorneys, stated emphatically that "Many Women are such good Lawyers, & of such quick understanding in the Fear of the Lord," that their legal abilities might well lead them into Heaven.[75]

Churches, too, began reflecting the somewhat egalitarian turn of the times. Andover townsmen appointed Rebecca Johnson a sexton, the first woman of record to secure that position in

New England.[76] In Boston, the merchant-dominated Brattle Street Church departed from the previously rigid franchise requirements. The last article of the Brattle Street Manifesto of November 17, 1699, stated explicitly, "Finally, we cannot confine the right of choosing a minister to the male communicants alone, but we think that every baptized adult person who contributes to the maintenance should have a vote in electing."[77] That provision at least gave self-supporting women an equal choice.

The Massachusetts General Court enacted several laws which made life easier for women, including the tax relief enactment of 1695, already mentioned. In 1692 the assemblymen directed that the widow's dower right be protected in the division of an insolvent estate; it further allowed the widow to receive one-third of her husband's realty, as had been the previous practice, but added to that one-half of his personalty. Six years later the assemblymen reduced the time which must pass before a deserted wife could petition for a divorce, from seven to three years.[78]

No longer did women appear as willing to marry or to play a nurturant maternal role. Although, even from earliest times, many a mother undoubtedly hoped her present conception would be her last, in the 1690s Cotton Mather became concerned over the increasing numbers of such women. These, Mather warned, would providentially have "multiplied and unhappy Miscarriages ever ofter."[79] At least a dozen women, eight of them single, appeared before the various colonial authorities on infanticide charges, easily setting a record for any decade of the century. One-third of all infanticidal mothers lived in the 1690s.[80] Seven of these were hanged, and the Massachusetts General Court in 1692 specified the death penalty for any mother who secretly buried her illegitimate infant's body and then, upon discovery, claimed the child had been stillborn.[81] Some evidence indicates that women, particularly younger women, had fewer children in the 1690s than had their predecessors, suggesting that couples practiced some form of birth control.[82] Husbands and wives may have used such partially effective means of contraception as coitus interruptus or the sheep-gut condom which was becoming so popular in England.[83] Some availability of birth control may have helped inspire many females to become sexually more assertive, for John Williams reported that too many maidens "inveigled" men by their "Eloquence." Such females, Williams maintained, cast aside a "Fear of Hell, a Religious Education," and any inhibiting sense of shame or fear of public reproach.[84] Often the popular dances and balls served as convenient meeting places where alluringly dressed maidens could entice young men.[85]

Apparently more unmarried couples were having sexual relations, [86] for despite the fact that the birth rate was on the downswing, relatively more women became pregnant prior to marriage.[87] Perhaps some of these had been seduced by secularized men, or had used sex to "trap" men into marriage, especially since parental consent to their choice of a partner was no longer considered so essential. However, many other female fornicators seemed to desire sex more than a wedding, even when it meant an illegitimate child. In the century's last decade proportionately more young mothers reacted like Hannah Souter of Marblehead, who "being questioned who was y[e] father of y[e] child . . . replyed shee would not tell however itt pleased god to deale wth her."[88] Often sexual affairs took place with transients (seamen, Indians, English soldiers) or persons with whom there was little chance of marriage (black slaves, servants who must first secure their masters' permission). Nor did female offenders argue that men seduced them, a plea which earlier fornicators often had used. In Massachusetts, Plymouth, and New Hampshire, fewer women now married the fathers of their offspring (see Chart 14.3). "Addicted" to "the infatuating and stupifying power of this brutish sin of uncleanness,"[89] Elizabeth Clements, Sarah Threenedles, Mary Bartlett, and Elizabeth Chase each had two or more illegitimate children.[90] Such fornicators may have been hoping that, when no father was designated to supply maintenance, their bastards would be "placed out" with a neighboring family almost at birth; the courts now often ordered the same. (Previously, the magistrates had directed that the child be kept with its mother until age five or seven, when it became eligible for apprenticeship.) The newer practice, designed to provide care for the child, had unintended benefits for those mothers who did not like being saddled with offspring.

People appeared less willing to enter traditional marital relationships. Some couples lived together without benefit of actual marriage.[91] There were women who had premarital intercourse regularly with the same man, including one who committed "hainous wickedness in lying with William Wogmans Negro man Jack many times."[92] In another case, John Russ, Jr., admitted having sex with Elizabeth Sessions "a Hundred times for ought he did know."[93] The women's opportunities to become self-supporting most nota-

bly through servitude and innkeeping, may have allowed some
to support their illegitimate children. If the mother failed to name
a father and could not find employment, the town in which she
resided usually put her on poor relief, whether or not she kept
the child.

Chart 14.3

Percentage of Women Who Did Not Marry After Discovering Pregnancy

Colony	Before 1690			1690–99		
	Married	Did Not Marry	% Not Marrying	Married	Did Not Marry	% Not Marrying
Massachusetts	202	310	60.5	58	134	69.8
Ct. Assts.	8	8	50.0	0	0	.0
Essex Co.	121	140	53.6	32	46	59.
Middlesex Co.	40	64	61.5	18	44	71.
Suffolk Co.	26	88	77.2	6	40	87.
Hampshire Co.	7	10	58.8	2	4	66.7
Maine	26	32	55.2	16	17	51.5
New Hampshire	35	37	51.4	3	48	94.1
Connecticut	55	86	61.	28	23	45.1
Plymouth	38	32	45.7	17	21	55.3

In part because of the welter of fornication cases, the percentage
of female criminal offenders exceeded that for any other decade,
approaching 30 percent in all areas save Connecticut, and exceeding
40 percent in Suffolk County, Massachusetts.[94] Even with fornicators excluded from the totals, the percentage of female offenders
increased in all colonies except war-torn New Hampshire and inland Connecticut.[95] The number of such criminals in Essex County
shot from an average of 12.5 women per annum between 1665
and 1689 to 17.4 in the 1690s. Figures for Suffolk County showed
a similar increase, from 9.8 to 12.5. Besides fornication, women
appeared in court most frequently for selling alcohol without a license, keeping a disorderly house, directing slanderous remarks
at neighbors, and refusing to show up for Sabbath services.

Emil Oberholzer has compiled a number of tables in his book
Delinquent Saints which suggest that more women were also punished by churches for fornication. Between 1620 and 1689, Massachusetts churches took action against only one such woman every
two years, but in 1690–1729 an average of four appeared before the
churches annually.[96] One traveler in 1695 reported that, in one Bay

Colony congregation, premarital sex "was followed in practically every marriage, while a church in Connecticut made a rule that seven-month children should be considered legitimate."[97] Prostitution had made inroads as well. In 1702 Cotton Mather would complain that Bostonians all too frequently tolerated brothel keepers and whores "for fear of being reputed ill neighbours."[98]

The behavior of these many women—whether as fornicators, well-dressed dames, attorneys, innkeepers, or members of the Brattle Street Church—clearly undermined the vitality of the dependent, unassertive, modest feminine ideal. No longer performing in a strictly dependent capacity, these nontraditional women carved out different lifestyles in New England's changing world. In that respect, they were assisted both by New World circumstances and by attitudes coming out of England. In the feminist outburst after England's Glorious Revolution, at least three men and three women published tracts calling for the extension of educational benefits to women, arguing woman's capacity for rule, describing the marriage institution as a petty tyranny, and celebrating the important role played by learned women in history. Scientific and educational magazines written for women had made their appearance, and no fewer than fourteen Englishwomen published books during the 1690s. In drama, a female character type had emerged who did not "consider herself merely an appendage of man."[99] We do know that some New Englanders liked to read the "sublime Devotion and Piety, as well as Ingenuity and Wit" appearing in the poetry of Philomena, the *nom de plume* of Elizabeth Singer of Agford.[100] (Note here the celebration of female ingenuity and wit, *along with* piety.) It seems very likely that feminist accounts would also have found their way across the Atlantic, especially since New Englanders conducted a thriving commerce in books.

News from England, the heterogeneity and materialism in New World urban centers, and the numbers of Maine refugees, coupled with the semi-licit or even illegal behavior of many women throughout the century, helped to create a societal mood which subtly legitimized more assertive activity on the part of good Puritan women. The journal kept by Sarah Knight offers us an opportunity to examine how one Boston gentledame, by no means a "rebel," was influenced by changes in the options available to women at late century. The widow of a London merchant's agent, Madame Knight maintained a shop and opened a school at Boston.[101] Possessed of much legal knowledge, she settled many of her own and her husband's civil affairs. On a journey to New York by horseback she apprehensively but singlemindedly braved the "hazzardous Rivers," "dolesome woods," tottering bridges, "steep and Rocky Hills and precipices" of the wilderness.[102] Although she had lapses of feminine weakness at river crossings and always traveled with one or more male companions, Madame Knight was able to laugh at her fears, at one point asserting that the least of the forest's dangers was also "enough to startle a more Masculine courage."[103] Once, when her horse dropped dead underneath her "in going up a very steep hill," she described the event with nonchalance, and without fear.[104]

While so many seventeenth-century journals became little more than narratives of the author's religious backsliding, Madame Knight's, by contrast, is almost entirely secular. Absorbed in her immediate surroundings, she did not concern herself with matters of religion. She stayed with Connecticut ministers and considered the colony's inhabitants morally indulgent, but did not write of any inner anguish, of daily prayers, or even of attending Sabbath services. Instead of taking a serious, essentially joyless approach to life, as did so many of her Puritan predecessors, Madame Knight wrote in a richly humorous, at times even earthy style. Speaking of the people of Norwalk, Connecticut, she observed, "They have aboundance of sheep, whose very Dung brings them great gain [as fertilizer], with part of which they pay their Parsons sallery. And they Grudge that, prefering their Dung before their Minister."[105] Sarah Knight was quite the secular lady—yet at the same time considered herself an orthodox Puritan.

Not all Puritans accepted the changes reflected in the behavior of secular women. Some, looking nostalgically back to the days of the patriarchal fathers and a carefully regulated authoritarian society, took steps to remind women that they had best toe the traditional line. In 1690 proper Bostonians authorized the publication of William Secker's *Directions to those men who want wives*, an English treatise which reiterated the theme that God had made woman for an inferior, dependent position in the world. Cotton Mather's *Ornaments for the Daughters of Zion*, printed in 1691 and again a year later, described "the vertuous and laudable Characters of holy Women."[106] John Cotton's *A Meet Help* urged the wife to "keep at home, educating of her children, keeping and improving what is got by the industry of the man" (1699).[107] After the founding of the Brattle Street Church, Increase Matter reminded his contemporaries that, though women may contribute to a minister's maintenance, "the Apostle [Paul] allows not their voting."[108] As divines indulged in much ancestor worship of the earlier, ostensibly more virtuous Puritan fathers, so too did some celebrate the ideal wives of such leaders, those humble souls "Trim'd with an High Neglect/Of Gay Things, but with Ancient Glories deck't."[109]

The ministers' propaganda effort may have returned some deviating women to the fold. The widely distributed publications probably caused other prospective "new" women to reconsider, with a good deal of personal discomfort, the wisdom of their impulses and behavior. The various ways in which fornicators attempted to justify their actions illustrated that religion still had some effect. According to John Williams, some fornicators hypocritically worked out their guilt by accusing other offenders with self-righteous severity. Some avoided taking responsibility for their "sin" by blaming the inebriating effect of alcohol; some expressed sorrow, not for their violation of God's law, but out of "Shame and fear of punishment." Others, despite their training and ministerial censure, failed to consider their behavior reprehensible in any way.[110]

Undoubtedly many women rejected the changed role symbolically offered to them in one form or another by secular, nontraditional women. In these polarizing times, female church membership stepped up, after a lull in the 1680s; but new female members did not keep pace with the population growth, at least in Roxbury, Dorchester, and Stonington. Women searching for stability during these confusing times found solace in the church. Young and married, these new church members may have been comforted by the increasing tendency of the clergy to elevate the status of religious women by describing the church as the bride of Christ. Sermons keynoted how the church and the church member should behave as the ideal wife in relation to her husband, avoiding his anger, observing his rules, and behaving humbly.[111] Such elevation, however, reaffirmed traditional values, at the same time that it inspired conversions. It did have psychological impact, helping church women to feel more important than they might in earlier decades. Still, not many women attended church. Nor could they—in Boston in 1690, there was pew space for just one-fourth of the population.[112] It was becoming quite apparent that those women who attended every Sabbath service, prayed diligently in their closets, dutifully obeyed their husbands, and hoped for limitless numbers of children were out of tune with contemporary trends. Many women were simply ceasing to respect, at least behaviorally, the female role praised in *Daughters of Zion* and other Puritan works. And they were, for the first time, capable of taking group action without needing to rely on the self-justifying impress of a heretical theology like Antinomianism, Anabaptism, or Quakerism. In 1707 such women would beat up a man who abused his wife.[113] In the same year they would greet the soldiers who had participated in a disastrous attack on Port Royal with the words, "Is your piss-pot charg'd neighbor? So-ho, souse the cowards. Salute Pt.-Royal."[114] Later in his life, Cotton Mather expressed grave concern that so many women failed to acknowledge his *Ornaments*. Instead, he wailed, "the female Sex have spitt more of their Venom at me than any other man." He questioned whether, in 1724, there existed twenty female Bostonians who had *not* "at some time or other spoken basely of me."[115]

Despite the outspokenness, occupational activity, and self-declarative appearance of large numbers of women in seacoast Massachusetts, there is no record of secular women forming support groups which then pressed for equal rights. These were not twentieth-century feminists. "Rebellious" maidens, goodwives, and widows of the 1690s did not look to intensified group activity to remedy the limitations they experienced as members of the "weaker sex"; nor did they examine all the dimensions of Puritan sex-role stereotyping, or consciously repudiate that stereotype. Still, the behavior of so many secularized women testified to the popularity of a number of individualized styles—all of which, to one degree or another, belied the conventional sex-role stereotype. No longer needing a political or religious philosophy to justify those same forms of rebellious behavior that nontraditional women had been expressing for decades, the secular woman of the 1690s helped

Chart 14.4

Change in Female Admissions to Church Membership, by Decade, 1660–99

	1660–69			1670–79			1680–89			1690–99		
	M	F	%F	M	F	%F	M	F	%F	M	F	%F
Roxbury	16	28	63.6	17	34	66.7	42	49	53.8	28	56	66.7
Dorchester	14	23	62.6	31	38	55.1	28	29	50.9	24	38	61.3
Boston First	52	102	66.2	65	116	64.1	32	58	64.4	53	165	75.7
Hartford 2d	xx	xx	xxxx	48	66	57.9	6	14	70.	23	30	56.6
Stonington	xx	xx	xxxx	19	17	47.2	8	15	65.2	23	23	50.
Milford	29	38	56.7	23	44	65.7	19	24	56.	29	60	67.4

erode the sharp edge of words like Virgin, Witch, Whore, or
Quaker. What was once hardly more than odd and isolated behavior was becoming altogether commonplace. Indeed, whereas once
the Puritan authorities had denounced those few women who
adopted a nontraditional style, by the early eighteenth century the
spokesmen for the Biblical Commonwealth had shifted their emphasis: instead of denouncing individual women, divines spoke
increasingly of deviant behavior by groups of women, or even of
allegedly disreputable activity by the female sex itself. Coupled with
this general denunciation of Woman, instead of certain women, was
ministerial praise for the ostensibly small number of women who
continued to lead properly feminine lives.

Evidence suggests that, outside of urban Massachusetts, larger
numbers of women were adopting aspects of a nontraditional style.
In Maine and New Hampshire, where throughout the century
women tended to be more roughhewn and assertive, Indian warfare required that numbers of men be kept on militia alert, which
made room for more women in usually male occupations. Women
participated more frequently in planting and harvesting, supervised small businesses, and became innkeepers. Maine women
sometimes picked up arms to repel Indian attackers. In rural Connecticut (according to Madame Knight, "this indulgent colony")
tradition had also lost some of its sting. Connecticut women dressed
plainly, but they had begun to give lip service to fashion.[116] In
Guilford, at least, women began reducing the size of their families,
by an average of 20 percent. Connecticut women did not find
employment in many occupations, although in 1695 the town of
Wallingford hired a "woman to teach in summer; and a man in
winter"—the first time a woman had been allowed to teach in the
colony in forty-four years.[117]

In many areas, the growing acceptability of a nontraditional lifestyle meshed with the materialism and individualism of a people
who, after decades of multifaceted turmoil, ardently wished to safe-
guard the twin values of "Liberty and Property" above the notion of the Biblical Commonwealth. Witchcraft accusations—once
an effective way to curb social deviation—had lost their credibility in a less rigid, more secular society, as they already had in
Europe. The punitive, patriarchal, oppressive, and repressive aspects of Puritanism still existed, to be sure, especially in the minds
of many ministers; but the concrete expression of that Puritanism
had been greatly modified. Although women could not vote in

church and colony, serve the community in a ministerial capacity, enter Harvard, or easily become self-supporting, they enjoyed opportunities virtually unknown to or unused by first-generation New Englanders.

Those ministers who objected so strongly to independent, assertive, sensual women continued to emphasize the sex-role stereotypes of their progenitors, both in England and in America. These latter-day divines reiterated the importance of rigid sex roles within a social system of superiors and inferiors, establishing a customary hierarchy in which their own feelings of powerlessness seemed less manifest. Having to cope with their own loss of prestige in more secular times, ministers like Cotton Mather, John Williams, and their contemporaries continued to view woman as the appropriately passive, modest, dependent, nurturant, non-intellectual, virginal sex, because such a perception enhanced their own egos. At the same time, it undoubtedly helped to foster a self-image of unassertiveness in many of the yet "uncorrupted" women of late century. From the 1620s through the 1690s, as in more recent times, man's search for power deprived many women of control over their own lives.

Preoccupied with their powerlessness before God, nature, the English authorities, contemporary status arrangements, and the anxieties of life in a New World, Puritans were hardly a "free and happy people" untroubled by the "inhibitions and prohibitions that have made latter-day Puritanism so unpopular."[118] Although some may have enjoyed very contented and tolerant lives, the thrust of Puritanism—given its obsession with the prevalence and awfulness of sin, its morbid introspection, its suppression of sexuality outside marriage, its profound fear of idleness and heresy—countered impulses for freedom and joy. A person like Anne Bradstreet could bridge the gap between the material and the spiritual, but many other Puritans indulged in a great deal of self-hatred, as their diaries readily attest, often feeling guiltily drawn by the material world's sinful allure.

Puritan attitudes about education, economic activity, sexuality, marital "love," and separation of the sexes checked, rather than fostered, progress for women. Puritanism became an important vehicle for keeping women locked into the role of weaker sex. Sex roles, so often detailed in sermons, letters, excommunication proceedings, and courtroom trials, could hardly be taken lightly; the authorities quite pointedly informed rebels like Anne Hutchinson and Anne Hibbins that they *were* violating their divinely prescribed position as inferior women. Such reminders, coupled with the threat of banishment, beating, or even death, were certainly calculated to curb any tendency toward female emancipation via religious leadership or any other route. A woman like Anne Hutchinson, then, was not merely heralding the liberation of women implicit within Puritanism, as some scholars have maintained. Rather, she was resisting an oppressive reality.

The case for the Puritan emancipation of women, argued most comprehensively by Roger Thompson,[119] does not hold up under careful analysis. One cannot, for example, reasonably argue that the circumscriptive female sex role posited by the divines and reinforced by society's institutions was countermanded by the Puritan stress on individualism, upon the right of all people to search for assurance of election. The authorities directed women to consult males for answers to their theological questions and deprived them of the right to speak or vote in church affairs. What happened in the isolation of the closet bore no relationship to the strict social conformity demanded in the world outside. When alternative behaviors became more common at late century, they did so not because Puritanism fostered such individualism, but because contact with non-Puritans, female rebelliousness, and the changed circumstances of life had weakened the impact of Calvinist teaching. Nor did recurrent labor shortages have an emancipating effect, since before 1690 very few women were employed in the professions or business; only the low-status, carefully regulated occupation of domestic servitude drew in large numbers of women. The Puritan celebration of love in marriage, instead of fostering equality, actually facilitated oppression by making female submission theoretically more tolerable. The law punishing spouse-beaters, a potentially liberating enactment, was voided in court by magistrates who rarely gave severe penalties to erring husbands. Puritans allowed wives the proprietory, tortious, and evidentiary rights denied them under English common law; but this constituted no real gain, since English customary and equity law guaranteed such rights as well. What appears to be a step forward merely represents a continuation of English local practice. The same holds true for divorce comparisons. Although officially procurable in the mother country only from the ecclesiastical courts (and, later, Parliament) on grounds of consanguinity, bigamy, or sexual incapacity, divorces were widely granted on a local level in pre-settlement times. Literally no evidence pres-ently exists to suggest that New World Puritan women fared any better than their English contemporaries. In fact, it can easily be argued that Puritans were, in some respects, more conservative than many Englishmen—for example, in their preoccupation with male dominance in marriage manuals, in their reluctance to employ farm wives at outside agricultural tasks, in their attacks on female vanity and pride, in their refusal to authorize female membership on juries, in their interest in witchcraft prosecutions after those had ceased to be popular in England, in their persecution of long-haired men and trousered women, in their sometime reminders to rebels like Anne Hutchinson and Anne Hibbins to maintain the expected submissive behavior, in their paltry legacies for daughters, and in their failure to recognize the legitimacy or importance of female sensuality. The one study which attempts to make a case for Puritan liberation of the "weaker sex," Thompson's *Women in Stuart England and America*, is long on impressionistic statements but short on substantive facts. More research is clearly needed in this vein.

Whatever the theoretical and practical differences between Englishmen and New England Calvinists, within New England itself considerable variation existed. Gortonists affirmed the "equal authority" of husband and wife, objected to corporal punishment as a viable way to keep boys and girls in line, and censured Puritans for believing in witches. Quakers held that women could preach, participate in church governance, and correct erring husbands. Antinomians supported the right of women to speak out publicly on religious matters. Women of the Maine–New Hampshire frontier were more inclined than their Puritan contemporaries to engage in active resistance to the authorities. Connecticut legitimized wills made by wives, usually appointed widows executors of their husbands' estates, and allowed prenuptial contracts, while Massachusetts was much less inclined to do so. Plymouth, more isolated than its neighbors, kept women in check more easily than any other colony. Massachusetts limited women's access to full participation in the state, the church, and the economy, rigorously prosecuting any "rebels"' who attempted to assert themselves. In contrast to Calvinist-dominated areas, Rhode Island provided more financial assistance to poor women, punished sexual offenders of both sexes equally, punished abusive husbands more severely than abusive wives, did not prosecute long-haired men, allowed women to preach and participate in political controversy, made divorce easier, and failed to use witchcraft prosecutions to check assertive women.

Less repressive and oppressive than bordering colonies, this "sewer of New England" served as the alternative colony for women, as well as for religious dissenters. Seventeenth-century New England was by no means a completely homogeneous society.

Of course, in all areas women were, to one extent or another, described as the "weaker sex," even though the patency of sex-role conditioning could not convert all women into proper gentledames. New England women did protest, both directly and indirectly, consciously and unconsciously, the limitations of the ideal female role. Puritan males, reacting both to tradition and to a multitude of insecurities, conventionally searched for power through their male-dominated social institutions, whereas these discontented women attempted to control their own destinies, to one degree or another, or to exercise power over others. When a husband tried to dominate his wife, in accordance with contemporary teaching, she could retaliate by withholding sex, disposing of "his" property without permission, committing adultery, physically abusing him, or running away. Through divorce petitions, efforts to open a business, and infanticide, women sought more control over their own lives. Some accentuated their weakness to gain influence or a desired end by covert manipulation; others had considerable impact on others by attaching themselves to the self-justifying power of God as heretical missionaries. A few tied themselves to the supernatural power of Satan and black magic. More than sixty adolescent girls and older women held numerous onlookers spellbound while they experienced hysterical fits. Numerous women stood up for their own point of view and heaped contempt or sharp words upon the authorities. In so many different ways, women struggled to assert themselves against the constrictive force of Puritanism.

It was an uphill struggle for much of the century. Burdened by the lack of a really effective form of contraception, by a long cultural tradition which equated womanhood with marriage and wifely dependency, by legal inequities and economic disadvantages, women in seventeenth-century New England—like their counterparts of more recent times—found self-assertion, or even self-awareness, difficult. Still, oppression bred frustration, and that in turn led to resistance, especially during the changing decades of late century. Most particularly in the materialistic, cosmopolitan world of the 1690s, the increasing numbers of female criminals, innkeepers, sexual rebels, well-dressed gentledames, and even suicides indicated how social conditioning often failed to mold the kind of women orthodox Puritans celebrated and required. Such "rebels" had a vital role to play in determining the quality of life in seventeenth-century New England. Their search for power, to one degree or another, had been successful.

"Herstory" is often not a very happy tale, and colonial scholars have only recently began piecing together its manifold parts. So much more waits to be discovered. We need to know, for example, how English customary and local law affected New England practice. Comparative examinations of woman's position in the Southern colonies, Quaker Pennsylvania, Dutch New Amsterdam, New Sweden, and French Canada might profitably be undertaken. The entire eighteenth century prior to the Revolution deserves fuller study, especially on a colony-by-colony basis. Only then can we reasonably determine how widespread the New England pattern (or, more appropriately, patterns) was, or how long the trend of the secular woman lasted.

Many unsubstantiated interpretations abound in the available literature. However, before we can come to grips with the nature and importance of sex roles in history, we must do some careful sifting and winnowing of primary materials—without preconceived notions about the direction of woman's history. (I actually began this study with the assumption—soon to be proven inaccurate —that Puritanism did, in some profound way, liberate the weaker sex.) Women in the past have often been shortchanged by their exclusion from history. One can only hope that future scholars can bring into fuller focus the complex dimensions of woman's roles and women's realities. Justice is long overdue.

1. The Connecticut authorities acquitted Hugh Crotia of witchcraft in 1693. Winifred Benham similarly received an acquittal from a New Haven County jury in 1692, then five years later fled to New York after renewed complaints against her. See J. Taylor, *Witchcraft Del. in Conn.*, pp. 118, 155; "New Haven Ct. Rec.," I, 202.

Massachusetts authorities did not try any witches after 1693, although neighbors made accusations against alleged witches far into the eighteenth century. Sam Sewall wrote on January 19, 1693/4, "This day Mrs. Prout dies after sore conflicts of mind, not without suspicion of witchcraft." In 1709, 61 of Mehitabel Warren's associates petitioned in her behalf after her accusation. No one faced prosecution in either instance, however. When three children at Littleton fell into hysterical fits in 1720 and designated a neighboring woman as their afflictor, rationalists explained their turmoil as due to distempered minds, dullwittedness, "perverse and wicked" behavior, physical maladies, and too much imagination. Still, the popular belief in witches continued long after. About 1760 a Billerica woman shot at three neighbors who came to her house to examine her for witch's teats. A few years later a Kennebunk (Maine) farmer beat a widow whom he thought had bewitched his cattle; he was appropriately punished for assault and battery. As late as 1789 Seth McFarlain fired at the specter of an "old hag," then explained she had dodged the bullet. See Sewall, *Diary*, I, 388; "Witchcraft in Hingham," p. 263; Turell, "Detection of Witchcraft"; Thacher, *Essay on Demon.*, pp. 198–204.

2. Breen, *Character of the Good Ruler*, pp. 180–203.

3. Dunn, *Puritans & Yankees*, pp. 286–335; "Gershom Bulkeley to [N.Y.] Governor Fletcher, Oct. 30, 1693," in Sainsbury & Headlam, eds., *Calendar of State Papers*, XIV, 197 (no. 650 xviii); Bushman, *From Puritan to Yankee*, pp. 41–72.

4. See Dunn, *Puritans & Yankees*, pp. 286–355.

5. Sainsbury & Headlam, eds., *Calendar of State Papers*, XV, 189–90 (no. 358); XVII, 449 (no. 817).

6. *Ibid.*, XV, 161–62 (no. 282).

7. *Ibid.*, XV, 367 (no. 729), 368–72 (no. 730).

8. *Ibid.*, XVI, 78–79 (no. 145), 91–92 (no. 186), 565–66 (no. 1022); XVII, 8 (no. 19), 18 (no. 34), 380 (no. 689), 426 (no. 769).

9. Quoted in Dunn, *Puritans & Yankees*, pp. 316–17.

10. Quoted in Breen, *Character of the Good Ruler*, p. 190.

11. Doyle, *Puritan Colonies*, II, 328; Sainsbury & Headlam, eds., *Calendar of State Papers*, XIV, 391 (no. 1467).

12. N. Hamp. "Ct. Papers," X (1693–94), 185.

13. "Rec., Ct. of Assts. & Sup. Ct., 1687–1715," in "Conn. Rec.," XLVIII, 27–28.

14. "Hartford Probate Rec.," V, 112, 120; N. Hamp. "Prov. Ct. Rec.—Ct. of Quarter Sessions," p. 41; Hamp. Ct. of "Gen. Sessions & Common Pleas, no. 1, 1677–1728," pp. 164–65.

15. N. Hamp. "Ct. Papers," X, 326; Dunn, *Puritans & Yankees*, p. 316.

16. N. Hamp. "Prov. Ct. Rec.—Ct. of Quarter Sessions," pp. 29, 34; N. Hamp. "Ct. Papers," X, 324–25; Hampshire Ct. of "Gen. Sessions & Common Pleas, no. 1, 1677–1728," p. 166; "Middlesex Ct. of Gen. Sessions, 1692–1723," n.p.

17. Hampshire "Ct. of Gen. Sessions & Common Pleas, no. 1, 1677–1728," p. 169; "Rec., Ct. of Assts. & Sup. Ct., 1687–1715," in "Conn. Rec.," XLVIII, 13; Bouton, ed., *N.-Hamp. Prov. Papers*, II, 198–99.

18. The Lords of Admiralty actually suggested that merchants send out "supernumerary seamen" on their ships to avoid "inconveniences arising from the impressment of seamen." Many impressed seamen deserted from English man-o'-wars, and some deserters became pirates. See Salisbury & Headlam, eds., *Calendar of State Papers*, XV, 297–98 (no. 567), 436 (no. 894).

19. Ziff, *Puritanism in Am.*, pp. 256, 258; "A Manifesto, 1699," in A. Vaughan, ed., *Puritan Trad. in Am.*, pp. 329–33.

20. Ziff, *Puritanism in Am.*, pp. 262–67.

21. In Roxbury the number of new church members increased from 44 in the 1660s to 51 in the 1670s and 91 in the 1680s, then decreased to 84 in the 1690s. At Dorchester the 1690s total (62) was only five higher than the 1680s and less than the 1670s ($N = 69$). In Hartford only 53 persons joined the

Second Church as full members, a decrease of 61 from the 1670s total. Of the six churches used in this study, only two, the Boston First Church and the First Congregational Church of Stonington, Connecticut, had significant increases. See Chart 14.; Pope, *Half-Way Covenant*, pp. 280, 285; Boston Rec. Cmrs., *Rep. Containing Roxbury Rec.*, pp. 101–2; *Rec. of Dorchester Church*, pp. 27–29; Parker, *Hist. of Hartford Second Church*, pp. 290–94; Wheeler, *Hist. of Stonington First Cong. Church*; Pierce, ed., *Rec. of Boston First Church*, I, 13–98; Moran, "Religious Renewal," p. 246.

22. Lucas, *Valley of Discord*, p. 244.

23. Quoted in Breen, *Character of the Good Ruler*, p. 187

24. *Ibid.*, pp. 164–67, 183, 201.

25. Craven, *Colonies in Transition*, p. 307.

26. Doyle, *Puritan Colonies*, II, 387–88; Ziff, *Puritanism in Am.*, p. 241.

27. Sainsbury & Headlam, eds., *Calendar of State Papers*, XV, 85 (no. 172), 339 (no. 653), 299–300 (no. 571); XVII, 416 (no. 746vii), 132 (no. 247).

28. *Ibid.*, XV, 214 (no. 396).

29. Dunn, *Puritans & Yankees*, p. 312.

30. Sainsbury & Headlam, eds., *Calendar of State Papers*, XVII, 38–39 (no. 73).

31. *Ibid.*, XVII, xlv, 71–72 (no. 116vii).

32. Greene & Harrington, *Am. Pop. Before Census of 1790*, pp. 14, 48, 70.

33. Dunn, *Puritans & Yankees*, p. 319.

34. Scottow, *Old Men's Tears*, p. 6.

35. *Mass. Acts & Laws, Nov. 20, 1695*, p. 143; C. Mather, *Bostonian Ebenezer*, p. 31.

36. C. Mather, quoted in Miller, *N. Eng. Mind: From Col. to Prov.*, p. 307.

37. C. Mather, *Religious Marriner*, pp. 5, 15–18.

38. Sewall, *Diary*, I, 498.

39. C. Mather, *Humiliations Follow'd with Deliverances*, p. 10; Ward, *Trip to N. Eng.*, pp. 54–55.

40. See Chart 11.3.

41. "N. Haven Ct. Rec.," II, 15.

42. *Their Majesties Col. of Conn. Vindicated*, p. 115.

43. Miller, *N. Eng. Mind: From Col. to Prov.*, pp. 171, 177.

44. Some continued to write jeremiads after 1692, but they were in the minority. E.g., C. Mather, *Bostonian Ebenezer* and *Reformation the Great Duty*; Walter, *Unfaithful Hearers Detected*; [W. Jameson,] *Remembrance of Former Times*; Willard, *Impenitent Sinners Warned*.

45. I. Mather, *Folly of Sinning*, p. 4; J. Williams, *Warning to Unclean*, p. 52.

46. Mass. *Acts & Laws, May 30, 1694–Feb. 27, 1695*, p. 101.

47. Traford, "Transformation of Mass. Education, 1670–1780," pp. 291–303; Lawson quoted in Hiner, "Cry of Sodom Enquired Into," p. 16.

48. Quoted in Morgan, *Puritan Family*, pp. 84–85.

49. J. Williams, *Warning to the Unclean*, p. 20; C. Mather, *Magnalia*, II, 576.

50. C. Mather, *Magnalia*, II, 576.

51. Slotkin, *Regeneration through Violence*, pp. 98, 100, 123; Coleman, "Story of Some N. Eng. Girls."

52. Slotkin, *Regeneration through Violence*, pp. 110, 128; Coleman, *N. Eng. Captives*, I, 172, 204–5.

53. Slotkin, *Regeneration through Violence*, pp. 47, 76, 109; Coleman, *N.*

Eng. Captives, I, 232.

54. J. Williams, *Redeemed Captive*, pp. 49–50, 55, 57.

55. Slotkin, *Regeneration through Violence*, pp. 128–39.

56. Vail, "Certain Ind., Captives in N. Eng.," p. 117.

57. Douglas, *Status of Women in N. Eng. & N. France*, p. 1. After considering the important position played by French women in Canada's religious and educational life, Douglas concludes his sixteen-page pamphlet with the words, "Though the womanhood of New England was undoubtedly as devout and unselfish, it was excluded by social habits and religious prejudice from exerting its influence as ostensibly and widely as these women of New France exerted theirs." Douglas may be right, but his pamphlet, however suggestive, is altogether too brief to prove his point.

The position of women in France has been more fully studied. Julia Kavanaugh believed that French women possessed a great deal of power in seventeenth-century society; their salons were centers of learning, and their advice was solicited and respected. More recently, Dorothy Backer has called these salonkeepers "a feminist phenomenon." The historian W. H. Lewis has described the opening of educational opportunities to French noblewomen in the 1680s, a time when women were expected to be familiar with reading, writing, arithmetic, contracts, seigneurial rights, "the receipt of rents, the law of inheritance, wills and donations." David Hunt has reported that throughout the century the "advancing importance of feminine initiative was evident outside the household . . . and . . . there were women writers, political leaders, and even generals."

A comparative study of women in seventeenth-century France and England remains to be done—I might add, by someone other than an ardent nationalist of either country. However, even if the condition of the "weaker sex" was substantially better in France (at least among the upper classes), New France had its own distinctive blend of native American and French culture. More research is needed on the status of women there before that area's appeal for New England captives can be realistically assessed.

See Kavanaugh, *Woman in France*, pp. 3–22; Backer, *Precious Women*, passim; Lewis, *Splendid Century*, pp. 241–62; Hunt, *Parents & Children in Hist.*, pp. 68–76.

58. Coleman, *N. Eng. Captives*, I, 198.

59. *Ibid.*, pp. 265–68.

60. *Ibid.*, p. 144.

61. T. Hutchinson, *Hist. of Mass. Bay*, II, 82.

62. Coleman, *N. Eng. Captives*, I, 193.

63. C. Mather, *Magnalia*, II, 534.

64. See ch. 7.

65. Miller, *N. Eng. Mind: From Col. to Prov.*, p. 307; [Jameson,] *Remembrance of Former Times*, p. 17; S. Knight, ed., *Private Journal*, pp. 42–43.

66. C. Mather, *Ornaments for Daughters of Zion*, p. 124.

67. Boston Rec. Cmrs., *Rep. Containing Boston Rec. 1660–1701*, p. 214; Boston Rec. Cmrs., *Rep. Containing Rec. of Boston Selectmen, 1701–15*, pp. 99, 165; Abbot, *Women in Ind.*, p. 15; *Acts & Resolves, Public & Private, of Mass.*, I, 213. The act rated working women at 2s., if they could pay it, while men were assessed at twice that amount.

68. S. Knight, ed., *Private Journal*, pp. 20, 38, 44–45, 47–48, 62.

69. Seybolt, *Private Schools of Col. Boston*, pp. 4–5.

70. Kilpatrick, *Dutch Schools, of N. Neth.*, p. 229; Lockridge, *Literacy in Col. N. Eng.*, p. 41.

71. Small, "Girls in Col. Schools," pp. 533–34.

72. Sainsbury & Headlam, eds., *Calendar of State Papers*, XVII, 512. In 1699 the New Hampshire General Assembly exempted Harvey from paying excises as long as she kept the post office.

73. See Chart 12.6.

74. Cases appear in Noble & Cronin, eds., *Rec. of Mass. Assts.*, I.

75. Sewall, "Selections from Sewall's Letter-Book," p. 383.

76. Brace, *Hist. Sketches of Andover*, p. 225n. Johnson spent eight months in prison as an accused witch during the Salem Village outbreak.

77. "A Manifesto, 1699," in A. Vaughan, ed., *Puritan Trad. in Am.*, p. 332.

78. *Acts & Resolves, Public & Private, of Mass.*, I, 48, 44, 53–54.

79. C. Mather, *Terribilia Dei*, p. 34.

80. See Appendix 4 for references.

81. *Acts & Laws, Passed by Gen. Ct. of Mass.* (1692), p. 23.

82. Smith, "Demographic Hist. of Col. N. Eng.," p. 177, Table 3, reports that the number of children per family in Hingham, Massachusetts, was 4.61 ($N = 84$ families) between 1691 and 1715, compared to a pre-1691 figure of 7.59 ($N = 97$ families). Harris, "Social Origins of Am. Leaders," p. 317, Table 14, gives a less significant decline in the average number of births per Harvard/Yale alumnus—from 5.96 ($N = 186$) in 1656–98 to 5.21 ($N = 289$) in 1699–1722.
Ned Ward implied that birth control was fairly widespread when he asserted, with characteristic overstatement, that Boston "Women have done bearing Children by that time they are four and twenty" (Ward, *Trip to N. Eng.*, p. 54).

83. See ch. 3, p. 83, for a discussion of contraceptive techniques.

84. J. Williams, *Warning to the Unclean*, p. 23.

85. C. Mather, *A Cloud of Witnesses*, p. 1.

86. It is impossible to find out how many persons actually appeared in court on fornication charges because many of the court records are partially missing for the 1690s. Moreover, after the mid-1680s increasing numbers of fornication cases were tried on a local level, by justices of the peace. Still, despite the missing records, much literary material and the extant cases indicate an upswing in premarital fornication.

87. Smith & Hindus, "Pre-marital Pregnancy in Am.," pp. 560–65, provide evidence for an increase in prenuptial pregnancy rates (i.e., "the number of first children born less than eight months after marriage as a percentage of the total number of legitimate [first-] births") at Hingham, Dedham, Watertown, and Salem.

88. "Essex Ct. Papers," XLIX, 121.

89. J. Williams, *Warning to the Unclean*, p. 6.

90. Sewall, *Diary*, I, 349; C. Mather, *Magnalia*, II, 364; "Ct. Files—Suffolk Co.," XLVII (1697–1700), no. 4565; N. Hamp. "Prov. Ct. Rec.," p. 2.

91. "Middlesex Ct. of Sessions, 1692–1723," pp. 89, 95; N. Hamp. "Prov. Ct. Rec.," p. 16.

92. "Middlesex Ct. of Sessions, 1692–1723," p. 89.

93. "Essex Ct. Papers," L, 62–63.

94. See Chart 12.1 for more complete statistics.

95. The percentage of female offenders (excluding fornicators from the total) by time interval is as follows:

Colony	1630–64	1665–89	1690–99
Maine	18.1	17.5	20.4
Massachusetts	16.0	16.5	16.7
Plymouth	9.0	5.6	10.1
Connecticut	11.6	12.0	10.1
New Hampshire	10.3	13.7	7.4
Martha's Vineyard	—	7.4	20.6

96. Oberholzer, *Delinquent Saints*, p. 255 (Table V).

97. J. Adams, *Prov. Society, 1690–1763*, p. 159.

98. C. Mather, *Magnalia*, I, 92.

99. Hilda Smith, "Private Tyranny"; Reynolds, *Learned Lady in Eng.*, pp. 271–323; Gagen, *The New Woman*, passim, esp. p. 11; Stenton, *Eng. Woman in Hist.*, pp. 209–30.

100. Sewall, *Diary*, I, 507; Turell, *Life & Character of Rev. Colman*, pp. 35–40.

101. S. Knight, *Private Journal*, pp. iv–vi.

102. *Ibid.*, pp. 12, 23, 61, 64.

103. *Ibid.*, pp. 9–10, 12–13, 28, 61.

104. *Ibid.*, p. 70.

105. *Ibid.*, p. 63.

106. C. Mather, *Diary*, II, 706.

107. J. Cotton, *A Meet Help*, p. 21.

108. Quoted in Paine, "Ungodly Carriages on Cape Cod," p. 183.

109. [Sewall,] *Mrs. Judith Hull of Boston*, broadside. See also J. Danforth, "A Poem upon Anne Eliot," pp. 64–65.

110. J. Williams, *Warning to the Unclean*, pp. 23–26, 35, 48.

111. Moran, "Religious Renewal," p. 251; *idem,* "'Sisters' in Christ"; Masson, "Typology of the Female"; E. Morgan, *Puritan Family*, pp. 161–65; Pope, *Halfway Covenant*, pp. 280–85; Ulrich, "Vertuous Women Found."

112. Bridenbaugh, *Cities in Wilderness*, p. 106.

113. Sewall, *Diary*, II, 194.

114. Quoted in Dunn, *Puritans & Yankees*, p. 344.

115. C. Mather, *Diary*, II, 706.

116. Madame Knight wrote, with reference to Connecticut people, "They are generaly very plain in their dress, throughout all ye Colony, as I saw, and follow one another in their mode; that you may know where they belong, especially the women, meet them where you will." See S. Knight, *Private Journal*, pp. 39, 42, 44.

117. Waters, "Family, Inheritance, & Migration," p. 9; C. Davis, *Hist. of Wallingford*, p. 311.

118. Morison, *Founding of Harvard*, pp. 155–56.

Appendixes

Appendix 1.

Petitions for Divorce in New England, 1620–99

MASSACHUSETTS BAY COLONY

	Date	Case	Cause Cited	Disposition	Source
1.	1636	Mrs. v. Richard Beggarly	Adultery	Unknown	Winthrop, *Journal*, I, 287
2.	1639	Second wife v. James Luxford	Bigamy	Granted	Noble & Cronin, eds., *Rec. Mass. Assts.*, II, 89
3.	1644	Anne v. Dennis Clarke	Desertion, adultery	Granted	*Ibid.*, II, 138
4.	1644	Elizabeth Frier v. John Richardson	Bigamy	Granted	*Ibid.*, II, 139
5.	1647	Sarah v. William Barnes	Adultery, desertion	Granted	Aspinwall, *Notarial Rec.*, 97
6.	1650	William v. Eleanor Palmer	Desertion, bigamy	Granted	Shurtleff, ed., *Mass. Rec.*, IV: I, 32
7.	1651	Margery v. William Norman*	Bigamy	Granted	Libby, Allen, & Moody, eds., *Maine Ct. Rec.*, I, 169
8.	1652	Dorothy v. William Pester	Long absence	Granted	Shurtleff, ed., *Mass. Rec.*, III, 277;IV: I, 89
9.	1654	Dorcas v. John Hall	Desertion, adultery?	Granted	*Ibid.*, III, 350; IV: I, 190
10.	1656	Samuel and Apphia Freeman	Unknown	Granted	"Ct. Files—Suffolk," II, #257
11.	1655–59	Joan v. George Halsell	Adultery	Granted	*Ibid.*, II, #257; Shurtleff, ed., *Mass. Rec.*, IV: I, 272, 380, 401
12.	1656	William v. Martha Clements	Unknown	Denied	Shurtleff, ed., *Mass. Rec.*, IV: I, 259, 269; "Mass. Arch.," IX, 25
13.	1656	Mary v. Stephen Batchelor*	Desertion, bigamy	Granted	Shurtleff, ed., *Mass. Rec.*, IV: I, 282
14.	1659	Anna v. Edward Lane	Impotence	Granted	Noble & Cronin, eds., *Rec. Mass. Assts.*, III, 67–68; "Mass. Arch.," IX, 25
15.	1661	Rachel v. Joseph Langton	Unknown	Granted	Shurtleff, ed., *Mass. Rec.*, IV: II, 8
16.	1662	Mary v. William Chichester	Desertion	Granted	"Mass. Arch.," IX, 41
17.	1663	Margaret Bennett for her daughter Mary v. Elias White	Impotence	Denied	*Ibid.*, 42–45; Shurtleff, ed., *Mass. Rec.*, IV: II, 91

No.	Year	Case	Grounds	Outcome	Citation
18.	1664	Sarah v. Edward Helwis	Bigamy, desertion	Granted	Noble & Cronin, eds., Rec. Mass. Assts., III, 142; "Ct. Files—Suffolk," V, #651
19.	1669	Christopher v. Elizabeth Lawson*	Adultery, cruelty to husband	Unknown	"Mass. Arch.," IX, 59; "Ct. Files—Suffolk," IX, #913
20.	1670	Elizabeth v. Henry Stevens	Desertion, adultery	Granted	Shurtleff, ed., Mass. Rec., IV: II, 465
21.	1672	Katherine v. Edward Naylor	Adultery, cruelty	Granted	Noble & Cronin, eds., Rec. Mass. Assts., I, 32; "Ct. Files—Suffolk," XIII, #1148
22.	1673	Hannah v. Thomas Herrick	Impotence	Granted	Dow, ed., Essex Ct. Rec., V, 252
23.	1675	Mary v. William Sanders	Desertion, bigamy	Granted	Noble & Cronin, eds., Rec. Mass. Assts., I, 30;" Ct. Files—Suffolk," XVI, #1360
24.	1673–7	Mary v. Hugh Drury	Impotence	Denied	Noble & Cronin, eds., Rec. Mass. Assts., I, 91; "Ct. Files—Suffolk," XVIII, #1644
25.	Between 1676 & 1685	Mary v. Thomas Litchfield	Unknown	Granted	Savage, Geneal. Dict. of N. Eng., III, 108
26.	1677	Rachel v. Laurence Clinton	Unknown	Denied	Dow, ed., Essex Ct. Rec., VI, 344
27.	1677	Philip v. Mary Wharton	Adulterous carriage	Granted	"Mass. Arch.," IX, 65–71
28.	1678	Hugh v. Dorcas Marsh	Bigamy	Denied	Noble & Cronin, eds., Rec. Mass. Assts., I, 127; Shurtleff, ed., Mass. Rec., V, 205; "Ct. Files—Suffolk," XX, #1741
29.	1678	Mary v. Henry Maddox	Long absence	Granted	Shurtleff, ed., Mass. Rec., V, 188
30.	1678	Hope v. Samuel Ambrose	Desertion, adultery	Granted	Noble & Cronin, eds., Rec. Mass. Assts., I, 127
31.	1679	Elizabeth v. Robert Lisby	Bigamy	Granted	Ibid., I, 131; "Mass. Arch.," IX, 74–83
32.	1679	Rebecca v. Richard Cooley	Adultery, neglect of family, endangering life when pregnant	Granted	Noble & Cronin, eds., Rec. Mass. Assts., I, 138; "Mass. Arch.," IX, 72

33.	1679	Mary v. Augustin Lyndon	Adultery	Granted	Shurtleff, ed., Mass. Rec., V, 248–49; "Mass. Arch.," IX, 88–102; "Ct. Files—Suffolk," XXI, #1807
34.	1679	Mary v. Job Bishop	Desertion, bigamy	Granted	Noble & Cronin, eds., Rec. Mass. Assts., I, 144
35.	1679	Mary v. Joseph White	Desertion	Granted	Ibid., I, 147; "Mass. Arch.," IX, 84–87
36.	1680	Susan v. Edward Goodwin	Desertion, failure to provide	Granted	Noble & Cronin, eds., Rec. Mass. Assts., I, 168
37.	1681	Samuel v. Mary Holton	Adultery, desertion	Granted	Ibid., I, 197
38.	1681	Dorcas v. Christopher Smith	Desertion, failure to provide	Granted	Ibid., I, 200
39.	1681	Rachel v. Lawrence Clinton	Adulterous carriage	Granted	Ibid., I, 208; "Mass. Arch.," IX, 204
40.	1682	Elizabeth v. Robert Street	Bigamy	Granted	Noble & Cronin, eds., Rec. Mass. Assts., I, 227
41.	1682	Sarah v. Hubartus Mattoon*	Adultery, desertion	Granted	Page, Judicial Beginnings of N. H., 162–63; Libby, Allen, & Moody, eds., Maine Ct. Rec., III, 87–88
42.	1683	Ann v. Mr. Perry	Impotence	Denied	Noble & Cronin, eds., Rec. Mass. Assts., I, 229
43.	1683	Elizabeth v. Nicholas Manning	Incest, desertion	Granted	Ibid., I, 240
44.	1684	Sarah v. Thomas Cooper	Desertion	Granted	Ibid., I, 256, 258
45.	1685	Thomas v. Rachel Windsor	Adultery	Granted	"Ct. Files—Suffolk," XXVII, #2347
46.	1685	Mary Litchfield for daughter Mary v. Henry Straight	Taking her clothing, nonsupport, beating & abusing her	Unknown	Morgan, Puritan Family, 38n
47.	1685	Hannah v. Benjamin Ayres	Desertion	Granted	"Mass. Arch.," IX, 114
48.	1690	Philip v. Hannah Goss	Desertion, bigamy	Granted	Noble & Cronin, eds., Rec. Mass. Assts., I, 326
49.	1690	Samuel and Rebecca Newton	Affinity (uncle's widow)	Marriage voided	Ibid., I, 342

50.	1691–5	Mary v. Samuel Stebbins	Adultery, desertion	Granted	Ibid., I, 242; "Mass. Arch.," IX, 146–47
51.	1691	Hannah and Josiah Owen	Affinity (brother's ex-wife)	Marriage voided	Noble & Cronin, eds., Rec. Mass. Assts., I, 361
52.	1693	Oliver v. Hannah Norris	Adultery	Granted	"Mass. Arch.," IX, 132–33
53.	1696	Richard v. Eunice Burt	Unknown	Unknown	Sainsbury & Headlam, eds., Calendar of State Papers, XV, 270
54.	1698	Rebecca v. Mr. Wansford	Bigamy	Granted	Ibid., XVI, 564

Petitions from wives = 39; petitions from husbands = 10; others or unknown = 5
*Petitions from Maine

PLYMOUTH COLONY

1.	1661	Elizabeth v. Thomas Burge	Adultery	Granted	Shurtleff & Pulsifer, eds., Plym. Rec., III, 221
2.	1664	William v. Mercy Tubbs	Adultery, desertion	Granted	Ibid., IV, 66, 187, 192
3.	1669	John v. Martha Hewitt	Incest with father	Unknown	Ibid., V, 21
4.	1670	Samuel v. Jane Halloway	Adultery	Unknown	Ibid., V, 32, 41–42
5.	1670	James v. Elizabeth Skiffe	Desertion, adultery	Granted	Ibid., V, 33
6.	1673	John v. Sarah Williams	Desertion	Granted	Ibid., V, 127
7.	1675	Edward Jenkins for his daughter Mary v. Marmaduke Atkinson	Desertion	Granted	Ibid., V, 159
8.	1680	Elizabeth v. Henry Stevens	Bigamy	Granted	Ibid., VI, 44–45
9.	1686	John v. Mary Glover	Adultery	Granted	Ibid., VI, 190

Petitions from wives = 2; petitions from husbands = 6; others = 1

NEW HAMPSHIRE COLONY

1.	1682	Sarah v. Hubartus Mattoon	Adultery, desertion	Referred to Maine jurisdiction	Page, Judicial Beginnings of N.H., 162–3
2.	1697	Elizabeth v. Mr. Smart	Desertion	Granted	Ibid., 163

Petitions from wives = 2

1.	1655	Goody v. Thomas Beckwith	Desertion	Granted	J. Trumbull, ed., Conn. Rec., I, 275
2.	1657	Robert v. Joan Wade	Refusal to have intercourse	Granted	Ibid., I, 301
3.	1660	Sarah v. Mr. North	Desertion	Granted	Ibid., I, 362
4.	1660	Ellen v. Jasper Clemens	Suspected bigamy	Separated	Ibid., I, 351
5.	1662	William Benfield v. Elizabeth Colson	Adultery, running away	Granted (?)	Wyllys Papers, 133–34
6.	1662	Bridget v. Thomas Baxter	Desertion	Granted	J. Trumbull, ed., Conn. Rec., I, 379
7.	1664	Samuel v. Rebecca Smith	Desertion, adultery	Denied	"Conn. Archives, Crimes," 1st ser., III, 194–210
8.	1665	Mrs. v. Robert Morris	Impotence	Granted	"Conn. Assts.," LVI, 36
9.	1667	Rebecca v. Samuel Smith	Desertion	Granted	Ibid., LVI, 63
10.	1668	Mary v. John Halloway	Impotence	Separated	Ibid., LVI, 72
11.	1669	Mary v. Charles Barnes	Adultery	Granted	Ibid., LIII, 1
12.	1669–72	Sarah v. Zachary Dibble	Desertion, adultery, cruelty	Granted	Ibid., LIII, 11; "Conn. Arch. Crimes," 1st, III, 211–4
13.	1670	Hannah v. Thomas Huit	Desertion	Granted	J. Trumbull, ed., Conn. Rec., I, 379
14.	1672	John v. Abigail Betts	Adultery	Granted	"Conn. Assts.," LIII, 12–3
15.	1673	Mary v. John Browne	Adultery, desertion	Granted	Ibid., LIII, 18
16.	1673	Elizabeth v. Robert Jarrad	Desertion	Granted	Ibid., LIII, 18
17.	1674	Elizabeth v. William Sedgwick	Desertion	Granted	Ibid., LIII, 15
18.	1676	Lydia v. William Moore	Desertion, adultery	Granted	Ibid., LIII, 20–21
19.	1676	Sarah v. Mr. Towle	Desertion	Granted	J. Trumbull, ed., Conn. Rec., II, 292
20.	1677	Elizabeth v. John Rogers	Heretical opinions, hard usage	Granted	Ibid., II, 292–23; "Conn. Assts.," LIII, 21
21.	1677	Mary v. Patrick Murrain	Desertion	Granted	J. Trumbull, ed., Conn. Rec., II, 322
22.	1677	Mercy v. John Niccolson	Desertion	Granted	Ibid., II, 327
23.	1677	Experience v. William Shepard	Desertion	Granted	Ibid., II, 327
24.	1678	Joanna v. Henry Pember	Desertion	Granted	Ibid., III, 23
25.	1680	John v. Martha Fish	Desertion, adultery	Granted	"Conn. Assts.," LIII, 30
26.	1680	James v. Alice Wakely	Refusal to accompany husband to Newport	Denied	"Conn. Arch. Crimes," 1st, III, 215–16
27.	1680	Alice v. James Wakely	Desertion	Unknown	Ibid., 215–16
28.	1682	Hugh v. Alice Macky	Cruelty, desertion, adultery	Granted	Ibid., 217–22

29.	1682	Mehittabel v. David Ensigne	Adultery	Granted	"Conn. Assts.," LIII, 45
30.	1683	Thomas v. Ruth Gutsell	Desertion	Granted	Ibid., LIII, 48
31.	1683–7	Mary v. Mr. Orgor	Desertion	Unknown	"Conn Arch Crimes," 1st, III, 227
32.	1685	Rebecca v. William Collins	Desertion	Granted	"Conn. Assts.," LIII, 55
33.	1685	Frances v. Henry Gordon	Desertion	Granted	Ibid., LIII, 60
34.	1686	Margaret v. George Hutchinson	Desertion	Granted	Ibid., LIII, 61
35.	1687	Thomas v. Martha Olmstead	Fraudulent contract	Granted	Ibid., LIII, 62–63; LVIII, 2; "Conn. Arch. Crimes," 1st, III, 228–34
36.	1689–91	Richard v. Elizabeth Edwards	Refusing sex, adultery	Denied	"Conn. Assts.," LVIII, 8; "Conn. Arch. Crimes," 1st, III, 235–39
37.	1691	Richard v. Elizabeth Rogers	Desertion	Granted	J. Trumbull, ed., Conn. Rec., IV, 37, 52–53, 59
38.	1692	Mercy v. Ebenezer Hill	Adultery	Granted	"Conn. Assts.," LVIII, 15
39.	1692–93	Nathaniel and Elizabeth Finch	Affinity (brother's ex-wife)	Annulled	"Conn. Arch. Crimes," 1st, III, 244–55
40.	1692	Susannah v. John Hodge	Adultery, desertion	Granted	"Conn. Assts.," LVIII, 15
41.	1693	Hannah v. Andrew Winton	Desertion	Granted	Ibid., LVIII, 18
42.	1693	Sarah v. John Dorman	Impotence	Unknown	Ibid., LVIII, 18; "Conn. Arch. Crimes," 1st, III, 242–43
43.	1694	John v. Lydia Ventrus	Fraudulent contract	Granted	"Conn. Assts.," LVIII, 24; "Conn. Arch. Crimes," 1st, III, 256–58
44.	1695	Joseph v. Mrs. Ingram	Desertion	Denied	"Conn. Assts.," LVIII, 32; "Conn. Arch. Crimes," 1st, III, 259
45.	1699–1704	Mary v. David Sage	Desertion	Granted	"Conn. Arch. Crimes," 1st, III, 272–73

Petitions from wives = 31; petitions from husbands = 13; other = 1

NEW HAVEN COLONY

1.	1656	Hannah v. John Uffit	Impotence	Granted	Hoadly, ed., N. Haven Rec., 1653–Union, 201–2
2.	1661	Mary v. William Andrews, Jr.	Bigamy	Granted	Ibid., 425–27

Petitions from wives = 2

RHODE ISLAND–PROVIDENCE PLANTATIONS COLONY

#	Year	Parties	Grounds	Outcome	Source
1.	1644?	John Hicks v. Horod Long	Adultery; loss of affection	Separated	Chapin, Doc. Hist. R.I., II, 152; Bartlett, ed., R.I. Col. Rec., II, 99
2.	1655	John and Elizabeth Coggeshall	Mutual consent	Separated	Bartlett, ed., R.I. Col. Rec., I, 319
3.	1655	Thomas v. Mrs. Jennings	Desertion	Unknown	Ibid., I, 392
4.	1664	Sarah v. Mr. Parker	Unknown	Left to next Gen. Assembly	Ibid., II, 82–83
5.	1665	Horod Long v. George Gardiner	"Much oppression of spirit"	Common law marriage split up	Ibid., II, 99–103
6.	1665	Margaret v. John Porter	Desertion	Separated	Ibid., II, 119–21
7.	1665	Peter v. Ann Talman	Adultery	Granted	Ibid., II, 122–24
8.	1667	Robert v. Margaret Colwell	Unknown	Granted	Ibid., II, 204
9.	1667	Mary v. Richard Pray	Unknown	Separated by Assembly; divorced by a magistrate 1672	Ibid., II, 188–89, 479; Calendar of State Papers, XVII, 546
10.	1669	Elizabeth v. Henry Stevens	Threats against her life	Separated	"Mass. Arch.," IX, 51
11.	1675	John and Mrs. Lewis	Mutual consent	Self-divorced	Muddy River & Brookline Rec., 69
12.	1676	John v. Hannah Belou	Husband's impotence	Granted	Bartlett, ed., R.I. Col. Rec., II, 543
13.	1680	James and Alice Wakeley	Unknown	Not granted	Savage, Geneal. Dict. of N. Eng., IV, 387
14.	1683	Ann v. John Warner	Adultery, personal violence	Granted?	Bartlett, ed., R.I. Col. Rec., III, 124
15.	1684	Phoebe v. John Cook	Desertion, bigamy, failure to provide	Granted	Ibid., III, 164
16.	1697	Daniel and Mary Wilcox	Unknown	Granted	Calendar of State Papers, XVII, 546

Petitions from wives = 7; petitions from husbands = 6; others = 3

Appendix 2.

Female Innkeepers and Liquor-Sellers in New England, 1620–99

	Year	Name	Locale	Marital status
1.	1643	William Knop's wife	Massachusetts	Md
2.	1647	Widow Clark	Salem, Mass.	Wid
3.	1661–75	Widow Upshaw	Boston, Mass.	Wid
4.	1661–62, 1664	Alice Thomas	Boston, Mass.	Wid
5.	1662, 1682	Patience Spencer	Saco, Maine Wells, Maine	Md Wid
6.	1662–7	Rachel Webster	Portsmouth, N. Hamp.	Wid
7.	1663	Lydia Garret	Scituate, Plym.	—
8.	1663	Martha Beamsley	Boston, Mass.	Wid
9.	1663, 1673–75	Joanna Courser	Boston, Mass.	Md
10.	1664	Johanna Tuck	Hampton, N. Hamp.	Wid
11.	1665	Widow Urin	Star Island, N. Hamp.	Wid
12.	1666	Widow Turner	Boston, Mass.	Wid
13.	1666	Elizabeth Sharrats	Haverhill, Mass.	Md
14.	1667	Sarah Abbot	Portsmouth, N. Hamp.	Wid
15.	1668	Sarah Morgan	Kittery, Maine	Md
16.	1669	Widow Snow	Boston, Mass.	Wid
17.	1670–80, 1684, 1690–91	Elizabeth Wardell	Boston, Mass.	Wid
18.	1672, 1677	Widow Hill	Malden, Mass.	Wid
19.	1673–82, 1690	Rebecca Winsor	Boston, Mass.	Wid
20.	1673–74	Elizabeth Connigrave	Boston, Mass.	Md
21.	1673–74, 1676–79	Ann Puglice or Puglace	Boston, Mass.	Md
22.	1673	Mrs. Johnson	Boston, Mass.	Md
23.	1673–74	Mrs. Jones	Boston, Mass.	Md
24.	1674	Ann Holliday	Boston, Mass.	Wid
25.	1676–79	Constance Mattocks	Boston, Mass.	—
26.	1676	Mrs. Rolfe	Boston, Mass.	Md
27.	1676–82	Elizabeth George	Dorchester, Mass.	Wid
28.	1677–78	Sarah Franckes	Boston, Mass.	Wid
29.	1677–81	Jane Bernard	Boston, Mass.	Wid
30.	1677–78	Elizabeth Belcher	Cambridge, Mass.	Wid
31.	1678	Mary Castle	Boston, Mass.	Wid
32.	1678	Hannah Edmunds	Charlestown, Mass.	—
33.	1678–81	Eleanor Phippany	Boston, Mass.	Wid
34.	1678	Amy Whitwell	Boston, Mass.	—
35.	1678–81	Phoebe Blanton	Boston, Mass.	Wid
36.	1678, 1681	Mary Williamson	Marshfield, Plym.	—
37.	1679	Rebecca Hawkins	Boston, Mass.	Wid
38.	1681	Widow Hudson	Boston, Mass.	Wid
39.	1681	Widow Sexton	Boston, Mass.	Wid

40.	1681	Widow Bosworth	Boston, Mass.	Wid
41.	1681–84	Mary Pray	Providence, R.I.	Wid
42.	1681–82	Ann Mosely	Boston, Mass.	—
43.	1682	Widow Martin	Boston, Mass.	Wid
44.	1682–88, 1690	Hannah Barrett	Charlestown, Mass.	Wid
45.	1683, 1695, 1698	Katherine Paul	Kittery, Maine	Wid
46.	1683–86	Margaret Murfree	Scituate, Plym.	—
47.	1683–84	Mary Combe	Middlebury, Plym.	—
48.	1684	Mary Long	Cambridge, Mass.	Md
49.	1686	Anne White	Newbury, Mass.	—
50.	1686	Edith Coman	Charlestown, Mass.	Md
51.	1686	Abigail Jones	Charlestown, Mass.	—
52.	1686	Mary Peachee	Charlestown, Mass.	Wid
53.	1686–88 1694, 1696–98	Mary Trumball	Charlestown, Mass.	Md
54.	1686–88	Elizabeth Edwards	Charlestown, Mass.	—
55.	1688	Mrs. Guilbert	Hartford, Conn.	Md
56.	1688	Hannah Rickland	Plymouth, Plym.	Wid
57.	1688	Sarah Davis	Charlestown, Mass.	Wid
58.	1688	Mary Sanford	Providence, R.I.	—
59.	1688	Sarah Blaney	Charlestown, Mass.	—
60.	1688–89	Anne Hooper	Marblehead, Mass.	—
61.	1690	Sarah Everton	Charlestown, Mass.	Wid
62.	1690	Mrs. Aaron Ludkin	Charlestown, Mass.	Md
63.	1690	Ann Pollard	Boston, Mass.	Wid
64.	1690	Mary Lawrence	Boston, Mass.	Wid
65.	1690–91	Martha Hewen	Boston, Mass.	Wid
66.	1690–91	Elizabeth Jackson	Boston, Mass.	Wid
67.	1690–91	Jane Heane	Boston, Mass.	Wid
68.	1690–91	Rebecca Stebbins	Boston, Mass.	Wid
69.	1690–91	Mary Hunt	Boston, Mass.	Wid
70.	1690–91	Sarah Hunt	Boston, Mass.	Wid
71.	1690–91	Hannah Mann	Boston, Mass.	—
72.	1690–91	Dorothy Gretian	Boston, Mass.	Wid
73.	1690–91	Sarah Harris	Boston, Mass.	Wid
74.	1690–91	Mercy Dowdon	Boston, Mass.	—
75.	1690	Elizabeth Barnes	Boston, Mass.	—
76.	1690	Ann Pierce	Boston, Mass.	—
77.	1690	Rebecca Charles	Boston, Mass.	—
78.	1690–91	Widow Beavis	Boston, Mass.	Wid
79.	1690, 1693	Mary Dafforne	Boston, Mass.	Wid
80.	1690–91	Elizabeth Stevens	Boston, Mass.	Wid

81.	1690–91, 1693–96	Sarah Robie	Boston, Mass.; Hampton, N. Hamp.	Wid
82.	1691	Elizabeth Winsor	Boston, Mass.	Wid
83.	1691, 1693	Elizabeth Watkins	Boston, Mass.	Wid
84.	1691	Widow Broughton	Boston, Mass.	Wid
85.	1691	Hannah Harris	Boston, Mass.	Wid
86.	1691	Mary Thatcher	Boston, Mass.	Wid
87.	1691	Widow Skinner	Boston, Mass.	Wid
88.	1691	Ann Griffin	Boston, Mass.	—
89.	1692–93, 1695–96	Hannah Frethy	York, Maine	Wid
90.	1692	Mary Dolliver	Marblehead, Mass.	—
91.	1692	Hannah Collins	Essex County, Mass.	—
92.	1692	Mary Gedney	Essex County, Mass.	—
93.	1692	Ann Collior	Salem, Mass.	—
94.	1692	Hannah Dyer	New Hampshire	—
95.	1692–93	Hannah Hull	New Hampshire	—
96.	1692–93, 1698–99	Ann Clark	Portsmouth, N. Hamp.	—
97.	1692	Elizabeth Elliot	Great Island, N. Hamp.	—
98.	1692–94	Mary Hoddy	Portsmouth, N. Hamp.	—
99.	1692–93, 1696	Katherine Johnson	Charlestown, Mass.	Md
100.	1692	Mary Davis	Essex County, Mass.	—
101.	1692	Hannah Shattock	Essex County, Mass.	—
102.	1692	Hannah Trask	Salem, Mass.	—
103.	1693	Joanna Hunlock	Boston, Mass.	—
104.	1693	Hannah Kent	Boston, Mass.	—
105.	1693	Mary Wright	Boston, Mass.	—
106.	1693	Susannah Gardner	Boston, Mass.	—
107.	1693	Deborah King	Boston, Mass.	—
108.	1693	Mary Pierce	Boston, Mass.	—
109.	1693	Sarah Baker	New Hampshire	—
110.	1693–94, 1698	Hannah Permut	New Hampshire	Md
111.	1693	Elinor Wilcomb	Isle of Shoals, N. Hamp.	—
112.	1693	Grace Tomling	Great Island, N. Hamp.	—
113.	1693–94	Joanna Hollicomb	New Hampshire	—
114.	1693–94	Rachel Mitchell	Great Island, N. Hamp.	—
115.	1693	Mrs. Cooper	Watertown, Mass.	Md
116.	1693, 1696–98	Ruth Baker	Charlestown, Mass.	Wid
117.	1694	Mary Barnwoll	New Hampshire	—
118.	1694	Joan Ameridith	Maine	Md

119.	1694–95	Anne Stevens	Ipswich, Mass.	—
120.	1694–95	Sarah Nason	Berwick, Maine	—
121.	1695–96	Mrs. Cutler	Charlestown, Mass.	Md
122.	1695	Mrs. Love Shearborn	Hampton, N. Hamp.	Md
123.	1695, 1698	Joanna Dearing	Maine	Wid
124.	1695, 1697	Joan Crafts	Kittery, Maine	Wid
125.	1696	Sarah Cutts	New Hampshire	—
126.	1696	Abigail Nichols	New Hampshire	—
127.	1696, 1698–99	Elizabeth Harvey	Portsmouth, N. Hamp.	—
128.	1696–98	Hannah Fosdick	Charlestown, Mass.	Wid
129.	1696–98	Sarah Bly	Charlestown, Mass.	Md
130.	1696–97	Elizabeth West	Newcastle, N. Hamp.	—
131.	1697	Hannah Stone	Taunton, Mass.	—
132.	1698	Elizabeth Redford	Portsmouth, N. Hamp.	Wid
133.	1698	Widow Bond	Charlestown, Mass.	Wid
134.	1698	Mary Ketted	Charlestown, Mass.	Wid
135.	1698	Sarah Cuttaslowd	New Hampshire	Md
136.	1698	Mary Frost	Maine	Md
137.	1698–99	Sarah Hopkins	Portsmouth, N. Hamp.	—
138.	1699	Abigail Partridge	Portsmouth, N. Hamp.	—
139.	1699	Mary Lidston	Maine	—

Total widows = 63; married women = 24; unknown = 52
By colony: Massachusetts = 96; New Hampshire = 26; Maine = 10;
   Plymouth = 5; Rhode Island = 2; Connecticut = 1

Appendix 2A.

Women on the 1687 Boston Tax List

	Name	Housing, Mills, Wharves	N Cows	From Trades & Estates	Value of Realty
1.	Widow Kellond	£40	0	£80*	£120
2.	Widow Hall	2	0	4*	6
3.	Widow Hunt	3	0	5*	8
4.	Widow Greenwood	3	0	5*	8
5.	Widow Gaurd	10	0	14*	24
6.	Widow Haneford	6	0	0	6
7.	Widow Cotter	6	0	0	6
8.	Widow Blackwell	6	0	0	6
9.	Widow Margaret Smith	6	0	0	6
10.	Widow Bell	6	0	0	6
11.	Widow Groves	6	0	0	6
12.	Widow Dowden	3	1(£3)	6*	12
13.	Widow Cundey	5	1(£3)	4*	12
14.	Widow Collicot	3	1(£3)	0	6
15.	Widow Joules	10	1(£3)	0	13
16.	Mrs. Winsley	20	1(£3)	15*	38
17.	Widow Warren	50	0	20*	70
18.	Susanah Oliver	15	0	10*	25
19.	Widow Carwithen alias Rolph	6	0	0	6
20.	Widow Keene	10	0	5*	15
21.	Widow Saxton	10	0	5*	15
22.	Mary Clarke	8	0	4*	12
23.	Widow Williams	6	0	0	6
24.	Widow Alice Thomas	12	0	0	12
25.	Widow Anderson	6	0	0	6
26.	Widow Baxter	6	0	0	6
27.	Deborah Prout	6	0	0	6
28.	Widow Webb	6	0	0	6
29.	Widow Ann Puglice	0	0	0	0
30.	Widow Martin	6	0	0	6
31.	Widow Everill	6	0	0	6
32.	Widow Manning	6	0	6	12
33.	Widow Elizabeth Thompson	8	0	8	16
34.	Widow Susannah Walker	6	0	15	21
35.	Widow Susanah Lendall	10	0	40	50
36.	Widow Winsor	6	0	6	12
37.	Widow Hannah Prouse	10	0	20	30
38.	Widow Mary Milam	6	0	6	12
39.	Widow Mary Lake	6	0	6	12
40.	Widow Ann Checkley	8	0	10	18
41.	Widow Turell	4	0	0	4
42.	Widow Rock	4	0	0	4
43.	Widow Newcombe	4	0	0	4
44.	Widow Whitwell	6	0	6	12
45.	Widow Emm Gepson	3	0	3	6
46.	Widow Dickerson	4	0	0	4

47.	Widow Edsell	6	0	6	12
48.	Sarah Barrett	6	0	6	12
49.	Mary Thatcher	12	0	0	12
50.	Widow Harrison	12	0	0	12
51.	Susanah Stokes	6	0	0	6
52.	Mary Lechfield	8	0	0	8
53.	Abigail Dudson	10	0	10	20
54.	Margaret Thatcher	20	0	20	40
55.	Mary Swett	15	1(£3)	20	38
56.	Mrs. Belingham	6	0	0	6
57.	Anne Hunt	10	0	0	10
58.	Mary Tyng	6	0	6	12
59.	Widow Smith	4	0	0	4
60.	Widow Gerish	4	0	8	12
61.	Widow Edgerton	4	0	8	12
62.	Widow Messinger	5	1(£3)	0	8
63.	Madam Leverett	37	0	5	42
64.	Widow Mary Stoddard	10	1(£3)	20	33
65.	Widow Mary Avery	16	0	30	46
66.	Widow Mann	20	0	4	24
67.	Widow Dudley	6	0	6	12
68.	Widow Judith Winslow	6	0	6	12
69.	Mrs. Lewes	6	0	0	6
70.	Widow Whetcombe	20	1(£3)	20	43
71.	Widow Frost	6	0	6	12
72.	Widow Langle	4	0	0	4
73.	Widow Cooke	6	0	0	6
74.	Widow Woody	6	0	0	6
75.	Widow Noyce	6	0	0	6
76.	Widow Hough	6	0	0	6
77.	Widow Stebbins	6	2(£6)	0	12
78.	Widow Sharpe	6	1(£3)	3	12
79.	Widow Ann Pollard	12	0	18	30
80.	Widow Parsons	20[†]	0	0	20
81.	Widow Elizabeth Winslow	0	0	0	0
82.	Elizabeth Barnes	10	0	20	30
83.	Widow Rainsford	6	1(£3)	15	24
84.	Widow Elliot	4	1(£3)	20	27
85.	Widow Daurs	4	0	0	4
86.	Widow Elgason	6	1(£3)	0	9
87.	Widow Barnard	6	0	6	12
88.	Florence Charty	5	1 Horse (£3)	5	13

*Indicates income from trades only
†For her warehouse at the dock

Appendix 2B.

Women on 1687 Tax Lists for Boston Suburbs

Name	Arable Land & Meadows	Pasture	Oxen	Cattle	Horses	Sheep	Swine	H‡	Total
MUDDY RIVER									
Widow Clarke	£2	£1	0	3(£7½)	1(£5)	0	0	£2	£17 10s.
RUMNEY MARSH									
Widow Maverick	20	20	2(£10)	6(£16½)	2(£10)	20(£10)	2(£2)	5	88 10s.
Aphra Bennett	0	0	0	0	0	0	0	0	0

‡Housing, Mills, and Wharves

Appendix 3.

Suicides in New England, 1620–1709

	Date	Party	Status	Locale	Means	Sources
1.	1620	Dorothy Bradford	Married to Wm. B.	Cape Cod Harbor	Drowning (Possible suicide)	Morison, "Intro." to W. Bradford, *Of Plym. Plant.*, xxiv
2.	1636	A man	Servant	Boston	Hanging	Hubbard, *Gen. Hist. N. Eng.*, V, 196
3.	1640	Richard Williams	Servant	Boston	Hanging	"Inquest on Body of Williams," 489–90
4.	1642	Mr. Turner	— —	Charlestown	Drowning	Winthrop, *Journal*, II, 55
5.	1645	One woman	— —	Saco, Maine	Drowning	"Thomas Jenner to John Winthrop, Mar. 28, 1645," in A. Forbes, ed., *Winthrop Papers*, V, 14
6.	1656	Thomas Johnson	— —	Boston	Drowning	"Ct. Files—Suffolk," II, no. 241
7.	1660	William Day	Servant	Plymouth Colony	Hanging	Shurtleff & Pulsifer, eds., *Plym. Rec.*, III, 213
8.	1660	Martha Coghan or Cogan	Widow	Massachusetts	Poison	Davenport, "Letter," 45
9.	1660	Goodwife Dwight	Married	Dedham	Drowning	Hull, "Memoir & Diaries," 195–96
10.	1661	Robert Allen	— —	Rehoboth	Unknown	Shurtleff & Pulsifer, eds., *Plym. Rec.*, IV, 13
11.	1661	John	Black servant	Salem	Shooting	Dow, ed., *Essex Ct. Rec.*, II, 421
12.	1664	Elizabeth Bishop	Widow	Ipswich	Drowning	Hull, "Memoir & Diaries," 214
13.	1664	Rebecca Sale	Married to Edward S.	Plymouth Colony	Hanging	Shurtleff & Pulsifer, eds., *Plym. Rec.*, IV, 83
14.	1664	Florence Bartoll	Married to John B.	Marblehead	Drowning	*Ibid.*, III, 223

	Year	Name	Status/Occupation	Place	Cause	Source
15.	1665	Henry Morrill	— —	New Haven	Drowning	F. Dexter, ed., *N. Hav. Town Rec. 1662–84*, 162
16.	1666	James Prist	— —	Salem	Hanging	Dow, ed., *Essex Ct. Rec.*, III, 298
17.	1668	Mr. Stratton	— —	Boston	Stabbing	S. Danforth, "Church Rec.," 298
18.	1672	John Solart	Married to Elizabeth S.	Wenham	Drowning	Boyer & Nissenbaum, eds., *Salem-Village Witchcraft*, 139
19.	1672	Florence Whitteridge	Married to Thomas W.	Ipswich	Drowning	W. & E. Adams, "Memoir," 17–18; Dow, ed., *Essex Ct. Rec.* V, 124
20.	1675	John Fallowell	— —	Plymouth Colony	Drowning	Shurtleff & Pulsifer, eds., *Plym. Rec.*, V, 182
21.	1677	John Wollacot, Jr.	— —	Manchester	Hanging	Dow, ed., *Essex Ct. Rec.*, VI, 397
22.	1677	John Tomlin	— —	Boston	Hanging	L. Hammond, "Diary," 169; Sewall, *Diary*, II, 14
23.	1677	Goodman Williams	Ferryman	Boston	Cut throat	L. Hammond, "Diary," 169
24.	1677	Abigail Claghorne	Married to James C.	Yarmouth	Hanging	*Ibid.*; Shurtleff & Pulsifer, eds., *Plym. Rec.*, V, 249–50
25.	1678	Hannah Checkley	Married to Anthony C.	Boston	Starvation	L. Hammond, "Diary," 169
26.	1678	Thomas Totman	— —	Plymouth Colony	Starvation	Shurtleff & Pulsifer, eds., *Plym. Rec.*, V, 262
27-28.	1678	Two Indians	Indians	Plymouth Colony	Unknown	L. Hammond, "Diary," 169
29-30.	1680	Black husband and wife	Slaves(?)	Boston	Unknown	Sewall, *Diary*, II, 14
31.	1680	A man	— —	Cambridge	Hanging	*Ibid.*, II, 14
32.	1681	Mistress Jackson	Married to Jonathan J.	Boston	Hanging	*Ibid.*, II, 17
33.	1681	Samuel Bliss	— —	Maine	Hanging	Libby, Allen, & Moody, eds., *Maine Ct. Rec.*, III, 74
34.	1682	William Taylor	Merchant	Boston	Hanging	Russell, "Diary," 56
35.	1682	Squando	Indian	— —	Unknown	I. Mather, "Diary," 409
36.	1684	John Miller	— —	Rehoboth	Cut throat	Shurtleff & Pulsifer, eds., *Plym. Rec.*, VI, 142

No.	Year	Name	Status	Location	Cause	Source
37.	1684	A maiden	Single	Salem	Shooting (Possible suicide)	Sewall, Diary, II, 19
38.	1685	Eleazer Westore	— — —	Hampshire County	Hanging	Hamp. Co. Ct. of "Gen. Sessions," 81
39.	1687	Elizabeth Jenkins	Married to Stephen J.	Oyster River, N. Hamp.	Drowning	"N. Hamp. Ct. Papers," XI, 327
40.	1687	Goody Trask	Married to Christian T.	Beverly	Cutting throat	"Salem Witchcraft—1692," I, n. p.
41.	1688	A tanner	— — —	Boston	Hanging	Sewall, Diary, I, 226
42.	1688	Hannah Marion	Married to Samuel M.	Boston	Hanging	Ibid., I, 208
43.	1688	Thomas	Indian servant	Boston	Hanging	Ibid., I, 229
44.	1690	An old man	— — —	Watertown	Hanging	Publick Occurences Both Foreign & Domestick, Sept. 25, 1690, in Weeks & Bacon, eds., Hist. Digest of Prov. Press, 29
45.	1693	Easter Burr	— — —	Suffolk County	Drowning	"Ct. Files—Suffolk," XXII, #2715
46.	1696	Samuel Powell	— — —	New Hampshire	Hanging	Page, Judicial Beginnings of N. Hamp., 132
47.	1696	Edward Rowe	— — —	New Hampshire	Hanging	Ibid.
48.	1697	William Howard	— — —	Bristol County	Shooting	Bristol Co. "Ct. of Gen. Sessions," 7
49.	1697	Mary Wilder	Married to Nathaniel W.	Lancaster	Unknown	Marshall, "Diary 1697–1709," 17
50.	1701	Mary Fuller	Married to Jonathan F.	Dedham	Drowning	Marshall, "Diary, 1697–1711," 155
51.	1701	A male prisoner in the Boston gaol	— — —	Boston	Hanging	Marshall, "Diary, 1697–1709," 20
52.	1702	Mary Bowtel	— — —	Cambridge	Burning	Sewall, Diary, II, 52
53.	1705	Susanna Griffin	— — —	Salisbury	Drowning—hanging	Boston News-Letter, Aug. 6–13, 1705, in Weeks & Bacon, eds., Hist. Digest of Prov. Press, 232

No.	Year	Name	Description	Location	Method	Source
54.	1705	Lydia Potter	——	Boston (?)	Cut throat	*Boston News-Letter*, July 16–23, 1705, in *ibid.*, 224
55.	1705	Thomas Thayer	——	——	Unknown	Marshall, "Diary, 1697–1709," 23
56.	1709	Joan Heiferman	——	Boston (?)	Drowning	Marshall, "Diary, 1697–1711," 160

33 men; 21 women; 2 possible female suicides

SUICIDES ATTEMPTED BUT NOT COMPLETED

No.	Year	Name	Description	Location	Method	Source
1.	1672	William Citterne	——	Suffolk County	Poison	*Rec. Suffolk Co. Ct.*, I, 189
2.	1682	Isack Heath	——	Roxbury	Unknown	Boston Rec. Cmrs., *Rep. Containing Roxbury Rec.*, 95
3.	1682	Mistress Saffing	Married	Boston	Unknown	Russell, "Diary," 56
4.	1682	Mr. Bernard	Cooper	Boston	Unknown	*Ibid.*
5.	1682	A woman	——	Dorchester	Drowning	*Ibid.*
6.	1693	Mary Watkins	Single; servant	Boston	Strangling	Watkins, "Discolored History," 168–70
7.	?	A man	Indian	Block Island	Shooting	Niles, "A Narrative," 199

4 men; 3 women

SUICIDES IN RHODE ISLAND

No.	Year	Name	Description	Location	Method	Source
1.	1683	John Crage	Scottish tailor	Portsmouth	Hanging	Brigham, ed., *Early Portsmouth Rec.*, 299–300
2.	1683	Elizur Collins	——	Warwick	Hanging	Austin, *Geneal. Dict. of R.I.*, 51
3.	1684	Indian lad of Widow Fish's	——	Portsmouth	Hanging	Brigham, ed., *Early Portsmouth Rec.*, 300

3 men

Appendix 4.

Suspected Killings of Children (Mostly Infants) by Their Mothers in New England, 1620–1700

	Date	Name	Status	Locale	Disposition	Sources
1.	1637	Dorothy Talby	Married	Salem, Mass.	Hanged	Dow, ed., *Essex Ct. Rec.*, I, 6, 9; Noble & Cronin, eds., *Rec. Mass. Assts.*, II, 78; Winthrop, *Journal*, I, 282–83
2.	1637	Anne Hett	Married	Hingham, Mass.	— —	Hubbard, *Gen. Hist. of N. Eng.*, VI, 422
3.	1642	Anne Hett	Married	Hingham, Mass.	Whipped, imprisoned	*Ibid.*; Noble & Cronin, eds., *Rec. Mass. Assts.*, II, 126; Winthrop, *Journal*, II, 60–61
4.	1647	Mary Martin	Single	Casco, Maine	Hanged	Winthrop, *Journal*, II, 317–18; C. Mather, *Magnalia*, II, 342
5.	1647	Mary Allen	Single	Black Point, Me.	Acquitted	Aspinwall, *Notarial Rec.*, 272
6.	1648	Alice Bishop	Married	Plymouth Colony	Hanged	Shurtleff & Pulsifer, eds., *Plym. Rec.*, II, 132
7.	1651	Mary Parsons	Married	Springfield, Mass.	Hanged	Drake, *Annals of Witchcraft*, 66–67
8.	1663	Zippora	Single; black servant	Boston, Mass.	Acquitted	"Ct. Files—Suffolk," V, #605
9.	1667	Ruth Briggs	Single	New Haven, Conn.	Hanged	"Conn. Arch.: Crimes," 1st, I, 32–33
10.	1668	Susanna Craford or Cravet	Single	Salem, Mass.	Hanged	S. Danforth, "Church Rec.," 299; Dow, ed., *Essex Ct. Rec.*, IV, 74, 84
11.	1668	A woman at Hartford	Married	Hartford, Conn.	Hanged	S. Bradstreet, "Journal," 44
12.	1672	Sarah Blacklock	— —	Suffolk Co., Mass.	— —	*Rec. Suffolk Co. Ct.*, I, 185–86
13.	1673	Elizabeth Oliver	Married	New Hampshire	30 lashes	O. Hammond, ed., *N. Hamp. Ct. Rec.*, 293

No.	Year	Name	Status	Location	Verdict	Source
14.	1674	Anna Negro	Single; black servant	Charlestown, Mass.	30 lashes; imprisoned	Noble & Cronin, eds., *Rec. Mass. Assts.*, I, 29
15.	1677	Marea	Single; Spanish Indian servant	Weymouth, Mass.	Acquitted	*Ibid.*, I, 115
16.	1678	Carden Drabston	Single	Watertown, Mass.	Acquitted	*Ibid.*, I, 125
17.	1678	Mary Hare	Married	Massachusetts	Acquitted	*Ibid.*, I, 126
18.	1683	Elizabeth Payne	Single	Massachusetts	20 lashes	*Ibid.*, I, 228
19.	1683	Betty Indian	Single	Plymouth Colony	Acquitted	Shurtleff & Pulsifer, eds., *Plym. Rec.*, VI, 113
20.	1685	Mary Flood	Married	Suffolk Co., Mass.	Acquitted	Noble & Cronin, eds., *Rec. Mass. Assts.*, I, 295; "Ct. Files—Suffolk," XXIX, #2388; Sewall, *Diary*, I, 123–24
21.	1685	Infant exposed to freezing by mother		Boston, Mass.	— —	Sewall, *Diary*, I, 103
22.	1688	An English maiden	Single	Bristol, Plym.	Hanged	*Ibid.*, I, 194
23.	1690	Mercy Brown	Married	Connecticut	Hanged	"Conn. Assts.," LVIII, 11–12, 19
24.	1691	Elizabeth Clements	Single	Haverhill, Mass.	Hanged	Sewall, *Diary*, I, 349
25.	1693	Grace	Single; slave or servant	Haverhill, Mass.	Hanged	"Mass. Arch.," LX, 279; C. Mather, *Magnalia*, II, 362
26.	1693	Elizabeth Emerson	Single	Haverhill, Mass.	Hanged	Sewall, *Diary*, I, 379; Noble & Cronin, eds., *Rec. Mass. Assts.*, I, 357
27.	1694	Welthian Thomas	— —	New Hampshire	Acquitted	"N. Hamp. Ct. Papers," X, 253
28.	1695	Susannah Andrews	Single	Lakenham, Plym.	Hanged	"Superiour Ct. of Judicature" (Mass.), 49
29.	1697	Hannah Turner	Widow	Duxbury, Mass.	Acquitted	*Ibid.*, 97
30.	1697	Mary Bartlett	Single	Massachusetts	— —	"Ct. Files—Suffolk," XLVII, #4565

31.	1698	Sarah Smith	Married	Deerfield, Mass.	Hanged	*Ibid.*, XLI, #3718; C. Mather, *Magnalia*, II, 364–65; J. Williams, *Warning to Unclean*; "Superiour Ct. of Judicature" (Mass.), pp. 193–94
32.	1698	Sarah Threenedles	Single	Boston, Mass.	Hanged	C. Mather, *Magnalia*, II, 364; Marshall, "Diary, 1697–1711," 153; "Superiour Ct. of Judicature" (Mass.), 199–200
33.	1699	Sarah Howland	Single	Massachusetts	Acquitted	"Superior Ct. of Judicature" (Mass.), 246
34.	1699	Amy Mun	Single	Farmington, Conn.	20 lashes	"Conn. Assts.," LVIII, 92
35.	1700	Hester Rogers	— — —	Newbury, Mass.	Hanged	John Pike, "Journal," 134; Marshall, "Diary, 1697–1711," 155

35 cases: 33 offenders, 16 hanged, 10 acquitted, 5 whipped, no record of final disposition in 4 cases

By colony: Massachusetts = 23; Connecticut = 4; Plymouth = 4; New Hampshire = 2; Maine = 2

Appendix 5.

Witches Accused in New England, 1620–99

	Name	Date	Profession (Social Status)*	Marital Status	Accusers	Victims
1.	Jane Hawkins	1638	Midwife-White Witch	Md. Thomas H.	Unknown	Various pregnant women
2.	Anne Hutchinson	1640	Midwife (Merchant)	Md. William H.	Unknown	One man
3.	Mary Parsons	1645, 1651	(Sawyer-bricklayer)	Md. Hugh P.	Neighbors	Her own and Rev. Moxon's childre
4.	Hugh Parsons	1645, 1651	Sawyer-bricklayer	Md. Mary P.	Neighbors & wife	Rev. Moxon's children
5.	Alse Young	1647	Unknown	Unknown	Unknown	Unknown
6.	Margaret Jones	1648	Herb-healer	Md. Thomas J.	Neighbor	Neighbor's children & othe
7.	Thomas Jones	1648	(Herb-healer)	Md. Margaret J.	Neighbor	Neighbor's children
8.	Mary Johnson	1648	Servant	Single	Master	Animals; her child
9.	Goodwife Marshfield	1649	Unknown	Widow	Mary Parsons	Rev. Moxon's children
10.	Mary Oliver	Before 1649	(Calinderer)	Md. Thomas O.	Unknown	Unknown
11.	Mrs. Henry Lake	1650	(Currier)	Md. Henry L.	Unknown	Unknown
12.	Jane James	1650–67	Unknown	Md. Erasmus J.	Unknown	Unknown
13.	Mrs. Robert Sawer	1650	Unknown	Md. Robert S.	Ralph Hall	Unknown
14.	Indian Powwaws	1651	— — —	— — —	Unknown	Sachem Uncas
15.	John Carrington	1651	Worth £23 11s. at death	Md. Joan C.	Unknown	Unknown
16.	Joan Carrington	1651	(Worth £23 11s. at death)	Md. John C.	Unknown	Unknown
17.	Goodwife Bassett	1651	(Shoemaker)	Md. Robert B.	Many people	Unknown
18.	Mistress Kendall	1651	Unknown	Unknown	Goodman Jenning's nurse	Goodman Jenning's child
19.	Elizabeth Godman	1651–60	Unknown	Md.	Many neighbors	Many neighbors, Stephen Goodyear's step-daughters, & several animals
20.	John Bradstreet	1652	Unknown	Single	Unknown	None
21.	Goodwife Knapp	1653	Unknown	Md. Roger K.	Roger Ludlow, Mistress Lockwood, 7 others	Several persons
22.	Mary Staplies	1653, 1692	Unknown	Md. Thomas S.	Roger Ludlow	Several persons
23.	John Godfrey	1653, 1659, 1669	Unknown	Unknown	Job, Moses, Mary Sr., Mary Jr. Tyler	Mary Tyler
24.	Jane Collins	1653	(Estate worth £422 in 1666)	Md. Christopher	Enoch Coldam	Unknown
25.	Grace Dutch	1653	Unknown	Md. Osmond D.	Edmond Marshall	Unknown
26.	Goody Vincent	1653	Unknown	Md. William V.	Edmond Marshall	Unknown
27.	Agnes Evans	1653	(Selectman)	Md. William E.	Edmond Marshall	Unknown
28.	Mistress Perkins	1653	Unknown	Unknown	Unknown	Unknown
29.	Lydia Gilbert	1654	Unknown	Md. William G.	Unknown	Henry Stiles
30.	Nicholas Bayly	1655	Unknown	Md. Eleanor B.	Several	Several
31.	Eleanor Bayly	1655	Unknown	Md. Nicholas B.	Several	Several

*Mate's profession or social status in parentheses

	Locale	Disposition of Case	Sources
1.	Boston, Mass.	Forbidden from meddling in religious or medical matters; banished	Winthrop, *Short Story*, 281; Shurtleff, ed., *Mass. Rec.*, I, 224, 329
2.	Portsmouth, R.I.	Charge made in Mass.; no prosecution	Winthrop, *Journal*, II, 8
3.	Springfield, Mass.	Acquitted by Gen. Ct.; later confessed witchcraft before hanging for infanticide	Shurtleff, ed., *Mass. Rec.*, IV: I, 47–48, 73; III, 229; E. Johnson, *Wonder-Working Prov.*, 237
4.	Springfield, Mass.	Acquitted at Gen. Ct., May 31, 1651	Shurtleff, ed., *Mass. Rec.*, IV: I, 96; Drake, *Witchcraft Annals*, 219–58
5.	Windsor, Conn.	Executed May 25, 1647	Winthrop, *Journal*, II, 323; J. Taylor, *Conn. Witch. Del.*, 35, 145–47
6.	Charlestown, Mass.	Executed June 15, 1648	Drake, *Witchcraft Annals*, 58–61
7.	Charlestown, Mass.	Arrested, possibly released	*Ibid.*, 59–61
8.	Wethersfield, Conn.	Executed at Hartford after Dec. 7, 1648	*Ibid.*, 62–63; C. Mather, *Magnalia*, II, 456–57
9.	Springfield, Mass.	Parsons to pay £3 in damages	Drake, *Witchcraft Annals*, 71–72; J. Smith, ed., *Pynchon Ct. Rec.*, 219–20
10.	Salem, Mass.	"Had the general reputation of a witch"	T. Hutchinson, *Witchcraft Delusion of 1692*, 6
11.	Dorchester, Mass.	Executed at Boston	*Ibid.*; J. Hale, *Modest Enquiry*, 17
12.	Marblehead, Mass.	Accused, but no prosecution	Dow, ed., *Essex Ct. Rec.*, I, 11, 84, 104, 199; III, 413; IV, 42
13.	Hampton, N. Hamp.	Slander suit initiated, then withdrawn	*Ibid.*, I, 202
14.	Connecticut	Inquiry by Cmrs. of United Colonies	Levermore, "Witch. in Conn.," 792–93
15.	Wethersfield, Conn.	Executed after Mar. 6, 1651	J. Taylor, *Conn. Witch. Del.*, 38, 147; *Rec. Conn. Particular Ct.*, 78; Manwaring, ed., *Digest of Conn. Probate Rec.*, 104
16.	Wethersfield, Conn.	Executed after Mar. 6, 1651	
17.	Stratford, Conn.	Executed	J. Taylor, *Conn. Witch. Del.*, 148–49; Drake, *Witchcraft Annals*, 73–74; J. Trumbull, ed., *Conn. Rec.*, I 220
18.	Cambridge, Mass.	Executed	J. Hale, *Modest Enquiry*, 18
19.	New Haven	Bond for good behavior taken	F. Dexter, ed., *N. Haven Town Rec.*, I, 249, 256–57; Hoadly, ed., *N. Haven Rec., 1653–Union*, 29–36, 151–52; J. Taylor, *Conn. Witch. Del.*, 85–96
20.	Rowley, Mass.	Fined 20s. or a whipping; fled in 1692	Dow, ed., *Essex Ct. Rec.*, I, 179, 188, 210, 234, 265, 332n
21.	Fairfield, N. Hav.	Executed at Fairfield	Hoadly, ed., *N. Haven Rec., 1653–Union*, 77, 80–81; J. Taylor, *Conn. Witch. Del.*, 132
22.	Fairfield, N. Hav.	Acquitted; Ludlow fined £25 for defam.	Hoadly, ed., *N. Haven Rec., 1653–Union*, 77–89; J. Taylor, *Conn. Witch. Del.*, 121–41; Wyllys, "Col. Suppl.," 36
23.	Andover, Mass.	Released	Drake, *Witchcraft Annals*, 87–88, 114–15
24.	Lynn (?), Mass.	Coldam pays for defamation	Dow, ed., *Essex Ct. Rec.*, I, 276; Savage, *Geneal. Dict. of N. Eng.*, I, 433–34
25.	Gloucester, Mass.	Defamation; Marshall	Dow, ed., *Essex Ct. Rec.*, I, 301
26.	Salem, Mass.	to make public	*Ibid.*
27.	Topsfield, Mass.	acknowledgment	*Ibid.*
28.	Essex Co., Mass.	Rumored a witch	*Ibid.*, I, 325
29.	Windsor, Conn.	Executed	J. Taylor, *Conn. Witch. Del.*, 148, 156; H. Stiles, *Hist. of Windsor*, 779
30.	New Haven	Advised to leave colony; went to Maine	J. Taylor, *Conn. Witch. Del.*, 149; F. Dexter, ed., *N. Haven Town Rec.*, I, 244–46, 256–58
31.	New Haven	Advised to leave colony; went to Maine; there accused in 1659	*Ibid.*; "Witch. in Maine," 195

32.	Mary Parsons	1656, 1675	(One of richest men in Northampton, Mass.)	Md. Joseph P.	A neighbor	Children; Mary Bartlett
33.	Anne Hibbins	1656	(Merchant, Assistant)	Widow (Md. Wm. H.)	Several	Unknown
34.	Thomas Turpin	1656	Fisherman	Md. Jane T.	Elizabeth Rowe	Unknown
35.	William Ham	1656	Unknown	Md.	Elizabeth Rowe	Unknown
36.	Jane Walford	1656–69	(Blacksmith)	Md. Thomas W.	Several	Nicholas Rowe; Robert Couch
37.	Eunice Cole	1656–80	Pauper (Carpenter)	Md. William C.	Several	Several
38.	Anne Austin	1656	Quaker missionary	Md.	Unknown	None
39.	Mary Fisher	1656	Ex-servant; Quaker miss.	Single	Unknown	None
40.	William Meaker	1657	Unknown	Unknown	Thomas Mullener	Mullener's pig
41.	Elizabeth Garlick	1658	Servant	Md. Joshua G.	A fellow servant	Servant's child
42.	Dorothy Waugh	1658	Quaker missionary	Unknown	Richard Bellingham	None
43.	Mary Tyler	1659	Unknown	Md. Job T.	John Godfrey	Unknown
44.	Elizabeth Kitchen	1660	(Shoemaker)	Md. John K.	Edmond Batter	Unknown
45.	Mary Wright	1660	Unknown	Single	Unknown	Unknown
46.	Alice Walton	1660?	(Prosperous Quaker)	Md. George W.	Unknown	Unknown
47.	Winifred Holman	1660	(Of "good estate")	Widow (Md. John H.)	Unknown	Rebecca Stearns
48.	Elizabeth Hooten	1661	Quaker missionary	Unknown	John Endicott	None
49.	Joan Brokesup	1661	Quaker missionary	Unknown	John Endicott	None
50.	Elizabeth Holmes	1661	Unknown	Md. William H.	Dinah Sylvester	Dinah Sylvester
51.	Wenlock Christianson	1661	Unknown	Unknown	John Endicott	None
52.	Nicholas Jennings	1661	Servant	Md. Margaret Poore	Unknown	Several
53.	Margaret Jennings	1661	Servant	Md. Nicholas J.	Unknown	Several
54.	John Redman	1661	Blacksmith	Unknown	None	None
55.	Rebecca Greensmith	1662	(Worth £137 14s. 1d.)	Md. Nathaniel G.	John Kelley's daughter, Anne Cole; William Ayres	Anne Cole & others
56.	Nathaniel Greensmith	1662	Worth £137 14s. ld. at death	Md. Rebecca G.	Kelley's daughter; Rebecca Greensmith	Anne Cole & others
57.	James Wakeley	1662	Unknown	Md. Alice Boosy	Kelley's daughter; Rebecca Greensmith	Anne Cole & others
58.	William Ayres	1662	Unknown	Md. Judith A.	Kelley's daughter	Anne Cole & others
59.	Judith Ayres	1662	Unknown	Md. William A.	Kelley's daughter	Anne Cole & others
60.	Judith Varlet	1662	(Father worth £205 14s. at his death in 1662)	Single	R. Greensmith; A. Cole; Kelley's daughter	Anne Cole & others
61.	Andrew Sanford	1662	(Fortuneteller)	Md. Mary S.	Kelley's daughter; A. Cole	Anne Cole & others
62.	Mary Sanford	1662	Fortuneteller	Md. Andrew S.	Kelley's daughter; A. Cole	Anne Cole & others
63.	Elizabeth Seager	1662–66	Unknown	Md. Richard S.	Anne Cole	Anne Cole
64.	Mary Tompkins	1662	Quaker missionary	Unknown	Great Isl. Men	None

32.	Northampton, Mass.	Acquitted by Assistants	James Trumbull, *Hist. of Northampton*, I, 43–51
33.	Salem, Mass.	Hanged June 19, 1656	Shurtleff, ed., *Mass. Rec.*, IV: I, 269; T. Hutchinson, *Hist. of Mass.*, I, 187–88; Drake, *Witchcraft Annals*, 98–99
34.	Strawberry Bank, N. Hamp.	Accused after his death	Drake, *Witchcraft Annals*, 107
35.	Strawberry Bank, N. Hamp.	Unknown	*Ibid.*
36.	Dover, N. Hamp.	Acquitted	Bouton, ed., *N. Hamp. Prov. Papers*, I, 217–19; Fogg, "Witch. in N. Hamp.," 181–83
37.	Hampton, N. Hamp.	Frequent complaints; acquitted	Noble & Cronin, eds., *Rec. Mass. Assts.*, III, 253; "Mass. Arch.," CXXXV, 2–15
38.	London, Eng. (Mass.)	Banished as Quaker	H. Norton, *N. Eng. Ensigne*, 6–7
39.	Yorkshire, Eng. (Mass.)	Banished as Quaker	*Ibid.*
40.	New Haven	Acquitted	J. Taylor, *Conn. Witch. Del.*, 149; Hoadly, ed., *N. Haven Rec., 1653–Union*, 224
41.	Easthampton, L.I. (Conn.)	Acquitted by Hartford Magistrates	J. Trumbull, ed., *Conn. Rec.*, I, 572; "Witch. on Long Island," 53
42.	Eng. (Mass.)	Banished as Quaker	H. Norton, *N. Eng. Ensigne*, 71
43.	Andover, Mass.	Unknown	Drake, *Witchcraft Annals*, 87–88
44.	Salem, Mass.	Not prosecuted	Dow, ed., *Essex Ct. Rec.*, II, 219
45.	Oyster Bay, L.I. (Mass.)	Acquitted; banished as Quaker	Drake, *Witchcraft Annals*, 117–18
46.	Great Island, N. Hamp.	Rumor; punished as Quaker	Bishop, *N. Eng. Judged*, 466–67
47.	Cambridge, Mass.	Two affidavits signed on her behalf	T. Hutchinson, *Witchcraft Del. of 1692*, 8n
48.	Eng. (Mass.)	Banished as Quaker	Bishop, *N. Eng. Judged*, 403–6
49.	Eng. (Mass.)	Banished as Quaker	*Ibid.*
50.	Scituate, Plym.	Acquitted	Drake, *Witchcraft Annals*, 113–19; Shurtleff & Pulsifer, eds., *Plym. Rec.*, III, 206
51.	Eng. (Mass.)	Banished as Quaker	Besse, *Col. of Quaker Sufferings*, II, 222
52.	Saybrook, Conn.	Acquitted by hung jury	J. Trumbull, ed., *Conn. Rec.*, I, 338; J. Taylor, *Conn. Witch. Del.*, 150, 156
53.	Saybrook, Conn.	Acquitted by hung jury	*Ibid.*
54.	Isles of Shoals, Maine	Confessed he "belonged" to Satan	Libby, Allen, & Moody, eds., *Maine Ct. Rec.*, II, 106
55.	Hartford, Conn.	Hanged Jan. 1663	J. Taylor, *Conn. Witch. Del.*, 98–99; I. Mather, *Essay for Recording Illustrious Prov.*, 136–37; Whiting, "Letter," 468
56.	Hartford, Conn.	Hanged Jan. 1663	*Ibid.*; Manwaring, ed., *Digest of Conn. Probate Rec.*, 121–22
57.	Hartford, Conn.	Fled to R.I.	Wyllys, "Col. Suppl.," 45
58.	Hartford, Conn.	Fled to R.I.	*Ibid.*; J. Taylor, *Conn. Witch. Del.*, 152
59.	Hartford, Conn.	Fled to R.I.	*Ibid.*
60.	Hartford, Conn.	Released at intervention of Gov. Peter Stuyvesant	J. Taylor, *Conn. Witch. Del.*, 150; Hoadly *Memorial*, 8; Manwaring, ed., *Digest of Conn. Probate Rec.*, 158
61.	Hartford, Conn.	Unknown	J. Taylor, *Conn. Witch. Del.*, 151
62.	Hartford, Conn.	Hanged after June 13, 1662	*Ibid.*
63.	Hartford, Conn.	Discharged three times by Assts.; removed to R.I.	*Ibid.*, 81; Wyllys, "Col. Suppl.," 45, 56–60; "Conn. Assts.," LVI, 35–36, 52
64.	Eng. (N. Hamp.)	Banished as Quaker	Bishop, *N. Eng. Judged*, 394

65.	Katherine Palmer	1662	Unknown	Md. Henry P.	Mrs. Robins, R. Greensmith, A. Cole	Anne Cole
66.	Mary Grant	1662	(Worth £50 13s. 6d. in 1681)	Md. Peter G.	Unknown	Unknown
67.	Mary Barnes	1662	Unknown	Md. Thomas B.	Unknown	Unknown
68.	Mistress Dayton	1663–93	Unknown	Unknown	Unknown	Unknown
69.	William Graves	1667	Unknown	Unknown	Samuel Debel's daughter	Debel's daughte... & one infant
70.	Mrs. John Tilerson	1667	Unknown	Md. John T.	Matthew Griswold	Unknown
71.	Widow Burt	1669	Potion doctress	Widow	Jacob Knight & others	Sarah Pearson & Sarah Townse...
72.	Katherine Harrison	1669	Fortuneteller (Merchant worth £929 6s. 9d. in 1666)	Widow (Md. John H.)	Unknown	Thomas Bray, J... Francis's chil... Mary Hale
73.	John Harrison	1669	Merchant (Fortuneteller)	Md. Katherine H.	Unknown	Unknown
74.	Susanna Martin	1669, 1674, 1692	(Blacksmith)	Md. George M.	William Sargeant, Salem Village girls	Salem Village girls
75.	Elizabeth Knap	1671	Unknown	Single	Unknown	None
76.	Anna Edmunds	1673	Unknown	Unknown	Samuel & Mrs. Bennit	Unknown
77.	John Parsons	1674	Unknown	Single	Unknown	Unknown
78.	Goodwife Tope	1674	Unknown	Unknown	Lawrence Carpenter	Unknown
79.	Mary Ingham	1677	(Shoemaker, weaver)	Md. Thomas I.	Mehittable Woodworth	Mehittable Woodworth
80.	Margaret Lord	1678	Servant	Single	Sarah Ross, John Hale's children	None
81.	Anis "Nancy" Hoar	1678	(Very poor)	Single	Three girls	Unknown
82.	Bridget Bishop	1680, 1692	Kept illegal inn (3d husband a sawyer)	Twice widowed; Md. to Edward B.	Wonn, a slave; several others	Salem Village girls & others
83.	Caleb Powell	1680	Astrologer, seaman	Single	Unknown	William Morse family
84.	Elizabeth Morse	1680	Midwife	Md. William M.	Several neighbors	Neighbors
85.	Rachel Fuller	1680	Unknown	Md. John F.	Unknown	John Godfrey's child
86.	Mary Prescott	1680	Unknown	Md. James P.	Rachel Fuller	Unknown
87.	Isabella Towle	1680	Unknown	Md. Philip T. (?)	Rachel Fuller	Unknown
88.	Grace Boulter	1680	Unknown	Md. Nathaniel B.	Rachel Fuller	Unknown
89.	Mrs. Benjamin Evans	1680	Unknown	Md. Benjamin E.	Rachel Fuller	Unknown
90.	Miss Evans	1680	Unknown	Single (daughters of Benjamin E.)	Rachel Fuller	Unknown
91.	Miss Evans	1680	Unknown		Rachel Fuller	Unknown
92.	Margaret Gifford	1680	(Lynn Iron-worker)	Md. John G.	Philip Read	Unknown
93.	Mary Hale	1680, 1682	Unknown	Widow	Unknown	Michael Smith, a child
94.	Sarah Wilds	1680s, 1692	(Carpenter)	Md. John	Salem Village girls, neighbors	Salem Village girls, neighbo...
95.	Lancelot Lafe	1680	Student	Single	George Penney	Unknown
96.	Elizabeth How	1682, 1692	(Farmer)	Md. James H.	Hannah Perley	Hannah Perley, Salem Village girls
97.	Hannah Jones	1682	Unknown	Md.	George Walton	George Walton
98.	Mary Webster	1683, 1685	Hog Reeve	Md. William W.	Unknown	Philip Smith
99.	James Fuller	1683	(Poor)	Unknown	Unknown	None
100.	Nicholas Disborough	1683	Farmer	Md. Elizabeth D.	Unknown	Disborough Fa...

65.	Wethersfield, Conn.	Unknown	Wyllys, "Col. Suppl.," 45, 55
66.	Hartford, Conn.	Unknown	*Ibid.*, 45; Manwaring, ed., *Digest of Conn. Probate Rec.*, 312
67.	Farmington, Conn.	Executed	J. Taylor, *Conn. Witch. Del.*, 151; Manwaring, ed., *Digest of Conn. Probate Rec.*, 401
68.	Massachusetts	Acquitted Feb. 1693	I. Mather, *Further Account of Trials*, 10
69.	Connecticut	Unknown	Wyllys, "Col. Suppl.," 39
70.	Saybrook, Conn.	Acquitted	"Hartford Co. Ct.," 63
71.	Essex County, Mass.	Acquitted	Woodward, ed., *Salem Witchcraft Rec.*, II, 262–65
72.	Weathersfield, Conn.	Released by Gen. Ct., May 20, 1670, provided she leave the colony	J. Taylor, *Conn. Witch. Del.*, 47–61; Manwaring, ed., *Digest of Conn. Probate Rec.*, 206
73.	Weathersfield, Conn.	Suspected, but died 1669 without being prosecuted	J. Taylor, *Conn. Witch. Del.*, 52
74.	Amesbury, Mass.	Acquitted by Assts., 1669; hanged July 19, 1692	Page, *Judicial Beginnings of N. Hamp.*, 93–94; "Ct. Files—Suffolk," XV, #1334; Woodward, ed., *Salem Witchcraft Rec.*, I, 197–226
75.	Groton, Mass.	Admitted signing Satan's Covenant	Willard, "A briefe Account," 8–18
76.	Massachusetts	Assts. threw case out	Noble & Cronin, eds., *Rec. Mass. Assts.*, I, 11
77.	Northampton, Mass.	Discharged for lack of evidence	James Trumbull, *Hist. of Northampton*, I, 234
78.	Isles of Shoals, N. Hamp.	Carpenter fined for lying about her	O. Hammond, ed., *N. Hamp. Ct. Rec.*, 304
79.	Scituate, Plym.	Acquitted by Gen. Ct., Mar. 6, 1676/7	Shurtleff & Pulsifer, eds., *Plym. Rec.*, V, 223
80.	Beverly, Mass.	Threatened to summon Satan to kill a fellow servant by using a magic book	Dow, ed., *Essex Ct. Rec.*, VII, 43–45, 49–50
81.	Beverly, Mass.	Allegedly possessed witch's puppet	*Ibid.*, VII, 49
82.	Salem Village, Mass.	Acquitted, 1680; hanged June 10, 1692	"Ct. Files—Suffolk," XXI, #1825; Woodward, ed., *Salem Witchcraft Rec.*, I, 148–69
83.	Newbury, Mass.	Held suspicious	Dow, ed., *Essex Ct. Rec.*, VII, 355
84.	Newbury, Mass.	Found guilty, but reprieved by Assts.	Noble & Cronin, eds., *Rec. Mass. Assts.*, I, 159; I. Mather, *Essay for Recording Illustrious Prov.*, 154–55
85.	Hampton, N. Hamp.	Acquitted	J. Dow, *Hist. of Hampton*, I, 85; *Cols. of N. Hamp. Hist. Soc.*, VIII, 45–46
86.	Hampton, N. Hamp.	Unknown	J. Dow, *Hist. of Hampton*, I, 85
87.	Hampton, N. Hamp.	Unknown	*Ibid.*
88.	Hampton, N. Hamp.	Unknown	*Ibid.*
89.	Hampton, N. Hamp.	Unknown	*Ibid.*
90.	Hampton, N. Hamp.	Unknown	*Ibid.*
91.	Hampton, N. Hamp.	Unknown	*Ibid.*
92.	Lynn, Mass.	Prosecuted, did not appear	Dow, ed., *Essex Ct. Rec.*, VIII, 23
93.	Boston, Mass.	Acquitted by Assts.	Noble & Cronin, eds., *Rec. Mass. Assts.*, I, 188–89
94.	Topsfield, Mass.	Rumors before 1692; hanged July 19, 1692	Woodward, ed., *Salem Witchcraft Rec.*, I, 181–89; Peterson & Clark, "Topsfield in Witchcraft Del.," 31
95.	Cambridge, Mass.	Penney to acknowledge his slander	Hist. Rec. Survey, *Suffolk Co. Ct. Rec.*, 25
96.	Topsfield, Mass.	Hanged July 19, 1692	Woodward, ed., *Salem Witchcraft Rec.*, II, 69–89
97.	Portsmouth, N. Hamp.	Council released her	C[hamberlain], "Lithobolia," 60–76; "N. Hamp. Ct. Papers," VI, 375, 381, 475
98.	Hadley, Mass.	Acquitted	M. Todd, "Witch. in N. Eng.," 174; Noble & Cronin, eds., *Rec. Mass. Assts.*, I, 233
99.	Springfield, Mass.	30 lashes & £5 fine	Noble & Cronin, eds., *Rec. Mass. Assts.*, I, 228–29
100.	Hartford, Conn.	Suspected but not prosecuted	J. Taylor, *Conn. Witch. Del.*, I, 153

101.	Goody Glover	1688	Washerwoman	Widow	John Goodwin Children	Goodwin Child[i]
102.	Abraham Ireland	1685	Unknown	Unknown	Unknown	Unknown
103.	Mary Randall	1691	Unknown	Single	Unknown	Unknown

WITCHES ACCUSED IN 1692 OUTBREAK

	Name	Profession (Social Status)	Marital Status	Relationship to Other Witches
104.	Nehemiah Abbott	Weaver, church deacon 1686	Md.	Neighbor of James & Elizabeth H[i] father of Nehemiah Jr.
105.	Nehemiah Abbott, Jr.	Weaver		Son of Nehemiah Sr.
106.	John Allen	Conn. Secretary, Asst., militia officer	Md. Ann Smith; 2d, Hannah Welles	
107.	John Alden	Commander of armed vessels in Mass.	Md. Elizabeth Phillips	
108.	Daniel Andrews	Bricklayer, schoolmaster, owned apothecary shop	Md. Sarah Porter	
109.	M. Andrews (Mistress)			
110.	Abigail Barker		Md. Ebenezer B.	Sister-in-law of Wm. B.; Aunt of Wm. Jr.
111.	Mary Barker		Single	Niece of Wm. B.
112.	William Barker	Poor husbandman	Md. Mary Dix	Father of Wm. Jr.; Brother-in-law Abigail B.
113.	William Barker, Jr.	Father a poor husbandman	Single	Son of Wm. B.
114.	Sarah Bassett	(Husbandman)	Md. William B.	Mother of Mary Derich
115.	Sarah Best			
116.	Sarah Bibber	Poor	Md.	
	Bridget Bishop (see no. 82, above)			
117.	Edward Bishop	Husbandman	Md. Sarah B.	Husband of Sarah B.
118.	Sarah Bishop	(Husbandman)	Md. Edward B.	Wife of Edward B.
119.	Mary Black	Slave of Nathaniel Putnam		
120.	Mary Bradbury	(Norfolk Co. Cmr., Associate Judge)	Md. Thomas B.	
121.	Ann Bradstreet	Member of Andover elite	Md. Dudley B.	Wife of Dudley B.; sister-in-law [of] John B.
122.	Dudley Bradstreet	Militia colonel; Councillor	Md. Ann Rice	Husband of Ann B.; brother of John B.
123.	John Bradstreet	Member of Andover elite	Md. Sarah Perkins	Brother of Dudley B.; Brother-in[-law] of Ann B.
124.	Mary Bridges	(Blacksmith)	Md. John B.	Mother of Mary & Sarah B.
125.	Mary Bridges, Jr.	Blacksmith's daughter	Single	Daughter of Mary B.; sister of Sarah B.
126.	Sarah Bridges		Single	Daughter of Mary; sister of Mary
127.	Hannah Bromidge		Md.	
128.	Mary Buckley or Whittredge	Daughter of shoemaker	Single (Md. Benj. Proctor 1694)	Daughter of Sarah B.; sister of Sarah B.
129.	Sarah Buckley	(Shoemaker)	Md. William B.	Mother of Mary & Sarah B.
130.	Sarah Buckley, Jr.	Daughter of shoemaker	Single	Daughter of Sarah B.; Sister of Mary B.
131.	George Burroughs	Minister at Falmouth, 1676, 1683–90; Salem Village, 1680–82; Wells, 1690–92	Md.; 2d Hannah B.	
132.	John Buxton	Constable	Md. Mary Small; 2d Elizabeth Holton	
133.	Candy	Black slave of Mary Hawkes	Single	

101.	Charlestown, Mass.	Suspected; 20 lashes	Hist. Rec. Sur., *Suffolk Co. Ct. Rec.*, 129
102.	Boston, Mass.	Hanged Nov. 16, 1688	C. Mather, *Memorable Prov.*, 1–12
103.	Springfield, Mass.	Suspected but not prosecuted	M. Todd, "Witch. in N. Eng.," 175

WITCHES ACCUSED IN 1692 OUTBREAK*

104.	Topsfield, Mass.	Dismissed after afflicted girls acquitted him	Upham, *Salem Witchcraft*, I, 128, 133–34
105.	Topsfield, Mass.		Woodward, ed., *Salem Witch. Rec.*, I, 180
106.	Hartford, Conn.	Accused; not prosecuted	*Ibid.*, II, 53; T. Hutchinson, *Witch. Del.*, 41n
107.	Boston, Mass.	Spent 15 wks. in jail; escaped; secreted at Duxbury	Woodward, ed., *Salem Witch. Rec.*, II, 196–97; Calef, *More Wonders*, 352–55; Sewall, *Diary*, I, 361–2n
108.	Salem Village, Mass.		Boyer & Nissenbaum, *Salem Possessed*, 120–22; Woodward, ed., *Salem Witch. Rec.*, I, 254
109.	Billerica, Mass.		
110.	Andover, Mass.	Acquitted	"Mass. Arch.," CXXXV, 51; Calef, *More Wonders*, 374–75
111.	Andover, Mass.	Acquitted May 1693	"Ct. Files—Suffolk," XXXII, #2678
112.	Andover, Mass.	Acquitted	"Mass. Arch.," CXXXV, 35
113.	Andover, Mass.	Acquitted May 1693	Noble, "Some Doc. Fragments," 25
114.	Lynn, Mass.	Ignoramus at Essex Co. Ct.	Woodward, ed., *Salem Witch. Rec.*, II, 47; "Ct. Files—Suffolk," #2701
115.	Reading, Mass.		"Mass. Arch.," CXXXV, 61
116.	Wenham, Mass.		Woodward, ed., *Salem Witch. Rec.*, II, 203–5
117.	Salem Village, Mass.	Broke prison & escaped	*Ibid.*, I, 135–48; Calef, *More Wonders*, 370; "Mass. Arch.," CXXXV, 117
118.	Salem Village, Mass.	Broke prison & escaped	Woodward, ed., *Salem Witch. Rec.*, I, 134–35; Calef, *More Wonders*, 370
119.	Salem Village, Mass.		Upham, *Salem Witchcraft*, II, 136; "Mass. Arch.," CXXXV, 18
120.	Salisbury, Mass.	Convicted Sept. 6, 1692; escaped	Woodward, ed., *Salem Witch. Rec.*, II, 160–64, 172–74; Upham, *Salem Witchcraft*, II, 226–28
121.	Andover, Mass.	Fled prosecution	Calef, *More Wonders*, 372
122.	Andover, Mass.	Fled prosecution	*Ibid.*
123.	Andover, Mass.	Fled to N. Hamp.	*Ibid.*
124.	Andover, Mass.	Acquitted Jan. 3, 1692/3	"Mass. Arch.," CXXXV, 57; Noble, "Some Doc. Fragments," 24
125.	Andover, Mass.	Acquitted May 1693	Noble, "Some Doc. Fragments," 25
126.	Andover, Mass.	Acquitted Jan. 3, 1692/3	"Mass. Arch.," CXXXV, 34; Noble, "Some Doc. Fragments," 24
127.	Haverhill, Mass.	Ignoramus at Essex Co. Ct.	"Ct. Files—Suffolk," XXXII, #2674
128.	Salem Village, Mass.	Acquitted Jan. 3, 1692/3	Noble, "Some Doc. Fragments," 23; Woodward, ed., *Salem Witch. Rec.*, I, 234; "Mass. Arch.," CXXXV, 19
129.	Salem Village, Mass.	Acquitted Jan. 3, 1692/3	Noble, "Some Doc. Fragments," 23; Woodward, ed., *Salem Witch. Rec.*, I, 234, 254; "Mass. Arch.," CXXXV, 20
130.	Salem Village, Mass.		Upham, *Salem Witchcraft*, II, 199
131.	Wells, Maine	Hanged Aug. 19, 1692	Woodward, ed., *Salem Witch. Rec.*, II, 109–27
132.	Salem Village, Mass.		
133.	Salem, Mass.	Acquitted Jan. 3, 1692/3	Noble, "Some Doc. Fragments," 23; Upham, *Salem Witchcraft*, II, 215; "Mass. Arch.," CXXXV, 29

*"Witches" with unspecified Sources appear in "Salem Witchcraft—1692."

134.	Elizabeth Carey	(Mariner)	Md. Nathaniel C.	Sister-in-law of Hannah C.
135.	Hannah Carey		Md. Jonathan C.	Sister-in-law of Elizabeth C.
136.	Hannah Carrell			
137.	Andrew Carrier	Son of husbandman	Single	Son of Martha & Thos. C.; sibling Richard & Sarah
138.	Martha (Allen) Carrier	(Husbandman)	Md. Thomas C.	Mother of Richard, Sarah, & Andrew; wife of Thomas C.; sister-in-law of Roger Toothaker
139.	Richard Carrier	Son of husbandman	Single	Son of Martha & Thos. C.; sibling Andrew & Sarah
140.	Sarah Carrier	Daughter of husbandman	Single	Daughter of Martha & Thomas C.; sister of Richard & Andrew C.
141.	Thomas Carrier	Husbandman	Md. Martha Allen	Father of Richard, Andrew, & Sarah C.; husband of Martha C.
142.	Bethiah Carter		Md. Joseph C.; Widow by Dec. 8	Mother of Bethiah Jr.
143.	Bethiah Carter, Jr.		Single	Daughter of Bethiah C.
144.	Sarah Cave		Md. Thomas C.	
145.	Rebecca Chamberlain		Md. William C.	
146.	Sarah Churchill	Servant of Geo. Jacobs	Single	Servant in Geo. Jacobs family (See nos. 219–23)
147.	Mary Clark		Md. Edward C.	
148.	Rachel Clinton	(Ex-servant)	Md. Lawrence C.	
149.	Peter Cloyse	Husbandman	Md. Sarah Bridges	Husband of Sarah C.; bro.-in-law of R. Nurse & Mary Easty; son-in-law of Mary Town
150.	Sarah Cloyse	(Husbandman)	Md. Edmund Bridges; 2d Peter Cloyse	Wife of Peter C.; sister of Rebecca Nurse & Mary Easty; daughter of Mary Town
151.	Mary Coffin			
152.	Sarah Cole	(Cooper)	Md. John C.	
153.	Susannah Cole	(Tailor)	Md. Abraham C.	
154.	Elizabeth Colson		Single	Daughter of Mary C.
155.	Mary Colson		Widow (Md. Adam C.)	Mother of Elizabeth C.
156.	Giles Corey	Carpenter	Md. Margaret C.; 2d Mary Britz; 3d Martha C.	Husband of Martha C.
157.	Martha Corey	(Carpenter)	Md. Giles C.	Wife of Giles C.
158.	Mary (Ingersoll) Cox	(Mariner)	Md. George C.	
159.	Hannah Dane	(Minister)	Md. Francis D.	Mother-in-law of Deliverance D.
160.	Deliverance Dane	(Member of Andover elite)	Md. Nathaniel D.	Daughter-in-law of Hannah D.
161.	Phebe (Wilds) Day	(Surgeon)	Md. Timothy Day	Daughter of Sarah Wilds; sister of Sarah Bishop
162.	Mary Derich or Derrill	(Husbandman)	Md. Michael D.	Daughter of Sarah Bassett
163.	Elizabeth Dicer		Md. William D.	
164.	Rebecca (Doliver) Dike		Md. Richard D.	
165.	Anne (Higginson) Doliver	(Militia captain)	Md. William D.	
166.	Mehitabel (Brabrook) Downing		Md. John D.	
167.	John Draper			
168.	Lydia Dustin		Widow (Md. Josiah D.)	
169.	Sarah Dustin		Single	
170.	Daniel Eames		Single	Son of Rebecca & Robert E.
171.	Rebecca Eames		Md. Robert E.	Wife of Robt. E.; mother of Daniel E.
172.	Robert Eames		Md. Rebecca E.	Husband of Rebecca E.; father of Daniel E.

134.	Charlestown, Mass.	Escaped to R.I.	Woodward, ed., *Salem Witch. Rec.*, II, 196; Calef, *More Wonders*, 349–52
135.	Haverhill, Mass.	Escaped to N.Y.	Upham, *Salem Witchcraft*, II, 215
136.	Salem, Mass.		
137.	Andover, Mass.		Woodward, ed., *Salem Witch. Rec.*, II, 141, 198; Calef, *More Wonders*, 363
138.	Andover, Mass.	Hanged Aug. 19, 1692	Woodward, ed., *Salem Witch. Rec.*, II, 54–68
139.	Andover, Mass.		*Ibid.*, II, 141, 198–99; Calef, *More Wonders*, 363
140.	Andover, Mass.	Confessed	Upham, *Salem Witchcraft*, II, 209–11
141.	Andover, Mass.		Boyer & Nissenbaum, eds., *Salem-Village Witch.*, 376
142.	Woburn, Mass.	Imprisoned at Woburn	Woodward, ed., *Salem-Village Witch.*, I, 254; II, 185; "Ct. Files—Suffolk," XXXII, #2697
143.	Woburn, Mass.		Woodward, ed., *Salem Witch. Rec.*, II, 185
144.	Andover, Mass.		
145.	Billerica, Mass.	Died in Cambridge prison Sept. 26, 1692	"Notes & Queries," 342
146.	Salem Village, Mass.	Imprisoned May 1692; confessed and, returned to accusing witches	Woodward, ed., *Salem Witch. Rec.*, II, 14; Upham, *Salem Witchcraft*, II, 166–69
147.	Haverhill, Mass.		Woodward, ed., *Salem Witch. Rec.*, I, 65
148.	Ipswich, Mass.		*Ibid.*, II, 213; "Ct. Files—Suffolk," XXXII, #2660
149.	Topsfield, Mass.	Ignoramus at Essex Co. Ct.	"Ct. Files—Suffolk," XXXII, #2677
150.	Topsfield, Mass.	Convicted Sept. 6; reprieved	Woodward, ed., *Salem Witch. Rec.*, I, 50; II, 47
151.	Gloucester, Mass.		
152.	Lynn, Mass.	Acquitted Feb. 1, 1692/3	Noble, "Some Doc. Fragments," 25; "Ct. Files—Suffolk," XXXII, #2712
153.	Salem, Mass.		"Mass. Arch.," CXXXV, 99
154.	Reading, Mass.		Woodward, ed., *Salem Witch. Rec.*, I, 254; II, 193
155.	Reading, Mass.		
156.	Salem Village, Mass.	Pressed to death Sept. 19, 1692	Woodward, ed., *Salem Witch. Rec.*, I, 50–56; II, 175–80; Upham, *Salem Witchcraft*, II, 334–43
157.	Salem Village, Mass.	Hanged Sept. 22, 1692	Woodward, ed., *Salem Witch. Rec.*, I, 50–59; Upham, *Salem Witchcraft*, II, 38–55
158.	Salem, Mass.		Upham, *Salem Witchcraft*, II, 198
159.	Andover, Mass.		
160.	Andover, Mass.		Woodward, ed., *Salem Witch. Rec.*, II, 229
161.	Gloucester, Mass.	Released on bond from Ipswich jail Sept. 24, 1692	W. Davis, "Wildes Family," 41
162.	Salem Village, Mass.		Woodward, ed., *Salem Witch. Rec.*, II, 47–48, 194
163.	Gloucester, Mass.		Boyer & Nissenbaum, eds., *Salem-Village Witch.*, 376
164.	Gloucester, Mass.		"Ct. Files—Suffolk," XXXII, #2689
165.	Gloucester, Mass.		Woodward, ed., *Salem Witch. Rec.*, II, 199–201
166.	Ipswich, Mass.		
167.	Andover, Mass.		Woodward, ed., *Salem Witch. Rec.*, II, 134
168.	Reading, Mass.	Acquitted Feb. 1, 1692/3	*Ibid.*, II, 183, 215; Noble, "Some Doc. Fragments," 25
169.	Reading, Mass.	Acquitted Feb. 1, 1692/3, but, unable to pay fees, died in prison	Woodward, ed., *Salem Witch. Rec.*, II, 184, 215
170.	Boxford, Mass.		Woodward, ed., *Salem Witch. Rec.*, II, 144–45
171.	Boxford, Mass.	Convicted Sept. 17, 1692; reprieved	*Ibid.*, II, 142–46
172.	Boxford, Mass.		

173.	Isaac Easty	Cooper; selectman; tithingman	Md. Mary Town	Husband of Mary E.; bro.-in-law (Rebecca Nurse and Sarah Cloys
174.	Mary (Town) Easty	(Cooper; selectman; tithingman)	Md. Isaac E.	Wife of Isaac E.; sister of Rebecca Nurse & Sarah Cloyse; daughte of Mary Town
175.	Esther (Dutch) Elwell		Md. Samuel E.	Daughter of Grace Dutch (See no. 25)
176.	Joseph Emens			
177.	Elizabeth Emerson		Single	
178.	Martha Emerson		Md. Joseph E.	Daughter of Roger Toothaker
179.	Mary English	(Merchant)	Md. Philip E.	Wife of Philip E.
180.	Philip English	Merchant	Md. Mary E.	Husband of Mary E.
181.	Thomas Farrar	Husbandman	Widower (Md. Eliz. F.)	
182.	Edward Farrington		Md. Martha Browne	
183.	Abigail (Dane) Faulkner	(Husbandman)	Md. Francis F.	Sister of Eliz. Johnson; aunt of E. Jr.; mother of Abigail and Doro
184.	Abigail Faulkner, Jr.	Husbandman's daughter	Single	Daughter of Abigail; sister of Dorothy
185.	Dorothy Faulkner	Husbandman's daughter	Single	Daughter of Abigail; sister of Abig Jr.
186.	John Flood	Militia captain	Md. Sarah F.	
187.	Elizabeth Fosdick	(Carpenter)	Md. John F.	Mother of Eliz. Jr.
188.	Elizabeth Fosdick, Jr.	Carpenter's daughter	Single	Daughter of Eliz. F.
189.	Ann Foster		Widow	Mother of Rose F. and Mary Lace
190.	Rose Foster		Single	Daughter of Ann F.; sister of Mar Lacey
191.	Philip Fowler		Md. Elizabeth Herrick	
192.	Nicholas Frost, Jr.	Mason		
193.	Eunice Frye	(Church deacon)	Md. John F.	
194.	Dorcas Good	Laborer's daughter	Single	Daughter of Sarah G.
195.	Sarah Good	(Poor laborer)	Md. Daniel Poole; 2d William Good	Mother of Dorcas G.
196.	Mary Greene	(Weaver)	Md. Peter G.	
197.	Sarah Hale	(Minister of Beverly)	Md. John Hale	
198.	Thomas Hardy		Md. Mercy Tenny	
199.	John Harrington		Md. Hannah Winter	
200.	Elizabeth Hart	(Husbandman)	Md. Isaac H.	
201.	Rachel Hatfield			
202.	Margaret Hawkes		Md.	
203.	Sarah Hawkes		Single (Later md. Francis Johnson, son of Eliz. & Stephen Johnsc	
204.	Dorcas Hoar	Estate worth only £8	Widow	
205.	Abigail Hobbs	Daughter of husbandman	Single	Daughter of William & Deliveranc H.
206.	Deliverance Hobbs	(Husbandman)	Md. William H.	Mother of Abigail H.; wife of William H.
207.	William Hobbs	Husbandman	Md. Deliverance H.	Father of Abigail H.; husband of Deliv.
208.	Abigail How	Daughter of husbandman	Single	Daughter of Elizabeth & James H. sister of Mary H.
	Elizabeth (Jackson) How (See no. 96)			
209.	James How	Husbandman	Md. Elizabeth Jackson	Father of Mary & Abigail H.; Husband of Eliz. H.
210.	Mary How	Daughter of husbandman	Single	Daughter of Jas. & Eliz.; Sister of Abig.
211.	John Howard, Jr.	Laborer	Single	

173.	Salem Village, Mass.		"Mass. Arch.," CXXXV, 115
174.	Salem Village, Mass.	Hanged Sept. 22, 1692	Woodward, ed., *Salem Witch. Rec.*, II, 27–47
175.	Gloucester, Mass.		"Ct. Files—Suffolk," XXXII, #2689
176.	Manchester, Mass.		Woodward, ed., *Salem Witch. Rec.*, II, 213
177.	Haverhill, Mass.	Later hanged for infanticide (1693)	
178.	Haverhill, Mass.	Ignoramus at Essex Co. Ct.	"Ct. Files—Suffolk," XXXII, #2708; Woodward, ed., *Salem Witch. Rec.*, II, 226
179.	Salem, Mass.	Broke jail and fled	Calef, *More Wonders*, 347, 371
180.	Salem, Mass.	Broke jail and fled	*Ibid.*; Woodward, ed., *Salem Witch. Rec.*, I, 189–92; "Mass. Arch.," CXXXV, 113
181.	Lynn, Mass.		Woodward, ed., *Salem Witch. Rec.*, I, 233; II, 201
182.	Andover, Mass.		"Mass. Arch.," CXXXV, 48
183.	Andover, Mass.	Convicted; plead pregnancy; reprieved	*Ibid.*, 44; Woodward, ed., *Salem Witch. Rec.*, II, 128–35
184.	Andover, Mass.		Woodward, ed., *Salem Witch. Rec.*, II, 134
185.	Andover, Mass.		*Ibid.*; "Mass. Arch.," CXXXV, 55
186.	Rumney Marsh, Mass.		Woodward, ed., *Salem Witch. Rec.*, II, 53
187.	Malden, Mass.		*Ibid.*, II, 106
188.	Malden, Mass.		Boyer & Nissenbaum, eds., *Salem-Village Witch.*, 377
189.	Andover, Mass.	Condemned; died in prison	Woodward, ed., *Salem Witch. Rec.*, II, 135–38
190.	Andover, Mass.		"Ct. Files—Suffolk," XXXII, #2702
191.	Andover, Mass.		
192.	Manchester, Mass.		
193.	Andover, Mass.	Acquitted May 1693	Brattle, "Letter," 180; "Mass. Arch.," CXXXV, 72; Noble, "Some Doc. Fragments" 25
194.	Salem Village, Mass.	Chained in dungeon 7 or 8 months	D. Lawson, *Brief Narrative*, 160; Woodward, ed., *Salem Witch. Rec.*, I, 74–76
195.	Salem Village, Mass.	Hanged July 19, 1692	Woodward, ed., *Salem Witch. Rec.*, I, 11–34; Boyer & Nissenbaum, *Salem Possessed*, 203–4
196.	Haverhill, Mass.		"Mass. Arch.," CXXXV, 71
197.	Beverly, Mass.	Not prosecuted	Calef, *More Wonders*, 369
198.	Great Island, N. Hamp.		
199.	Andover, Mass.		
200.	Lynn, Mass.	Ignoramus at Essex Co. Ct.	"Mass. Arch.," CXXXV, 60; Woodward, ed., *Salem Witch. Rec.*, I, 233, 254; "Ct. Files—Suffolk," XXXII, #2668
201.			
202.	Salem, Mass.		Upham, *Salem Witchcraft*, II, 216
203.	Salem, Mass.	Acquitted Jan. 3, 1692/3	Woodward, ed., *Salem Witch. Rec.*, II, 230; Noble, "Some Doc. Fragments," 24
204.	Beverly, Mass.	Convicted Sept. 6, 1692; reprieved	Woodward, ed., *Salem Witch. Rec.*, I, 189, 235–53
205.	Topsfield, Mass.	Convicted Sept. 6, 1692; reprieved	*Ibid.*, I, 23, 176–80
206.	Topsfield, Mass.		*Ibid.*, I, 180–92
207.	Topsfield, Mass.		*Ibid.*, I, 180, 182–86; "Mass. Arch.," CXXXV, 69
208.	Topsfield, Mass.		"Mass. Arch.," CXXXV, 116
209.	Topsfield, Mass.		M. Perley, "James Howe," 85–86
210.	Topsfield, Mass.		"Mass. Arch.," CXXXV, 116
211.	Rowley, Mass.		Woodward, ed., *Salem Witch. Rec.*, II, 213; "Ct. Files—Suffolk," XXXII, #2705

212.	Elizabeth Hubbard	Servant	Single	
213.	Francis Hutchens		Md.	Husband of Mrs. Hutchens
214.	Mrs. Francis Hutchens		Widow (Md. Francis H.)	Wife of Francis H.
215.	Sarah Ingersoll		Md. Samuel I. Later Md. Philip English	
216.	Mary Ireson	(Husbandman)	Md. Benjamin I.	
217.	John Jackson	Laborer	Md. Susanna Jokes	Father of John, Jr.; brother of Eliz. How
218.	John Jackson, Jr.	Laborer		Son of John J.; nephew of Eliz. How
219.	George Jacobs	Husbandman; moderately wealthy (estate worth £79 13s.)	Md. Martha J.	Father of George; Husband of Martha J.; Grandfather of Margaret; father-in-law of Rebecca J.
220.	George Jacobs, Jr.	Husbandman	Md. Rebecca J.	Husband of Rebecca J.; son of George & Martha J.; father of Margaret J.
221.	Margaret Jacobs	Husbandman's daughter	Single	Daughter of George Jr.; granddaughter of George & Martha; daughter of Rebecca
222.	Martha Jacobs	(Husbandman)	Md. George J.	Wife of George J.; mother-in-law of Rebecca J.; mother of Geo. Jr.; grandmother of Margaret J.
223.	Rebecca (Frost) Jacobs	(Husbandman)	Md. George J. Jr.	Wife of Geo. Jr.; daughter-in-law of Geo. & Martha J.; mother of Margaret J.
224.	John Indian	Barbadian Indian slave	Md. Tituba	Husband of Tituba
225.	Abigail Johnson		Single	Daughter of Eliz. J.; sister of Eliz. Jr. & Stephen J.
226.	Elizabeth (Dane) Johnson		Md. Stephen J.	Stepdaughter of Hannah Dane; sister of Abigail Faulkner; mother of Abigail, Eliz. Jr., & Stephen Jr.
227.	Elizabeth Johnson, Jr.		Single	Daughter of Eliz.; sister of Abigail & Stephen Jr.
228.	Rebecca Johnson		Widow	Mother of Mary Post
229.	Stephen Johnson, Jr.		Single	Son of Eliz.; bro. of Abigail & Eliz. Jr.
230.	Mary (Foster) Lacey	(Husbandman)	Md. Lawrence L.	Daughter of Ann Foster; mother of Mary Jr.
231.	Mary Lacey, Jr.	Husbandman's daughter	Single	Daughter of Mary L.
232.	John Lee		Single	
233.	Mercy Lewis	Servant of Thomas Putnam, Jr.	Single	
234.	Jane Lilly		Single	
235.	Mary Marston			Niece of Mary Osgood
	Susannah Martin (see no. 74)		Widow in 1692	
236.	Maria Mather	(Minister of Boston)	Md. Increase M.	
237.	Sarah (Clough) Merrill		Md. Daniel M.	
238.	Mistress Moody	(Minister of Boston)	Md. Joshua M.	
239.	Mary Morey		Single	
240.	Rebecca (Town) Nurse	(Wealthy traymaker)	Md. Francis N.	Sister of Mary Easty & Sarah Cloyse; sister-in-law of Isaac Easty & Peter Cloyse; daughter of Mary Town
241.	Mary Obinson	(Tanner)	Md. William O.	
242.	Sarah (Warren) Osborne		Md. Sam'l Prince; 2d William Osborne	
243.	Mary Osgood	(Church deacon; militia captain)	Md. John O.	Aunt of Mary Marston
244.	Alice Parker	(Fisherman)	Md. John P.	
245.	Mary Parker	(Tanner)	Md. John P.	
246.	William Parker			

212.	Salem Village, Mass.		Woodward, ed., *Salem Witch. Rec.*, II, 205
213.	Haverhill, Mass.	Died while trials in progress	
214.	Haverhill, Mass.		"Mass. Arch.," CXXXV, 74
215.	Salem, Mass.	Confessed	Upham, *Salem Witch. Rec.*, II, 169–71
216.	Lynn, Mass.		Woodward, ed., *Salem Witch. Rec.*, II, 108
217.	Rowley, Mass.		Upham, *Salem Witchcraft*, II, 223
218.	Rowley, Mass.		*Ibid.*; "Ct. Files—Suffolk," XXXII, #2704
219.	Salem, Mass.	Hanged Aug. 19, 1692	Woodward, ed., *Salem Witch. Rec.*, I, 254–65; "Mass. Arch.," CXXXV, 89
220.	Salem Village, Mass.		Woodward, ed., *Salem Witch. Rec.*, I, 254
221.	Salem, Mass.	Acquitted Jan. 3, 1692/3	*Ibid.*, II, 203; "Mass. Arch.," CXXXV, 91; Noble, "Some Doc. Fragments," 23
222.	Salem, Mass.		
223.	Salem Village, Mass.	Acquitted Jan. 3, 1692/3	Woodward, ed., *Salem Witch. Rec.*, II, 23–24; "Mass. Arch.," CXXXV, 89; Noble, "Some Doc. Fragments," 23
224.	Salem Village, Mass.		
225.	Andover, Mass.		Boyer & Nissenbaum, eds., *Salem-Village Witch.*, 377
226.	Andover, Mass.	Acquitted Jan. 3, 1692/3	Woodward, ed., *Salem Witch. Rec.*, II, 68; "Mass. Arch.," CXXXV, 32; Noble, "Some Doc. Fragments," 23
227.	Andover, Mass.	Convicted Jan. 3, 1692/3; reprieved	Woodward, ed., *Salem Witch. Rec.*, II, 68; Noble, "Some Doc. Fragments," 24
228.	Andover, Mass.		"Ct. Files—Suffolk," XXXII, #2707
229.	Andover, Mass.		"Mass. Arch.," CXXXV, 39
230.	Andover, Mass.	Convicted Sept. 6, 1692; reprieved	*Ibid.*, 54; Woodward, ed., *Salem Witch. Rec.*, II, 39–42
231.	Andover, Mass.	Acquitted Jan. 3, 1692/3	Woodward, ed., *Salem Witch. Rec.*, 141; Noble, "Some Doc. Fragments," 24
232.	Andover, Mass.		
233.	Salem Village, Mass.		Chever, "Remarks on Salem Commerce"
234.	Malden, Mass.	Acquitted Feb. 1, 1692/3	"Ct. Files—Suffolk," XXXII, #2714
235.	Andover, Mass.	Acquitted Jan. 3, 1692/3	"Mass. Arch.," CXXXV, 44; Noble, "Some Doc. Fragments," 23
236.	Boston, Mass.	Not prosecuted	J. Whiting, *Truth & Innocency*, 140
237.	Beverly, Mass.		Woodward, ed., *Salem Witch. Rec.*, I, 189; Upham, *Salem Witchcraft*, II, 140, 144
238.	Boston, Mass.	Not prosecuted	
239.	Beverly, Mass.		Boyer & Nissenbaum, eds., *Salem-Village Witch.*, 377
240.	Salem Village, Mass.	Hanged July 19, 1692	Woodward, ed., *Salem Witch. Rec.*, I, 76–97
241.	Boston, Mass.	Not prosecuted	Brattle, "Letter," 179–80
242.	Salem Village, Mass.	Died in jail May 10, 1692	Woodward, ed., *Salem Witch. Rec.*, I, 35–41; Boyer & Nissenbaum, *Salem Possessed*, 193–94
243.	Andover, Mass.	Acquitted Jan. 3, 1692/3	Brattle, "Letter," 180; Calef, *More Wonders*, 374–75; "Mass. Arch.," CXXXV, 73; Noble, "Some Doc. Fragments," 24
244.	Salem, Mass.	Hanged Sept. 22, 1692	Upham, *Salem Witchcraft*, II, 179–85, 324
245.	Andover, Mass.	Hanged Sept. 22, 1692	Woodward, ed., *Salem Witch. Rec.*, II, 153–60; "Mass. Arch.," CXXXV, 63
246.	Andover, Mass.		Boyer & Nissenbaum, eds., *Salem-Village Witch.*, 377

247.	Elizabeth Payne	(Husbandman)	Md. Stephen P.	
248.	Sarah Pease	(Weaver)	Md. Robert P.	
249.	Joan Peney		Widow	
250.	Thomas Pharoh	Husbandman	Widower	
251.	Mary Phips	(Governor)	Md. William P.	
252.	Hannah Post		Single	
253.	Mary Post		Single	Daughter of Rebecca Johnson
254.	Sarah Post			
255.	Susannah Post		Single	
256.	Margaret Prince		Widow (Md. Thomas P.)	
257.	Benjamin Proctor	Husbandman's son	Single (Md. Mary Whittredge 1694)	Son of John & Eliz. P.; brother of Sarah & William P.
258.	Elizabeth Proctor	(Husbandman)	Md. John P.	Wife of John P.; mother of Wm., Benj., & Sarah P.
259.	John Proctor	Husbandman	Md. Elizabeth P.	Husband of Eliz. P.; father of Wm., Benj., & Sarah P.
260.	Sarah Proctor	Husbandman's daughter	Single	Daughter of John & Eliz.; sister of Wm. & Benjamin P.
261.	William Proctor	Husbandman's son	Single	Son of John & Eliz.; bro. of Benj. & Sarah
262.	Ann Pudeator	(Blacksmith)	Widow (Md. Jacob P.)	
263.	Wilmot Reed	(Fisherman)	Md. Samuel R.	
264.	Sarah Rice		Md. Nicholas R.	
265.	Sarah Riste			
266.	Abigail Roe		Single	Daughter of Mary R.
267.	Mary Roe		Md. Hugh R.	Mother of Abigail R.
268.	Susanna Roote		Widow (Md. Josiah R.)	
269.	Henry Salter	Husbandman		
270.	Nathaniel Saltonstall	Militia major; Councillor; witch judge	Md. Elizabeth Ward	
271.	John Sawdry	Apprentice	Single	
272.	Margaret Scott	Very poor	Widow	
273.	Ann Sears		Md. John S.	
274.	Abigail Somes		Single	
275.	Martha Sparks	Soldier's daughter	Single	
276.	Mr. Stevens			
277.	Mary Taylor		Md. Seabred T.	
278.	Margaret Thatcher	(Minister)	Widow (Md. Thos. T.)	Mistress of no. 279
279.	Margaret Thatcher's maid	Servant	Single	Servant of Margaret Thatcher
280.	Tituba	Slave	Md. John Indian	Wife of John Indian
281.	Jason Toothaker			Son(?) of Roger & Mary T.
282.	Mary Toothaker	(Doctor)	Widow (Md. Roger T.)	Sister of Martha Carrier; wife of Roger T.; mother of Margaret & Jason(?)
283.	Roger Toothaker	Doctor	Md. Mary T.	Bro.-in-law of Martha Carrier; husband of Mary T.; father of Jason & Marg.
284.	Margaret Toothaker	Doctor's daughter	Single	Daughter of Mary & Roger T.; sister of Jason(?); niece of Martha Carrier
285.	Mary Town	(Husbandman)	Widow (Md. Wm. T.)	Mother of Mary Easty, Sarah Cloys, Rebecca Nurse
286.	Job Tukey	Laborer, fisherman	Single	

247.	Charlestown, Mass.		Woodward, ed., *Salem Witch. Rec.*, II, 106–7
248.	Salem, Mass.		*Ibid.*, II, 47, 195
249.	Gloucester, Mass.		Boyer & Nissenbaum, eds., *Salem-Village Witch.*, 377
250.	Lynn, Mass.	Ignoramus at Essex Co. Ct.	Woodward, ed., *Salem Witch. Rec.*, II, 201–2; "Ct. Files—Suffolk," XXXII, #2667
251.	Boston, Mass.	Not prosecuted	J. Whiting, *Truth & Innocency*, 140; Calef, *More Wonders*, 377n
252.	Boxford, Mass.	Acquitted Jan. 3, 1692/3	Noble, "Some Doc. Fragments," 24
253.	Rowley, Mass.	Convicted Jan. 3, 1692/3; reprieved	Noble, "Some Doc. Fragments," 24
254.	Andover, Mass.		
255.	Andover, Mass.	Acquitted May 1693	Noble, "Some Doc. Fragments," 25; "Ct. Files—Suffolk," XXXII, #2705
256.	Gloucester, Mass.	Ignoramus at Essex Co. Ct.	"Ct. Files—Suffolk," XXXII, #2676; "Mass. Arch.," CXXXV, 70
257.	Salem Village, Mass.		Woodward, ed., *Salem Witch. Rec.*, II, 47
258.	Salem Village, Mass.	Convicted; plead pregnancy	*Ibid.*, I, 99–117, 127–30
259.	Salem Village, Mass.	Hanged Aug. 19, 1692	*Ibid.*, I, 60–73
260.	Salem Village, Mass.		*Ibid.*, II, 47–48, 51–52
261.	Salem Village, Mass.	Ignoramus at Essex Co. Ct.	*Ibid.*, II, 53, 89–97; "Ct. Files—Suffolk," XXXII, #2705
262.	Salem, Mass.	Hanged Sept. 22, 1692	Woodward, ed., *Salem Witch. Rec.*, II, 12–23
263.	Marblehead, Mass.	Hanged Sept. 22, 1692	*Ibid.*, II, 97–105
264.	Reading, Mass.		*Ibid.*, II, 53, 195
265.	Beverly, Mass.		
266.	Gloucester, Mass.		
267.	Gloucester, Mass.	Released on bonds from Ipswich jail Sept. 24, 1692	W. Davis, "Wildes Family," 41
268.	Beverly, Mass.		Woodward, ed., *Salem Witch. Rec.*, I, 47, 52–53
269.	Andover, Mass.		"Ct. Files—Suffolk," XXXII, #2702
270.	Haverhill, Mass.	Not prosecuted	Sewall, *Diary*, I, 373
271.	Andover, Mass.		"Mass. Arch.," CXXXV, 52
272.	Rowley, Mass.	Hanged Sept. 22, 1692	Woodward, ed., *Salem Witch. Rec.*, II, 181–82; Upham, *Salem Witchcraft*, II, 324–25
273.	Woburn, Mass.		Woodward, ed., *Salem Witch. Rec.*, II, 185; "Ct. Files—Suffolk," XXXII, #2694
274.	Gloucester, Mass.	Ignoramus at Essex Co. Ct.	Woodward, ed., *Salem Witch. Rec.*, II, 193; "Ct. Files—Suffolk," XXXII, #2703
275.	Chelmesford, Mass.	Jailed at Boston	"Ct. Files—Suffolk," XXXII, #2696; "Mass. Arch.," CXXXV, 62
276.	Andover, Mass.	Accused; fled	Brattle, "Letter," 180
277.	Reading, Mass.	Acquitted Feb. 1, 1692/3	Noble, "Some Doc. Fragments," 25; "Ct. Files—Suffolk," XXXII, #2710
278.	Boston, Mass.	Not prosecuted	Brattle, "Letter," 177
279.	Boston, Mass.		Upham, *Salem Witchcraft*, II, 255
280.	Salem Village, Mass.		*Ibid.*, II, 23, 32, 255; Woodward, ed., *Salem Witch. Rec.*, I, 41–50
281.	Billerica, Mass.		Woodward, ed., *Salem Witch. Rec.*, II, 202
282.	Billerica, Mass.	Acquitted Feb. 1, 1692/3	*Ibid.*, II, 53; Noble, "Some Doc. Fragments," 25; "Ct. Files—Suffolk," XXXII, #2713
283.	Billerica, Mass.	Died in jail in June, 1692	"Ct. Files—Suffolk," XXXII, #2690; Woodward, ed., *Salem Witch. Rec.*, II, 25–27
284.	Billerica, Mass.		Woodward, ed., *Salem Witch. Rec.*, II, 53
285.	Topsfield, Mass.		Woodward, ed., *Salem Witch. Rec.*, II, 39–40
286.	Beverly, Mass.	Acquitted Jan. 3, 1692/3	"Mass. Arch.," CXXXV, 31; Upham, *Salem Witchcraft*, II, 223–24; "Ct. Files—Suffolk," XXXII, #2670; Noble, "Some Doc. Fragments," 23

287.	Hannah Tyler	Blacksmith's daughter	Single	Daughter of Mary T.; sister of Joanna T.
288.	Joanna Tyler	Blacksmith's daughter	Single	Daughter of Mary T.; sister of Hannah T.
289.	Martha Tyler	Balcksmith's daughter (?)	Single	Another daughter of Mary T. (?)
290.	Mary Tyler	(Blacksmith)	Md. Hopestill T.	Mother of Joanna, Hannah, and Martha T.
291.	Hezekiah Usher	Merchant	Md. Bridget Hoar	
292.	Rachel Vincent		Widow	
293.	Mary Wardwell			
294.	Mercy Wardwell	Carpenter's daughter	Single	Daughter of Samuel & Sarah W.
295.	Samuel Wardwell	Carpenter	Md. Sarah W.	Father of Mercy W.; husband of Sarah W.
296.	Sarah Wardwell	(Carpenter)	Md. Samuel W.	Mother of Mercy W.; wife of Samuel W.
297.	Mary Warren	Servant	Single	
298.	Mary Watkins	Servant	Single	
299.	Mistress White,		Md.	
	Sarah Wilds (see no. 94)			
300.	Ruth Wilford			
301.	John Willard	Farmer of "Comfortable" estate; deputy constable	Md. Margaret Knight	
302.	Samuel Willard	Minister of Boston	Md. Abigail Sherman; 2d Eunice Tyng	
303.	Sarah Wilson		Md. Joseph W.	Mother of Sarah Jr.
304.	Sarah Wilson, Jr.		Single	Daughter of Sarah W.

OTHER WITCHES ACCUSED, 1692–99

	Name	Date	Profession (Social Status)	Marital Status	Accusers	Victims
305.	Goody Miller	1692	Unknown	Unknown	Catherine Branch	Catherine Branch
306.	Mary Harvey	1692	Unknown	Md. Josiah H.	Catherine Branch	Catherine Branch
307.	Hannah Harvey	1692	Unknown	Single	Catherine Branch	Catherine Branch
308.	Mercy Disborough	1692	Unknown	Md. Thomas D.	Catherine Branch	Catherine Branch
309.	Elizabeth Clawson	1692	Unknown	Md. Stephen C.	Catherine Branch	Catherine Branch
310.	Winifred (King) Benham	1692, 1697	Unknown	Md. Joseph B.	Some children	Some children
311.	Hugh Crotia	1693	Unknown	Unknown	Eben Booth's girl	Eben Booth's girl
312.	Dame Swift	1693	Unknown	Unknown	Mary Watkins	Mary Watkins
313.	A female fortune-teller	1693	Fortuneteller	Unknown	Margaret Rule	Unknown
314.	Wenlock Curtis	1695	Sailor	Unknown	Self-accused	Other sailors
315.	Winifred Benham, Jr.	1697	Unknown	Single	Some children	Some children

287.	Andover, Mass.	Acquitted Jan. 3, 1692/3	"Mass. Arch.," CXXXV, 50; Calef, *More Wonders*, 374–75; Noble, "Some Doc. Fragments," 23
288.	Andover, Mass.		Woodward, ed., *Salem Witch. Rec.*, II, 134; "Mass. Arch.," CXXXV, 98
289.	Andover, Mass.		"Mass. Arch.," CXXXV, 98
290.	Andover, Mass.	Acquitted Jan. 3, 1692/3	Woodward, ed., *Salem Witch. Rec.*, II, 134; Calef, *More Wonders*, 374–75; Noble, "Some Doc. Fragments," 23
291.	Boston, Mass.	Fled prosecution	Brattle, "Letter," 178
292.	Gloucester, Mass.	Released on bonds from Ipswich Jail Sept. 24, 1692	W. Davis, "Wildes Family," 41
293.	Andover, Mass.		
294.	Andover, Mass.	Acquitted Jan. 3, 1692/3	"Mass. Arch.," CXXXV, 92; Noble, "Some Doc. Fragments," 24
295.	Andover, Mass.	Hanged Sept. 22, 1692	Woodward, ed., *Salem Witch. Rec.*, II, 146–53
296.	Andover, Mass.	Convicted Jan. 3, 1692/3; reprieved	*Ibid.*, II, 228; Noble, "Some Doc. Fragments," 24
297.	Salem Village, Mass.		Woodward, ed., *Salem Witch. Rec.*, I, 123–35
298.	Milton, Mass.	Acquitted April 25, 1693	Calef, *More Wonders*, 383–84
299.	Salem, Mass.		Woodward, ed., *Salem Witch. Rec.*, I, 193
300.	Haverhill, Mass.		Boyer & Nissenbaum, eds., *Salem-Village Witch.*, 378
301.	Salem Village, Mass.	Fled, retaken, hanged Aug. 19, 1692	Woodward, ed., *Salem Witch. Rec.*, I, 266–79; II, 1–12
302.	Boston, Mass.	Not prosecuted	Brattle, "Letter,"177–78
303.	Andover, Mass.		Woodward, ed., *Salem Witch. Rec.*, II, 134; Calef, *More Wonders*, 374–75; "Mass. Arch.," CXXXV, 97
304.	Andover, Mass.		"Mass. Arch.," CXXXV, 97

OTHER WITCHES ACCUSED, 1692–99

305.	Fairfield, Conn.	Acquitted	Wyllys, "Col. Suppl.," 17; J. Taylor, *Conn. Witch. Del.*, 154
306.	Fairfield, Conn.	Grand jury found no true bill	Wyllys, "Col. Suppl.," 5–6; J. Taylor, *Conn. Witch. Del.*, 154
307.	Fairfield, Conn.	Grand jury found no true bill	*Ibid.*
308.	Campo, Conn.	Convicted Oct. 28, 1692; reprieved 1693	Wyllys, "Col. Suppl.," 5–37; J. Taylor, *Conn. Witch. Del.*, 63–78, 116
309.	Stamford, Conn.	Acquitted Oct. 28, 1692	J. Taylor, *Conn. Witch. Del.*, 73, 102, 116; Wyllys, "Papers," 19–21
310.	Wallingford, Conn.	Acquitted; fled upon renewed complaints	J. Taylor, *Conn. Witch. Del.*, 155; Calef, *More Wonders*, 385
311.	Stratford, Conn.	Acquitted	J. Taylor, *Conn. Witch. Del.*, 118; "Conn. Assts.," LVIII, 19
312.	Salem Village, Mass.		Calef, *More Wonders*, 383–84
313.	Boston, Mass.	Not prosecuted	*Ibid.*, 311
314.	Aboard ship bound for Barbados	Had visions of Devil; died strangely aboard ship	C. Mather, *Magnalia*, II, 403–4
315.	Wallingford, Conn.	Fled to N.Y. with mother	J. Taylor, *Conn. Witch. Del.*, 155; Calef, *More Wonders*, 385

Bibliography

Records of Colony, Town, Church, and Court

CONNECTICUT-NEW HAVEN

The Book of General Laws for the People within the Jurisdiction of Connecticut . . . . Cambridge: Samuel Peters, 1673.

Burr, John Chandler, ed. *Lyme Records, 1667–1730: A Literal Transcription of the Town Meetings* . . . . Stonington, Conn.: Pequot Press, 1968.

"Connecticut Archives: Court Papers, 1649–1709." Connecticut State Library, Hartford.

"Connecticut Archives: Crimes and Misdemeanors," ser. 1, v. I; ser. 2, v. III. Connecticut State Library, Hartford.

Connecticut "Court of Assistants, 1665–1677." In "Records of the Colony of Connecticut," LVI. Connecticut State Library, Hartford.

Connecticut "Court of Assistants, 1669–1686, 1696–1701." In "Records of the Colony of Connecticut," LIII. Connecticut State Library, Hartford.

Dexter, Franklin Bowditch, ed. *New Haven Town Records, 1649–1662.* Ancient Town Records, I. New Haven: New Haven Historical Society, 1917.

———. *New Haven Town Records, 1662–1684.* Ancient Town Records, II. New Haven: New Haven Historical Society, 1917.

"Hartford County, Connecticut. County Court Records, 1666–1677." In "Records of the Colony of Connecticut," LVI. Connecticut State Library, Hartford.

Hartford "County Court Records, 1677–1706." In "Hartford Probate Records," IV, V, & VI. Connecticut State Library, Hartford.

Hartford Town Votes, I (1635–1716). Collections of the Connecticut Historical Society, VI (1897).

Hoadly, Charles J., ed. *Records of the Colony and Plantation of New Haven, 1638–1649.* Hartford: Case, Lockwood, 1857.

————. *Records of the Colony and Plantation of New Haven from May 1653 to the Union*. Hartford: Case, Lockwood, 1858.

Manwaring, Charles William, ed. *A Digest of the Early Connecticut Probate Records, I. Hartford District, 1635–1700*. Hartford: R. S. Peck, 1904.

"New Haven County, Connecticut. County Court Records, 1666–1855," I & II. Connecticut State Library, Hartford.

"New London County, Connecticut. County Court Records, 1661–1855," I–VII. Connecticut State Library, Hartford.

"Papers Relating to the Controversy in the Church in Hartford, 1656–1659."*Collections of the Connecticut Historical Society*, II (1870): 51–125.

"Particular Court Records, 1663–1665." In "Records of the Colony of Connecticut," LVI. Connecticut State Library, Hartford.

Powers, Jonas, ed. *New Haven Town Records, 1684–1769*. Ancient Town Records, III. New Haven: New Haven Historical Society, 1962.

"Records, Court of Assistants and Superior Court, 1687–1715." In "Records of the Colony of Connecticut," LVIII. Connecticut State Library, Hartford.

Records of the Particular Court of Connecticut, 1639–1663. Collections of the Connecticut Historical Society, XXII (1928).

"Trial of Ezekiel Cheever Before the Church at New Haven." *Collections of the Connecticut Historical Society*, I (1860): 22–51.

T[rumbull], A[nnie] E. *Records of the Particular Court of the Colony of Connecticut During the Administration of Sir Edmond Andros, Royal Governor, 1687–1688*. Hartford: n.p., 1935.

Trumbull, J. Hammond, ed. *Public Records of the Colony of Connecticut*. 4 vols. Hartford: Brown & Parson (I); F.A. Brown (II); Case, Lockwood & Brainerd (III & IV), 1850–68.

Wyllys, Samuel. "Samuel Wyllys Collections. Supplement. Witchcraft in Connecticut, 1662–1693." Connecticut State Library, Hartford.

————. "Samuel Wyllys Papers. Depositions on Cases of Witchcraft, Assault, Theft, Drunkenness, and Other Crimes in Connecticut, 1663–1728." Connecticut State Library, Hartford.

MAINE

Libby, Charles Thornton; Allen, Neal W.; and Moody, Robert E., eds. *Province and Court Records of Maine*. 5 vols. Portland: Maine Historical Society, 1928–64.

"York County Records," Book B. York County Court House, Alfred, Maine.

MASSACHUSETTS

Acts and Laws, May 30, 1694–February 27, 1695. Boston: Bartholomew Green, 1695.

Acts and Laws, Passed by the Great and General Court or Assembly of Their Majesties Province of the Massachusetts-Bay in New-England. . . . Boston: Benjamin Harris, 1692.

Acts and Laws, Passed by the Great and General Court or Assembly of Their Majesties Province of the Massachusetts-Bay in New-England. . . . Boston: Bartholomew Green, 1694.

The Acts and Laws, Public and Private, of the Province of the Massachusetts Bay . . ., I. Boston: Wright & Potter, 1869.

Acts & Laws, through November 20, 1695. Boston: Bartholomew Green & John Allen, 1695.

Boston Record Commissioners. *First Report of the Record Commissioners of the City of Boston.* 1876.

————. *Fourth Report of the Record Commissioners of the City of Boston, Containing the Dorchester Town Records.* 1881.

————. *A Report of the Record Commissioners of the City of Boston, Containing the Boston Records from 1660 to 1701.* VII, 1881.

————. *A Report of the Record Commissioners of the City of Boston, Containing Miscellaneous Papers.* X, 1886.

————. *A Report of the Record Commissioners of the City of Boston, Containing Records of Boston Selectmen, 1701–1715.* XI, 1884.

————. *A Report of the Record Commissioners of the City of Boston, Containing Roxbury Land and Church Records.* VI, 1884.

————. *Second Report of the Record Commissioners of the City of Boston, Containing Boston Records 1634–1660 and the Book of Possessions.* 1881.

By the Governor and General Court of the Colony of the Massachusetts Bay in New-England, March 13, 1689/90. Cambridge: Samuel Green, 1690.

A Confession of Faith Owned and Consented unto by the Elders and Messengers of the Churches. Boston: John Foster, 1680.

"A Coppie of the Liberties of the Massachusets [sic] Colonie in New England." *Collections of the Massachusetts Historical Society,* ser. 3, VIII (1843): 216–37.

Cotton, John. *An Abstract of the Lawes of New England, As They Are Now Established.* London: For F. Coules & W. Ley, 1641.

"Court Files—Suffolk County." 48 vols. Suffolk County Court House, Boston.

"Court Records. I. Dukes County, 1665–1715." Dukes County Court House, Edgartown, Mass.

Danforth, Samuel. "Rev. Samuel Danforth's Records of the First Church in Roxbury, Massachusetts." *New England Historical and Genealogical Register,* XXXIV (1880): 84–89, 162–66, 297–301, 359–63.

"Danvers Church Records." *New England Historical and Genealogical Register,* XI (1857): 131–35, 316–21.

Dow, George Francis, ed. *Records and Files of the Quarterly Courts of Essex County, Massachusetts.* 8 vols. Salem, Mass.: Essex Institute, 1911–21.

"Dukes County Court Records, 1673–1819." New England Historic and Genealogical Society, Boston.

Essex "County Court. Ipswich, September 1682–April 1686." Essex County Court House, Salem.

Essex "County Court. Ipswich, 1682–1692." Essex County Court House, Salem.

Essex "County Court. Salem, September 1679–November 1691." Essex County Court House, Salem.

Essex "County Court. Salem, June 1682–November 1685." Essex County Court House, Salem.

"Essex County Court of General Sessions, 1686–1689, 1692–1723." Essex County Court House, Salem.

Essex County "Court of Pleas and Sessions, 1688–1689." Essex County Court House, Salem.

"Essex County Court Papers." 57 vols. Essex County Court House, Salem.

Essex County "General Sessions of the Peace, July 1692–September 1769." Essex County Court House, Salem.

"The Examination of Mrs. Anne Hutchinson at the Court at Newtown." In David D. Hall, ed., *The Antinomian Controversy, 1636–1638: A Documentary History*, pp. 311–48. Middletown, Conn.: Wesleyan University Press, 1968.

"General Sessions of the Peace, Essex County, Massachusetts, 1692–1695." Essex County Court House, Salem.

Hampshire County Court of "General Sessions and Common Pleas, no. 1, 1677–1728." Hampshire County Court House, Northampton.

Historical Records Survey. *Abstract and Index of the Inferiour Court of Pleas (Suffolk County Court) Held at Boston, 1680–1698.* Boston: Historical Records Survey, 1940.

McLaughlin, William G., and Davidson, Martha Whiting, eds. "The Baptist Debate of April 14–15, 1668." *Proceedings of the Massachusetts Historical Society*, LXXV (1964): 101–33.

"A Manifesto or Declaration Set Forth by the Undertakers of the New Church Now Erected in Boston in New England, November 17th, 1699." In Alden T. Vaughan, ed., *The Puritan Tradition in America, 1620–1730*, pp. 329–33. New York: Harper & Row, 1972.

"Massachusetts Archives. VIII: Depositions, 1662–1766." Massachusetts State Archives, Boston.

"Massachusetts Archives. XXX: Indians, 1639–1705." Massachusetts State Archives, Boston.

"Massachusetts Archives. LX: Maritime Affairs, 1641–1671." Massachusetts State Archives, Boston.

"Massachusetts Archives. CXXXV: Witchcraft." Massachusetts State Archives, Boston.

"Middlesex Court of General Sessions, 1692–1723." Middlesex County Court House, Cambridge.

"Middlesex Court Records," folios 1–303, 1X–120X, 1A–200A, 13B–27B, 251B. Middlesex County Court House, Cambridge.

Muddy River and Brookline Records, 1634–1838. Boston: J. E. Farwell, 1875.

Noble, John A., and Cronin, Joseph F., eds. *Records of the Court of Assistants of the Colony of Massachusetts Bay*. 3 vols. Boston: Massachusetts Historical Society, 1901–28.

"Photostatic Copy of Records of the County Court, Suffolk, 1680–1692, Pt. I." Suffolk County Court House, Boston.

Pierce, Richard D., ed. *The Records of the First Church in Boston, 1630–1838. Publications of the Colonial Society of Massachusetts*, XXXIX–XLI (1961–63).

"Proceedings of Excommunication against Mistress Ann Hibbens of Boston (1640)." In John Demos, ed., *Remarkable Providences, 1600–1760*, pp. 221–39. New York: George Braziller, 1972.

"Proceedings of the Boston Church against the Exiles." In David D. Hall, ed., *The Antinomian Controversy, 1636–1638: A Documentary History*, pp. 389–95. Middletown, Conn.: Wesleyan University Press.

Pulsifer, David S., transcriber. "Records of the County of Middlesex in the Commonwealth of Massachusetts," I, III, IV. Middlesex County Court House, Cambridge.

"Records of a Speciall Court of Oyer and Terminer, a Court of Appeals, a Superiour Court, Assizes, and a Superiour Court Held at Boston in 1686–1687." Suffolk County Court House, Boston.

Records of the First Church at Dorchester in New England, 1636–1734. Boston: G. H. Ellis, 1891.

"Records of the Massachusetts Council under Joseph Dudley, 1686." In *Proceedings of the Massachusetts Historical Society*, ser. 2, XIII (1899): 226–86.

Records of the Suffolk County Court, 1671–1680. Publications of the Colonial Society of Massachusetts, XXIX & XXX (1930).

Records of the Town of Cambridge (Formerly New-Towne), Massachusetts, 1630–1703. . . . Cambridge: City Council, 1901.

"A Report of the Trial of Mrs. Anne Hutchinson before the Church in Boston." In David D. Hall, ed., *The Antinomian Controversy, 1636–1638: A Documentary History*, pp. 349–88. Middletown, Conn.: Wesleyan University Press, 1968.

"Salem Witchcraft—1692 in Three Volumes: Verbatim Transcription of Salem Witchcraft Papers." Essex County Court House, Salem.

Shurtleff, Nathaniel B., ed. *Records of the Governor and Company of the Massachusetts Bay in New England*. 5 vols. Boston: W. White, 1853–54.

Smith, Joseph H., ed. *Colonial Justice in Massachusetts (1639–1702): The Pynchon Court Record*, Cambridge: Harvard University Press, 1961.

Suffolk Deeds. 12 vols. Boston: Rockwell & Churchill, 1880–1902.

"Superiour Court of Judicature, Etc., 1686–1700." Suffolk County Court House, Boston.

"Tax List and Schedules—1687." In *First Report of the Record Commissioners of the City of Boston*, pp. 91–127. Boston Record Commissioners.

"Town Records of Salem, 1634–1695." *Historical Collections of the Essex Institute*, IX (1869): 5–232; XL (1904): 97–128, 273–96, 337–52; XLI (1905): 117–40, 293–308; XLII (1906): 41–64, 257–72; XLIII (1907): 33–48, 145–60, 257–72; XLVIII (1912): 17–40, 149–72, 229–44, 341–56; XLIX (1913): 65–80,

145–60, 257–74; LXII (1926): 81–96, 177–92, 257–72; LXIII (1927): 65–80; LXIV (1928): 65–80, 201–8; LXV (1929): 25–40; LXVI (1930): 209–24, 505–20; LXVII (1931): 233–48, 385–400; LXVIII (1932): 33–48, 153–68, 209–24, 305–20; LXIX (1933): 65–80, 137–54; LXXXIII (1947): 67–82, 273–88; LXXXV (1949): 181–96, 369–92; LXXXVI (1950): 183–98; LXXXVIII (1952): 367–90.

Watertown Third Book of Records. Watertown: City Council, 1838.

Whitmore, William H., ed. *The Colonial Laws of Massachusetts. Reprinted from the Edition of 1672, with the Supplements through 1686*. Boston: Rockwell & Churchill, 1887.

Woodward, W. Elliot, ed. *Records of Salem Witchcraft, Copied from the Original Records*. Roxbury, Mass.: W. E. Woodward, 1864.

NEW HAMPSHIRE

Acts and Laws, Passed by the General Court or Assembly of His Majesties Province of New Hampshire in New England. Boston: B. Green, 1716.

Batchellor, Albert Stillman, ed. "Records of the President and Council, 1679–1682." New Hampshire State Papers Series, XIX, 647–91. Concord N.H.: John B. Clarke, 1891.

Bouton, Nathaniel, ed. *Provincial Papers. Documents and Records Relating to the Province of New-Hampshire from the Earliest Period of Its Settlement*. New Hampshire State Papers Series, I & II. Concord, N.H.: E. Jenks, 1867–68.

Collections of the New-Hampshire Historical Society, Containing Province Records and Court Papers, From 1680 to 1692, VIII (1866).

Hammond, Otis G., ed. *New Hampshire Court Records 1640–1692, Court Papers 1652–1668*. New Hampshire State Papers Series, XL. Concord, N.H.: State of New Hampshire, 1943.

"New Hampshire Court of Quarter Sessions, 1686–1699." New Hampshire State Archives, Concord.

"New Hampshire Court Papers." 11 vols. New Hampshire State Archives, Concord.

New Hampshire "Provincial Court Records—Court of Quarter Sessions: Inferior Court of Common Pleas 1692–June 1704; Supreme Court of Judicature April–October 1694." New Hampshire State Archives, Concord.

"Norfolk County Court Records, 1649–1679." In George Francis Dow, ed., *Records and Files of the Quarterly Courts of Essex County, Massachusetts*. 8 vols. Salem, Mass.: Essex Institute, 1911–21.

Pulsifer, David S., transcriber. "Records of the County Courts of Norfolk, Salisbury, and Hampton, in the Colony of Massachusetts, 1648–1654," I, pt. 1 (1852). Essex County Court House, Salem, Mass.

"Records of the President and Council of New Hampshire." *Proceedings of the Massachusetts Historical Society*, 1st ser., XVI (1878): 261–79.

PLYMOUTH

Bristol County "Court of General Sessions, 1697–1701." Bristol County Court House, Taunton, Mass.

"Minutes of the Sandwich Men's Monthly Meeting, 1672–1754." Friend's Library, Rhode Island Historical Society, Providence.

Plymouth Church Records, 1620–1859, I. *Publications of the Colonial Society of Massachusetts,* XXII (1920).

"Records, Sessions of the Peace. Plymouth County, 1686–1721." Old Colony Historical Society, Plymouth.

Shurtleff, Nathaniel B., and Pulsifer, David S., eds. *Records of the Colony of New Plymouth.* 12 vols. Boston: W. White, 1855–61.

RHODE ISLAND-PROVIDENCE PLANTATIONS

Acts and Laws of His Majesties Colony of Rhode-Island and Providence Plantations in America. Boston: John Allen, 1719.

"Aquidneck Quarter Court Records (1641–1646)." In Howard M. Chapin, *Documentary History of Rhode Island,* pp. 132–65. Providence: Preston & Rounds, 1919.

Bartlett, John Russell, ed. *Records of the Colony of Rhode Island and Providence Plantations, in New England.* 3 vols. Providence: A. Crawford Greene & Bro., 1856–58.

Brigham, Clarence S., ed. *The Early Records of the Town of Portsmouth.* Providence: E. L. Freeman & Sons, 1901.

Capwell, Helen, transcriber. *Records of the Court of Trials of the Town of Warwick, 1659–1674.* Providence: n.p., 1922

Chapin, Howard M., ed. *The Early Records of the Town of Warwick.* Providence: E. A. Johnson, 1926.

"General Court of Trials. Newport County, 1671–1724." Newport County Court House, Newport.

Klyberg, Albert T., ed. *Rhode Island Land Evidences, v. I, 1648–1696.* Baltimore: Genealogical Publishers, 1970. [Originally published in 1921.]

"Records of the Men's Rhode Island Monthly Meeting, 1676–1773." Friend's Library, Rhode Island Historical Society, Providence.

"Records of the Monthly Meeting of Women Friends for Rhode Island, 1690–1801." Friend's Library, Rhode Island Historical Society, Providence.

"Records of the Quarterly Meetings for Rhode Island from 1681 to 1746." Friend's Library, Rhode Island Historical Society, Providence.

Rhode Island Court Records: Records of the Court of Trials of the Colony of Providence Plantations, 1647–1670. 2 vols. Providence: n.p., 1920.

Rogers, Horatio, and Field, Edward, eds. *Early Records of the Town of Providence.* 21 vols. Providence: Snow and Farnham Co., 1892–1915.

Other Primary and Secondary Accounts

Abbott, Edith. *Women in Industry: A Study in American Economic History*. New York: D. Appleton, 1910.

Adams, Herbert B. "Allotments of Land in Salem to Men, Women, and Maids." *Historical Collections of the Essex Institute*, XIX (1882): 167–75.

Adams, James Truslow. *The Founding of New England*. Boston: Atlantic Monthly Press, 1921.

―――. *Provincial Society, 1690–1763*. New York: Macmillan, 1927.

Adams, Ruth, and Murray, Frank. *Minerals: Kill or Cure?* New York: Larchmont Books, 1974.

Adams, William and Eliphalet. "Memoir of the Rev. William Adams of Dedham, Massachusetts, and of the Rev. Eliphalet Adams of New London, Connecticut." *Collections of the Massachusetts Historical Society*, ser. 4, I (1852): 1–51.

Adburgham, Alison. *Women in Print: Writing Women and Women's Magazines from the Restoration to the Accession of Victoria*. London: G. Allen & Unwin, 1972.

Alexander, Franz. *Fundamentals of Psychoanalysis*. New York: W. W. Norton, 1948.

Allport, Floyd H. "The J-Curve Hypothesis of Conforming Behavior." *Journal of Social Psychology*, V (1934): 141–83.

Allport, Gordon W. *Personality and Social Encounter*. Boston: Beacon Press, 1964.

Amir, Menachim. *Patterns in Forcible Rape*. Chicago: University of Chicago Press, 1971.

"Ancient Marriage Contract." *New England Historical and Genealogical Register*, XII (1858): 353.

Andrews, Charles M. *The Colonial Period of American History*. 4 vols. New Haven: Yale University Press, 1934.

"An Apologetical Reply to an invective petition, May 30, 1665." *Collections of the Rhode Island Historical Society*, II (1853): 233–46.

Aristotle's Compleat Masterpiece. N.p., 1755 [Originally published in 1684].

Asch, Stuart S. "Depression: Three Clinical Variations." *Psychoanalytic Study of the Child*, XXI (1966): 150–71.

Ashley, Maurice. *The Stuarts in Love, with Some Reflections on Love and Marriage in the Sixteenth and Seventeenth Centuries*. New York: Macmillan, 1964.

Aspinwall, William. *A Volume Relating to the Early History of Boston, Containing the Aspinwall Notarial Records from 1644 to 1651*. Boston: Record Commissioners, XXXII, 1903.

Austin, John Osborne. *A Genealogical Dictionary of Rhode Island. . . .* Albany: Joel Munsell's Sons, 1885.

Axtell, James. *The School upon a Hill: Education and Society in Colonial New England*. New Haven: Yale University Press, 1974.

———. "The Vengeful Women of Marblehead: Robert Roule's Deposition of 1677." *William and Mary Quarterly*, ser. 3, XXXI (1974): 647–52.

Bach, Bert C. "Self-Depreciation in Edward Taylor's *Sacramental Meditations*." *Cithara*, VI (1966): 45–59.

Backer, Dorothy Anne Liot. *Precious Women: A Feminist Phenomenon in the Age of Louis XIV*. New York: Basic Books, 1974.

Bacon, Margaret. *The Quiet Rebels: The Story of the Quakers in America*. New York: Basic Books, 1969.

Bailey, Sarah Loring. *Historical Sketches of Andover, Comprising the Present Towns of North Andover and Andover*. Boston: Houghton Mifflin, 1956.

Baily, John. "Diary of John Baily." In Cotton Mather, *Magnalia Christi Americana: Or, the Ecclesiastical History of New England, from its First Planting in the Year 1620, unto the Year of Our Lord, 1698*. Hartford: Silas Andrus, Roberts, & Burr, 1820, I, 504–7. [Originally published in 1702.]

Baily, Samuel. "The Colledge ferula being a reply to ye country mans ap[o]crypha, 1697." In "Samuel Baily Papers, 1671–1906." Rhode Island Historical Society, Providence.

Bailyn, Bernard. *The New England Merchants in the Seventeenth Century*. Cambridge: Harvard University Press, 1955.

Baker, Catharine S. "Rape in Seventeenth Century Massachusetts." Paper delivered at Third Berkshire Conference on the History of Women, June 10, 1976, Bryn Mawr, Penna.

Banks, Charles Edward. *The Planters of the Commonwealth: A Study of the Emigrants and Emigrations in Colonial Times. . . .* Boston: Houghton Mifflin, 1930.

———. "Scotch Prisoners Deported to New England by Cromwell, 1651–1652." *Proceedings of the Massachusetts Historical Society*, LXI (1927): 14–29.

Barnard, John. "Autobiography of the Rev. John Barnard." *Collections of the Massachusetts Historical Society*, ser. 3, V (1836).

Baroja, Julio Caro. *The World of the Witches*. Trans. O. N. V. Glendinning. Chicago: University of Chicago Press, 1964.

Battis, Emery. *Saints and Sectaries: Anne Hutchinson and the Antinomian Controversy in the Massachusetts Bay Colony*. Chapel Hill: University of North Carolina Press, 1962.

Baumrind, Diana. "From Each According to Her Ability." *School Review*, LXXX (1972): 161–97.

Baxter, James Phinney, ed. *Documentary History of the State of Maine. Collections of the Maine Historical Society*, ser. 2, III, IV, & VI (1884–1900).

Baxter, Richard. *Reasons of the Christian Religion. . . .* London: R. White for Francis Titon, 1667.

Baylie, Robert. *A Dissuasive from the Errours of the Time*. London: for Samuel Gellibrand, 1645.

Beacon, Joseph. "Solitary Meditations; ye Sence on many of y^m borrowed from Bishop Hall, but ye words mostly mine own." In "Miscellanies on various Subjects. Translations and Collections out of Diverse Authors

(1688)." Houghton Library, Harvard University.

Beales, Ross W., Jr. "The Half-Way Covenant and Religious Scrupulosity: The First Church of Dorchester, Massachusetts, as a Test Case." *William and Mary Quarterly*, ser. 3, XXXI (1974): 465–80.

Bednarski, Joyce. "The Salem Witch-Scare Viewed Sociologically." In Maxwell G. Marwick, ed., *Witchcraft and Sorcery: Selected Readings*, pp. 151–63. Baltimore: Penguin Books, 1970.

Beedy, Helen Coffin. *Mothers of Maine*. Portland: Thurston Printers, 1895.

Beidelman, T. O. "Witchcraft in Ukaguru." In John Middleton and E. H. Winter, eds., *Witchcraft and Sorcery in East Africa*, pp. 57–98. London: Routledge and Kegan Paul, 1963.

Belcher, Joseph. *Duty of Parents and Early Seeking of Christ: Two Sermons Preached in Dedham, New England. . . .* Boston: B. Green for Samuel Phillips, 1710.

Belknap, Jeremy. *The History of New Hampshire*. 3 vols. Philadelphia: Robert Aitken, 1784–92.

Bell, Charles H. *History of the Town of Exeter, New Hampshire*. Exeter: J. E. Farwell, 1888.

Benam, Silvio; Horder, John; and Anderson, Jennifer. "Hysterical Epidemic in a Classroom." *Psychological Medicine*, III (1973): 366–73.

Benedict, David. *A General History of the Baptist Denomination in America and Other Parts of the World*. New York: Sheldon, 1855.

Benson, Mary Sumner. *Women in Eighteenth Century America: A Study of Opinions and Social Usage*. New York: Columbia University Press, 1935.

Benson, Ralph C. *Handbook of Obstetrics and Gynecology*. Los Altos, Calif.: Lange Medical Publications, 1971.

[Bentley, William.] "A Description and History of Salem by the Reverend William Bentley." *Collections of the Massachusetts Historical Society*, ser. 1, VI (1799): 212–88.

Benton, Josiah Henry. *Early Census Making in Massachusetts. . . .* Boston: C. E. Goodspeed, 1905.

———. *Warning Out in New England, 1656–1817*. Boston: W. B. Clarke, 1911.

Berkowitz, L., and Green, J. "The Stimulus Qualities of the Scapegoat." *Journal of Abnormal and Social Psychology*, LXIV (1962): 293–301.

———, and Holmes, D. S. "The Generalization of Hostility to Disliked Objects." *Journal of Personality*, XXVII (1959): 565–77.

Berryman, John. *Homage to Mistress Bradstreet*. New York: Farrar, Straus, 1956.

Besse, Joseph. *A Collection of the Sufferings of the People Called Quakers. . . .* London: L. Hinde, 1753.

Bibb, Richard C., and Guze, Samuel B. "Hysteria (Briquet's Syndrome) in a Psychiatric Hospital: The Significance of Secondary Depression." *American Journal of Psychiatry*, CXXIX (1972): 224–28.

Bishop, George. *New-England Judged, by the Spirit of the Lord*. London: T. Sowle, 1703. [Originally published in 1661.]

Bissell, Linda Auwers. "From One Generation to Another: Mobility in Seventeenth-Century Windsor, Connecticut." *William and Mary Quarterly*, ser. 3, XXXI (1974): 79–110.

Blackstone, Sir William. *Commentaries on the Laws of England*, ed. John L. Wendell. 4 vols. New York: Harper & Bros., 1858.

Bliss, Robert M. "A Secular Revival: Puritanism in Connecticut, 1675–1708." *Journal of American Studies*, VI (1972): 129–52.

Bliss, William Root. *Side Glimpses from the Colonial Meeting House*. Boston: Houghton Mifflin, 1894.

Bloch, Dorothy, "Feelings That Kill: The Effect of the Wish for Infanticide in Neurotic Depression." *Psychoanalytic Review*, LII (1965): 51–66.

Bogart, Dodd. "Demonism as a Function of Status Certainty Loss." Ph.D. dissertation, University of Michigan, 1967.

Boston Women's Health Book Collective. *Our Bodies, Ourselves: A Book by and for Women*. New York: Simon and Schuster, 1973.

Bourne, Edward E. *The History of Wells and Kennebunk . . .* Portland, Maine: B. Thurston, 1875.

Bowen, Richard Le Baron. "The 1690 Tax Revolt of Plymouth Colony Towns." *New England Historical and Genealogical Register*, CXII (1958): 4–14.

Boyer, Paul, and Nissenbaum, Stephen. *Salem Possessed: The Social Origins of Witchcraft*. Cambridge: Harvard University Press, 1974.

———, eds. *Salem–Village Witchcraft: A Documentary Record of Local Conflict in Colonial New England*. Belmont, Calif.: Wadsworth, 1972.

Bradford, Gamaliel. *Elizabethan Women*. Boston: Houghton Mifflin, 1936.

Bradford, William. "A Descriptive and Historical Account of New England in Verse." *Collections of the Massachusetts Historical Society*, ser. 1, III (1794): 77–84.

———. *Of Plymouth Plantation, 1620–1647*, ed. Samuel Eliot Morison. New York: Alfred A. Knopf, 1952.

———, and Allerton, Isaac. "Letter of September 8, 1623." *American Historical Review*, VIII (1903): 294–301.

[Bradstreet, Anne.] *The Tenth Muse Lately Sprung Up in America, Or Several Poems Compiled with Great Variety of Witt and Learning*. London: For Steven Bowtell, 1650.

———. *The Works of Anne Bradstreet*, ed. Jeannine Hensley. Cambridge: Belknap Press of Harvard University Press, 1967.

Bradstreet, Simon. "Governor Simon Bradstreet and Council to the Agents, November 29, 1690." In William H. Whitmore, ed., *Andros Tracts: Being a Collection of Pamphlets and Official Papers Issued During the Period Between the Overthrow of the Andros Government and the Establishment of the Second Charter of Massachusetts*, III, 52–57. *Publications of the Prince Society*, VII (1874).

———. "Simon Bradstreet's Journal, 1664–1683." *Historical and Genealogical Register*, IX (1855): 43–51.

Brattle, Thomas. "Letter, 1692." In George Lincoln Burr, ed., *Narratives of the Witchcraft Cases, 1648–1706*, pp. 165–90. New York: Charles Scribner's Sons, 1914.

Breen, Timothy H. *The Character of the Good Ruler: A Study of Puritan Political Ideas in New England, 1630–1730.* New Haven: Yale University Press, 1970.

———. "Persistent Localism: English Social Change and the Shaping of New England Institutions." *William and Mary Quarterly*, ser. 3, XXXII (1975): 3–18.

———, and Foster, Stephen. "The Puritan's Greatest Achievement: A Study of Social Cohesion in Seventeenth-Century Massachusetts." *Journal of American History*, LX (1973): 5–22.

Brenton, Myron. *The American Male.* Greenwich, Conn.: Fawcett, 1970.

Bridenbaugh, Carl. *Cities in the Wilderness: The First Century of Urban Life in America 1625–1742.* New York: Capricorn Books, 1964. [Originally published in 1938.]

———. *Fat Mutton and Liberty of Conscience: Society in Rhode Island, 1636–1690.* Providence: Brown University Press, 1974.

———, "The New England Town: A Way of Life." *Proceedings of the American Antiquarian Society*, n.s., LVI (1946): 19–48.

———. *Vexed and Troubled Englishmen, 1590–1642.* New York: Oxford University Press, 1968.

Brinton, Howard H. *Friends for Three Hundred Years.* Wallingford,: Pendle Hill, 1972.

Bristol, Roger Patrell. *Supplement to Charles Evans' American Bibliography.* Charlottesville: University Press of Virginia, 1970.

Brock, John. "The Autobiographical Memoranda of John Brock, 1636–1659," ed. Clifford K. Shipton. *Proceedings of the American Antiquarian Society*, n.s., LIII (1943): 96–105.

Brown, B. Katherine. "Puritan Democracy in Dedham, Massachusetts: Another Case Study." *William and Mary Quarterly*, ser. 3, XXIV (1967): 378–96.

Brownmiller, Susan. *Against Our Will: Men, Women and Rape.* New York: Simon & Schuster, 1975.

Bulkeley, Gershom. *The People's Right to Election or Alteration of Government in Connecticut, Argued in a Letter.* Philadelphia, 1689. In William H. Whitmore, ed., *Andros Tracts: Being a Collection of Pamphlets and Official Papers Issued During the Period Between the Overthrow of the Andros Government and the Establishment of the Second Charter of Massachusetts*, II, 83–110. *Publications of the Prince Society*, VI (1869).

———. *Will and Doom, or The Miseries of Connecticut by and under an Usurped and Arbitary Power.* Philadelphia, 1692. In *Collections of the Connecticut Historical Society*, III (1895): 69–269.

Bullivant, Benjamin. "Benjamin Bullivant's Journal, 1690." *Proceedings of the Massachusetts Historical Society*, XVI (1878): 103–8.

Burnyeat, John. *The Truth Exalted in the Writings of That Eminent and Faithful Servant of Christ John Burnyeat.* London: For Thomas Northcott, 1691.

Burr, George Lincoln, ed. *Narratives of the Witchcraft Cases, 1648–1706*. New York: Charles Scribner's Sons, 1914.

[Burrough, Edward.] *A Declaration of the Sad and Great Persecution and Martyrdom of the People of God, Called Quakers, in New-England, for the Worshipping of God*. London: For Robert Wilson, 1660.

Bushman, Richard L. *From Puritan to Yankee: Character and the Social Order in Connecticut, 1690–1765*. New York: W. W. Norton, 1970.

Buxton, Jean. "Mandari Witchcraft." In John Middleton and E. H. Winter, eds., *Witchcraft and Sorcery in East Africa*, pp. 99–121. London: Routledge & Kegan Paul, 1963.

Byfield, Nathaniel. *An Account of the Late Revolution in N.E. Together with the Declaration of the Gentlemen, Merchants, and Inhabitants of Boston, and the Country Adjacent, April 18, 1689*. London: For Richard Chiswell, 1689.

Cadbury, Henry J. "Early Quakers at Cambridge." *Proceedings of the Cambridge Historical Society*, XXIV (1938): 67–82.

Calef, Robert. *More Wonders of the Invisible World*. London, 1700. Excerpted in George Lincoln Burr, ed., *Narratives of the Witchcraft Cases, 1648–1706*, pp. 289–393. New York: Charles Scribner's Sons, 1914.

Calhoun, Arthur C. *A Social History of the American Family*. 3 vols. New York: Arthur H. Clark, 1917–19.

Calvin, John. *Commentary on the First Epistle to the Corinthians*. Edinburgh: Calvin Translation Society, 1848.

———. *Institutes of the Christian Religion*. Trans. John Allen. 2 vols. Philadelphia: Presbyterian Board of Christian Education, 1936. [Originally published in 1536.]

Campbell, Helen. *Anne Bradstreet and Her Times*. Boston: D. Lathrop, 1891.

Cartland, Barbara. *Woman the Enigma*. New York: Pyramid Books, 1974.

Caulfield, Ernest. "Infant Feeding in Colonial America." *Journal of Pediatrics*, XLI (1952): 673–87.

———."Pediatric Aspects of the Salem Witchcraft Tragedy: A Lesson on Mental Health." *American Journal of Diseases of Children*, LXV (1943): 788–802.

Caulkins, Frances M. *History of New London, Connecticut, From the First Survey of the Coast in 1612, to 1852*. Hartford: Case, Lockwood, 1860.

Chalkley, Thomas. *A Journal or Historical Account of the life, travels, and Christian Experiences, of that antient, faithful servant of Jesus Christ, Thomas Chalkley. . . .* Philadelphia: James Chattin, 1754.

C[hamberlain], R[ichard]. *Lithobolia: or the Stone-Throwing Devil*. London, 1698. In George Lincoln Burr, ed., *Narratives of the Witchcraft Cases, 1648–1706*, pp. 58–77. New York: Charles Scribner's Sons, 1914.

Chandos, John, ed. *In God's Name: Examples of Preaching in England from the Act of Supremacy to the Act of Uniformity, 1534–1662*. Indianapolis: Bobbs-Merrill, 1971.

Chapman, A. K. "Obsessions of Infanticide." *American Medical Association Archives of General Psychiatry*, I (1959): 12–16.

Chever, George E. "Some Remarks on the Commerce of Salem from 1626 to 1740—With a Sketch of Philip English—A Merchant in Salem from about 1670 to about 1733–4."*Historical Collections of the Essex Institute*, I (1859): 67–91, 117–43, 157–81; II (1860): 21–32, 73–85, 133–44, 185–204, 237–48, 261–72; III (1861): 17–28, 67–79, 111–120.

Chicago Tribune, July 3, 1972, sec. II, p. 3. [Dorothy Gates on women's liberation and crime.]

Chodoff, Paul. "A Re-examination of Some Aspects of Conversion Hysteria." *Psychiatry*, XVII (1954): 75–81.

———, and Lyons, Henry. "Hysteria, the Hysterical Personality, and 'Hysterical' Conversion." *American Journal of Psychiatry*, CIV, pt. II (1958): 734–40.

Cianfrani, Theodore. *A Short History of Obstetrics and Gynecology*. Springfield, Ill.: Thomas, 1960.

Cincinnati Enquirer, June 23, 1974, p. 4–H. [FBI Uniform Crime Reports.]

Clap, Roger. "Roger Clap's Memoirs." In Alexander Young, ed., *Chronicles of the First Planters of the Colony of Massachusetts Bay, from 1623 to 1636*. pp. 343–67. Boston: C. C. Little & J. Brown, 1846.

Clark, Alice. *Working Life of Women in the Seventeenth Century*. London: Frank Cass, 1919.

Clark, John. *Ill Newes from New England. . . .* London, 1652. In *Collections of the Massachusetts Historical Society*, ser. 4, II (1853): 1–113.

Cleaver, Robert. *A godlie forme of householde government. . . .* London: T. Crede for T. Man, 1598.

Cobbett, Thomas. *A Fruitfull and Usefull Discourse touching the Honour due from Children to Parents and the Duty of Parents towards their Children*. London: S. G. for John Rothwell, 1656.

Cobbledick, M. Robert. "The Property Rights of Women in Puritan New England." In George Peter Murdock, ed., *Studies in the Science of Society Presented to Albert Galloway Keller . . .* , pp. 107–17. New Haven: Yale University Press, 1937.

Coffin, Allen. *The Life of Tristam Coffyn, of Nantucket, Massachusetts: Founder of the Family Line in America*. Nantucket: Hussey & Robinson, 1881.

Coffin, Joshua. *A Sketch of the History of Newbury, Newburyport, and West Newbury from 1635 to 1845*. Boston: S. G. Drake, 1845.

Cohen, Ronald A. "Church and State in Seventeenth Century Massachusetts: Another Look at the Antinomian Controversy." *Journal of Church and State*, XII (1970): 475–94.

———. *The Family in Colonial America*. St. Charles, Mo.: Forum Press, 1976.

Coit, Mehetabel Chandler. *Mehetabel Chandler Coit. Her Book, 1714*. Norwich, Conn.: Norwich Bulletin Printers. 1895.

Coleman, Emma L. *New England Captives Carried to Canada Between 1677 and 1760 During the French and Indian Wars*. Portland: Southworth Press, 1925.

———. "The Story of Some New England Girls Who Were Captured by

Indians and Taken to Canada." *Old Time New England*, ser. #65, XXII, no. 1 (July 1931): 23–30.

Collinson, Patrick. *The Elizabethan Puritan Movement*. Berkeley: University of California Press, 1967.

Colman, Benjamin. *The Duty and Honour of Aged Women. A Sermon on the Death of Madame Abigail Foster*. Boston: B. Green, 1711.

Committee of the Dorchester Antiquarian and Historical Society. *History of the Town of Dorchester, Massachusetts*. Boston: E. Clapp, Jr., 1859.

Compleat Midwifes Practice Enlarged. London: for Nathaniel Brooke, 1656.

Corey, Deloraine Pendre. *The History of Malden, Massachusetts, 1633–1785*. Malden: By the author, 1899.

Cotton, John. *The Bloudy Tenent Washed and Made White in the bloud of the Lambe. . . .* London: Matthew Symmons for Hannah Allen, 1647.

———. *A Discourse about Civil Government*. Cambridge: Samuel Green & Marmaduke Johnson, 1663.

———. "Letter to Francis Hutchinson." *Collections of the Massachusetts Historical Society*, ser. 2, X (1823): 184–86.

———. *A Practical Commentary, or An Exposition with Observations, Reasons, and Uses upon the First Epistle Generall of John*. London: R. I. & E. C. for Thomas Parkhurst, 1656.

———. "Psalm Singing a Godly Exercise" (from *Singing of Psalmes a Gospel Ordinance . . .*, London, 1650). In Edmund Clarence Stedman and Ellen MacKay Hutchinson, eds., *A Library of American Literature from the Earliest Settlement to the Present Time*, I, 254–60. New York: W. E. Benjamin, 1894.

———. *Spiritual Milk for Boston Babes in Either England. Drawn out of the Breasts of Both Testaments for the Souls Nourishment*. Boston: Samuel Green for Hezekiah Usher, 1656.

———. *A Treatise of the Covenant of Grace, as it is despensed to the Elect Seed, effectually unto Salvation*. 3rd ed. London: For Peter Parker, 1671.

———. *The Way of Congregational Churches Cleared*. London: Matthew Simmons for John Bellamie, 1648.

Cotton, John [II]. *A Meet Help: Or, A Wedding Sermon, Preached at New-Castle in New England, June .9, 1694*. Boston: B. Green & J. Allen, 1699.

Cotton, Josiah. "Some Observations—Concerning Witches, Spirits, and Apparitions Collected from Diverse Authors—Together with a Remarkable Discovery of a Notorious Imposture in the County of Middlesex in New England (1733)." Houghton Library, Harvard University.

Craven, Wesley Frank. *The Colonies in Transition, 1660–1713*. New York: Harper & Row, 1968.

Croese, Gerard. *The General History of the Quakers*. London: For John Dunton, 1696.

Cudworth, James. "Letter at Scituate, December 1658." In C[harles] F[rancis] Swift, *Genealogical Notes of Barnstable Families, Being a Reprint of the Amos Otis Papers, Originally Published in the Barnstable Patriot*. Barnstable,

Mass.: F. B. & F. P. Goss, 1888–90.

Culpeper, Nicholas. *A Directory for Midwives: Or, A Guide for Women*. London: Peter Cole, 1651.

————. *A Directory for Midwives: Or, A Guide for Women, the Second Part*. London: Peter Cole, 1662.

Curtis, Edith. *Anne Hutchinson: A Biography*. Cambridge: Washburn & Thomas, 1930.

Cyrano de Bergerac, Savinien. "Lettre contre sorciers, 1654." In Frederic Lachevre, ed., *Les Oeuvres Libertines de Cyrano de Bergerac*, II, 211–18. Paris: Libraire Honore, 1912.

D., C. *New-England's Faction Discovered, Or a Brief and True Account of Their Persecution of the Church of England*. . . . London, 1690. In William H. Whitmore, ed., *Andros Tracts: Being a Collection of Pamphlets and Official Papers Issued During the Period Between the Overthrow of the Andros Government and the Establishment of the Second Charter of Massachusetts*, II, 203–22. *Publications of the Prince Society*, VI (1869).

Danckaerts, Jasper. *Journal of Jasper Danckaerts, 1679–1680*, ed. Bartlett Burleigh James and J. Franklin Jameson. New York: Charles Scribner's Sons, 1913.

Danforth, John. "A Poem upon the Triumphant Translation of a Mother in Our Israel, viz. Mrs. Anne Eliot. From This Life to a Better. On March 24th 1687. *Aetatis Suae* 84." In John Danforth, *Kneeling to God, at Parting with Friends*, pp. 64–65. Boston: B. Green & J. Allen, 1697.

Danforth, Samuel. *The Cry of Sodom Enquired Into*. . . . Cambridge: Marmaduke Johnson, 1674.

Davenport, John. "Letter to John Winthrop, Jr., November 27, 1660." *Collections of the Massachusetts Historical Society*, ser. 3, X (1849): 44–46.

Davies, Reginald Thorne. *Four Centuries of Witch-Beliefs, with Special Reference to the Great Rebellion*. London: B. Blom, 1972.

Davis, Adelle. *Let's Get Well*. New York: New American Library, 1965.

Davis, Charles H.S. *History of Wallingford*. . . . Meriden, Conn.: By the author, 1870.

Davis, Elizabeth Gould. *The First Sex*. Baltimore: Penguin Books, 1971.

Davis, Thomas M. "Edward Taylor's 'Occasional Meditations.'" *Early American Literature*, V, no. 3 (1971): 17–29.

Davis, Walter, Jr. "The Wildes Family of Essex County, Massachusetts." *Historical Collections of the Topsfield Historical Society*, XI (1906): 24–29.

Deane, Charles. "Notice of Samuel Gorton." *New England Historical and Genealogical Register*, IV (1850): 201–21.

Debrunner, H. *Witchcraft in Ghana: A Study on the Belief in Destructive Witches and Its Effect on the Akan Tribes*. Accra: Presbyterian Book Depot, 1961.

Defoe, Daniel. *Conjugal Lewdness: or, Matrimonial Whoredom*. London: For T. Warner, 1727.

DeLee, Joseph B., and Greenhill, J. P. *The Principles and Practice of Obstetrics*. Philadelphia: W. B. Saunders, 1943.

de Mause, Lloyd. "The Evolution of Childhood." In de Mause, ed., *The History of Childhood*, pp. 1–73. New York: Psychohistory Press, 1974.

Demos, John. *A Little Commonwealth: Family Life in Plymouth Colony*. New York: Oxford University Press, 1970.

———. "Notes on Life in Plymouth Colony." *William and Mary Quarterly*, ser. 3, XXII (1965): 264–86.

———. "Underlying Themes in the Witchcraft of Seventeenth-Century New England." *American Historical Review*, LXXV (1970): 1311–26.

De Normandie, James. "Manners, Morals, and Laws of the Piscataqua Colony." *Proceedings of the Massachusetts Historical Society*, ser. 2, XIX (1905): 169–77.

Dent, Arthur. *The Plaine Man's Path-way to Heauen*. London: R. Dexter, 1601.

Derbyshire, Robert C. *Medical Licensure and Discipline in the United States*. Baltimore: Johns Hopkins Press, 1969.

Deutsch, Helene. *Psychology of Women: A Psychoanalytic Interpretation*. New York: Grune & Stratton, 1944–45.

Dexter, Elisabeth A. *Colonial Women of Affairs: A Study of Women in Business and the Professions in America Before 1776*. Boston: Houghton Mifflin, 1924.

Digby, Kenelme. "Letter to John Winthrop, Jr., January 1655/56." *Collections of the Massachusetts Historical Society*, ser. 3, X (1849): 15–18.

Douglas, James. *The Status of Women in New England and New France*. Kingston, Ontario: Jackson Press, 1912.

Dow, George Francis. *Everyday Life in the Massachusetts Bay Colony*. Boston: Society for the Preservation of New England Antiquities, 1935.

———. *The Pirates of the New England Coast, 1630–1730*. Salem, Mass.: Marine Research Society, 1923.

Dow, Henry. "Extracts from Capt. Henry Dow's Journal." In Joseph Dow, *History of the Town of Hampton, New Hampshire*, I, 578. Salem, Mass.: Salem Press, 1893.

Dow, Joseph. *History of the Town of Hampton, New Hampshire, 1638–1892*. 2 vols. Salem: Salem Press, 1893.

Downing, Lucy. "Letters to John Winthrop, 1636–1650." *Collections of the Massachusetts Historical Society*, ser. 5, I (1871): 14–42.

Doyle, John Andrew. *The Puritan Colonies*, II. New York: H. Holt, 1889.

Drake, Samuel G. *Annals of Witchcraft in New England, and Elsewhere in the United States, from their First Settlement. . . .* New York: W. E. Woodward, 1869.

———, ed. *The Witchcraft Delusion in New-England*. Roxbury, Mass.: W. E. Woodward, 1866.

Dudley, Thomas. *Letter to the Countess of Lincoln, March 1631*. In Peter Force, comp., *Tracts and Other Papers, Relating Principally to the Origin, Settlement, and Progress of the Colonies in North America, From the Discovery to the Year 1776*, II, no. IV. Washington: Peter Force, 1838.

Duffy, John. *Epidemics in Colonial America*. Baton Rouge: Louisiana State University Press, 1953.

Dunham, H. W. *Crucial Issues in the Treatment and Control of Sex Deviation in the Community: A Report.* Lansing: Michigan State Psychiatric Research Clinic, 1951.

Dunn, Richard S. *Puritans and Yankees: The Winthrop Dynasty of New England, 1630–1717.* Princeton: Princeton University Press, 1962.

Dunton, John. *Letters Written from New England, A. D. 1686,* ed. William H. Whitmore. *Publications of the Prince Society,* IV (1867).

———. *The Life and Errors of John Dunton, Citizen of London. . . .* London: J. Nichols, Son, & Bentley, 1818.

Durkheim, Emile. *Suicide: A Study in Sociology.* Translated by John A. Spaulding and George Simpson. Glencoe, Ill.: Free Press, 1951. [Originally published in 1897].

Dusinberre, Juliet. *Shakespeare and the Nature of Women.* New York: Barnes & Noble, 1975.

Earle, Alice Morse. *Child-Life in Colonial Days.* New York: Macmillan, 1899.

———. *Colonial Dames and Good Wives.* New York: Ungar, 1962.

———. *Curious Punishments of By-Gone Days.* Chicago: For H. S. Stone, 1896.

———. *Customs and Fashions in Old New England.* New York: Charles Scribner's Sons, 1894.

———. *Home Life in Colonial Days.* New York: Macmillan, 1898.

———. *Margaret Winthrop, 1591–1647.* New York: Charles Scribner's Sons, 1895.

———. *The Sabbath in Puritan New England.* New York: Macmillan, 1893.

———. *Stage-Coach and Tavern Days.* New York: Macmillan, 1900.

Early, Eleanor. *New-England Sampler.* Boston: Waverly House, 1940.

Eaton, Theophilus. "Letter to John Winthrop, Jr., July 21, 1648." *Collections of the Massachusetts Historical Society,* ser. 4, VI (1863): 348–50.

Edwards, Mrs. Henry W. "Lady Deborah Moody." *Historical Collections of the Essex Institute,* XXXI (1894): 96–102.

Eliot, John. *The Harmony of the Gospels.* Boston: John Foster, 1678.

Elliot, Emory. *Power and the Pulpit in Puritan New England.* Princeton: Princeton University Press, 1975.

Ellis, George E. "Life of Anne Hutchinson with a Sketch of the Antinomian Controversy." In Jared Sparks, ed., *The Library of American Biography,* ser. 2, VI (1849): 169–376.

Erikson, Erik. *Identity, Youth and Crisis.* New York: W. W. Norton, 1968.

Erikson, Kai T. *Wayward Puritans: A Study in the Sociology of Deviance.* New York: John Wiley & Sons, 1966.

Ernst, George. *New England Miniature: A History of York, Maine.* Freeport, Maine: Bond Wheelwright Co., 1961.

Evans, Charles. *American Bibliography; A Chronological Dictionary of All Books, Pamphlets, and Periodical Publications Printed in the United States from the Genesis of Printing in 1639 Down to and Including the Year 1820.* 14 vols. Chicago: Blakely Press, 1903–59.

Evans-Pritchard, Edward Evan. *Witchcraft, Oracles and Magic among the Azande.* Oxford: Clarendon Press, 1937.

Facetiae . . . also Wits Recreations. 2 vols. London: n.p., 1640.

Feinstein, Howard M. "The Prepared Heart: A Comparative Study of Puritan Theology and Psychoanalysis." *American Quarterly*, XXIII (1970): 167–76.

Felt, Joseph B. *Annals of Salem, Massachusetts.* 2nd ed. 2 vols. Salem, Mass.: W. & S. B. Ives, 1845–49.

Findley, Palmer. *Priests of Lucina: The Story of Obstetrics.* Boston: Little, Brown, 1939.

Fisk, John. *The Beginnings of New England, or the Puritan Theocracy in Its Relations to Civil and Religious Liberty.* Boston: Houghton Mifflin, 1889.

Fiske, John. *The Notebook of the Reverend John Fiske, 1644–1675,* ed. Robert G. Pope. *Publications of the Colonial Society of Massachusetts,* XLVII (1974).

———. *The Watering of the Olive Plant in Christ's Garden: Or a Short Catechism for the First Entrance of Our Chelmesford Children.* Boston: Samuel Green, 1657.

Fitch, James. *An Explanation of the Solemn Advice Recommended by the Council in the Jurisdiction, Respecting the Reformation of Those Evils, Which Have Been the Procuring Cause of the Late Judgements upon New-England.* Boston: Samuel Green for I. Usher, 1683.

———. *The First Principles of the Doctrine of Christ. . . .* Boston: John Foster, 1679.

———. *An Holy Connection. . . .* Cambridge: Samuel Green, 1674.

———. "Letter to Increase Mather, July 1, 1684." *Collections of the Massachusetts Historical Society,* ser. 4, VIII (1868): 475–76.

Flexner, Eleanor. *Century of Struggle: The Woman's Rights Movement in the United States.* New York: Atheneum, 1972.

Flynt, Josiah. "Manuscript of Rev. Josiah Flynt, of Braintree and Dorchester." *Dedham Historical Register,* X (1899): 19–25.

Fogg, John S. H. "Witchcraft in New Hampshire in 1656." *New England Historical and Genealogical Register,* XLIII (1889): 181–83.

Fontaus, Nicholas. *The Womans Doctour: or, an exact and distinct Explanation of all such Diseases as are peculiar to that Sex with Choise and Experimentall Remedies against the Same.* London: For John Blague and Samuel Howes, 1652.

Forbes, Allyn B., ed. *The Winthrop Papers.* 5 vols. Boston: Massachusetts Historical Society, 1929–47.

Forbes, Thomas Rogers. *The Midwife and the Witch.* New Haven: Yale University Press, 1966.

———. "Midwifery and Witchcraft." *Journal of the History of Medicine and Allied Sciences,* XVII (1962): 264–83.

———. "The Regulation of English Midwives in the Sixteenth and Seventeenth Centuries." *Medical History,* VII (1964): 235–44.

Ford, Worthington C. "Mather-Calef Paper on Witchcraft." *Proceedings of the Massachusetts Historical Society,* XLVII (1914): 240–68.

Fowler, Samuel P. "Biographical Sketches of Rev. Joseph Green, Rev. Peter Clark, and Rev. Benjamin Wadsworth, D. D., Ministers of Salem Village

(Now Danvers)." *Historical Collections of the Essex Institute*, I (1859): 56–66.

Fox, Claire Elizabeth. "Pregnancy, Childbirth and Early Infancy in Anglo-American Culture, 1675–1830." Ph.D. dissertation, University of Pennsylvania, 1966.

Fox, George. *A New-England Fire-Brand Quenched*. London: n.p., 1678.

Fox, Sanford J. *Science and Justice: The Massachusetts Witchcraft Trials*. Baltimore: Johns Hopkins Press, 1968.

Foxcroft, Francis. "Letter, October 6, 1692." *New England Historical and Genealogical Register*, XXXIV (1880): 80–81.

Francois, Martha Ellis. "Women's Activities Against the Law, Essex County, England, 1550–1660." Paper delivered at Second Berkshire Conference on the History of Women, June 1974, Cambridge, Mass.

Frere, Walter Howard. *The English Church in the Reigns of Elizabeth and James I (1558–1625)*. New York: AMS Press, 1967. [Originally published in 1904.]

———, ed. *Puritan Manifestoes: A Study of the Origin of the Puritan Revolt*. London: For Church Historical Society, 1954.

Friedman, Stanford B. "Conversion Symptoms in Adolescents." *Pediatric Clinics of North America*, XX (1973): 873–82.

Frost, J. William. *The Quaker Family: A Portrait of the Society of Friends*. New York: St. Martin's Press, 1973.

Gagen, Jean Elisabeth. *The New Woman: Her Emergence in English Drama, 1600–1730*. New York: Twayne, 1954.

Gallop, Hannah. "Letter to John Winthrop, Jr., May 6, 1672." *Collections of the Massachusetts Historical Society*, ser. 5, I (1871): 104–5.

Gataker, Thomas. *A Good Wife Gods Gift*. London: J. Haviland for F. Clifton, 1623.

———. *Marriage Dvties Briefly Covched Together*. London: W. Jones for W. Bladen, 1619.

———. *A Wife Indeed*. London: J. Haviland for F. Clifton, 1623.

Gershon, Elliot G.; Dunner, David L.; and Goodwin, Frederick K. "Toward a Biology of Affective Disorders." *Archives of General Psychiatry*, XIV (1971): 1–15.

Gibbs, Jack, and Martin, Walter T. *Status Integration and Suicide*. Eugene: University of Oregon Books, 1964.

Glanvill, Joseph. *Saducismus Triumphatus: Or, Full and Plain Evidence Concerning Witches and Apparitions*. 3rd ed. London: For S. L., 1689.

Godwin, George. "The Scandal of the Witch-Doctor." *Saturday Review*, CLVII (1934): 410–11.

Goebel, Julius, Jr. "King's Law and Local Custom in Seventeenth Century New England." *Columbia Law Review*, XXXI (1931): 416–48.

Good News from New England, with An exact Relation of the First planting of that Countrey. London, 1648. *Collections of the Massachusetts Historical Society*, ser. 4, I (1852): 195–218.

Goodell, William. "When and Why Were Male Physicians Employed as Accoucheurs?" *American Journal of Obstetrics and Diseases of Women and*

Children, IX (1876): 381–90.

Goodman, William B. "Edward Taylor Writes His Love." *New England Quarterly*, XXVII (1954): 510–14.

Goodspeed, Charles Eliot. "Extortion, Captain Turner, and the Widow Stolion." *Publications of the Colonial Society of Massachusetts*, XXXVIII (1959): 60–79.

Gorton, Samuel. *An Antidote Against the Common Plague of the World*. London: J. M. for A. Crook, 1657.

————. *An Incorruptible Key*. London: n.p., 1647.

————. *Letter to Nathaniel Morton, June 30, 1669*. In *Tracts and Other Papers, Relating Principally to the Origin, Settlement, and Progress of the Colonies in North America, From the Discovery to the Year 1776*, comp. Peter Force. IV, no. VII. Washington: William Q. Force, 1846.

————. *Saltmarsh Returned from the Dead, In Amico Philalethe. Or, the Resurrection of James the Apostle*. London: For Giles Calvert, 1655.

————. *Simplicities Defence Against Seven-Headed Policy*. London, 1647. *Collections of the Rhode-Island Historical Society*, II (1835).

Gouge, William. *Of Domesticall Dvties*. London: J. Haviland for W. Bladen, 1622.

Grabo, Norman S. *Edward Taylor*. New York: Twayne, 1961.

Gray, Elizabeth Janet. *Contributions of the Quakers*. Pendle Hill Pamphlet no. 34. Wallingford, Conn.: Pendle Hill, 1947.

Green, Samuel A. "Slavery at Groton in Provinciall Times." *Proceedings of the Massachusetts Historical Society*, XLII (1909): 196–202.

Greene, Evarts B., and Harrington, Virginia. *American Population Before the Federal Census of 1790*. New York: Columbia University Press, 1932.

Greenough, Chester N. "John Dunton's Letters from New England." *Publications of the Colonial Society of Massachusetts*, XIV (1912): 212–57.

Greer, Germaine. *The Female Eunuch*. New York: McGraw-Hill, 1971.

Greven, Philip J. *Four Generations: Population, Land, and Family in Colonial Andover, Massachusetts*. Ithaca: Cornell University Press, 1970.

Groome, Samuel. *A Glass for the People of New-England, in which they may see themselves and Spirits and if not too late, Repent and Turn from their Abominable Ways and Cursed Contrivances*. London, 1676. Reprinted in *The Magazine of History* (Tarrytown, N.Y.) no. 147 (1929).

Guillemeau, Jacques. *Child-Birth*. London: A. Hatfield, 1612.

Gummere, Amelia Mott. *Witchcraft and Quakerism: A Study in Social History*. Philadelphia: Biddle Press, 1908.

Hair, Paul, ed. *Before the Bawdy Court: Selections from Church Court and Other Records Relating to the Correction of Moral Offences in England, Scotland and New England, 1300–1800*. London: Paul Elek Books Ltd., 1972.

Hale, John. *A Modest Inquiry into the Nature of Witchcraft. . . .* Boston: B. Green & J. Allen for Benjamin Eliot, 1702.

Hale, Matthew. *History of the Pleas of the Crown. . . .* Philadelphia: R. H. Small, 1847.

Hall, David D., ed. *The Antinomian Controversy, 1636–1638: A Documentary History*. Middletown, Conn.: Wesleyan University Press, 1968.

Haller, William. *The Rise of Puritanism . . . . 1570–1643*. New York: Columbia University Press, 1938.

————, and Haller, Malleville. "The Puritan Art of Love." *Huntington Library Quarterly*, V (1942): 235–72.

Hammond, Laurence. "Diary, 1674–1694." *Proceedings of the Massachusetts Historical Society*, ser. 2, VII (1892): 144–72.

Hansen, Chadwick. *Witchcraft at Salem*. New York: New American Library, 1970.

Harris, P. M. G. "The Social Origins of American Leaders: The Demographic Foundations." *Perspectives in American History*, III (1969): 159–346.

Hartman, Franz. *The Life and Teachings of Philippus Theophratus Bombast of Hohenheim (Paracelsus) 1493–1541*. London: n.p., 1841.

Harvey, William. *Anatomical Excitations, Concerning the Generation of Living Creatures*. London: Francis Leach for Richard Lowndes, 1653.

Haskins, George Lee. *Law and Authority in Early Massachusetts: A Study in Tradition and Design*. New York: Macmillan, 1960.

Hastings, James, ed. *Encyclopedia of Religion and Ethics*. New York: Charles Scribner's Sons, 1908–26.

Hawthorne, Nathaniel. "Young Goodman Brown." In Norman Holmes Pearson, ed., *The Complete Novels and Selected Tales of Nathaniel Hawthorne*, pp. 1033–42. New York: Modern Library, 1965.

Hayman, Charles R.; Lanza, Charlene; Fuentes, Roberto; and Algor, Kathe. "Rape in the District of Columbia." *American Journal of Obstetrics and Gynecology*, CXIII (1972): 91–97.

Haynes, John. "Letters to John Winthrop, Jr., 1649–53." *Collections of the Massachusetts Historical Society*, ser. 4, VII (1865), 452–65; VI (1863), 359–60.

Heinrich, Joachim. "Die Frauenfrage bei Steele und Addision." *Palaestra*, CLXVIII (1930): 1–50.

Henretta, James A. "Economic Development and Social Structure in Colonial Boston." *William and Mary Quarterly*, ser. 3, XXII (1965): 75–92.

Herschberger, Ruth. *Adam's Rib*. New York: Harper & Row, 1948.

Hertz, Marguerite R. "Further Study of Suicidal Configurations in Rorschach Records." *Journal of Projective Techniques*, XIII (1948): 44–73.

Higginson, Thomas Wentworth. *A History of the Public School System of Rhode Island*. Providence: n.p., 1876.

Hill, Christopher. *The World Turned Upside Down: Radical Ideas during the English Revolution*. London: Temple Smith, 1972.

Himes, Norman E. *Medical History of Contraception*. New York: Schocken Books, 1970. [Originally published in 1936.]

————. "Note on the Early History of Contraception in America." *New England Journal of Medicine*, CCV (1931): 438–40.

Hinchman, Lydia S. *Early Settlers of Nantucket: Their Associates and Descendants*. Philadelphia: J. B. Lippincott, 1901.

Hiner, N. Ray. "The Cry of Sodom Enquired Into: Educational Analysis of Seventeenth Century New England." *History of Education Quarterly*, XIII (1973): 3–22.

Hirsch, J. "Methods and Fashions of Suicide." *Mental Hygiene*, XLIV (1960): 3–11.

History of Education Quarterly: The Journal of Psychohistory, III (1976): 462. [Brief description of poll conducted by Ann Landers in one "From the Sources" section.]

Hoadly Memorial: Early Letters and Documents Relating to Connecticut 1643–1709. Collections of the Connecticut Historical Society, XXIV (1932).

Holden, Randall. "Letter to the Massachusetts General Court, September 15, 1643." *Collections of the Massachusetts Historical Society*, ser. 3, I (1825): 5–15.

Holdsworth, Sir William Searle. *A History of English Law*. 12 vols. Boston: Little, Brown, 1922–38.

Hole, Christina. *Witchcraft in England*. London: Collier-Macmillan, 1970.

Hollender, Marc H. "Conversion Hysteria: A Post-Freudian Reinterpretation of Nineteenth Century Psycho-Social Data." *Archives of General Psychiatry*, XXVI (1972): 311–14.

Holman, Mabel Cassine. "A Story of Early American Womanhood." *Connecticut Magazine*, XI (1907): 251–54.

Holwell, John. *Holwell's Predictions: Of Remarkable Things which May Probably Come to Pase. . . .* Cambridge: S. Green for Benjamin Harris, 1690.

Hooker, Samuel. *Righteousness Rained from Heaven. . . .* Cambridge: Samuel Green, 1677.

Hooker, Thomas. *The Application of Redemption by the Effectual Work of the Word, and Spirit of Christ. . . .* 2nd ed. London: Peter Cole, 1659.

———. *The Soules' Humiliation. . . .* London: J. Legatt for A. Crooke, 1637.

Howard, George Elliott. *A History of Matrimonial Institutions*. 3 vols. Chicago: University of Chicago Press, 1904.

Hubbard, William. *A General History of New England from the Discovery to MDCLXXX. Collections of the Massachusetts Historical Society*, ser. 2, V & VI (1815).

Hughes, Langston. "Dream Deferred." In Langston Hughes, *The Panther and the Lash: Poems of Our Time*, p. 14. New York: Alfred A. Knopf, 1967.

Hughes, Pennethorne. *Witchcraft*. Baltimore: Penguin Books, 1970.

Hull, John. "Memoir and Diaries." *Archaeologia Americana: Transactions and Collections of the American Antiquarian Society*, III (1857): 117–265.

Hunt, David. *Parents and Children in History: The Psychology of Family Life in Early Modern France*. New York: Harper & Row, 1972.

Hurd-Mead, Kate Campbell. *A History of Women in Medicine: A Short History of the Pioneer Medical Women of America and a Few of Their Colleagues in England*. Haddam, Conn.: Froben Press, 1938.

Hutchinson, Frances. *An Historical Essay Concerning Witchcraft. . . .* London For R. Knaplock, 1720.

Hutchinson, Thomas, ed. *A Collection of Original Papers Relative to the History of the Colony of Massachusetts-Bay*. . . . Boston: Thomas & John Fleet, 1769.

————. *The History of the Colony and Province of Massachusetts Bay*, ed. Lawrence Shaw Mayo. 3 vols. Cambridge: Harvard University Press, 1936. [Originally published in 1764.]

————. *The Witchcraft Delusion of 1692*. . . . Boston: n.p., 1870.

Inhabitants of Boston. *The Revolution in New-England Justified*. . . . Boston, 1691. In William H. Whitmore, ed., *Andros Tracts: Being a Collection of Pamphlets and Official Papers Issued During the Period Between the Overthrow of the Andros Government and the Establishment of the Second Charter of Massachusetts*, I, 63–132. Publications of the Prince Society, V (1868).

"Inquest on the Body of Richard Williams, 1640." *Collections of the Massachusetts Historical Society*, ser. 5, I (1871): 489–90.

James, Edward T.; James, Janet Wilson; and Boyer, Paul S., eds. *Notable American Women 1607–1950: A Biographical Dictionary*. 3 vols. Cambridge: Belknap Press of Harvard University, 1971.

Jameson, Edwin M. "Eighteenth Century Obstetrics and Obstetricians in the United States." *Annals of Medical History*, n.s., X (1938): 413–28.

[Jameson, William.] *A Remembrance of Former Times for This Generation and Our Degeneracy Lamented*. Boston: B. Green & J. Allen for Duncan Campbel, 1697.

Janeway, Elizabeth. *Man's World, Woman's Place: A Study in Social Mythology*. New York: William Morrow, 1971.

Janeway, James. *A Token for Children, Being an Exact Account of the Conversion, Holy and Exemplary Lives and Joyful Deaths of Several Young Children*. Boston: For Nicholas Boone, 1700.

Jantz, Harold S. "The First Century of New England Verse." *Proceedings of the American Antiquarian Society*, n.s., LIII (1943): 219–508.

Jenkins, R. L. H. "The Making of Sex Offenders." *Focus*, XXX (1951): 129–31.

Jenness, John Scribner. *The Isles of Shoals: An Historical Sketch*. . . . New York: Hurd & Houghton, 1873.

Jennings, Francis. *The Invasion of America: Indians, Colonialism, and the Cant of Conquest*. Chapel Hill: University of North Carolina Press, 1975.

Johnson, B. D. "Durkheim's One Cause of Suicide." *American Sociological Review*, XXX (1965): 875–86.

Johnson, Edward. *Johnson's Wonder-Working Providence, 1628–1651*, ed. J. Franklin Jameson. New York: Charles Scribner's Sons, 1910.

Jones, Hannah. "Letter to Increase Mather, 1681." *Collections of the Massachusetts Historical Society*, ser. 4, VIII (1866): 604–7.

Josselyn, John. *An Account of Two Voyages to New England*. London: For G. Widdowes, 1674.

Katachadourian, Herant A., and Lunde, Donald T. *Fundamentals of Human Sexuality*. New York: Holt, Rinehart and Winston, 1972.

Kavanaugh, Julia. *Women in France During the Eighteenth Century*. New York: Putnam, 1893.

Keayne, Robert. *The Apologia of Robert Keayne: The Last Will and Testament of Me, Robert Keayne, All of It Written with My Own Hands and Began by Me, Mo: 6:1:1653, Commonly Called August: The Self-Portrait of a Puritan Merchant,* ed. Bernard Bailyn. New York: Harper & Row, 1964.

Kenyon, Theda. *Scarlet Anne.* New York: Doubleday, Doran, 1939.

Keyssar, Alexander. "Widowhood in Eighteenth-Century Massachusetts: A Problem in the History of the Family." In Donald Fleming and Bernard Bailyn, eds., *Perspectives in American History,* VIII (1974): 81–119. Cambridge: Charles Warren Center for Studies in American History, Harvard University.

Kilpatrick, William Heard. *The Dutch Schools of New Netherlands and Colonial New York.* Washington: Government Printing Office, 1912.

Kittredge, George Lyman. "A Harvard Salutary Oration of 1662." *Publications of the Colonial Society of Massachusetts,* XXVIII (1935): 1–24.

Kluckhohn, Clyde. *Navaho Witchcraft.* Boston: Beacon Press, 1970.

Knappen, Marshall Mason. *Tudor Puritanism: A Chapter in the History of Idealism.* Chicago: University of Chicago Press, 1939.

Knight, James A.; Friedman, Theodore; and Sulianti, Julie. "Epidemic Hysteria: A Field Study." *American Journal of Public Health and the Nation's Health,* LV (1965): 858–65.

Knight, Sarah. *The Private Journal of a Journey from Boston to New York, in the Year 1704.* Albany: F. H. Little, 1865.

Koehler, Lyle. "The Case of the American Jezebels: Anne Hutchinson and Female Agitation during the Years of Antinomian Turmoil, 1636–1640." *William and Mary Quarterly,* ser. 3, XXXI (1974): 55–78.

———. "Letter." *William and Mary Quarterly,* ser. 3, XXXII (1975): 170–78.

Kraditor, Aileen S., ed. *Up from the Pedestal: Selected Writings in the History of American Feminism.* Chicago: University of Chicago Press, 1970.

La Fontaine, Jean. "Witchcraft in Bugisi." In John Middleton and E. H. Winter, eds., *Witchcraft and Sorcery in East Africa,* pp. 187–220. London: Routledge & Kegan Paul, 1963.

Langdon, George D., Jr. "The Franchise and Political Democracy in Plymouth Colony." *William and Mary Quarterly,* ser. 3, XX (1963): 513–26.

———. *Pilgrim Colony: A History of New Plymouth, 1620–1691.* New Haven: Yale University Press, 1966.

Langer, William L. "Infanticide: A Historical Survey." In Lloyd de Maude, ed., *The New Psychohistory,* pp. 55–67. New York: Psychohistory Press, 1975.

Lawrence, Marion B. "Cure-alls of the Past." *Vermont Quarterly,* n.s., XX (1952): 35–38.

Lawson, Christopher. "Petition, 1669." *Proceedings of the Massachusetts Historical Society,* XLVI (1913): 479–84.

Lawson, Deodat. *A Brief and True Narrative of some Remarkable Passages Relating to Sundry Persons Afflicted by Witchcraft. . . .* Boston, 1692. In George Lincoln Burr, ed., *Narratives of the Witchcraft Cases, 1648–1706,* pp. 145–64. New York: Charles Scribner's Sons, 1914.

————. *Christ's Fidelity the Only Shield against Satan's Malignity, asserted in a Sermon Deliver'd at Salem-Village the 24th of March, 1692.* Boston: Benjamin Harris, 1693.

————. *The Duty and Propriety of a Religious Householder. . . .* Boston: Bartholomew Green, 1693.

Lechford, Thomas. *Plain Dealing: Or, Newes from New England.* London, 1642. In *Collections of the Massachusetts Historical Society*, ser. 3, III (1833): 55–128.

Leonard, Calista. *Understanding and Preventing Suicide.* Springfield, Ill.: Thomas, 1967.

Lester, Gene and David. *Suicide: The Gamble with Death.* Englewood Cliffs, N.J.: Prentice-Hall, 1971.

Levermore, C. H. "Witchcraft in Connecticut, 1647–1697." *New Englander and Yale Review*, XLIV (1885): 792–815.

Lewinsohn, Richard. *A History of Sexual Customs.* Trans. Alexander Mayce. Greenwich, Conn.: Fawcett, 1958.

Lewis, Alonzo, and Newhall, James R. *History of Lynn, Essex County, Massachusetts, Including Lynnfield, Saugus, Swampscot, and Nahant.* Boston: J. L. Shorey, 1865.

Lewis, I. M. *Ecstatic Religion: An Anthropological Study of Spirit Possession and Shamanism.* Harmondworth, England: Penguin Books, 1971.

Lewis, W. H. *The Splendid Century.* New York: William Morrow, 1954.

Lewis, William. *The New Dispensatory. . . .* 5th ed. London: n.p., 1785.

Leynse, James P. *Preceding the Mayflower: The Pilgrims in England and in the Netherlands.* New York: Fountainhead, 1972.

Lindey, Alexander. *Plagiarism and Originality.* New York: Harper, 1952.

Linton, Ralph. *The Effects of Culture on Mental and Emotional Processes. Research Publications of the Association for Research in Nervous and Mental Disease*, XIX (1939).

Lloyd, Arnold. *Quaker Social History 1669–1738.* New York: Longmans Green, 1950.

Lockridge, Kenneth. "Land, Population, and the Evolution of New England Society, 1630–1730." *Past and Present*, no. 39 (1968): 62–80.

————. *Literacy in Colonial New England.* New York: Norton, 1974.

————. "The Population of Dedham, Massachusetts, 1636–1736." *Economic History Review*, ser. 2, XIX (1966): 318–44.

————, and Kreider, Alan. "The Evolution of Massachusetts Town Government." *William and Mary Quarterly*, ser. 3, XXIII (1966): 549–74.

Lovejoy, David S. *The Glorious Revolution in America.* New York: Harper & Row, 1972.

Lucas, Paul R. "Church versus Town: The Half-Way Covenant and the Problem of Authority in Early Connecticut." Paper delivered at the Conference on Puritanism in Old and New England, April 21, 1975, Thomas More College, Ft. Mitchell , Ky.

————. *Valley of Discord: Church and Society along the Connecticut River, 1636–1725.* Hanover, N.H.: University Press of New England, 1976.

Lundberg, Ferdinand, and Farnham, Marynia F. "The Destruction of Women's Legal Rights." In Lundberg and Farnham, *Modern Woman; The Lost Sex,* pp. 422–41. New York: Harper & Row, 1947.

MacDonald, John. *Rape: Offenders and Their Victims.* Springfield, Ill.: Thomas, 1971.

McCary, James Leslie. *Human Sexuality: Physiological and Psychological Factors of Sexual Behavior.* New York: Van Nostrand Reinhold, 1967.

McCoy, Raymond F. "Hygienic Recommendations of *The Ladies Library.*" *Bulletin of the Institute of the History of Medicine,* IV (1936): 367–72.

McEvedy, Colin P.; Griffith, Alwyn; and Hall, Thomas. "Two School Epidemics." *British Medical Journal,* II (1966): 1300–1312.

MacFarlane, Alan. *Witchcraft in Tudor and Stuart England.* New York: Harper & Row, 1970.

Maddux, Hilary C. *Menstruation.* New Canaan, Conn.: Tobey, 1975.

Malmquist, Charles F. "Hysteria in Childhood." *Postgraduate Medicine,* L, no. 2 (August 1971): 112–17.

Man, Samuel. "Rev. Samuel Man, First Minister of Wrentham, Massachusetts. His Advice to his children, who were Soon to Enter the Married State. Written in 1704." *New England Historical and Genealogical Register,* X (1852): 39–41.

Marmor, Judd. "Orality in the Hysterical Personality." *American Psychoanalytic Association Journal,* I (1953): 656–71.

Marshall, John. "Diary, 1697–1709." *Proceedings of the Massachusetts Historical Society,* ser. 2, XIV (1900): 13–34.

————. "Diary, 1697–1711." *Proceedings of the Massachusetts Historical Society,* ser. 2, I (1884): 148–61.

Marvin, Abijah P. *The Life and Times of Cotton Mather, D. D., F. R. S., or A Boston Minister of Two Centuries Ago, 1663–1728.* Boston: Congregation Sunday School & Publishing Society, 1892.

Marwick, Maxwell G. *Sorcery in Social Setting: A Study of the Northern Rhodesian Cewa.* Manchester, England: Manchester University Press, 1965.

————, ed. *Witchcraft and Sorcery: Selected Readings.* Baltimore: Penguin Books, 1970.

Masson, Margaret W. "The Typology of the Female as a Model for the Regenerate: Puritan Preaching, 1690–1730." *Signs,* II (1976): 304–15.

Masters, R. E. L. *Eros and Evil: The Sexual Psychopathology of Witchcraft.* New York: Julian Press, 1962.

————, and Lea, Eduard, eds. *The Anti-Sex.* New York: Julian Press, 1964.

Masters, William H., and Johnson, Virginia E. *Human Sexual Response.* Boston: Little, Brown, 1966.

Mather, Cotton. *The Bostonian Ebenezer. Some Historical Remarks on the State of Boston. . . .* Boston: B. Green & J. Allen for Samuel Phillips, 1698.

————. *A Brand Pluck'd Out of the Burning.* Boston, 1693. In George Lincoln

Burr, ed., *Narratives of the Witchcraft Cases, 1648–1706*. pp. 253–87. New York: Charles Scribner's Sons, 1914.

———. *A Christian at His Calling*. . . . Boston: B. Green & J. Allen for Samuel Sewall, 1701.

———. *A Cloud of Witnesses—Against Balls and Dances*. Boston: B. Green & J. Allen, 1700.

———. *Decennium Luctuosom. An History of Remarkable Occurrences in the Long War, Which New-England Had with the Indian Savages, from the Year 1688 to the Year 1698*. Boston: B. Green & J. Allen for Samuel Phillips, 1699.

———. *Diary*, ed. Worthington C. Ford. *Collections of the Massachusetts Historical Society*, ser. 7, VII & VIII (1911–12).

———. *Early Religion, Urged in a Sermon*. . . . Boston: B. Harris for Michael Perry, 1694.

———. *Elizabeth in Her Holy Retirement. An Essay to Prepare a Pious Woman for Her Lying-In*. . . . Boston: B. Green, 1710.

[———.] *Eureka the Vertuous Woman Found. An Essay on the Death of Mrs. Mary Brown*. Boston: B. Green & J. Allen, 1703.

———. *Fair Weather*. . . . Boston: Bartholomew Green & John A. Allen for Benjamin Harris, 1691.

———. *A Family Well-Ordered: or an Essay to Render Parents and Children Happy in One Another*. Boston: B. Green & J. Allen for Michael Perry, 1699.

———. *Help for Distressed Parents*. . . . Boston: John Allen, 1695.

———. *Humiliations Follow'd with Deliverances*. . . . Boston: B. Green & J. Allen for Samuel Phillips, 1697.

———. "Letter to John Cotton, November 1678." *Collections of the Massachusetts Historical Society*, ser. 4, VIII (1868): 383–84.

———. "Letter to John Richards, May 31, 1692." *Collections of the Massachusetts Historical Society*, ser. 4, VIII (1868): 391–97.

———. "Letter to John Richards, September 5, 1693." *Collections of the Massachusetts Historical Society*, ser. 4, VIII (1868): 401–2.

———. *Magnalia Christi Americana: Or, the Ecclesiastical History of New-England, from its First Planting in the Year 1620, unto the Year of Our Lord, 1698*. Hartford: Silas Andrus, Roberts, & Burr, 1820. [Originally published in 1702.]

———. *Memorable Providences, Relating to Witchcrafts and Possessions*. . . . Boston: R. Pierce, 1689.

———. *Memorials of Early Piety Occurring in the Holy Life and Joyful Death of Mrs. Jerusha Oliver*. . . . Boston: T. Green, 1711.

———. *The Negro Christianized*. . . . Boston: B. Green, 1706.

———. *Ornaments for the Daughters of Zion. Or the Character and Happiness of a Vertuous Woman*. . . . Cambridge: S. & B. Green, 1692.

———. *Parentator: Memoirs of Remarkables in the Life and Death of the Ever Memorable Doctor Increase Mather*. Boston: B. Green for Nathaniel Belknap, 1724.

———. *Reformation the Great Duty of an Afflicted People*. Boston: Bartholomew Green, 1694.

———. *The Religious Marriner*. . . . Boston: B. Green & J. Allen, 1700.

———. *Selected Letters of Cotton Mather*, ed. Kenneth Silverman. Baton Rouge: Louisiana State University Press, 1971.

———. *Terribilia Dei*. . . . Boston: B. Green & J. Allen, 1697.

———. *A Warning to the Flocks Against Wolves in Sheep's Clothing*. Boston: B. Green & J. Allen, 1700.

———. *Warnings from the Dead*. . . . Boston: Bartholomew Green for Samuel Phillips, 1693.

———. *The Way to Prosperity*. Boston: Richard Pierce for Benjamin Harris, 1690.

———. *Wonders of the Invisible World*. . . . Boston: Benjamin Harris for Samuel Phillips, 1693.

Mather, Increase. *An Arrow Against Profane and Promiscuous Dancing, Drawn Out of the Quiver of the Scriptures*. Boston: Samuel Green, 1684.

———. "Autobiography," ed. M. G. Hall. *Proceedings of the American Antiquarian Society*, n.s., LXXI (1961): 271–360.

———. *Cases of Conscience Concerning Evil Spirits Personating Men, Witchcrafts, Infallible Proofs of Guilt in Such as Are Accused with That Crime*. Boston: Benjamin Harris, 1693.

———. "Diary." In *Proceedings of the Massachusetts Historical Society*, ser. 2, XII (1900): 340–74, 398–411.

———. *An Earnest Exhortation for the Inhabitants of New-England, To hearken to the Voice of God in his late and present Dispensations*. Boston: John Foster, 1676.

———. *An Essay for the Recording of Illustrious Providences*. Boston: Samuel Green for Joseph Browning, 1684.

———. *The Folly of Sinning, Opened and Applyed*. . . . Boston: B. Green & J. Allen for Michael Perry, 1699.

———. *A Further Account of the Tryals of the New-England Witches*. London: For John Dunton, 1693.

———. *The Life and Death of that Reverend Man of God, Mr. Richard Mather, Teacher of the Church in New England*. Cambridge: S. Green & M. Johnson, 1670.

[———.] *The Necessity of Reformation . . . Agreed upon by the Elders and Messengers of the Churches Assembled in Synod at Boston in New-England. September 10, 1679*. Boston: John Foster, 1679.

———. *Practical Truths Tending to Promote the Power of Godliness*. Boston: Samuel Green, 1682.

Mather, Nathaniel. "Letter to Increase Mather, December 31, 1679." *Collections of the Massachusetts Historical Society*, ser. 4, VIII (1868): 22–28.

———. "Letter to Increase Mather, December 31, 1684." *Collections of the Massachusetts Historical Society*, ser. 4, VIII (1868): 58–61.

Matthews, Albert. "Family Tradition and History." *Proceedings of the Massachusetts Historical Society*, ser. 3, II (1909): 193–95.

Matthews, William. *American Diaries: An Annotated Bibliography of American Diaries Written Prior to the Year 1861*. Boston: J. S. Canner, 1959.

[Maule, Thomas] Thomas Philalethes. *New-England Persecutors Mauled with their own Weapons*. . . . New York: William Bradford, 1697.

———. *Truth Held Forth and Maintained according to the Testimony of the Holy Prophets, Christ and His Apostles*. . . . New York: William Bradford, 1695.

May, Rollo. *Power and Innocence: A Search for the Sources of Violence*. New York: W. W. Norton, 1972.

Mayer, Philip. "Witches." In Maxwell G. Marwick, ed., *Witchcraft and Sorcery: Selected Readings*, pp. 45–64. Baltimore: Penguin Books, 1970.

Medea, Andrea, and Thompson, Kathleen. "How Much Do You Really Know about Rapists?" *Ms.*, III, no. 1 (July 1974): 113–15.

Mengert, William F. "The Origin of the Male Midwife." *Annals of Medical History*, n.s., IV (1932): 453–65.

Meserole, Harrison T., ed. *Seventeenth Century American Poetry*. Garden City, N.Y.: Doubleday, 1968.

Mettler, Cecilia C. and Fred A. *History of Medicine*. Philadelphia: Blakiston, 1947.

Middlemore, Merell. "The Treatment of Bewitchment in a Puritan Community." *International Journal of Psycho-Analysis*, XV (1934): 41–58.

Midelfort, H. C. Erick. *Witch Hunting in Southwestern Germany 1562–1684*. Stanford: Stanford University Press, 1972.

Miller, Perry. *The New England Mind: From Colony to Province*. Boston: Beacon Press, 1961.

———. *The New England Mind: The Seventeenth Century*. Boston: Beacon Press, 1961.

———, and Johnson, Thomas H., eds. *The Puritans: A Sourcebook of Their Writings*. New York: Harper & Row, 1938.

Moller, Herbert. "Sex Composition and Correlated Culture Patterns of Colonial America." *William and Mary Quarterly*, ser. 3, II (1945): 113–53.

Monter, E. William. "Witchcraft in Geneva, 1537–1662." *Journal of Modern History*, XLIII (1971): 179–204.

Mood, Fulmer, "Biography of John Josselyn." In Dumas Malone, ed., *Dictionary of American Biography*, X, 219. New York, 1933.

Moody, Joshua. "Letter to Samuel Nowell, November 19, 1688." *Collections of the Massachusetts Historical Society*, ser. 4, VIII (1868): 371–73.

Moran, Gerald F. "Religious Renewal, Puritan Tribalism, and the Family in Seventeenth-Century Milford, Connecticut." *William and Mary Quarterly*, ser. 3, XXXVI (1979): 236–54.

———. "'Sisters' in Christ: Women and the Church in Seventeenth-Century New England." Unpublished manuscript.

Morgan, Edmund S. "Light on the Puritans from John Hull's Notebooks." *New England Quarterly*, XV (1942): 95–101.

———. *The Puritan Dilemma: The Story of John Winthrop*. Boston: Little, Brown, 1958.

———.*The Puritan Family: Religion and Domestic Relations in Seventeenth-Century New England*. New York: Harper & Row, 1944.

———. "The Puritans and Sex." *New England Quarterly*, XV (1942): 591–607.

———. *Visible Saints: The History of a Puritan Idea*. Ithaca: Cornell University Press, 1972.

Morgan, Forrest; Hart, Samuel; Trumbull, Jonathan; Holmes, Frank R.; and Bartlett, Ellen Strong. *Connecticut as a Colony and as a State: or, One of the Original Thirteen*. 4 vols. Hartford: Publishing Society of Connecticut, 1904.

Morison, Samuel Eliot. *The Founding of Harvard College*. Cambridge: Harvard University Press, 1935.

———. *Harvard College in the Seventeenth Century*. Cambridge: Harvard University Press, 1936.

———. *The Story of the "Old Colony" of New Plymouth (1620–1692)*. New York: Alfred A. Knopf, 1956.

Morris, Desmond. *The Naked Ape*. New York: McGraw-Hill, 1969.

Morris, Richard B. *Studies in the History of American Law, with Special Reference to the Seventeenth and Eighteenth Centuries*. Philadelphia: I. M. Mitchell, 1959.

Morton, Nathaniel. *New-England's Memorial. . . .* Cambridge: S. Green & M. Johnson for John Usher, 1669.

Mourt's Relation, or a Journal of the Plantation of Plymouth. London: For John Bellamie, 1622.

Murdock, Kenneth B., ed. *Handkerchiefs from Paul: Being Pious and Consolatory Verses of Puritan Massachusetts, Including Unpublished Poems by Benjamin Tompson, John Wilson, and Anna Hayden*. Cambridge: Harvard University Press, 1927.

———. *Increase Mather: The Foremost American Puritan*. Cambridge: Harvard University Press, 1925.

Murphy, Geraldine Joanne. "Massachusetts Bay Colony: The Role of Government in Massachusetts." Ph.D. dissertation, Radcliffe College, 1960.

Murray, Harry Alexander. *Explorations in Personality. . . .* New York: Oxford University Press, 1938.

Nadel, Siegfried Frederick. *Nupe Religion*. London: Routledge & Kegan Paul, 1954.

Nevins, Winfield. *Witchcraft in Salem Village in 1692*. Salem: North Shore, 1892.

New England Primer. In Leslie A. Fiedler and Arthur Ziegler, eds., *O Brave New New World: American Literature from 1600 to 1840*, I, 381–84. New York: Dell, 1968.

Newes for New-England: A Letter Written to a Person of Quality. London: For John Dunton, 1690.

Niccoles, Alexander. *Discourse on Marriage and Wiving*. London: N. Okes for

L. Becket, 1615.

Niles, Samuel. "A Summary Historical Narrative of the Wars in New-England with the French and Indians, in the several Parts of the Country." *Collections of the Massachusetts Historical Society*, ser. 3, VI (1837): 154–279.

Noble, John. "The Case of Maria in the Court of Assistants in 1681." *Publications of the Colonial Society of Massachusetts*, VI (1904): 323–36.

———. "Some Documentary Fragments Touching the Witchcraft Episode of 1692." *Publications of the Colonial Society of Massachusetts*, X (1907): 12–26.

[Norton, Humphrey.] *New-England's Ensigne: It Being the Account of Cruelty, the Professors Pride, and the Articles of Their Faith*. London: T. L. for G. Calvert, 1659.

Norton, John. *Abel Being Dead Yet Speaketh*. . . . London: Thomas Newcomb for Lodowick Lloyd, 1658.

[———.] "The Negative Vote, June 22, 1643." *Proceedings of the Massachusetts Historical Society*, VI (1913): 281–84.

Norton, Susan L. "Population Growth in Colonial America: A Study of Ipswich, Massachusetts." *Population Studies*, XXV (1971): 433–52.

"Notes and Queries." *New England Historical and Genealogical Register*, XXXII (1878): 342.

Notestein, Wallace. *The English People on the Eve of Colonization, 1602–1630*. New York: Harper & Row, 1962.

———. "The English Woman, 1580–1650." In John Harold Plumb, ed., *Studies in Social History: A Tribute to G. M. Trevelyan*, pp. 69–107. Freeport, N.Y.: Books for Libraries Press, 1969.

Novak, Emil. "Historical Review of Physiology of the Reproductive Organs (Exclusive of Pregnancy)." In Arthur Hale Curtis, ed., *Obstetrics and Gynecology*, I (1933): 279–82. Philadelphia: W. B. Saunders, 1933.

———. "The Superstition and Folklore of Menstruation." *John Hopkins Hospital Bulletin*, XXVII (1916): 270–74.

Noyes, James. *A Short Catechism*. . . . Cambridge: Samuel Green, 1661.

Noyes, Nicholas. "Letter to Cotton Mather, 1706." *Proceedings of the Massachusetts Historical Society*, ser. 1, IX (1866): 484–85.

Nye, Russell. *The Unembarrassed Muse: The Popular Arts in America*. New York: Dial Press, 1970.

Oberholzer, Emil, Jr. *Delinquent Saints: Disiplinary Action in the Early Congregational Churches of Massachusetts*. New York: Columbia University Press, 1955.

O'Callaghan, Edmund Bailey. *History of New Netherlands: or, New York Under the Dutch*. 2 vols. New York: D. Appleton, 1846–48.

O'Faolain, Julia, and Martines, Lauro, eds. *Not in God's Image: Women in History from the Greeks to the Victorians*. New York: Harper & Row, 1973.

Oliver, John. *A Present for Teeming Women*. . . . Boston: Benjamin Harris, 1694.

Omoyajowo, J. A. *Witches? A Study of the Belief in Witchcraft and of Its Future in Modern African Society*. Ibadan, Nigeria: Daystar Press, 1971.

Osol, Arthur, and Farrar, George E., Jr. *The Dispensatory of the United States of America*. Philadelphia: J. B. Lippincott, 1947.

O[xenbridge], J[ohn]. *New-England Freemen Warned and Warmed, To Be Free indeed, having an Eye to God in their Elections*. Boston: n.p., 1673.

Packard, Francis R. *History of Medicine in the United States*. New York: P. B. Hoeber, 1931.

Page, Elwin Lawrence. *Judicial Beginnings of New Hampshire, 1640–1700*. Concord: New Hampshire Historical Society, 1959.

Pain, Philip. *Daily Meditations: Or, Quotidian Preparations For, and Considerations of, Death and Eternity*. . . . Cambridge: S. Green & M. Johnson, 1670.

Paine, Gustavus Swift. "Ungodly Carriages on Cape Cod." *New England Quarterly*, XXV (1952): 181–98.

Palmer, John. *An Impartial Account of the State of New England*. London, 1690. In William H. Whitmore, ed., *Andros Tracts: Being a Collection of Pamphlets and Official Papers Issued During the Period Between the Overthrow of the Andros Government and the Establishment of the Second Charter of Massachusetts*, I, 21–62. Publications of the Prince Society, V (1868).

Parker, Edwin Pond. *History of the Second Church of Christ in Hartford, 1670–1892*. Hartford: Belknap & Warfield, 1892.

Parker, Thomas. *The Coppy of a Letter Written* . . . *to His Sister*. London: John Field for Edmund Paxton, 1650.

Parkin, Michael. "Suicide and Culture in Fairbanks: A Comparison of Three Cultural Groups in a Small City of Interior Alaska" *Psychiatry*, XXXVII (1974): 60–67.

Patai, Raphael. *Sex and Family in the Bible and Middle East*. Garden City, N.Y. Doubleday, 1959.

Paull, Harry Major. *Literary Ethics: A Study in the Growth of the Literary Conscience*. London: T. Butterworth, 1928.

Peckham, Howard M. *Captured by Indians: True Tales of Pioneer Survivors*. New Brunswick, N.J.: Rutgers University Press, 1954.

Perkins, William. *Oeconomie: Or, Houshold-Government: A Short Survey of the Right Manner of Erecting and Ordering a Family, according to the Scriptures*. London, 1631. In *The Workes of that Famovs and Worthy Minister of Christ in the Vniuersitie of Cambridge, Mr. William Perkins*, II, 667–700. 2 vols. London: For Iohn Legatt, 1626–31.

Perley, M. V. B. "James Howe of Ipswich and Some of His Descendants." *Historical Collections of the Topsfield Historical Society*, XXII (1918): 81–96.

Perley, Sidney. *History of Salem, Massachusetts, 1638–1716*. 3 vols. Salem: By the author, 1926.

Peter, Hugh. *A Dying Father's Last Legacy to An Only Child: Or, Mr. Hugh Peter's Advice to His Daughter*. Boston: B. Green for Benjamin Eliot, 1717.

Pettit, Norman. *The Heart Prepared: Grace and Conversion in Puritan Spiritual*

Life. New Haven: Yale University Press, 1966.

Phips, Sir William. "Letters to William Blathwayt, October 12, 1692, and February 21, 1692/3." In George Lincoln Burr, ed., *Narratives of the Witchcraft Cases, 1648–1706*, pp. 191–202. New York: Charles Scribner's Sons, 1914.

Piercy, Josephine K. *Anne Bradstreet*. New York: Twayne, 1964.

Pike, James Shepherd. *The New Puritan: New England Two Hundred Years Ago*. New York: Harper, 1879.

Pike, John. "Journal of the Rev. John Pike, 1678–1709." *Proceedings of the Massachusetts Historical Society*, ser. 1, XIV (1875): 144–72.

Pinchbeck, Ivy, and Hewitt, Margaret. *Children in English Society*. London: Routledge & Kegan Paul, 1969.

Polishook, Irwin H., ed. *Roger Williams, John Cotton, and Religious Freedom: A Controversy in New and Old England*. Englewood Cliffs, N.J.: Prentice-Hall, 1967.

Pope, Charles Henry. *The Pioneers of Maine and New Hampshire, 1623 to 1660. . . .* Baltimore: Genealogical Publishing, 1965.

Pope, Robert G. *The Half-Way Covenant: Church Membership in Puritan New England*. Princeton: Princeton University Press, 1969.

Porterfield, Austin L. "The Problem of Suicide." In Jack P. Gibbs, ed., *Suicide*, pp. 31–57. New York: Harper & Row, 1968.

Postell, William D. "Medicinal Education and Medical Schools in Colonial America." In Felix Marti-Ibanez, ed., *History of American Medicine: A Symposium*, pp. 48–54. New York: MD Publications, 1959.

Powell, Chilton Latham. *English Domestic Relations, 1487–1653. . . .* New York: Columbia University Press, 1917.

Powell, Sumner Chilton. *Puritan Village: The Formation of a New England Town*. Middletown, Conn.: Wesleyan University Press, 1963.

Powers, Edwin. *Crime and Punishment in Early Massachusetts, 1620–1692: A Documentary History*. Boston: Beacon Press, 1966.

"Pownall Epitaphs." *Vermont History*, n.s., XXIV (1956): 184.

Pricke, Robert. *The Doctrine of Superioritie, and of Subjection*. London: For T. Downes & E. Dawson, 1609.

The Problemes of Aristotle, with Other Philosophers and Phisitians. . . . Edinborough: R. Waldegraue, 1595.

Protestant Episcopal Historical Collections, I (1851), xx. [George Kieth quotation].

Putnam, Emily James. *The Lady: Studies of Certain Significant Phases in Her History*. Chicago: University of Chicago Press, 1970. [Originally published in 1910.]

Rado, Sandor. "An Adaptational View of Sexual Behavior." In Paul H. Hoch and Joseph Zubin, eds., *Psychosexual Development in Health and Disease*, pp. 159–89. New York: Grune & Stratton, 1949.

"Recantation of Confessors of Witchcraft." *Collections of the Massachusetts Historical Society*, ser. 2, III (1815): 221–25.

Reckless, Walter C. *American Criminology: New Directions.* New York: Appleton-Century-Crofts, 1973.

———, and Shoham, Shlomo. "Norm Containment Theory as Applied to Delinquency and Crime." *Excerpta Criminologia,* III (1963): 637–44.

Reynolds, Myra. *The Learned Lady in England.* Gloucester, Mass.: P. Smith, 1920.

Rheingold, Joseph C. *The Fear of Being a Woman: A Theory of Maternal Destructiveness.* New York: Grune & Stratton, 1964.

———. *The Mother, Anxiety, and Death: The Catastrophic Death Complex.* Boston: Little, Brown, 1967.

Richardson, John. *An Account of that Ancient Servant of Jesus Christ, John Richardson. . . .* Philadelphia: Joseph Crukshank, 1783.

Richardson, William. "Newport Account Book, 1662–1669." Rhode Island Historical Society, Providence.

Richman, Irving Berdine. *Rhode Island: Its Making and Meaning.* Boston: Houghton Mifflin, 1905.

Riverius, Lazarius. *The Practice of Physick. . . .* Trans. Nicholas Culpeper, Abdiah Cole, and William Rowland. London: John Streater, 1672.

Robbins, Russell Hope. *The Encyclopedia of Witchcraft and Demonology.* New York: Crown, 1959.

Robinson, John. *Observations of Knowledge and Virtue.* London: n.p., 1625.

———. *The Works of John Robinson, Pastor of the Pilgrim Fathers,* ed. Robert Ashton. London: J. Snow, 1851.

Roeburt, John. *The Wicked and the Banned.* New York: Macfadden-Bartell, 1963.

Rogers, Horatio. "Mary Dyer Did Hang as a Flag." In Jessamyn West, ed., *The Quaker Reader,* pp. 168–75. New York: Viking Press, 1969.

Rogers, John. *A Mid-Night-Cry from the Temple of God to the Ten Virgins Slumbering and Sleeping, Awake, Awake, Arise and Gird Your Loyns, and Trim Your Lamps, For Behold the Bridegroom Cometh Go Ye Therefore Out to Meet Him. . . .* New York: William Bradford, 1705.

Rogers, Katharine M. *The Troublesome Helpmate: A History of Misogyny in Literature.* Seattle: University of Washington Press, 1966.

Rosenman, Stanley. "The Witch-Hunter." *Psychoanalysis,* III (1954): 3–18.

Rosenmeier, Jesper. "New England's Perfection: The Image of Adam and the Image of Christ in the Antinomian Crisis, 1634 to 1638." *William and Mary Quarterly,* ser. 3, XXVII (1970): 435–59.

Ross, C. "Calvinism and the Witchcraft Prosecutions in England." *Journal of the Presbyterian Historical Society of England,* XII (1960): 22–27.

Rowse, Alfred Leslie. *The England of Elizabeth: The Structure of Society.* London: Macmillan, 1950.

Rubincam, Milton. "Lydia Wright and Her Sister: The Quaker Maidens Who Defied the Stern Puritans." *Proceedings of the New Jersey Historical Society,* LVIII (1940): 103–18.

Rugg, Winifred. *Unafraid: A Life of Anne Hutchinson.* Boston: Houghton

Mifflin, 1930.

"Rules and Regulations for the Government of the New Haven Hopkins Grammar School." In Elwood P. Cubberly, ed., *Readings in the History of Education: A Collection of Sources and Readings to Illustrate the Development of Educational Practice, Theory, and Organization,* pp. 296–98. Boston: Houghton Mifflin, 1920.

Russell, Noahdiah. "Copy of the Diary of Noahdiah Russell, Tutor at Harvard College, Beginning Anno Domini, 1682." *New England Historical and Genealogical Register,* VII (1853): 53–59.

Rutman, Darrett Bruce. *Winthrop's Boston.* Chapel Hill: University of North Carolina Press, 1965.

Ryan, William B. *Infanticide: Its Law, Prevalence, Prevention, and History.* London: Churchill, 1862.

Saffin, John. "Cankers touch fairest fruites." In Kenneth Silverman, ed., *Colonial American Poetry,* pp. 92–93. New York: Hafner, 1968.

———. "The Painters Premonition." In Kenneth Silverman, ed., *Colonial American Poetry,* p. 93. New York: Hafner, 1968.

Sainsbury, W. Noel, and Headlam, Cecil, eds. *Calendar of State Papers, Colonial Series, America and West Indies.* 18 vols. London: Public Record Office, 1862–1910.

Sanford, Elizabeth. *Woman, in Her Social and Domestic Character.* London: Longman, 1831.

Savage, James. *A Genealogical Dictionary of the First Settlers of New England, Shewing Three Generations of Those Who Came Before May 1692 On the Basis of Farmer's Register.* 4 vols. Boston: Little, Brown, 1860–62.

———. "More Gleanings from New England History." *Collections of the Massachusetts Historical Society,* ser. 4, I (1852): 91–101.

Savelle, Max. *Seeds of Liberty: The Genesis of the American Mind.* New York: Alfred A. Knopf, 1948.

Scales, John, ed. *Historical Memoranda Concerning Persons and Places in Old Dover, New Hampshire. . . .* Dover: n.p., 1900.

Scheick, William J. "The Widower Narrator in Nathaniel Ward's *The Simple Cobler of Agawam in America.*" *New England Quarterly,* XLVII (1974): 87–96.

Schenck, Elizabeth Hubbell. *The History of Fairfield, Fairfield County, Connecticut, From the Settlement of the Town in 1639 to 1818.* 2 vols. New York: By the author, 1889–1905.

Schlatter, Richard B. *The Social Ideas of Religious Leaders, 1660–1688.* London: Oxford University Press, 1940.

Schmidt, Edwin H.; O'Neal, Patricia; and Robins, Eli. "Evaluation of Suicide Attempts as a Guide to Therapy." *Journal of the American Medical Association,* CLV (1954): 549–57.

Schnucker, Robert V. "Elizabethan Birth Control and Puritan Attitudes." *Journal of Interdisciplinary History,* V (1975): 655–67.

Schuler, E. A., and Parenton, V. J. "A Recent Epidemic of Hysteria in a

Louisiana Medical Hospital." *Journal of Social Psychology*, XVII (1943): 221–35.

Scott, Katherine. "Letter to John Winthrop, Jr., 1658." *Collections of the Massachusetts Historical Society*, ser. 5, I (1871): 96–97.

Scott, Major. "From Majr. Scott's Mouth." *Proceedings of the Massachusetts Historical Society*, ser. 1, XIII (1873): 132.

Scottow, Joshua. *Old Men's Tears for their Own Declensions.* . . . Boston: Benjamin Harris & John Allen, 1691.

Seaver, James Edward. "The Two Settlements of Taunton, Massachusetts." *Collections of the Old Colony Historical Society*, no. VII, pp. 106–34. Taunton, 1909.

Secker, William. *A Wedding ring for the finger, the salve of divinity on the sore of Humanity. Directions to those men who want wives, how to choose.* Boston: Samuel Green for Benjamin Harris, 1690.

Segal, Bernard E., and Humphrey, John. "A Comparison of Suicide Victims and Suicide Attempters in New Hampshire." *Diseases of the Nervous System*, XXXI (1970): 830–38.

Seligman, Martin. *Helplessness: On Depression, Development, and Death.* San Francisco: W. H. Freeman, 1975.

Sewall, Samuel. *Diary*, I–III. *Collections of the Massachusetts Historical Society*, ser. 5, V–VII (1878–82).

———. *Letter-Book. Collections of the Massachusetts Historical Society*, ser. 6, I (1886).

———. *Mrs. Judith Hull of Boston, in N. E.* . . . Boston: Bartholomew Green, 1695.

———. "Selections from the Letter-Book of Samuel Sewall." *Proceedings of the Massachusetts Historical Society*, ser. 1, XII (1873): 358–85.

———. "The Selling of Joseph, 1700." In George H. Moore, *Notes on Slavery in Massachusetts*. New York: Negro Universities Press, 1968. [Originally published in 1866.]

"Sewall and Noyes on Wigs." *Publications of the Colonial Society of Massachusetts*, XX (1917): 109–28.

Sewel, William. *The History of the Rise, Increase and Progress of the Christian People Called Quakers.* 4th ed. 2 vols. London: n.p., 1795. [Originally published in 1722.]

Seybolt, Robert Francis. *The Private Schools of Colonial Boston.* Cambridge: Harvard University Press, 1935.

———. *The Public Schools of Colonial Boston.* Cambridge: Harvard University Press, 1935.

Shakespeare, William. *Troilus and Cressida.* In G. B. Harrison, ed., *Shakespeare: The Complete Works*, pp. 973–1017. New York: Harcourt, Brace & World, 1952.

[Shepard, Hetty.] "A Puritan Maiden's Diary," ed. Adeline E. H. Slicer. *New England Magazine and Illustrated Monthly*, XI (1894): 20–24.

[Shepard, Thomas.] T. S. Philomathemat. *A Almanack for the Year of Our Lord 1656*. Cambridge: Samuel Green, 1656.

———. *The Clear Sun-shine of the Gospel Breaking Forth upon the Indians in New-England*. London, 1649. In *Collections of the Massachusetts Historical Society*, ser. 3, IV (1834): 25–68.

[———.] *God's Plot: The Paradoxes of Puritan Piety, Being the Autobiography and Journal of Thomas Shepard*, ed. Michael McGiffert. Amherst: University of Massachusetts Press, 1972.

———. "Letter to His Son at His admission into the College." *Publications of the Colonial Society of Massachusetts*, XIV (1913): 191–98.

———. *The Parable of the Ten Virgins Opened and Applied*. London: I. H. for John Rothwell & Samuel Thomson, 1660.

Shneidman, Edwin S., and Farberow, Norman L. "Statistical Comparisons between Attempted and Committed Suicide." In Shneidman and Farberow, eds., *The Cry for Help*, pp 19–47. New York: McGraw-Hill, 1961.

Shryock, Richard Harrison. *Medical Licensing in America, 1650–1965*. Baltimore: Johns Hopkins Press, 1967.

Shurtleff, Nathaniel B. *A Topographical and Historical Description of Boston*. Boston: By request of City Council, 1871.

Sibley, John Langdon, and Shipton, Clifford K. *Biographical Sketches of Graduates of Harvard University in Cambridge, Massachusetts*. 11 vols. Cambridge: Harvard University Press, 1873–1960.

Silverman, Samuel. "The Role of Aggressive Drives in the Conversion Process." In Felix Deutsch, ed., *On the Mysterious Leap from the Mind to the Body: A Workshop Study on the Theory of Conversion*, pp. 110–30. New York: International Universities Press, 1959.

Simmons, Richard C. "Richard Sadler's Account of the Massachusetts Churches." *New England Quarterly*, XLII (1969): 411–25.

Simpson, Alan. *Puritanism in Old and New England*. Chicago: University of Chicago Press, 1955.

Sinclair, Andrew. *The Emancipation of the American Woman*. New York: Harper & Row, 1966.

Slafter, Carlos. *A Record of Education: The Schools and Teachers of Dedham, Massachusetts, 1644–1904*. Dedham: Dedham Transcript Press, 1905.

Slotkin, Richard. *Regeneration through Violence: The Myth of the American Frontier, 1600–1860*. Middletown, Conn.: Wesleyan University Press, 1973.

Small, Walter Herbert. *Early New England Schools*, ed. W. H. Eddy. New York: Ginn, 1969. [Originally published in 1914.]

———. "Girls in Colonial Schools." *Education*, XXII (1902): 532–37.

Smith, Abbot Emerson. *Colonists in Bondage: White Servitude and Convict Labor in America, 1607–1776*. Chapel Hill: University of North Carolina Press, 1947.

Smith, Daniel Scott. "The Demographic History of Colonial New England." *Journal of Economic History*, XXXII (1972): 165–83.

———. "Underregistration and Bias in Probate Records: An Analysis of

Data from Eighteenth Century Hingham, Massachusetts." *William and Mary Quarterly*, ser. 3, XXXII (1975): 100–10.

——, and Hindus, Michael S. "Premarital Pregnancy in America, 1640–1971: An Overview and Interpretation." *Journal of Interdisciplinary History*, V (1975): 537–70.

Smith, Henry. *Sermons*. London: F. Kingston for T. Man. 1599.

Smith, Hilda. "Gynecology and Ideology in Seventeenth-Century England." In Berenice A. Carroll, ed., *Liberating Women's History: Theoretical and Critical Essays*, pp. 97–114. Urbana: University of Illinois Press, 1976.

——. "A Private Tyranny: The Vision of Seventeenth Century English Feminists on Marital Power Relationships." Paper delivered at Conference on Women in World and American History, April 22, 1976, Thomas More College, Ft. Mitchell, Ky.

Smith, Page. *Daughters of the Promised Land: Women in American History*. Boston: Little, Brown, 1970.

Spencer, Herbert R. *The History of British Midwifery from 1650 to 1800*. . . . London: John Bale, sons & Danielsson, 1927.

Sperling, Melitta. "Conversion Hysteria and Conversion Symptoms: A Revision of Classification and Concepts." *American Psychoanalytic Association Journal*, XXI (1973): 745–71.

Sprenger, Jakob, and Kramer, Heinrich. *Malleus Maleficarum*, ed. Montague Summers. London: Pushkin, 1948. [Originally published in 1486.]

Sprott, S. E. *The English Debate on Suicide: From Donne to Hume*. La Salle, Ill.: Open Court, 1961.

——. "The Puritan Problem of Suicide." *Dalhousie Review*, XXXVIII (1958): 222–33.

Spruill, Julia Cherry. *Women's Life and Work in the Southern Colonies*. Chapel Hill: University of North Carolina Press, 1938.

Stannard, David. "Death and Dying in Puritan New England." *American Historical Review*, LVIII (1973): 1305–30.

——. "Death and the Puritan Child." *American Quarterly*, XXVI (1974): 456–77.

Starkey, Marion L. *The Congregational Way: The Role of the Pilgrims and their Heirs in Shaping America*. Garden City, N.Y.: Doubleday, 1966.

——. *The Devil in Massachusetts: A Modern Enquiry into the Salem Witch Trials*. Garden City, N.Y.: Doubleday, 1969.

Steadman, John M. "Eve's Dream and Witchcraft Conventions." *Journal of the History of Ideas*, XXVI (1965): 567–74.

Stearns, Raymond P., ed. "The Correspondence of John Woodbridge, Jr., and Richard Baxter." *New England Quarterly*, X (1937): 557–83.

Stengel, E. *Suicide and Attempted Suicide*. Harmondsworth, England: Penguin Books, 1964.

Stenton, Doris Mary. *The English Woman in History*. London: Allen & Unwin, 1957.

Stevenson, Noel C. "Marital Rights in the Colonial Period." *New England*

Historical and Genealogical Register, CIX (1955): 84–91.

Stiles, Ezra. *The Literary Diary of Ezra Stiles, D.D., LL. D.*, ed. Franklin B. Dexter. New York: Charles Scribner's Sons, 1910.

Stiles, Henry Reed. *The History and Genealogies of Ancient Windsor, Connecticut, Including East Windsor, South Windsor, Bloomfield, Windsor Locks, and Ellington, 1635–1891*. 2 vols. Hartford: Case, Lockwood & Brainard, 1891–92.

Stoddard, Solomon. *The Doctrine of Instituted Churches, Explained and Proved by the Word of God*. London: For Ralph Smith, 1700.

Story, Thomas. *A Journal of the Life of Thomas Story*. . . . London: n.p., 1704.

Stubbes, Philip. *Anatomy of Abuses*. London: R. Jones, 1583.

Szasz, Thomas. *The Manufacture of Madness*. New York: Dell, 1970.

Taylor, Edward. "Letter to Increase Mather, Mar. 22, 1682/3." *Collections of the Massachusetts Historical Society*, ser. 4, VIII (1868): 629–31.

———. *The Poems of Edward Taylor*, ed. Donald E. Stanford. New Haven: Yale University Press, 1960.

———. *Treatise Concerning the Lord's Supper*, ed. Norman S. Grabo. East Lansing: Michigan State University Press, 1966.

Taylor, F. Kraupl, and Hunter, R. C. A. "Observation of a Hysterical Epidemic in a Hospital Ward: Thoughts on the Dynamics of Mental Epidemics." *Psychiatric Quarterly*, XXXII (1958): 821–39.

———, and Rey, J. H. "The Scapegoat Motif in Society and Its Manifestations in a Therapeutic Group." *International Journal of Psycho-Analysis*, XXXIV (1953): 253–64.

Taylor, John M. *The Witchcraft Delusion in Colonial Connecticut 1647–1697*. New York: Grafton Press, 1908.

Teall, John L. "Witchcraft and Calvinism in Elizabethan England." *Journal of the History of Ideas*, XXIII (1962): 21–36.

Thacher, James. *An Essay on Demonology, Ghosts and Apparitions and Popular Superstitions. Also, an Account of the Witchcraft Delusion at Salem in 1692*. Boston: Carter & Hendee, 1831.

Their Majesties Colony of Connecticut in New-England Vindicated. . . . Boston, 1694. In *Collections of the Connecticut Historical Society*, I (1860): 83–130.

Thomas, G. E. "Puritans, Indians and the Concept of Race." *New England Quarterly*, XLVII (1975): 3–27.

Thomas, Isaiah. *The History of Printing in America*. New York: Weathervane Press, 1970.

Thomas, Keith. "Women and the Civil War Sects." *Past and Present*, XIII (1958): 42–62.

Thompson, Roger. "Review Article: Salem Revisited." *Journal of American Studies*, VI (1972): 317–36.

———. "Seventeenth-Century English and Colonial Sex Ratios: A Postscript." *Population Studies*, XXVIII (1974): 153–65.

———. *Women in Stuart England and America*. London: Routledge & Kegan Paul, 1974.

Thoms, Herbert. "The Beginnings of Obstetrics in America." *Yale Journal of Biology and Medicine*, IV (1932): 665–75.

Todd, Barbara H. "'In Her Free Widowhood': Succession to Property and Remarriage in Rural England, 1540–1800." Paper delivered at Third Berkshire Conference on the History of Women, June 11, 1976, Bryn Mawr, Penna.

Todd, Mabel Loomis. "Witchcraft in New England." *Papers and Proceedings of the Connecticut Valley Historical Society*, IV (1912): 165–83.

Thompson, Benjamin. "On a Fortification at Boston begun by Women, 1676." In Harrison T. Meserole, ed., *Seventeenth-Century American Poetry*, pp. 235–36. Garden City, N.Y.: Doubleday, 1968.

Towne, Abbie Peterson, and Clark, Marietta. "Topsfield in the Witchcraft Delusion." *Historical Collections of the Topsfield Historical Society*, XIII (1908): 23–38.

Towner, Lawrence. "'A Fondness for Freedom': Servant Protest in Puritan Society." *William and Mary Quarterly*, ser. 3, XIX (1962): 201–19.

Traford, Jon. "The Transformation of Massachusetts Education, 1670–1780." *History of Education Quarterly*, X (1970): 287–307.

Troyer, Howard William. *Ned Ward of Grub Street: A Story of Sub-Literary Literature in the Eighteenth Century*. London: Cass, 1968.

Trumbull, Benjamin. *A Complete History of Connecticut*. . . . New Haven: Maltby, Goldsmith, 1818.

Trumbull, James Russell. *History of Northampton, Massachusetts, From Its Settlement in 1654*. 2 vols. Northampton: Northampton Press of Gazette Printing Co., 1898–1902.

Tuke, Thomas. *A Treatise against Painting and Tincturing of Men and Women: Against Murther and Poysoning: Pride and Ambition: Adulterie and Witchcraft*. London: T. Credd & B. Allsope for E. Merchant, 1616.

Turell, Ebenezer. "Detection of Witchcraft, 1720." *Collections of the Massachusetts Historical Society*, ser. 2, X (1824): 6–22.

————. *The Life and Character of the Reverend Benjamin Colman, D.D.; late Paster of a Church in Boston, New-England, who deceased August 29th 1747*. Boston: Rogers & Fowle, 1749.

Twombly, Robert C., and Moore, Robert H. "Black Puritan: The Negro in Seventeenth Century Massachusetts." *William and Mary Quarterly*, ser. 3, XXIV (1967): 224–42.

Ulrich, Laurel Thatcher. "'A Friendly Neighbor': Social Dimensions of Housework in Northern Colonial New England." Paper delivered at Fourth Berkshire Conference on the History of Women, August 24, 1978, South Hadley, Mass.

————. "Vertuous Women Found: New England Ministerial Literature, 1668–1735." *American Quarterly*, XXVIII (1976): 20–40.

Underhill, John. "Letter to John Winthrop, Jr., Mar. 28, 1664." *Collections of the Massachusetts Historical Society*, ser. 4, VII (1865): 188–89.

————. *Newes from America: or a New and Experimentall Discoverie of New*

England. . . . London, 1638. In *Collections of the Massachusetts Historical Society*, ser. 3, VI (1837): 1–28.

United States. Department of Heath, Education, and Welfare. *Vital Statistics of the United States, II—Mortality, Part A*. Washington: Government Printing Office, 1969.

Upham, Charles. *Salem Witchcraft*. . . . Boston: Wiggin & Lunt, 1867.

———. "Salem Witchcraft and Cotton Mather." *Historical Magazine*, ser. 2, VI (1869): 129–219.

Vail, Robert W. G. "Certain Indian Captives in New England." *Proceedings of the Massachusetts Historical Society*, LXVIII (1946): 113–31.

Van Swieten, Geerard. *The Commentaries upon the Aphorisms of Dr. Herman Boerhaave*. . . . 18 vols. London: Robert Horsfield & Thomas Longman, 1744–73.

Vaughan, Alden T., ed. *The Puritan Tradition in America; 1620–1730*. New York: Harper & Row, 1972.

Vaughan, Thomas. *Anthroposophia Theomagica: or a Discourse*. London: T. W. H. for Blunden, 1650.

Vieth, Ilza. *Hysteria: The Story of a Disease*. Chicago: University of Chicago Press, 1965.

Vindication of New England. London, 1689. In William H. Whitmore, ed., *Andros Tracts: Being a Collection of Pamphlets and Official Papers Issued During the Period Between the Overthrow of the Andros Government and the Establishment of the Second Charter of Massachusetts*, II, 19–78. *Publications of the Prince Society*, VI (1869).

W., J. *Letter from New-England, Concerning their Customs, Manners, and Religion*. . . . London, 1682. In George Parker Winship, ed., *Boston in 1682 and 1699: A Trip to New-England by Edward Ward and A Letter from New-England by J. W.* Publication of the Club for Colonial Reprints of Providence, R.I., no. 2, pt. 2, pp. 1–9. New York: B. Franklin, 1970. [Originally published in 1905.]

Wadsworth, Benjamin. "The Nature of Early Piety." In Cotton Mather et al., *A Course of Sermons on Early Piety*, pp. 1–30. Boston: S. Kneeland for N. Buttolph, 1721.

———. *The Well-Ordered Family*. . . . Boston: B. Green, 1712.

Walley, Thomas. *Balm in Gilead to Heal Sion's Wounds*. . . . Cambridge: S. Green & M. Johnson, 1669.

Walter, Nehemiah. *Unfaithful Hearers Detected and Warned*. . . . Boston: B. Green & J. Allen, 1696.

Ward, Edward. *A Trip to New-England*. . . . London, 1699. In George Parker Winship, ed., *Boston in 1682 and 1699: A Trip to New-England by Edward Ward and A Letter from New-England by J. W.* Publication of the Club for Colonial Reprints of Providence, R.I., no. 2, pt. 1, pp. 29–70. New York: B. Franklin, 1970. [Originally published in 1905.]

Ward, Harry M. *Statism in Plymouth Colony*. Port Washington, N.Y.: Kennikat Press, 1973.

[Ward, Nathaniel.] *The Simple Cobler of Agawam in America*. London, 1647. In Peter Force, comp., *Tracts and Other Papers, Relating Principally to the Origin, Settlement, and Progress of the Colonies in North America, From the Discovery to the Year 1776*, III, no. 8. Washington: P. Force, 1844.

Warren, Austin. *The New England Conscience*. Ann Arbor: University of Michigan Press, 1967.

Waters, John J. "Family, Inheritance, and Migration in Colonial New England." Paper delivered at the Organization of American Historians annual meeting, April 12, 1979, New Orleans. La.

Watkins, Walter C. "A Discolored History of Witchcraft, Cleansed by Modern Research." *New England Historical and Genealogical Register*, XLIV (1890): 168–70.

Weeden, William B. *Economic and Social History of New England, 1620–1789*. Boston: Houghton Mifflin, 1890.

Weeks, Lyman Horace, and Bacon, Edwin M., eds. *An Historical Digest of the Provincial Press*. Boston: Society for Americana, 1911.

Welde, Thomas. *Answer to W. R. His Narration*. London: Thomas Paine for H. Overton, 1644.

Wendell, Barrett. "Were the Salem Witches Guiltless?" *Historical Collections of the Essex Institute*, XXIX (1892): 129–47.

Wertenbacker, Thomas Jefferson. *The Puritan Oligarchy: The Founding of American Civilization*. New York: Charles Scribner's Sons, 1947.

Wertheimer, Barbara Mayer. *We Were There: The Story of Working Women in America*. New York: Pantheon Books, 1977.

Westgate, John. "Letter to Increase Mather, May 8, 1677." *Collections of the Massachusetts Historical Society*, ser. 4, VIII (1868): 577–81.

Wheeler, Richard A. *History of the First Congregational Church, Stonington, Connecticut, 1674–1874*. . . . Norwich, Conn.: T. H. Davis, 1875.

Wheelright, John. *John Wheelwright: His Writings* . . .,ed. Charles H. Bell. *Publications of the Prince Society*, IX (1876).

White, Elizabeth. *The Experience of God's gracious Dealing with Mrs. Elizabeth White*. Boston: n.p., 1741.

White, Elizabeth Wade. *Anne Bradstreet: The Tenth Muse*. New York: Oxford University Press, 1971.

————. "The Tenth Muse—A Tercentenary Appraisal of Anne Bradstreet." *William and Mary Quarterly*, ser. 3, VIII (1951): 355–77.

White, Robert W., and Farber, M. L. "Motivation Reconsidered." *Psychological Review*, XVI (1909): 297–333.

Whiting, John. "Letter to Increase Mather, 1682." *Collections of the Massachusetts Historical Society*, ser. 4, VIII (1868): 466–69.

————. *Truth and Innocency Defended, against Falshood and Envy: and the Martyrs of Jesus, and Sufferers for His Sake Vindicated. In Answer to Cotton Mather (a Priest of Boston) his Calumnies, Lyes and Abuses of the People Called Quakers, in his Late Church-History of New-England*. London: T. Soule, 1702.

————. *The Way of Israel's Welfare*. . . . Boston: Samuel Green, 1686.

Whiting, Samuel. *Abraham's Humble Intercession for Sodom.* . . . Cambridge: Samuel Green, 1666.

Whitmore, William H., ed. *Andros Tracts: Being a Collection of Pamphlets and Official Papers Issued During the Period Between the Overthrow of the Andros Government and the Establishment of the Second Charter of Massachusetts,* I–III. *Publications of the Prince Society,* V–VII (1868–74).

Wickes, Ian G. "A History of Infant Feeding." *Archives of Disease in Childhood,* XXVIII (1953): 151–58, 232–40, 332–40, 416–22, 495–502.

Wigglesworth, Michael. *Diary,* ed. Edmund S. Morgan. *Publications of the Colonial Society of Massachusetts,* XXXV (1951).

———. "Letter to Mrs. Samuel Avery, Mar. 23, 1691." *New England Historical and Genealogical Register,* XVII (1863): 140–42.

[———.] "On the Wearing of the Hair." *New England Historical and Genealogical Register,* I (1847): 368–71.

Willard, Samuel. "A briefe Account of the strange & unusuall Providence of God befallen to Elizabeth Knap of Groton, 1672." In Samuel A. Green, *Groton in Witchcraft Times.* pp. 4–21. Cambridge: J. Wilson & Son, 1883.

———. *Impenitent Sinners Warned of their Misery and Summoned to Judgement.* . . . Boston: B. Green & J. Allen, 1698.

Williams, John. *The Redeemed Captive Returning to Zion.* . . . Boston: Samuel Hall, 1795.

———. *Warning to the Unclean: A Discourse Preacht at Springfield Lecture August 25, 1698, at the Execution of Sarah Smith.* Boston: B. Green & J. Allen for M. Perry, 1699.

Williams, Roger. *The Complete Writings of Roger Williams,* ed. Perry Miller. 7 vols. New York: Russell & Russell, 1963.

———. *George Fox Digg'd Out of His Burrowes.* Boston: John Foster, 1676.

Williamson, William. *The History of the State of Maine.* . . . Hallowell, Me.: Glazier, Masters, 1832.

Wilson, Monica. *Reaction to Conquest: Effects of Contact with Europeans on the Pondo of South Africa.* London: Oxford University Press for the International African Institute, 1961.

Winship, George Parker. "Introduction" to *Boston in 1682 and 1699: A Trip to New-England by Edward Ward and A Letter from New-England by J. W.,* pp, ix–xxviii. Publication of the Club for Colonial Reprints of Providence, R.I., no. 2. New York: B. Franklin, 1970. [Originally published in 1905.]

Winslow, Edward. *Hypocrisie Unmasked: a true relation of the Proceedings of the Governor and Company of the Massachusetts against Samuel Gorton of Rhode Island.* New York: B. Franklin, 1968. [Originally published in 1646.]

Winslow, Ola Elizabeth. *Meetinghouse Hill, 1630–1783.* New York: Macmillan, 1952.

Winthrop, John. *A Short Story of the Rise, reign, and ruine of the Antinomians, Familists, and Libertines.* London, 1644. In David D. Hall, ed., *The Antinomian Controversy, 1636–1638: A Documentary History,* pp. 199–310. Middletown, Conn.: Wesleyan University Press, 1968.

———. *Winthrop's Journal "History of New England" 1630–1649*, ed. James Kendall Hosmer. 2 vols. New York: Charles Scribner's Sons, 1908.

Winthrop, John, Jr. "Letter to Fitz-John Winthrop, Sept. 9, 1658." *Collections of the Massachusetts Historical Society*, ser. 5, VIII (1882): 45–49.

"Witchcraft in Hingham." *New England Historical and Genealogical Register*, V (1851): 263.

"Witchcraft in Maine." *New England Historical and Genealogical Register*, XIII (1859): 193–96.

"Witchcraft on Long Island." *Historical Magazine*, ser. 1, VI (1862): 53.

Wood, Pamela Lakes. "The Victim in a Forcible Rape Case: A Feminist View." *American Criminal Law Review*, XI (1973): 335–54.

Woody, Thomas. *A History of Women's Education in the United States*. 2 vols. New York: Science Press, 1929.

Wright, Louis B. *Middle-Class Culture in Elizabethan England*. Ithaca: Cornell University Press for the Folger Shakespeare Library, 1958.

Wrigley, E. A. "Family Limitation in Pre-Industrial England." In Orest and Patricia Ranum, eds., *Popular Attitudes toward Birth Control in Pre-Industrial France and England*, pp. 53–99. New York: Harper & Row, 1972.

The Wyllys Papers. . . . Collections of the Connecticut Historical Society, XXI (1924).

Youngs, William T. "Congregational Clericalism: New England Ordinations before the Great Awakening." *William and Mary Quarterly*, ser. 3, XXXI (1974): 481–90.

Ziegler, Frederick J. "Hysterical Conversion Reactions." *Postgraduate Medicine*, XLVII, no. 5 (1970): 174–78.

Ziff, Larzer. *Puritanism in America: New Culture in a New World*. New York: Viking Press, 1973.

Index